Blackstone's

Magistrates' Court Handbook 2014

Blackstone's
Magistrates' Court Handbook 2014

Anthony Edwards

OXFORD
UNIVERSITY PRESS

OXFORD
UNIVERSITY PRESS

Great Clarendon Street, Oxford, OX2 6DP,
United Kingdom

Oxford University Press is a department of the University of Oxford.
It furthers the University's objective of excellence in research, scholarship,
and education by publishing worldwide. Oxford is a registered trade mark of
Oxford University Press in the UK and in certain other countries

Published in the United States of America by Oxford University Press
198 Madison Avenue, New York, NY 10016, United States of America

British Library Cataloguing in Publication Data
Data available

ISBN 978-0-19-967763-4

Printed by
L.E.G.O. S.p.A.–Lavis TN

Preface to the 2014 Edition

This book owes its origin to the inspiration of Andrew Keogh to whom the profession owes a huge debt. It aims to provide a portable resource to busy criminal lawyers seeking answers to the common—and some not so common—issues that arise at court. The balance between portability and content is a fine one and, like Andrew, I apologise in advance for those topics which have had to be sacrificed.

I welcome feedback on this book, both formally and informally. The text must meet the needs of the practising lawyer, and your experiences do not always reflect mine, so please do not hesitate to continue the dialogue that Andrew began. Inevitably I do not agree with him on every part and have made changes that seem to me to be desirable; and to make it part of a series of books that will help practitioners in the police station and in the youth, magistrates', and Crown courts. The intention is that it will continue to be the most easily accessed source of answers to questions that arise pre-trial at the magistrates' court level. The law is cited as at 31 May 2013.

I wish to acknowledge the help given by District Judge Naomi Redhouse and my colleague Mark Ashford in relation to youths; by my colleague William Bergstrom in writing the section on extradition; by Philip Houlden, Clerk to the Justices, for the inspiration behind the diagram at the start of the section on bail; and to Fiona Sinclair of Oxford University Press for her extraordinary skills and patience in the preparation of this edition of the *Handbook*. The remaining mistakes are my responsibility alone.

Anthony Edwards
London

Contents

Part A Procedure and Evidence

Contents

Part B Youths in the Adult Court

Part C Offences

Part D Sentencing

Contents

Icons List

The following icons are used throughout this book:

DO Dangerous Offender

EW Either Way

Sentence

SO Summary Only

Cross-reference to *Blackstone's Criminal Practice 2014*

Table of Cases

Table of Cases

Table of Cases

Table of Cases

Table of Cases

Table of Cases

Table of Cases

Table of Cases

Table of Primary Legislation

Table of Primary Legislation

Table of Primary Legislation

Table of Primary Legislation

Table of Primary Legislation

Table of Primary Legislation

Table of Secondary Legislation

Table of Secondary Legislation

Table of Conventions

Table of Practice Directions

Part A
Procedure and Evidence

A1 **Abuse of Process**

A1.1 **Introduction**

Abuse of process is something so unfair and wrong with the prosecution that the court should not allow a prosecutor to proceed with what is, in all other respects, a regular proceeding: *Hui-chi Ming v R* [1992] 1 AC 34.

A stay on these grounds falls into two main categories:

- where a fair trial of the particular defendant is impossible (eg due to loss of evidence);
- where there is a misuse of court process (where it offends the court's sense of justice and propriety to be asked to try the accused in the circumstances of the particular case). In relation to this category of case, the magistrates' court does not have jurisdiction to determine the issue and proceedings ought therefore to be adjourned in order that the defence may seek a judicial review.

A stay of proceedings based on an abuse of process will be rare and should be allowed only in exceptional circumstances (see *Attorney-General's Reference No 1 of 1990* (1992) 95 Cr App R 296); and if the court process can compensate for any unfairness or wrongs, so as to allow for a fair trial, that is the way in which it should proceed.

On an application to stay for abuse of process, it is for the defendant to satisfy the court on a balance of probabilities that no fair trial is possible. The application should be decided on material adduced by prosecution and defence, with both parties having the right (subject to usual judicial discretion) to call evidence (*R v Clerkenwell Magistrates' Court, ex p Bell* [1991] Crim LR 468).

A1.2 **Relevant grounds**

A1.2.1 *Missing evidence*

The issues identified in *R v Dobson* [2001] EWCA Crim 1606 are as follows:

- What was the duty of the police?
- Did the police fail in their duty by not obtaining or retaining the appropriate (material)?
- If so, was there serious prejudice which rendered a fair trial impossible in the light of such failure?

- Alternatively, did the police failure result from such bad behaviour, in the sense of bad faith or serious fault, as to render it unfair that the accused should be tried at all?

There is no *general* duty on the prosecution to retain CCTV evidence that might have given insight into whether a warning was given to a detainee during a breath test procedure (*Morris v Director of Public Prosecutions* [2008] EWHC 2788 (Admin)). This decision follows the leading case of *R v Feltham Magistrates' Court and another, ex p Ebrahim* [2001] EWHC Admin 130.

That case emphasizes the early identification of the significance of the relevant material is a key factor to ensure that the prosecution are under a duty, not least under the code of practice made under the Criminal Procedure and Investigations Act 1996.

A1.2.2 *Failure to supply initial details of the prosecution case*

There is no jurisdiction to stay proceedings for failures in service of initial details of the prosecution case under Part 10 of the Criminal Procedure Rules; the appropriate remedy is to adjourn (*R v Leeds Youth Court, ex p P(A)* [2001] EWHC 215 (Admin)), although repeated failure to comply with the rules may provide for a stay in truly exceptional circumstances (*R v Willesden Magistrates' Court, ex p Clemmings* (1988) 152 JPN 46). A threat to stay a prosecution if there were further disclosure breaches did not give rise to any legitimate expectation on the part of the defendant so as to require the court to carry through its threat on the next occasion (*R v Leeds Youth Court, ex p AP and others* [2001] EWHC 215 (Admin)).

A1.2.3 *Improper motive*

The fact that there was a mixed motive for launching a private prosecution will justify a stay only if the conduct of the prosecutor is truly oppressive, as it was obvious that many private prosecutions would be brought with mixed motives (*Dacre v City of Westminster Magistrates' Court* [2009] 1 Cr App R 6).

In *Nembhard v Director of Public Prosecutions* [2009] EWHC 194 (Admin), the court ruled that a magistrates' court was correct to refuse to stay proceedings on the ground that a request to produce traffic documents was motivated by improper considerations—namely a desire to harass the defendant. In such cases the proper course of action would be either to stay the prosecution pending determination of the issue by the High Court, or to apply for judicial review of the decision to prosecute. This case is an important reminder that in instances where an abuse of state power is being alleged, a magistrates' court has no jurisdiction to stay proceedings (*R v Horseferry Road Magistrates' Court, ex p Paul James Bennett* [1994] 1 AC 42).

A1.2.4 *Delay*

In the absence of other compelling reasons, a lengthy delay, in itself, does not justify a stay of criminal proceedings (*Spiers v Ruddy* [2008] 1 AC 873, PC).

In *Ali v Crown Prosecution Service* [2007] EWCA Crim 691, proceedings brought seven years after the incident should have been stayed, as important documentary evidence, relevant to assessing the victim's credibility, had been lost. The court emphasized that:

> this is a rare case where prejudice following from the delay was not alleviated and probably could never have been cured during the course of the trial.

In *R (Flaherty) v City of Westminster Magistrates' Court* [2008] EWHC 2589 (Admin), the last two years of a ten-year delay in enforcing a confiscation order were attributable to the prosecution. The proceedings ought to have been stayed, as confiscation proceedings must be determined within a reasonable time.

Earlier cases, such as *R v Clerk to the Medway Justices, ex p DHSS* [1986] Crim LR 686, DC, in which a prosecution was stayed where the prosecution laid the information on the last day before it was time-barred, should be treated with extreme caution in the light of considerable and more recent appellate-level scrutiny of the principles that apply. It is almost inconceivable that the *Medway* case would be decided similarly today.

A1.2.5 *Legitimate expectation*

The prosecution of a person who has received a promise, an undertaking, or a representation from the police that he will not be prosecuted is capable of being an abuse of process (*Croydon Justices, ex p Dean* [1993] QB 769). So too will be the prosecution of a person denied a caution by the failure of the police to make appropriate disclosure to enable legal advice to be given (*DPP v Ara* [2001] EWHC 493 (Admin)). The administration of a caution may make it an abuse for there to be a later prosecution (*Jones v Whalley* [2007] 1 AC 63). The Crown may in appropriate cases, where there is a proper basis, change its mind as to how to proceed. However, the Crown is required, absent a change of circumstances, to proceed in a single prosecution with all the charges it proposes to bring arising out of the same incident (*Connelly v DPP* [1964] AC 1254).

  See *Blackstone's Criminal Practice 2014* **D3**

A2 **Adjournments**

A2.1 Time limits applicable to adjournments

It should be noted that remand limits apply to remands under the Magistrates' Courts Act 1980 (eg ss 5, 10, 11, 17, 130, etc). Therefore, when a person is sent for trial to the Crown Court, the eight-clear-day limit on initial remand (if in custody) does not apply as the court has not remanded the case.

Adjournment during trial	No limit (MCA 1980, s 10)
Adjournment after conviction but before sentence—for the purpose of reports/inquiries	Maximum four weeks, unless the defendant is in custody, when it is then three weeks.
Prior to conviction following remand into custody	Maximum eight clear days for first remand. On a subsequent remand the maximum period is 28 days, provided that it will be possible for the next stage in the proceedings (not simply an onward remand) to be completed. A defendant can consent to onward remands in his absence, and this will often be done when the proceedings cannot be progressed materially within a four-week period.
Prior to conviction—on bail	Maximum eight days unless defendant and prosecution consent (MCA 1980, s 128(6)).

A2.2 Principles to be applied

Part 3 of the Criminal Procedure Rules requires active case management. This includes discouraging delay, and dealing with as many aspects of the case as possible on the same occasion and avoiding unnecessary hearings (r 3.2(2)(f)). At every hearing, if the case cannot be concluded there and then, the court must give directions so that it can be concluded at the next hearing or as soon as possible after that (r 3.8(1)). Unless it has been done already, the court must take the defendant's plea (r 3.8(2)(b)). This obligation does not depend on the extent of advance information, service of evidence, disclosure of unused material, or the grant of legal aid. This is an aim generally shared by both defence and prosecution alike, but there are still many instances where an adjournment is required. In such instances advocates can expect those applications to be closely scrutinized (*R v Hereford Magistrates Court, ex p Rowland* [1998] QB 110).

In *Crown Prosecution Service v Picton* [2006] EWHC 1108 (Admin), the court laid down the following general approach:

- A decision whether to adjourn is a decision within the discretion of the trial court. An appellate court will interfere only if very clear grounds for doing so are shown.
- Magistrates should pay great attention to the need for expedition in the prosecution of criminal proceedings; delays are scandalous; they bring the law into disrepute; summary justice should be speedy justice; an application for an adjournment should be rigorously scrutinized.
- Where an adjournment is sought by the prosecution, magistrates must consider both the interest of the defendant in getting the matter dealt with, and the interest of the public that criminal charges should be adjudicated upon: the guilty convicted as well as the innocent acquitted. With a more serious charge, the public interest that there be a trial will carry greater weight.
- Where an adjournment is sought by the accused, the magistrates must consider whether, if it is not granted, the accused will be able fully to present his defence and, if he will not be able to do so, the degree to which his ability to do so is compromised.
- In considering the competing interests of the parties, the magistrates should examine the likely consequences of the proposed adjournment, in particular, its likely length, and the need to decide the facts while recollections are fresh.
- The reason that the adjournment is required should be examined and, if it arises through the fault of the party asking for the adjournment, that is a factor against granting the adjournment, carrying weight in accordance with the gravity of the fault. If that party was not at fault then that may favour an adjournment. Likewise, if the party opposing the adjournment has been at fault then that will favour an adjournment.
- The magistrates should take appropriate account of the history of the case, and whether there have been earlier adjournments and at whose request and why.
- Lastly, of course, the factors to be considered cannot be comprehensively stated but depend upon the particular circumstances of each case, and they will often overlap. The court's duty is to do justice between the parties in the circumstances as they have arisen.

In *Aravinthan Visvaratnam v Brent Magistrates' Court* [2009] EWHC 3017 (Admin), the court made these observations:

> The prosecution must not think that they are always allowed at least one application to adjourn the case. If that idea were to gain currency, no trial would ever start on the first date set for trial.

> So these are the competing considerations. I have no doubt that there is a high public interest in trials taking place on the date set for trial, and that trials should not be adjourned unless there is a good and compelling reason to do so. The sooner the prosecution understand this—that they cannot rely

on their own serious failures properly to warn witnesses—the sooner the efficiency in the Magistrates' Court system improves. An improvement in timeliness and the achievement of a more effective and efficient system of criminal justice in the Magistrates' Court will bring about great benefits to victims and to witnesses and huge savings in time and money.

A2.2.1 *Legal aid*

A common issue that arises is in relation to adjournments for the purposes of legal aid being granted. Much will depend on the circumstances, and in particular, how much time the defendant has had, if any, to arrange appropriate representation. The court will also be mindful of payments that can be made to firms if legal aid is refused—thereby diluting the force of any argument that work would otherwise be unfunded. That said, support can be found for an adjournment in the case of *Berry Trade Ltd v Moussavi* [2002] 1 WLR 1910:

> The question which the judge had to ask was a different question, whether Mr Moussavi had had an effective opportunity for applying for public funding. The weight to be accorded to giving him this opportunity must, in these circumstances, outweigh other considerations, such as the convenience to other parties and the use of court resources.

Any submission by the court that this is a civil case and therefore has no relevance to a criminal case does not withstand scrutiny, particularly in light of the extradition case of *Stopya v District Court of Lublin Poland* [2012] EWHC 1787 (Admin), which held that 'delays occasioned by means testing which are not occasioned by the fault of the requested person or his legal advisers cannot be held against the requested person'.

A2.2.2 *Absence of the defendant*

A trial may take place in the absence of the defendant only in exceptional circumstances (*R (Drinkwater) v Solihull Magistrates' Court* [2012] EWHC 765 (Admin), applying *R v Jones* [2002] UKHL 5). A failure to make proper inquiry into a defendant's absence which, had it been carried out, would have led to the adjournment of the matter, will result in 'any resulting conviction following trial in absence being quashed' (*R (James) v Tower Bridge Magistrates' Court*, unreported, 9 June 2009, DC).

Where a defendant provides a medical note in relation to non-attendance, a court should give reasons for finding such medical excuses spurious, it being rarely, if ever, appropriate to reject a medical certificate (even if not meeting the normal requirements as to information required) without first giving the defendant an opportunity to respond (*Evans v East Lancashire Magistrates' Court* [2010] EWHC 2108 (Admin)).

In *R v Bolton Magistrates' Court, ex p Merna* [1991] Crim LR 848, the court said:

> if the court suspects the [medical] grounds to be spurious or believes them to be inadequate, the court should ordinarily express its doubts and thereby give the defendant an opportunity to seek to resolve the doubts. It may call for better evidence, require further inquiries to be made or adopt any other expedient fair to both parties. The ultimate test must always be one of fairness and if a defendant claims to be ill with apparently responsible professional support for his claim, the court should not reject that claim and proceed to hear the case in a defendant's absence without satisfying itself that the claim may properly be rejected and that no unfairness will thereby be done.

The issues were re-examined and confirmed in *Killick v West London Magistrates' Court* [2012] EWHC 3864 (Admin):

> Section 11(1)(b) and (2A) of the Magistrates' Courts Act 1980 allow the court to proceed in the absence of a defendant unless it appears contrary to the interests of justice, but it should not do so if it considers that there is an acceptable reason for his failure to attend. The jurisdiction must be exercised with the utmost care and caution. The case should not proceed without the court satisfying itself that the claim for an adjournment may properly be rejected and that no unfairness will thereby be done.

> Where a defendant wished to resist a criminal charge and is shown by medical evidence to be unfit to attend court either as a result of involuntary illness or incapacity, it would be very rarely, if ever, right for the court to exercise its discretion in favour of proceeding. If the court suspects the grounds to be spurious or inadequate, it should express its doubts to give the defence a chance to resolve them. The court must distinguish genuine grounds from those that are spurious and designed to frustrate the process. If the court concludes the latter is the case, it may proceed as if there is a truly compelling reason for doing so, notwithstanding the justified non-attendance.

> If a court proceeds, it should set aside the order under section 142 of the Magistrates' Court Act 1980 if compelling medical evidence is then produced.

A2.2.3 *Witnesses*

Where a party was unable, through no fault of his own, to call an important witness, an adjournment should be granted to give an opportunity for that witness to be traced and steps taken to secure attendance (*Khurshied v Peterborough Magistrates' Court* [2009] EWHC 1136 (Admin) and *Nadour v Chester Magistrates* [2009] EWHC 1505 (Admin)). In *Essen v Director of Public Prosecutions* [2005] EWHC 1077 (Admin), the court was concerned with a failure of the CPS, due to administrative error, to warn its witnesses for trial. The court held that in the absence of some other counterprevailing factor an adjournment ought not to be granted. The fact that a crime may go unpunished is not sufficient as:

> in that case no prosecutor, however dilatory, need attend to the requirement to be ready for trial on the set date ... The prejudice to the defendant [of an

adjournment in those circumstances] was manifest. The CPS had no ground for seeking clemency. It was the sole author of its own misfortune.

A prosecutor should always be given some time to make inquiries as to why a witness is not present (*R v Swansea Justices, ex p Director of Public Prosecutions* The Times, 30 March 1990).

A2.2.4 *Disclosure*

If the prosecution have failed to carry out their statutory duties in relation to disclosure under the Criminal Procedure and Investigations Act 1996, an adjournment should be granted (on the Crown's application) to the defence (*Swash v Director of Public Prosecutions* [2009] EWHC 803 (Admin)). If, as is increasingly common, the Crown's application is refused, it is professionally improper for a lawyer to prosecute a case where there has been a breach of the duty to disclose, and courts may exclude all prosecution evidence under section 78 of the Police and Criminal Evidence Act 1984 as it may then be unfair in the proceedings to admit that evidence alone at trial.

A2.2.5 *Ambush defence*

If a defendant raises matters for the first time in the proceedings (so-called 'ambush defences'), the court is fully justified in adjourning the matter in order to allow the prosecution to deal with them properly (eg *R (Lawson) v Stratford Magistrates' Court* [2007] EWHC 2490 (Admin), where compliance with signage regulations in relation to a prosecution for speeding was raised for the first time in cross-examination). The general principles are established by the series of decisons in *R v Gleeson* [2003] EWCA Crim 3357, *R v Chorley Justices* [2006] EWHC 1795 (Admin), and *Malcolm v Director of Public Prosecutions* [2007] EWHC 363 (Admin).

In *R (Taylor) v Southampton Magistrates' Court* [2008] EWHC 3006 (Admin), it was held that during a trial for failing to comply with a notice under section 172 of the Road Traffic Act 1988, a District Judge was right to adjourn the case in order for the prosecution to be able to gather evidence (if such evidence existed) to prove service of the notice. There was no question of bias, even though the court acted of its own motion. In this case there was no issue of 'ambush', the prosecution having not only been put to proof of all issues but the specific issue having been raised. That was not enough for the court in this instance, in the absence of a positive defence case that the notice had not in fact been served.

 See *Blackstone's Criminal Practice 2014* **D4**

A3 **Admissibility and Exclusion of Evidence**

A3.1 **Admissibility and exclusion**

Given that magistrates deal with questions of both fact and law, the voir dire procedure adopted in the Crown Court is not always appropriate in summary proceedings when issues of admissibility arise. The timing of any challenge is a matter for the court, and there is no right to have issues of admissibility determined as a preliminary issue (*R v Epping and Ongar Justices, ex p Manby* [1986] Crim LR 555). It has been ruled that a court has no power to delegate issues of admissibility to another bench (*R v Ormskirk Justices, ex p Davies* (1994) 158 JP 1145); however, section 8A of the Magistrates' Courts Act 1980 now provides for pre-trial rulings on issues of admissibility (see **A3.2**). Previous rulings on admissibility can be reversed, but this should happen only exceptionally (see **A.9** for relevant cases).

When a party is seeking to exclude evidence under section 76 of the Police and Criminal Evidence Act 1984, a voir dire will be required as there is no discretion under section 76 (as opposed to section 78) and the prosecution carry the burden of disproving unfairness (*Vel v Owen* [1987] Crim LR 496).

Police and Criminal Evidence Act 1984, s 76

76 Confessions

(1) In any proceedings a confession made by an accused person may be given in evidence against him in so far as it is relevant to any matter in issue in the proceedings and is not excluded by the court in pursuance of this section.

(2) If, in any proceedings where the prosecution proposes to give in evidence a confession made by an accused person, it is represented to the court that the confession was or may have been obtained—

(a) by oppression of the person who made it; or

(b) in consequence of anything said or done which was likely, in the circumstances existing at the time, to render unreliable any confession which might be made by him in consequence thereof,

the court shall not allow the confession to be given in evidence against him except in so far as the prosecution proves to the court beyond reasonable doubt that the confession (notwithstanding that it may be true) was not obtained as aforesaid.

(3) In any proceedings where the prosecution proposes to give in evidence a confession made by an accused person, the court may of its own motion

---

require the prosecution, as a condition of allowing it to do so, to prove that the confession was not obtained as mentioned in subsection (2) above.

(4) The fact that a confession is wholly or partly excluded in pursuance of this section shall not affect the admissibility in evidence—

    (a) of any facts discovered as a result of the confession; or

    (b) where the confession is relevant as showing that the accused speaks, writes or expresses himself in a particular way, of so much of the confession as is necessary to show that he does so.

(5) Evidence that a fact to which this subsection applies was discovered as a result of a statement made by an accused person shall not be admissible unless evidence of how it was discovered is given by him or on his behalf.

(6) Subsection (5) above applies—

    (a) to any fact discovered as a result of a confession which is wholly excluded in pursuance of this section; and

    (b) to any fact discovered as a result of a confession which is partly so excluded, if the fact is discovered as a result of the excluded part of the confession.

(7) Nothing in Part VII of this Act shall prejudice the admissibility of a confession made by an accused person.

(8) In this section 'oppression' includes torture, inhuman or degrading treatment, and the use or threat of violence (whether or not amounting to torture).

(9) Where the proceedings mentioned in subsection (1) above are proceedings before a magistrates' court inquiring into an offence as examining justices this section shall have effect with the omission of—

    (a) in subsection (1) the words 'and is not excluded by the court in pursuance of this section', and

    (b) subsections (2) to (6) and (8).

When a party is inviting a court to exercise its discretion to exclude evidence under section 78 of the Police and Criminal Evidence Act 1984, the court has a choice as to whether to deal with the issue when it arises or once all evidence has been heard. The voir dire procedure is appropriate to such applications, as an accused may otherwise be denied the opportunity to remain silent in relation to the substantive matter. In *Halawa v Federation Against Copyright Theft* [1995] 1 Cr App R 496, the court laid down the following principles:

- Absent a good reason, the defendant is entitled to a voir dire on the issue of exclusion under section 78.
- If section 78 is being argued as an alternative to section 76, a voir dire should be held.
- It will generally be appropriate to hear all of the prosecution evidence before embarking on a voir dire in relation to the disputed parts.
- If the argument is only to the circumstances in which evidence was gathered, a voir dire may not be necessary. If, however, the defendant contradicts the evidence, it is more likely that a voir dire is appropriate.

- The defence must be in a position to assist the court in determining the extent of any challenge.

Police and Criminal Evidence Act 1984, s 78

(1) In any proceedings the court may refuse to allow evidence on which the prosecution proposes to rely to be given if it appears to the court that, having regard to all the circumstances, including the circumstances in which the evidence was obtained, the admission of the evidence would have such an adverse effect on the fairness of the proceedings that the court ought not to admit it.

(2) Nothing in this section shall prejudice any rule of law requiring a court to exclude evidence.

(3) This section shall not apply in the case of proceedings before a magistrates' court inquiring into an offences as examining justices.

A3.2 Pre-trial rulings

Sections 8A and 8B of the Magistrates' Courts Act 1980 provide:

Magistrates' Courts Act 1980, ss 8A and 8B

8A Power to make rulings at pre-trial hearing

(1) For the purposes of this section a hearing is a pre-trial hearing if—
   (a) it relates to an information—
      (i) which is to be tried summarily, and
      (ii) to which the accused has pleaded not guilty, and
   (b) it takes place before the start of the trial.

(2) [...]

(3) At a pre-trial hearing, a magistrates' court may make a ruling as to any matter mentioned in subsection (4) if—
   (a) the condition in subsection (5) is met,
   (b) the court has given the parties an opportunity to be heard, and
   (c) it appears to the court that it is in the interests of justice to make the ruling.

(4) The matters are—
   (a) any question as to the admissibility of evidence;
   (b) any other question of law relating to the case.

(5) [...]

(6) A ruling may be made under this section—
   (a) on an application by a party to the case, or
   (b) of the court's own motion.

(7) For the purposes of this section and section 8B, references to the prosecutor are to any person acting as prosecutor, whether an individual or body.

8B Effect of rulings at pre-trial hearing

(1) Subject to subsections (3) and (6), a ruling under section 8A has binding effect from the time it is made until the case against the accused or, if there is more than one, against each of them, is disposed of.

(2) The case against an accused is disposed of if—

      (a) he is acquitted or convicted,

      (b) the prosecutor decides not to proceed with the case against him, or

      (c) the information is dismissed.

(3) A magistrates' court may discharge or vary (or further vary) a ruling under section 8A if—

      (a) the condition in section 8A(5) is met,

      (b) the court has given the parties an opportunity to be heard, and

      (c) it appears to the court that it is in the interests of justice to do so.

(4) The court may act under subsection (3)—

      (a) on an application by a party to the case, or

      (b) of its own motion.

(5) No application may be made under subsection (4)(a) unless there has been a material change of circumstances since the ruling was made or, if a previous application has been made, since the application (or last application) was made.

(6) A ruling under section 8A is discharged in relation to an accused if—

      (a) the magistrates' court commits or sends him to the Crown Court for trial for the offence charged in the information, or

      (b) a count charging him with the offence is included in an indictment by virtue of section 40 of the Criminal Justice Act 1988.

 See *Blackstone's Criminal Practice 2014* **F1–F2**

A4 **Allocation and Plea Before Venue**

A4.1 Cases that may be sent to the Crown Court

The court must send the case to the Crown Court if:

- there is an indictable only offence (see **Appendix 3**);
- a notice has been served under section 51B (serious fraud) or section 51C (children) of the Crime and Disorder Act 1998; or
- the offence is related to an indictable/notice offence for which the defendant or another defendant is sent for trial (unless the defendant appears on a subsequent occasion when there is a discretion);
- the defendant is charged with an either way offence or relevant (imprisonable or disqualifiable) summary offence, and is or has been sent to the Crown Court for a related offence;
- the defendant is jointly charged with another defendant who is or has been sent to the Crown Court for a related offence;
- the defendant is jointly charged or is charged with a related offence with a youth defendant who is or has been sent to the Crown Court for trial.

In each case where there is a co-defendant, the duty exists when the defendants appear on the same occasion, but becomes a discretion if this defendant appears on a subsequent occasion.

A plea before venue is conducted for all other either way offences. The defendant is asked to indicate a plea.

A4.2 Where there is a guilty plea

If the indication of plea is guilty, the court proceeds to sentence, and this may include committal for sentence if Crown Court powers are required to deal with the defendant. It shall commit for sentence if the offence is a specified offence (see **Appendix 5**) and the dangerous offender provisions apply on the facts of the particular case.

A4.3 Not guilty or no indication of plea

If the indication of plea is not guilty, or there is no indication of plea, the court proceeds to allocation.

The court receives representations from the Crown, which may include details of previous convictions of the defendant, and from the defence.

The court determines, in accordance with section 19 of the Magistrates' Courts Act 1980 and the Allocation Guidelines, whether the case is more suitable for summary trial or trial on indictment.

A4.4 Court declines jurisdiction

If the court declines jurisdiction, it must send the case to the Crown Court.

A4.5 Court accepts jurisdiction

If the court accepts jurisdiction, the defendant may request an indication whether the court is considering a custodial sentence. If the court is willing to give an indication, the defendant must be invited to reconsider his plea. If the indication was non-custodial and a plea of guilty is indicated, the court may not impose a custodial sentence or commit for sentence.

The defence must otherwise be asked if they consent to summary trial. If the defence elect trial on indictment, the case must be sent to the Crown Court.

If the defence consent to summary trial, the Crown may make further representations that the trial should be on indictment if new factors become relevant. However, there can be no change of venue once the trial has begun or an application in relation to the trial has been made.

If the case remains summary there is a trial, and in the event of a conviction the court may sentence within its own powers only, unless:

- there is a specified offence and the requirements for an extended sentence are met by the facts of the particular case; or
- wholly exceptional new factors have arisen during the trial, making the initial decision to accept jurisdiction inappropriate. This follows the case law on 'expectation' preventing a court from changing its mind (*R v Nottingham Magistrates' Court, ex p Davidson* [2000] 1 Cr App R (S) 167). Under these procedures the court will have been fully advised about the defendant's previous convictions, and as the Crown will have had opportunities to emphasize particular seriousness, it will therefore be very difficult for the court to say that the decision to accept summary jurisdiction did not give rise to a legitimate expectation of disposal within magistrates' court powers (*Sheffield Magistrates' Court, ex p Ojo* (2000) 164 JP 659). The power to commit for sentence in these circumstances would require an acceptance of jurisdiction that was so perverse as to be unlawful (*R (Nicholas) v Chester Magistrates' Court* [2009] EWHC 1504 (Admin)) or in total disregard of the relevant sentencing guideline (*Thornton v CPS* [2012] EWHC 346 (Admin)); or that there have

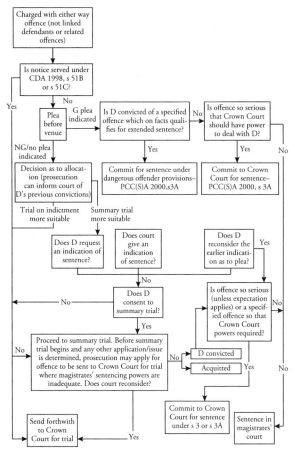

Figure 1 Allocation Procedure for Adults

been new convictions since the allocation hearing; or the facts at trial were clearly more serious than originally described so that Crown Court sentencing powers are required.

A4.6 Either way offences that must be tried summarily

The court must determine venue for either way offences. Some either way offences have venue dictated by value (criminal damage, save arson and aggravated vehicle-taking). If the value of damage is less than £5,000, only summary trial will be offered. For multiple offences, the aggregate value must be considered (Magistrates' Courts Act 1980, s 22(11)). A court has a discretion but not a duty to hear evidence in relation to value (*R v Canterbury Justices, ex p Klisiak* [1981] 2 All ER 129). Value does not include consequential loss flowing from destruction (*R v Colchester Magistrates' Court, ex p Abbott* [2001] Crim LR 564). Where it is not clear whether or not the value exceeds £5,000, the defendant will be permitted, if he so wishes, to elect Crown Court trial. Section 22 of the Magistrates' Courts Act 1980 provides:

Magistrates' Courts Act 1980, s 22(1)–(11)

22 Certain offences triable either way to be tried summarily if value involved is small

(1) If the offence charged by the information is one of those mentioned in the first column of Schedule 2 to this Act (in this section referred to as 'scheduled offences') then, subject to subsection 7 below, the court shall, before proceeding in accordance with section 19 above, consider whether, having regard to any representations made by the prosecutor or the accused, the value involved (as defined in subsection (10) below) appears to the court to exceed the relevant sum. For the purposes of this section the relevant sum is £5,000.

(2) If, where subsection (1) above applies, it appears to the court clear that, for the offence charged, the value involved does not exceed the relevant sum, the court shall proceed as if the offence were triable only summarily, and sections 19 to 21 above shall not apply.

(3) If, where subsection (1) above applies, it appears to the court clear that, for the offence charged, the value involved exceeds the relevant sum, the court shall thereupon proceed in accordance with section 19 above in the ordinary way without further regard to the provisions of this section.

(4) If, where subsection (1) above applies, it appears to the court for any reason not clear whether, for the offence charged, the value involved does or does not exceed the relevant sum, the provisions of subsections (5) and (6) below shall apply.

(5) The court shall cause the charge to be written down, if this has not already been done, and read to the accused, and shall explain to him in ordinary language—

    (a) that he can, if he wishes, consent to be tried summarily for the offence and that if he consents to be so tried, he will definitely be tried in that way; and

    (b) that if he is tried summarily and is convicted by the court, his liability to imprisonment or a fine will be limited as provided in section 33 below.

(6) After explaining to the accused as provided by subsection (5) above the court shall ask him whether he consents to be tried summarily and—

    (a) if he so consents, shall proceed in accordance with subsection (2) above as if that subsection applied;

    (b) if he does not so consent, shall proceed in accordance with subsection (3) above as if that subsection applied.

(7) [repealed]

(8) Where a person is convicted by a magistrates' court of a scheduled offence, it shall not be open to him to appeal to the Crown Court against the conviction on the ground that the convicting court's decision as to the value involved was mistaken.

(9) If, where subsection (1) above applies, the offence charged is one with which the accused is charged jointly with a person who has not attained the age of 17, the reference in that subsection to any representations made by the accused shall be read as including any representations made by the person under 18.

(10) In this section 'the value involved', in relation to any scheduled offence, means the value indicated in the second column of Schedule 2 to this Act, measured as indicated in the third column of that Schedule; and in that Schedule 'the material time' means the time of the alleged offence.

(11) Where—

    (a) the accused is charged on the same occasion with two or more scheduled offences and it appears to the court that they constitute or form part of a series of two or more offences of the same or a similar character; or

    (b) the offence charged consists in incitement to commit two or more scheduled offences,

this section shall have effect as if any reference in it to the value involved were a reference to the aggregate of the values involved.

A4.7 Allocation in the absence of the defendant

An advocate can indicate a plea on a defendant's behalf if that defendant has been removed for unruly behaviour, or the defendant is a company.

Section 17A of the Magistrates' Courts Act 1980 provides:

Magistrates' Courts Act 1980, s 17A

17A Initial procedure: accused to indicate intention as to plea

(1) This section shall have effect where a person who has attained the age of 18 years appears or is brought before a magistrates' court on an information charging him with an offence triable either way.

(2) Everything that the court is required to do under the following provisions of this section must be done with the accused present in court.

(3) The court shall cause the charge to be written down, if this has not already been done, and to be read to the accused.

(4) The court shall then explain to the accused in ordinary language that he may indicate whether (if the offence were to proceed to trial) he would plead guilty or not guilty, and that if he indicates that he would plead guilty—

   (a) the court must proceed as mentioned in subsection (6) below; and

   (b) he may (unless section 17D(2) below were to apply) be committed for sentence to the Crown Court under section 3 or (if applicable) 3A of the Powers of Criminal Courts (Sentencing) Act 2000 if the court is of such opinion as is mentioned in subsection (2) of the applicable section.

(5) The court shall then ask the accused whether (if the offence were to proceed to trial) he would plead guilty or not guilty.

(6) If the accused indicates that he would plead guilty the court shall proceed as if—

   (a) the proceedings constituted from the beginning the summary trial of the information; and

   (b) section 9(1) above was complied with and he pleaded guilty under it.

(7) If the accused indicates that he would plead not guilty section 18(1) below shall apply.

(8) If the accused in fact fails to indicate how he would plead, for the purposes of this section and section 18(1) below he shall be taken to indicate that he would plead not guilty.

(9) Subject to subsection (6) above, the following shall not for any purpose be taken to constitute the taking of a plea—

   (a) asking the accused under this section whether (if the offence were to proceed to trial) he would plead guilty or not guilty;

   (b) an indication by the accused under this section of how he would plead.

(10) If in respect of the offence the court receives a notice under section 51B or 51C of the Crime and Disorder Act 1998 (which relate to serious or complex fraud cases and to certain cases involving children respectively), the preceding provisions of this section and the provisions of section 17B below shall not apply, and the court shall proceed in relation to the offence in accordance with section 51 or, as the case may be, section 51A of that Act.

A4.8 Sentence discount for early indication of plea

In *R v Caley* [2012] EWCA Crim 2821 the court appears to indicate that the same discount will be given for a plea of guiilty in the magistrates' court, followed by a committal for sentence, as for an indication given immediately, or immediately after, the case is sent to the Crown Court.

A4.9 Allocation procedure

The court must hear representations from all parties before considering whether jurisdiction ought to be accepted or declined. In a case with more than one defendant, each defendant has an individual right of election (*R v Wigan Magistrates' Court, ex p Layland* (1995) 160 JP 223). A court can in limited circumstances change its election decision, provided the defendant consents (Magistrates' Courts Act 1980, s 25). A defendant can change from summary trial to sending proceedings only if he can establish that he did not understand the nature and significance of the election decision (*R v Birmingham Justices, ex p Hodgson and another* [1985] 2 WLR 630).

Section 19 of the Magistrates' Courts Act 1980 provides:

Magistrates' Courts Act 1980, s 19(1)–(6)

19 Court to begin by considering which mode of trial appears more suitable

(1) The court shall decide whether the offence appears to it more suitable for summary trial or for trial on indictment.

(2) Before making a decision under this section, the court—

    (a) shall give the prosecution an opportunity to inform the court of the accused's previous convictions (if any); and

    (b) shall give the prosecution and the accused an opportunity to make representations as to whether summary trial or trial on indictment would be more suitable.

(3) In making a decision under this section, the court shall consider—

    (a) whether the sentence which a magistrates' court would have power to impose for the offence would be adequate; and

    (b) any representations made by the prosecution or the accused under subsection (2)(b) above,

and shall have regard to any allocation guidelines (or revised allocation guidelines) issued as definitive guidelines under section 170 of the Criminal Justice Act 2003.

(4) Where—

    (a) the accused is charged with two or more offences; and

    (b) it appears to the court that the charges for the offences could be joined in the same indictment or that the offences arise out of the same or connected circumstances,

subsection (3)(a) above shall have effect as if references to the sentence which a magistrates' court would have power to impose for the offence were a reference to the maximum aggregate sentence which a magistrates' court would have power to impose for all of the offences taken together.

(5) In this section any reference to a previous conviction is a reference to—

    (a) a previous conviction by a court in the United Kingdom; or

    (b) a previous finding of guilt in—

        (i) any proceedings under the Army Act 1955, the Air Force Act 1955 or the Naval Discipline Act 1957 (whether before a court-martial

---

> or any other court or person authorised under any of those Acts to
> award a punishment in respect of any offence); or
>   (ii) any proceedings before a Standing Civilian Court.
> (6) If, in respect of the offence, the court receives a notice under section 51B
> or 51C of the Crime and Disorder Act 1998 (which relate to serious or
> complex fraud cases and to certain cases involving children respectively),
> the preceding provisions of this section and sections 20, 20A and 21 below
> shall not apply, and the court shall proceed in relation to the offence in
> accordance with section 51(1) of that Act.

A4.10 Allocation guidelines

The Sentencing Council has issued a definitive guideline in relation to the allocation of cases between the magistrates' court and
Crown Court.

There is a presumption in favour of summary trial, but generally
speaking the Magistrates' Court Sentencing Guidelines will be used to
determine whether the court's sentencing powers are sufficient. Both
prosecution and defence will make representations; neither is given
priority—the court must balance the representations made.

See *Blackstone's Criminal Practice 2014* **D6**

A5 **Amending Charge**

A5.1 Amendment within the time limit

It should not be thought that prosecutors have an unfettered right to seek to amend charges that are not subject to any limitation of time (ie indictable and indictable only charges). Amendments should be granted only where the application is judged to be proper and appropriate (*R v Redbridge Justices, ex p Whitehouse* (1992) 94 Cr App R 332).

In *Director of Public Prosecutions v Hammerton* [2009] EWHC 921 (Admin), the court applauded a refusal to amend a charge alleging an either way offence to one triable summarily only, when the application had been made on the day that the original offence was due to be committed to the Crown Court for trial. However, with all proceedings being sent to the Crown Court, such opportunities will not exist in the future.

A5.2 Amendment outside the time limit

An amendment outside the time limit, in order to allow the prosecution to proceed with a summary only offence which would otherwise be time-barred, may be permitted, provided that the new offence is based on the 'same misdoing' and that it is in the interests of justice to allow the amendment (*R v Scunthorpe Justices, ex p McPhee and Gallagher* (1998) 162 JP 635, DC).

The following principles emerge from *Scunthorpe Justices*:

- The purpose of the six-month time limit imposed by section 127 of the 1980 Act is to ensure that summary offences are charged and tried as soon as reasonably practicable after their alleged commission.
- Where an information has been laid within the six-month period it can be amended after the expiry of that period.
- An information can be amended after the expiry of the six-month period, even to allege a different offence or different offences, provided that:
  - the different offence or offences allege the 'same misdoing' as the original offence; and
  - the amendment can be made in the interests of justice.

The phrase 'same misdoing' should not be construed too narrowly. It means that the new offence should arise out of the same (or substantially the same) facts as gave rise to the original offence.

A5 Amending Charge

In *Shaw v Director of Public Prosecutions* [2007] EWHC 207 (Admin), the court ruled that an amendment to charge an offence which was based on similar misdoing ought not to have been permitted, as the original offence carried only a financial penalty whereas the new offence carried imprisonment. The court ruled similarly in *R (Crown Prosecution Service) v Everest* [2005] EWHC 1124 (Admin), observing that the new offence carried a higher penalty, had a statutory defence that the defence had to establish, and that the defendant was not legally represented.

The amendment of a charge to substitute failing to provide a specimen of breath with failing to provide a specimen of urine was held to be proper in *Williams v Director of Public Prosecutions* [2009] EWHC 2354 (Admin), although the court did allow the appeal as the alteration had not been made in a timely fashion (applying *Hammerton*—see **A5.1**). In *Crann v CPS* [2013] EWHC 552 (Admin), a very late amendment was allowed as the offence was no more serious and had been anticipated. The imposition of a higher fine (if convicted of the new charge) would not in itself be enough to justify the refusal of an otherwise sound amendment (*R v Newcastle Upon Tyne Justices, ex p Pound-stretcher*, unreported, 2 March 1998).

An out-of-time amendment to allege a different defendant is not permissible (*Sainsbury's Supermarkets Ltd v HM Courts Service* [2006] EWHC 1749 (Admin)).

A6 **Appeals and Reopening**

A6.1 **Appeals**

An appeal against conviction and/or sentence lies as of right to the Crown Court. A notice of appeal must be served within 21 days of final disposal of the case.

It is not the normal practice to grant bail pending an appeal, and there is no statutory right to bail. Where the appeal is against conviction and the defendant was convicted after trial, many courts will look more favourably on bail pending appeal, particularly when the custodial sentence is short. In *R v Imdad Shah* (1980) 144 JP 460, the court rejected an argument that bail should be granted where the sentence was a short one and there was a risk that the sentence would be served prior to the appeal being heard. The court ruled that in such cases an early listing should be sought. By way of contrast, in *R (G) v Inner London Crown Court* [2003] EWHC 2715 (Admin) the applicant successfully judicially reviewed a decision by a Crown Court to refuse bail in a 'short sentence' case.

Section 108 of the Magistrates' Courts Act 1980 provides:

Magistrates' Courts Act 1980, s 108

108 Right of appeal to the Crown Court

(1) A person convicted by a magistrates' court may appeal to the Crown Court—
   (a) if he pleaded guilty, against his sentence;
   (b) if he did not, against the conviction or sentence.

(1A) Section 14 of the Powers of Criminal Courts (Sentencing) Act 2000 (under which a conviction of an offence for which an order for conditional or absolute discharge is made is deemed not to be a conviction except for certain purposes) shall not prevent an appeal under this Act, whether against conviction or otherwise.

(2) A person sentenced by a magistrates' court for an offence in respect of which an order for conditional discharge has been previously made may appeal to the Crown Court against the sentence.

(3) In this section 'sentence' includes any order made on conviction by a magistrates' court, not being—
   (b) an order for the payment of costs;
   (c) an order under section 37(1) of the Animal Welfare Act 2006 (which enables a court to order the destruction of an animal); or
   (d) an order made in pursuance of any enactment under which the court has no discretion as to the making of the order or its terms
   and also includes a declaration of relevance, within the meaning of section 23 of the Football Spectators Act 1989.

---

(4) Subsection (3)(d) above does not prevent an appeal against a surcharge imposed under section 161A of the Criminal Justice Act 2003.

A6.2 Reopening cases

A6.2.1 *Jurisdiction*

Magistrates' Courts Act 1980, s 142

142 Power of magistrates' court to re-open cases to rectify mistakes etc

(1) A magistrates' court may vary or rescind a sentence or other order imposed or made by it when dealing with an offender if it appears to the court to be in the interests of justice to do so, and it is hereby declared that this power extends to replacing a sentence or order which for any reason appears to be invalid by another which the court has power to impose or make.

(1A) The power conferred on a magistrates' court by subsection (1) above shall not be exercisable in relation to any sentence or order imposed or made by it when dealing with an offender if—

    (a) the Crown Court has determined an appeal against—

        (i) that sentence or order;

        (ii) the conviction in respect of which that sentence or order was imposed or made; or

        (iii) any other sentence or order imposed or made by the magistrates' court when dealing with the offender in respect of that conviction (including a sentence or order replaced by that sentence or order); or

    (b) the High Court has determined a case stated for the opinion of that court on any question arising in any proceeding leading to or resulting from the imposition or making of the sentence or order.

(2) Where a person is convicted by a magistrates' court and it subsequently appears to the court that it would be in the interests of justice that the case should be heard again by different justices, the court may so direct.

(2A) The power conferred on a magistrates' court by subsection (2) above shall not be exercisable in relation to a conviction if—

    (a) the Crown Court has determined an appeal against—

        (i) the conviction; or

        (ii) any sentence or order imposed or made by the magistrates' court when dealing with the offender in respect of the conviction; or

    (b) the High Court has determined a case stated for the opinion of that court on any question arising in any proceeding leading to or resulting from the conviction.

(3) Where a court gives a direction under subsection (2) above—

    (a) the conviction and any sentence or other order imposed or made in consequence thereof shall be of no effect; and

    (b) section 10(4) above shall apply as if the trial of the person in question had been adjourned.

(4) [repealed]

(5) Where a sentence or order is varied under subsection (1) above, the sentence or other order, as so varied, shall take effect from the beginning of the day on which it was originally imposed or made, unless the court otherwise directs.

A6.2.2 *Principles*

Section 142 of the Magistrates' Courts Act 1980 relates to criminal proceedings and has no application to other areas of magistrates' court jurisdiction such as liability orders (*Liverpool City Council v Plemora Distribution Ltd* [2002] EWHC 2467 (Admin)) and detention and forfeiture in relation to proceeds of crime. Further, the court enjoys no common law jurisdiction to reopen civil matters such as an anti-social behaviour order (*Samuda v Birmingham Justices* [2008] EWHC 205 (Admin)). Persons made subject to a hospital order under section 37(3) of the Mental Health Act 1983 fall within the definition of 'offender', and a person can use section 142 to reopen a hearing determining the issue under the Mental Health Act (*R (Bartram) v Southend Magistrates' Court* [2004] EWHC 2691 (Admin)). An order to commit an offender to prison for non-satisfaction of a confiscation order made under the Proceeds of Crime Act 2002 in the Crown Court is capable of being reopened.

The court has power to revisit the issue of a warrant following non-payment of fines. A court does not have the power to rescind a costs order made in favour of a defendant who was not convicted as the section related only to orders post-conviction (*Coles v East Penwith Justices* The Times, 27 July 1998).

The nature of the remedy afforded under this Act is akin to a 'slip rule', allowing a court to rectify a clear mistake or injustice. An applicant who entered an unequivocal plea of guilty cannot apply to reopen a plea under this section (*R v Croydon Youth Court, ex p Director of Public Prosecutions* [1997] 2 Cr App R 411), unless the plea was inappropriate and so now equivocal; however, this did not apply where the allegation was of professional impropriety by the defendant's legal representative as this did not fall within the word 'mistake' (*Williamson v City of Westminster Magistrates' Court* [2012] EWHC 1444 (Admin)).

Section 142 should not be used to advance new arguments, neither should it be used as an 'appeal' mechanism against an earlier decision (*Zykin v Crown Prosecution Service* [2009] EWHC 1469 (Admin); *R v Chajed* [2013] EWHC 188 (Admin)). Applications based on a change of law between conviction and application should not be entertained, under normal principles of finality of judgment.

A prosecutor cannot apply to reopen proceedings that have previously been withdrawn (*R (Green and Green Scaffolding Ltd) v Staines Magistrates' Court* (2008) 172 JP 353).

A6.2.3 *Applications*

An application may be made orally or in writing; the applicant does not have to attend the hearing. All parties must be given notice of the application and be heard if they so wish. Section 142(1A) and (2A) of the 1980 Act set out the instances when a remedy under this provision is denied on account of an alternative avenue of appeal having been taken.

There is no statutory time limit on reopening, but the former 28-day rule should act as a salutary guideline. Applications made much beyond this date might properly be refused on interests of justice grounds, as '[d]elay in matters of this sort is always harmful, memories fade, records may be lost and the essence of doing justice is that it should be done expeditiously' (*R v Ealing Magistrates' Court, ex p Sahota* The Times, 9 December 1997). It is not, however, a decisive factor. It is not enough for the magistrates simply to say that the length of time is such that it is no longer proper to open the case under section 142. More substantial reasoning than that has to be given, so that the applicant (and any court on appeal) can understand why it is no longer proper to deal with the matter.

Applications may be made by both defence and prosecution, but the exercise of such discretion in favour of a prosecutor will be rare, and can never extend to the overturning of an acquittal. A prosecutor could properly make an application to reopen where the court had erroneously failed to impose penalty points or some other appropriate order. Similarly, if the court had been unaware of factors relevant to sentence, it could be invited to reopen sentence, even if that meant a risk that it would be increased. However, if it is appropriate for the powers under section 142 to be used to increase sentence then the power must be exercised very speedily (*R (Holme) v Liverpool Magistrates' Court* [2004] EWHC 3131 (Admin), where the court declined to allow the prosecution to exercise the power; advocates facing this type of application should refer to the full judgment).

A defendant who had been convicted in absence can properly attempt to reopen under this section. Culpability on the part of the offender is relevant to whether it is in the interests of justice to reopen, but it is not determinative. It will normally be in the interests of justice for a defendant to be able to defend himself, and unless the evidence indicates that his absence from trial is deliberate and voluntary, a rehearing would normally be the appropriate course (*R (Morsby) v Tower Bridge Magistrates' Court* [2007] EWHC 2766 (Admin)). Any inconvenience to the court in allowing a reopening can never outweigh the interests of justice (*R (Blick) v Doncaster Magistrates' Court* (2008) 172 JP 651).

A6.2.4 *Interests of justice*

Justices are given wide discretion in determining what are relevant factors in relation to interests of justice, but decisions must be based on sound judicial reasoning. A defendant's late arrival at court was held not to be a proper ground, in itself, to refuse a rehearing (*R v Camberwell Green Magistrates' Court, ex p Ibrahim* (1984) 148 JP 400). Factors a court ought to consider include:

• why the convicted person did not appear at the original trial (if that was the case);
• timeliness of the application;
• reason for any delay;
• importance of the decision being questioned—note that the importance to all parties, including defendant, prosecution, and other interested parties (such as victim), should be assessed;
• inconvenience and prejudice caused to opposing parties;
• whether a more appropriate appeal remedy is available. It will not be appropriate to allow a reopening where a defendant is denied a right of appeal due to an unequivocal guilty plea (*R v Croydon Youth Court, ex p Director of Public Prosecutions* [1997] 2 Cr App R 411).

In addition, the court must always consider rule 1 of the Criminal Procedure Rules and the overriding objective.

 See *Blackstone's Criminal Practice 2014* **D29**

A6.2.5 *Effect of reopening*

A conviction will be set aside, as will any sentence or ancillary orders flowing from it. The matter is treated as adjourned for trial. Justices who sat on the original hearing, or the hearing to reopen, cannot sit on the adjourned trial. The prosecution retain the right to offer no evidence and the court lacks power to insist that a prosecutor proceeds with the case (*R (Rhodes-Presley) v South Worcestershire Magistrates' Court* [2008] EWHC 2700 (Admin)).

If a sentence or order is reopened, the court may vary or rescind the original finding and substitute any other lawful sentence or order that would have been available to the court at the original hearing. The new orders take effect from the date of the old order unless the court directs otherwise. A court must be careful not to offend against any legitimate expectation given to the offender (*Jane v Broome* The Times, 2 November 1988).

A6.3 Reopening of guilty plea

> ### Criminal Procedure Rules, r 37.9
>
> *Application to withdraw a guilty plea*
>
> (1) This rule applies where the defendant wants to withdraw a guilty plea.
> (2) The defendant must apply to do so—
>   (a) as soon as practicable after becoming aware of the reasons for doing so; and
>   (b) before sentence.
> (3) Unless the court otherwise directs, the application must be in writing and the defendant must serve it on—
>   (a) the court officer; and
>   (b) the prosecutor.
> (4) The application must—
>   (a) explain why it would be unjust not to allow the defendant to withdraw the guilty plea;
>   (b) identify—
>   (i) any witness that the defendant wants to call, and
>   (ii) any other proposed evidence; and
>   (c) say whether the defendant waives legal professional privilege, giving any relevant name and date.

The following principles emerge from the authorities:

- The fact that the defendant was not legally represented when he entered his guilty plea is not on its own grounds for allowing a change of plea (*R v South Tameside Magistrates' Court, ex p Rowland* [1983] 3 All ER 689).
- A misunderstanding as to the nature of the charge being pleaded to may justify a change of plea (and may well be an equivocal plea in any event) (*P Foster Haulage Ltd v Roberts* [1978] 2 All ER 751).
- Evidence of the previous guilty plea may be adduced at any later trial, although its probative value will generally be so low that a court ought to decline to admit it (*R v Rimmer* [1972] 1 WLR 268).

In *S (An Infant) v Recorder of Manchester* [1971] AC 481, the court held:

- the power to reopen plea was a discretionary one;
- the power ought to be used sparingly;
- the power is available up until sentence has been passed;
- the question for the court is whether justice requires the change of plea to be permitted.

A7 **Bad Character**

A7.1 **Introduction**

The admissibility of bad character is regulated by sections 98–113 of the Criminal Justice Act 2003. The common law rules are now subsidiary to the statutory regime. The Act is concerned with the admission of bad character in relation to:

- the defendant;
- any co-defendant;
- a person other than a defendant in the case.

The Criminal Procedure Rules provide a strict regime for the admission of evidence of bad character. The court has the power to exclude otherwise admissible evidence of bad character on the grounds of non-compliance, if the effect would be to prejudice a party, for example by way of ambush defence (*R v Musone* [2007] EWCA Crim 1237). Provided that there is no prejudice, a court is free to admit evidence of bad character if to do so would satisfy the overriding objective of rule 1 of the Criminal Procedure Rules. Attempts to argue that evidence ought to be admitted following procedural non-compliance only in exceptional cases have been rejected (*R (Robinson) v Sutton Coldfield Magistrates' Court* [2006] EWHC 307 (Admin)). In *Robinson*, the court did say, however, that:

> a court would ordinarily wish to know when the relevant enquiries had been initiated, and in broad terms why they have not been completed within the time allowed. Any application for an extension will be closely scrutinised by the court. A party seeking an extension cannot expect the indulgence of the court unless it clearly sets out the reasons why it is seeking that indulgence.

Rule 35 of the Criminal Procedure Rules 2012 regulates the admission of bad character evidence.

A7.2 **What is bad character?**

The Act defines 'bad character' as the commission of an offence or other 'reprehensible behaviour'. It is important to note the effect of section 98 (see **A7.3**), which has the effect of excluding much bad-character evidence from the statutory scheme, allowing for its admissibility subject only to the normal rules of probity and relevance.

In considering whether or not a party has committed an offence, regard can be had to:

- previous convictions;
- previous police cautions or youth cautions;

- offences for which the person has not been tried;
- offences for which the person has been acquitted (*R v Z* [2000] 2 AC 483) or found unfit to be tried (*R v Renda* [2005] EWCA Crim 2826).

Other examples include telling lies, taking illegal drugs (*R v AJC* [2006] EWCA Crim 284), being sexually promiscuous (*R v Ball* [2005] EWCA Crim 2826), and collecting photographs of people being violently attacked (*R v Saleem* [2007] EWCA Crim 1923).

The Act also covers those with a disposition towards reprehensible conduct, for example an admission that a person is sexually attracted to children (*R v S* [2007] EWCA Crim 1387; but see also *R v Fox* [2009] EWCA Crim 653, where such evidence ought not to be admitted).

It is important to note that a defendant is entitled to dispute that he is guilty of a matter that has resulted in conviction (or caution); the procedure for doing so is discussed in *R v C* [2010] EWCA Crim 2971.

There are some particular considerations at play when admitting police cautions as evidence of bad character. In *R v Olu and others* [2010] EWCA Crim 2975, the court held:

> We accept the submission that there is a very considerable difference not only between a caution and a conviction for the reasons given in the authorities to which we have referred, but there is also a very considerable difference between an admission contained in a caution without legal advice having been given and an admission made in a caution after legal advice or before a court by a plea. In such circumstances, the giving of legal advice or the formality of a court appearance will have made clear to the person the consequences of his admission. The processes that lead to a caution can differ widely between police area and police area; a court would be shutting its eyes to reality if it assumed that, where a person was not legally represented, the consequences of admitting an offence and accepting a caution were fully explained to a person in a manner that he understood the serious adverse consequences that would follow and what he was giving up by not exercising his right to legal advice—namely that what he was admitting would give him a criminal record, that the caution would be maintained on his PNC record for very many years and that it would be used against his interests in certain circumstances.

Penalty notices for disorder cannot, in themselves, be adduced as evidence of bad character (*R v Hamer* [2010] EWCA Crim 2053), neither can unsubstantiated allegations contained in crime reports (*R v Braithwaite* [2010] EWCA Crim 1082).

A7.3 Bad character excluded from application

Section 98 provides:

Criminal Justice Act 2003, s 98

98 'Bad character'

References in this Chapter to evidence of a person's 'bad character' are to evidence of, or of a disposition towards, misconduct on his part, other than evidence which—

(a) has to do with the alleged facts of the offence with which the defendant is charged, or

(b) is evidence of misconduct in connection with the investigation or prosecution of that offence.

At a more obvious level this means that the allegation itself (obviously of misconduct) does not need to be subject to an application to admit bad character. It also covers the following:

- evidence of a previous conviction that might be a component of the offence alleged (eg a conviction for assault against a child in relation to a cruelty charge concerning that same child: *R v R* [2006] EWCA Crim 3196);
- preparatory acts (eg purchase of a murder weapon);
- background evidence (eg an act that provided motive for the offence: *R v Saleem* [2007] EWCA Crim 1923 and *R v McNeill* [2007] EWCA Crim 2927);
- a temporal connection is not essential for the evidence to be 'to do' with the offence if it goes to provide the motive, but it is otherwise if it is being used as evidence of propensity (*R v Sule* [2012] EWCA Crim 1130).

A7.4 Non-defendant's bad character

Section 100 provides:

Criminal Justice Act 2003, s 100

100 Non-defendant's bad character

(1) In criminal proceedings evidence of the bad character of a person other than the defendant is admissible if and only if—

(a) it is important explanatory evidence,

(b) it has substantial probative value in relation to a matter which—

(i) is a matter in issue in the proceedings, and

(ii) is of substantial importance in the context of the case as a whole, or

(c) all parties to the proceedings agree to the evidence being admissible.

(2) For the purposes of subsection (1)(a) evidence is important explanatory evidence if—

    (a) without it, the court or jury would find it impossible or difficult properly to understand other evidence in the case, and

    (b) its value for understanding the case as a whole is substantial.

(3) In assessing the probative value of evidence for the purposes of subsection (1)(b) the court must have regard to the following factors (and to any others it considers relevant)—

    (a) the nature and number of the events, or other things, to which the evidence relates;

    (b) when those events or things are alleged to have happened or existed;

    (c) where—

        (i) the evidence is evidence of a person's misconduct, and

        (ii) it is suggested that the evidence has probative value by reason of similarity between that misconduct and other alleged misconduct,

    the nature and extent of the similarities and the dissimilarities between each of the alleged instances of misconduct;

    (d) where—

        (i) the evidence is evidence of a person's misconduct,

        (ii) it is suggested that that person is also responsible for the misconduct charged, and

        (iii) the identity of the person responsible for the misconduct charged is disputed,

    the extent to which the evidence shows or tends to show that the same person was responsible each time.

(4) Except where subsection (1)(c) applies, evidence of the bad character of a person other than the defendant must not be given without leave of the court.

A7.5 Defendant's bad character

Section 101 provides:

Criminal Justice Act 2003, s 101

101 Defendant's bad character

(1) In criminal proceedings evidence of the defendant's bad character is admissible if, but only if—

    (a) all parties to the proceedings agree to the evidence being admissible,

    (b) the evidence is adduced by the defendant himself or is given in answer to a question asked by him in cross-examination and intended to elicit it,

    (c) it is important explanatory evidence,

    (d) it is relevant to an important matter in issue between the defendant and the prosecution,

    (e) it has substantial probative value in relation to an important matter in issue between the defendant and a co-defendant,

    (f) it is evidence to correct a false impression given by the defendant, or

    (g) the defendant has made an attack on another person's character.

(2) Sections 102 to 106 contain provision supplementing subsection (1).
(3) The court must not admit evidence under subsection (1)(d) or (g) if, on an application by the defendant to exclude it, it appears to the court that the admission of the evidence would have such an adverse effect on the fairness of the proceedings that the court ought not to admit it.
(4) On an application to exclude evidence under subsection (3) the court must have regard, in particular, to the length of time between the matters to which that evidence relates and the matters which form the subject of the offence charged. . .

A7.6 Important explanatory evidence

Section 102 provides:

Criminal Justice Act 2003, s 102

102 'Important explanatory evidence'

For the purposes of section 101(1)(c) evidence is important explanatory evidence if—
(a) without it, the court or jury would find it impossible or difficult properly to understand other evidence in the case, and
(b) its value for understanding the case as a whole is substantial.

A case which is truly one of propensity cannot and must not be dressed up as a case of important explanatory evidence. To say the evidence fills out the picture is not the same as saying that the rest of the picture is either impossible or difficult to see without it (*R v Lee* [2012] EWCA Crim 316).

A7.7 Matter in issue between defendant and prosecution

Section 103 provides:

Criminal Justice Act 2003, s 103

103 Matter in issue between the defendant and the prosecution

(1) For the purposes of section 101(1)(d) the matters in issue between the defendant and the prosecution include—
(a) the question whether the defendant has a propensity to commit offences of the kind with which he is charged, except where his having such a propensity makes it no more likely that he is guilty of the offence;
(b) the question whether the defendant has a propensity to be untruthful, except where it is not suggested that the defendant's case is untruthful in any respect.

(2) Where subsection (1)(a) applies, a defendant's propensity to commit offences of the kind with which he is charged may (without prejudice to any other way of doing so) be established by evidence that he has been convicted of—
   (a) an offence of the same description as the one with which he is charged, or
   (b) an offence of the same category as the one with which he is charged.
(3) Subsection (2) does not apply in the case of a particular defendant if the court is satisfied, by reason of the length of time since the conviction or for any other reason, that it would be unjust for it to apply in his case.
(4) For the purposes of subsection (2)—
   (a) two offences are of the same description as each other if the statement of the offence in a written charge or indictment would, in each case, be in the same terms;
   (b) two offences are of the same category as each other if they belong to the same category of offences prescribed for the purposes of this section by an order made by the Secretary of State.
(5) A category prescribed by an order under subsection (4)(b) must consist of offences of the same type.
(6) Only prosecution evidence is admissible under section 101(1)(d).

A7.8 Matter in issue between the defendant and a co-defendant

Section 104 provides:

Criminal Justice Act 2003, s 104

104 'Matter in issue between the defendant and a co-defendant'

(1) Evidence which is relevant to the question whether the defendant has a propensity to be untruthful is admissible on that basis under section 101(1) only if the nature or conduct of his defence is such as to undermine the co-defendant's defence.
(2) Only evidence—
   (a) which is to be (or has been) adduced by the co-defendant, or
   (b) which a witness is to be invited to give (or has given) in cross-examination by the co-defendant, is admissible under section 101(1)(e).

A7.9 Evidence to correct a false impression

Section 105 provides:

Criminal Justice Act 2003, s 105

105 'Evidence to correct a false impression'
(1) For the purposes of section 101(1)(f)—

(a) the defendant gives a false impression if he is responsible for the making of an express or implied assertion which is apt to give the court or jury a false or misleading impression about the defendant;

(b) evidence to correct such an impression is evidence which has probative value in correcting it.

(2) A defendant is treated as being responsible for the making of an assertion if—

    (a) the assertion is made by the defendant in the proceedings (whether or not in evidence given by him),

    (b) the assertion was made by the defendant—

        (i) on being questioned under caution, before charge, about the offence with which he is charged, or

        (ii) on being charged with the offence or officially informed that he might be prosecuted for it,

    and evidence of the assertion is given in the proceedings,

    (c) the assertion is made by a witness called by the defendant,

    (d) the assertion is made by any witness in cross-examination in response to a question asked by the defendant that is intended to elicit it, or is likely to do so, or

    (e) the assertion was made by any person out of court, and the defendant adduces evidence of it in the proceedings.

(3) A defendant who would otherwise be treated as responsible for the making of an assertion shall not be so treated if, or to the extent that, he withdraws it or disassociates himself from it.

(4) Where it appears to the court that a defendant, by means of his conduct (other than the giving of evidence) in the proceedings, is seeking to give the court or jury an impression about himself that is false or misleading, the court may if it appears just to do so treat the defendant as being responsible for the making of an assertion which is apt to give that impression.

(5) In subsection (4) 'conduct' includes appearance or dress.

(6) Evidence is admissible under section 101(1)(f) only if it goes no further than is necessary to correct the false impression.

(7) Only prosecution evidence is admissible under section 101(1)(f).

A7.10 Attack on another person's character

Section 106 provides:

Criminal Justice Act 2003, s 106

106 'Attack on another person's character'

(1) For the purposes of section 101(1)(g) a defendant makes an attack on another person's character if—

    (a) he adduces evidence attacking the other person's character,

    (b) he (or any legal representative appointed under section 38(4) of the Youth Justice and Criminal Evidence Act 1999 (c. 23) to cross-examine a witness in his interests) asks questions in cross-examination that are intended to elicit such evidence, or are likely to do so, or

   (c) evidence is given of an imputation about the other person made by the defendant—

     (i) on being questioned under caution, before charge, about the offence with which he is charged, or

     (ii) on being charged with the offence or officially informed that he might be prosecuted for it.

(2) In subsection (1) 'evidence attacking the other person's character' means evidence to the effect that the other person—

   (a) has committed an offence (whether a different offence from the one with which the defendant is charged or the same one), or

   (b) has behaved, or is disposed to behave, in a reprehensible way;

and 'imputation about the other person' means an assertion to that effect.

(3) Only prosecution evidence is admissible under section 101(1)(g).

 See *Blackstone's Criminal Practice 2014* **F12**

A8 **Bail**

A8.1 **Introduction**

The starting point is that there is a presumption in favour of bail (often described as a right to bail) being granted in criminal proceedings (see **A8.2** for the position in relation to defendants charged with murder appearing before a magistrates' court). The exceptions to that right under Schedule 1 to the Bail Act 1976 are summarized below:

Exception	Imprisonable— Pt I	Imprisonable— Pt IA triable only summarily	Non-imprisonable— Pt II
Fail to answer bail	Yes, but where there is a real likelihood of custody (para 2(1)(a))	Previously failed to answer bail in criminal proceedings and consequently court believes will fail to answer if bailed now, but only where real likelihood of custody (para 2)	Previously failed to answer bail in criminal proceedings and consequently court believes will fail to answer bail now (para 2)
Offend whilst on bail	Yes, but where real likelihood of custody (para 2(1)(b))	On bail at the date of the offence and consequently court believes would commit an offence on bail, but only if a real likelihood of custody (para 3)	NA
Interfere with witnesses or obstruct course of justice	Yes, but where real likelihood of custody (para 2(1)(c))	NA	NA
Substantial grounds for believing that if released on bail would commit an offence likely to cause physical or mental injury to an associated person, or cause an associated person to fear physical or mental injury	Yes (para 2ZA)	Yes (para 4)	NA

A8 Bail

Exception	Imprisonable— Pt I	Imprisonable— Pt IA triable only summarily	Non-imprisonable— Pt II
Arrested for breach of bail in same proceedings and substantial grounds to believe would fail to appear, commit offences, or interfere with witnesses or obstruct the course of justice	Yes, but must be a real likelihood of custody; if offence carries a life term the court may not grant bail unless satisfied there is no significant risk of failure to appear (para 6)	Yes, but must be real likelihood of custody (para 7)	Yes, including committing the offence by engaging in conduct likely to cause physical or mental injury to an associated person (paras 5 and 6)
Indictable or either way offence and defendant on bail at the time of the offence	Yes, but note that if the offence carries a life term the court may not grant bail unless it is satisfied that there is no significant risk of an offence on bail. Must be a real likelihood of custody (para 2A)	NA	NA
Own protection or welfare	Yes (para 3)	Yes (para 5)	Yes (para 3)
Serving sentence	Yes (para 4)	Yes (para 6)	Yes (para 4)
Insufficient information	Yes (para 5)	Yes (para 8)	NA
Reports	Yes (para 7)	NA	NA
Drugs scheme	Yes (para 6A)	Yes (para 9)	NA
Homicide or rape	No bail unless exceptional circumstances justified if charged or convicted of a CJPOA 1994, s 25 offence and previous convictions for a s 25 offence	NA	NA
Murder	Not in the magistrates' court	NA	NA

A8.1.1 *General exceptions*

That presumption does not apply in the following cases:

- in extradition proceedings where the person is alleged to have been convicted of the offence or in connection with a warrant issued in the Republic of Ireland;
- following committal to the Crown Court for sentence or for breach of a Crown Court order;
- after conviction, unless the proceedings are adjourned for inquiries to be made or a report to be prepared for sentence;
- on appeal against conviction or sentence.

Where a defendant aged 18 or over has tested positive for heroin, cocaine, or crack cocaine, and is unwilling to undergo an assessment into his drug misuse and/or any proposed follow-up treatment, different rules apply. The defendant cannot be granted bail unless the court is satisfied that there is no significant risk of an offence being committed on bail.

Schedule 1, paragraph 6A to the Bail Act 1976 provides:

Bail Act 1976, Sch 1, paras 6A, 6B, and 6C

6A Subject to paragraph 6C below, a defendant who falls within paragraph 6B below may not be granted bail unless the court is satisfied that there is no significant risk of his committing an offence while on bail (whether subject to conditions or not).

6B (1) A defendant falls within this paragraph if—

(a) he is aged 18 or over;

(b) a sample taken—

(i) under section 63B of the Police and Criminal Evidence Act 1984 (testing for presence of Class A drugs) in connection with the offence; or

(ii) under section 161 of the Criminal Justice Act 2003 (drug testing after conviction of an offence but before sentence),

has revealed the presence in his body of a specified Class A drug;

(c) either the offence is one under section 5(2) or (3) of the Misuse of Drugs Act 1971 and relates to a specified Class A drug, or the court is satisfied that there are substantial grounds for believing—

(i) that misuse by him of any specified Class A drug caused or contributed to the offence; or

(ii) (even if it did not) that the offence was motivated wholly or partly by his intended misuse of such a drug; and

(d) the condition set out in sub-paragraph (2) below is satisfied or (if the court is considering on a second or subsequent occasion whether or not to grant bail) has been, and continues to be, satisfied.

---

(2) The condition referred to is that after the taking and analysis of the sample—

   (a) a relevant assessment has been offered to the defendant but he does not agree to undergo it; or

   (b) he has undergone a relevant assessment, and relevant follow-up has been proposed to him, but he does not agree to participate in it.

(3) In this paragraph and paragraph 6C below—

   (a) 'Class A drug' and 'misuse' have the same meaning as in the Misuse of Drugs Act 1971;

   (b) 'relevant assessment' and 'relevant follow-up' have the meaning given by section 3(6E) of this Act;

   (c) 'specified' (in relation to a Class A drug) has the same meaning as in Part 3 of the Criminal Justice and Court Services Act 2000.

6C Paragraph 6A above does not apply unless—

   (a) the court has been notified by the Secretary of State that arrangements for conducting a relevant assessment or, as the case may be, providing relevant follow-up have been made for the local justice area in which it appears to the court that the defendant would reside if granted bail; and

   (b) the notice has not been withdrawn.

Bail may be granted only in exceptional circumstances where a defendant is charged with or convicted of an offence of:

- murder, or
- attempted murder, or
- manslaughter, or
- rape, or
- attempted rape,

and the defendant has been previously convicted in the United Kingdom of any such offence or of culpable homicide. (If the previous conviction was manslaughter or culpable homicide, the provision applies only if the defendant received a sentence of imprisonment/long-term detention.) Convictions in EU Member States can be taken into account.

Bail need not be granted to a person on bail at the time of committing an indictable offence (Bail Act 1976, Sch 1, para 2A).

Sections 14 and 15 of the Criminal Justice Act 2003 are partially in force and currently apply *only* to those charged with offences carrying life imprisonment. Offences carrying life imperisonment appear in **Appendix 3** to this book.

Criminal Justice Act 2003, s 14

14 Offences committed on bail

(1) For paragraph 2A of Part 1 of Schedule 1 to the 1976 Act (defendant need not be granted bail where he was on bail on date of offence) there is substituted—

'2A(1) If the defendant falls within this paragraph he may not be granted bail unless the court is satisfied that there is no significant risk of his committing an offence while on bail (whether subject to conditions or not).

(2) The defendant falls within this paragraph if—
(a) he is aged 18 or over, and
(b) it appears to the court that he was on bail in criminal proceedings on the date of the offence.'

(2) After paragraph 9 of that Part there is inserted—

'9AA(1) This paragraph applies if—
(a) the defendant is a child or young person, and
(b) it appears to the court that he was on bail in criminal proceedings on the date of the offence.

(2) In deciding for the purposes of paragraph 2(1) of this Part of this Schedule whether it is satisfied that there are substantial grounds for believing that the defendant, if released on bail (whether subject to conditions or not), would commit an offence while on bail, the court shall give particular weight to the fact that the defendant was on bail in criminal proceedings on the date of the offence.'

Criminal Justice Act 2003, s 15(1) and (2)

15 Absconding by persons released on bail

(1) For paragraph 6 of Part 1 of Schedule 1 to the 1976 Act (defendant need not be granted bail if having been released on bail he has been arrested in pursuance of section 7) there is substituted—

'6(1) If the defendant falls within this paragraph, he may not be granted bail unless the court is satisfied that there is no significant risk that, if released on bail (whether subject to conditions or not), he would fail to surrender to custody.

(2) Subject to sub-paragraph (3) below, the defendant falls within this paragraph if—
(a) he is aged 18 or over, and
(b) it appears to the court that, having been released on bail in or in connection with the proceedings for the offence, he failed to surrender to custody.

(3) Where it appears to the court that the defendant had reasonable cause for his failure to surrender to custody, he does not fall within this paragraph unless it also appears to the court that he failed to surrender to custody at the appointed place as soon as reasonably practicable after the appointed time.

> (4) For the purposes of sub-paragraph (3) above, a failure to give to the defendant a copy of the record of the decision to grant him bail shall not constitute a reasonable cause for his failure to surrender to custody.'
>
> (2) After paragraph 9AA of that Part (inserted by section 14(2)) there is inserted—
>
> > '9AB(1) Subject to sub-paragraph (2) below, this paragraph applies if—
> >
> > > (a) the defendant is a child or young person, and
> > >
> > > (b) it appears to the court that, having been released on bail in or in connection with the proceedings for the offence, he failed to surrender to custody
> >
> > (2) Where it appears to the court that the defendant had reasonable cause for his failure to surrender to custody, this paragraph does not apply unless it also appears to the court that he failed to surrender to custody at the appointed place as soon as reasonably practicable after the appointed time.
> >
> > (3) In deciding for the purposes of paragraph 2(1) of this Part of this Schedule whether it is satisfied that there are substantial grounds for believing that the defendant, if released on bail (whether subject to conditions or not), would fail to surrender to custody, the court shall give particular weight to—
> >
> > > (a) where the defendant did not have reasonable cause for his failure to surrender to custody, the fact that he failed to surrender to custody, or
> > >
> > > (b) where he did have reasonable cause for his failure to surrender to custody, the fact that he failed to surrender to custody at the appointed place as soon as reasonably practicable after the appointed time.
> >
> > (4) For the purposes of this paragraph, a failure to give to the defendant a copy of the record of the decision to grant him bail shall not constitute a reasonable cause for his failure to surrender to custody.'

A8.2 Right to apply for bail

An application for bail may be made at the first hearing of the case before a magistrates' court, save in respect of a defendant facing a charge of murder (or murder and any other charge(s)), in which case the issue of bail must be resolved before a Crown Court judge within 48 hours (excluding public holidays) beginning the day after the defendant's appearance in the magistrates' court (Coroners and Justice Act 2009, s 115). If bail is refused, an application may be made at the subsequent hearing, and may be based on the same grounds as the first. A refusal of bail on the grounds of insufficient information should not be counted as a decision to refuse bail, thereby exhausting one of the two attempts (*R v Calderdale Justices, ex p Kenedy* The Times, 18 February 1992). Similarly, a remand in absence should be discounted (*R v Dover and East Kent Justices, ex p Dean* The Times, 22 August 1991).

Note, however, that if a fully-argued application is not made by the defendant at the first hearing, the effect is that one opportunity to argue for bail is lost, meaning that if bail is refused at the subsequent hearing, the two opportunities for bail are spent. Similarly, if an argument is made at the first hearing but not at the second hearing, there is no right to a second application for bail at the third hearing. Advocates should always obtain certificates of full argument in order to support any further Crown Court bail application (Bail Act 1976, s 5(6A)).

Following two refusals to grant bail, further applications may be made if there are new arguments as to fact or law (Bail Act 1976, Sch 1, Pt IIA). This includes but is not limited to a change in circumstances, for example:

- change in the case alleged against the defendant (*R v Reading Crown Court, ex p Malik* [1981] QB 451 and *R v Slough Justices, ex p Duncan* [1981] QB 451);
- increased surety (*R v Isleworth Crown Court, ex p Commissioners of Customs and Excise* The Times, 27 July 1990);
- passage of time (*Neumeister v Austria (No 1)* (1979–80) 1 EHRR 91).

In *R (B) v Brent Youth Court* [2010] EWHC 1893 (Admin), the court held that a change of address presented for residence purposes amounted to a change of circumstances. It was not necessary that any new factor be exceptional in nature. The correct test is whether there are any new considerations which were not before the court when the accused was last remanded in custody. Similarly, an argument that the prosecution case against the defendant was significantly weaker than at first presented would qualify as a new argument. The court ended by saying that:

> even if the Bench had been entitled to form the view that each and every argument as to fact or law was an argument which it had heard previously, it manifestly failed to go on to consider whether, notwithstanding that, it should nonetheless consider substantively a bail application, given the provisions of Section 44 [Children and Young Persons Act 1933], having regard to the welfare of a child or young person.

A8.3 Grounds for refusing bail

The seriousness of the offence (and the likely penalty) cannot of itself justify a refusal of bail on the inference that the person is likely to abscond (*Lettelier v France* (1992) 14 EHRR 83), although a judge is perfectly entitled to regard that as a significant factor (*R (Thompson) v Central Criminal Court* [2005] EWHC 2345 (Admin)). Before bail can be refused on the grounds of interfering with witnesses or obstructing justice, the prosecution must point to an identifiable risk and provide supporting evidence (*Clooth v Belgium* (1991) 14 EHRR 717). The court should not take the prosecution case at its highest, but rather follow the statute and consider the strength overall of the prosecution evidence (*R (E) v Wood Green Crown Court* [2013] EWHC 1869 (Admin)).

In deciding whether to refuse bail the relevant considerations include (Bail Act 1976, Sch 1, para 9):

- the nature and seriousness of the offence or default (and the probable method of dealing with the defendant for it);
- the character, antecedents, associations, and community ties of the defendant;
- the defendant's record as respects the fulfilment of his obligations under previous grants of bail in criminal proceedings;
- except in the case of a defendant whose case is adjourned for inquiries or a report, the strength of the evidence of his having committed the offence or having defaulted, as well as to any other considerations which appear to be relevant.

Section 114 of the Coroners and Justice Act 2009 amends the Bail Act 1976 with the following consequences (although in practice they add very little):

- If the defendant is charged with murder, the defendant may not be granted bail unless the court is of the opinion that there is no significant risk of the defendant committing, while on bail, an offence that would, or would be likely to, cause physical or mental injury to any person other than the defendant.
- If the defendant faces an imprisonable offence and the court is satisfied that there are substantial grounds for believing that the defendant, if released on bail (whether subject to conditions or not), would commit an offence while on bail, it is a relevant consideration that there is a risk that the defendant may do so by engaging in conduct that would, or would be likely to, cause physical or mental injury to any person other than the defendant.

A8.3.1 *Classifying the offence*

There are three categories of offences to consider:

- indictable imprisonable offences (Sch 1, Pt 1);
- summary only imprisonable offences (which includes offences triable summarily only due to the value of the offence, eg criminal damage) (Sch 1, Pt 1A); and
- summary only non-imprisonable offences (Sch 1, Pt II).

A8.4 Indictable imprisonable offences

Bail cannot be refused if there is no real prospect that the defendant will be sentenced to a custodial sentence in the proceedings.

A court may refuse bail on the grounds:

- that the defendant is already a serving prisoner (para 4 remand); or
- that there is insufficient information on which to base a decision (para 5 remand).

Refusal of bail can be based upon the defendant's own protection or, for a defendant under 18 years of age, his own welfare (para 3 remand).

Bail may be refused if there are substantial grounds for believing that, if released on bail, the defendant would:

- fail to surrender;
- commit further offences;
- commit an offence on bail by engaging in conduct that would or would be likely to cause physical or mental injury to an associated person, or an associated person would fear physical or mental injury. Under section 62 of the Family Law Act 1996, 'associated person' includes:
  - those who are or have been married to each other or in a civil partnership,
  - present or former cohabitants,
  - those who live or have lived in the same household other than as employees, tenants, or lodgers,
  - relatives,
  - those who are or have been engaged to marry or enter into a civil partnership,
  - those who have or have had intimate personal relationships of significant duration,
  - the parents of children and those with parental responsibility,
  - parties to the same family proceedings; or
- interfere with witnesses or otherwise obstruct the course of justice.

Bail may also be refused if the offender was:

- on bail at the time of the offence;
- arrested for breach of bail in the same proceedings and there are substantial grounds to believe he would fail to appear, commit offences, or interfere with witnesses or obstruct the course of justice.

A8.5 Summary only imprisonable offences

Bail cannot be refused if there is no real prospect that the defendant will be sentenced to a custodial sentence in the proceedings.

Bail can be refused on one or more of the following grounds only:

- failure to surrender (if the defendant has previously failed to surrender);
- commission of further offences (if the instant offence was committed on bail);
- fear of commission of offences likely to cause an associated person to suffer or fear physical or mental injury;
- the defendant's own protection (for his own welfare if aged under 18);
- the defendant is serving custody;
- fear of failure to surrender, commission of offences, interference with witnesses, or obstruction of justice (if the defendant has been arrested for breach of bail in respect of the instant offence); and
- lack of sufficient information.

A8.6 Summary only non-imprisonable offences (Sch 1, Pt II)

Bail can be denied only if there has been a previous failure to surrender in the proceedings and the court believes that if granted bail he would fail to surrender again, or:

- for the defendant's own protection (for his own welfare if aged under 18);
- where the defendant is already in custody;
- following a breach of bail, or the defendant absconding, there are substantial grounds for believing that if released on bail the defendant would:
  - fail to surrender,
  - commit further offences, or
  - interfere with witnesses or otherwise obstruct the course of justice.

A8.7 Conditional bail

Conditional bail may be imposed if the court believes there to be a risk that:

- the defendant will fail to surrender;
- the defendant will commit an offence while on bail;
- the defendant would interfere with witnesses or obstruct justice;
- the defendant would not cooperate with the making of pre-sentence or other reports; or
- the defendant would not attend appointments with his legal adviser.

A person granted bail on a charge of murder must be required to undergo a psychiatric examination (Bail Act 1976, s 3(6A)).

A8.8 Electronic monitoring

Section 3AB of the Bail Act 1976 deals with electronic monitoring for adults; and section 3AC is applicable to all defendants.

Bail Act 1976, ss 3AB and 3AC(1) and (2)

3AB Conditions for the imposition of electronic monitoring requirements: other persons

(1) A court may not impose electronic monitoring requirements on a person who has attained the age of eighteen unless each of the following conditions is met.

(2) The first condition is that the court is satisfied that without the electronic monitoring requirements the person would not be granted bail.

(3) The second condition is that the court is satisfied that the necessary provision for dealing with the person concerned can be made under arrangements for the electronic monitoring of persons released on bail that are currently available in each local justice area which is a relevant area.

3AC Electronic monitoring: general provisions

(1) Where a court imposes electronic monitoring requirements as a condition of bail, the requirements must include provision for making a person responsible for the monitoring.

(2) A person may not be made responsible for the electronic monitoring of a person on bail unless he is of a description specified in an order made by the Secretary of State.

A8.9 Prosecution appeals against the grant of bail

The Bail (Amendment) Act 1993 allows a prosecutor to appeal the grant of bail in any case where the offence is imprisonable. The prosecution must have objected to bail, and following the grant of bail, must orally in court state their intention to appeal the decision. A written notice must be served on both the court and defendant within two hours of the oral notice having been given. A delay of five minutes in giving an oral indication to the court (and after the defendant had been taken from the courtroom) was deemed to comply with the Act in *R v Isleworth Crown Court, ex p Clarke* [1998] 1 Cr App R 257. In *R (Jeffrey) v Crown Court at Warwick* [2003] Crim LR 190, a written notice was served three minutes late due to no fault on the part of the prosecutor. A challenge to the validity of that service failed and the court suggested that section 1(7) of the Act should have read into it the following words:

unless such failure was caused by circumstances outside the control of the prosecution and not due to any fault on its part.

Service of the written notice on a jailer who hands the notice to a defendant suffices, and solicitors who accept such notices do so on the implicit understanding that they will be immediately communicated to the defendant.

A8.10 Breach of bail

Following an alleged breach of bail, the defendant must be brought before a magistrates' court within 24 hours of arrest. This means that the hearing must commence at court within those 24 hours, and any delay must result in the defendant's automatic release from custody (*R v Governor of Glen Parva Young Offender Institution, ex p G (A Minor)* [1998] 2 Cr App R 349). A court can, however, bring a defendant into the dock and then adjourn the hearing until later in the court list (*R (Hussein) v Derby Magistrates' Court* [2001] 1 WLR 254). A magistrates' court has no power simply to commit an offender to the Crown Court in order for the breach to be decided (*R v Teeside Magistrates' Court, ex p Ellison* (2001) 165 JP 355).

Only one magistrate need deal with an alleged bail breach, and there is no requirement for formal evidence to be called by prosecution or defence. There is no defence of 'reasonable excuse' in relation to the breaking of bail conditions (*R (Vickers) v West London Magistrates' Court* [2004] Crim LR 63), although the reasons for breach would be relevant to the determination of whether or not to grant bail again.

In *R v Liverpool Justices, ex p Director of Public Prosecutions* (1992) 95 Cr App R 222, the court laid down the following guidance for a court to follow when considering bail breaches:

- strict rules of evidence did not apply and hearsay was admissible;
- the court must consider the type of evidence called and take account of the fact that there had been no cross-examination;
- the prosecution and defence can call witnesses if they so wish, and the other party has the right to cross-examine;
- the defendant has a right to give oral evidence.

In practice a statement will be read to the court. It follows as a result of the above that no issue in relation to hearsay arises (*R (Thomas) v Greenwich Magistrates' Court* [2009] EWHC 1180 (Admin)).

If the breach is not proved, the defendant must be released on the same conditions as existed previously. If the breach is proved, that does not mean an automatic remand into custody; *R (DPP) v Havering*

Magistrates' Court [2001] 1 WLR 805 confirms that it is simply a factor to be considered when the court decides whether or not it should re-bail the defendant.

A8.11 Criminal Procedure Rules applicable to the grant of bail

Part 19 of the Criminal Procedure Rules 2012 applies to bail.

A8.12 Provision of bail for youths

The rules relating to the provision of bail for youths are discussed in **B2**.

A8.13 Appeals in relation to bail

A8.13.1 *Appeal against conditional bail*

If a defendant is dissatisfied with the conditions of bail he may appeal to the Crown Court, provided that he has first applied to a magistrates' court to vary those conditions and has been unsuccessful. An appeal lies only in relation to the following conditions:

- residence (but not in relation to any bail hostel);
- surety or security;
- curfew;
- non-contact.

In other circumstances it may be necessary to apply for a judicial review.

A8.13.2 *Appeal against refusal of bail*

Following full argument in the magistrates' court (and a certificate of full argument having been issued) an appeal lies as of right to the Crown Court.

There is no longer any appeal route to the High Court, save in an exceptional case by way of judicial review.

 See *Blackstone's Criminal Practice 2014* **D7**

A9 **Binding Rulings**

Section 8B of the Magistrates' Courts Act 1980 allows a magistrates' court to make binding rulings. Section 8B provides:

Magistrates' Courts Act 1980, s 8B

8B Effect of rulings at pre-trial hearing

(1) Subject to subsections (3) and (6), a ruling under section 8A has binding effect from the time it is made until the case against the accused or, if there is more than one, against each of them, is disposed of.

(2) The case against an accused is disposed of if—
    (a) he is acquitted or convicted,
    (b) the prosecutor decides not to proceed with the case against him, or
    (c) the information is dismissed.

(3) A magistrates' court may discharge or vary (or further vary) a ruling under section 8A if—
    (a) the condition in section 8A(5) is met,
    (b) the court has given the parties an opportunity to be heard, and
    (c) it appears to the court that it is in the interests of justice to do so.

(4) The court may act under subsection (3)—
    (a) on an application by a party to the case, or
    (b) of its own motion.

(5) No application may be made under subsection (4)(a) unless there has been a material change of circumstances since the ruling was made or, if a previous application has been made, since the application (or last application) was made.

(6) A ruling under section 8A is discharged in relation to an accused if—
    (a) the magistrates' court commits or sends him to the Crown Court for trial for the offence charged in the information, or
    (b) a count charging him with the offence is included in an indictment by virtue of section 40 of the Criminal Justice Act 1988.

Because of the binding nature of these rulings, it is not open to a later bench simply to reverse the ruling because it would have reached a different conclusion.

In *Brett v Director of Public Prosecutions* [2009] EWHC 440 (Admin), the court took a far less restrictive approach than that taken in previous cases in holding a judge to have erred in feeling that he was bound by a previous ruling under section 8A of the Magistrates' Courts Act 1980. What is certainly clear from pre- and post-section 8A case law, is that a later court cannot simply annul a previous decision on the sole ground that it simply disagrees with it (*Crown Prosecution Service v Gloucester Justices and Loveridge* [2008] EWHC 1488 (Admin)). In *R (Jones) v South East Surrey Local Justice Area* [2010] EWHC 916

(Admin), the court, having previously disallowed a prosecution application to adjourn, later granted it due to the fact that the information presented on the renewed application was different and that it was in the interests of justice that the previous ruling be reversed.

Where the court acts of its own motion to vary a previous ruling, the grounds for discharge or variation are simply the interests of justice; and where an application is made by a party, there is an additional requirement for proof of material change of circumstances (*Crown Prosecution Service v Gloucester Justices and Alan Loveridge* [2008] EWHC 1488 (Admin)).

 See *Blackstone's Criminal Practice 2014* **D21**

A10 **Case Management**

A10.1 **Overview**

All parties are expected to manage cases proactively through the system. Courts take on a supervisory responsibility to ensure that justice is achieved in a cost-effective way. The most notable impact has been in relation to so-called 'ambush defences' and the widely held view among criminal lawyers that there is no duty to declare their hand in advance. That notion has been exploded through a number of cases (see **A10.5**), and all advocates can now expect robust challenges to that type of practice. However, a strong defendant, aware of the risks, is still able to put the Crown to proof.

For information on the completion of the case management form and standard time limits, see **Appendix 1**.

A10.2 **Application of the rules to civil proceedings**

The Criminal Procedure Rules have no application in relation to civil procedure in the magistrates' court, and the Civil Procedure Rules do not apply either.

Rule 3A of the Magistrates' Courts Rules 1981 (as inserted by SI 2009/3362) provides the court with case management powers identical to those enjoyed in relation to criminal cases.

A10.3 **The overriding objective and case management**

Rules 1 and 3 deal with the overriding objective and case management powers. Extracts from rules 1 and 3 are reproduced in **Appendix 2**.

A10.4 **Defence witnesses—notification of intention to call**

Section 6C of the Criminal Procedure and Investigations Act 1996 imposes duties on a defendant proposing to call defence witnesses at trial. Failure to comply is most likely to result in an adjournment and wasted costs, so solicitors should ensure that they have taken all reasonable steps to ensure that a defendant is made aware of his obligations to provide such information. It is likely that the prosecution will take advantage of any information supplied and supply it to the police, resulting in witness statements being produced. A code of practice governing this is available at <http://www.legislation.gov.uk/ukpga/1996/25/pdfs/ukpgacop_19960025_en.pdf>.

A10.4.1 *Duty to provide details and keep disclosure under review*

Within 14 days of the prosecutor's complying with initial disclosure:

Criminal Procedure and Investigations Act 1996, s 6C

6C Notification of intention to call defence witnesses

(1) The accused must give to the court and the prosecutor a notice indicating whether he intends to call any persons (other than himself) as witnesses at his trial and, if so—

   (a) giving the name, address and date of birth of each such proposed witness, or as many of those details as are known to the accused when the notice is given;

   (b) providing any information in the accused's possession which might be of material assistance in identifying or finding any such proposed witness in whose case any of the details mentioned in paragraph (a) are not known to the accused when the notice is given.

(2) Details do not have to be given under this section to the extent that they have already been given under section 6A(2). [Alibi witness details included in any defence statement.]

(3) The accused must give a notice under this section during the period which, by virtue of section 12, is the relevant period for this section. [Set as 14 days by virtue of SI 2010/214.]

(4) If, following the giving of a notice under this section, the accused—

   (a) decides to call a person (other than himself) who is not included in the notice as a proposed witness, or decides not to call a person who is so included, or

   (b) discovers any information which, under subsection (1), he would have had to include in the notice if he had been aware of it when giving the notice,

he must give an appropriately amended notice to the court and the prosecutor.

A10.4.2 *Time limits*

Criminal Procedure and Investigations Act 1996 (Defence Disclosure Time Limits) Regulations 2011, regs 2 and 3

2. (1) The relevant period for section 5 (compulsory disclosure), section 6 (voluntary disclosure) and section 6C (notification of intention to call defence witnesses) begins with the day on which the prosecutor complies or purports to comply with section 3 (initial duty of the prosecutor to disclose).

---

(2) In a case where Part 1 applies by virtue of section 1(1) (application of Part 1 in respect of summary proceedings), the relevant period for section 6 and section 6C expires at the end of 14 days beginning with the first day of the relevant period.

(3) In a case where Part 1 applies by virtue of section 1(2) (application of Part 1 in respect of Crown Court proceedings), the relevant period for section 5 and section 6C expires at the end of 28 days beginning with the first day of the relevant period.

(4) Where the relevant period would expire on a Saturday, Sunday, Christmas Day, Good Friday or any day that under the Banking and Financial Dealings Act 1971 is a bank holiday in England and Wales, the relevant period is treated as expiring on the next day that is not one of those days.

(5) Paragraphs (2) and (3) are subject to regulation 3.

3. (1) The court may by order extend (or further extend) the relevant period by so many days as it specifies.

(2) The court may only make such an order—
   (a) on an application by the accused; and
   (b) if it is satisfied that it would be unreasonable to require the accused to give a defence statement under section 5 or section 6, or give notice under section 6C, as the case may be, within the relevant period.

(3) Such an application must—
   (a) be made within the relevant period;
   (b) specify the grounds on which it is made; and
   (c) state the number of days by which the accused wishes the relevant period to be extended.

(4) There is no limit on the number of applications that may be made under paragraph (2)(a).

A10.5 Case law

There has been a constant stream of case law in relation to case management, and the courts deprecate any attempts to take a tactical advantage.

In *Writtle v Director of Public Prosecutions* [2009] EWHC 236 (Admin), the court held:

(1) the present regime of case management should in general ensure that the issues in the case are identified well before a hearing. There will, of course, be cases where something occurs in the course of a trial which may properly give rise to a new issue, but this was not such a case. The days when the defence can assume that they will be able successfully to ambush the prosecution are over.

(2) A challenge to the way a procedure was carried out (in this case in relation to evidential samples) was more than merely factual such that the defence were doing nothing more than putting the prosecution to proof.

The court adopted the earlier ruling in *Malcolm v Director of Public Prosecutions* [2007] EWHC 363 (Admin), in which Burnton J stated that it is the duty of the defence to make clear to the prosecution and the court at an early stage both the defence and the issues it raises:

> In my judgment, [counsel's] submissions, which emphasised the obligation of the prosecution to prove its case in its entirety before closing its case, and certainly before the end of the final speech for the defence, had an anachronistic, and obsolete, ring. Criminal trials are no longer to be treated as a game, in which each move is final and any omission by the prosecution leads to its failure. It is the duty of the defence to make its defence and the issues it raises clear to the prosecution and to the court at an early stage. That duty is implicit in rule 3.3 of the Criminal Procedure Rules, which requires the parties actively to assist the exercise by the court of its case management powers, the exercise of which requires early identification of the real issues. Even in a relatively straightforward trial such as the present, in the magistrates' court (where there is not yet any requirement of a defence statement or a pre-trial review), it is the duty of the defence to make the real issues clear at the latest before the prosecution closes its case.

In *Director of Public Prosecutions v Bury Magistrates' Court* [2007] EWHC 3256 (Admin), the court deprecated the practice of the defence of failing to notify the court of prosecution failures when certifying a case ready for trial, in order to take a tactical advantage. Further, that defence breach of the rules may have an impact on the amount of any costs to be recovered (in this case wasted costs).

In *R (Lawson) v Stratford Magistrates' Court* [2007] EWHC 2490 (Admin), it was held that a court was correct to allow a prosecution adjournment in order to address issues raised for the first time by the defence during a closing speech. The issues related to signage and device calibration.

A10.6 Essential case management: apply the Criminal Procedure Rules

Magistrates have been issued with the following guidance:

- It is important to note that all participants in criminal cases, including magistrates, District Judges, and Justices' Clerks, must follow and apply the Criminal Procedure Rules. The Rules are not mere guidance. Compliance is compulsory.
- The expression 'court' includes magistrates, District Judges, and Justices' Clerks exercising judicial powers (Crim PR 2.2(1)).
- Exceptions to the rule requiring the plea to be taken are rare and must be strictly justified.

(A) Generally

- The court must further the Overriding Objective of the Rules by actively managing each case (Crim PR 3.2(1)).
- The parties must actively assist the court in this without being asked (Crim PR 3.3(a)).
- But at every hearing, including a trial, it is the personal responsibility of the magistrates or District Judge to manage the case actively (Crim PR 3.2).
- Unnecessary hearings should be avoided by dealing with as many aspects of the case as possible at the same time (Crim PR 3.2(2)(f)).

(B) The first hearing taking the plea

At every hearing, (however early):

- Unless it has been done already, the court must take the defendant's plea (Crim PR 3.8(2)(b)). This obligation does not depend on the extent of initial disclosure or service of evidence, disclosure of unused material, or the grant of legal aid.
- If the plea really cannot be taken, or if the alleged offence is indictable only, the court must find out what the plea is likely to be (Crim PR 3.8(2)(b)).

(C) If the plea is 'guilty'

- The court should pass sentence on the same day, if at all possible (unless committing for sentence).
- If information about the defendant is needed from the Probation Service, it may be that a report prepared for earlier proceedings will be sufficient, or (depending on local arrangements) a 'fast delivery' report (oral or written) may be made that day.
- If a *'Newton'* hearing is needed, the court, with the active assistance of the parties, must identify the disputed issue (Crim PR 3.2(2)(a); 3.3(a)) and either, if possible, determine it there and then or, if it really cannot be determined, give directions specifically relating to that disputed issue so that the next hearing is the last.

(D) If the plea is 'not guilty'

- The key to effective case management is the early identification by the court of the relevant disputed issues (Crim PR 3.2(2)(a)).
- From the start, the parties must identify those issues and tell the court what they are (Crim PR 3.3(a)). If the parties do not tell the court, the court must require them to do so.
- The relevant disputed issues must be explicitly identified, and the case must be managed by the court so that the 'live' evidence at trial is confined to those issues.

- The parties must complete the prescribed case progression form (Crim PR 3.11; Consolidated Practice Direction V.56.2), and the court must rigorously consider each entry on the form in order to comply with its duty to manage the case actively by making properly informed directions specific to each case. Whilst this form is admissible hearsay in relation to any statements it contains, the content should be excluded from use at trial, under section 78 of the Police and Criminal Evidence Act 1984, provided the case is conducted in accordance with the letter and spirit of the Criminal Procedure Rules (*R v Newell* [2012] EWCA Crim 650).
- Only those witnesses who are really needed in relation to genuinely disputed, relevant issues should be required to attend. The court must take responsibility for this (not simply leave it to the parties) in order to comply with the Overriding Objective of the Rules (Crim PR 1.1(2)(d), (e)). However, for a defendant prepared to take the consequences there is no power under the Rules to make hearsay statements admissible other than by a proper application of the hearsay provisions of the Criminal Justice Act 2003. *T v R* [2012] EWCA Crim 2358 confirms that a failure to comply with procedural rules could not affect the law on the admissibility of evidence.
- The court's directions must include a timetable for the progress of the case (which can include a timetable for the trial itself) (Crim PR 3.8(2)(c)).
- The time estimate for the trial should be made by considering, individually, how long each 'live' witness will take, having regard to the relevant disputed issue(s).

(E) The parties' obligations to prepare for trial

The parties' obligations to prepare for trial include:

- getting witnesses to court (Crim PR 3.9(2)(b));
- making arrangements for the efficient presentation of written evidence/other material (Crim PR 3.9(2)(c));
- promptly warning the court and other parties of any problems (Crim PR 3.9(2)(d)).

(F) At trial

Before the trial begins, the court must establish, with the active assistance of the parties, what disputed issues they intend to explore (Crim PR 3.10(a)).

The court may require the parties to provide:

- a timed, 'batting order' of live witnesses (Crim PR 3.10(b)(i), (ii), (ix));
- details of any admissions/written evidence/other material to be adduced (Crim PR 3.10(b)(vi), (vii));

- warning of any point of law (Crim PR 3.10(b)(viii));
- a timetable for the whole case (Crim PR 3.10(b)(ix)).

During the trial the court must ensure that the 'live' evidence, questions, and submissions are strictly directed to the relevant disputed issues.

A10.7 Law Society Practice Note

All advocates should have access to the Law Society Practice Note in relation to the Criminal Procedure Rules.

A10.8 Sanctions

Failure to abide by the rules brings sanctions specified by statute (eg adverse inferences). A failure by a defendant to serve a defence statement did not amount to a contempt of court on either the part of the advocate or defendant. *Joseph Hill & Co* [2013] EWCA Crim 775 confirms that an alibi notice is required if the defendant believes that a witness may be able to assist his defence. Because it is based on belief, not actuality, it is not proper to wait until there is a signed proof from the witness in question. In *SKS Solicitors* [2012] EWCA Crim 319, a wasted costs order was upheld in a case where the solicitors were said to be complicit in their client's disobedience of the rules. The court stated (albeit obiter) that a solicitor faced with such a scenario should withdraw from the case.

 See *Blackstone's Criminal Practice 2014* **D4**

A11 **Commencing Proceedings**

A11.1 **Consent to prosecute**

Section 25 of the Prosecution of Offences Act 1985 provides:

Prosecution of Offences Act 1985, s 25

25 Consents to prosections etc

(1) This section applies to any enactment which prohibits the institution or carrying on of proceedings for any offence except—
  (a) with the consent (however expressed) of a Law Officer of the Crown or the Director; or
  (b) where the proceedings are instituted or carried on by or on behalf of a Law Officer of the Crown or the Director;
  and so applies whether or not there are other exceptions to the prohibition (and in particular whether or not the consent is an alternative to the consent of any other authority or person).
(2) An enactment to which this section applies—
  (a) shall not prevent the arrest without warrant, or the issue or execution of a warrant for the arrest, of a person for any offence, or the remand in custody or on bail of a person charged with any offence; and
  (b) shall be subject to any enactment concerning the apprehension or detention of children or young persons.
(3) In this section 'enactment' includes any provision having effect under or by virtue of any Act; and this section applies to enactments whenever passed or made.

It is by no means clear, but highly likely, that were proceedings to have been commenced without the requisite authority, they will be a nullity (*R v Clarke and McDaid* [2008] 1 WLR 338, HL). Consent must be obtained by the time the charge is entered into the court register (*R v Lambert* [2009] 2 Cr App R 523 (32)).

A Crown Prosecutor can give consent where the consent of the Director of Public Prosecutions is required (Prosecution of Offences Act 1985, s 1(7)).

Section 26 of the 1985 Act deals with proof of consent:

Prosecution of Offences Act 1985, s 26

26 Consents to be admissible in evidence

Any document purporting to be the consent of a Law Officer of the Crown, the Director or a Crown Prosecutor for, or to—
(a) the institution of any criminal proceedings; or
(b) the institution of criminal proceedings in any particular form;

and to be signed by a Law Officer of the Crown, the Director or, as the case may be, a Crown Prosecutor shall be admissible as prima facie evidence without further proof.

A11.2 Time limits

A11.2.1 *Overview*

Generally speaking, summary proceedings must be started within six months of the criminality complained of.

Section 127 of the Magistrates' Courts Act 1980 provides:

> **Magistrates' Courts Act 1980, s 127**
>
> **127 Limitation of time**
> (1) Except as otherwise expressly provided by any enactment and subject to subsection (2) below, a magistrates' court shall not try an information or hear a complaint unless the information was laid, or the complaint made, within 6 months from the time when the offence was committed, or the matter of complaint arose.
> (2) Nothing in—
>   (a) subsection (1) above; or
>   (b) subject to subsection (4) below, any other enactment (however framed or worded) which, as regards any offence to which it applies, would but for this section impose a time-limit on the power of a magistrates' court to try an information summarily or impose a limitation on the time for taking summary proceedings,
>   shall apply in relation to any indictable offence.
> (3) …
> (4) …

The following principles emerge from the case law:

- The date of the offence is excluded from the time calculation (*Radcliffe v Bartholomew* [1892] 1 QB 161).
- In relation to a continuing offence, it is the date of the last act that is relevant (*Director of Public Prosecutions v Baker* [2004] EWHC 2782 (Admin)).
- Month means calendar month.
- Limitation ends at midnight on the last day.
- If there is doubt as to whether an information has been laid in time, it must be resolved in favour of the defendant (*Lloyd v Young* [1963] Crim LR 703).

See **A5** for the rules relating to amendment of a charge to substitute an offence that would otherwise be time-barred.

A11.2.2 *Exceptions*

A large number of offences that can be tried only summarily are, in certain circumstances, exempt from the six-month time bar.

In relation to some offences time runs only from when an offence is 'discovered' by the prosecutor, which means when there was a reasonable belief that an offence had been committed (*Tesco Stores Ltd v London Borough of Harrow* (2003) 167 JP 657, DC). Where the relevant statute provides for a certificate to be signed by a prosecutor as to when he first had knowledge of the relevant facts, and there is a defence challenge to such a certificate, the matter should be dealt with by an application to stay the case for abuse (*Lamont-Perkins v RSPCA* [2012] EWHC 1002 (Admin)).

 See *Blackstone's Criminal Practice 2014* **D2**

A12 **Constitution and Jurisdiction**

A12.1 **The magistrates' court**

The magistrates' court (which includes a youth court) is a creature of statute created under the Magistrates' Courts Act 1980.

> ### Magistrates' Courts Act 1980, s 148
>
> #### 148 'Magistrates' court'
>
> (1) In this Act the expression 'magistrates' court' means any justice or justices of the peace acting under any enactment or by virtue of his or their commission or under the common law.
> (2) Except where the contrary is expressed, anything authorised or required by this Act to be done by, to or before the magistrates' court by, to or before which any other thing was done, or is to be done, may be done by, to or before any magistrates' court acting in the same local justice area as that court.

A12.2 **Constitution and place of sitting**

> ### Magistrates' Courts Act 1980, s 121
>
> #### 121 Constitution and place of sitting of court
>
> (1) A magistrates' court shall not try an information summarily or hear a complaint except when composed of at least 2 justices unless the trial or hearing is one that by virtue of any enactment may take place before a single justice.
> (2) A magistrates' court shall not hold an inquiry into the means of an offender for the purposes of section 82 above or determine under that section at a hearing at which the offender is not present whether to issue a warrant of commitment except when composed of at least 2 justices.
> (4) Subject to the provisions of any enactment to the contrary, a magistrates' court must sit in open court if it is—
>   (a) trying summarily an information for an indictable offence,
>   (b) trying an information for a summary offence,
>   (c) imposing imprisonment,
>   (d) hearing a complaint, or
>   (e) holding an inquiry into the means of an offender for the purposes of section 82.
> (5) A magistrates' court composed of a single justice shall not impose imprisonment for a period exceeding 14 days or order a person to pay more than £1.
> (6) Subject to the provisions of subsection (7) below, the justices composing the court before which any proceedings take place shall be present during the whole of the proceedings; but if during the course of the proceedings any justice absents himself, he shall cease to act further therein and, if the

remaining justices are enough to satisfy the requirements of the preceding provisions of this section, the proceedings may continue before a court composed of those justices.

(7) Where the trial of an information is adjourned after the accused has been convicted and before he is sentenced or otherwise dealt with, the court which sentences or deals with him need not be composed of the same justices as that which convicted him; but, where among the justices composing the court which sentences or deals with an offender there are any who were not sitting when he was convicted, the court which sentences or deals with the offender shall before doing so make such inquiry into the facts and circumstances of the case as will enable the justices who were not sitting when the offender was convicted to be fully acquainted with those facts and circumstances.

A12.3 Territorial jurisdiction

The court has jurisdiction over:

- offences committed in England and Wales;
- offences committed elsewhere when statute so prescribes;
- offences committed by an English citizen aboard a UK ship, or any foreign ship where he does not belong (Merchant Shipping Act 1995, s 281(a));
- offences committed by a non-UK citizen aboard any UK ship on the high seas (Merchant Shipping Act 1995, s 281(b));
- offences committed on an aircraft in flight over the United Kingdom.

 See *Blackstone's Criminal Practice 2014* **D3**

A12.4 Diplomatic immunity

A member of a diplomatic mission, their staff, and families enjoy diplomatic immunity from prosecution, provided that their arrival into the United Kingdom has been notified under the Vienna Convention on Diplomatic Relations. A failure to notify presence in the United Kingdom prevents the defendant from claiming immunity (*R v Lambeth Justices, ex p Yusufu* [1985] Crim LR 510). There is no duty on the accused to raise immunity, although it would clearly be sensible to do so at the earliest stage. Any prosecution and proceedings, save where a waiver has been granted by the chief representative (or his agent) of the mission concerned, is void (*R v Madan* [1961] Crim LR 253). It remains unclear as to whether a waiver can be granted retrospectively.

A12.5 **Prosecutions by local government**

In some instances prosecutions commenced by local government bodies can be brought only for offences committed within their local area, unless authority to prosecute has been delegated to them by the other relevant local body. If in doubt as to the authority to prosecute, consideration should be given to sections 101 and 202 of the Local Government Act 1972 and the cases of *Brighton and Hove County Council v Woolworths* [2002] EWHC 2656 (Admin) and *R (Donnachie) v Cardiff Magistrates' Court* [2009] EWHC 489 (Admin).

 See *Blackstone's Criminal Practice 2014* **A8.25** and **D2.20**

A13 **Costs (Defendants)**

A13.1 **Statutory basis for awarding defence costs**

Section 16(1) of the Prosecution of Offences Act 1985 provides:

> ### Prosecution of Offences Act 1985, s 16(1)
>
> **16 Defence costs**
> (1) Where—
>   (a) an information laid before a justice of the peace for any area, charging any person with an offence, is not proceeded with;
>   (b) a magistrates' court dealing summarily with an offence dismisses the information;
>   that court or, in a case falling within paragraph (a) above, a magistrates' court for that area, may make an order in favour of the accused for a payment to be made out of central funds in respect of his costs (a 'defendant's costs order').

Section 16(1) does not apply to proceedings in respect to breach of community penalty as the information does not charge a person with an offence. Similarly, the provision has no application in relation to civil proceedings (eg in relation to anti-social behaviour orders; see **A13.3** for other provisions).

Costs should generally be awarded to a defendant who can satisfy section 16(1). This includes:

- where the case is withdrawn so that a caution can be administered (*R (Stoddard) v Oxford Magistrates' Court* (2005) 169 JP 683);
- where there is a stay for abuse of process (*R (RE Williams & Sons (Wholesale) Ltd) v Hereford Magistrates' Court* [2008] EWHC 2585 (Admin));
- where a case is resolved by way of bind over (*Emohare v Thames Magistrates' Court* [2009] EWHC 689 (Admin)).

In *R (Spiteri) v Basildon Crown Court* [2009] EWHC 665 (Admin), the applicant successfully appealed a refusal to make a defendant's costs order on the grounds that he was acquitted on a 'technicality'. It was held that a costs order could not be refused on the sole ground that the applicant had brought the proceedings upon himself, as more was required, such as the defendant's having misled the prosecution as to the strength of the case against him. A similar point arose in *Dowler v MerseyRail* [2009] EWHC 558 (Admin), where the court ruled that when refusing costs, courts should give reasons for the refusal contemporaneously with the ruling. In *R (Guney) v Central Criminal Court* [2011] EWHC 767 (Admin), a case involving the making of a Recovery of Defence Costs Order following an acquittal, the court discusses further the issue of a defendant who brings the proceedings upon himself and misleads the prosecution as to the strength of the case against him. The same principles will apply when a court is considering refusing a defence costs order.

In *Brewer v Secretary of State for Justice* [2009] EWHC 987 (QB), the court held that a publicly funded defendant was able to recover, as out-of-pocket expenses, payments made to a third party for professional services. Whether such costs would be recoverable depended upon (a) the profession of the person instructed and the services provided, (b) the reason why it was necessary and reasonable to incur the expenditure, and (c) why the work was not paid for under the representation order in force. In cases where the expenditure claimed was outside the norm, the person claiming should assist the court by providing full details of the heads of expenditure.

It is not appropriate to award costs on an appeal to the Crown Court where the appeal was allowed as an act of mercy (*R (Pluckrose) v Snaresbrook Crown Court*, unreported, 9 June 2009). In *R (Rees) v Snaresbrook Crown Court* [2012] EWHC 3879 (Admin), the court left open the possibility of refusing a defence cost order where the defendant had committed perjury or succeeded by ambushing the Crown.

A13.2 Practice Direction: Costs in Criminal Proceedings

Part 2.1 of the Practice Direction: Costs in Criminal Proceedings states:

Practice Direction on Costs in Criminal Proceedings, Part 2.1

2.1 In a Magistrates' Court

2.1.1

Where an information laid before a Justice of the Peace charging a person with an offence is not proceeded with, a Magistrates' Court inquiring into an indictable offence as examining Justices determines not to commit the accused for trial, or a Magistrates' Court dealing summarily with an offence dismisses the information, the court may make a defendant's costs order. An order under Section 16 of the Act may also be made in relation to breach of bind-over proceedings in a Magistrates' Court or the Crown Court (Regulation 14(4) of the General Regulations). As is the case with the Crown Court ... such an order should normally be made unless there are positive reasons for not doing so.

For example, where the defendant's own conduct has brought suspicion on himself and has misled the prosecution into thinking that the case against him was stronger than it was, the defendant can be left to pay his own costs. In the case of a partial acquittal the court may make a part order...

2.1.2

Whether to make such an award is a matter in the discretion of the court in the light of the circumstances of each particular case.

A13.3 Costs in relation to civil complaints

Section 64 of the Magistrates' Courts Act 1980 provides:

Magistrates' Courts Act 1980, s 64

64 Power to award costs and enforcement of costs

(1) On the hearing of a complaint, a magistrates' court shall have power in its discretion to make such order as to costs—

(a) on making the order for which the complaint is made, to be paid by the defendant to the complainant;

(b) on dismissing the complaint, to be paid by the complainant to the defendant,

as it thinks just and reasonable; but if the complaint is for an order for the periodical payment of money, or for the revocation, revival or variation of such an order, or for the enforcement of such an order, the court may, whatever adjudication it makes, order either party to pay the whole or any part of the other's costs.

(2) The amount of any sum ordered to be paid under subsection (1) above shall be specified in the order, or order of dismissal, as the case may be.

The discretion here is narrower than under section 16 of the Prosecution of Offences Act 1985 (see **A13.1**), and can be invoked only if the court either makes an order or dismisses the complaint. Accordingly, where the applicant withdraws proceedings, no costs can follow. Applicants may also rely upon *Baxendale-Walker v Law Society* [2007] 3 All ER 330 (and other similar cases) to avoid costs on the basis that they are public bodies acting in the wider public interest and should not be exposed to the risk of adverse costs orders. This principle has been upheld in two further cases:

• in relation to civil proceedings commenced under Part 2 of the Proceeds of Crime Act 2002 (*Perinpanathan v City of Westminster Magistrates' Court* [2010] EWCA Civ 40) in relation to cash seizure cases that have been successfully defended;

• in relation to proceedings under section 1 of the Crime and Disorder Act 1998 (ASBO application) (*Manchester City Council v Manchester Magistrates' Court* [2009] EWHC 1866 (Admin)).

A13.4 **Costs in relation to witnesses**

Costs in relation to character witnesses' attendance at court can be recovered only when the court has certified that the interests of justice required the witnesses' attendance (Costs in Criminal Cases (General) Regulations 1986 (SI 1986/1335), reg 15). Advocates should ensure that an application is made to the court either prior to or immediately after the witnesses' attendance.

 See *Blackstone's Criminal Practice 2014* **D33**

A14 **Court-Appointed Legal Representatives**

A14.1 Overview

In certain circumstances a defendant is prohibited from cross-examining witnesses. In the event that the defendant has declined or is not eligible for legal funding, the court has power to appoint a legal representative to carry out this function on behalf of the court.

Fees for this work are authorized under section 19 of the Prosecution of Offences Act 1985 and are as agreed by the court or allowed following taxation at private client rates. Solicitors should not agree to fees that are less than those that would be allowed for in line with civil guideline costs rates.

 See *Blackstone's Criminal Practice 2014* **F7.2** and **F7.3**

A15 **Custody Time Limits**

A15.1 **Overview**

Category	Time limit
Cases sent to the Crown Court	An overall time limit of 182 days applies, which includes any time spent in custody at the magistrates' court.
Either way offences	Maximum 56 days from first appearance to hearing evidence in a summary trial (unless case was originally destined for sending and court reverts to summary trial after 56 days have elapsed, in which case the limit is 70 days).
Summary only offences	56 days to start of summary trial.
Youths	As above, save that indictable only cases that are tried summarily in the youth court are subject to the same time limits as either way cases (*R v Stratford Youth Court, ex p S (A Minor)* [1998] 1 WLR 1758).

A15.2 **Exceptions**

Defendants who abscond from prison, or who have been released on bail following expiry of a custody time limit, but are then remanded following a breach of bail, do not enjoy the protections offered by custody time limits.

If a person is granted bail and is then later remanded into custody, the earlier period on remand will count towards the custody time limit.

Custody time limits start at the end of the first day of remand and expire at midnight on the last day. A time limit expiring on one of the following days will be treated as having expired on the next preceding day which is not one of those days: Saturday, Sunday, Christmas Day, Good Friday, and bank holidays.

A15.3 **Extending custody time limits**

The case law on extending custody time limits is voluminous, and since applications will generally be made on notice, this topic is not covered in this book (see instead *Blackstone's Criminal Practice*). In general the following considerations are relevant.

- The prosecution should give two days' notice of an intention to apply, but lack of notice is not fatal to the application and the court retains a discretion to extend the time limits (*R v Governor of Canterbury Prison, ex p Craig* [1991] 2 QB 195).

- There is no power to extend once a time limit has lapsed (*R v Sheffield Justices, ex p Turner* [1991] 2 WLR 987).
- The court must be satisfied, on a balance of probabilities, that the need for the extension is due to the illness or absence of the accused, a necessary witness, a judge, or magistrate; or a postponement which is occasioned by the ordering of separate trials, or some other good and sufficient cause; and that the prosecution have acted with all due diligence and expedition.
- The following have been held not to amount to good and sufficient cause, certainly in cases that are routine (*R (McAuley) v Coventry Crown Court* [2012] EWHC 680 (Admin) and *R (Raeside) v Luton Crown Court* [2012] EWHC 1064 (Admin)): lack of court time, listing difficulties due to the nature of the case, lack of a suitably experienced judge (or lack of any judge at all). Absent exceptional circumstances, resource difficulties do not amount to a good and sufficient cause.

 See *Blackstone's Criminal Practice 2014* **D15.7–D15.38**

A16 **Disclosure**

A16.1 Overview

Prosecution disclosure of unused material following a not guilty plea is regulated under section 3(1)(a) of the Criminal Procedure and Investigations Act 1996:

> ### Criminal Procedure and Investigations Act 1996, s 3(1)(a)
>
> **3 Initial duty of prosecutor to disclose**
>
> (1) The prosecutor must—
>> (a) disclose to the accused any prosecution material which has not previously been disclosed to the accused and which might reasonably be considered capable of undermining the case for the prosecution against the accused or of assisting the case for the accused . . .

In the magistrates' court there is no duty to serve a defence case statement, but in the absence of one a prosecutor may not be able adequately or at all to discover which information might be disclosable.

A failure to disclose in accordance with the statutory scheme should lead to an adjournment (and possibly in an extreme case an argument in relation to abuse of process) (*Swash v Director of Public Prosecutions* [2009] EWHC 803 (Admin)). In *Swash* the court emphasized the court's case management powers, and also rejected a prosecution argument that the court had no jurisdiction to adjourn—the defence remedy in relation to defects in disclosure being restricted to a section 8 application (see **A16.2**). In the alternative, courts are now excluding all prosecution evidence under section 78 of the Police and Criminal Evidence Act 1984 where there has been a failure in accordance with statutory time limits to provide initial or further disclosure.

A16.2 Section 8 disclosure applications

A party aggrieved in relation to prosecution disclosure can apply to the court under section 8 of the 1996 Act, which provides:

> ### Criminal Procedure and Investigations Act 1996, s 8
>
> **8 Application by accused for disclosure**
>
> (1) This section applies where the accused has given a defence statement under section 5, 6 or 6B and the prosecutor has complied with section 7A(5) or purported to comply with it or has failed to comply with it.

(2) If the accused has at any time reasonable cause to believe that there is prosecution material which is required by section 7A to be disclosed to him and has not been, he may apply to the court for an order requiring the prosecutor to disclose it to him.

(3) For the purposes of this section prosecution material is material—

    (a) which is in the prosecutor's possession and came into his possession in connection with the case for the prosecution against the accused.

    (b) which, in pursuance of a code operative under Part II, he has inspected in connection with the case for the prosecution against the accused, or

    (c) which falls within subsection (4).

(4) Material falls within this subsection if in pursuance of a code operative under Part II the prosecutor must, if he asks for the material, be given a copy of it or be allowed to inspect it in connection with the case for the prosecution against the accused.

(5) Material must not be disclosed under this section to the extent that the court, on an application by the prosecutor, concludes it is not in the public interest to disclose it and orders accordingly.

(6) Material must not be disclosed under this section to the extent that it is material the disclosure of which is prohibited by section 17 of the Regulation of Investigatory Powers Act 2000.

 See *Blackstone's Criminal Practice 2014* **D9**

A17 **Evidence in Civil Cases**

A17.1 **Hearsay**

Civil behaviour orders are now commonplace in criminal courts, but very often involve issues of hearsay and the like. Hearsay evidence in civil proceedings is not regulated by the Criminal Justice Act 2003 but by Part 50 of the Criminal Procedure Rules, in so far as it relates to ancillary orders in criminal proceedings.

A17.2 **Challenging the weight to be attached to hearsay evidence**

Regard should be had to section 4 of the Civil Evidence Act 1995, which provides:

Civil Evidence Act 1995, s 4

4 Considerations relevant to weighing of hearsay evidence

(1) In estimating the weight (if any) to be given to hearsay evidence in civil proceedings the court shall have regard to any circumstances from which any inference can reasonably be drawn as to the reliability or otherwise of the evidence.

(2) Regard may be had, in particular, to the following—

  (a) whether it would have been reasonable and practicable for the party by whom the evidence was adduced to have produced the maker of the original statement as a witness;

  (b) whether the original statement was made contemporaneously with the occurrence or existence of the matters stated;

  (c) whether the evidence involves multiple hearsay;

  (d) whether any person involved had any motive to conceal or misrepresent matters;

  (e) whether the original statement was an edited account, or was made in collaboration with another or for a particular purpose;

  (f) whether the circumstances in which the evidence is adduced as hearsay are such as to suggest an attempt to prevent proper evaluation of its weight.

A17.3 **Credibility and previous inconsistent statements**

Sections 5(2) and 6 of the Civil Evidence Act 1995 provide:

Civil Evidence Act 1995, ss 5(2) and 6

5 Competence and credibility

(2) Where in civil proceedings hearsay evidence is adduced and the maker of the original statement, or of any statement relied upon to prove another statement, is not called as a witness—

(a) evidence which if he had been so called would be admissible for the purpose of attacking or supporting his credibility as a witness is admissible for that purpose in the proceedings; and

(b) evidence tending to prove that, whether before or after he made the statement, he made any other statement inconsistent with it is admissible for the purpose of showing that he had contradicted himself. Provided that evidence may not be given of any matter of which, if he had been called as a witness and had denied that matter in cross-examination, evidence could not have been adduced by the cross-examining party.

6 Previous statements of witness

(1) Subject as follows, the provisions of this Act as to hearsay evidence in civil proceedings apply equally (but with any necessary modifications) in relation to a previous statement made by a person called as a witness in the proceedings.

(2) A party who has called or intends to call a person as a witness in civil proceedings may not in those proceedings adduce evidence of a previous statement made by that person, except—

(a) with the leave of the court, or

(b) for the purpose of rebutting a suggestion that his evidence has been fabricated.

This shall not be construed as preventing a witness statement (that is, a written statement of oral evidence which a party to the proceedings intends to lead) from being adopted by a witness in giving evidence or treated as his evidence.

(3) Where in the case of civil proceedings section 3, 4 or 5 of the Criminal Procedure Act 1865 applies, which make provision as to—

(a) how far a witness may be discredited by the party producing him,

(b) the proof of contradictory statements made by a witness, and

(c) cross-examination as to previous statements in writing,

this Act does not authorise the adducing of evidence of a previous inconsistent or contradictory statement otherwise than in accordance with those sections.

This is without prejudice to any provision made by rules of court under section 3 above (power to call witness for cross-examination on hearsay statement).

(4) Nothing in this Act affects any of the rules of law as to the circumstances in which, where a person called as a witness in civil proceedings is cross-examined on a document used by him to refresh his memory, that document may be made evidence in the proceedings.

(5) Nothing in this section shall be construed as preventing a statement of any description referred to above from being admissible by virtue of section 1 as evidence of the matters stated.

A18 **Extradition**

A18.1 **Jurisdiction**

The Extradition Act 2003 sets out the procedures to be adopted during the extradition process. The power to extradite rests with the Senior Magistrate and authorized District Judges, and cases are generally heard only at City of Westminster Magistrates' Court. This section details the most important initial checks that a solicitor or barrister should make when seized of the case for the first time. Unless absolutely satisfied that extradition can proceed properly unopposed under Part 1 of the Act, recourse should be had to the detailed practitioner works and to specialist practitioners, as well as fast-developing case law.

Countries issuing extradition requests are divided into category 1 (Part 1 Extraditions) and category 2 countries (Part 2 Extraditions). Category 1 states utilize the European Arrest Warrant (EAW) procedure, and extradition will generally be ordered save in the most exceptional defined circumstances. More robust evidential protections are in place in relation to most category 2 states. The United Kingdom also has special arrangements in place with certain states, for example the United States of America.

A18.2 **The arrest warrant**

A18.2.1 *Part 1 Extradition*

The following states have been designated under Part 1 of the 2003 Act: Austria, Belgium, Bulgaria, Croatia, Cyprus, Czech Republic, Denmark, Estonia, Finland, France, Germany, Gibraltar, Greece, Hungary, Ireland, Italy, Latvia, Lithuania, Luxembourg, Malta, the Netherlands, Poland, Portugal, Romania, Slovakia, Slovenia, Spain, and Sweden.

Following the issuing of an arrest warrant, the police will execute that warrant and bring the individual before the court.

The arrest warrant should be in the standard format and detail the statutory particulars as required under section 2 of the Act.

A18.2.2 *Part 2 Extradition*

A request for an arrest warrant is made to the Secretary of State, who must issue to the court a certicate, unless certain exceptions apply, if a valid extradition request is received (s 70). This will result in the wanted person being brought before the court pursuant to an arrest warrant being issued by the court (s 71).

A18.3 Funding

Extradition work is funded under the Standard Crime Contract, and an application for representation should be made in the usual way. Extradition proceedings are the only proceedings in the magistrates' court that allow for representation by Queen's Counsel. It is rare for legal aid to be refused on merits, but means inquiries can cause considerable difficulty and delay. Extradition should not proceed in the absence of a representation order if the requested person and his representatives have been guilty of no fault (*Stopya v District Court of Lublin Poland* [2012] EWHC 1787 (Admin)).

A18.4 Timing of appearance and time limits

In the case of a provisional arrest under Part 1 of the Act, where a constable has reasonable grounds to believe that a warrant is being or will be issued, the first appearance must be within 48 hours of arrest (weekends and holidays excepted). In all other cases the appearance must be as soon as is practicable. A failure to comply should lead to the person's discharge.

In Part 1 cases where there has been a provisional arrest, section 4(2) requires service of the warrant, failure of which may result in a discharge at the discretion of the District Judge.

The initial hearing may be adjourned to a later date.

If consent to extradition is not given, the judge will set the appropriate timetable, the limits of which may be extended by the District Judge:

- Under Part 1—21 days from arrest, or a later date if it is in the interests of justice (Extradition Act 2003, s 8).
- Under Part 2—not later than two months from first appearance, or a later date if it is in the interests of justice (Extradition Act 2003, s 75).

A18.5 Statutory bars to extradition

The statutory bars to extradition are:

- age (s 15)—the fugitive must not be under 10 years old at the date of the crime;
- double jeopardy (ss 12, 80) (so that a defendant is not prosecuted twice for the same offence in different jurisdictions, etc);
- earlier extradition (Part 1, ss 18, 19) (prohibition of defendant's extradition where he has already been extradited to the United Kingdom from a category 1 or non-category 1 territory, and certain other circumstances apply);
- extraneous considerations (ss 13, 81) (eg disguised extradition request and the defendant is in reality wanted on account of his

political opinions, race, religion, nationality, gender, or sexual orientation, etc, or if the defendant would be prejudiced at his trial, or punished or detained because of such extraneous considerations);

- hostage taking (ss 16, 83) (see Art 9 of the International Covention against the Taking of Hostages);
- passage of time (ss 14, 82) (if it appears that it would be 'unjust or oppressive' to extradite by reason of passage of time since the defendant allegedly committed the extradition offence or became unlawfully at large, in accordance with the meaning of that phrase in *Kakis v Cyprus* [1978] 1 WLR 779, 782 and subsequent case law). 'Unjust' may include risk of prejudice to the accused in the conduct of the trial itself, for example if defence witnesses or other evidence would have disappeared due to lapse of time. 'Oppressive' includes hardship to the accused resulting from change in circumstances that has occurred during the period to be taken into consideration (eg if the client has set up a family in the United Kingdom and would suffer serious hardship). It should be noted that this ground cannot be used if it can be shown the defendant is a fugitive (ie he knew about the case and fled the country);
- speciality (ss 17, 95) (the burden is on the defendant to show that there are not adequate speciality arrangements in place, etc);
- asylum claim pending (ss 39, 40, 121);
- competing claims for extradition (ss 24, 90);
- convictions in absence (ss 20, 86) (if the defendant was convicted in absentia, did not deliberately absent himself from trial, and if he would not be entitled to a re-trial, etc);
- domestic UK criminal proceedings taking precedence (ss 22, 88). These forum provisons are clarified upon implementation on 29 July 2013 of the Crime and Courts Act 2013;
- person serving prison sentence(s) in the United Kingdom (ss 23, 89);
- physical or mental health (ss 25, 91) (if such that it would be unjust or oppressive to extradite the defendant, in accordance with the meaning in the case law). If physical illness is raised as an objection, that is, it would be unjust or oppressive to extradite, it would have to be very serious. If so, and if a treatment plan is in place in the United Kingdom, this may justify an adjournment to explore it by further inquiry. With mental health issues and a potential risk of suicide, a real and substantial risk of suicide must be shown, but the court looks at the measures in place to prevent suicide while the requested person is in the United Kingdom, while being transferred to the requesting state, and when received by the requesting state. It is only in a very rare case that a requested person would be likely to establish that measures to prevent a substantial risk of suicide would not be effective (see *Wolkowicz v Poland* [2013] EWHC 102 (Admin));

- human rights considerations (ss 21, 87) (if ordering extradition would be incompatible with the defendant's Convention rights within the meaning of the Human Rights Act 1998—most commonly raised are Arts 2, 3, 5, 6, 8).

A18.6 Human rights

A18.6.1 *Articles 2 and 3 ECHR*

Right to life (Art 2) and prohibition of inhuman or degrading treatment or punishment (Art 3).

- These rights may be argued if it can be shown that there are 'substantial grounds for believing there is a real risk of breach'. This is a high test, but can be explored if the client instructs that his life is in danger in the requesting state.
- If it is alleged that there is a risk of breach due to the actions of non-state agents, such as a gang of organized criminals, it must be shown that there is inadequate protection available from the requesting state. The court presumes that an EU Member State will be able to comply with its obligations as a member.

A18.6.2 *Articles 5 and 6 ECHR*

'Flagrant denial of justice in requesting state' (Art 5) and 'real risk that defendant will suffer a flagrant denial of a fair trial' (Art 6).

There is a presumption that an EU Member State will honour its treaty obligations, and these rights are guaranteed.

A18.6.3 *Article 8 ECHR*

Right to respect for private and family life. See *R (on the application of HH) v Westminster City Magistrates' Court* [2012] UKSC 25.

A18.7 Procedure in category 2 cases

Applicable where the defendant is wanted by a non-EU country:

- The prosecution will serve either a provisional request (warrant) with limited information about the crime for which the defendant is wanted, or full extradition papers. Section 74 of the Extradition Act 2003 applies if the defendant has been arrested under a provisional warrant. The warrant must be shown to the defendant upon arrest, or as soon as practicable after his arrest (s 74(2)). The defendant must also be brought before the appropriate judge as soon as practicable (s 74(3)), unless the defendant is granted bail by police, or the Secretary of State decides under section 126 that the request is not to be proceeded with. If these requirements are not complied with and the defendant applies to be discharged, the judge must order his discharge (s 74(5)).

- The judge must give the defendant information in accordance with section 74(7), which is that he is accused of the commission of an offence in a category 2 territory or that he is alleged to be unlawfully at large after conviction of an offence by a court in a category 2 territory, and the required information about consent (ie that the requested person may consent to his extradition, the effect of consent, and the procedure that will apply if he gives consent, and that the consent must be given in writing and is irrevocable).
- If section 70(9) has been complied with (ie the judge has received the request and certificate), the judge must fix a hearing date, which must not be later than two months starting with the date on which the judge receives the documents. This period may be extended under section 76(4).
- The court may seek to identify the potential issues that will be raised against extradition.
- The judge must remand the requested person in custody or on bail. See further **A18.9**.

A18.8 Procedure in category 1 cases

Applicable where the defendant is wanted by a country within the EAW system.

The court may wish to proceed with the extradition hearing forthwith but will adjourn, for example, upon request of the defence to obtain and present evidence in relation to a bar that has been raised. Well-reasoned arguments on sound grounds are required. The following matters must be considered.

A18.8.1 *The contents of the EAW*

A technically valid warrant must contain certain specific information, the absence of which will may make it invalid and the requested person must be discharged.

A18.8.1.1 Accusation case

The EAW must contain:

- a statement that defendant is wanted for the purpose of prosecution (rather than mere investigation);
- the defendant's identity (ie personal details);
- details of any other warrants issued for same offence;
- details of the alleged offence, date, place. The offence must constitute an extradition offence, that is, an offence over which the

United Kingdom takes jurisdiction (framework, dual criminality, or recognized by international law), and be punishable with at least 12 months' imprisonment;

- the maximum sentence, which must be 12 months' imprisonment or more to extradite.

A18.8.1.2 Conviction case

The EAW must contain:

- a statement that the defendant is wanted for the purpose of sentencing or serving a sentence of imprisonment;
- the defendant's identity;
- particulars of conviction, date, court;
- any other warrants issued for the same offence;
- the sentence that has been imposed—which must be four months' custody or over to extradite if the requested person is alleged to be unlawfully at large after conviction, and has been sentenced for an offence over which the United Kingdom takes jurisdiction.

A18.8.2 *Extradition offences*

The offence outlined in the warrant must be an extradition offence. This generally means that it must have dual criminality with an offence in the United Kingdom, must be one that carries a sentence of imprisonment of over 12 months in an accusation case, or one for which a sentence of four months or more has been imposed in a conviction case. The offence will also qualify if it is a specified offence included in the schedule to the EAW or recognized by international law, etc.

A18.8.3 *Identity*

If identity is not admitted, the requesting state must be in a position to prove it (Extradition Act 2003, s 7). Some examples of identification methods include:

- photographic or video evidence;
- possession of (or proximity to) papers bearing the same or essentially the same details;
- unusual name;
- fingerprints;
- admissions.

The defendant at court must be the person named in the EAW.

The court will decide this issue on the balance of probabilities, taking into account the information available to the court at the initial hearing.

A18.8.4 *Requirement regarding production at court*

If the defendant is not produced as soon as practicable at court, the judge must discharge (Extradition Act 2003, s 4(3) and (5)).

A18.8.5 *Requirement of service of the warrant*

The requested person must be given a copy of the warrant as soon as practicable after his arrest, if not the judge has a discretion to discharge, though seldom exercised (Extradition Act 2003, s 4(2) and (4)).

A18.8.6 *Consent*

A person who is legally represented (or is ineligible for legal aid, has declined it, or has had it withdrawn) may consent to extradition; such consent cannot be revoked.

Consenting to extradition might be advisable only if the requested person expressly wishes to give consent, and should be given only when the legal adviser is satisfied that none of the statutory or other bars to extradition is at issue.

The court will ask if the defendant will be consenting to his or her extradition. By indicating consent, the requested person waives appeal rights and speciality protection, that is, a legal protection that guarantees that the requested person may be prosecuted only for conduct that appears in the EAW.

The court will seek to identify any bars or arguments against the extradition request. If any realistically arguable bars or arguments are raised, the usual procedure is for the court to open the extradition hearing and to adjourn to allow for preparation or gathering of evidence. The court may also fix a timetable in relation to filing and service of evidence, skeleton arguments, etc.

If the extradition is not challenged (even though the defendant has not consented), the court will proceed with an uncontested extradition hearing, which is usually resolved within a short time. The result of such uncontested hearing will be an order for the defendant's extradition. The order for extradition is subject to a right of appeal to the Administrative Court. The appeal procedure is subject to a statutory time limit of seven days (including the date of the order for extradition), which is absolute in relation to the filing and service requirements. Only specialist practitioners should undertake such appeals.

A18.9 Bail

The court will invariably consider bail, whether or not the extradition hearing is adjourned or the defendant's extradition is ordered.

Usual Bail Act considerations apply, although there is no presumption in favour of bail in conviction cases. A security is often required.

 See *Blackstone's Criminal Practice 2014* **D31**

A19 Handcuffs Applications

A19.1 Introduction

There is no statutory authority for the handcuffing of defendants at court, but common law authority exists to support its legality where there is shown to be a danger of escape or a violent breach of the peace. These are the only two factors that are relevant when considering such applications (*R v Vrastides* [1998] Crim LR 251, CA). Only in the most exceptional case should handcuffs be permitted while a defendant is giving evidence.

The court has no jurisdiction over defendants who have not arrived at court and are in transit, that being a matter for the police or prison authorities. The fact that a prisoner has arrived in handcuffs does not remove the need for the court to consider the matter afresh (*R v Cambridge Justices, ex p Peacock* (1992) 161 JP 113, DC) (save where it has already heard argument on the issue and there is no change in circumstances).

The fact that these applications are becoming commonplace does not dilute the fact that important human rights are engaged. Whether Convention rights are breached is a matter of fact and degree in each case, but advocates should have their eye on the overriding principle, namely:

> Article 3 does not bite if handcuffing has been imposed in connection with lawful detention, provided the force and public exposure does not exceed that which is reasonably considered necessary by the public authority carrying out the handcuffing. (*R (JB) v GSL Ltd* [2007] EWHC 2227 (Admin))

A19.2 Applications

Applications should be decided before the defendant is brought into court as the decision is that of the court and the court alone, and should always be heard *inter partes* (*R v Rollinson* (1996) 161 JP 107, CA). It is for the applicant to show that reasonable grounds exist for the use of handcuffs. A response that 'it was usual practice' to make an application when the prisoner had an escape marker recorded against him was not acceptable; the court should either be given detailed information on which to make a decision, or in its absence should request it (*R v Horden* [2009] EWCA Crim 288).

The CPS has issued the following guidance to prosecutors:

> The rights of the suspects need to be balanced against public safety, and legitimate reasons put forward for handcuffing in court. Any derogations from these principles must be strictly justified. Consistent with this approach, other

methods of countering any risk of escape or violence should be explored to ensure the least risk of prejudice to the suspect. This may include, for example, the presence of covertly armed police officers in court or a use of a specially protected dock. Applications for handcuffs are becoming common. It is the role of the prosecutor to make representations to the court for the hand-cuffing of a prisoner based on information provided by the police or court security officers. It would not be appropriate for a prosecutor to comment upon the decision to seek an order or to advise on the safety of a particular person, other than to advise on the legal parameters of the court's discretion. Therefore, a prosecutor should not advise whether a particular defendant should be handcuffed but may refuse to assist the police or security staff where an application would be outside the court's discretion. A prosecutor may also refuse to make an application where s/he is not satisfied about the nature or extent of information provided by the police or Securicor when requested to make an application.

It is not appropriate for anyone other than the prosecutor to make a direct application to the court.

To maintain consistency of approach, all requests should be channelled through the prosecutor, and the application should be made, wherever possible, before the defendant is brought into court. However, there is nothing to prevent an application being made once the court is sitting or the suspect is in the dock.

Prosecutors need to examine carefully requests to make applications for handcuffs to be worn in court, and to ensure that there are sufficient grounds for making such applications.

A court is not bound to consider the application afresh at each subsequent hearing (*R v Cambridge Justices, ex p Peacock* (1992) 156 JP 895), but if there has been a change in circumstances, such as a defendant withdrawing his initial consent following a change of representation, the court should consider the matter afresh (*R v Monk* [2004] EWCA Crim 1256).

 See *Blackstone's Criminal Practice 2014* **D1.8**

A20 **Hearsay**

A20.1 Overview

Hearsay evidence in criminal proceedings is regulated by sections 114–126 of the Criminal Justice Act 2003. The main legislative provisions are set out in **A20.3.**

A20.2 Criminal Procedure Rules

Part 34 of the Criminal Procedure Rules regulates the admission of hearsay evidence.

A20.3 Legislative scheme

Sections 114–120 of the Criminal Justice Act 2003 are the main statutory provisions.

Criminal Justice Act 2003, s 114

114 Admissibility of hearsay evidence

(1) In criminal proceedings a statement not made in oral evidence in the proceedings is admissible as evidence of any matter stated if, but only if—
   (a) any provision of this Chapter or any other statutory provision makes it admissible,
   (b) any rule of law preserved by section 118 makes it admissible,
   (c) all parties to the proceedings agree to it being admissible, or
   (d) the court is satisfied that it is in the interests of justice for it to be admissible.

(2) In deciding whether a statement not made in oral evidence should be admitted under subsection (1)(d), the court must have regard to the following factors (and to any others it considers relevant)—
   (a) how much probative value the statement has (assuming it to be true) in relation to a matter in issue in the proceedings, or how valuable it is for the understanding of other evidence in the case;
   (b) what other evidence has been, or can be, given on the matter or evidence mentioned in paragraph (a);
   (c) how important the matter or evidence mentioned in paragraph (a) is in the context of the case as a whole;
   (d) the circumstances in which the statement was made;
   (e) how reliable the maker of the statement appears to be;
   (f) how reliable the evidence of the making of the statement appears to be;
   (g) whether oral evidence of the matter stated can be given and, if not, why it cannot;
   (h) the amount of difficulty involved in challenging the statement;
   (i) the extent to which that difficulty would be likely to prejudice the party facing it.

---

(3) Nothing in this Chapter affects the exclusion of evidence of a statement on grounds other than the fact that it is a statement not made in oral evidence in the proceedings.

It will rarely be appropriate to use section 114 in order to circumvent section 116 (cases where a witness is unavailable) (*R v Ibrahim* [2010] EWCA Crim 1176). This principle takes on a particular importance in the magistrates' court in relation to 'missing' or reluctant witnesses (eg in so-called domestic violence cases). Section 114 should not be used simply to bypass other procedures available to the prosecution, for example the witness summons. In *R v Freeman* [2010] EWCA Crim 1997, the court quashed a conviction where section 114 was used in relation to a witness who had retracted his previous statement.

Regard must be had to all of the criteria in section 114(2), although not all factors need be decided in favour of admissibility.

Section 114(2)(e) requires the court to consider the reliability of the maker of the statement. The principles were considered further in *R v Riat and others* [2012] EWCA Crim 1509. The court must:

- be satisfied that there is proper statutory basis for admitting hearsay;
- identify if there is any material assisting in the test of credibility (s 124);
- consider as appropriate any interests of justice test;
- if there is no specific gateway, consider section 144(1)(d);
- consider any application to exclude under section 78 of the Police and Criminal Evidence Act 1984 or section 126 of the Criminal Justice Act 2003.

The criteria in section 114(2) are a useful aide-memoire in identifying the relevant issues.

A focused decision must be made considering:

- the importance of the evidence in the case;
- the risks of unreliability;
- issues as to whether the reliability of the maker of the statement can be tested and assessed. Of particular relevance are:
  - the circumstances of the making of the hearsay statement,
  - interest or disinterest of the maker,
  - the existence of supporting evidence,
  - information on the reliability of the maker,
  - any means of testing reliability.

Criminal Justice Act 2003, ss 115 and 116

115 Statements and matters stated

(1) In this Chapter references to a statement or to a matter stated are to be read as follows.

(2) A statement is any representation of fact or opinion made by a person by whatever means; and it includes a representation made in a sketch, photofit or other pictorial form.

(3) A matter stated is one to which this Chapter applies if (and only if) the purpose, or one of the purposes, of the person making the statement appears to the court to have been—

   (a) to cause another person to believe the matter, or

   (b) to cause another person to act or a machine to operate on the basis that the matter is as stated.

Principal categories of admissibility

116 Cases where a witness is unavailable

(1) In criminal proceedings a statement not made in oral evidence in the proceedings is admissible as evidence of any matter stated if—

   (a) oral evidence given in the proceedings by the person who made the statement would be admissible as evidence of that matter,

   (b) the person who made the statement (the relevant person) is identified to the court's satisfaction, and

   (c) any of the five conditions mentioned in subsection (2) is satisfied.

(2) The conditions are—

   (a) that the relevant person is dead;

   (b) that the relevant person is unfit to be a witness because of his bodily or mental condition;

   (c) that the relevant person is outside the United Kingdom and it is not reasonably practicable to secure his attendance;

   (d) that the relevant person cannot be found although such steps as it is reasonably practicable to take to find him have been taken;

   (e) that through fear the relevant person does not give (or does not continue to give) oral evidence in the proceedings, either at all or in connection with the subject matter of the statement, and the court gives leave for the statement to be given in evidence.

(3) For the purposes of subsection (2)(e) 'fear' is to be widely construed and (for example) includes fear of the death or injury of another person or of financial loss.

(4) Leave may be given under subsection (2)(e) only if the court considers that the statement ought to be admitted in the interests of justice, having regard—

   (a) to the statement's contents,

   (b) to any risk that its admission or exclusion will result in unfairness to any party to the proceedings (and in particular to how difficult it will be to challenge the statement if the relevant person does not give oral evidence),

   (c) in appropriate cases, to the fact that a direction under section 19 of the Youth Justice and Criminal Evidence Act 1999 (c. 23) (special measures for the giving of evidence by fearful witnesses etc) could be made in relation to the relevant person, and

(d) to any other relevant circumstances.

(5) A condition set out in any paragraph of subsection (2) which is in fact satisfied is to be treated as not satisfied if it is shown that the circumstances described in that paragraph are caused—

(a) by the person in support of whose case it is sought to give the state in evidence, or

(b) by a person acting on his behalf,

in order to prevent the relevant person giving oral evidence in the proceedings (whether at all or in connection with the subject matter of the statement).

In considering whether it is reasonably practicable to secure the attendance of a witness, the court must consider what steps have, and have not, been taken. The reasonableness will be judged in relation to many factors, including the resources available to the party (*R v Maloney* [1994] Crim LR 525).

Even where the attendance of a witness is not practicable (or some other factor in s 116 is present), the court should then go on to consider section 126 of the Act and section 78 of the Police and Criminal Evidence Act 1984 in order to decide whether the evidence ought, in fairness, to be admitted.

Criminal Justice Act 2003, ss 117–120

117 Business and other documents

(1) In criminal proceedings a statement contained in a document is admissible as evidence of any matter stated if—

(a) oral evidence given in the proceedings would be admissible as evidence of that matter,

(b) the requirements of subsection (2) are satisfied, and

(c) the requirements of subsection (5) are satisfied, in a case where subsection (4) requires them to be.

(2) The requirements of this subsection are satisfied if—

(a) the document or the part containing the statement was created or received by a person in the course of a trade, business, profession or other occupation, or as the holder of a paid or unpaid office,

(b) the person who supplied the information contained in the statement (the relevant person) had or may reasonably be supposed to have had personal knowledge of the matters dealt with, and

(c) each person (if any) through whom the information was supplied from the relevant person to the person mentioned in paragraph (a) received the information in the course of a trade, business, profession or other occupation, or as the holder of a paid or unpaid office.

(3) The persons mentioned in paragraphs (a) and (b) of subsection (2) may be the same person.

(4) The additional requirements of subsection (5) must be satisfied if the statement—
   (a) was prepared for the purposes of pending or contemplated criminal proceedings, or for a criminal investigation, but
   (b) was not obtained pursuant to a request under section 7 of the Crime (International Co-operation) Act 2003 (c. 32) or an order under paragraph 6 of Schedule 13 to the Criminal Justice Act 1988 (c. 33) (which relate to overseas evidence).

(5) The requirements of this subsection are satisfied if—
   (a) any of the five conditions mentioned in section 116(2) is satisfied (absence of relevant person etc), or
   (b) the relevant person cannot reasonably be expected to have any recollection of the matters dealt with in the statement (having regard to the length of time since he supplied the information and all other circumstances).

(6) A statement is not admissible under this section if the court makes a direction to that effect under subsection (7).

(7) The court may make a direction under this subsection if satisfied that the statement's reliability as evidence for the purpose for which it is tendered is doubtful in view of—
   (a) its contents,
   (b) the source of the information contained in it,
   (c) the way in which or the circumstances in which the information was supplied or received, or
   (d) the way in which or the circumstances in which the document concerned was created or received.

118 Preservation of certain common law categories of admissibility

(1) The following rules of law are preserved.
   Public information etc
   (1) Any rule of law under which in criminal proceedings—
      (a) published works dealing with matters of a public nature (such as histories, scientific works, dictionaries and maps) are admissible as evidence of facts of a public nature stated in them,
      (b) public documents (such as public registers, and returns made under public authority with respect to matters of public interest) are admissible as evidence of facts stated in them,
      (c) records (such as the records of certain courts, treaties, Crown grants, pardons and commissions) are admissible as evidence of facts stated in them, or
      (d) evidence relating to a person's age or date or place of birth may be given by a person without personal knowledge of the matter.
   Reputation as to character
   (2) Any rule of law under which in criminal proceedings evidence of a person's reputation is admissible for the purpose of proving his good or bad character.
   [Note. The rule is preserved only so far as it allows the court to treat such evidence as proving the matter concerned.]

Reputation or family tradition

(3) Any rule of law under which in criminal proceedings evidence of reputation or family tradition is admissible for the purpose of proving or disproving—

   (a) pedigree or the existence of a marriage,

   (b) the existence of any public or general right, or

   (c) the identity of any person or thing.

[*Note*: The rule is preserved only so far as it allows the court to treat such evidence as proving or disproving the matter concerned.]

Res gestae

(4) Any rule of law under which in criminal proceedings a statement is admissible as evidence of any matter stated if—

   (a) the statement was made by a person so emotionally overpowered by an event that the possibility of concoction or distortion can be disregarded,

   (b) the statement accompanied an act which can be properly evaluated as evidence only if considered in conjunction with the statement, or

   (c) the statement relates to a physical sensation or a mental state (such as intention or emotion).

Confessions etc

(5) Any rule of law relating to the admissibility of confessions or mixed statements in criminal proceedings.

Admissions by agents etc

(6) Any rule of law under which in criminal proceedings—

   (a) an admission made by an agent of a defendant is admissible against the defendant as evidence of any matter stated, or

   (b) a statement made by a person to whom a defendant refers a person for information is admissible against the defendant as evidence of any matter stated.

Common enterprise

(7) Any rule of law under which in criminal proceedings a statement made by a party to a common enterprise is admissible against another party to the enterprise as evidence of any matter stated.

Expert evidence

(8) Any rule of law under which in criminal proceedings an expert witness may draw on the body of expertise relevant to his field.

(2) With the exception of the rules preserved by this section, the common law rules governing the admissibility of hearsay evidence in criminal proceedings are abolished.

119 Inconsistent statements

(1) If in criminal proceedings a person gives oral evidence and—

   (a) he admits making a previous inconsistent statement, or

   (b) a previous inconsistent statement made by him is proved by virtue of section 3, 4 or 5 of the Criminal Procedure Act 1865 (c. 18),

   the statement is admissible as evidence of any matter stated of which oral evidence by him would be admissible.

(2) If in criminal proceedings evidence of an inconsistent statement by any person is given under section 124(2)(c), the statement is admissible as evidence of any matter stated in it of which oral evidence by that person would be admissible.

120 Other previous statements of witnesses

(1) This section applies where a person (the witness) is called to give evidence in criminal proceedings.

(2) If a previous statement by the witness is admitted as evidence to rebut a suggestion that his oral evidence has been fabricated, that statement is admissible as evidence of any matter stated of which oral evidence by the witness would be admissible.

(3) A statement made by the witness in a document—
    (a) which is used by him to refresh his memory while giving evidence,
    (b) on which he is cross-examined, and
    (c) which as a consequence is received in evidence in the proceedings,
is admissible as evidence of any matter stated of which oral evidence by him would be admissible.

(4) A previous statement by the witness is admissible as evidence of any matter stated of which oral evidence by him would be admissible, if—
    (a) any of the following three conditions is satisfied, and
    (b) while giving evidence the witness indicates that to the best of his belief he made the statement, and that to the best of his belief it states the truth.

(5) The first condition is that the statement identifies or describes a person, object or place.

(6) The second condition is that the statement was made by the witness when the matters stated were fresh in his memory but he does not remember them, and cannot reasonably be expected to remember them, well enough to give oral evidence of them in the proceedings.

(7) The third condition is that—
    (a) the witness claims to be a person against whom an offence has been committed,
    (b) the offence is one to which the proceedings relate,
    (c) the statement consists of a complaint made by the witness (whether to a person in authority or not) about conduct which would, if proved, constitute the offence or part of the offence,
    (d) [repealed]
    (e) the complaint was not made as a result of a threat or a promise, and
    (f) before the statement is adduced the witness gives oral evidence in connection with its subject matter.

(8) For the purposes of subsection (7) the fact that the complaint was elicited (for example, by a leading question) is irrelevant unless a threat or a promise was involved.

 See *Blackstone's Criminal Practice 2014* **A7.92–A7.98** and **F16**

A21 **Identification Evidence**

A21.1 *Turnbull* direction

In *R v Turnbull* (1976) 63 Cr App R 132, the court laid down the following guidance:

First, whenever the case against an accused depends wholly or substantially on the correctness of one or more identifications of the accused which the defence alleges to be mistaken, the judge should warn the jury of the special need for caution before convicting the accused in reliance on the correctness of the identification or identifications. In addition he should instruct them as to the reason for the need for such a warning and should make some reference to the possibility that a mistaken witness can be a convincing one and that a number of such witnesses can all be mistaken. Provided this is done in clear terms the judge need not use any particular form of words.

Secondly, the judge should direct the jury to examine closely the circumstances in which the identification by each witness came to be made. How long did the witness have the accused under observation? At what distance? In what light? Was the observation impeded in any way, as for example, by passing traffic or a press of people? Had the witness ever seen the accused before? How often? If only occasionally, had he any special reason for remembering the accused? How long elapsed between the original observation and the subsequent identification to the police? Was there any material discrepancy between the description of the accused given to the police by the witness when first seen by them and his actual appearance? If in any case, whether it is being dealt with summarily or on indictment, the prosecution has reason to believe that there is such a material discrepancy it should supply the accused or his legal advisers with particulars of the description the police were first given. In all cases if the accused asks to be given particulars of such descriptions, the prosecution should supply them. Finally, he should remind the jury of any specific weaknesses which had appeared in the identification evidence.

Recognition may be more reliable than identification of a stranger; but even when the witness is purporting to recognise someone whom he knows, the jury should be reminded that mistakes in recognition of close relatives and friends are sometimes made.

All these matters go to the quality of the identification evidence. If the quality is good and remains good at the close of the accused's case, the danger of a mistaken identification is lessened; but the poorer the quality, the greater the danger.

In our judgment when the quality is good as for example when the identification is made after a long period of observation, or in satisfactory conditions by a relative, a neighbour, a close friend, a workmate and the like, the jury can safely be left to assess the value of the identifying evidence even though there is no other evidence to support it: provided always, however, that an adequate warning has been given about the special need for caution.

A21 Identification Evidence

Were the Courts to adjudge otherwise, affronts to justice would frequently occur. A few examples, taken over the whole spectrum of criminal activity, will illustrate what the effects upon the maintenance of law and order would be if any law were enacted that no person could be convicted on evidence of visual identification alone.

For the protections necessary when there is evidence of voice recognition, reference should be made to *Flynn and St John* [2008] EWCA Crim 970. In Facebook identifcation cases, reference should be made to *R v Alexander and McGill* [2012] EWCA Crim 2768.

 See *Blackstone's Criminal Practice 2014* **F18**

A22 Initial Details of the Prosecution Case

A22.1 Summary

The term 'advance information' is no longer strictly accurate as the Criminal Procedure Rules refer only to initial details of the prosecution case. Rule 10 of the Criminal Procedure Rules 2013 requires that if litigators advise the CPS of their interest in a case, initial disclosure should be available at the start of the day of the first hearing.

Rule 10 provide for disclosure of such information in relation to all cases that can be tried in a magistrates' court, so curing the previous anomaly that denied the defendant disclosure in relation to summary only matters.

It can be seen from rule 10 (see **A22.2**) that prosecutors enjoy a wide discretion as to what is served prior to plea.

Frequent problems arise in relation to the service of video and other recorded evidence. If the Crown is not relying on the undisclosed video evidence then no issue in relation to initial disclosure arises. In *R v Calderdale Magistrates' Court, ex p Donahue and others* [2001] Crim LR 141, it was accepted by the prosecution that a video was a document for the purposes of the then advance information rules. In a later case the prosecution declined to make the same concession, and the matter may have to be litigated again, as delays in entering plea due to awaiting video evidence may be thought by some to fly in the face of the streamlined process, and in some areas courts are increasingly reluctant to order service of such items: see *R v Croydon Magistrates' Court, ex p Director of Public Prosecutions* [2001] EWHC Admin 552. In any event the prosecution are under a duty to serve only a summary of their case, not the case in its entirety. The defendant's remedy is to enter a not guilty plea and put the Crown to proof.

A22.2 Extent of disclosure

Rule 10 of the Criminal Procedure Rules provides:

Criminal Procedure Rules 2013, Part 10

10.1 When this Part applies

(1) This Part applies in a magistrates' court, where the offence is one that can be tried in a magistrates' court.

(2) The court may direct that, for a specified period, this Part will not apply—

    (a) to any case in that court; or

    (b) to any specified category of case.

10.2 Providing initial details of the prosecution case

(1) The prosecutor must serve initial details of the prosecution case on the court officer—

    (a) as soon as practicable; and

    (b) in any event, no later than the beginning of the day of the first hearing.

(2) Where a defendant requests those details, the prosecutor must serve them on the defendant—

    (a) as soon as practicable; and

    (b) in any event, no later than the beginning of the day of the first hearing.

(3) Where a defendant does not request those details, the prosecutor must make them available to the defendant at, or before, the beginning of the day of the first hearing.

10.3 Content of initial details

Initial details of the prosecution case must include—

    (a) a summary of the evidence on which that case will be based; or

    (b) any statement, document or extract setting out facts or other matters on which that case will be based; or

    (c) any combination of such a summary, statement, document or extract; and

    (d) the defendant's previous convictions.

 See *Blackstone's Criminal Practice 2014* **D5**

A23 Legal Advisers Retiring with Justices

The Consolidated Criminal Practice Direction provides:

Consolidated Criminal Practice Direction, Part V.55

(V.55.1)

A justices' clerk is responsible for:

(a) the legal advice tendered to the justices within the area;

(b) the performance of any of the functions set out below by any member of his staff acting as legal adviser;

(c) ensuring that competent advice is available to justices when the justices' clerk is not personally present in court; and

(d) the effective delivery of case management and the reduction of unnecessary delay.

(V.55.2)

Where a person other than the justices' clerk (a 'legal adviser'), who is authorised to do so, performs any of the functions referred to in this direction he will have the same responsibilities as the justices' clerk. The legal adviser may consult the justices' clerk or other person authorised by the justices' clerk for that purpose before tendering advice to the bench. If the justices' clerk or that person gives any advice directly to the bench, he should give the parties or their advocates an opportunity of repeating any relevant submissions prior to the advice being given.

(V.55.3)

It shall be the responsibility of the legal adviser to provide the justices with any advice they require properly to perform their functions, whether or not the justices have requested that advice, on:

(a) questions of law (including European Court of Human Rights jurisprudence and those matters set out in section 2(1) of the Human Rights Act 1998);

(b) questions of mixed law and fact;

(c) matters of practice and procedure;

(d) the range of penalties available;

(e) any relevant decisions of the superior courts or other guidelines;

(f) other issues relevant to the matter before the court; and

(g) the appropriate decision-making structure to be applied in any given case.

In addition to advising the justices it shall be the legal adviser's responsibility to assist the court, where appropriate, as to the formulation of reasons and the recording of those reasons.

(V.55.4)

A justices' clerk or legal adviser must not play any part in making findings of fact, but may assist the bench by reminding them of the evidence, using any notes of the proceedings for this purpose.

(V.55.5)

A justices' clerk or legal adviser may ask questions of witnesses and the parties in order to clarify the evidence and any issues in the case. A legal adviser has a duty to ensure that every case is conducted fairly.

(V.55.6)

When advising the justices the justices' clerk or legal adviser, whether or not previously in court, should:
(a) ensure that he is aware of the relevant facts; and
(b) provide the parties with the information necessary to enable the parties to make any representations they wish as to the advice before it is given.

(V.55.7)

At any time justices are entitled to receive advice to assist them in discharging their responsibilities. If they are in any doubt as to the evidence which has been given, they should seek the aid of their legal adviser, referring to his notes as appropriate. This should ordinarily be done in open court. Where the justices request their adviser to join them in the retiring room, this request should be made in the presence of the parties in court. Any legal advice given to the justices other than in open court should be clearly stated to be provisional and the adviser should subsequently repeat the substance of the advice in open court and give the parties an opportunity to make any representations they wish on that provisional advice. The legal adviser should then state in open court whether the provisional advice is confirmed or if it is varied the nature of the variation.

(V.55.8)

The performance of a legal adviser may be appraised by a person authorised by the magistrates' courts committee to do so. For that purpose the appraiser may be present in the justices' retiring room. The content of the appraisal is confidential, but the fact that an appraisal has taken place, and the presence of the appraiser in the retiring room, should be briefly explained in open court.

(V.55.9)

The legal adviser is under a duty to assist unrepresented parties to present their case, but must do so without appearing to become an advocate for the party concerned.

(V.55.10)

The role of legal advisers in fine default proceedings or any other proceedings for the enforcement of financial orders, obligations or penalties is to assist the court. They must not act in an adversarial or partisan manner. With the agreement of the justices a legal adviser may ask questions of the defaulter to elicit information which the justices will require to make an adjudication, for example to facilitate his explanation for the default. A legal adviser may also advise the justices in the normal way as to the options open to them in dealing with the case. It would be inappropriate for the legal adviser to set out to establish wilful refusal or neglect or any other type of culpable behaviour, to offer an opinion on the facts, or to urge a particular course of action upon the justices. The duty of impartiality is the paramount consideration for the legal adviser at all times, and this takes precedence over any role he may have as a collecting officer. The appointment of other staff to 'prosecute' the case for the collecting officer is not essential to ensure compliance with the law, including the Human Rights Act 1998. Whether to make such appointments is a matter for the justices' chief executive.

 See *Blackstone's Criminal Practice 2014* **D22.72**

A24 Legal Aid

A24.1 Overview

Legal aid is available for criminal proceedings. These are defined by the Legal Aid Sentencing and Punishment of Offenders Act 2012 as including the following:

Legal Aid, Sentencing and Punishment of Offenders Act 2012, s 14

14 Criminal proceedings

In this Part 'criminal proceedings' means—

(a) proceedings before a court for dealing with an individual accused of an offence,

(b) proceedings before a court for dealing with an individual convicted of an offence, including proceedings in respect of a sentence or order,

(c) proceedings for dealing with an individual under the Extradition Act 2003,

(d) proceedings for binding an individual over to keep the peace or to be of good behaviour under section 115 of the Magistrates' Courts Act 1980 and for dealing with an individual who fails to comply with an order under that section,

(e) proceedings on an appeal brought by an individual under section 44A of the Criminal Appeal Act 1968 (appeal in case of death of appellant),

(f) proceedings on a reference under section 36 of the Criminal Justice Act 1972 on a point of law following the acquittal of an individual on indictment,

(g) proceedings for contempt committed, or alleged to have been committed, by an individual in the face of a court, and

(h) such other proceedings, before any court, tribunal or other person, as may be prescribed.

The proceedings referred to in section 14(h) are set out at regulation 9 of the Criminal Legal Aid (General) Regulations 2013 (SI 2013/9):

Criminal Legal Aid (General) Regulations 2013, reg 9

Criminal proceedings

9. The following proceedings are criminal proceedings for the purposes of section 14(h) of the Act (criminal proceedings)—

(a) civil proceedings in a magistrates' court arising from a failure to pay a sum due or to obey an order of that court where such failure carries the risk of imprisonment;

(b) proceedings under sections 14B, 14D, 14G, 14H, 21B and 21D of the Football Spectators Act 1989 in relation to banning orders and references to a court;

(c) proceedings under section 5A of the Protection from Harassment Act 1997 in relation to restraining orders on acquittal;

(d) proceedings under sections 1, 1D and 4 of the Crime and Disorder Act 1998 in relation to anti-social behaviour orders;

(e) proceedings under sections 1G and 1H of the Crime and Disorder Act 1998 in relation to intervention orders, in which an application for an anti-social behaviour order has been made;

(f) proceedings under section 8(1)(b) of the Crime and Disorder Act 1998 in relation to parenting orders made where an anti-social behaviour order or a sex offender order is made in respect of a child;

(g) proceedings under section 8(1)(c) of the Crime and Disorder Act 1998 in relation to parenting orders made on the conviction of a child;

(h) proceedings under section 9(5) of the Crime and Disorder Act 1998 to discharge or vary a parenting order made as set out in sub-paragraph (f) or (g);

(i) proceedings under section 10 of the Crime and Disorder Act 1998 in relation to an appeal against a parenting order made as set out in sub-paragraph (f) or (g);

(j) proceedings under Part 1A of Schedule 1 to the Powers of Criminal Courts (Sentencing) Act 2000 in relation to parenting orders for failure to comply with orders under section 20 of that Act;

(k) proceedings under sections 2, 5 and 6 of the Anti-social Behaviour Act 2003 in relation to closure orders;

(l) proceedings under sections 20, 22, 26 and 28 of the Anti-social Behaviour Act 2003 in relation to parenting orders—
  (i) in cases of exclusion from school; or
  (ii) in respect of criminal conduct and anti-social behaviour;

(m) proceedings under sections 97, 100 and 101 of the Sexual Offences Act 2003 in relation to notification orders and interim notification orders;

(n) proceedings under sections 104, 108, 109 and 110 of the Sexual Offences Act 2003 in relation to sexual offences prevention orders and interim sexual offences prevention orders;

(o) proceedings under sections 114, 118 and 119 of the Sexual Offences Act 2003 in relation to foreign travel orders;

(p) proceedings under sections 123, 125, 126 and 127 of the Sexual Offences Act 2003 in relation to risk of sexual harm orders and interim risk of sexual harm orders;

(q) proceedings under sections 3, 5, 9 and 10 of the Violent Crime Reduction Act 2006 in relation to drinking banning orders and interim drinking banning orders;

(r) proceedings under section 13 of the Tribunals, Courts and Enforcement Act 2007 on appeal against a decision of the Upper Tribunal in proceedings in respect of—
  (i)   a decision of the Financial Conduct Authority
  (ia) a decison of the Prudential Regulation Authority;
  (ii) a decision of the Bank of England; or
  (iii) a decision of a person in relation to the assessment of any compensation or consideration under the Banking (Special Provisions) Act 2008 or the Banking Act 2009;

(s) proceedings before the Crown Court or the Court of Appeal in relation to serious crime prevention orders under sections 19, 20, 21 and 24 of the Serious Crime Act 2007;

(t) proceedings under sections 100, 101, 103, 104 and 106 of the Criminal Justice and Immigration Act 2008 in relation to violent offender orders and interim violent offender orders;

(u) proceedings under sections 26, 27 and 29 of the Crime and Security Act 2010 in relation to—

  (i) domestic violence protection notices; or
  (ii) domestic violence protection orders; and

(v) any other proceedings that involve the determination of a criminal charge for the purposes of Article 6(1) of the European Convention on Human Rights.

In the magistrates' court, legal aid is subject to a merits test and means assessment in some cases. There is no means assessment:

- for those under 18 years;
- for those in receipt of income support;
- for those in receipt of income-based employment and support allowance (ESA);
- for those in receipt of income-based job-seeker's allowance (JSA); or
- for those in receipt of guaranteed state pension credit.

Legal aid extends automatically to the Crown Court if the case is committed for sentence (note that there is no additional contribution payable in respect to these Crown Court proceedings).

Legal aid automatically extends, without a merits test, to any case sent to the Crown Court, but proceedings in the Crown Court are subject to a contribution dependent on means.

Appeals to the Crown Court require a fresh legal aid application to be lodged, and are subject to interests of justice and means criteria. A contribution may be payable in the Crown Court, dependent on means.

A24.2 The interests of justice test

When assessing whether the grant of representation is in the interests of justice, regard should be had to the provisions of section 17(2) of the Legal Aid, Sentencing and Punishment of Offenders Act 2012 (the *Widgery* criteria). The defendant must be able to demonstrate one or more of the following:

- It is likely that I will lose my liberty.
- I have been given a sentence that is suspended or non-custodial. If I break this, the court may be able to deal with me for the original offence.

- It is likely that I will lose my livelihood.
- It is likely that I will suffer serious damage to my reputation.
- A substantial question of law may be involved.
- I may not be able to understand the court proceedings or present my own case.
- I may need witnesses to be traced or interviewed on my behalf.
- The proceedings may involve expert cross-examination of a prosecution witness.
- It is in the interests of another person that I am represented.
- Any other reasons.

Refusal on the basis of the interests of justice test can be appealed to justices or an officer of the Crown Court (Criminal Legal Aid (General) Regulations 2013 (SI 2013/9), regs 29 and 30), and regard should be had to the following cases:

- Regard should be had to the likely penalty, not the theoretical maximum: *R v Highgate Justices, ex p Lewis* [1977] Crim LR 611.
- In *R (Punatar) v Horseferry Road Magistrates' Court* [2002] EWHC 1196 (Admin), the solicitor attended court to defend an imprisonable matter and submitted an application for representation at the end of those proceedings. At that stage the imprisonable matter had been replaced by a non-imprisonable one and legal aid was refused. The court held that the refusal was wrong in law; the court should not apply hindsight but instead look at what was in the mind of the solicitor when he made the decision to attend court.
- A 16-year-old would not have the skills to cross-examine a police officer effectively: *Scunthorpe Justices, ex p S* The Times, 5 March 1998.
- In *R (GKR Law Solicitors) v Liverpool Magistrates' Court* [2008] EWHC 2974 (Admin), the court held that it was appropriate to grant representation to a defendant in relation to a special reasons hearing, where a witness in the case was the defendant's 12-year-old son. The child was a witness entitled to and requiring special measures, and consideration would need to be given to video-interviewing the young witness in order to ensure best evidence was given; such measures would be outside the competence and resources of the defendant
- In *R v Chester Magistrates' Court, ex p Ball* (1999) 163 JP 757, it was said that any defendant of previous good character pleading not guilty to a charge equal to, or more significant than, section 5 of the Public Order Act 1986 in terms of nature and seriousness, should be granted legal aid regardless of his social or professional standing. This is very unlikely to include non-imprisonable road traffic or regulatory offences.

A24.3 Transfer of representation

The law is now contained in regulation 14 of the Criminal Legal Aid (Determinations by a Court and Choice of Representative) Regulations 2013 (SI 2013/614):

> ### Criminal Legal Aid (Determinations by a Court and Choice of Representative) Regulations 2013, reg 14
>
> #### Change of provider
>
> 14.—(1) Subject to paragraph (2), where an individual has selected a provider in criminal proceedings, the right conferred by section 27(4) of the Act does not include a right to select a provider in place of the original provider.
>
> (2) The relevant court may determine that the individual can select a provider in place of the original provider in the circumstances set out in paragraphs (3) or (4).
>
> (3) The circumstances are that the relevant court determines that—
>
>   (a) there has been a breakdown in the relationship between the individual and the original provider such that effective representation can no longer be provided by the original provider; or
>
>   (b) there is some other compelling reason why effective representation can no longer be provided by the original provider.
>
> (4) The circumstances are that the relevant court determines that—
>
>   (a) the original provider—
>
>   (i) considers there to be a duty to withdraw from the case in accordance with the provider's professional rules of conduct; or
>
>   (ii) is no longer able to represent the individual through circumstances outside the provider's control; and
>
>   (b) the original provider has supplied the relevant court with details as to—
>
>   (i) the nature of any such duty to withdraw from the case; or
>
>   (ii) the particular circumstances that render the provider unable to represent the individual.

In *Ashgar Khan* (unreported, 10 July 2001, Birmingham Crown Court), the court emphasized the requirement to satisfy the Regulations, and in particular the need to show good cause for the transfer:

> I should add this: the court will insist on strict compliance with the [Regulation]. In other words, the grounds of the application and the full particulars of how it comes within the [Regulation] should be specified.... [A] substantial compelling reason, if relied on, needs to be specified. It will not generally be sufficient to allege a lack of care or competence of existing representatives. Only in extremely rare circumstances, and where full particulars are given in the application, will a general ground of loss of confidence or incompetence be entertained. It must be further pointed out that it will

not be sufficient simply to say that there is a breakdown in the relationship between solicitor and client. Many breakdowns are imagined rather than real or as the result of proper advice. This court will want to look to see what the cause of that is.

 See *Blackstone's Criminal Practice 2014* **D32**

A25 **Mental Disorder**

A25.1 **Fitness to plead**

In a strict legal sense the issue of fitness to plead does not arise in the magistrates' court as the relevant legislation does not provide for any summary procedures.

If the offence is an either way offence the court may decline jurisdiction, but the defendant will not be able to consent to summary trial. However, if the accused is being tried for an imprisonable offence, and it is shown that the accused did the act or made the omission charged, *Lincoln (Kesteven) Justices, ex p O'Connor* [1983] 1 WLR 335 confirms that he can be made subject to a hospital order under section 37(3) of the Mental Health Act 1983. The same provisions apply to the youth court (*R (P) v Barking Youth Court* [2002] EWHC 734 (Admin)).

Subject to having obtained two satisfactory reports (the court can remand under s 35 of the Mental Health Act 1983 for that purpose), the court can then go on to make a hospital order under section 37(3). The stages are:

• Issue of mental disorder raised.
• Prove that the accused did the act or made the omission charged.
• Obtain requisite medical assessment.
• Make hospital order.

The prosecution will be required to prove only the actus reus of the offence (*R v Antoine* [2000] 2 All ER 208, HL). If the prosecution cannot prove the act or omission, the defendant must be discharged.

In the alternative, if the Crown will not follow that route, the defendant can plead not guilty and put the Crown to proof of the mental element.

The procedure under section 37(3) of the Mental Health Act 1983 is not available for indictable only offences.

A25.2 **Insanity**

Insanity is available as a defence in the magistrates' court, but the defendant does not have an absolute right to have the issue determined at trial if the court feels that a disposal under section 37(3) of the Mental Health Act 1983 might be more appropriate (*R (Singh) v Stratford Magistrates' Court* [2007] EWHC 1582 (Admin)).

A25.3 Medical reports

In order to decide whether the person should be tried or made subject to the fitness to plead procedure, the court may need to consider the report of a medical practitioner, and a remand to hospital under section 11 of the Powers of Criminal Courts (Sentencing) Act 2000 may be ordered.

Powers of Criminal Courts (Sentencing) Act 2000, s 11

11 Remand by magistrates' court for medical examination

(1) If, on the trial by a magistrates' court of an offence punishable on summary conviction with imprisonment, the court—
   (a) is satisfied that the accused did the act or made the omission charged, but
   (b) is of the opinion that an inquiry ought to be made into his physical or mental condition before the method of dealing with him is determined,
   the court shall adjourn the case to enable a medical examination and report to be made, and shall remand him.

(2) An adjournment under subsection (1) above shall not be for more than three weeks at a time where the court remands the accused in custody, nor for more than four weeks at a time where it remands him on bail.

(3) Where on an adjournment under subsection (1) above the accused is remanded on bail, the court shall impose conditions under paragraph (d) of section 3(6) of the Bail Act 1976 and the requirements imposed as conditions under that paragraph shall be or shall include requirements that the accused—
   (a) undergo medical examination by a registered medical practitioner or, where the inquiry is into his mental condition and the court so directs, two such practitioners; and
   (b) for that purpose attend such an institution or place, or on such practitioner, as the court directs and, where the inquiry is into his mental condition, comply with any other directions which may be given to him for that purpose by any person specified by the court or by a person of any class so specified.

A25.4 Diversion

The Crown Prosecution Service has issued the following guidance which is to be considered before prosecuting an offender (or if the prosecution has commenced, before dealing further with the offender):

The Code for Crown Prosecutors states that alternatives to prosecution should be considered when deciding whether a case should be prosecuted. Rehabilitative, reparative and restorative processes can be considered, and alternatives to prosecution for adult offenders include a simple caution and conditional caution.

A25 Mental Disorder

The National Standards for Cautioning require that the following conditions are met before a simple caution may be administered by the police:

- there is a realistic prospect of conviction;
- the offender admits the offence; and
- the offender (or appropriate adult) understands the significance of a caution and gives informed consent to being cautioned.

The National Standards for Conditional Cautioning require that the following conditions are met before a conditional caution may be administered:

- there is enough evidence to bring charges and it is in the public interest to do so;
- the offender has admitted the offence and is aged 18 or over;
- the offender agrees to accept the caution and to carry out the conditions;
- the most likely outcome of attending court would have been a small fine, compensation, conditional discharge or a community penalty at the lower end of the scale; and
- the use of reparative or rehabilitative conditions is felt to be the most effective way of dealing with the offending behaviour and/or recompensing the victim.

A caution or conditional caution will not be appropriate if there is any doubt about the reliability of any admissions made or if the defendant's level of understanding prevents him or her from understanding the significance of the caution or conditional caution and giving informed consent. It should not be assumed that all mentally disordered offenders are ineligible for cautioning or conditional cautioning, but there is no definition of or restriction on the particular form of mental or psychological condition or disorder that may make an admission unreliable (*R v Walker* [1998] Crim LR 211).

Where a caution or conditional caution is inappropriate, the only alternative to prosecution is to take no further action. In considering whether the public interest requires a prosecution, prosecutors should inquire whether:

- the police or Social Serrices have used their powers under sections 135 or 136 Mental Health Act 1983;
- the defendant has been admitted to hospital for assessment or treatment under sections 2 or 3 Mental Health Act 1983;
- the defendant is receiving supervised community treatment under a Community Treatment Order made under section 17A Mental Health Act 1983;
- the offender has been admitted to hospital as an informal patient under section 131 Mental Health Act 1983; or
- an order for guardianship under section 7 Mental Health Act 1983 has been made.

However, the existence of a mental disorder is only one of the factors to be taken into account when deciding whether the public interest requires a prosecution. The seriousness or the persistence of the offending behaviour, the views of the victim and any responsible clinician should also be considered.

The fact that a person is receiving compulsory treatment under the Mental Health Act 1983, or as an informal patient under section 131 Mental Health Act 1983, does not prevent a prosecution. However, a prosecution must not be pursued solely to treat and manage a mental disorder. The decision to prosecute or divert a patient receiving treatment under the Mental Health Act 1983 should be informed by additional information, including:

medical reports from the responsible clinician to explain the nature and degree of the disorder or disability, and any relationship between the disorder and the treatment and behaviour of the offender; and

any other relevant information from hospital staff about the treatment and behaviour of the patient, including the treatment regime and any history of similar and recent behaviour.

Where the patient is alleged to have assaulted a member of staff, prosecutors should refer to the NHS/SMS/CPS Memorandum of Understanding on the effective prosecution of cases involving violence and abuse against any member of NHS staff.

 See *Blackstone's Criminal Practice 2014* **D20.27** and **E22**

A26 **Misbehaviour at Court**

A26.1 Misbehaviour during allocation and summary trial

Section 18(3) of the Magistrates' Courts Act 1980 provides:

> ## Magistrates' Courts Act 1980, s 18(3)
>
> **18 Initial procedure on information against adult for offence triable either way**
>
> …
>
> (3) The court may proceed in the absence of the accused in accordance with such of the provisions of sections 19 to 22 below as are applicable in the circumstances if the court considers that by reason of his disorderly conduct before the court it is not practicable for the proceedings to be conducted in his presence; and subsections (3) to (5) of section 23 below, so far as applicable, shall have effect in relation to proceedings conducted in the absence of the accused by virtue of this subsection (references in those subsections to the person representing the accused being for this purpose read as references to the person, if any, representing him).
>
> …

A26.2 Contempt of Court Act 1981

Section 12 of the Contempt of Court Act 1981 provides:

> ## Contempt of Court Act 1981, s 12
>
> **12 Offences of contempt of magistrates' courts**
>
> (1) A magistrates' court has jurisdiction under this section to deal with any person who—
>   (a) wilfully insults the justice or justices, any witness before or officer of the court or any solicitor or counsel having business in the court, during his or their sitting or attendance in court or in going to or returning from the court; or
>   (b) wilfully interrupts the proceedings of the court or otherwise misbehaves in court.
>
> (2) In any such case the court may order any officer of the court, or any constable, to take the offender into custody and detain him until the rising of the court; and the court may, if it thinks fit, commit the offender to custody for a specified period not exceeding one month or impose on him a fine not exceeding £2,500, or both.
>
> (2A) A fine imposed under subsection (2) above shall be deemed, for the purposes of any enactment, to be a sum adjudged to be paid by a conviction.

(3) A magistrates' court may at any time revoke an order of committal made under subsection (2) and, if the offender is in custody, order his discharge.

(4) Section 135 of the Powers of Criminal Courts (Sentencing) Act 2000 (limit on fines in respect of young persons) and the following provisions of the Magistrates' Courts Act 1980 apply in relation to an order under this section as they apply in relation to a sentence on conviction or finding of guilty of an offence; and those provisions of the Magistrates' Courts Act 1980 are section 36 (restriction on fines in respect of young persons); sections 75 to 91 (enforcement); section 108 (appeal to Crown Court); section 136 (overnight detention in default of payment); and section 142(1) (power to rectify mistakes).

It should be noted that there is no power to adjourn, and the matter must be dealt with before the end of the court day. There will be few cases that cannot be handled adequately by a suitable apology. See also Part 62 of the Criminal Procedure Rules.

 See *Blackstone's Criminal Practice 2014* **B14.79–B14.129**

A27 Presence of Defendant in Court

A27.1 General principles

If a defendant has been bailed to attend court, his presence is mandatory unless and until it is excused by the court. Where a defendant on bail fails to appear, a warrant may be issued for his arrest.

On summons and certain other matters, the defendant may be represented by a legal representative.

Section 122 of the Magistrates' Courts Act 1980 provides:

> **Magistrates' Courts Act 1980, s 122**
>
> **122 Appearance by counsel or solicitor**
> (1) A party to any proceedings before a magistrates' court may be represented by a legal representative.
> (2) Subject to subsection (3) below, an absent party so represented shall be deemed not to be absent.
> (3) Appearance of a party by legal representative shall not satisfy any provision of any enactment or any condition of a recognizance expressly requiring his presence.

A27.2 Defendant's presence at trial

Section 11 of the Magistrates' Courts Act 1980 details the court's powers when a defendant does not appear for trial:

> **Magistrates' Courts Act 1980, s 11**
>
> **11 Non-appearance of accused: general provisions**
> (1) Subject to the provisions of this Act, where at the time and place appointed for the trial or adjourned trial of an information the prosecutor appears but the accused does not—
>   (a) if the accused is under 18 years of age, the court may proceed in his absence; and
>   (b) if the accused has attained the age of 18 years, the court shall proceed in his absence unless it appears to the court to be contrary to the interests of justice to do so.
>   This is subject to subsections (2), (2A), (3) and (4).
> (2) Where a summons has been issued, the court shall not begin to try the information in the absence of the accused unless either it is proved to the satisfaction of the court, on oath or in such other manner as may be prescribed, that the summons was served on the accused within what appears

to the court to be a reasonable time before the trial or adjourned trial or the accused has appeared on a previous occasion to answer to the information.

(2A) The court shall not proceed in the absence of the accused if it considers that there is an acceptable reason for his failure to appear.

(3) In proceedings to which this subsection applies, the court shall not in a person's absence sentence him to imprisonment or detention in a detention centre or make a detention and training order or an order under paragraph 8(2)(a) or (b) of Schedule 12 to the Criminal Justice Act 2003 that a suspended sentence passed on him shall take effect.

(3A) But where a sentence or order of a kind mentioned in subsection (3) is imposed or given in the absence of the offender, the offender must be brought before the court before being taken to a prison or other institution to begin serving his sentence (and the sentence or order is not to be regarded as taking effect until he is brought before the court).

(4) In proceedings to which this subsection applies, the court shall not in a person's absence impose any disqualification on him, except on resumption of the hearing after an adjournment under section 10(3) above; and where a trial is adjourned in pursuance of this subsection the notice required by section 10(2) above shall include notice of the reason for the adjournment.

(5) Subsections (3) and (4) apply to—

(a) proceedings instituted by an information, where a summons has been issued; and

(b) proceedings instituted by a written charge.

(6) Nothing in this section requires the court to enquire into the reasons for the accused's failure to appear before deciding whether to proceed in his absence.

(7) The court shall state in open court its reasons for not proceeding under this section in the absence of an accused who has attained the age of 18 years; and the court shall cause those reasons to be entered in its register of proceedings.

In deciding whether or not to proceed in the defendant's absence, the court has to have regard to the following principles (*R v Jones and others* [2002] UKHL 5; *Shirzadeh v Maidstone Magistrates' Court* [2003] EWHC 2216 (Admin)):

- the nature and circumstances of the defendant's behaviour in absenting himself from the trial or disrupting it, as the case may be, and in particular, whether his behaviour was deliberate, voluntary, and such as plainly waived his right to appear;
- (in the case of a defendant aged under 18 years) whether an adjournment might result in the defendant being caught or attending voluntarily and/or not disrupting the proceedings;
- (in the case of a defendant aged under 18 years) the likely length of such an adjournment;
- whether the defendant, though absent, is, or wishes to be, legally represented at the trial or has, by his conduct, waived his right to representation;

- whether an absent defendant's legal representatives are able to receive instructions from him during the trial and the extent to which they are able to present his defence;
- the extent of the disadvantage to the defendant in not being able to give his account of events, having regard to the nature of the evidence against him;
- the risk of the jury reaching an improper conclusion about the absence of the defendant;
- the seriousness of the offence, which affects defendant, victim, and public;
- the general public interest and the particular interest of victims and witnesses that a trial should take place within a reasonable time of the events to which it relates;
- the effect of delay on the memories of witnesses;
- where there is more than one defendant and not all have absconded, the undesirability of separate trials, and the prospects of a fair trial for the defendants who are present.

The court in *Shirzadeh* identified four additional factors relevant to trial in the magistrates' court:

> [first] that there ought to be less risk from either a trained lay justice or a district judge in drawing an impermissible inference from a defendant's absence; secondly, in a magistrates' court the finder of fact may ask its own questions and test the evidence of prosecution witnesses; thirdly, a defendant in summary proceedings can apply to set aside any resulting conviction under section 142 of the Magistrates' Courts Act 1980; and fourthly, a defendant in summary proceedings has an automatic right of appeal to the Crown Court.

The decision to try a person in his absence must be exercised with great care and only in exceptional circumstances, such as cases where the absence was a deliberate absconding (*R (Drinkwater) v Solihull Magistrates' Court* [2012] EWHC 765 (Admin)). (See also **A2**.)

A27.3 Statutory declarations

Where a defendant is convicted in absence, having not known of the summons or proceedings, he may apply to the court for the conviction to be set aside. Section 14 of the Magistrates' Courts Act 1980 provides:

> ### Magistrates' Courts Act 1980, s 14
>
> **14 Proceedings invalid where accused did not know of them**
>
> (1) Where a summons has been issued under section 1 above and a magistrates' court has begun to try the information to which the summons relates, then, if—

    (a) the accused, at any time during or after the trial, makes a statutory declaration that he did not know of the summons or the proceedings until a date specified in the declaration, being a date after the court has begun to try the information; and

    (b) within 21 days of that date the declaration is served on the designated officer for the court,

without prejudice to the validity of the information, the summons and all subsequent proceedings shall be void.

(2) For the purposes of subsection (1) above a statutory declaration shall be deemed to be duly served on the designated officer if it is delivered to him, or left at his office, or is sent in a registered letter or by the recorded delivery service addressed to him at his office.

(3) If on the application of the accused it appears to a magistrates' court (which for this purpose may be composed of a single justice) that it was not reasonable to expect the accused to serve such a statutory declaration as is mentioned in subsection (1) above within the period allowed by that subsection, the court may accept service of such a declaration by the accused after that period has expired; and a statutory declaration accepted under this subsection shall be deemed to have been served as required by that subsection.

(4) Where any proceedings have become void by virtue of subsection (1) above, the information shall not be tried again by any of the same justices.

 See *Blackstone's Criminal Practice 2014* **D22**

A28 Remand Periods

A28.1 Prior to conviction

- Remand to police cells for three days.
- Remand to custody for maximum of eight clear days on first remand.
- Subsequent remand to custody for up to 28 clear days, provided the next stage in the proceedings will be dealt with. If it is known that the next stage cannot be dealt with in that period then eight-day remands will have to follow, until such time as completion of the next stage within 28 days is achievable.
- Subsequent remand to custody for 28 clear days if the defendant is already in custody serving a sentence and will not be released before that date.
- Remand on bail for eight days, or longer if the defendant consents.
- Following a sending to the Crown Court, the magistrates have the power to adjourn for a period up to the date of trial (so the normal eight-day limit on first remand does not apply). It is important to note that the expression 'remand' has a particular meaning within the 1980 Act, and the court is not remanding a person when it sends someone for trial—therefore when a court sends a person for trial during his first appearance, it can do so in custody for a period in excess of eight days.

Section 129 of the Magistrates' Courts Act 1980 allows for the remands of persons not produced before the court due to illness or accident. The court must have 'solid grounds' to justify an opinion that failure to be produced was due to illness or accident (*R v Liverpool Justices, ex p Grogan* The Times, 8 October 1990).

A28.2 Post conviction

- Maximum three weeks if in custody, four weeks if on bail.

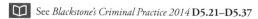 See *Blackstone's Criminal Practice 2014* **D5.21–D5.37**

A29 **Reporting Restrictions**

A29.1 **Youths**

Proceedings in the adult court in relation to youths are protected under section 39 of the Children and Young Persons Act 1933. Section 39 provides a discretionary power for such courts to protect the identity of children (whether a party or otherwise connected with the proceedings).

> ### Children and Young Persons Act 1933, s 39
>
> **39 Power to prohibit publication of certain matter in newspapers**
>
> (1) In relation to any proceedings in any court, the court may direct that—
>
> (a) no newspaper report of the proceedings shall reveal the name, address or school, or include any particulars calculated to lead to the identification, of any child or young person concerned in the proceedings, either as being the person by or against or in respect of whom the proceedings are taken, or as being a witness therein:
>
> (b) no picture shall be published in any newspaper as being or including a picture of any child or young person so concerned in the proceedings as aforesaid;
>
> except in so far (if at all) as may be permitted by the direction of the court.
>
> (2) Any person who publishes any matter in contravention of any such direction shall on summary conviction be liable in respect of each offence to a fine not exceeding level 5 on the standard scale.

The Judicial College has issued the following guidance in its *ASBO Guidance for the Judiciary* (3rd edn):

- The court has the discretion to hear media representations on whether it should make or lift a section 39 order. Courts have discretion to hear reporters in person, as well as their legal representatives. Indeed, many courts have formally reconsidered orders or purported restrictions after media representations by letter or discussion with the clerk to the justices.
- There must be good reason to make a section 39 order. There is a clear distinction between the automatic ban on identification of children involved in youth court proceedings under section 49 and the discretion to impose an order under section 39 of the 1933 Act: *R v Lee* [1993] 1 WLR 103; *R v Central Criminal Court, ex p W, B, and C* [2001] Cr App R 2. Age alone is insufficient to justify the order. Courts have accepted that very young children cannot be harmed by publicity of which they will be unaware and therefore

section 39 orders are unnecessary. Orders cannot be made in respect of dead children. Naming a young offender who has been convicted might act as a deterrent to others, or the public might wish to know the outcome of the trial in serious cases.

- The order must be restricted to the terms of section 39. The court cannot ban the naming of any adult, nor make any order relating to any child or young person who is not involved in the proceedings. The court can give guidance on the practical effect of the order and what, in its view, might and might not be caught by the order. However, this can only be guidance, which is not binding on the media.

- If a reporting restriction is imposed, the justices must make it clear in court that a formal order has been made. The order should use the words of section 39 and identify the child or children involved with clarity. A written copy should be drawn up as soon as possible after the order has been made orally.

- The order only applies to the proceedings in the court by which it was made, but is not limited as to time.

In its *ASBO Guidance for the Judiciary* (3rd edn), the Judicial College outlines that in relation to anti-social behaviour orders, the following considerations apply:

> Applications for anti-social behaviour orders (ASBOs) pursuant to section 1 of the Crime and Disorder Act 1998 are civil proceedings (*R (McCann) v Crown Court at Manchester* [2001] 1 WLR 1084 (CA); *B v Chief Constable of Avon and Somerset Constabulary* [2001] 1 WLR 340). Since the Youth Court has no civil jurisdiction, all such applications will be heard by the Magistrates' Court. The Magistrates' Court is open to the general public; no automatic restrictions will apply to prevent public and press access or to prevent reporting of the proceedings or to protect the identity of any adult or juvenile who are defendants as the subject of an application.

> The court would have to have good reason, aside from age alone, to impose any discretionary order under section 39 of the Children and Young Persons Act 1933 to prevent the identification of any child or young person concerned in the proceedings (see *R v Lee* (1993) 96 Cr App R 188 applied by the Divisional Court in *R v Central Criminal Court, ex p W, B, and C* [2001] Cr App R 2).

Although any request for reporting restrictions to be imposed is for the court to decide, the applicant may resist a call from the defendant's representatives for such restrictions if the effectiveness of the ASBO will largely depend on a wider community knowing the details. Given the nature of the proceedings, that is, that the under-18-year-old is being accused of anti-social behaviour in the community, it is in the community interest that any order will be enforced in order to protect the community. Unless the nuisance is extremely localized, enforcement of the order will normally depend upon the general public being aware of the order and of the identity of the person against whom it is made.

Effective enforcement may require the publication of photographs of the subjects, as well as their names and addresses. The magistrates dealing with a youth in ASBO proceedings may be called upon to balance the interests of the community with that of the young person against whom the order has been made.

Breach of an ASBO without reasonable excuse is an offence punishable on conviction on indictment with five years' imprisonment and/or a fine, and on summary conviction by six months' imprisonment and/or a fine up to the statutory maximum. Again, no automatic restrictions upon press and public access or upon media reporting will apply to criminal proceedings before the magistrates' court (or the Crown Court). There would have to be good reason to impose any restrictions to prevent media reports' identification of any under-18-year-old involved in the proceedings under section 39 of the Children and Young Persons Act 1933 or its replacement, section 45 of the Youth Justice and Criminal Evidence Act 1999, when in force.

If the defendant is under 18 and is the subject of criminal proceedings before the youth court for the alleged breach of an ASBO, the automatic restrictions upon public, but not press, access to the proceedings and upon identification of the alleged offender will apply. The press will have the right to attend the proceedings under section 47 of the Children and Young Persons Act 1933 and the right to report the proceedings, subject to the automatic restrictions upon identification of the under-18-year-old involved under section 49 of the Children and Young Persons Act 1933.

As outlined in the two Home Office/Lord Chancellor's Department publications, Circular 1998, *Opening Up the Youth Court* and *Youth Court 2001—The Changing Culture of the Youth Court: Good Practice Guide*, the youth court has the discretion to admit the public and to lift the automatic reporting restrictions. The joint publications suggest relevant considerations.

The High Court in *McKerry v Teesdale and Wear Justices* [2000] Crim LR 594 considered factors to be taken into account by youth courts in lifting section 49 restrictions. (Note that this case did not directly relate to imposition of discretionary restrictions under section 39 and the court was not referred to the Court of Appeal's judgment in *R v Lee—McKerry* was considered but not followed by the Divisional Court in *R v Central Crown Court, ex p W B, and C* [2001] Cr App R 2, which re-emphasized Parliament's distinction between treatment of juveniles appearing in youth courts and juveniles appearing in adult courts.) The factors included the great care, caution, and circumspection which had to be exercised; the need for the statutory public interest test to be satisfied; the background of international law and practice, including the competing principles of Articles 8 and 10 of the European Convention on Human Rights; the collision between the hallowed principle that justice was administered in public, open to full and fair reporting of court proceedings so that the public might be informed about the justice administered in their name, and the important principle of protection of juveniles' privacy in legal proceedings, great weight being given to their welfare; and inappropriateness of dispensing with a juvenile's prima facie right to privacy as an additional punishment.

The High Court also made clear that there was nothing to preclude the justices from hearing a representative of the press, either orally or in writing, on whether reporting restrictions should be lifted, and that could be a valuable process, since the reporter might well have a legitimate point to make and one which would save the court from falling into error.

The following principles were set out in *R (Y) v Aylesbury Crown Court* [2012] EWHC 1140 (Admin):

- The defendant had to satisfy the court that there was a good reason for restriction.
- The good reason for a young person would in most cases be his welfare. Publicity would have significant effects on the young person's prospects and opportunities.
- The court must have regard to Article 10 ECHR. A restriction order must be necessary and proportionate, and for a pressing social need. There was a public interest in knowing the outcome of proceedings.
- There is a balance to be struck. Prior to conviction it was unlikely that there should be publicity. After conviction, the age of the defendant and seriousness of the crime would be particularly relevant.
- Partial publicity was possible.
- If there was an even balance there should be no publicity.

In appropriate cases consideration should be given to section 46 of the Youth Justice and Criminal Evidence Act 1999 if the evidence of a witness may be affected by fear that the identity of her children may become known. *Re ITN News*, 21 April 2013 (Admin), confirms that this does not follow automatically from a special measures direction but requires a separate fact-finding exercise.

A29.2 **Adults**

Section 4(2) of the Contempt of Court Act 1981 provides:

Contempt of Court Act 1981, s 4(2)

4 Contemporary reports of proceedings

...

(2) In any such proceedings the court may, where it appears to be necessary for avoiding a substantial risk of prejudice to the administration of justice in those proceedings, or in any other proceedings pending or imminent, order that the publication of any report of the proceedings, or any part of the proceedings, be postponed for such period as the court thinks necessary for that purpose.

...

A30 **Sending and Transfer for Trial**

A30.1 Overview

In the following instances the court may decline or be deprived of jurisdiction to try a matter:

- indictable only matters—sent to the Crown Court;
- either way matters where jurisdiction is declined or the defendant has elected Crown Court trial—sent to the Crown Court; transfer cases—transferred to the Crown Court;
- voluntary bill of indictment (not covered in this book).

Method	Notes
Sending. Section 51 of the Crime and Disorder Act 1998	The court will send any indictable only matter, along with any related either way matters. This may involve sending one or more co-defendants. *Note*: A sending is not a remand within the meaning of MCA 1980, ss 128, 128A, and therefore the initial eight-day limitation on a remand in custody does not apply.
	An either way offence is related to an indictable offence if the charge for the either way offence could be joined in the same indictment as the charge for the indictable offence.
	A summary offence is related to an indictable offence if it arises out of circumstances which are the same as or connected with those giving rise to the indictable offence. The court can send related summary offences if they are imprisonable or carry discretionary or obligatory disqualification from driving. It does not matter that all matters are not sent on the same occasion.
	In the case of a youth charged with an adult (not necessarily on the same occasion), the youth will be sent if it is in the interests of justice to try him with the adult. There is no power to send a case to the Crown Court in the absence of a defendant, even if that person is legally represented.
Transfer cases. *Note*: See ss 51B and 51C of the Crime and Disorder Act 1998	Applicable to fraud cases and child cases.

Where a person is arrested for an either way offence and commits a summary only assault whilst at the police station, there is no basis for dealing with the summary only matter at the Crown Court; it did not arise out of the same facts, neither was it part of a series of offences, so section 40(1) of the Criminal Justice Act 1988 did not apply (*R v Walton* [2011] EWCA Crim 2832).

A30.2 Relevant legislation

Crime and Disorder Act 1998, ss 50A–51E

50A Order of consideration for either-way offences

(1) Where an adult appears or is brought before a magistrates' court charged with an either-way offence (the 'relevant offence'), the court shall proceed in the manner described in this section.

(2) If notice is given in respect of the relevant offence under section 51B or 51C below, the court shall deal with the offence as provided in section 51 below.

(3) Otherwise—

(a) if the adult (or another adult with whom the adult is charged jointly with the relevant offence) is or has been sent to the Crown Court for trial for an offence under section 51(2)(a) or 51(2)(c) below—

  (i) the court shall first consider the relevant offence under subsection (3), (4), (5) or, as the case may be, (6) of section 51 below and, where applicable, deal with it under that subsection;

  (ii) if the adult is not sent to the Crown Court for trial for the relevant offence by virtue of sub-paragraph (i) above, the court shall then proceed to deal with the relevant offence in accordance with sections 17A to 23 of the 1980 Act;

(b) in all other cases—

  (i) the court shall first consider the relevant offence under sections 17A to 20 (excluding subsections (8) and (9) of section 20) of the 1980 Act;

  (ii) if, by virtue of sub-paragraph (i) above, the court would be required to proceed in relation to the offence as mentioned in section 17A(6), 17B(2)(c) or 20(7) of that Act (indication of guilty plea), it shall proceed as so required (and, accordingly, shall not consider the offence under section 51 or 51A below);

  (iii) if sub-paragraph (ii) above does not apply—

   (a) the court shall consider the relevant offence under sections 51 and 51A below and, where applicable, deal with it under the relevant section;

   (b) if the adult is not sent to the Crown Court for trial for the relevant offence by virtue of paragraph (a) of this sub-paragraph, the court shall then proceed to deal with the relevant offence as contemplated by section 20(9) or, as the case may be, section 21 of the 1980 Act.

(4) Subsection (3) above is subject to any requirement to proceed as mentioned in subsections (2) or (6)(a) of section 22 of the 1980 Act (certain offences where value involved is small).

(5) Nothing in this section shall prevent the court from committing the adult to the Crown Court for sentence pursuant to any enactment, if he is convicted of the relevant offence.

51 Sending cases to the Crown Court: adults

(1) Where an adult appears or is brought before a magistrates' court ('the court') charged with an offence and any of the conditions mentioned in

subsection (2) below is satisfied, the court shall send him forthwith to the Crown Court for trial for the offence.

(2) Those conditions are—

   (a) that the offence is an offence triable only on indictment other than one in respect of which notice has been given under section 51B or 51C below;

   (b) that the offence is an either-way offence and the court is required under section 20(9)(b), 21, 23(4)(b) or (5) or 25(2D) of the Magistrates' Courts Act 1980 to proceed in relation to the offence in accordance with subsection (1) above;

   (c) that notice is given to the court under section 51B or 51C below in respect of the offence.

(3) Where the court sends an adult for trial under subsection (1) above, it shall at the same time send him to the Crown Court for trial for any either-way or summary offence with which he is charged and which—

   (a) (if it is an either-way offence) appears to the court to be related to the offence mentioned in subsection (1) above; or

   (b) (if it is a summary offence) appears to the court to be related to the offence mentioned in subsection (1) above or to the either-way offence, and which fulfils the requisite condition (as defined in subsection (11) below).

(4) Where an adult who has been sent for trial under subsection (1) above subsequently appears or is brought before a magistrates' court charged with an either-way or summary offence which—

   (a) appears to the court to be related to the offence mentioned in subsection (1) above; and

   (b) (in the case of a summary offence) fulfils the requisite condition, the court may send him forthwith to the Crown Court for trial for the either-way or summary offence.

(5) Where—

   (a) the court sends an adult ('A') for trial under subsection (1) or (3) above;

   (b) another adult appears or is brought before the court on the same or a subsequent occasion charged jointly with A with an either-way offence; and

   (c) that offence appears to the court to be related to an offence for which A was sent for trial under subsection (1) or (3) above,

the court shall where it is the same occasion, and may where it is a subsequent occasion, send the other adult forthwith to the Crown Court for trial for the either-way offence.

(6) Where the court sends an adult for trial under subsection (5) above, it shall at the same time send him to the Crown Court for trial for any either-way or summary offence with which he is charged and which—

   (a) (if it is an either-way offence) appears to the court to be related to the offence for which he is sent for trial; and

   (b) (if it is a summary offence) appears to the court to be related to the offence for which he is sent for trial or to the either-way offence, and which fulfils the requisite condition.

(7) Where—

   (a) the court sends an adult ('A') for trial under subsection (1), (3) or (5) above; and

(b) a child or young person appears or is brought before the court on the same or a subsequent occasion charged jointly with A with an indictable offence for which A is sent for trial under subsection (1), (3) or (5) above, or an indictable offence which appears to the court to be related to that offence,

the court shall, if it considers it necessary in the interests of justice to do so, send the child or young person forthwith to the Crown Court for trial for the indictable offence.

(8) Where the court sends a child or young person for trial under subsection (7) above, it may at the same time send him to the Crown Court for trial for any indictable or summary offence with which he is charged and which—

(a) (if it is an indictable offence) appears to the court to be related to the offence for which he is sent for trial; and

(b) (if it is a summary offence) appears to the court to be related to the offence for which he is sent for trial or to the indictable offence, and which fulfils the requisite condition.

(9) Subsections (7) and (8) above are subject to sections 24A and 24B of the Magistrates' Courts Act 1980 (which provide for certain cases involving children and young persons to be tried summarily).

(10) The trial of the information charging any summary offence for which a person is sent for trial under this section shall be treated as if the court had adjourned it under section 10 of the 1980 Act and had not fixed the time and place for its resumption.

(11) A summary offence fulfils the requisite condition if it is punishable with imprisonment or involves obligatory or discretionary disqualification from driving.

(12) In the case of an adult charged with an offence—

(a) if the offence satisfies paragraph (c) of subsection (2) above, the offence shall be dealt with under subsection (1) above and not under any other provision of this section or section 51A below;

(b) subject to paragraph (a) above, if the offence is one in respect of which the court is required to, or would decide to, send the adult to the Crown Court under—

(i) subsection (5) above; or

(ii) subsection (6) of section 51A below,

the offence shall be dealt with under that subsection and not under any other provision of this section or section 51A below.

(13) The functions of a magistrates' court under this section, and its related functions under section 51D below, may be discharged by a single justice.

51A Sending cases to the Crown Court: children and young persons

(1) This section is subject to sections 24A and 24B of the Magistrates' Courts Act 1980 (which provide for certain offences involving children or young persons to be tried summarily).

(2) Where a child or young person appears or is brought before a magistrates' court ('the court') charged with an offence and any of the conditions mentioned in subsection (3) below is satisfied, the court shall send him forthwith to the Crown Court for trial for the offence.

(3) Those conditions are—

   (a) that the offence falls within subsection (12) below;

   (b) that the offence is such as is mentioned in subsection (1) of section 91 of the Powers of Criminal Courts (Sentencing) Act 2000 (other than one mentioned in paragraph (d) below in relation to which it appears to the court as mentioned there) and the court considers that if he is found guilty of the offence it ought to be possible to sentence him in pursuance of subsection (3) of that section;

   (c) that notice is given to the court under section 51B or 51C below in respect of the offence;

   (d) that the offence is a specified offence (within the meaning of section 224 of the Criminal Justice Act 2003) and it appears to the court that if he is found guilty of the offence the criteria for the imposition of a sentence under section 226B of that Act would be met.

(4) Where the court sends a child or young person for trial under subsection (2) above, it may at the same time send him to the Crown Court for trial for any indictable or summary offence with which he is charged and which—

   (a) (if it is an indictable offence) appears to the court to be related to the offence mentioned in subsection (2) above; or

   (b) (if it is a summary offence) appears to the court to be related to the offence mentioned in subsection (2) above or to the indictable offence, and which fulfils the requisite condition (as defined in subsection (9) below).

(5) Where a child or young person who has been sent for trial under subsection (2) above subsequently appears or is brought before a magistrates' court charged with an indictable or summary offence which—

   (a) appears to the court to be related to the offence mentioned in subsection (2) above; and

   (b) (in the case of a summary offence) fulfils the requisite condition,

the court may send him forthwith to the Crown Court for trial for the indictable or summary offence.

(6) Where—

   (a) the court sends a child or young person ('C') for trial under subsection (2) or (4) above; and

   (b) an adult appears or is brought before the court on the same or a subsequent occasion charged jointly with C with an either-way offence for which C is sent for trial under subsection (2) or (4) above, or an either-way offence which appears to the court to be related to that offence,

the court shall where it is the same occasion, and may where it is a subsequent occasion, send the adult forthwith to the Crown Court for trial for the either-way offence.

(7) Where the court sends an adult for trial under subsection (6) above, it shall at the same time send him to the Crown Court for trial for any either-way or summary offence with which he is charged and which—

   (a) (if it is an either-way offence) appears to the court to be related to the offence for which he was sent for trial; and

   (b) (if it is a summary offence) appears to the court to be related to the offence for which he was sent for trial or to the either-way offence, and which fulfils the requisite condition.

(8) The trial of the information charging any summary offence for which a person is sent for trial under this section shall be treated as if the court had adjourned it under section 10 of the 1980 Act and had not fixed the time and place for its resumption.

(9) A summary offence fulfils the requisite condition if it is punishable with imprisonment or involves obligatory or discretionary disqualification from driving.

(10) In the case of a child or young person charged with an offence—

    (a) if the offence satisfies any of the conditions in subsection (3) above, the offence shall be dealt with under subsection (2) above and not under any other provision of this section or section 51 above;

    (b) subject to paragraph (a) above, if the offence is one in respect of which the requirements of subsection (7) of section 51 above for sending the child or young person to the Crown Court are satisfied, the offence shall be dealt with under that subsection and not under any other provision of this section or section 51 above.

(11) The functions of a magistrates' court under this section, and its related functions under section 51D below, may be discharged by a single justice.

(12) An offence falls within this subsection if—

    (a) it is an offence of homicide;

    (b) each of the requirements of section 51A(1) of the Firearms Act 1968 would be satisfied with respect to—

        (i) the offence; and

        (ii) the person charged with it,

    if he were convicted of the offence; or

    (c) section 29(3) of Violent Crime Reduction Act 2006 (minimum sentences in certain cases of using someone to mind a weapon) would apply if he were convicted of the offence.

51B Notices in serious or complex fraud cases

(1) A notice may be given by a designated authority under this section in respect of an indictable offence if the authority is of the opinion that the evidence of the offence charged—

    (a) is sufficient for the person charged to be put on trial for the offence; and

    (b) reveals a case of fraud of such seriousness or complexity that it is appropriate that the management of the case should without delay be taken over by the Crown Court.

(2) That opinion must be certified by the designated authority in the notice.

(3) The notice must also specify the proposed place of trial, and in selecting that place the designated authority must have regard to the same matters as are specified in paragraphs (a) to (c) of section 51D(4) below.

(4) A notice under this section must be given to the magistrates' court at which the person charged appears or before which he is brought.

(5) Such a notice must be given to the magistrates' court before any summary trial begins.

(6) The effect of such a notice is that the functions of the magistrates' court cease in relation to the case, except—

    (a) for the purposes of section 51D below;

    (b) as provided by paragraph 2 of Schedule 3 to the Access to Justice Act 1999; and

    (c) as provided by section 52 below.

(7) The functions of a designated authority under this section may be exercised by an officer of the authority acting on behalf of the authority.

(8) A decision to give a notice under this section shall not be subject to appeal or liable to be questioned in any court (whether a magistrates' court or not).

(9) In this section 'designated authority' means—

    (a) the Director of Public Prosecutions;

    (b) the Director of the Serious Fraud Office;

    (c) the Director of Revenue and Customs Prosecutions;

    (d) [repealed]

    (e) the Secretary of State.

51C Notices in certain cases involving children

(1) A notice may be given by the Director of Public Prosecutions under this section in respect of an offence falling within subsection (3) below if he is of the opinion—

    (a) that the evidence of the offence would be sufficient for the person charged to be put on trial for the offence;

    (b) that a child would be called as a witness at the trial; and

    (c) that, for the purpose of avoiding any prejudice to the welfare of the child, the case should be taken over and proceeded with without delay by the Crown Court.

(2) That opinion must be certified by the Director of Public Prosecutions in the notice.

(3) This subsection applies to an offence—

    (a) which involves an assault on, or injury or a threat of injury to, a person;

    (b) under section 1 of the Children and Young Persons Act 1933 (cruelty to persons under 16);

    (c) under the Sexual Offences Act 1956, the Protection of Children Act 1978 or the Sexual Offences Act 2003;

    (d) of kidnapping or false imprisonment, or an offence under section 1 or 2 of the Child Abduction Act 1984;

    (e) which consists of attempting or conspiring to commit, or of aiding, abetting, counselling, procuring or inciting the commission of, an offence falling within paragraph (a), (b), (c) or (d) above.

(4) Subsections (4), (5) and (6) of section 51B above apply for the purposes of this section as they apply for the purposes of that.

(5) The functions of the Director of Public Prosecutions under this section may be exercised by an officer acting on behalf of the Director.

(6) A decision to give a notice under this section shall not be subject to appeal or liable to be questioned in any court (whether a magistrates' court or not).

(7) In this section 'child' means—

    (a) a person who is under the age of 17; or

    (b) any person of whom a video recording (as defined in section 63(1) of the Youth Justice and Criminal Evidence Act 1999) was made when he was under the age of 17 with a view to its admission as his evidence in chief in the trial referred to in subsection (1) above.

51D Notice of offence and place of trial

(1) The court shall specify in a notice—

    (a) the offence or offences for which a person is sent for trial under section 51 or 51A above; and

    (b) the place at which he is to be tried (which, if a notice has been given under section 51B above, must be the place specified in that notice).

(2) A copy of the notice shall be served on the accused and given to the Crown Court sitting at that place.

(3) In a case where a person is sent for trial under section 51 or 51A above for more than one offence, the court shall specify in that notice, for each offence—

    (a) the subsection under which the person is so sent; and

    (b) if applicable, the offence to which that offence appears to the court to be related.

(4) Where the court selects the place of trial for the purposes of subsection (1) above, it shall have regard to—

    (a) the convenience of the defence, the prosecution and the witnesses;

    (b) the desirability of expediting the trial; and

    (c) any direction given by or on behalf of the Lord Chief Justice with the concurrence of the Lord Chancellor under section 75(1) of the Supreme Court Act 1981.

51E Interpretation of sections 50A to 51D

For the purposes of sections 50A to 51D above—

(a) 'adult' means a person aged 18 or over, and references to an adult include a corporation;

(b) 'either-way offence' means an offence triable either way;

(c) an either-way offence is related to an indictable offence if the charge for the either-way offence could be joined in the same indictment as the charge for the indictable offence;

(d) a summary offence is related to an indictable offence if it arises out of circumstances which are the same as or connected with those giving rise to the indictable offence.

 See *Blackstone's Criminal Practice 2014* **D10**

A31 Special Measures and Vulnerable Witnesses

A31.1 Special measures

Sections 16 and 17 of the Youth Justice and Criminal Evidence Act 1999 provide for special measures. Those aged under 18 may always benefit, as well as those meeting the requirements for incapacity (s 16). Witnesses who seek assistance may always benefit if the allegation is of an offence listed in **Appendix 4**, as well as those who otherwise meet the criteria (s 17). Under Part 3 of the Criminal Procedure Rules, the courts are required to facilitate the participation of anyone taking part, both witnesses and the defendant.

Youth Justice and Criminal Evidence Act 1999, ss 16 and 17

16 Witnesses eligible for assistance on grounds of age or incapacity

(1) For the purposes of this Chapter a witness in criminal proceedings (other than the accused) is eligible for assistance by virtue of this section—

    (a) if under the age of 18 at the time of the hearing; or

    (b) if the court considers that the quality of evidence given by the witness is likely to be diminished by reason of any circumstances falling within subsection (2).

(2) The circumstances falling within this subsection are—

    (a) that the witness—

        (i) suffers from mental disorder within the meaning of the Mental Health Act 1983, or

        (ii) otherwise has a significant impairment of intelligence and social functioning;

    (b) that the witness has a physical disability or is suffering from a physical disorder.

(3) In subsection (1)(a) 'the time of the hearing', in relation to a witness, means the time when it falls to the court to make a determination for the purposes of section 19(2) in relation to the witness.

(4) In determining whether a witness falls within subsection (1)(b) the court must consider any views expressed by the witness.

(5) In this Chapter references to the quality of a witness's evidence are to its quality in terms of completeness, coherence and accuracy; and for this purpose 'coherence' refers to a witness's ability in giving evidence to give answers which address the questions put to the witness and can be understood both individually and collectively.

---

17 Witnesses eligible for assistance on grounds of fear or distress about testifying

(1) For the purposes of this Chapter a witness in criminal proceedings (other than the accused) is eligible for assistance by virtue of this subsection if the court is satisfied that the quality of evidence given by the witness is likely to be diminished by reason of fear or distress on the part of the witness in connection with testifying in the proceedings.

(2) In determining whether a witness falls within subsection (1) the court must take into account, in particular—

    (a) the nature and alleged circumstances of the offence to which the proceedings relate;

    (b) the age of the witness;

    (c) such of the following matters as appear to the court to be relevant, namely—

        (i) the social and cultural background and ethnic origins of the witness,

        (ii) the domestic and employment circumstances of the witness, and

        (iii) any religious beliefs or political opinions of the witness;

    (d) any behaviour towards the witness on the part of—

        (i) the accused,

        (ii) members of the family or associates of the accused, or

        (iii) any other person who is likely to be an accused or a witness in the proceedings.

(3) In determining that question the court must in addition consider any views expressed by the witness.

(4) Where the complainant in respect of a sexual offence is a witness in proceedings relating to that offence (or to that offence and any other offences), the witness is eligible for assistance in relation to those proceedings by virtue of this subsection unless the witness has informed the court of the witness' wish not to be so eligible by virtue of this subsection.

(5) A witness in proceedings relating to a relevant offence (or to a relevant offence and any other offences) is eligible for assistance in relation to those proceedings by virtue of this subsection unless the witness has informed the court of the witness's wish not to be so eligible by virtue of this subsection.

(6) For the purposes of subsection (5) an offence is a relevant offence if it is an offence described in Schedule 1A.

(7) The Secretary of State may by order amend Schedule 1A.

The following special measures are available in the magistrates' court:

	Section 16 witnesses (children and vulnerable adults)	Section 17 witnesses (intimidated/fear or distress)
Section 23 screening witness from accused	Full availability	Full availability
Section 24 evidence via live link	Full availability	Full availability

	Section 16 witnesses (children and vulnerable adults)	Section 17 witnesses (intimidated/fear or distress)
Section 25 evidence given in private	Full availability	Full availability
Section 26 removal of wigs/gowns	Not applicable	Not applicable
Section 27 video recorded evidence-in-chief	Full availability	Not available
Section 28 video recorded cross-examination and re-examination	Not available	Not available
Section 29 examination through an intermediary	Full availability	Not applicable
Section 30 aids to communication	Full availability	Not applicable

A31.2 Witness anonymity

The Coroners and Justice Act 2009 provides for the making and discharge of witness anonymity orders. These are to be regarded as a special mesaure of last practicable resort (*R v Mayers* [2008] EWCA Crim 2989).

Coroners and Justice Act 2009, ss 86–89, 91, and 95

86 Witness anonymity orders

(1) In this Chapter a 'witness anonymity order' is an order made by a court that requires such specified measures to be taken in relation to a witness in criminal proceedings as the court considers appropriate to ensure that the identity of the witness is not disclosed in or in connection with the proceedings.

(2) The kinds of measures that may be required to be taken in relation to a witness include measures for securing one or more of the following—

    (a) that the witness's name and other identifying details may be—

        (i) withheld;

        (ii) removed from materials disclosed to any party to the proceedings;

    (b) that the witness may use a pseudonym;

    (c) that the witness is not asked questions of any specified description that might lead to the identification of the witness;

    (d) that the witness is screened to any specified extent;

    (e) that the witness's voice is subjected to modulation to any specified extent.

(3) Subsection (2) does not affect the generality of subsection (1).

(4) Nothing in this section authorises the court to require—
  (a) the witness to be screened to such an extent that the witness cannot be seen by—
    (i) the judge or other members of the court (if any), or
    (ii) the jury (if there is one);
  (b) the witness's voice to be modulated to such an extent that the witness's natural voice cannot be heard by any persons within paragraph (a)(i) or (ii).

(5) In this section 'specified' means specified in the witness anonymity order concerned.

87 Applications

(1) An application for a witness anonymity order to be made in relation to a witness in criminal proceedings may be made to the court by the prosecutor or the defendant.

(2) Where an application is made by the prosecutor, the prosecutor—
  (a) must (unless the court directs otherwise) inform the court of the identity of the witness, but
  (b) is not required to disclose in connection with the application—
    (i) the identity of the witness, or
    (ii) any information that might enable the witness to be identified, to any other party to the proceedings or his or her legal representatives.

(3) Where an application is made by the defendant, the defendant—
  (a) must inform the court and the prosecutor of the identity of the witness, but
  (b) (if there is more than one defendant) is not required to disclose in connection with the application—
    (i) the identity of the witness, or
    (ii) any information that might enable the witness to be identified, to any other defendant or his or her legal representatives.

(4) Accordingly, where the prosecutor or the defendant proposes to make an application under this section in respect of a witness, any relevant material which is disclosed by or on behalf of that party before the determination of the application may be disclosed in such a way as to prevent—
  (a) the identity of the witness, or
  (b) any information that might enable the witness to be identified, from being disclosed except as required by subsection (2)(a) or (3)(a).

(5) 'Relevant material' means any document or other material which falls to be disclosed, or is sought to be relied on, by or on behalf of the party concerned in connection with the proceedings or proceedings preliminary to them.

(6) The court must give every party to the proceedings the opportunity to be heard on an application under this section.

(7) But subsection (6) does not prevent the court from hearing one or more parties in the absence of a defendant and his or her legal representatives, if it appears to the court to be appropriate to do so in the circumstances of the case.

(8) Nothing in this section is to be taken as restricting any power to make rules of court.

88 Conditions for making order

(1) This section applies where an application is made for a witness anonymity order to be made in relation to a witness in criminal proceedings.

(2) The court may make such an order only if it is satisfied that Conditions A to C below are met.

(3) Condition A is that the proposed order is necessary—

   (a) in order to protect the safety of the witness or another person or to prevent any serious damage to property, or

   (b) in order to prevent real harm to the public interest (whether affecting the carrying on of any activities in the public interest or the safety of a person involved in carrying on such activities, or otherwise).

(4) Condition B is that, having regard to all the circumstances, the effect of the proposed order would be consistent with the defendant receiving a fair trial.

(5) Condition C is that the importance of the witness's testimony is such that in the interests of justice the witness ought to testify and—

   (a) the witness would not testify if the proposed order were not made, or

   (b) there would be real harm to the public interest if the witness were to testify without the proposed order being made.

(6) In determining whether the proposed order is necessary for the purpose mentioned in subsection (3)(a), the court must have regard (in particular) to any reasonable fear on the part of the witness—

   (a) that the witness or another person would suffer death or injury, or

   (b) that there would be serious damage to property, if the witness were to be identified.

89 Relevant considerations

(1) When deciding whether Conditions A to C in section 88 are met in the case of an application for a witness anonymity order, the court must have regard to—

   (a) the considerations mentioned in subsection (2) below, and

   (b) such other matters as the court considers relevant.

(2) The considerations are—

   (a) the general right of a defendant in criminal proceedings to know the identity of a witness in the proceedings;

   (b) the extent to which the credibility of the witness concerned would be a relevant factor when the weight of his or her evidence comes to be assessed;

   (c) whether evidence given by the witness might be the sole or decisive evidence implicating the defendant;

   (d) whether the witness's evidence could be properly tested (whether on grounds of credibility or otherwise) without his or her identity being disclosed;

   (e) whether there is any reason to believe that the witness—

      (i) has a tendency to be dishonest, or

      (ii) has any motive to be dishonest in the circumstances of the case, having regard (in particular) to any previous convictions of the witness and to any relationship between the witness and the defendant or any associates of the defendant;

    (f) whether it would be reasonably practicable to protect the witness by any means other than by making a witness anonymity order specifying the measures that are under consideration by the court.

90 ...

91 Discharge or variation of order

(1) A court that has made a witness anonymity order in relation to any criminal proceedings may in those proceedings subsequently discharge or vary (or further vary) the order if it appears to the court to be appropriate to do so in view of the provisions of sections 88 and 89 that apply to the making of an order.

(2) The court may do so—
    (a) on an application made by a party to the proceedings if there has been a material change of circumstances since the relevant time, or
    (b) on its own initiative.

(3) The court must give every party to the proceedings the opportunity to be heard—
    (a) before determining an application made to it under subsection (2);
    (b) before discharging or varying the order on its own initiative.

(4) But subsection (3) does not prevent the court hearing one or more of the parties to the proceedings in the absence of a defendant in the proceedings and his or her legal representatives, if it appears to the court to be appropriate to do so in the circumstances of the case.

(5) 'The relevant time' means—
    (a) the time when the order was made, or
    (b) if a previous application has been made under subsection (2), the time when the application (or the last application) was made.

92 ...

93 ...

94 ...

95 Public interest immunity

Nothing in this Chapter affects the common law rules as to the withholding of information on the grounds of public interest immunity.

 See *Blackstone's Criminal Practice 2014* **D14**

A32 **Submission of No Case**

A32.1 **Test for no case to answer**

In *R v Galbraith* (1981) 73 Cr App R 124, the court laid down the following test:

(1) If there is no evidence that the crime alleged has been committed by the defendant, there is no difficulty. The judge will of course stop the case.

(2) The difficulty arises where there is some evidence but it is of a tenuous character, for example because of inherent weakness or vagueness or because it is inconsistent with other evidence. (a) Where the judge comes to the conclusion that the prosecution evidence, taken at its highest, is such that a jury properly directed could not properly convict upon it, it is his duty, upon a submission being made, to stop the case. (b) Where however the prosecution evidence is such that its strength or weakness depends on the view to be taken of a witness's reliability, or other matters which are generally speaking within the province of the jury and where on one possible view of the facts there is evidence upon which a jury could properly come to the conclusion that the defendant is guilty, then the judge should allow the matter to be tried by the jury. It follows that we think the second of the two schools of thought is to be preferred.

 See *Blackstone's Criminal Practice 2014* **D16.54–D16.73**

A33 Transfer/Remittal of Criminal Cases

Section 27A of the Magistrates' Courts Act 1980 provides:

Magistrates' Courts Act 1980, s 27A

27A Power to transfer criminal proceedings

(1) Where a person appears or is brought before a magistrates' court—
   (a) to be tried by the court for an offence, or
   (b) for the court to inquire into the offence as examining justices, the court may transfer the matter to another magistrates' court.
(2) The court may transfer the matter before or after beginning the trial or inquiry.
(3) But if the court transfers the matter after it has begun to hear the evidence and the parties, the court to which the matter is transferred must begin hearing the evidence and the parties again.
(4) The power of the court under this section to transfer any matter must be exercised in accordance with any directions given under section 30(3) of the Courts Act 2003.

A33.1 Remittal of convicted defendants

Provision is made for the remittal of convicted defendants by section 10 of the Powers of Criminal Courts (Sentencing) Act 2000:

Powers of Criminal Courts (Sentencing) Act 2000, s 10

10 Power of magistrates' court to remit case to another magistrates' court for sentence

(1) Where a person aged 18 or over ('the offender') has been convicted by a magistrates' court ('the convicting court') of an offence to which this section applies ('the instant offence') and—
   (a) it appears to the convicting court that some other magistrates' court ('the other court') has convicted him of another such offence in respect of which the other court has neither passed sentence on him nor committed him to the Crown Court for sentence nor dealt with him in any other way, and
   (b) the other court consents to his being remitted under this section to the other court,
   the convicting court may remit him to the other court to be dealt with in respect of the instant offence by the other court instead of by the convicting court.
(2) This section applies to—
   (a) any offence punishable with imprisonment; and

(b) any offence in respect of which the convicting court has a power or duty to order the offender to be disqualified under section 34, 35 or 36 of the Road Traffic Offenders Act 1988 (disqualification for certain motoring offences).

See *Blackstone's Criminal Practice 2014* **D21.5**

A34 **Video Links**

Sections 57A–57F of the Crime and Disorder Act 1998 provide for the use of live links in relation to preliminary hearings and sentence (see **A31** for special measure provisions):

Crime and Disorder Act 1998, ss 57A–57F

57A Introductory

(1) This Part—
  (a) applies to preliminary hearings and sentencing hearings in the course of proceedings for an offence and enforcement hearings relating to confiscation orders; and
  (b) enables the court in the circumstances provided for in sections 57B, 57C, 57E and 57F to direct the use of a live link for securing the accused's attendance at a hearing to which this Part applies.

(2) The accused is to be treated as present in court when, by virtue of a live link direction under this Part, he attends a hearing through a live link.

(3) In this Part—

'confiscation order' means an order made under—
  (a) section 71 of the Criminal Justice Act 1988;
  (b) section 2 of the Drug Trafficking Act 1994; or
  (c) section 6 of the Proceeds of Crime Act 2002;

'custody'—
  (a) includes local authority accommodation to which a person is remanded or committed by virtue of section 23 of the Children and Young Persons Act 1969; but
  (b) does not include police detention;

'enforcement hearing' means a hearing under section 82 of the Magistrates' Courts Act 1980 to consider the issuing of a warrant of committal or to inquire into a person's means;

'live link' means an arrangement by which a person (when not in the place where the hearing is being held) is able to see and hear, and to be seen and heard by, the court during a hearing (and for this purpose any impairment of eyesight or hearing is to be disregarded);

'police detention' has the meaning given by section 118(2) of the Police and Criminal Evidence Act 1984;

'preliminary hearing' means a hearing in the proceedings held before the start of the trial (within the meaning of subsection (11A) or (11B) of section 22 of the 1985 Act) including, in the case of proceedings in the Crown Court, a preparatory hearing held under—
  (a) section 7 of the Criminal Justice Act 1987 (cases of serious or complex fraud); or
  (b) section 29 of the Criminal Procedure and Investigations Act 1996 (other serious, complex or lengthy cases);

'sentencing hearing' means any hearing following conviction which is held for the purpose of—

(a) proceedings relating to the giving or rescinding of a direction under section 57E;

(b) proceedings (in a magistrates' court) relating to committal to the Crown Court for sentencing; or

(c) sentencing the offender or determining how the court should deal with him in respect of the offence.

57B Use of live link at preliminary hearings where accused is in custody

(1) This section applies in relation to a preliminary hearing in a magistrates' court or the C rown Court.

(2) Where it appears to the court before which the preliminary hearing is to take place that the accused is likely to be held in custody during the hearing, the court may give a live link direction under this section in relation to the attendance of the accused at the hearing.

(3) A live link direction under this section is a direction requiring the accused, if he is being held in custody during the hearing, to attend it through a live link from the place at which he is being held.

(4) If a hearing takes place in relation to the giving or rescinding of such a direction, the court may require or permit a person attending the hearing to do so through a live link.

(5) The court shall not give or rescind such a direction (whether at a hearing or otherwise) unless the parties to the proceedings have been given the opportunity to make representations.

(6) If in a case where it has power to do so a magistrates' court decides not to give a live link direction under this section, it must—

(a) state in open court its reasons for not doing so; and

(b) cause those reasons to be entered in the register of its proceedings.

(7) The following functions of a magistrates' court under this section may be discharged by a single justice—

(a) giving a live link direction under this section;

(b) rescinding a live link direction before a preliminary hearing begins; and

(c) requiring or permitting a person to attend by live link a hearing about a matter within paragraph (a) or (b).

57C Use of live link at preliminary hearings where accused is at police station

(1) This section applies in relation to a preliminary hearing in a magistrates' court.

(2) Where subsection (3) or (4) applies to the accused, the court may give a live link direction in relation to his attendance at the preliminary hearing.

(3) This subsection applies to the accused if—

(a) he is in police detention at a police station in connection with the offence; and

(b) it appears to the court that he is likely to remain at that station in police detention until the beginning of the preliminary hearing.

(4) This subsection applies to the accused if he is at a police station in answer to live link bail in connection with the offence.

(5) A live link direction under this section is a direction requiring the accused to attend the preliminary hearing through a live link from the police station.

(6) But a direction given in relation to an accused to whom subsection (3) applies has no effect if he does not remain in police detention at the police station until the beginning of the preliminary hearing.

(6A) A live link direction under this section may not be given unless the court is satisfied that it is not contrary to the interests of justice to give the direction.

(8) A magistrates' court may rescind a live link direction under this section at any time during a hearing to which it relates.

(9) A magistrates' court may require or permit—

[. . .]

(b) any party to the proceedings who wishes to make representations in relation to the giving or rescission of a live link direction under this section to do so through a live link.

(10) Where a live link direction under this section is given in relation to an accused person who is answering to live link bail he is to be treated as having surrendered to the custody of the court (as from the time when the direction is given).

(11) In this section, 'live link bail' means bail granted under Part 4 of the Police and Criminal Evidence Act 1984 subject to the duty mentioned in section 47(3)(b) of that Act.

57D Continued use of live link for sentencing hearing following a preliminary hearing

(1) Subsection (2) applies where—

(a) a live link direction under section 57B or 57C is in force;

(b) the accused is attending a preliminary hearing through a live link by virtue of the direction;

(c) the court convicts him of the offence in the course of that hearing (whether by virtue of a guilty plea or an indication of an intention to plead guilty); and

(d) the court proposes to continue the hearing as a sentencing hearing in relation to the offence.

(2) The accused may continue to attend through the live link by virtue of the direction if—

(a) the hearing is continued as a sentencing hearing in relation to the offence; and

(c) the court is satisfied that the accused continuing to attend through the live link is not contrary to the interests of justice.

(3) But the accused may not give oral evidence through the live link during a continued hearing under subsection (2) unless—

[. . .]

(b) the court is satisfied that it is not contrary to the interests of justice for him to give it in that way.

57E Use of live link in sentencing hearings

(1) This section applies where the accused is convicted of the offence.

(2) If it appears to the court by or before which the accused is convicted that it is likely that he will be held in custody during any sentencing hearing for the

offence, the court may give a live link direction under this section in relation to that hearing.

(3) A live link direction under this section is a direction requiring the accused, if he is being held in custody during the hearing, to attend it through a live link from the place at which he is being held.

(4) Such a direction—
   (a) may be given by the court of its own motion or on an application by a party; and
   (b) may be given in relation to all subsequent sentencing hearings before the court or to such hearing or hearings as may be specified or described in the direction.

(5) The court may not give such a direction unless—
   [. . .]
   (b) the court is satisfied that it is not contrary to the interests of justice to give the direction.

(6) The court may rescind such a direction at any time before or during a hearing to which it relates if it appears to the court to be in the interests of justice to do so (but this does not affect the court's power to give a further live link direction in relation to the offender).
   The court may exercise this power of its own motion or on an application by a party.

(7) The offender may not give oral evidence while attending a hearing through a live link by virtue of this section unless—
   [. . .]
   (b) the court is satisfied that it is not contrary to the interests of justice for him to give it in that way.

(8) The court must—
   (a) state in open court its reasons for refusing an application for, or for the rescission of, a live link direction under this section; and
   (b) if it is a magistrates' court, cause those reasons to be entered in the register of its proceedings.

57F Use of live link in certain enforcement hearings

(1) This section applies where—
   (a) a confiscation order is made against a person; and
   (b) the amount required to be paid under the order is not paid when it is required to be paid.

(2) If it appears to the court before which an enforcement hearing relating to the confiscation order is to take place that it is likely that the person will be held in custody at the time of the hearing, the court may give a live link direction under this section in relation to that hearing.

(3) A live link direction under this section is a direction requiring the person, if the person is being held in custody at the time of the hearing, to attend it through a live link from the place at which the person is being held.

(4) Such a direction—
   (a) may be given by the court of its own motion or on an application by a party; and
   (b) may be given in relation to all subsequent enforcement hearings before the court or to such hearing or hearings as may be specified or described in the direction.

(5) The court may rescind a live link direction under this section at any time before or during a hearing to which it relates.

(6) The court may not give or rescind a live link direction under this section (whether at a hearing or otherwise) unless the parties to the proceedings have been given the opportunity to make representations.

(7) If a hearing takes place in relation to the giving or rescinding of such a direction, the court may require or permit any party to the proceedings who wishes to make representations in relation to the giving or rescission of a live link direction under this section to do so through a live link.

(8) The person may not give oral evidence while attending a hearing through a live link by virtue of this section unless the court is satisfied that it is not contrary to the interests of justice for the person to give it that way.

(9) If in a case where it has power to do so a court decides not to give a live link direction under this section, it must—

   (a) state in open court its reasons for not doing so; and

   (b) cause those reasons to be entered in the register of its proceedings.

(10) The following functions of a magistrates' court under this section may be discharged by a single justice—

   (a) giving a live link direction under this section;

   (b) rescinding a live link direction before a preliminary hearing begins; and

   (c) requiring or permitting a person to attend by live link a hearing about a matter within paragraph (a) or (b).

 See *Blackstone's Criminal Practice 2014* **D5.38–D5.41**

A35 **Warrants**

Sections 1 and 13 of the Magistrates' Courts Act 1980 provide for the issue of warrants to secure a person's attendance before the court:

Magistrates' Courts Act 1980, ss 1 and 13

1 Issue of summons to accused or warrant for his arrest

(1) On an information being laid before a justice of the peace that a person has, or is suspected of having, committed an offence, the justice may issue—

    (a) a summons directed to that person requiring him to appear before a magistrates' court to answer the information, or

    (b) a warrant to arrest that person and bring him before a magistrates' court.

(3) No warrant shall be issued under this section unless the information is in writing.

(4) No warrant shall be issued under this section for the arrest of any person who has attained the age of 18 years unless—

    (a) the offence to which the warrant relates is an indictable offence or is punishable with imprisonment, or

    (b) the person's address is not sufficiently established for a summons to be served on him.

(6) Where the offence charged is an indictable offence, a warrant under this section may be issued at any time notwithstanding that a summons has previously been issued.

(7) A justice of the peace may issue a summons or warrant under this section upon an information being laid before him notwithstanding any enactment requiring the information to be laid before two or more justices.

13 Non-appearance of accused: issue of warrant

(1) Subject to the provisions of this section, where the court, instead of proceeding in the absence of the accused, adjourns or further adjourns the trial, the court may issue a warrant for his arrest.

(2) Where a summons has been issued, the court shall not issue a warrant under this section unless the condition in subsection (2A) below or that in subsection (2B) below is fulfilled.

(2A) The condition in this subsection is that it is proved to the satisfaction of the court, on oath or in such other manner as may be prescribed, that the summons was served on the accused within what appears to the court to be a reasonable time before the trial or adjourned trial.

(2B) The condition in this subsection is that—

    (a) the adjournment now being made is a second or subsequent adjournment of the trial,

    (b) the accused was present on the last (or only) occasion when the trial was adjourned, and

    (c) on that occasion the court determined the time for the hearing at which the adjournment is now being made.

(3) A warrant for the arrest of any person who has attained the age of 18 shall not be issued under this section unless—

   (a) the offence to which the warrant relates is punishable with imprisonment, or

   (b) the court, having convicted the accused, proposes to impose a disqualification on him.

(3A) A warrant for the arrest of any person who has not attained the age of 18 shall not be issued under this section unless—

   (a) the offence to which the warrant relates is punishable, in the case of a person who has attained the age of 18, with imprisonment, or

   (b) the court, having convicted the accused, proposes to impose a disqualification on him.

(4) This section shall not apply to an adjournment on the occasion of the accused's conviction in his absence under subsection (5) of section 12 above or to an adjournment required by subsection (9) of that section.

See *Blackstone's Criminal Practice 2014* **D5.44**

A36 **Witnesses, Issue of Summons or Warrant**

A36.1 **Power to require attendance**

Magistrates' Courts Act 1980, s 97

97 Summons to witness and warrant for his arrest

(1) Where a justice of the peace is satisfied that—

    (a) any person in England or Wales is likely to be able to give material evidence, or produce any document or thing likely to be material evidence, at the summary trial of an information or hearing of a complaint or of an application under the Adoption and Children Act 2002 (c. 38) by a magistrates' court, and

    (b) it is in the interests of justice to issue a summons under this subsection to secure the attendance of that person to give evidence or produce the document or thing,

the justice shall issue a summons directed to that person requiring him to attend before the court at the time and place appointed in the summons to give evidence or to produce the document or thing.

(2) If a justice of the peace is satisfied by evidence on oath of the matters mentioned in subsection (1) above, and also that it is probable that a summons under that subsection would not procure the attendance of the person in question, the justice may instead of issuing a summons issue a warrant to arrest that person and bring him before such a court as aforesaid at a time and place specified in the warrant; but a warrant shall not be issued under this subsection where the attendance is required for the hearing of a complaint or of an application under the Adoption and Children Act 2002 (c. 38).

(2A) A summons may also be issued under subsection (1) above if the justice is satisfied that the person in question is outside the British Islands but no warrant shall be issued under subsection (2) above unless the justice is satisfied by evidence on oath that the person in question is in England or Wales.

(2B) A justice may refuse to issue a summons under subsection (1) above in relation to the summary trial of an information if he is not satisfied that an application for the summons was made by a party to the case as soon as reasonably practicable after the accused pleaded not guilty.

(2C) In relation to the summary trial of an information, subsection (2) above shall have effect as if the reference to the matters mentioned in subsection (1) above included a reference to the matter mentioned in subsection (2B) above.

(3) On the failure of any person to attend before a magistrates' court in answer to a summons under this section, if—

    (a) the court is satisfied by evidence on oath that he is likely to be able to give material evidence or produce any document or thing likely to be material evidence in the proceedings; and

(b) it is proved on oath, or in such other manner as may be prescribed, that he has been duly served with the summons, and that a reasonable sum has been paid or tendered to him for costs and expenses; and

(c) it appears to the court that there is no just excuse for the failure,

the court may issue a warrant to arrest him and bring him before the court at a time and place specified in the warrant.

(4) If any person attending or brought before a magistrates' court refuses without just excuse to be sworn or give evidence, or to produce any document or thing, the court may commit him to custody until the expiration of such period not exceeding one month as may be specified in the warrant or until he sooner gives evidence or produces the document or thing or impose on him a fine not exceeding £2,500 or both.

Conduct money should be served with any summons sufficient to enable the person to attend court.

The power to compel production of documents relates only to material evidence, and should not be used to compel the production of documents solely for the purpose of cross-examination (*R v Skegness Magistrates' Court, ex p Cardy* [1985] RTR 49). See also Part 28 of the Criminal Procedure Rules.

 See *Blackstone's Criminal Practice 2014* **D21.27–D21.33**

Part B
Youths in the Adult Court

B1 Age of Offender and the Position of Those Attaining 18

It is the duty of a court to determine age when a young person is brought before the court. In most cases there is no dispute and a simple confirmation of the youth's date of birth will suffice. The court is, however, able to hear evidence on the issue. If the age is later found to be incorrect, this has no bearing on any orders made by the court. Section 99 of the Children and Young Persons Act 1933 provides:

Children and Young Persons Act 1933, s 99

99 Presumption and determination of age

(1) Where a person, whether charged with an offence or not, is brought before any court otherwise than for the purpose of giving evidence, and it appears to the court that he is a child or young person, the court shall make due inquiry as to the age of that person, and for that purpose shall take such evidence as may be forthcoming at the hearing of the case, but an order or judgment of the court shall not be invalidated by any subsequent proof that the age of that person has not been correctly stated to the court, and the age presumed or declared by the court to be the age of the person so brought before it shall, for the purposes of this Act, be deemed to be the true age of that person, and, where it appears to the court that the person so brought before it has attained the age of eighteen years, that person shall for the purposes of this Act be deemed not to be a child or young person.

(2) Where in any charge or indictment for any offence under this Act or any of the offences mentioned in the First Schedule to this Act except as provided in that Schedule, it is alleged that the person by or in respect of whom the offence was committed was a child or young person or was under or had attained any specified age, and he appears to the court to have been at the date of the commission of the alleged offence a child or young person, or to have been under or to have attained the specified age, as the case may be, he shall for the purposes of this Act be presumed at that date to have been a child or young person or to have been under or to have attained that age, as the case may be, unless the contrary is proved.

(3) Where, in any charge or indictment for any offence under this Act or any of the offences mentioned in the First Schedule to this Act, it is alleged that the person in respect of whom the offence was committed was a child or was a young person, it shall not be a defence to prove that the person alleged to have been a child was a young person or the person alleged to have been a young person was a child in any case where the acts constituting the alleged offence would equally have been an offence if committed in respect of a young person or child respectively.

(4) Where a person is charged with an offence under this Act in respect of a person apparently under a specified age it shall be a defence to prove that the person was actually of or over that age.

B1.1 Youth becoming an adult during course of proceedings

B1.1.1 *Attaining 18 before first court appearance*

Notwithstanding the defendant's age at the date of allegation or charge, where a defendant is 18 years of age at the date of the first court appearance the hearing is in the adult magistrates' court. Section 24(1) of the Magistrates' Courts Act 1980 ('summary trial of information against child or young person for indictable offence') applies only to those who are under 18 years at the date of the first appearance in court. The youth court has no jurisdiction (*R v Amersham Juvenile Court, ex p Wilson* [1981] 2 All ER 315). This applies where the defendant does not appear and a warrant is issued prior to the defendant's 18th birthday. The charge must be laid again in the adult court (*R v Uxbridge Youth Court, ex p H* [1998] EWHC (Admin) 341).

B1.1.2 *Attaining 18 during court proceedings*

The relevant date is the date on which the plea is taken and/or venue is determined. If the defendant attains 18 after the first appearance at court and the offence is indictable, and no plea has been taken/venue has not been determined, the adult sending and venue procedures apply. This includes the right to elect trial by jury (*Re Daley* [1983] 1 AC 327; *R v West London Justices, ex p Siley-Winditt* [2000] Crim LR 926).

Where the prosecution, during the course of the proceedings, seek to lay a new charge based on the same facts, the new charge must be laid in the adult court (*R v Chelsea Justices, ex p Director of Public Prosecutions* [1963] 3 All ER 657).

B1.1.3 *Sentence*

For the purposes of sentence, the relevant age is the age of the defendant at the date of conviction or guilty plea (*R v Danga* [1992] QB 476).

The starting point is the sentence the defendant would have been likely to receive if he had been sentenced at the date of the commission of the offence (*R v Ghafoor* [2002] EWCA Crim 1857):

> It will rarely be necessary for a court even to consider the passing of a sentence which is more severe than the maximum it would have had jurisdiction to pass at the time of the commission of the offence.

The defendant's age is a powerful, but not the sole, determining factor (*R v Bowker* [2007] EWCA Crim 1608):

> Whilst therefore it is clearly right that a person who has committed an offence whilst under the age of 18 should be sentenced on the basis that his culpability is to be judged by reference to his age at the time of the offence,

nonetheless, the necessary sentencing disposal has to take account of the matters set out in section 142(1) [of the Criminal Justice Act 2003] if he is convicted after he has reached the age of 18. When sentencing those under 18, the court will generally focus more on their requirements and their rehabilitation. Section 142 suggests that for those over the age of 18, however, more general public policy considerations, in particular deterrence, can play a greater part.

The age of the offender for the purposes of determining which of the statutory regimes under the Criminal Justice Act 2003 applies (dangerousness) is his age at date of conviction (*R v Robson* [2006] EWCA Crim 1414).

SGC Guideline: Overarching Principles—Sentencing Youths, para 5

5. Crossing a significant age threshold between commission of an offence and sentence

5.1 There will be occasions when an increase in the age of an offender 15 will result in the maximum sentence on the date of conviction being greater than that available on the date on which the offence was committed.

5.2 In such circumstances, the approach should be:

- where an offender crosses a relevant age threshold between the date on which the offence was committed and the date of conviction or sentence, a court should take as its starting point the sentence likely to have been imposed on the date on which the offence was committed;

- where an offender attains the age of 18 after committing the offence but before conviction, section 142 of the Criminal Justice Act 2003 applies (whilst section 37 of the 1998 Act and section 44 of the 1933 Act...apply to those aged under 18) and the sentencing disposal has to take account of the matters set out in that section;

- it will be rare for a court to have to consider passing a sentence more severe than the maximum it would have had jurisdiction to pass at the time the offence was committed even where an offender has subsequently attained the age of 18;

- however, a sentence at or close to that maximum may be appropriate, especially where a serious offence was committed by an offender close to the age threshold.

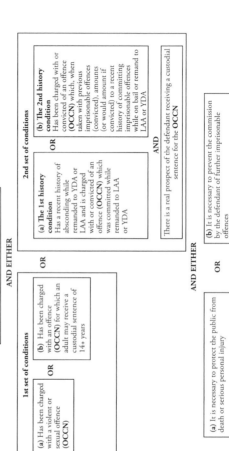

Figure 2 Remand to Youth Detention Accommodation

Be aged between 12–17

AND

Satisfy the legal representation conditions

AND EITHER

1st set of conditions

(a) Has been charged with a violent or sexual offence (**OCCN**)

OR

(b) Has been charged with an offence (**OCCN**) for which an adult may receive a custodial sentence of 14+ years

OR

2nd set of conditions

(a) The 1st history condition
Has a recent history of absconding while remanded to YDA or LAA and is charged with or convicted of an offence (**OCCN**) which was committed while remanded to LAA or YDA

OR

(b) The 2nd history condition
Has been charged with or convicted of an offence (**OCCN**) which, when taken with previous imprisonable offences (convicted), amounts (or would amount if convicted) to a recent history of committing imprisonable offences while on bail or remand to LAA or YDA

AND

There is a real prospect of the defendant receiving a custodial sentence for the **OCCN**

AND EITHER

(a) It is necessary to protect the public from death or serious personal injury

OR

(b) It is necessary to prevent the commission by the defendant of further imprisonable offences

With the following exceptions, the bases on which the Crown may oppose bail, and on which an application for bail, whether unconditional or conditional, may be made for a youth appearing in the adult court, are the same as for an adult (see **A8**).

If, under transitional arrangments, the offence carries a sentence of life imprisonment and at the time of the offence the defendant was on bail, Schedule 1, paragraphs 9AA and 9AB to the Bail Act 1976 (as amended) provide:

Bail Act 1976, Sch 1, paras 9AA and 9AB

9AA (1) This paragraph applies if—
    (a) the defendant is a child or young person, and
    (b) it appears to the court that he was on bail in criminal proceedings on the date of the offence.
  (2) In deciding for the purposes of paragraph 2(1) of this Part of this Schedule whether it is satisfied that there are substantial grounds for believing that the defendant, if released on bail (whether subject to conditions or not), would commit an offence while on bail, the court shall give particular weight to the fact that the defendant was on bail in criminal proceedings on the date of the offence.

9AB (1) Subject to sub-paragraph (2) below, this paragraph applies if—
    (a) the defendant is a child or young person, and
    (b) it appears to the court that, having been released on bail in or in connection with the proceedings for the offence, he failed to surrender to custody.
  (2) Where it appears to the court that the defendant had reasonable cause for his failure to surrender to custody, this paragraph does not apply unless it also appears to the court that he failed to surrender to custody at the appointed place as soon as reasonably practicable after the appointed time.
  (3) In deciding for the purposes of paragraph 2(1) of this Part of this Schedule whether it is satisfied that there are substantial grounds for believing that the defendant, if released on bail (whether subject to conditions or not), would fail to surrender to custody, the court shall give particular weight to—
    (a) where the defendant did not have reasonable cause for his failure to surrender to custody, the fact that he failed to surrender to custody, or
    (b) where he did have reasonable cause for his failure to surrender to custody, the fact that he failed to surrender to custody at the appointed place as soon as reasonably practicable after the appointed time.
  (4) …

If electronic monitoring is to be a condition of bail, the court must comply with sections 3AA and 3AC of the Bail Act 1976:

Bail Act 1976, ss 3AA(1)–(5) and 3AC(1) and (2)

3AA Conditions for the imposition of electronic monitoring requirements: children and young persons

(1) A court may not impose electronic monitoring requirements on a child or young person unless each of the following conditions is met.

(2) The first condition is that the child or young person has attained the age of twelve years.

(3) The second condition is that—

  (a) the child or young person is charged with or has been convicted of a violent or sexual offence, or an offence punishable in the case of an adult with imprisonment for a term of fourteen years or more; or

  (b) he is charged with or has been convicted of one or more imprisonable offences which, together with any other imprisonable offences of which he has been convicted in any proceedings—

  (i) amount, or

  (ii) would, if he were convicted of the offences with which he is charged, amount,

  to a recent history of repeatedly committing imprisonable offences while remanded on bail or to local authority accommodation.

(4) The third condition is that the court is satisfied that the necessary provision for dealing with the person concerned can be made under arrangements for the electronic monitoring of persons released on bail that are currently available in each local justice area which is a relevant area.

(5) The fourth condition is that a youth offending team has informed the court that in its opinion the imposition of electronic monitoring requirements will be suitable in the case of the child or young person.

3AC Electronic monitoring: general provisions

(1) Where a court imposes electronic monitoring requirements as a condition of bail, the requirements must include provision for making a person responsible for the monitoring.

(2) A person may not be made responsible for the electronic monitoring of a person on bail unless he is of a description specified in an order made by the Secretary of State.

B2.1 Refusal of bail

If a youth is refused bail, the Legal Aid, Sentencing and Punishment of Offenders Act 2012, Part 3, Chapter 3 provides for an entirely different regime (see **B2.1.9** for ss 91–102 in full).

It should be noted that remands both to local authority accommodation and to youth detention accommodation are custodial remands, and that time limits for such remands and custody time limits apply.

In the case of a youth charged with murder, where the court has no power to grant bail, the court will still determine where the youth is to be remanded (*R (A) v Lewisham Youth Court* [2011] EWHC 1193 (Admin)) and there is no limit under the Bail Act 1976 to the number of occasions on which consideration can be given to this issue.

B2.1.1 *Youth remands*

Where a youth is not released on bail, section 91 of the Legal Aid, Sentencing and Punishment of Offenders Act 2012 requires the court to remand the child to local authority accommodation in accordance with section 92, unless one of the sets of conditions set out in sections 98 to 101 are fulfilled (see **B2.1.9**), in which case the court may instead remand the child to youth detention accommodation. Under section 92(2), a court that remands a child to local authority accommodation must designate the local authority that is to receive the child.

B2.1.2 *Remand to local authority accommodation*

The remand may be without conditions, but if appropriate, under section 93 of the Legal Aid, Sentencing and Punishment of Offenders Act 2012, after consultation with the designated local authority, the court may require:

- the child to comply with any conditions that could be imposed under section 3(6) of the Bail Act 1976;
- the child to comply with any conditions required for the purpose of securing compliance with electronic monitoring;
- the designated local authority to comply with any requirements to secure the child's compliance with a condition; and
- the designated local authority not to place the child with a named person.

An application may be made to the court in respect of a child who has been remanded to local authority accommodation to impose, vary, or revoke conditions.

B2.1.3 *Electronic monitoring as a condition of bail whilst remanded to local authority accommodation*

The court may not impose electronic monitoring of a child's compliance with a condition imposed under section 93 unless the conditions set out in section 94 (see **B2.1.9**) are satisfied.

B2.1.4 *Failure to surrender*

Where a child who is remanded on bail fails to surrender to court without reasonable cause, section 6 of the Bail Act 1976 will apply (see **C3**).

B2.1.5 *Breach of conditions of remand to local authority accommodation*

Under section 97 of the Legal Aid, Sentencing and Punishment of Offenders Act 2012, a constable may arrest a child without a warrant if the child has been remanded to local authority accommodation with conditions and the constable has reasonable grounds to suspect that the child has broken any of those conditions. The child must be brought before the court as soon as practicable and within 24 hours of the child's arrest. Where that 24-hour period includes the time appointed for the child's original court appearance then the child should appear before that same court.

If the court is of the opinion that a child has broken any of the conditions of a remand to local authority accommodation, the court may once again consider the conditions of bail and may attach new conditions to the remand to local authority accommodation or, if the conditions in sections 98 to 101 are met, remand the child to youth detention accommodation.

If the court is not of the opinion that the child has broken any of the conditions of his remand to local authority accommodation, it must remand the child subject to the original conditions imposed.

B2.1.6 *10–11-year-olds*

A child aged 10 to 11 years may only be remanded on bail or to local authority accommodation. If a child reaches the age of 12 during the course of a remand, it is possible that he may then be remanded to youth detention accommodation at the next court appearance should the relevant conditions (Legal Aid, Sentencing and Punishment of Offenders Act 2012, ss 98–101) be met.

B2.1.7 *Secure accommodation*

A child aged between 10 and 17 years who is remanded to local authority accommodation may be placed in secure local authority accommodation if the designated local authority obtains a court order permitting this under section 25 of the Children Act 1989 (as modified by the Children (Secure Accommodation) Regulations 1991 (SI 1991/1505)).

Section 25 of the Children Act 1989 provides:

Children Act 1989, s 25

25 Use of accommodation for restricting liberty

(1) Subject to the following provisions of this section, a child who is being looked after by a local authority may not be placed, and, if placed, may not be kept, in accommodation provided for the purpose of restricting liberty ('secure accommodation') unless it appears—

   (a) that—

      (i) he has a history of absconding and is likely to abscond from any other description of accommodation; and

      (ii) if he absconds, he is likely to suffer significant harm; or

   (b) that if he is kept in any other description of accommodation he is likely to injure himself or other persons.

(2) The appropriate national authority may by regulations—

   (a) specify a maximum period—

      (i) beyond which a child may not be kept in secure accommodation without the authority of the court; and

      (ii) for which the court may authorise a child to be kept in secure accommodation;

   (b) empower the court from time to time to authorise a child to be kept in secure accommodation for such further period as the regulations may specify; and

   (c) provide that applications to the court under this section shall be made only by local authorities.

(3) It shall be the duty of a court hearing an application under this section to determine whether any relevant criteria for keeping a child in secure accommodation are satisfied in his case.

(4) If a court determines that any such criteria are satisfied, it shall make an order authorising the child to be kept in secure accommodation and specifying the maximum period for which he may be so kept.

(5) On any adjournment of the hearing of an application under this section, a court may make an interim order permitting the child to be kept during the period of the adjournment in secure accommodation.

(6) No court shall exercise the powers conferred by this section in respect of a child who is not legally represented in that court unless, having been informed of his right to apply for representation funded by the Legal Aid Authority as part of the Civil Legal Aid or Criminal Legal Aid and having had the opportunity to do so, he refused or failed to apply.

(7) The appropriate national authority may by regulations provide that—

   (a) this section shall or shall not apply to any description of children specified in the regulations;

   (b) this section shall have effect in relation to children of a description specified in the regulations subject to such modifications as may be so specified;

(c) such other provisions as may be so specified shall have effect for the purpose of determining whether a child of a description specified in the regulations may be placed or kept in secure accommodation.

(8) The giving of an authorisation under this section shall not prejudice any power of any court in England and Wales or Scotland to give directions relating to the child to whom the authorisation relates.

(9) This section is subject to section 20(8).

B2.1.8 *Children who turn 18 years of age during their remand*

Where a child turns 18 during the course of his remand, he will remain in youth detention accommodation until he is released or returned to court.

B2.1.9 *The statutory remand scheme*

Legal Aid, Sentencing and Punishment of Offenders Act 2012, ss 91–102

91 Remands of children otherwise than on bail

(1) This section applies where—
   (a) a court deals with a child charged with or convicted of one or more offences by remanding the child, and
   (b) the child is not released on bail.

(2) This section also applies where—
   (a) a court remands a child in connection with extradition proceedings, and
   (b) the child is not released on bail.

(3) Subject to subsection (4), the court must remand the child to local authority accommodation in accordance with section 92.

(4) The court may instead remand the child to youth detention accommodation in accordance with section 102 where—
   (a) in the case of a child remanded under subsection (1), the first or second set of conditions for such a remand (see sections 98 and 99) is met in relation to the child, or
   (b) in the case of a child remanded under subsection (2), the first or second set of conditions for such a remand in an extradition case (see sections 100 and 101) is met in relation to the child.

(5) This section is subject to section 128(7) of the Magistrates' Courts Act 1980 (remands to police detention for periods of not more than 3 days); but that provision has effect in relation to a child as if for the reference to 3 clear days there were substituted a reference to 24 hours.

(6) In this Chapter, 'child' means a person under the age of 18.

(7) References in this Chapter (other than in relation to extradition proceedings) to the remand of a child include a reference to—
   (a) the sending of a child for trial, and
   (b) the committal of a child for sentence, and related expressions are to be construed accordingly.

(8) Before the insertion of section 51A of the Crime and Disorder Act 1998 (sending cases to the Crown Court: children and young persons) by Schedule 3 to the Criminal Justice Act 2003 is fully in force, subsection (7) has effect as if it also referred to the committal of a child for trial.

(9) Subsection (7) also applies to any provision of an Act other than this Act that refers (directly or indirectly) to the remand of a child under this section.

92 Remands to local authority accommodation

(1) A remand to local authority accommodation is a remand to accommodation provided by or on behalf of a local authority.

(2) A court that remands a child to local authority accommodation must designate the local authority that is to receive the child.

(3) That authority must be—
   (a) in the case of a child who is being looked after by a local authority, that authority, and
   (b) in any other case, the local authority in whose area it appears to the court that the child habitually resides or the offence or one of the offences was committed.

(4) The designated authority must—
   (a) receive the child, and
   (b) provide or arrange for the provision of accommodation for the child whilst the child is remanded to local authority accommodation.

(5) Where a child is remanded to local authority accommodation, it is lawful for any person acting on behalf of the designated authority to detain the child.

93 Conditions etc on remands to local authority accommodation

(1) A court remanding a child to local authority accommodation may require the child to comply with any conditions that could be imposed under section 3(6) of the Bail Act 1976 if the child were then being granted bail.

(2) The court may also require the child to comply with any conditions imposed for the purpose of securing the electronic monitoring of the child's compliance with the conditions imposed under subsection (1) if—
   (a) in the case of a child remanded under section 91(1) (proceedings other than extradition proceedings), the requirements in section 94 are met, or
   (b) in the case of a child remanded under section 91(2) (extradition proceedings), the requirements in section 95 are met.

(3) A court remanding a child to local authority accommodation may impose on the designated authority—
   (a) requirements for securing compliance with any conditions imposed on the child under subsection (1) or (2), or
   (b) requirements stipulating that the child must not be placed with a named person.

(4) A court may only impose a condition under subsection (1) or (2), or a requirement under subsection (3), after consultation with the designated authority.

(5) Where a child has been remanded to local authority accommodation, a relevant court—

    (a) may, on the application of the designated authority, impose on that child any conditions that could be imposed under subsection (1) or (2) if the court were then remanding the child to local authority accommodation, and

    (b) where it does so, may impose on the authority requirements for securing compliance with the conditions imposed under paragraph (a).

(6) Where a child has been remanded to local authority accommodation, a relevant court may, on the application of the designated authority or that child, vary or revoke any conditions or requirements imposed under this section (including as previously varied under this subsection).

(7) A court that imposes conditions on a child under this section or varies conditions so imposed—

    (a) must explain to the child in open court and in ordinary language why it is imposing or varying those conditions, and

    (b) if the court is a magistrates' court, must cause a reason given under paragraph (a) to be specified in the warrant of commitment and entered in the register.

(8) In this section 'relevant court'—

    (a) in relation to a child remanded to local authority accommodation by virtue of section 91(1) (proceedings other than extradition proceedings), means—

       (i) the court by which the child was so remanded, or

       (ii) any magistrates' court that has jurisdiction in the place where the child is for the time being;

    (b) in relation to a child remanded to local authority accommodation by virtue of section 91(2) (extradition proceedings), means the court by which the child was so remanded.

(9) References in this section to consultation are to such consultation (if any) as is reasonably practicable in all the circumstances of the case.

94 Requirements for electronic monitoring

(1) The requirements referred to in section 93(2)(a) (requirements for imposing electronic monitoring condition: non-extradition cases) are those set out in subsections (2) to (6).

(2) The first requirement is that the child has reached the age of twelve.

(3) The second requirement is that the offence mentioned in section 91(1), or one or more of those offences, is an imprisonable offence.

(4) The third requirement is that—

    (a) the offence mentioned in section 91(1), or one or more of those offences, is a violent or sexual offence or an offence punishable in the case of an adult with imprisonment for a term of 14 years or more, or

    (b) the offence or offences mentioned in section 91(1), together with any other imprisonable offences of which the child has been convicted in any proceedings, amount or would, if the child were convicted of that offence or those offences, amount to a recent history of committing imprisonable offences while on bail or subject to a custodial remand.

(5) The fourth requirement is that the court is satisfied that the necessary provision for electronic monitoring can be made under arrangements currently available in each local justice area which is a relevant area.

(6) The fifth requirement is that a youth offending team has informed the court that, in its opinion, the imposition of an electronic monitoring condition will be suitable in the child's case.

(7) For the purposes of this section, a local justice area is a relevant area in relation to a proposed electronic monitoring condition if the court considers that it will not be practicable to secure the electronic monitoring in question unless electronic monitoring arrangements are available in that area.

(8) In this Chapter—

'electronic monitoring condition' means a condition imposed on a child remanded to local authority accommodation for the purpose of securing the electronic monitoring of the child's compliance with conditions imposed under section 93(1) or (5);

'imprisonable offence' means—

(a) an offence punishable in the case of an adult with imprisonment, or

(b) in relation to an offence of which a child has been accused or convicted outside England and Wales, an offence equivalent to an offence that, in England and Wales, is punishable in the case of an adult with imprisonment;

'sexual offence' means an offence specified in Part 2 of Schedule 15 to the Criminal Justice Act 2003;

'violent offence' means murder or an offence specified in Part 1 of Schedule 15 to the Criminal Justice Act 2003;

'youth offending team' means a team established under section 39 of the Crime and Disorder Act 1998.

(9) References in this Chapter to a child being subject to a custodial remand are to the child being—

(a) remanded to local authority accommodation or youth detention accommodation, or

(b) subject to a form of custodial detention in a country or territory outside England and Wales while awaiting trial or sentence in that country or territory or during a trial in that country or territory.

(10) The reference in subsection (9) to a child being remanded to local authority accommodation or youth detention accommodation includes—

(a) a child being remanded to local authority accommodation under section 23 of the Children and Young Persons Act 1969, and

(b) a child being remanded to prison under that section as modified by section 98 of the Crime and Disorder Act 1998 or under section 27 of the Criminal Justice Act 1948.

95 Requirements for electronic monitoring: extradition cases

(1) The requirements referred to in section 93(2)(b) (requirements for imposing electronic monitoring condition: extradition cases) are those set out in subsections (2) to (6).

(2) The first requirement is that the child has reached the age of twelve.

(3) The second requirement is that the offence to which the extradition proceedings relate, or one or more of those offences, is an imprisonable offence.

(4) The third requirement is that—

(a) the conduct constituting the offence to which the extradition proceedings relate, or one or more of those offences, would, if committed in England and Wales, constitute a violent or sexual offence or an offence punishable in the case of an adult with imprisonment for a term of 14 years or more, or

(b) the offence or offences to which the extradition proceedings relate, together with any other imprisonable offences of which the child has been convicted, amount or would, if the child were convicted of that offence or those offences, amount to a recent history of committing imprisonable offences while on bail or subject to a custodial remand.

(5) The fourth requirement is that the court is satisfied that the necessary provision for electronic monitoring can be made under arrangements currently available in each local justice area which is a relevant area.

(6) The fifth requirement is that a youth offending team has informed the court that, in its opinion, the imposition of an electronic monitoring condition will be suitable in the child's case.

(7) For the purposes of this section, a local justice area is a relevant area in relation to a proposed electronic monitoring condition if the court considers that it will not be practicable to secure the electronic monitoring in question unless electronic monitoring arrangements are available in that area.

96 Further provisions about electronic monitoring

(1) Where a court imposes an electronic monitoring condition, the condition must include provision making a person responsible for the monitoring.

(2) A person who is made responsible by virtue of subsection (1) must be of a description specified in an order made by the Secretary of State.

(3) The Secretary of State may make rules for regulating—

(a) the electronic monitoring of compliance with conditions imposed under section 93(1) or (5), and

(b) in particular, the functions of persons made responsible by virtue of subsection (1) of this section.

(4) Rules under this section may make different provision for different cases.

(5) Any power of the Secretary of State to make an order or rules under this section is exercisable by statutory instrument.

(6) A statutory instrument containing rules under this section is subject to annulment in pursuance of a resolution of either House of Parliament.

97 Liability to arrest for breaking conditions of remand

(1) A child may be arrested without warrant by a constable if—

(a) the child has been remanded to local authority accommodation,

(b) conditions under section 93 have been imposed in respect of the child, and

(c) the constable has reasonable grounds for suspecting that the child has broken any of those conditions.

(2) Subject to subsection (3), a child arrested under subsection (1) must be brought before a justice of the peace—

(a) as soon as practicable, and

(b) in any event within the period of 24 hours beginning with the child's arrest.

(3) If the child was arrested during the period of 24 hours ending with the time appointed for the child to appear before the court in pursuance of the

remand, the child must be brought before the court before which the child was to have appeared.

(4) In reckoning a period of 24 hours for the purposes of subsection (2) or (3), no account is to be taken of Christmas Day, Good Friday or any Sunday.

(5) If a justice of the peace before whom a child is brought under subsection (2) is of the opinion that the child has broken any condition imposed in respect of the child under section 93, the justice of the peace must remand the child.

(6) Section 91 applies to a child in relation to whom subsection (5) applies as if—
   (a) except in a case within paragraph (b), the child was then charged with or convicted of the offence for which the child had been remanded, or
   (b) in the case of a child remanded in connection with extradition proceedings, the child was then appearing before the justice of the peace in connection with those proceedings.

(7) If a justice of the peace before whom a child is brought under subsection (2) is not of the opinion mentioned in subsection (5), the justice of the peace must remand the child to the place to which the child had been remanded at the time of the child's arrest subject to the same conditions as those which had been imposed on the child at that time.

98 First set of conditions for a remand to youth detention accommodation

(1) For the purposes of section 91(4)(a), the first set of conditions for a remand to youth detention accommodation is met in relation to a child if each of the following is met in relation to the child—
   (a) the age condition (see subsection (2)),
   (b) the offence condition (see subsection (3)),
   (c) the necessity condition (see subsection (4)), and
   (d) the first or second legal representation condition (see subsections (5) and (6)).

(2) The age condition is that the child has reached the age of twelve.

(3) The offence condition is that the offence mentioned in section 91(1), or one or more of those offences—
   (a) is a violent or sexual offence, or
   (b) is an offence punishable in the case of an adult with imprisonment for a term of 14 years or more.

(4) The necessity condition is that the court is of the opinion, after considering all the options for the remand of the child, that only remanding the child to youth detention accommodation would be adequate—
   (a) to protect the public from death or serious personal injury (whether physical or psychological) occasioned by further offences committed by the child, or
   (b) to prevent the commission by the child of imprisonable offences.

(5) The first legal representation condition is that the child is legally represented before the court.

(6) The second legal representation condition is that the child is not legally represented before the court and—
   (a) representation was provided to the child under Part 1 of this Act for the purposes of the proceedings, but was withdrawn—
      (i) because of the child's conduct, or

(ii) because it appeared that the child's financial resources were such that the child was not eligible for such representation,

(b) the child applied for such representation and the application was refused because it appeared that the child's financial resources were such that the child was not eligible for such representation, or

(c) having been informed of the right to apply for such representation and having had the opportunity to do so, the child refused or failed to apply.

99 Second set of conditions for a remand to youth detention accommodation

(1) For the purposes of section 91(4)(a), the second set of conditions for a remand to youth detention accommodation is met in relation to a child if each of the following is met in relation to the child—

(a) the age condition (see subsection (2)),

(b) the sentencing condition (see subsection (3)),

(c) the offence condition (see subsection (4)),

(d) the first or second history condition or both (see subsections (5) and (6)),

(e) the necessity condition (see subsection (7)), and

(f) the first or second legal representation condition (see subsections (8) and (9)).

(2) The age condition is that the child has reached the age of twelve.

(3) The sentencing condition is that it appears to the court that there is a real prospect that the child will be sentenced to a custodial sentence for the offence mentioned in section 91(1) or one or more of those offences.

(4) The offence condition is that the offence mentioned in section 91(1), or one or more of those offences, is an imprisonable offence.

(5) The first history condition is that—

(a) the child has a recent history of absconding while subject to a custodial remand, and

(b) the offence mentioned in section 91(1), or one or more of those offences, is alleged to be or has been found to have been committed while the child was remanded to local authority accommodation or youth detention accommodation.

(6) The second history condition is that the offence or offences mentioned in section 91(1), together with any other imprisonable offences of which the child has been convicted in any proceedings, amount or would, if the child were convicted of that offence or those offences, amount to a recent history of committing imprisonable offences while on bail or subject to a custodial remand.

(7) The necessity condition is that the court is of the opinion, after considering all the options for the remand of the child, that only remanding the child to youth detention accommodation would be adequate—

(a) to protect the public from death or serious personal injury (whether physical or psychological) occasioned by further offences committed by the child, or

(b) to prevent the commission by the child of imprisonable offences.

(8) The first legal representation condition is that the child is legally represented before the court.

(9) The second legal representation condition is that the child is not legally represented before the court and—

(a) representation was provided to the child under Part 1 of this Act for the purposes of the proceedings, but was withdrawn—
   (i) because of the child's conduct, or
   (ii) because it appeared that the child's financial resources were such that the child was not eligible for such representation,
(b) the child applied for such representation and the application was refused because it appeared that the child's financial resources were such that the child was not eligible for such representation, or
(c) having been informed of the right to apply for such representation and having had the opportunity to do so, the child refused or failed to apply.

(10) In this Chapter 'custodial sentence' means a sentence or order mentioned in section 76(1) of the Powers of Criminal Courts (Sentencing) Act 2000.

(11) The reference in subsection (5)(b) to a child being remanded to local authority accommodation or youth detention accommodation includes—
   (a) a child being remanded to local authority accommodation under section 23 of the Children and Young Persons Act 1969, and
   (b) a child being remanded to prison under that section as modified by section 98 of the Crime and Disorder Act 1998 or under section 27 of the Criminal Justice Act 1948.

100 First set of conditions for a remand to youth detention accommodation: extradition cases

(1) For the purposes of section 91(4)(b), the first set of conditions for a remand to youth detention accommodation in an extradition case is met in relation to a child if each of the following is met in relation to the child—
   (a) the age condition (see subsection (2))
   (b) the offence condition (see subsection (3))
   (c) the necessity condition (see subsection (4)) and
   (d) the first or second legal representation condition (see subsections (5) and (6)).

(2) The age condition is that the child has reached the age of twelve.

(3) The offence condition is that the conduct constituting the offence to which the extradition proceedings relate, or one or more of those offences, would, if committed in England and Wales, constitute—
   (a) a violent or sexual offence, or
   (b) an offence punishable in the case of an adult with imprisonment for a term of 14 years or more.

(4) The necessity condition is that the court is of the opinion, after considering all the options for the remand of the child, that only remanding the child to youth detention accommodation would be adequate—
   (a) to protect the public from death or serious personal injury (whether physical or psychological) occasioned by further offences committed by the child, or
   (b) to prevent the commission by the child of imprisonable offences.

(5) The first legal representation condition is that the child is legally represented before the court.

(6) The second legal representation condition is that the child is not legally represented before the court and—
   (a) representation was provided to the child under Part 1 of this Act for the purposes of the proceedings, but was withdrawn—

      (i)   because of the child's conduct, or

      (ii) because it appeared that the child's financial resources were such that the child was not eligible for such representation,

(b) the child applied for such representation and the application was refused because it appeared that the child's financial resources were such that the child was not eligible for such representation, or

(c) having been informed of the right to apply for such representation and having had the opportunity to do so, the child refused or failed to apply.

101 Second set of conditions for a remand to youth detention accommodation: extradition cases

(1) For the purposes of section 91(4)(b), the second set of conditions for a remand to youth detention accommodation in an extradition case is met in relation to a child if each of the following is met in relation to the child—

(a) the age condition (see subsection (2)),

(b) the sentencing condition (see subsection (3)),

(c) the offence condition (see subsection (4)),

(d) the first or second history condition or both (see subsections (5) and (6)),

(e) the necessity condition (see subsection (7)), and

(f) the first or second legal representation condition (see subsections (8) and (9)).

(2) The age condition is that the child has reached the age of twelve.

(3) The sentencing condition is that it appears to the court that, if the child were convicted in England and Wales of an offence equivalent to the offence to which the extradition proceedings relate or one or more of those offences, there would be a real prospect that the child would be sentenced to a custodial sentence for that offence or those offences.

(4) The offence condition is that the offence to which the extradition proceedings relate, or one or more of those offences, is an imprisonable offence.

(5) The first history condition is that—

(a) the child has a recent history of absconding while subject to a custodial remand, and

(b) the offence to which the extradition proceedings relate, or one or more of those offences, is alleged to be or has been found to have been committed while the child was subject to a custodial remand.

(6) The second history condition is that the offence or offences to which the extradition proceedings relate, together with any other imprisonable offences of which the child has been convicted, amount or would, if the child were convicted of that offence or those offences, amount to a recent history of committing imprisonable offences while on bail or subject to a custodial remand.

(7) The necessity condition is that the court is of the opinion, after considering all the options for the remand of the child, that only remanding the child to youth detention accommodation would be adequate—

(a) to protect the public from death or serious personal injury (whether physical or psychological) occasioned by further offences committed by the child, or

(b) to prevent the commission by the child of imprisonable offences.

(8) The first legal representation condition is that the child is legally represented before the court.

(9) The second legal representation condition is that the child is not legally represented before the court and—

    (a) representation was provided to the child under Part 1 of this Act for the purposes of the proceedings, but was withdrawn—

        (i) because of the child's conduct, or

        (ii) because it appeared that the child's financial resources were such that the child was not eligible for such representation,

    (b) the child applied for such representation and the application was refused because it appeared that the child's financial resources were such that the child was not eligible for such representation, or

    (c) having been informed of the right to apply for such representation and having had the opportunity to do so, the child refused or failed to apply.

102 Remands to youth detention accommodation

(1) A remand to youth detention accommodation is a remand to such accommodation of a kind listed in subsection (2) as the Secretary of State directs in the child's case.

(2) Those kinds of accommodation are—

    (a) a secure children's home,

    (b) a secure training centre,

    (c) a young offender institution, and

    (d) accommodation, or accommodation of a description, for the time being specified by order under section 107(1)(e) of the Powers of Criminal Courts (Sentencing) Act 2000 (youth detention accommodation for purposes of detention and training order provisions).

(3) A child's detention in one of those kinds of accommodation pursuant to a remand to youth detention accommodation is lawful.

(4) Where a court remands a child to youth detention accommodation, the court must—

    (a) state in open court that it is of the opinion mentioned in section 98(4), 99(7), 100(4) or 101(7) (as the case may be), and

    (b) explain to the child in open court and in ordinary language why it is of that opinion.

(5) A magistrates' court must ensure a reason that it gives under subsection (4)(b)—

    (a) is specified in the warrant of commitment, and

    (b) is entered in the register.

(6) Where a court remands a child to youth detention accommodation, the court must designate a local authority as the designated authority for the child for the purposes of—

    (a) subsection (8),

    (b) regulations under section 103 (arrangements for remands), and

    (c) section 104 (looked after child status).

(7) That authority must be—

    (a) in the case of a child who is being looked after by a local authority, that authority, and

    (b) in any other case, the local authority in whose area it appears to the court that the child habitually resides or the offence or one of the offences was committed.

(8) Before giving a direction under subsection (1), the Secretary of State must consult the designated authority.

(9) A function of the Secretary of State under this section (other than the function of making regulations) is exercisable by the Youth Justice Board for England and Wales concurrently with the Secretary of State.

(10) The Secretary of State may by regulations provide that subsection (9) is not to apply, either generally or in relation to a particular description of case.

(11) In this Chapter 'secure children's home' means accommodation which is provided in a children's home, within the meaning of the Care Standards Act 2000—

   (a) which provides accommodation for the purposes of restricting liberty, and

   (b) in respect of which a person is registered under Part 2 of that Act.

(12) Before the coming into force in relation to England of section 107(2) of the Health and Social Care (Community Health and Standards) Act 2003, subsection (11) has effect as if it defined 'secure children's home' in relation to England as accommodation which—

   (a) is provided in a children's home, within the meaning of the Care Standards Act 2000, in respect of which a person is registered under Part 2 of that Act, and

   (b) is approved by the Secretary of State for the purpose of restricting the liberty of children.

B3 Breach of Orders, and New Offences Committed During an Order

See Powers of Criminal Courts (Sentencing) Act 2000, Schedule 1, Part 1, paragraphs 1–7.

B3.1 Referral orders

B3.1.1 *Which court will handle the case?*

> **Powers of Criminal Courts (Sentencing) Act 2000, Sch 1, Pt 1, para 1(2)**
>
> (2) ...the appropriate court is—
>
> (a) in the case of an offender aged under 18 at the time when (in pursuance of the referral back) he first appears before the court, a youth court acting in the local justice area in which it appears to the youth offender panel that the offender resides or will reside; and
>
> (b) otherwise, a magistrates' court (other than a youth court) acting in that area.

B3.1.2 *Powers of the court*

In dealing with the offender for such an offence, the appropriate court 'may deal with him in any way in which (assuming section 16 of this Act had not applied) he could have been dealt with for that offence by the court which made the order' (Sch 1, Pt 1, para 5(5)(a)). This provision disapplies the obligation to impose a referral order.

The court must be satisfied that the youth offender panel was entitled to make the finding of breach of the referral order, or that any discretion was exercised reasonably up to a maximum of 12 months. Where a court is revoking and re-sentencing an offender, the court has the powers of the youth court, whatever the age of the defendant. The contract period may be increased up to a maximum of 12 months, and the court must have regard to the circumstances of the referral back and the extent of any compliance with it. The court may take no action.

B3.1.3 *Conviction whilst subject to a referral order*

See Powers of Criminal Courts (Sentencing) Act 2000, Schedule 1, Part 1, paragraphs 11–14.

The court sentencing for the new offence may extend the compliance period of the referral order. The total period may not exceed 12 months. If sentencing for the new offence in any other way (other than by an absolute discharge), the referral order must be revoked. The court may, if it is in the interests of justice, deal with the offender in any manner in which the offender could have been dealt with by the original court. The extent of any compliance must be taken into account.

B3.2 Youth rehabilitation order—breach proceedings

B3.2.1 *Which court will handle the case?*

> **Criminal Justice and Immigration Act 2008, Sch 2, para 5(3)**
>
> (3) ... 'appropriate court' means—
>   (a) if the offender is aged under 18, a youth court acting in the relevant local justice area, and
>   (b) if the offender is aged 18 or over, a magistrates' court (other than a youth court) acting in that local justice area.

In a youth rehabilitation order (YRO) case, a warning is required if the supervising officer finds there is a failure to comply without reasonable excuse. If, following a further second warning, within the 12-month 'warned period', there is then a third failure to comply without reasonable excuse, the officer must refer the case to court for breach proceedings, although Youth Offender Teams will have additional discretion in exceptional circumstances following a third failure to comply. The officer also has the discretion to refer the case to court at an earlier warning stage.

B3.2.2 *Powers of the court*

When dealing with the breach of a YRO, the court has the following options:

- no action;
- a fine of up to £2,500;
- amend the YRO, but not with Intensive Supervision and Surveillance Requirement (ISSR) or Intensive Fostering, unless that already applies;
- revoke the YRO and resentence, within the powers of the original (sentencing) court.

Custody is an option for breach of a YRO only if the original offence is imprisonable or, in the case of a non-imprisonable offence, if, following 'wilful and persistent' (Criminal Justice and Immigration Act 2008, Sch 2) non-compliance, a YRO with an ISSR or Intensive Fostering provision is made and that further YRO is then also subject to non-compliance. The court, if passing a custodial sentence, must state that a YRO with an ISSR or Intensive Fostering provision is not appropriate and the reasons why. This is in addition to meeting the existing criteria, that is, the court forming the opinion that the offence(s) is so serious that a community sentence cannot be justified.

Paragraph 6 provides:

Criminal Justice and Immigration Act 2008, Sch 2, para 6

6 (1) This paragraph applies where—
   (a) an offender appears or is brought before a youth court or other magistrates' court under paragraph 5, and
   (b) it is proved to the satisfaction of the court that the offender has failed without reasonable excuse to comply with the youth rehabilitation order.

(2) The court may deal with the offender in respect of that failure in any one of the following ways—
   (a) by ordering the offender to pay a fine of an amount not exceeding— £2,500
   (b) by amending the terms of the youth rehabilitation order so as to impose any requirement which could have been included in the order when it was made—
      (i) in addition to, or
      (ii) in substitution for, any requirement or requirements already imposed by the order;
   (c) by dealing with the offender, for the offence in respect of which the order was made, in any way in which the court could have dealt with the offender for that offence (had the offender been before that court to be dealt with for it).

(3) Sub-paragraph (2)(b) is subject to sub-paragraphs (6) to (9).

(4) In dealing with the offender under sub-paragraph (2), the court must take into account the extent to which the offender has complied with the youth rehabilitation order.

(5) A fine imposed under sub-paragraph (2)(a) is to be treated, for the purposes of any enactment, as being a sum adjudged to be paid by a conviction.

(6) Any requirement imposed under sub-paragraph (2)(b) must be capable of being complied with before the date specified under paragraph 32(1) of Schedule 1.

(7) Where—

    (a) the court is dealing with the offender under sub-paragraph (2)(b), and

    (b) the youth rehabilitation order does not contain an unpaid work requirement,

paragraph 10(2) of Schedule 1 applies in relation to the inclusion of such a requirement as if for '40' there were substituted '20'.

(8) The court may not under sub-paragraph (2)(b) impose—

    (a) an extended activity requirement, or

    (b) a fostering requirement,

if the order does not already impose such a requirement.

(9) Where—

    (a) the order imposes a fostering requirement (the 'original requirement'), and

    (b) under sub-paragraph (2)(b) the court proposes to substitute a new fostering requirement ('the substitute requirement') for the original requirement,

paragraph 18(2) of Schedule 1 applies in relation to the substitute requirement as if the reference to the period of 12 months beginning with the date on which the original requirement first had effect were a reference to the period of 18 months beginning with that date.

(10) Where—

    (a) the court deals with the offender under sub-paragraph (2)(b), and

    (b) it would not otherwise have the power to amend the youth rehabilitation order under paragraph 13 (amendment by reason of change of residence),

that paragraph has effect as if references in it to the appropriate court were references to the court which is dealing with the offender.

(11) Where the court deals with the offender under sub-paragraph (2)(c), it must revoke the youth rehabilitation order if it is still in force.

(12) Sub-paragraphs (13) to (15) apply where—

    (a) the court is dealing with the offender under sub-paragraph (2)(c), and

    (b) the offender has wilfully and persistently failed to comply with a youth rehabilitation order.

(13) The court may impose a youth rehabilitation order with intensive supervision and surveillance notwithstanding anything in section 1(4)(a) or (b).

(14) If—

    (a) the order is a youth rehabilitation order with intensive supervision and surveillance, and

    (b) the offence mentioned in sub-paragraph (2)(c) was punishable with imprisonment,

the court may impose a custodial sentence notwithstanding anything in section 152(2) of the Criminal Justice Act 2003 (c. 44) (general restrictions on imposing discretionary custodial sentences).

(15) If—

    (a) the order is a youth rehabilitation order with intensive supervision and surveillance which was imposed by virtue of sub-paragraph (13) or paragraph 8(12), and

    (b) the offence mentioned in sub-paragraph (2)(c) was not punishable with imprisonment, for the purposes of dealing with the offender under sub-paragraph (2)(c), the court is to be taken to have had power to deal with the offender for that offence by making a detention and training order for a term not exceeding 4 months.

(16) An offender may appeal to the Crown Court against a sentence imposed under sub-paragraph (2)(c).

B3.3 Youth rehabilitation orders made in the Crown Court

B3.3.1 *Powers of the court*

Criminal Justice and Immigration Act 2008, Sch 1, para 36

36 (1) Where the Crown Court makes a youth rehabilitation order, it may include in the order a direction that further proceedings relating to the order be in a youth court or other magistrates' court (subject to paragraph 7 of Schedule 2).

   (2) In sub-paragraph (1), 'further proceedings', in relation to a youth rehabilitation order, means proceedings—
      (a) for any failure to comply with the order within the meaning given by paragraph 1(2)(b) of Schedule 2, or
      (b) on any application for amendment or revocation of the order under Part 3 or 4 of that Schedule.

Criminal Justice and Immigration Act 2008, Sch 2, para 7

7 (1) Sub-paragraph (2) applies if—
      (a) the youth rehabilitation order was made by the Crown Court and contains a direction under paragraph 36 of Schedule 1, and
      (b) a youth court or other magistrates' court would (apart from that sub-paragraph) be required, or has the power, to deal with the offender in one of the ways mentioned in paragraph 6(2).

   (2) The court may instead—
      (a) commit the offender in custody, or
      (b) release the offender on bail,
      until the offender can be brought or appear before the Crown Court.

   (3) Where a court deals with the offender's case under sub-paragraph (2) it must send to the Crown Court—
      (a) a certificate signed by a justice of the peace certifying that the offender has failed to comply with the youth rehabilitation order in the respect specified in the certificate, and
      (b) such other particulars of the case as may be desirable;
      and a certificate purporting to be so signed is admissible as evidence of the failure before the Crown Court.

B3.3.2 *Conviction whilst subject to a youth rehabilitation order*

If the defendant is convicted of a new offence whilst subject to a YRO, the court has power to revoke the sentence and resentence. If the sentence was imposed in the Crown Court, it must commit to the Crown Court for sentence, unless the Crown Court made an order allowing the magistrates' court to deal with any breach under paragraph 36 of Schedule 1 to the Criminal Justice and Inmmigration Act 1998.

Paragraph 18 of Schedule 2 to the Criminal Justice and Immigration Act 2008 provides:

Criminal Justice and Immigration Act 2008, Sch 2, para 18

18 (1) This paragraph applies where—
    (a) a youth rehabilitation order is in force in respect of an offender, and
    (b) the offender is convicted of an offence (the 'further offence') by a youth court or other magistrates' court ('the convicting court').

(2) Sub-paragraphs (3) and (4) apply where—
    (a) the youth rehabilitation order—
       (i) was made by a youth court or other magistrates' court, or.
       (ii) was made by the Crown Court and contains a direction under paragraph 36 of Schedule 1, and
    (b) the convicting court is dealing with the offender for the further offence.

(3) The convicting court may revoke the order.

(4) Where the convicting court revokes the order under sub-paragraph (3), it may deal with the offender, for the offence in respect of which the order was made, in any way in which it could have dealt with the offender for that offence (had the offender been before that court to be dealt with for the offence).

(5) The convicting court may not exercise its powers under sub-paragraph (3) or (4) unless it considers that it would be in the interests of justice to do so, having regard to circumstances which have arisen since the youth rehabilitation order was made.

(6) In dealing with an offender under sub-paragraph (4), the sentencing court must take into account the extent to which the offender has complied with the order.

(7) A person sentenced under sub-paragraph (4) for an offence may appeal to the Crown Court against the sentence.

(8) Sub-paragraph (9) applies where—
    (a) the youth rehabilitation order was made by the Crown Court and contains a direction under paragraph 36 of Schedule 1, and
    (b) the convicting court would, but for that sub-paragraph, deal with the offender for the further offence.

(9) The convicting court may, instead of proceeding under sub-paragraph (3)—
    (a) commit the offender in custody, or

(b) release the offender on bail,

until the offender can be brought before the Crown Court.

(10) Sub-paragraph (11) applies if the youth rehabilitation order was made by the Crown court and does not contain a direction under paragraph 36 of Schedule 1.

(11) The convicting court may—.

(a) commit the offender in custody, or

(b) release the offender on bail,

until the offender can be brought or appear before the Crown Court.

B3.4 Detention and training order: breach of the supervision requirements

B3.4.1 *Which court handles the case?*

The Powers of Criminal Courts (Sentencing) Act 2000, section 104(1) provides that such matters must be dealt with by the youth court, even if the defendant has reached the age of 18 years.

B.3.4.2 *Detention and training order—new offences*

Powers of Criminal Courts (Sentencing) Act 2000, s 105(1)–(4)

105 Offences during currency of order

(1) This section applies to a person subject to a detention and training order if—

(a) after his release and before the date on which the term of the order ends, he commits an offence punishable with imprisonment in the case of a person aged 21 or over ('the new offence'); and

(b) whether before or after that date, he is convicted of the new offence.

(2) Subject to section 8(6) above (duty of adult magistrates' court to remit young offenders to youth court for sentence), the court by or before which a person to whom this section applies is convicted of the new offence may, whether or not it passes any other sentence on him, order him to be detained in such youth detention accommodation as the Secretary of State may determine for the whole or any part of the period which—

(a) begins with the date of the court's order; and

(b) is equal in length to the period between the date on which the new offence was committed and the date mentioned in subsection (1) above.

(3) The period for which a person to whom this section applies is ordered under subsection (2) above to be detained in youth detention accommodation—

(a) shall, as the court may direct, either be served before and be followed by, or be served concurrently with, any sentence imposed for the new offence; and

(b) in either case, shall be disregarded in determining the appropriate length of that sentence.

(4) Where the new offence is found to have been committed over a period of two or more days, or at some time during a period of two or more days, it shall be taken for the purposes of this section to have been committed on the last of those days.

...

See *Blackstone's Criminal Practice 2014* **E7.15–E7.25**

B4 Jurisdiction of the Adult Magistrates' Court over Youths

B4.1 Youths in the adult court alone

A child or young person, who is not jointly charged with an adult and who is refused bail at the police station, may appear in an adult court where no youth court is sitting. The adult court may deal with the young person only for the purposes of making a decision with regard to a remand. It must then remit the young person to the next available youth court (Children and Young Persons Act 1933, s 46(2)) (see further **B7**).

B4.2 Jointly charged with an adult

A child or young person *must* appear before the adult court if jointly charged with an adult.

A child or young person *may* appear before the adult court if:

- charged with aiding or abetting an adult;
- an adult is charged with aiding or abetting the child or young person;
- charged with an offence arising out of the same circumstances as those giving rise to proceedings against an adult.

Children and Young Persons Act 1933, s 46

46 Assignment of certain matters to youth courts

(1) Subject as hereinafter provided, no charge against a child or young person, and no application whereof the hearing is by rules made under this section assigned to youth courts, shall be heard by a magistrates' court which is not a youth court:

Provided that—

(a) a charge made jointly against a child or young person and a person who has attained the age of eighteen years shall be heard by a magistrates' court other than a youth court; and

(b) where a child or young person is charged with an offence, the charge may be heard by a magistrates' court which is not a youth court if a person who has attained the age of eighteen years is charged at the same time with aiding, abetting, causing, procuring, allowing or permitting that offence; and

(c) where, in the course of any proceedings before any magistrates' court other than a youth court, it appears that the person to whom the proceedings relate is a child or young person, nothing in this subsection shall be construed as preventing the court, if it thinks fit so to do, from proceeding with the hearing and determination of those proceedings.

Children and Young Persons Act 1963, s 18

18 Jurisdiction of magistrates' courts in certain cases involving children and young persons

Notwithstanding section 46(1) of the principal Act (which restricts the jurisdiction of magistrates' courts which are not youth courts in cases where a child or young person is charged with an offence) a magistrates' court which is not a youth court may hear an information against a child or young person if he is charged—

(a) with aiding, abetting, causing, procuring, allowing or permitting an offence with which a person who has attained the age of eighteen is charged at the same time; or

(b) with an offence arising out of circumstances which are the same as or connected with those giving rise to an offence with which a person who has attained the age of eighteen is charged at the same time.

B4.2.1 *What is a joint charge?*

It is not necessary for the charge to specify that the offence was committed 'jointly' or 'together with' the adult concerned (*R v Rowlands* [1972] 1 All ER 306).

Where there is a charge of taking a motor vehicle without consent or aggravated vehicle-taking, the driver and any passengers charged with allowing themselves to be carried are jointly charged (*R v Peterborough Justices, ex p Allgood* (1995) 159 JP 627, QBD).

B4.3 Severance of a youth from an adult

B4.3.1 *Sendings*

When the court sends the adult but is not obliged to send the youth, it shall, after following the plea before venue procedures (see **B5**), send the youth too if it considers it necessary in the interests of justice to do so (Crime and Disorder Act 1998, s 51(7)).

Relevant issues have been identified by the Sentencing Council in two Guidelines:

Allocation Guideline

Linked cases

Where a youth and an adult are jointly charged, the youth must be tried summarily unless the court considers it to be in the interests of justice for both the youth and the adult to be committed to the Crown Court for trial. Examples of factors that should be considered when deciding whether to separate the youth and adult defendants include:

- whether separate trials can take place without causing undue inconvenience to witnesses or injustice to the case as a whole;
- the young age of the defendant, particularly where the age gap between the adult and youth offender is substantial;
- the immaturity of the youth;
- the relative culpability of the youth compared with the adult and whether or not the role played by the youth was minor; and
- the lack of previous convictions on the part of the youth.

Guideline Overeaching Principles—Youth Sentencing, paras 12.15–12.18

Jointly charged with an adult

12.15 A further exception to the presumption in favour of summary trial arises where a young person is charged jointly with a person aged 18 or over; if the court considers it necessary to commit them both for trial it will have the power to commit the young person to the Crown Court for trial.

12.16 Any presumption in favour of sending a youth to the Crown Court to be tried jointly with an adult must be balanced with the general presumption that young offenders should be dealt with in a youth court.

12.17 When deciding whether to separate the youth and adult defendants, a court must consider:

- the young age of the offender, particularly where the age gap between the adult and youth is substantial,
- the immaturity and intellect of the youth,
- the relative culpability of the youth compared with the adult and whether or not the role played by the youth was minor, and
- any lack of previous convictions on the part of the youth compared with the adult offender.

12.18 A very significant factor will be whether the trial of the adult and youth could be severed without inconvenience to witnesses or injustice to the case as a whole, including whether there are benefits in the same tribunal sentencing all offenders. In most circumstances, a single trial of all issues is likely to be most in the interests of justice.

In *Newham Justices, ex p Knight* [1976] Crim LR 323, it was stated:

The advantage of committing the child or young person for trial is that he/she and the adult will be tried together in the Crown Court. Those charged with committing an offence jointly should generally be jointly tried. The disadvantage of such a committal/sending is that the Crown Court is now not generally thought to be the best place for the trial of young people, unless the offence is unusually serious. In deciding whether to commit the young person the magistrates should exercise their discretion judicially and should not automatically send him/her to the Crown Court just because he/she is jointly charged with an adult.

B4.4 Summary trials

If an adult and the youth plead not guilty to a joint charge, the trial must take place in the adult court (Children and Young Persons Act 1933, s 46(1)(a)). It may do so if the allegation is of aiding and abetting, or arises out of the same circumstances (Children and Young Persons Act 1933, s 46(1)(b); Children and Young Person Act 1963, s 18(a) and (b)). (See **B4.2**.)

If the youth pleads guilty or is found guilty, the adult court may sentence under its limited powers or remit to the youth court (Powers of Criminal Courts (Sentencing) Act 2000, s 8(6)).

If the adult pleads guilty and the youth not guilty, it is to be expected that the court will remit to the youth court for trial (Magistrates' Courts Act 1980, s 29(2)) (see **B7**).

B4.5 Remittal

All cases not sent to the Crown Court, sentenced within the limited powers of the adult court (see **B9**) or listed for trial with an adult will be remitted to the youth court (see **B7**).

B5 **Managing the Case**

In order to handle the case appropriately, the steps shown in **Figure 3** must be followed.

Figure 3 Allocation Procedure for Youths

B5.1 Sendings to the Crown Court

The court *must* forthwith send the case to the Crown Court if the youth is charged with:

- homicide;
- an offence attracting a minimum sentence under section 51A of the Firearms Act 1968 or section 29(3) of the Violent Crime Reduction Act 2006, provided the youth was aged at least 16 at the date of the offence;
- a specified offence (see **Appendix 5**) and on the facts of the case an extended sentence may be required (so that for youths, a minimum sentence of four years would be required); *or*
- if notice has been given by the Crown under section 51B (serious fraud) or section 51C (children) of the Crime and Disorder Act 1998 (see **B5.5**).

When a child or young person is sent for trial, the court may also send for trial any either way or summary offence for which he is charged if:

- it appears to the court to be related to the indictable only offence; and
- in the case of a summary offence, it is punishable with imprisonment or involves obligatory or discretionary disqualification from driving (Crime and Disorder Act 1998, s 51(6) and (11)—see **B5.5**).

B5.1.1 Key points

- An offence of murder, attempted murder, manslaughter, causing or allowing the death of a child or vulnerable adult, or infanticide must be sent to the Crown Court for trial (Magistrates' Courts Act 1980, s 24(1)), along with any other offences with which the defendant is charged at the same time, if the charges for both offences could be joined in the same indictment (Magistrates' Courts Act 1980, s 24(1A)).
- The relevant offences under the Firearms Act 1968 are set out in section 51A of that Act:

Firearms Act 1968, s 51A

51A Minimum sentence for certain offences under s 5

(1) This section applies where—
    (a) an individual is convicted of—

    (i) an offence under section 5(1)(a), (ab), (aba), (ac), (ad), (ae), (af) or of this Act,

    (ii) an offence under section 5(1A)(a) of this Act, or

    (iii) an offence under any of the provisions of this Act listed in subsection (1A) in respect of a firearm or ammunition specified in section 5(1)(a), (ab), (aba), (ac), (ad), (ae), (af) or (c) or section 5(1A) (a) of this Act, and

  (b) the offence was committed after the commencement of this section and at a time when he was aged 16 or over.

(1A) The provisions are—

  (a) section 16 (possession of firearm with intent to injure);

  (b) section 16A (possession of firearm with intent to cause fear of violence);

  (c) section 17 (use of firearm to resist arrest);

  (d) section 18 (carrying firearm with criminal intent);

  (e) section 19 (carrying a firearm in a public place);

  (f) section 20(1) (trespassing in a building with firearm).

(2) The court shall impose an appropriate custodial sentence (or order for detention) for a term of at least the required minimum term (with or without a fine) unless the court is of the opinion that there are exceptional circumstances relating to the offence or to the offender which justify its not doing so.

(3) Where an offence is found to have been committed over a period of two or more days, or at some time during a period of two or more days, it shall be taken for the purposes of this section to have been committed on the last of those days.

(4) In this section 'appropriate custodial sentence (or order for detention)' means—

  (a) in relation to England and Wales—

    (i) in the case of an offender who is aged 18 or over when convicted, a sentence of imprisonment, and

    (ii) in the case of an offender who is aged under 18 at that time, a sentence of detention under section 91 of the Powers of Criminal Courts (Sentencing) Act 2000;

  (b) . . .

(5) In this section 'the required minimum term' means—

  (a) in relation to England and Wales—

    (i) in the case of an offender who was aged 18 or over when he committed the offence, five years, and

    (ii) in the case of an offender who was under 18 at that time, three years . . .

  (b) . . .

B5.2 Either way and summary matters

The court must proceed to plea before venue if the case could be sent; or take a plea if it is summary only offence. This applies even when appearing jointly with an adult, though if both plead not guilty the court will have to consider whether it is appropriate to join the cases.

Tottenham Youth Court, ex p Fawzy [1999] 1 WLR 1350 confirms that the adult court must make the decision on venue under section 24. There is no power to remit the youth to the youth court for that court to make the mode of trial decision.

B5.3 Guilty plea indications

If a guilty plea is indicated, the court should proceed to sentence if the court's powers are sufficient (see **B9**) or remit to the youth court (see **B7**) *unless*:

- the offence is a specifed offence (see **Appendix 5**) and on the developing facts an extended sentence may be required, in which case it *must* commit to the Crown Court for sentence;
- the offence is related to an offence which is being sent that day, or related to a matter which has already been sent, in which case it *may* commit to the Crown Court for sentence;
- the offence is capable of being a grave crime, in which case it *may* commit for sentence if on the facts the offence might attract a sentence of long-term detention.

If the youth pleads guilty and the adult is committed for sentence under section 4 of the Powers of Criminal Courts (Sentencing) Act 2000, he must be remitted for sentence to the youth court, unless either he is committed to the Crown Court for seriousness or dangerousness, or the court imposes a discharge, referral order, financial penalty, or bind over under section 8 of the 2000 Act.

B5.3.1 Key points

- Offences are *grave crimes* if they comprise:
  - an offence punishable in the case of a person aged 21 or over with imprisonment for 14 years or more, not being an offence the sentence for which is fixed by law; or
  - an offence under section 3 of the Sexual Offences Act 2003 ('the 2003 Act') (sexual assault); or
  - an offence under section 13 of the 2003 Act (child sex offences committed by children or young persons); or
  - an offence under section 25 of the 2003 Act (sexual activity with a child family member); or
  - an offence under section 26 of the 2003 Act (inciting a child family member to engage in sexual activity); or

- an offence under subsection (1)(a), (ab), (aba), (ac), (ad), (ae), (af), or (c) of section 5 of the Firearms Act 1968 (prohibited weapons), or under subsection (1A)(a) of that section; or
- an offence under section 51A(1A)(b), (e), or (f) of the Firearms Act 1968, which was committed in respect of a firearm or ammunition specified in section 5(1), (ab), (aba), (ac), (ad), (ae), (af), or (c), or section 5(1A)(a) of that Act; or
- an offence under section 28 of the Violent Crime Reduction Act 2006 (using someone to mind a weapon).

- An offence should attract a sentence of long-term detention if it should exceed two years:
  - In determining whether a sentence of more than two years would be imposed, the court should ask itself what sentence was realistically possible, bearing in mind the sentencing range (*Crown Prosecution Service v Newcastle Upon Tyne Youth Court* [2010] EWHC 2773 (Admin)).
  - The overarching guideline on sentencing youths issued by the Sentencing Council states, in relation to the use of long-term detention:

Overarching Guideline—Youth Sentencing, paras 12.10 and 12.11

12.10 This general power should be used rarely since:
    i) it is the general policy of Parliament that those under 18 should be tried in the youth court wherever possible;
    ii) trial in the Crown Court under this provision should be reserved for the most serious cases, recognising the greater formality of the proceedings and the greatly increased number of people involved;
    iii) offenders aged under 15 will rarely attract a period of detention under this provision and those under 12 even more rarely.

12.11 Accordingly,
    i) a young person aged 10 or 11 (or aged 12–14 but not a persistent offender) should be committed to the Crown Court under this provision only where charged with an offence of such gravity that, despite the normal prohibition on a custodial sentence for a person of that age, a sentence exceeding two years is a realistic possibility; R(D) v Manchester City Youth Court [2001] EWHC Admin 860
    ii) a young person aged 12–17 (for which a detention and training order could be imposed) should be committed to the Crown Court under this provision only where charged with an offence of such gravity that a sentence substantially beyond the 2 year maximum for a detention and training order is a realistic possibility; C & D v Sheffield Youth Court [2003] EWHC Admin 35 confirming the relevance of undisputed personal mitigation

 See *Blackstone's Criminal Practice 2014* **D24.25**

B5.4 Not guilty and no plea indications

- If a youth is jointly charged with an adult who has been sent to the Crown Court, the court must first consider if the offence is a grave crime which on the facts should attract a sentence of long-term detention; and if it is, the court *must* send for trial.
- If the youth has not been sent for that reason but it is necessary in the interests of justice to send the youth to the Crown Court for trial, the court must then send the youth for that reason.
- If the defendant is charged with an offence related to an offence which is sent that day or has already been sent, the court *may* send to the Crown Court for trial.
- In all other cases the court should proceed to summary trial or, if there is to be no effective trial of the adult, remit to the youth court (see **B7**).

B5.5 Statutory provisions

Magistrates' Courts Act 1980, ss 24A–24C

24A Child or young person to indicate intention as to plea in certain cases

(1) This section applies where—

    (a) a person under the age of 18 years appears or is brought before a magistrates' court on an information charging him with an offence other than one falling within section 51A(12) of the Crime and Disorder Act 1998 ('the 1998 Act'); and

    (b) but for the application of the following provisions of this section, the court would be required at that stage, by virtue of section 51(7) or (8) or 51A(3)(b), (4) or (5) of the 1998 Act to determine, in relation to the offence, whether to send the person to the Crown Court for trial (or to determine any matter, the effect of which would be to determine whether he is sent to the Crown Court for trial).

(2) Where this section applies, the court shall, before proceeding to make any such determination as is referred to in subsection (1)(b) above (the 'relevant determination'), follow the procedure set out in this section.

(3) Everything that the court is required to do under the following provisions of this section must be done with the accused person in court.

(4) The court shall cause the charge to be written down, if this has not already been done, and to be read to the accused.

(5) The court shall then explain to the accused in ordinary language that he may indicate whether (if the offence were to proceed to trial) he would plead guilty or not guilty, and that if he indicates that he would plead guilty—

    (a) the court must proceed as mentioned in subsection (7) below; and

    (b) (in cases where the offence is one mentioned in section 91(1) of the Powers of Criminal Courts (Sentencing) Act 2000) he may be sent to the Crown Court for sentencing under section 3B or (if applicable) 3C of that Act if the court is of such opinion as is mentioned in subsection (2) of the applicable section.

(6) The court shall then ask the accused whether (if the offence were to proceed to trial) he would plead guilty or not guilty.

(7) If the accused indicates that he would plead guilty, the court shall proceed as if—

    (a) the proceedings constituted from the beginning the summary trial of the information; and

    (b) section 9(1) above was complied with and he pleaded guilty under it,

and, accordingly, the court shall not (and shall not be required to) proceed to make the relevant determination or to proceed further under section 51 or (as the case may be) section 51A of the 1998 Act in relation to the offence.

(8) If the accused indicates that he would plead not guilty, the court shall proceed to make the relevant determination and this section shall cease to apply.

(9) If the accused in fact fails to indicate how he would plead, for the purposes of this section he shall be taken to indicate that he would plead not guilty.

(10) Subject to subsection (7) above, the following shall not for any purpose be taken to constitute the taking of a plea—

    (a) asking the accused under this section whether (if the offence were to proceed to trial) he would plead guilty or not guilty;

    (b) an indication by the accused under this section of how he would plead.

24B Intention as to plea by child or young person: absence of accused

(1) This section shall have effect where—

    (a) a person under the age of 18 years appears or is brought before a magistrates' court on an information charging him with an offence other than one falling within section 51A(12) of the Crime and Disorder Act 1998;

    (b) but for the application of the following provisions of this section, the court would be required at that stage to make one of the determinations referred to in paragraph (b) of section 24A(1) above ('the relevant determination');

    (c) the accused is represented by a legal representative;

    (d) the court considers that by reason of the accused's disorderly conduct before the court it is not practicable for proceedings under section 24A above to be conducted in his presence; and

    (e) the court considers that it should proceed in the absence of the accused.

(2) In such a case—

    (a) the court shall cause the charge to be written down, if this has not already been done, and to be read to the representative;

    (b) the court shall ask the representative whether (if the offence were to proceed to trial) the accused would plead guilty or not guilty;

    (c) if the representative indicates that the accused would plead guilty the court shall proceed as if the proceedings constituted from the

> beginning the summary trial of the information, and as if section 9(1) above was complied with and the accused pleaded guilty under it;
>
> (d) if the representative indicates that the accused would plead not guilty the court shall proceed to make the relevant determination and this section shall cease to apply.

(3) If the representative in fact fails to indicate how the accused would plead, for the purposes of this section he shall be taken to indicate that the accused would plead not guilty.

(4) Subject to subsection (2)(c) above, the following shall not for any purpose be taken to constitute the taking of a plea—

(a) asking the representative under this section whether (if the offence were to proceed to trial) the accused would plead guilty or not guilty;

(b) an indication by the representative under this section of how the accused would plead.

24C Intention as to plea by child or young person: adjournment

(1) A magistrates' court proceeding under section 24A or 24B above may adjourn the proceedings at any time, and on doing so on any occasion when the accused is present may remand the accused.

(2) Where the court remands the accused, the time fixed for the resumption of proceedings shall be that at which he is required to appear or be brought before the court in pursuance of the remand or would be required to be brought before the court but for section 128(3A) below.

Crime and Disorder Act 1998, ss 50A–51C

50A Order of consideration for either-way offences

(1) Where an adult appears or is brought before a magistrates' court charged with an either-way offence (the 'relevant offence'), the court shall proceed in the manner described in this section.

(2) If notice is given in respect of the relevant offence under section 51B or 51C below, the court shall deal with the offence as provided in section 51 below.

(3) Otherwise—

(a) if the adult (or another adult with whom the adult is charged jointly with the relevant offence) is or has been sent to the Crown Court for trial for an offence under section 51(2)(a) or 51(2)(c) below—

(i) the court shall first consider the relevant offence under subsection (3), (4), (5) or, as the case may be, (6) of section 51 below and, where applicable, deal with it under that subsection;

(ii) if the adult is not sent to the Crown Court for trial for the relevant offence by virtue of sub-paragraph (i) above, the court shall then proceed to deal with the relevant offence in accordance with sections 17A to 23 of the 1980 Act;

(b) in all other cases—

(i) the court shall first consider the relevant offence under sections 17A to 20 (excluding subsections (8) and (9) of section 20) of the 1980 Act;

(ii) if, by virtue of sub-paragraph (i) above, the court would be required to proceed in relation to the offence as mentioned in section 17A(6), 17B(2)(c) or 20(7) of that Act (indication of guilty plea), it shall proceed as so required (and, accordingly, shall not consider the offence under section 51 or 51A below);

(iii) if sub-paragraph (ii) above does not apply—

    (a) the court shall consider the relevant offence under sections 51 and 51A below and, where applicable, deal with it under the relevant section;

    (b) if the adult is not sent to the Crown Court for trial for the relevant offence by virtue of paragraph (a) of this sub-paragraph, the court shall then proceed to deal with the relevant offence as contemplated by section 20(9) or, as the case may be, section 21 of the 1980 Act.

(4) Subsection (3) above is subject to any requirement to proceed as mentioned in subsections (2) or (6)(a) of section 22 of the 1980 Act (certain offences where value involved is small).

(5) Nothing in this section shall prevent the court from committing the adult to the Crown Court for sentence pursuant to any enactment, if he is convicted of the relevant offence.

51 Sending cases to the Crown Court: adults

(1) Where an adult appears or is brought before a magistrates' court ('the court') charged with an offence and any of the conditions mentioned in subsection (2) below is satisfied, the court shall send him forthwith to the Crown Court for trial for the offence.

(2) Those conditions are—

    (a) that the offence is an offence triable only on indictment other than one in respect of which notice has been given under section 51B or 51C below;

    (b) that the offence is an either-way offence and the court is required under section 20(9)(b), 21, 23(4)(b) or (5) or 25(2D) of the Magistrates' Courts Act 1980 to proceed in relation to the offence in accordance with subsection (1) above;

    (c) that notice is given to the court under section 51B or 51C below in respect of the offence.

(3) Where the court sends an adult for trial under subsection (1) above, it shall at the same time send him to the Crown Court for trial for any either-way or summary offence with which he is charged and which—

    (a) (if it is an either-way offence) appears to the court to be related to the offence mentioned in subsection (1) above; or

    (b) (if it is a summary offence) appears to the court to be related to the offence mentioned in subsection (1) above or to the either-way offence, and which fulfils the requisite condition (as defined in subsection (11) below).

(4) Where an adult who has been sent for trial under subsection (1) above subsequently appears or is brought before a magistrates' court charged with an either-way or summary offence which—

    (a) appears to the court to be related to the offence mentioned in subsection (1) above; and

    (b) (in the case of a summary offence) fulfils the requisite condition, the court may send him forthwith to the Crown Court for trial for the either-way or summary offence.

(5) Where—

    (a) the court sends an adult ('A') for trial under subsection (1) or (3) above;

    (b) another adult appears or is brought before the court on the same or a subsequent occasion charged jointly with A with an either-way offence; and

    (c) that offence appears to the court to be related to an offence for which A was sent for trial under subsection (1) or (3) above,

the court shall where it is the same occasion, and may where it is a subsequent occasion, send the other adult forthwith to the Crown Court for trial for the either-way offence.

(6) Where the court sends an adult for trial under subsection (5) above, it shall at the same time send him to the Crown Court for trial for any either-way or summary offence with which he is charged and which—

    (a) (if it is an either-way offence) appears to the court to be related to the offence for which he is sent for trial; and

    (b) (if it is a summary offence) appears to the court to be related to the offence for which he is sent for trial or to the either-way offence, and which fulfils the requisite condition.

(7) Where—

    (a) the court sends an adult ('A') for trial under subsection (1), (3) or (5) above; and

    (b) a child or young person appears or is brought before the court on the same or a subsequent occasion charged jointly with A with an indictable offence for which A is sent for trial under subsection (1), (3) or (5) above, or an indictable offence which appears to the court to be related to that offence,

the court shall, if it considers it necessary in the interests of justice to do so, send the child or young person forthwith to the Crown Court for trial for the indictable offence.

(8) Where the court sends a child or young person for trial under subsection (7) above, it may at the same time send him to the Crown Court for trial for any indictable or summary offence with which he is charged and which—

    (a) (if it is an indictable offence) appears to the court to be related to the offence for which he is sent for trial; and

    (b) (if it is a summary offence) appears to the court to be related to the offence for which he is sent for trial or to the indictable offence, and which fulfils the requisite condition.

(9) Subsections (7) and (8) above are subject to sections 24A and 24B of the Magistrates' Courts Act 1980 (which provide for certain cases involving children and young persons to be tried summarily).

(10) The trial of the information charging any summary offence for which a person is sent for trial under this section shall be treated as if the court had adjourned it under section 10 of the 1980 Act and had not fixed the time and place for its resumption.

(11) A summary offence fulfils the requisite condition if it is punishable with imprisonment or involves obligatory or discretionary disqualification from driving.

(12) In the case of an adult charged with an offence—
- (a) if the offence satisfies paragraph (c) of subsection (2) above, the offence shall be dealt with under subsection (1) above and not under any other provision of this section or section 51A below;
- (b) subject to paragraph (a) above, if the offence is one in respect of which the court is required to, or would decide to, send the adult to the Crown Court under—
  - (i) subsection (5) above; or
  - (ii) subsection (6) of section 51A below,

  the offence shall be dealt with under that subsection and not under any other provision of this section or section 51A below.

(13) The functions of a magistrates' court under this section, and its related functions under section 51D below, may be discharged by a single justice.

51A Sending cases to the Crown Court: children and young persons

(1) This section is subject to sections 24A and 24B of the Magistrates' Courts Act 1980 (which provide for certain offences involving children or young persons to be tried summarily).

(2) Where a child or young person appears or is brought before a magistrates' court ('the court') charged with an offence and any of the conditions mentioned in subsection (3) below is satisfied, the court shall send him forthwith to the Crown Court for trial for the offence.

(3) Those conditions are—
- (a) that the offence falls within subsection (12) below;
- (b) that the offence is such as is mentioned in subsection (1) of section 91 of the Powers of Criminal Courts (Sentencing) Act 2000 (other than one mentioned in paragraph (d) below in relation to which it appears to the court as mentioned there) and the court considers that if he is found guilty of the offence it ought to be possible to sentence him in pursuance of subsection (3) of that section;
- (c) that notice is given to the court under section 51B or 51C below in respect of the offence;
- (d) that the offence is a specified offence (within the meaning of section 224 of the Criminal Justice Act 2003) and it appears to the court that if he is found guilty of the offence the criteria for the imposition of a sentence under section 226B of that Act would be met.

(4) Where the court sends a child or young person for trial under subsection (2) above, it may at the same time send him to the Crown Court for trial for any indictable or summary offence with which he is charged and which—
- (a) (if it is an indictable offence) appears to the court to be related to the offence mentioned in subsection (2) above; or
- (b) (if it is a summary offence) appears to the court to be related to the offence mentioned in subsection (2) above or to the indictable offence, and which fulfils the requisite condition (as defined in subsection (9) below).

(5) Where a child or young person who has been sent for trial under subsection (2) above subsequently appears or is brought before a magistrates' court charged with an indictable or summary offence which—

      (a) appears to the court to be related to the offence mentioned in subsection (2) above; and

      (b) (in the case of a summary offence) fulfils the requisite condition,

the court may send him forthwith to the Crown Court for trial for the indictable or summary offence.

(6) Where—

      (a) the court sends a child or young person ('C') for trial under subsection (2) or (4) above; and

      (b) an adult appears or is brought before the court on the same or a subsequent occasion charged jointly with C with an either-way offence for which C is sent for trial under subsection (2) or (4) above, or an either-way offence which appears to the court to be related to that offence,

the court shall where it is the same occasion, and may where it is a subsequent occasion, send the adult forthwith to the Crown Court for trial for the either-way offence.

(7) Where the court sends an adult for trial under subsection (6) above, it shall at the same time send him to the Crown Court for trial for any either-way or summary offence with which he is charged and which—

      (a) (if it is an either-way offence) appears to the court to be related to the offence for which he was sent for trial; and

      (b) (if it is a summary offence) appears to the court to be related to the offence for which he was sent for trial or to the either-way offence, and which fulfils the requisite condition.

(8) The trial of the information charging any summary offence for which a person is sent for trial under this section shall be treated as if the court had adjourned it under section 10 of the 1980 Act and had not fixed the time and place for its resumption.

(9) A summary offence fulfils the requisite condition if it is punishable with imprisonment or involves obligatory or discretionary disqualification from driving.

(10) In the case of a child or young person charged with an offence—

      (a) if the offence satisfies any of the conditions in subsection (3) above, the offence shall be dealt with under subsection (2) above and not under any other provision of this section or section 51 above;

      (b) subject to paragraph (a) above, if the offence is one in respect of which the requirements of subsection (7) of section 51 above for sending the child or young person to the Crown Court are satisfied, the offence shall be dealt with under that subsection and not under any other provision of this section or section 51 above.

(11) The functions of a magistrates' court under this section, and its related functions under section 51D below, may be discharged by a single justice.

(12) An offence falls within this subsection if—

      (a) it is an offence of homicide;

      (b) each of the requirements of section 51A(1) of the Firearms Act 1968 would be satisfied with respect to—

         (i) the offence; and

         (ii) the person charged with it,

      if he were convicted of the offence; or

(c) section 29(3) of Violent Crime Reduction Act 2006 (minimum sentences in certain cases of using someone to mind a weapon) would apply if he were convicted of the offence.

51B Notices in serious or complex fraud cases

(1) A notice may be given by a designated authority under this section in respect of an indictable offence if the authority is of the opinion that the evidence of the offence charged—
   (a) is sufficient for the person charged to be put on trial for the offence; and
   (b) reveals a case of fraud of such seriousness or complexity that it is appropriate that the management of the case should without delay be taken over by the Crown Court.

(2) That opinion must be certified by the designated authority in the notice.

(3) The notice must also specify the proposed place of trial, and in selecting that place the designated authority must have regard to the same matters as are specified in paragraphs (a) to (c) of section 51D(4) below.

(4) A notice under this section must be given to the magistrates' court at which the person charged appears or before which he is brought.

(5) Such a notice must be given to the magistrates' court before any summary trial begins.

(6) The effect of such a notice is that the functions of the magistrates' court cease in relation to the case, except—
   (a) for the purposes of section 51D below;
   (b) as provided by paragraph 2 of Schedule 3 to the Access to Justice Act 1999; and
   (c) as provided by section 52 below.

(7) The functions of a designated authority under this section may be exercised by an officer of the authority acting on behalf of the authority.

(8) A decision to give a notice under this section shall not be subject to appeal or liable to be questioned in any court (whether a magistrates' court or not).

(9) In this section 'designated authority' means—
   (a) the Director of Public Prosecutions;
   (b) the Director of the Serious Fraud Office;
   (c) the Commissioners of the Inland Revenue;
   (d) the Commissioners of Customs and Excise; or
   (e) the Secretary of State.

51C Notices in certain cases involving children

(1) A notice may be given by the Director of Public Prosecutions under this section in respect of an offence falling within subsection (3) below if he is of the opinion—
   (a) that the evidence of the offence would be sufficient for the person charged to be put on trial for the offence;
   (b) that a child would be called as a witness at the trial; and
   (c) that, for the purpose of avoiding any prejudice to the welfare of the child, the case should be taken over and proceeded with without delay by the Crown Court.

(2) That opinion must be certified by the Director of Public Prosecutions in the notice.

(3) This subsection applies to an offence—

    (a) which involves an assault on, or injury or a threat of injury to, a person;

    (b) under section 1 of the Children and Young Persons Act 1933 (cruelty to persons under 16);

    (c) under the Sexual Offences Act 1956, the Protection of Children Act 1978 or the Sexual Offences Act 2003;

    (d) of kidnapping or false imprisonment, or an offence under section 1 or 2 of the Child Abduction Act 1984;

    (e) which consists of attempting or conspiring to commit, or of aiding, abetting, counselling, procuring or inciting the commission of, an offence falling within paragraph (a), (b), (c) or (d) above.

(4) Subsections (4), (5) and (6) of section 51B above apply for the purposes of this section as they apply for the purposes of that.

(5) The functions of the Director of Public Prosecutions under this section may be exercised by an officer acting on behalf of the Director.

(6) A decision to give a notice under this section shall not be subject to appeal or liable to be questioned in any court (whether a magistrates' court or not).

(7) In this section 'child' means—

    (a) a person who is under the age of 17; or

    (b) any person of whom a video recording (as defined in section 63(1) of the Youth Justice and Criminal Evidence Act 1999) was made when he was under the age of 17 with a view to its admission as his evidence in chief in the trial referred to in subsection (1) above.

B6 **Parents and Guardians**

B6.1 Definition of parent/guardian

B6.1.1 *Parent*

There is no definition of who is a 'parent', but it is likely to include a person with parental responsibility under the Children Act 1989.

B6.1.2 *Guardian*

Children and Young Persons Act 1933, s 107(1)

107 Interpretation

'Guardian', in relation to a child or young person, includes any person who, in the opinion of the court having cognisance of any case in relation to the child or young person or in which the child or young person is concerned, has for the time being the care of the child or young person . . .

B6.2 Requiring attendance at court

Children and Young Persons Act 1933, s 34A

34A Attendance at court of parent or guardian

(1) Where a child or young person is charged with an offence or is for any other reason brought before a court, the court—
   (a) may in any case; and
   (b) shall in the case of a child or a young person who is under the age of sixteen years,
   require a person who is a parent or guardian of his to attend at the court during all the stages of the proceedings, unless and to the extent that the court is satisfied that it would be unreasonable to require such attendance, having regard to the circumstances of the case.

(2) In relation to a child or young person for whom a local authority have parental responsibility and who—
   (a) is in their care; or
   (b) is provided with accommodation by them in the exercise of any functions (in particular those under the Children Act 1989) which are social service functions within the meaning of the Local Authority Social Services Act 1970,
   the reference in subsection (1) above to a person who is a parent or guardian of his shall be construed as a reference to that authority or, where he is allowed to live with such a person, as including such a reference.
   In this subsection 'local authority' and 'parental responsibility' have the same meanings as in the Children Act 1989.

In the sentencing guideline, Overarching Principles—Sentencing Youths (to which the court must have regard), it is stated:

Overarching Principles—Sentencing Youths

The statutory framework clearly envisages the attendance of an adult with a degree of responsibility for the young person; this obligation reflects the principal aim of reducing offending, recognising that that is unlikely to be achieved by the young person alone. A court must be aware of a risk that a young person will seek to avoid this requirement either by urging the court to proceed in the absence of an adult or in arranging for a person to come to court who purports to have (but in reality does not have) the necessary degree of responsibility. Insistence on attendance may produce a delay in the case before the court; however, it is important that this obligation is maintained and that it is widely recognised that a court will require such attendance, especially when imposing sentence.

The Criminal Procedure Rules 2012, rule 7.4(9) provides:

Criminal Procedure Rules 2012, r 7.4(9)

7.4 Summons, warrant and requisition

(9) A summons or requisition issued to a defendant under 18 may require that defendant's parent or guardian to attend the court with the defendant, or a separate summons or requisition may be issued for that purpose.

B6.3 Responsibility for financial orders

Where the defendant is aged under 16 years, the court must order the parent or guardian to pay the fine, costs, surcharge, and compensation if ordered unless:

- he cannot be found; or
- it would be unreasonable to make an order for payment having regard to the circumstances of the case.

Where the defendant is aged 16 or 17 years, the court may order the parent or guardian to pay the fine, costs, surcharge, and compensation if ordered unless:

- he cannot be found; or
- it would be unreasonable to make an order for payment having regard to the circumstances of the case.

The court may make such an order in the absence of the parent or guardian where the court has required attendance but they have not attended.

Section 137 of the Powers of Criminal Courts (Sentencing) Act 2000 states that before making a financial order against a parent or guardian, the court may require details of their circumstances through a financial circumstances order. If there is no cooperation with this inquiry, the court may make such determination as it thinks fit.

Courts need not order parents to pay the victim surcharge if they are the victims of the crime. The liability may be delayed, possibly until the youth reaches 18 (see Ministry of Justice Circular 18/13).

B6.3.1 *When is it 'unreasonable' to make a financial order?*

- In *R v Sheffield Crown Court, ex p Clarkson* [1986] Cr App R (S) 454, a compensation order payable by a mother who 'had done what she could to keep her son from criminal ways' was quashed. She was also of limited means, and the order meant that it would have taken her more than two years to pay.
- In *TA v DPP* [1997] 1 Cr App R (S) 1, [1996] Crim LR 606, QBD, the parent of a child accommodated by the local authority under section 20 of the Children Act 1989 was not reasonably to be ordered to pay a financial penalty.
- In *R (M) v Inner London Crown Court* [2003] EWHC 301 (Admin), the policy underlying the legislation meant that it was in the public interest that the financial order be recovered from the parent unless there were special circumstances which made that inappropriate.
- In *R v JB* [2004] EWCA Crim 14, there seems to be an assumption that in the absence of parental fault it would be unreasonable to order the parent to pay.

B6.4 Local authorities

A local authority is responsible for payment of financial orders where the authority has parental responsibility for the defendant and the defendant is in the authority's care or is accommodated by it (Powers of Criminal Courts (Sentencing) Act 2000, s 137(8)).

An order remanding a young person to the care of the local authority does not confer parental responsibility on the local authority. Parental responsibility is acquired only with a full care order (*North Yorkshire County Council v Selby Youth Court* [1994] 1 All ER 991, QBD).

B6.4.1 *When is it 'unreasonable' to make a financial order?*

- In *D and R v DPP* [1995] 16 Cr App R (S) 1040, [1995] Crim LR 748, a local authority that had done everything it reasonably and properly could to protect the public from the criminal behaviour of a young person in its care, could not be expected to assume responsibility for financial orders.

- In *Bedfordshire County Council v DPP* [1996] 1 Cr App R (S) 322, [1995] Crim LR 962, the court stated that a causal link between the authority's lack of care and the offending needs to be established before the court should order payment of the financial penalty by the authority.
- In *Marlowe Child and Family Services Ltd v DPP* [1998] Crim LR 594, a company contracted by the local authority to look after the young person could not be ordered to pay a financial order.

B6.5 Parental bind overs

Since the introduction of parenting orders, the imposition of parental bind overs has declined.

The making of a bind over requires consideration of its terms and the consent of the person being bound over.

Powers of the Criminal Courts (Sentencing) Act 2000, s 150

150 Binding over of parent or guardian

(1) Where a child or young person (that is to say, any person aged under 18) is convicted of an offence, the powers conferred by this section shall be exercisable by the court by which he is sentenced for that offence, and where the offender is aged under 16 when sentenced it shall be the duty of that court—

    (a) to exercise those powers if it is satisfied, having regard to the circumstances of the case, that their exercise would be desirable in the interests of preventing the commission by him of further offences; and

    (b) if it does not exercise them, to state in open court that it is not satisfied as mentioned in paragraph (a) above and why it is not so satisfied;

but this subsection has effect subject to section 19(5) above and paragraph 13(5) of Schedule 1 to this Act (cases where referral orders made or extended).

(2) The powers conferred by this section are as follows—

    (a) with the consent of the offender's parent or guardian, to order the parent or guardian to enter into a recognizance to take proper care of him and exercise proper control over him; and

    (b) if the parent or guardian refuses consent and the court considers the refusal unreasonable, to order the parent or guardian to pay a fine not exceeding £1,000;

and where the court has passed on the offender a sentence which consists of or includes a youth rehabilitation order, it may include in the recognizance a provision that the offender's parent or guardian ensure that the offender complies with the requirements of that sentence.

(3) An order under this section shall not require the parent or guardian to enter into a recognizance for an amount exceeding £1,000.

(4) An order under this section shall not require the parent or guardian to enter into a recognizance—

(a) for a period exceeding three years; or

(b) where the offender will attain the age of 18 in a period shorter than three years, for a period exceeding that shorter period.

Article 7 Convention rights are engaged and the procedure set out in Part III.31 of the Consolidated Criminal Practice Direction must be followed. This includes:

Consolidated Criminal Practice Direction

III.31.17 Where a court is considering binding over a parent or guardian under section 150 of the Powers of Criminal Courts (Sentencing) Act 2000 to enter into a recognisance to take proper care of and exercise proper control over a child or young person, the court should specify the actions which the parent or guardian is to take.

Where a bind over is not made, the court must explain its reasons in open court.

Where the court makes a referral order, it cannot impose a parental bind over (Powers of the Criminal Courts (Sentencing) Act 2000, s 19).

The parent who is made subject to a bind over has the right of appeal to the Crown Court from the youth court or adult magistrates' court, and to the Court of Appeal from the Crown Court.

B6.6 Parenting orders

A parenting order may be made by any criminal court—youth court, adult magistrates' court, or Crown Court. It may also be made by a Family Proceedings Court and an adult magistrates' court in the exercise of its civil jurisdiction.

Crime and Disorder Act 1998, s 8(1)–(4)

8 Parenting orders

(1) This section applies where, in any court proceedings—

(a) a child safety order is made in respect of a child or the court determines on an application under section 12(6) below that a child has failed to comply with any requirement included in such an order;

(aa) a parental compensation order is made in relation to a child's behaviour;

    (b) an anti-social behaviour order or sexual offences prevention order is made in respect of a child or young person;

    (c) a child or young person is convicted of an offence, except in a case where section 8A below applies (parenting order on breach of anti-social behaviour order); or

    (d) a person is convicted of an offence under section 443 (failure to comply with school attendance order) or section 444 (failure to secure regular attendance at school of registered pupil) of the Education Act 1996.

(2) Subject to subsection (3) and section 9(1) below . . . , if in the proceedings the court is satisfied that the relevant condition is fulfilled, it may make a parenting order in respect of a person who is a parent or guardian of the child or young person or, as the case may be, the person convicted of the offence under section 443 or 444 ('the parent').

(3) A court shall not make a parenting order unless it has been notified by the Secretary of State that arrangements for implementing such orders are available in the area in which it appears to the court that the parent resides or will reside and the notice has not been withdrawn.

(4) A parenting order is an order which requires the parent—

    (a) to comply, for a period not exceeding twelve months, with such requirements as are specified in the order, and

    (b) subject to subsection (5) below, to attend, for a concurrent period not exceeding three months, such counselling or guidance programme as may be specified in directions given by the responsible officer.

A parenting order is an order requiring a parent or guardian to comply with requirements that the court considers desirable:

- in criminal proceedings, in the interests of preventing the commission of further offences;
- in civil proceedings, to prevent the behaviour which led to the making of a particular order.

Where an offender is aged under 16 years, the court must make a parenting order if it considers it desirable as above. If the court is not so satisfied, it must state this in open court and give reasons.

Where an offender is aged 16 or 17 years, the court has a discretionary power to make an order.

Before making an order, the court shall obtain and consider information about the family circumstances and the likely effect of the order on them. Where the court is considering making a referral order and a parenting order, this information shall be in a report by an appropriate officer.

B6.6.1 *Terms of the order*

The order will last for up to 12 months, and must include a requirement to attend a parenting programme for a period not exceeding three months and not more than once a week. It may be a residential course if it is likely to be more effective than a non-residential course and the likely interference with family life is proportionate.

The order must specify a responsible officer who may be:

- a probation officer;
- a social worker;
- a person nominated by the local education authority;
- a member of the youth offending team.

B6.6.2 *Breach*

Breach of the order, without reasonable excuse, is punishable on conviction by a fine not exceeding level 3.

B6.6.3 *Variation, discharge, and appeal*

The responsible officer or parent may apply to the court which made the order to vary or discharge the order.

Appeal against an order made in the adult magistrates' court is to the Crown Court.

B7 Remittal to the Youth Court for Trial/Sentence

The magistrates' court may remit to:

- a youth court acting for the same place as the remitting court; or
- a youth court acting for the place where the young offender habitually resides.

It is generally good practice to remit for sentence to the young person's local court.

The powers to remit arise under section 46 of the Children and Young Persons Act 1933

Children and Young Persons Act 1933, s 46

46 Assignment of certain matters to youth courts

(1) Subject as hereinafter provided, no charge against a child or young person, and no application whereof the hearing is by rules made under this section assigned to youth courts, shall be heard by a magistrates' court which is not a youth court:
Provided that—

(a) a charge made jointly against a child or young person and a person who has attained the age of eighteen years shall be heard by a magistrates' court other than a youth court; and

(b) where a child or young person is charged with an offence, the charge may be heard by a magistrates' court which is not a youth court if a person who has attained the age of eighteen years is charged at the same time with aiding, abetting, causing, procuring, allowing or permitting that offence; and

(c) where, in the course of any proceedings before any magistrates' court other than a youth court, it appears that the person to whom the proceedings relate is a child or young person, nothing in this subsection shall be construed as preventing the court, if it thinks fit so to do, from proceeding with the hearing and determination of those proceedings.

(1A) If a notification that the accused desires to plead guilty without appearing before the court is received by the designated officer for a court in pursuance of section 12 of the Magistrates' Courts Act 1980 and the court has no reason to believe that the accused is a child or young person, then, if he is a child or young person he shall be deemed to have attained the age of eighteen for the purposes of subsection (1) of this section in its application to the proceedings in question.

(2) No direction, whether contained in this or any other Act, that a charge shall be brought before a youth court shall be construed as restricting the powers of any justice or justices to entertain an application for bail or for a remand, and to hear such evidence as may be necessary for that purpose.

A power to remit is granted under section 29 of the Magistrates' Courts Act 1980 where there will be no effective trial of an adult in relation to a joint charge:

Magistrates' Courts Act 1980, s 29

29 Power of magistrates' court to remit a person under 17 for trial to a youth court in certain circumstances

(1) Where—

    (a) a person under the age of 18 years ('the juvenile') appears or is brought before a magistrates' court other than a youth court on an information jointly charging him and one or more other persons with an offence; and

    (b) that other person, or any of those other persons, has attained that age, subsection (2) below shall have effect notwithstanding proviso (a) in section 46(1) of the Children and Young Persons Act 1933 (which would otherwise require the charge against the juvenile to be heard by a magistrates' court other than a youth court).

    In the following provisions of this section 'the older accused' means such one or more of the accused as have attained the age of 18 years.

(2) If—

    (a) the court proceeds to the summary trial of the information in the case of both or all of the accused, and the older accused or each of the older accused pleads guilty; or

    (b) the court—

        (i) in the case of the older accused or each of the older accused, sends him to the Crown Court for trial under section 51 or 51A of the Crime and Disorder Act 1998; and

        (ii) in the case of the juvenile, proceeds to the summary trial of the information,

    then, if in either situation the juvenile pleads not guilty, the court may before any evidence is called in his case remit him for trial to a youth court acting for the same place as the remitting court or for the place where he habitually resides.

(3) A person remitted to a youth court under subsection (2) above shall be brought before and tried by a youth court accordingly.

(4) Where a person is so remitted to a youth court—

    (a) he shall have no right of appeal against the order of remission; and

    (b) the remitting court may, subject to section 25 of the Criminal Justice and Public Order Act 1994, give such directions as appear to be necessary with respect to his custody or for his release on bail until he can be brought before the youth court.

A duty to remit exists under section 8 of the Powers of Criminal Courts (Sentencing) Act 2000, for sentencing where the adult court powers are not regarded as sufficient:

Powers of Criminal Courts (Sentencing) Act 2000, s 8

8 Power and duty to remit young offenders to youth courts for sentence

(1) Subsection (2) below applies where a child or young person (that is to say, any person aged under 18) is convicted by or before any court of an offence other than homicide.

(2) The court may and, if it is not a youth court, shall unless satisfied that it would be undesirable to do so, remit the case—

   (a) if the offender was sent to the Crown Court for trial under section 51 or 51A of the Crime and Disorder Act 1998, to a youth court acting for the place where he was sent to the Crown Court for trial;

   (b) in any other case, to a youth court acting either for the same place as the remitting court or for the place where the offender habitually resides;

   but in relation to a magistrates' court other than a youth court this subsection has effect subject to subsection (6) below.

(3) Where a case is remitted under subsection (2) above, the offender shall be brought before a youth court accordingly, and that court may deal with him in any way in which it might have dealt with him if he had been tried and convicted by that court.

(4) A court by which an order remitting a case to a youth court is made under subsection (2) above—

   (a) may, subject to section 25 of the Criminal Justice and Public Order Act 1994 (restrictions on granting bail), give such directions as appear to be necessary with respect to the custody of the offender or for his release on bail until he can be brought before the youth court; and

   (b) shall cause to be transmitted to the designated officer for the youth court a certificate setting out the nature of the offence and stating—

   (i) that the offender has been convicted of the offence; and

   (ii) that the case has been remitted for the purpose of being dealt with under the preceding provisions of this section.

(5) Where a case is remitted under subsection (2) above, the offender shall have no right of appeal against the order of remission, but shall have the same right of appeal against any order of the court to which the case is remitted as if he had been convicted by that court.

(6) Without prejudice to the power to remit any case to a youth court which is conferred on a magistrates' court other than a youth court by subsections (1) and (2) above, where such a magistrates' court convicts a child or young person of an offence it must exercise that power unless the case falls within subsection (7) or (8) below.

(7) The case falls within this subsection if the court would, were it not so to remit the case, be required by section 16(2) below to refer the offender to a youth offender panel (in which event the court may, but need not, so remit the case).

(8) The case falls within this subsection if it does not fall within subsection (7) above but the court is of the opinion that the case is one which can properly be dealt with by means of—

   (a) an order discharging the offender absolutely or conditionally, or

    (b) an order for the payment of a fine, or

    (c) an order (under section 150 below) requiring the offender's parent or guardian to enter into a recognizance to take proper care of him and exercise proper control over him,

  with or without any other order that the court has power to make when absolutely or conditionally discharging an offender.

 (9) In subsection (8) above 'care' and 'control' shall be construed in accordance with section 150(11) below.

(10) A document purporting to be a copy of an order made by a court under this section shall, if it purports to be certified as a true copy by the justices' chief executive for the court, be evidence of the order.

B8 **Reporting Restrictions**

In the adult court, unlike the youth court, discretionary provisions apply. The court must specifically apply the restrictions which relate to the identification of victims, other witnesses, and defendants by stating in open court that it is doing so. The conflicting demands of Articles 8 and 10 of the European Convention on Human Rights must be balanced (see **A29.1**).

Children and Young Persons Act 1933, s 39

39 Power to prohibit publication of certain matter in newspapers

(1) In relation to any proceedings in any court, the court may direct that—
   (a) no newspaper report of the proceedings shall reveal the name, address or school, or include any particulars calculated to lead to the identification, of any child or young person concerned in the proceedings, either as being the person by or against or in respect of whom the proceedings are taken, or as being a witness therein[;]
   (b) no picture shall be published in any newspaper as being or including a picture of any child or young person so concerned in the proceedings as aforesaid;
   except in so far (if at all) as may be permitted by the direction of the court.
(2) Any person who publishes any matter in contravention of any such direction shall on summary conviction be liable in respect of each offence to a fine not exceeding level 5 on the standard scale.

B9 Sentencing

B9.1 Overview of section 8 of the Powers of Criminal Courts (Sentencing) Act 2000

Only the following sentencing options are available in relation to young offenders appearing in the adult court. Any case requiring a greater sentence must be remitted to the youth court. See **B7**.

Age (last birthday)	10–13	14	15	16–17
Absolute discharge	Yes	Yes	Yes	Yes
Conditional discharge (note that a conditional discharge cannot be imposed if the offender has received a final warning/youth caution in the previous 24 months unless exceptional circumstances are found). A conditional discharge in respect to a youth can be for a maximum period of 3 years.	Yes	Yes	Yes	Yes
Fine	Yes: maximum £250. Order must be made against parent/guardian unless unreasonable in the circumstances	Yes: maximum £1,000. Order must be made against parent/guardian unless unreasonable in the circumstances	Yes: maximum £1,000. Order must be made against parent/guardian unless unreasonable in the circumstances	Yes: maximum £1,000
Referral order	Yes	Yes	Yes	Yes

B9.2 Victim surcharge

If a conditional discharge or a fine is imposed, the court must add the relevant victim surcharge which for youths are as follows:

- Conditional discharge—£10
- Fine—£15.

B9.3 Referral orders

The adult court may (but need not) make a referral order in circumstances where, in the youth court, such an order must be made. This obligation arises under section 17(1) of the Powers of Criminal Courts (Sentencing) Act 2000, where:

- the offence is punishable with imprisonment;
- the offender has pleaded guilty to the offence(s);
- the court is not imposing an absolute or conditional discharge, a hospital order, or a custodial sentence;
- the offender has never previously been convicted (in the United Kingdom) of an offence or bound over.

B9.4 Ancillary powers

In additon to exercising these powers, the court may make ancillary orders such as:

- an order (under section 150 of the Powers of Criminal Courts (Sentencing) Act 2000) binding over a parent or guardian to take proper care of the youth and exercise proper care over him, or a parenting order (see **B6**);
- ancillary orders such as disqualification from driving, endorsement of a driving licence, and to pay compensation and costs.

 See *Blackstone's Criminal Practice 2014* **D24.113** and **D24.114**

B10 Summary Trials Involving Youths

Before the trial of a youth in the adult court can begin, it is necessary to check the ability of the youth to understand the procedure.

B10.1 Capacity of the youth to take part

It is necessary to consider the youth's intellectual capacity to understand the proceedings.

There have been a number of cases where the defence have sought to raise a capacity issue, namely, that the defendant, whether due to immaturity or mental capacity, is unable to understand the proceedings, such that it would be an abuse of process to continue on the ground that he could not have a fair trial.

The elements of a fair trial (in this regard) are:

- the defendant had to understand what he is said to have done wrong;
- the court had to be satisfied that the defendant, when he had done wrong by act or omission, had the means of knowing that was wrong;
- he had to understand what, if any, defences were available to him;
- he had to have a reasonable opportunity to make relevant representations if he wished;
- he had to have the opportunity to consider what representation he wished to make once he understood the issues involved;
- he had, therefore, to be able to give proper instructions and to participate by way of providing answers to questions and suggesting questions to his lawyers in the circumstances of the trial as they arose.

The following guidance on how to approach the issue was issued by the court in *Crown Prosecution Service v P* [2007] EWHC 946 (Admin):

- The fitness to plead procedure (in so far as it applies in the magistrates' court—see **A25.1**) does not provide a complete answer to the defendant who lacks capacity as there are fair trial issues to consider under Article 6 ECHR.
- In an exceptional case there may be grounds to stay a case as an abuse of process if the youth lacks capacity.
- Medical evidence on the issue is not decisive.
- Before considering a stay, the court should consider conducting a fact-finding exercise with a view to a medical disposal under the Mental Health Act 1983 in appropriate cases.

It can be seen, therefore, that only in cases where the capacity issue is not linked to mental health, or a mental health disposal is not appropriate, will a court consider a stay of proceedings.

B10.2 Assistance to the defendant

B10.2.1 *Live link direction for vulnerable young defendants*

The court has power to allow a vulnerable young defendant to give evidence via live link (Youth Justice and Criminal Evidence Act 1999, s 33A):

Youth Justice and Criminal Evidence Act 1999, s 33A

33A Live link directions

(1) This section applies to any proceedings (whether in a magistrates' court or before the Crown Court) against a person for an offence.

(2) The court may, on the application of the accused, give a live link direction if it is satisfied—

    (a) that the conditions in subsection (4) or, as the case may be, subsection are met in relation to the accused, and

    (b) that it is in the interests of justice for the accused to give evidence through a live link.

(3) A live link direction is a direction that any oral evidence to be given before the court by the accused is to be given through a live link.

(4) Where the accused is aged under 18 when the application is made, the conditions are that—

    (a) his ability to participate effectively in the proceedings as a witness giving oral evidence in court is compromised by his level of intellectual ability or social functioning, and

    (b) use of a live link would enable him to participate more effectively in the proceedings as a witness (whether by improving the quality of his evidence or otherwise).

(5) Where the accused has attained the age of 18 at that time, the conditions are that—

    (a) he suffers from a mental disorder (within the meaning of the Mental Health Act 1983) or otherwise has a significant impairment of intelligence and social function,

    (b) he is for that reason unable to participate effectively in the proceedings as a witness giving oral evidence in court, and

    (c) use of a live link would enable him to participate more effectively in the proceedings as a witness (whether by improving the quality of his evidence or otherwise).

(6) While a live link direction has effect the accused may not give oral evidence before the court in the proceedings otherwise than through a live link.

(7) The court may discharge a live link direction at any time before or during any hearing to which it applies if it appears to the court to be in the interests

---

of justice to do so (but this does not affect the power to give a further live link direction in relation to the accused).

The court may exercise this power of its own motion or on an application by a party.

(8) The court must state in open court its reasons for—

(a) giving or discharging a live link direction, or

(b) refusing an application for or for the discharge of a live link direction,

and, if it is a magistrates' court, it must cause those reasons to be entered in the register of its proceedings.

B10.2.2 *Examination of accused through intermediary*

In *R (C) v Sevenoaks Youth Court* [2009] EWHC 3088 (Admin), the court held that an intermediary could be appointed under the court's common law power to ensure a fair trial process, until such time as statutory provisions are brought into force. In *R (AS) v Great Yarmouth Youth Court* [2011] EWHC 2059 (Admin), the court held that it was irrational to ignore the need for an intermediary of a youth suffering from ADHD.

B10.3 **Further assistance**

The Consolidated Criminal Practice Direction gives further assistance:

> ### **Consolidated Criminal Practice Direction, paras III.30.1–III.30.18**
>
> #### **III.30 TREATMENT OF VULNERABLE DEFENDANTS**
>
> #### **III.30.1**
>
> This direction applies to proceedings in the Crown Court and in magistrates' courts on the trial, sentencing or (in the Crown Court) appeal of (a) children and young persons under 18 or (b) adults who suffer from a mental disorder within the meaning of the Mental Health Act 1983 or who have any significant impairment of intelligence and social function.1 In this direction, such defendants are referred to collectively as 'vulnerable defendants'. The purpose of this direction is to extend to proceedings in relation to such persons in the adult courts procedures analogous to those in use in youth courts.
>
> #### **III.30.2**
>
> The steps which should be taken to comply with paragraphs III.30.3 to III.30.17 should be judged, in any given case, taking account of the age, maturity and development (intellectual, social and emotional) of the defendant concerned and all other circumstances of the case.

The overriding principle

III.30.3

A defendant may be young and immature, or may have a mental disorder within the meaning of the Mental Health Act 1983, or some other significant impairment of intelligence and social function such as to inhibit his understanding of and participation in the proceedings. The purpose of criminal proceedings is to determine guilt, if that is in issue, and decide on the appropriate sentence if the defendant pleads guilty or is convicted. All possible steps should be taken to assist a vulnerable defendant to understand and participate in those proceedings. The ordinary trial process should, so far as necessary, be adapted to meet those ends. Regard should be had to the welfare of a young defendant as required by section 44 of the Children and Young Persons Act 1933, and generally to Parts 1 and 3 of The Criminal Procedure Rules (the overriding objective and the court's powers of case management).

Before the trial, sentencing or appeal

III.30.4

If a vulnerable defendant, especially one who is young, is to be tried jointly with one who is not, the court should consider at the plea and case management hearing, or at a case management hearing in a magistrates' court, whether the vulnerable defendant should be tried on his own and should so order unless of the opinion that a joint trial would be in accordance with Part 1 of The Criminal Procedure Rules (the overriding objective) and in the interests of justice. If a vulnerable defendant is tried jointly with one who is not, the court should consider whether any of the modifications set out in this direction should apply in the circumstances of the joint trial and, so far as practicable, make orders to give effect to any such modifications.

III.30.5

At the plea and case management hearing, or at a case management hearing in a magistrates' court, the court should consider and so far as practicable give directions on the matters covered in paragraphs III.30.9 to III.30.17.

III.30.6

It may be appropriate to arrange that a vulnerable defendant should visit, out of court hours and before the trial, sentencing or appeal hearing, the courtroom in which that hearing is to take place so that he can familiarise himself with it.

III.30.7

If any case against a vulnerable defendant has attracted or may attract widespread public or media interest, the assistance of the police should be enlisted to try and ensure that the defendant is not, when attending the court, exposed to intimidation, vilification or abuse. Section 41 of the Criminal Justice Act 1925 prohibits the taking of photographs of defendants and witnesses (among others) in the court building or in its precincts, or when entering or leaving those precincts. A direction informing media representatives that the prohibition will be enforced may be appropriate.

III.30.8

The court should be ready at this stage, if it has not already done so, where relevant to make a reporting restriction under section 39 of the Children and Young Persons Act 1933 or, on an appeal to the Crown Court from a youth court, to remind media representatives of the application of section 49 of that Act. Any such order, once made, should be reduced to writing and copies should on request be made available to anyone affected or potentially affected by it.

The trial, sentencing or appeal hearing

III.30.9

Subject to the need for appropriate security arrangements, the proceedings should, if practicable, be held in a courtroom in which all the participants are on the same or almost the same level.

III.30.10

A vulnerable defendant, especially if he is young, should normally, if he wishes, be free to sit with members of his family or others in a like relationship, and with some other suitable supporting adult such as a social worker, and in a place which permits easy, informal communication with his legal representatives. The court should ensure that a suitable supporting adult is available throughout the course of the proceedings.

III.30.11

At the beginning of the proceedings, the court should ensure that what is to take place has been explained to a vulnerable defendant in terms he can understand and, at trial in the Crown Court, it should ensure in particular that the role of the jury has been explained. It should remind those representing the vulnerable defendant and the supporting adult of their responsibility to explain each step as it takes place and, at trial, to explain the possible consequences of a guilty verdict. Throughout the trial the court should continue to ensure, by any appropriate means, that the defendant understands what is happening and what has been said by those on the bench, the advocates and witnesses.

III.30.12

A trial should be conducted according to a timetable which takes full account of a vulnerable defendant's ability to concentrate. Frequent and regular breaks will often be appropriate. The court should ensure, so far as practicable, that the trial is conducted in simple, clear language that the defendant can understand and that cross-examination is conducted by questions that are short and clear.

III.30.13

A vulnerable defendant who wishes to give evidence by live link, in accordance with section 33A of the Youth Justice and Criminal Evidence Act 1999, may apply for a direction to that effect. Before making such a direction, the court must be satisfied that it is in the interests of justice to do so and that the use of a live link would enable the defendant to participate more effectively as a witness in the proceedings. The direction will need to deal with the practical arrangements to be made, including the room from which the defendant will give evidence, the identity of the person or persons who will accompany him, and how it will be arranged for him to be seen and heard by the court.

III.30.14

(Crown Court)

III.30.15

The court should be prepared to restrict attendance by members of the public in the court room to a small number, perhaps limited to those with an immediate and direct interest in the outcome. The court should rule on any challenged claim to attend.

III.30.16

Facilities for reporting the proceedings (subject to any restrictions under section 39 or 49 of the Children and Young Persons Act 1933) must be provided. But the court may restrict the number of reporters attending in the courtroom to such number as is judged practicable and desirable. In ruling on any challenged claim to attend in the court room for the purpose of reporting, the court should be mindful of the public's general right to be informed about the administration of justice.

III.30.17

Where it has been decided to limit access to the courtroom, whether by reporters or generally, arrangements should be made for the proceedings to be relayed, audibly and if possible visually, to another room in the same court complex to which the media and the public have access if it appears that there will be a need for such additional facilities. Those making use of such a facility should be reminded that it is to be treated as an extension of the court room and that they are required to conduct themselves accordingly.

III.30.18

Where the court is called upon to exercise its discretion in relation to any procedural matter falling within the scope of this practice direction but not the subject of specific reference, such direction should be exercised having regard to the principles in paragraph III.30.3.

. . .

 See *Blackstone's Criminal Practice 2014* **D14.21**

Part C
Offences

C1 **Animal Offences**

C1.1 **Animal cruelty**

Sections 4, 5, 6, 7, 8, and 9 of the Animal Welfare Act 2006 provide for offences in relation to unnecessary suffering, mutilation, docking of dogs' tails, administration of poisons, and fighting.

Animal Welfare Act 2006, ss 4(1)–(2), 5(1)–(2), (6), 6(1)–(12), 7, 8, and 9

4 Unnecessary suffering

(1) A person commits an offence if—
  (a) an act of his, or a failure of his to act, causes an animal to suffer,
  (b) he knew, or ought reasonably to have known, that the act, or failure to act, would have that effect or be likely to do so,
  (c) the animal is a protected animal, and
  (d) the suffering is unnecessary.

(2) A person commits an offence if—
  (a) he is responsible for an animal,
  (b) an act, or failure to act, of another person causes the animal to suffer,
  (c) he permitted that to happen or failed to take such steps (whether by way of supervising the other person or otherwise) as were reasonable in all the circumstances to prevent that happening, and
  (d) the suffering is unnecessary . . .

5 Mutilation

(1) A person commits an offence if—
  (a) he carries out a prohibited procedure on a protected animal;
  (b) he causes such a procedure to be carried out on such an animal.

(2) A person commits an offence if—
  (a) he is responsible for an animal,
  (b) another person carries out a prohibited procedure on the animal, and
  (c) he permitted that to happen or failed to take such steps (whether by way of supervising the other person or otherwise) as were reasonable in all the circumstances to prevent that happening.

[. . .]

(6) Nothing in this section applies to the removal of the whole or any part of a dog's tail.

6 Docking of dogs' tails

(1) A person commits an offence if—
  (a) he removes the whole or any part of a dog's tail, otherwise than for the purpose of its medical treatment;
  (b) he causes the whole or any part of a dog's tail to be removed by another person, otherwise than for the purpose of its medical treatment.

(2) A person commits an offence if—
  (a) he is responsible for a dog,

    (b) another person removes the whole or any part of the dog's tail, otherwise than for the purpose of its medical treatment, and

    (c) he permitted that to happen or failed to take such steps (whether by way of supervising the other person or otherwise) as were reasonable in all the circumstances to prevent that happening.

(3) Subsections (1) and (2) do not apply if the dog is a certified working dog that is not more than 5 days old.

(4) For the purposes of subsection (3), a dog is a certified working dog if a veterinary surgeon has certified, in accordance with regulations made by the appropriate national authority, that the first and second conditions mentioned below are met.

(5) The first condition referred to in subsection (4) is that there has been produced to the veterinary surgeon such evidence as the appropriate national authority may by regulations require for the purpose of showing that the dog is likely to be used for work in connection with—

    (a) law enforcement,

    (b) activities of Her Majesty's armed forces,

    (c) emergency rescue,

    (d) lawful pest control, or

    (e) the lawful shooting of animals.

(6) The second condition referred to in subsection (4) is that the dog is of a type specified for the purposes of this subsection by regulations made by the appropriate national authority.

(7) It is a defence for a person accused of an offence under subsection (1) or to show that he reasonably believed that the dog was one in relation to which subsection (3) applies.

(8) A person commits an offence if—

    (a) he owns a subsection (3) dog, and

    (b) fails to take reasonable steps to secure that, before the dog is 3 months old, it is identified as a subsection (3) dog in accordance with regulations made by the appropriate national authority.

(9) A person commits an offence if—

    (a) he shows a dog at an event to which members of the public are admitted on payment of a fee,

    (b) the dog's tail has been wholly or partly removed (in England and Wales or elsewhere), and

    (c) removal took place on or after the commencement day.

(10) Where a dog is shown only for the purpose of demonstrating its working ability, subsection (9) does not apply if the dog is a subsection (3) dog.

(11) It is a defence for a person accused of an offence under subsection (9) to show that he reasonably believed—

    (a) that the event was not one to which members of the public were admitted on payment of an entrance fee,

    (b) that the removal took place before the commencement day, or

    (c) that the dog was one in relation to which subsection (10) applies.

(12) A person commits an offence if he knowingly gives false Information to a veterinary surgeon in connection with the giving of a certificate for the purposes of this section.

7 Administration of poisons etc

(1) A person commits an offence if, without lawful authority or reasonable excuse, he—

    (a) administers any poisonous or injurious drug or substance to a protected animal, knowing it to be poisonous or injurious, or

    (b) causes any poisonous or injurious drug or substance to be taken by a protected animal, knowing it to be poisonous or injurious.

(2) A person commits an offence if—

    (a) he is responsible for an animal,

    (b) without lawful authority or reasonable excuse, another person administers a poisonous or injurious drug or substance to the animal or causes the animal to take such a drug or substance, and

    (c) he permitted that to happen or, knowing the drug or substance to be poisonous or injurious, he failed to take such steps (whether by way of supervising the other person or otherwise) as were reasonable in all the circumstances to prevent that happening.

(3) In this section, references to a poisonous or injurious drug or substance include a drug or substance which, by virtue of the quantity or manner in which it is administered or taken, has the effect of a poisonous or injurious drug or substance.

8 Fighting etc

(1) A person commits an offence if he—

    (a) causes an animal fight to take place, or attempts to do so;

    (b) knowingly receives money for admission to an animal fight;

    (c) knowingly publicises a proposed animal fight;

    (d) provides information about an animal fight to another with the intention of enabling or encouraging attendance at the fight;

    (e) makes or accepts a bet on the outcome of an animal fight or on the likelihood of anything occurring or not occurring in the course of an animal fight;

    (f) takes part in an animal fight;

    (g) has in his possession anything designed or adapted for use in connection with an animal fight with the intention of its being so used;

    (h) keeps or trains an animal for use for in connection with an animal fight;

    (i) keeps any premises for use for an animal fight.

(2) A person commits an offence if, without lawful authority or reasonable excuse, he is present at an animal fight.

(3) A person commits an offence if, without lawful authority or reasonable excuse, he—

    (a) knowingly supplies a video recording of an animal fight,

    (b) knowingly publishes a video recording of an animal fight,

    (c) knowingly shows a video recording of an animal fight to another, or

    (d) possesses a video recording of an animal fight, knowing it to be such a recording, with the intention of supplying it.

(4) Subsection (3) does not apply if the video recording is of an animal fight that took place—

    (a) outside Great Britain, or

    (b) before the commencement date.

(5) Subsection (3) does not apply—

    (a) in the case of paragraph (a), to the supply of a video recording for inclusion in a programme service;

    (b) in the case of paragraph (b) or (c), to the publication or showing of a video recording by means of its inclusion in a programme service;

    (c) in the case of paragraph (d), by virtue of intention to supply for inclusion in a programme service.

...

(7) In this section—

'animal fight' means an occasion on which a protected animal is placed with an animal, or with a human, for the purpose of fighting, wrestling or baiting;

    ...

'programme service' has the same meaning as in the Communications Act 2003 (c. 21);

'video recording' means a recording, in any form, from which a moving image may by any means be reproduced and includes data stored on a computer disc or by other electronic means which is capable of conversion into a moving image.

(8) In this section—

    (a) references to supplying or publishing a video recording are to supplying or publishing a video recording in any manner, including, in relation to a video recording in the form of data stored electronically, by means of transmitting such data;

    (b) references to showing a video recording are to showing a moving image reproduced from a video recording by any means.

9 Duty of person responsible for animal to ensure welfare

(1) A person commits an offence if he does not take such steps as are reasonable in all the circumstances to ensure that the needs of an animal for which he is responsible are met to the extent required by good practice.

(2) For the purposes of this Act, an animal's needs shall be taken to include—

    (a) its need for a suitable environment,

    (b) its need for a suitable diet,

    (c) its need to be able to exhibit normal behaviour patterns,

    (d) any need it has to be housed with, or apart from, other animals, and

    (e) its need to be protected from pain, suffering, injury and disease.

(3) The circumstances to which it is relevant to have regard when applying subsection (1) include, in particular—

    (a) any lawful purpose for which the animal is kept, and

    (b) any lawful activity undertaken in relation to the animal.

(4) Nothing in this section applies to the destruction of an animal in an appropriate and humane manner.

SO But note that a magistrates' court may try an Information relating to an offence under this Act if the information is laid:

    (a) before the end of the period of three years beginning with the date of the commission of the offence; and

(b) before the end of the period of six months beginning with the date on which evidence which the prosecutor thinks is sufficient to justify the proceedings comes to his knowledge.

 £20,000 fine and/or 6 months' imprisonment (ss 4, 5, 6(1) and (2), 7, and 8).

 Level 5 fine and/or 6 months' imprisonment (s 9).

C1.1.1 *Sentencing*

Offence seriousness (culpability and harm)		
A. Identify the appropriate starting point		
Starting points based on first-time offender pleading not guilty		
Examples of nature of activity	**Starting point**	**Range**
One impulsive act causing little or no injury; short-term neglect	Band C fine	Band B fine to medium level community order
Several incidents of deliberate ill-treatment/frightening animal(s); medium-term neglect	High level community order	Medium level community order to 12 weeks' custody
Attempt to kill/torture; animal baiting/conducting or permitting cock-fighting etc; prolonged neglect	18 weeks' custody	12 to 26 weeks' custody

Offence seriousness (culpability and harm)	
B. Consider the effect of aggravating and mitigating factors (other than those within examples above)	
The following may be particularly relevant but these lists are not exhaustive	
Factors indicating higher culpability	**Factors indicating lower culpability**
1. Offender in position of special responsibility	1. Offender induced by others
2. Adult involves children in offending	2. Ignorance of appropriate care
3. Animal(s) kept for livelihood	3. Offender with limited capacity
4. Use of weapon	
5. Offender ignored advice/warnings	
6. Offence committed for commercial gain	
Factors indicating greater degree of harm	
1. Serious injury or death	
2. Several animals affected	

C1.1.2 *Deprivation order*

Section 33 of the Animal Welfare Act 2006 provides for a convicted person to be deprived of his animals:

Animal Welfare Act 2006, s 33

33 Deprivation

(1) If the person convicted of an offence under any of sections 4, 5, 6(1) and (2), 7, 8 and 9 is the owner of an animal in relation to which the offence was committed, the court by or before which he is convicted may, instead of or in addition to dealing with him in any other way, make an order depriving him of ownership of the animal and for its disposal.

(2) Where the owner of an animal is convicted of an offence under section 34(9) because ownership of the animal is in breach of a disqualification under section 34(2), the court by or before which he is convicted may, instead of or in addition to dealing with him in any other way, make an order depriving him of ownership of the animal and for its disposal.

(3) Where the animal in respect of which an order under subsection (1) or (2) is made has any dependent offspring, the order may include provision depriving the person to whom it relates of ownership of the offspring and for its disposal.

(4) Where a court makes an order under subsection (1) or (2), it may—

    (a) appoint a person to carry out, or arrange for the carrying out of, the order;

    (b) require any person who has possession of an animal to which the order applies to deliver it up to enable the order to be carried out;

    (c) give directions with respect to the carrying out of the order;

    (d) confer additional powers (including power to enter premises where an animal to which the order applies is being kept) for the purpose of, or in connection with, the carrying out of the order;

    (e) order the offender to reimburse the expenses of carrying out the order.

(5) Directions under subsection (4)(c) may—

    (a) specify the manner in which an animal is to be disposed of, or

    (b) delegate the decision about the manner in which an animal is to be disposed of to a person appointed under subsection (4)(a).

(6) Where a court decides not to make an order under subsection (1) or (2) in relation to an offender, it shall—

    (a) give its reasons for the decision in open court, and

    (b) if it is a magistrates' court, cause them to be entered in the register of its proceedings.

(7) Subsection (6) does not apply where the court makes an order under section 34(1) in relation to the offender.

(8) In subsection (1), the reference to an animal in relation to which an offence was committed includes, in the case of an offence under section 8, an animal which took part in an animal fight in relation to which the offence was committed.

(9) In this section, references to disposing of an animal include destroying it.

C1.1.3 *Disqualification order*

Section 34 of the Animal Welfare Act 2006 provides for disqualification orders to be made against convicted persons, thereby making it an offence for them to be involved with owning, keeping, or otherwise being involved in the control of animals:

Animal Welfare Act 2006, s 34

34 Disqualification

(1) If a person is convicted of an offence to which this section applies, the court by or before which he is convicted may, instead of or in addition to dealing with him in any other way, make an order disqualifying him under any one or more of subsections (2) to (4) for such period as it thinks fit.

(2) Disqualification under this subsection disqualifies a person—

    (a) from owning animals,

    (b) from keeping animals,

    (c) from participating in the keeping of animals, and

    (d) from being party to an arrangement under which he is entitled to control or influence the way in which animals are kept.

(3) Disqualification under this subsection disqualifies a person from dealing in animals.

(4) Disqualification under this subsection disqualifies a person—

    (a) from transporting animals, and

    (b) from arranging for the transport of animals.

(5) Disqualification under subsection (2), (3) or (4) may be imposed in relation to animals generally, or in relation to animals of one or more kinds.

(6) The court by which an order under subsection (1) is made may specify a period during which the offender may not make an application under section 43(1) for termination of the order.

. . .

(9) A person who breaches a disqualification imposed by an order under subsection (1) commits an offence [carrying a level 5 fine and/or 6 months' imprisonment (s 32(2))].

(10) This section applies to an offence under any of sections 4, 5, 6(1) and (2), 7, 8, 9 and 13(6) and subsection (9).

C1.1.4 *Destruction orders*

Sections 37 and 38 of the Animal Welfare Act 2006 allow for destruction orders to be made in appropriate cases:

Animal Welfare Act 2006, ss 37 and 38

37 Destruction in the interests of the animal

(1) The court by or before which a person is convicted of an offence under any of sections 4, 5, 6(1) and (2), 7, 8(1) and (2) and 9 may order the destruction of an animal in relation to which the offence was committed if it is satisfied,

---

on the basis of evidence given by a veterinary surgeon, that it is appropriate to do so in the interests of the animal.

(2) A court may not make an order under subsection (1) unless—
   (a) it has given the owner of the animal an opportunity to be heard, or
   (b) it is satisfied that it is not reasonably practicable to communicate with the owner.

(3) Where a court makes an order under subsection (1), it may—
   (a) appoint a person to carry out, or arrange for the carrying out of, the order;
   (b) require a person who has possession of the animal to deliver it up to enable the order to be carried out;
   (c) give directions with respect to the carrying out of the order (including directions about how the animal is to be dealt with until it is destroyed);
   (d) confer additional powers (including power to enter premises where the animal is being kept) for the purpose of, or in connection with, the carrying out of the order;
   (e) order the offender or another person to reimburse the expenses of carrying out the order.

(4) Where a court makes an order under subsection (1), each of the offender and, if different, the owner of the animal may—
   (a) in the case of an order made by a magistrates' court, appeal against the order to the Crown Court;
   (b) in the case of an order made by the Crown Court, appeal against the order to the Court of Appeal.

(5) Subsection (4) does not apply if the court by which the order is made directs that it is appropriate in the interests of the animal that the carrying out of the order should not be delayed.

(6) In subsection (1), the reference to an animal in relation to which an offence was committed includes, in the case of an offence under section 8(1) or (2), an animal which took part in an animal fight in relation to which the offence was committed.

38 Destruction of animals involved in fighting offences

(1) The court by or before which a person is convicted of an offence under section 8(1) or (2) may order the destruction of an animal in relation to which the offence was committed on grounds other than the interests of the animal.

(2) A court may not make an order under subsection (1) unless—
   (a) it has given the owner of the animal an opportunity to be heard, or
   (b) it is satisfied that it is not reasonably practicable to communicate with the owner.

(3) Where a court makes an order under subsection (1), it may—
   (a) appoint a person to carry out, or arrange for the carrying out of, the order;
   (b) require a person who has possession of the animal to deliver it up to enable the order to be carried out;
   (c) give directions with respect to the carrying out of the order (including directions about how the animal is to be dealt with until it is destroyed);

(d) confer additional powers (including power to enter premises where the animal is being kept) for the purpose of, or in connection with, the carrying out of the order;

(e) order the offender or another person to reimburse the expenses of carrying out the order.

(4) Where a court makes an order under subsection (1) in relation to an animal which is owned by a person other than the offender, that person may—

(a) in the case of an order made by a magistrates' court, appeal against the order to the Crown Court;

(b) in the case of an order made by the Crown Court, appeal against the order to the Court of Appeal.

(5) In subsection (1), the reference to an animal in relation to which the offence was committed includes an animal which took part in an animal fight in relation to which the offence was committed.

C1.1.5 Key points

- The six-month limitation period for summary offences under this Act can be disapplied in certain circumstances (see section 31 of the 2006 Act and *RSPCA v Johnson* [2009] EWHC 2702 (Admin)).
- References to a person responsible for an animal are to a person responsible for an animal whether on a permanent or a temporary basis.
- References to being responsible for an animal include being in charge of it.
- A person who owns an animal shall always be regarded as being a person who is responsible for it.
- A person shall be treated as responsible for any animal for which a person under the age of 16 years of whom he has actual care and control is responsible.
- Protected animal refers to an animal commonly domesticated in the British Isles, under the control of man, or not living in a wild state.

The considerations to which it is relevant to have regard when determining for the purposes of this section whether suffering is unnecessary include:

- whether the suffering could reasonably have been avoided or reduced;
- whether the conduct which caused the suffering was in compliance with any relevant enactment or any relevant provisions of a licence or code of practice issued under an enactment;
- whether the conduct which caused the suffering was for a legitimate purpose, such as:
  - the purpose of benefiting the animal, or
  - the purpose of protecting a person, property, or another animal;

- whether the suffering was proportionate to the purpose of the conduct concerned;
- whether the conduct concerned was in all the circumstances that of a reasonably competent and humane person.

Nothing in this section applies to the destruction of an animal in an appropriate and humane manner.

When considering making a disqualification order under section 4 of the Act, regard can be had to any previous convictions (*Ward v RSPCA*, unreported, 29 January 2010).

C1.1.6 *Animal welfare: section 9*

The welfare offence in this section extends to non-farmed animals; similar provisions as are found in the Welfare of Farmed Animals (England) Regulations 2000 (SI 2000/1870) (made under Part 1 of the Agriculture (Miscellaneous Provisions) Act 1968), which ensure the welfare of livestock situated on agricultural land. A duty to ensure welfare will therefore apply to all animals for which someone is responsible, as defined in section 3. Where someone is responsible for an animal, he has a duty to take steps that are reasonable in all the circumstances to ensure its needs are met to the extent required by good practice (s 9(1)).

Section 9(3) specifies certain matters to which the courts should have regard when considering whether a person has committed an offence under this section. The provision recognizes that some otherwise lawful practices may prevent or hinder a person from ensuring that all of the welfare needs specified in section 9(2) can be met, and requires the courts to take this into account when considering what is reasonable in the circumstances of the case.

C1.2 Dangerous dogs

Dangerous Dogs Act 1991, s 1

1 Dogs bred for fighting

(1) This section applies to—
  (a) any dog of the type known as the pit bull terrier;
  (b) any dog of the type known as the Japanese tosa; and
  (c) any dog of any type designated for the purposes of this section by an order of the Secretary of State, being a type appearing to him to be bred for fighting or to have the characteristics of a type bred for that purpose.
(2) No person shall—
  (a) breed, or breed from, a dog to which this section applies;

(b) sell or exchange such a dog or offer, advertise or expose such a dog for sale or exchange;

(c) make or offer to make a gift of such a dog or advertise or expose such a dog as a gift;

(d) allow such a dog of which he is the owner or of which he is for the time being in charge to be in a public place without being muzzled and kept on a lead; or

(e) abandon such a dog of which he is the owner or, being the owner or for the time being in charge of such a dog, allow it to stray.

(3) After [30 November 1991] no person shall have any dog to which this section applies in his possession or custody except—

(a) in pursuance of the power of seizure conferred by the subsequent provisions of this Act; or

(b) in accordance with an order for its destruction made under those provisions;

but the Secretary of State shall by order make a scheme for the payment to the owners of such dogs who arrange for them to be destroyed before that day of sums specified in or determined under the scheme in respect of those dogs and the cost of their destruction.

(4) Subsection (2)(b) and (c) above shall not make unlawful anything done with a view to the dog in question being removed from the United Kingdom before the day appointed under subsection (3) above.

(5) The Secretary of State may by order provide that the prohibition in subsection (3) above shall not apply in such cases and subject to compliance with such conditions as are specified in the order and any such provision may take the form of a scheme of exemption containing such arrangements (including provision for the payment of charges or fees) as he thinks appropriate.

(6) A scheme under subsection (3) or (5) above may provide for specified functions under the scheme to be discharged by such persons or bodies as the Secretary of State thinks appropriate.

(7) Any person who contravenes this section is guilty of an offence and liable on summary conviction to imprisonment for a term not exceeding six months or a fine not exceeding level 5 on the standard scale or both except that a person who publishes an advertisement in contravention of subsection (2)(b) or (c)—

(a) shall not on being convicted be liable to imprisonment if he shows that he published the advertisement to the order of someone else and did not himself devise it; and

(b) shall not be convicted if, in addition, he shows that he did not know and had no reasonable cause to suspect that it related to a dog to which this section applies.

Dangerous Dogs Act 1991, s 3

3 Keeping dogs under proper control

(1) If a dog is dangerously out of control in a public place—

(a) the owner; and

(b) if different, the person for the time being in charge of the dog,

is guilty of an offence, or, if the dog while so out of control injures any person, an aggravated offence, under this subsection.

(2) In proceedings for an offence under subsection (1) above against a person who is the owner of a dog but was not at the material time in charge of it, it shall be a defence for the accused to prove that the dog was at the material time in the charge of a person whom he reasonably believed to be a fit and proper person to be in charge of it.

(3) If the owner or, if different, the person for the time being in charge of a dog allows it to enter a place which is not a public place but where it is not permitted to be and while it is there—

(a) it injures any person; or

(b) there are grounds for reasonable apprehension that it will do so,

he is guilty of an offence, or, if the dog injures any person, an aggravated offence, under this subsection.

(4) A person guilty of an offence under subsection (1) or (3) above other than an aggravated offence is liable on summary conviction to imprisonment for a term not exceeding six months or a fine not exceeding level 5 on the standard scale or both; and a person guilty of an aggravated offence under either of those subsections is liable—

(a) on summary conviction, to imprisonment for a term not exceeding six months or a fine not exceeding the statutory maximum or both;

(b) on conviction on indictment, to imprisonment for a term not exceeding two years or a fine or both.

(5) It is hereby declared for the avoidance of doubt that an order under section of the Dogs Act 1871 (order on complaint that dog is dangerous and not kept under proper control)—

(a) may be made whether or not the dog is shown to have injured any person; and

(b) may specify the measures to be taken for keeping the dog under proper control, whether by muzzling, keeping on a lead, excluding it from specified places or otherwise.

(6) If it appears to a court on a complaint under section 2 of the said Act of 1871 that the dog to which the complaint relates is a male and would be less dangerous if neutered the court may under that section make an order requiring it to be neutered.

(7) The reference in section 1(3) of the Dangerous Dogs Act 1989 (penalties) to failing to comply with an order under section 2 of the said Act of 1871 to keep a dog under proper control shall include a reference to failing to comply with any oth order made under that section; but no order shall be made under that section by virtue of subsection (6) above where the matters complained of arose before the coming into force of that subsection.

🎫 Level 5 fine and/or 6 months' imprisonment

Aggravated offence under either section 3(1) or (3) is either way—level 5 fine and/or 6 months'/2 years' imprisonment on indictment.

An offence is aggravated if the dog injures a person.

In relation to an offence under section 1(2)(b) or (c), see section 1(7) which limits sentence in certain circumstances.

C1.2.1 *Sentencing Guidelines*

DANGEROUS DOG OFFENCES

Owner or Person in Charge of a Dog Dangerously Out of Control in a Public Place, Injuring any Person

Dangerous Dogs Act 1991 (section 3(1))

Owner or Person in Charge Allowing a Dog to be in a Private Place Where the Dog is not Permitted to be, Injuring any Person

Dangerous Dogs Act 1991 (section 3(3)(a))

Triable either way

Maximum: 2 years' custody

Offence range: Discharge — 18 months' custody

STEP ONE Determining the offence category

The court should determine the offence category using the table below.

Category 1	Greater harm **and** higher culpability
Category 2	Greater harm **and** lower culpability; **or** lesser harm **and** higher culpability
Category 3	Lesser harm **and** lower culpability

The court should determine culpability and harm caused or intended, by reference only to the factors below, which comprise the principal factual elements of the offence. Where an offence does not fall squarely into a category, individual factors may require a degree of weighting before making an overall assessment and determining the appropriate offence category.

Factors indicating greater harm	**Factors indicating lower culpability**
Serious injury (which includes disease transmission and/or psychological harm) Sustained or repeated attack Victim is a child or otherwise vulnerable because of personal circumstances	Attempts made to regain control of dog and/or intervene Provocation of dog without fault of the offender Evidence of safety or control measures having been taken Mental disorder or learning disability, where linked to the commission of the offence
Factor indicating lesser harm	
Minor injury	
Factors indicating higher culpability	
Statutory aggravating factors: Offence racially or religiously aggravated Offence motivated by, or demonstrating, hostility to the victim based on his or her sexual orientation (or presumed sexual orientation)	

C1 Animal Offences

Offence motivated by, or demonstrating, hostility to the victim based on the victim's disability (or presumed disability) **Other aggravating factors:** Failure to respond to warnings or concerns expressed by others about the dog's behaviour Goading, or allowing goading, of dog Dog used as weapon or to intimidate victim Offence motivated by, or demonstrating, hostility based on the victim's age, sex, gender identity (or presumed gender identity)	

STEP TWO Starting point and category range

Having determined the category, the court should use the corresponding starting points to reach a sentence within the category range below. The starting point applies to all offenders irrespective of plea or previous convictions. A case of particular gravity, reflected by multiple features of culpability or harm in step 1, could merit upward adjustment from the starting point before further adjustment for aggravating or mitigating features, set out [below].

Offence Category	Starting Point (Applicable to all offenders)	Category Range (Applicable to all offenders)
Category 1	6 months' custody	Medium level community order – 18 months' custody
Category 2	Medium level community order	Band B fine – 6 months' custody
Category 3	Band B fine	Discharge – Band C fine

The table below contains a **non-exhaustive** list of additional factual elements providing the context of the offence and factors relating to the offender. Identify whether any combination of these, or other relevant factors, should result in an upward or downward adjustment from the starting point. In some cases, having considered these factors, it may be appropriate to move outside the identified category range.

When sentencing **category 1 or 2** offences, the court should also consider the custody threshold as follows:

- has the custody threshold been passed?
- if so, is it unavoidable that a custodial sentence be imposed?
- if so, can that sentence be suspended?

When sentencing **category 2** offences, the court should also consider the community order threshold as follows:

- has the community order threshold been passed?

Factors increasing seriousness	Factors reducing seriousness or reflecting personal mitigation
Statutory aggravating factors: Previous convictions, having regard to a) the nature of the offence to which the conviction relates and its relevance to the current offence; and b) the time that has elapsed since the conviction Offence committed whilst on bail **Other aggravating factors include:** Location of the offence Ongoing effect upon the victim and/or others Failure to take adequate precautions to prevent dog escaping Allowing person insufficiently experienced or trained, to be in charge of dog Ill treatment or failure to ensure welfare needs of dog, where not charged separatelyDog known to be prohibited Lack or loss of control of dog due to the influence of alcohol or drugs Offence committed against those working in the public sector or providing a service to the public Established evidence of community impact Failure to comply with current court orders Offence committed whilst on licence	No previous convictions or no relevant/recent convictions Isolated incident No previous complaints against, or incidents involving, the dog Remorse Good character and/or exemplary conduct Evidence of responsible ownership Determination and/or demonstration of steps taken to address addiction or offending behaviour Serious medical conditions requiring urgent, intensive or long-term treatment Age and/or lack of maturity where it affects the responsibility of the offender Mental disorder or learning disability, where not linked to the commission of the offence Sole or primary carer for dependent relatives

STEP THREE Consider any factors which indicate a reduction, such as assistance to the prosecution

The court should take into account sections 73 and 74 of the Serious Organised Crime and Police Act 2005 (assistance by defendants: reduction or review of sentence) and any other rule of law by virtue of which an offender may receive a discounted sentence in consequence of assistance given (or offered) to the prosecutor or investigator.

STEP FOUR Reduction for guilty pleas

The court should take account of any potential reduction for a guilty plea in accordance with section 144 of the Criminal Justice Act 2003 and the *Guilty Plea* guideline.

STEP FIVE Compensation and ancillary orders

In all cases, the court should consider whether to make a compensation order and/or other ancillary orders.

Compensation order

The court should consider compensation orders in all cases where personal injury, loss or damage has resulted from the offence. The court must give reasons if it decides not to award compensation in such cases.

C1 Animal Offences

Other ancillary orders available include:

Disqualification from having custody of a dog

The court may disqualify the offender from having custody of a dog. The test the court should consider is whether the offender is a fit and proper person to have custody of a dog.

Destruction order/contingent destruction order

In any case where the offender is not the owner of the dog, the owner must be given an opportunity to be present and make representations to the court.

The court **shall** make a destruction order unless the court is satisfied that the dog would not constitute a danger to public safety.

In reaching a decision, the court should consider the relevant circumstances which include:

- the incident — what degree of harm was caused by the dog's behaviour?
- past behaviour of the dog — is this an isolated incident or have there been previous warnings or incidents? and
- owner's character — is the owner a fit and proper person to own this particular dog?

If the court is satisfied that the dog would not constitute a danger to public safety, it shall make a contingent destruction order imposing certain available conditions. A contingent destruction order should specify the measures to be taken by the owner for keeping the dog under proper control, which include:

- muzzling;
- keeping on a lead;
- neutering in appropriate cases; and
- excluding it from a specified place.

Where the court makes a destruction order, it may order the offender to pay what it determines to be the reasonable expenses of destroying the dog and of keeping it pending its destruction.

Owner or Person in charge of a Dog Dangerously out of Control in a Public Place

Dangerous Dogs Act 1991 (section 3(1))

Owner or Person in Charge Allowing a Dog to be in a Private Place Where the Dog is not Permitted to be, Which Makes a Person Fear Injury

Dangerous Dogs Act 1991 (section 3(3)(b))

Triable summarily only

Maximum: 6 months' custody

Offence range: Discharge — 6 months' custody

STEP ONE Determining the offence category

The court should determine the offence category using the table below.

Category 1	Greater harm **and** higher culpability
Category 2	Greater harm **and** lower culpability; **or** lesser harm **and** higher culpability
Category 3	Lesser harm **and** lower culpability

The court should determine culpability and harm caused or intended, by reference **only** to the factors below, which comprise the principal factual elements of the offence. Where an offence does not fall squarely into a category, individual factors may require a degree of weighting before making an overall assessment and determining the appropriate offence category.

Factors indicating greater harm	**Factors indicating lesser harm**
Presence of children or others who are vulnerable because of personal circumstances Injury to another animal(s)	Low risk to the public
Factors indicating higher culpability	**Factors indicating lower culpability**
Statutory aggravating factors: Offence racially or religiously aggravated Offence motivated by, or demonstrating, hostility to the victim based on his or her sexual orientation (or presumed sexual orientation) Offence motivated by, or demonstrating, hostility to the victim based on the victim's disability (or presumed disability) **Other aggravating factors:** Failure to respond to warnings or concerns expressed by others about the dog's behaviour Goading, or allowing goading, of dog Dog used as weapon or to intimidate victim Offence motivated by, or demonstrating, hostility based on the victim's age, sex, gender identity (or presumed gender identity)	Attempts made to regain control of dog and/or intervene Provocation of dog without fault of the offender Evidence of safety or control measures having been taken Mental disorder or learning disability, where linked to the commission of the offence

STEP TWO Starting point and category range

Having determined the category, the court should use the corresponding starting points to reach a sentence within the category range below. The starting point applies to all offenders irrespective of plea or previous convictions. A case of particular gravity, reflected by multiple features of culpability or harm in step 1, could merit upward adjustment from the starting point before further adjustment for aggravating or mitigating features, set out [below].

C1 Animal Offences

Offence Category	Starting Point (Applicable to all offenders)	Category Range (Applicable to all offenders)
Category 1	Medium level community order	Band C fine – 6 months' custody
Category 2	Band B fine	Band A fine – Low level community order
Category 3	Band A fine	Discharge – Band B fine

The table below contains a **non-exhaustive** list of additional factual elements providing the context of the offence and factors relating to the offender. Identify whether any combination of these, or other relevant factors, should result in an upward or downward adjustment from the starting point. In some cases, having considered these factors, it may be appropriate to move outside the identified category range.

When sentencing **category 1** offences, the court should also consider the custody threshold as follows:

- has the custody threshold been passed?
- if so, is it unavoidable that a custodial sentence be imposed?
- if so, can that sentence be suspended?

When sentencing **category 1 or 2** offences, the court should also consider the community order threshold as follows:

- has the community order threshold been passed?

Factors increasing seriousness	Factors reducing seriousness or reflecting personal mitigation
Statutory aggravating factors: Previous convictions, having regard to a) the nature of the offence to which the conviction relates and its relevance to the current offence; and b) the time that has elapsed since the conviction Offence committed whilst on bail **Other aggravating factors include:** Injury to another animal(s) Location of the offence Ongoing effect upon the victim and/or others Failure to take adequate precautions to prevent dog escaping Allowing person insufficiently experienced or trained, to be in charge of dog Ill treatment or failure to ensure welfare needs of dog, where not charged separately Dog known to be prohibited Lack or loss of control of dog due to influence of alcohol or drugs	No previous convictions or no relevant/recent convictions Isolated incident No previous complaints against, or incidents involving, the dog Remorse Good character and/or exemplary conduct Evidence of responsible ownershipDetermination and/or demonstration of steps taken to address addiction or offending behaviour Serious medical conditions requiring urgent, intensive or long-term treatment Age and/or lack of maturity where it affects the responsibility of the offender Mental disorder or learning disability, where not linked to the commission of the offence Sole or primary carer for dependent relatives

Offence committed against those working in the public sector or providing a service to the public Established evidence of community impact Failure to comply with current court orders Offence committed whilst on licence	

[Steps Three to Eight are almost identical to those applicable to Owner or person in charge of a dog dangerously out of control in a public place, injuring any person, but differ in relation to Destruction order/contingent destruction order. Step 5 deals with ancillary orders.]

Destruction order/contingent destruction order

In any case where the offender is not the owner of the dog, the owner must be given an opportunity to be present and make representations to the court.

The court **may** make a destruction order. Alternatively, it **may** make a contingent destruction order imposing certain available conditions. A contingent destruction order should specify the measures to be taken by the owner for keeping the dog under proper control, which include:

- muzzling;
- keeping on a lead;
- neutering in appropriate cases; and
- excluding it from a specified place.

In reaching a decision, the court should consider the relevant circumstances which include:

- the incident — what degree of harm was caused by the dog's behaviour?
- past behaviour of the dog — is this an isolated incident or have there been previous warnings or incidents? and
- owner's character — is the owner a fit and proper person to own this particular dog?

Where the court makes a destruction order, it **may** order the offender to pay what it determines to be the reasonable expenses of destroying the dog and of keeping it pending its destruction.

Possession of a Prohibited Dog

Dangerous Dogs Act 1991 (section 1(3))

Breeding, Selling, Exchanging or Advertising a Prohibited Dog

Dangerous Dogs Act 1991 (section 1(2))

Triable only summarily

Maximum: 6 months' custody

Offence range: Discharge — 6 months' custody

C1 Animal Offences

STEP ONE Determining the offence category

The court should determine the offence category using the table below.

Category 1	Greater harm **and** higher culpability
Category 2	Greater harm **or** higher culpability
Category 3	**Neither** greater harm **nor** higher culpability

The court should determine culpability and harm caused or intended, by reference **only** to the factors below, which comprise the principal factual elements of the offence. Where an offence does not fall squarely into a category, individual factors may require a degree of weighting before making an overall assessment and determining the appropriate offence category.

Factors indicating greater harm	Factors indicating higher culpability
Injury to person Injury to another animal(s)	Possessing a dog known to be prohibited Breeding from a dog known to be prohibited Selling, exchanging or advertising a dog known to be prohibited Offence committed for gain Dog used to threaten or intimidate Permitting fighting Training and/or possession of paraphernalia for dog fighting

STEP TWO Starting point and category range

Having determined the category, the court should use the corresponding starting points to reach a sentence within the category range below. The starting point applies to all offenders irrespective of plea or previous convictions. A case of particular gravity, reflected by multiple features of culpability or harm in step 1, could merit upward adjustment from the starting point before further adjustment for aggravating or mitigating features, set out [below].

Offence Category	Starting Point (Applicable to all offenders)	Category Range (Applicable to all offenders)
Category 1	Medium level community order	Band C fine – 6 months' custody*
Category 2	Band C fine	Band A fine – Medium level community order
Category 3	Band A fine	Discharge – Band B fine

* Imprisonment is not available if the provisions of s 1(7) Dangerous Dogs Act 1991 apply

The table below contains a **non-exhaustive** list of additional factual elements providing the context of the offence and factors relating to the offender. Identify whether any combination of these, or other relevant factors, should result in an upward or downward adjustment from the starting point. In some cases, having considered these factors, it may be appropriate to move outside the identified category range.

When sentencing **category 1** offences, the court should also consider the custody threshold as follows:

- has the custody threshold been passed?
- if so, is it unavoidable that a custodial sentence be imposed?
- if so, can that sentence be suspended?

When sentencing **category 1 or 2** offences, the court should also consider the community order threshold as follows:

- has the community order threshold been passed?

Factors increasing seriousness	Factors reducing seriousness or reflecting personal mitigation
Statutory aggravating factors: Previous convictions, having regard to a) the nature of the offence to which the conviction relates and its relevance to the current offence; and b) the time that has elapsed since the conviction Offence committed whilst on bail **Other aggravating factors include:** Presence of children or others who are vulnerable because of personal circumstances Ill treatment or failure to ensure welfare needs of dog, where not charged separately Established evidence of community impact Failure to comply with current court orders Offence committed whilst on licence	No previous convictions **or** no relevant/recent convictions Unaware that dog was prohibited type despite reasonable efforts to identify type Evidence of safety or control measures having been taken by owner Prosecution results from owner notification Remorse Good character and/or exemplary conduct Evidence of responsible ownership Determination and/or demonstration of steps taken to address addiction or offending behaviour Serious medical conditions requiring urgent, intensive or long-term treatment Age and/or lack of maturity where it affects the responsibility of the offender Lapse of time since the offence where this is not the fault of the offender Mental disorder or learning disability Sole or primary carer for dependent relatives

[Steps Three to Eight are almost identical to those applicable to Owner or person in charge of a dog dangerously out of control in a public place, injuring any person, but differ in relation to Destruction order/contingent destruction order. Step 5 deals with ancillary powers.]

Destruction order/contingent destruction order

The court **shall** make a destruction order unless the court is satisfied that the dog would not constitute a danger to public safety.

C1 Animal Offences

In reaching a decision, the court should consider the relevant circumstances which include:

- danger to the public — what is the potential risk of harm posed by the dog?
- behaviour of the dog — have there been any warnings or incidents involving the dog? and
- owner's character — is the owner a fit and proper person to own this particular dog?

If the court does not make a destruction order, the court **shall** make a contingent destruction order providing that unless the dog is exempted from the prohibition within two months it shall be destroyed. Statutory procedures and conditions automatically apply to exempted dogs and no other conditions can be imposed. Where the offender is the owner of the dog, it would not normally be appropriate to make a contingent destruction order in conjunction with a disqualification order.

Furthermore, the court **must not** transfer ownership of the dog to another.

Where the court makes a destruction order, it **may** order the offender to pay what it determines to be the reasonable expenses of destroying the dog and of keeping it pending its destruction.

On conviction there is power under section 4 of the 1991 Act to make destruction and disqualification orders:

Dangerous Dogs Act 1991, ss 4(1)–(3) and 4A

4 Destruction and disqualification orders

(1) Where a person is convicted of an offence under section 1 or 3(1) or (3) above or of an offence under an order made under section 2 above the court—

    (a) may order the destruction of any dog in respect of which the offence was committed and, subject to subsection (1A) below, shall do so in the case of an offence under section 1 or an aggravated offence under section 3(1) or (3) above; and

    (b) may order the offender to be disqualified, for such period as the court thinks fit, for having custody of a dog.

(1A) Nothing in subsection (1)(a) above shall require the court to order the destruction of a dog if the court is satisfied—

    (a) that the dog would not constitute a danger to public safety; and

    (b) where the dog was born before 30th November 1991 and is subject to the prohibition in section 1(3) above, that there is a good reason why the dog has not been exempted from that prohibition.

(2) Where a court makes an order under subsection (1)(a) above for the destruction of a dog owned by a person other than the offender, the owner may appeal to the Crown Court against the order.

(3) A dog shall not be destroyed pursuant to an order under subsection (1)(a) above—

    (a) until the end of the period for giving notice of appeal against the conviction or, against the order; and

---

(b) if notice of appeal is given within that period, until the appeal is determined or withdrawn,

unless the offender and, in a case to which subsection (2) above applies,
the owner of the dog give notice to the court that made the order that
there is to be no appeal

...

4A Contingent destruction orders

(1) Where—
    (a) a person is convicted of an offence under section 1 above or an aggra-
        vated offence under section 3(1) or (3) above;
    (b) the court does not order the destruction of the dog under section
        4(1)(a) above; and
    (c) in the case of an offence under section 1 above, the dog is subject to the
        prohibition in section 1(3) above,

    the court shall order that, unless the dog is exempted from that prohibition
    within the requisite period, the dog shall be destroyed.

(2) Where an order is made under subsection (1) above in respect of a dog, and
    the dog is not exempted from the prohibition in section 1(3) above within
    the requisite period, the court may extend that period.

(3) Subject to subsection (2) above, the requisite period for the purposes of
    such an order is the period of two months beginning with the date of
    the order.

(4) Where a person is convicted of an offence under section 3(1) or (3) above,
    the court may order that, unless the owner of the dog keeps it under proper
    control, the dog shall be destroyed.

(5) An order under subsection (4) above—
    (a) may specify the measures to be taken for keeping the dog under proper
        control, whether by muzzling, keeping on a lead, excluding it from
        specified places or otherwise; and
    (b) if it appears to the court that the dog is a male and would be less dan-
        gerous if neutered, may require it to be neutered.

(6) Subsections (2) to (4) of section 4 above shall apply in relation to an order
    under subsection (1) or (4) above as they apply in relation to an order under
    subsection (1)(a) of that section.

C1.2.2 Key points

- For 'type' see *Crown Court at Knightsbridge, ex p Dune* [1993] 4 All
  ER 491.
- 'Dangerously out of control' is defined under section 10(3) of
  the Act:

Dangerous Dogs Act 1991, s 10(3)

10 Short title, interpretation, commencement and extent

(3) For the purposes of this Act a dog shall be regarded as dangerously out of control on any occasion on which there are grounds for reasonable apprehension that it will injure any person, whether or not it actually does so, but references to a dog injuring a person or there being grounds for reasonable apprehension that it will do so do not include references to any case in which the dog is being used for a lawful purpose by a constable or a person in the service of the Crown.

- Regard must be had to the behaviour of the dog and the degree of control exercised by its handler. The fact that the dog has not displayed any previous bad traits was of relevance but not conclusive (*R v Gedminintaite* [2008] EWCA Crim 814).
- It is sufficient that the danger is only to other dogs (*Briscoe v Shattock* (1998) 163 JP 201), but a dog hunting and killing rabbits and other small animals is part of a dog's nature and does not make it dangerous (*Sansom v Chief Constable of Kent* [1981] Crim LR 617).
- The owner of the dog has a defence under section 3(2) if another fit and proper person was in charge of the dog at the material time. Whether a person is a fit and proper person will depend on all of the circumstances. The dog must have been left with an identifiable person; it was not sufficient merely to say that different members of a family looked after the dog at different times (*R v Huddart* [1999] Crim LR 568).
- It is irrelevant that the owner did not anticipate the behaviour of the dog (*R v Bezzina* (1994) 158 JP 671).
- A person who relinquishes physical control of a dog by passing the lead to another may remain in joint control of the dog (*L v Crown Prosecution Service*, unreported, 10 February 2010). Plain evidence is required to demonstrate that control has been passed to another (*R v Huddart* [1999] Crim LR 568).
- 'Public place' includes the inside of a vehicle which is itself in a public place (*Bates v Director of Public Prosecutions* (1993) 157 JP 1004).
- There are no defences in relation to section 1 (see *Director of Public Prosecutions v Kellett* (1994) 158 JP 1138 (intoxication) and *Cichon v Director of Public Prosecutions* [1994] Crim LR (welfare of the animal—unmuzzling to allow the dog to be sick).
- In relation to destruction orders, see the guidance issued by the Court of Appeal in *R v Flack* [2008] Cr App R (S) 395 and *R v Davies* [2010] 174 JP 514, CA, reviewed in *Kelleher v DPP* [2012] 176 JP 729, QBD.

Essentially the court must consider whether the dog constitues a danger to the public. If it does not then no order is made. If it does, the court must consider whether a contingent destruction order would remove that danger. In the case of an aggravated offence, the burden of proof to show that the dog does not represent a danger is on the defence. The normal burden of proof applies in non-aggravated cases.

 See *Blackstones' Criminal Practice 2014* **B20**

C1.3 Dog worrying livestock

Dogs (Protection of Livestock) Act 1953, s 1

1 Penalty where dog worries livestock on agricultural land

(1) Subject to the provisions of this section, if a dog worries livestock on any agricultural land, the owner of the dog, and, if it is in the charge of a person other than its owner, that person also, shall be guilty of an offence under this Act.

(2) For the purposes of this Act worrying livestock means—

  (a) attacking livestock, or

  (b) chasing livestock in such a way as may reasonably be expected to cause injury or suffering to the livestock or, in the case of females, abortion, or loss of or diminution in their produce, or

  (c) being at large (that is to say not on a lead or otherwise under close control) in a field or enclosure in which there are sheep.

(2A) Subsection (2)(c) of this section shall not apply in relation to—

  (a) a dog owned by, or in the charge of, the occupier of the field or enclosure or the owner of the sheep or a person authorised by either of those persons; or

  (b) a police dog, a guide dog, trained sheep dog, a working gun dog or a pack of hounds.

(3) A person shall not be guilty of an offence under this Act by reason of anything done by a dog, if at the material time the livestock are trespassing on the land in question and the dog is owned by, or in the charge of, the occupier of that land or a person authorised by him, except in a case where the said person causes the dog to attack the livestock.

(4) The owner of a dog shall not be convicted of an offence under this Act in respect of the worrying of livestock by the dog if he proves that at the time when the dog worried the livestock it was in the charge of some other person, whom he reasonably believed to be a fit and proper person to be in charge of the dog.

SO

Fine level 3

C1.4 Guard dogs

Guard Dogs Act 1975, ss 1 and 7

1 Control of guard dogs

(1) A person shall not use or permit the use of a guard dog at any premises unless a person ('the handler') who is capable of controlling the dog is present on the premises and the dog is under the control of the handler at all times while it is being so used except while it is secured so that it is not at liberty to go freely about the premises.

(2) The handler of a guard dog shall keep the dog under his control at all times while it is being used as a guard dog at any premises except—
   (a) while another handler has control over the dog; or
   (b) while the dog is secured so that it is not at liberty to go freely about the premises.

(3) A person shall not use or permit the use of a guard dog at any premises unless a notice containing a warning that a guard dog is present is clearly exhibited at each entrance to the premises.

7 Interpretation

In this Act, unless the context otherwise requires—

. . .

'guard dog' means a dog which is being used to protect—
   (a) premises; or
   (b) property kept on the premises; or
   (c) a person guarding the premises or such property;

. . .

SO

▦ Fine level 3

▥ See *Blackstone's Criminal Practice 2014* **B20.141**

C2 Anti-Social Behaviour Order, Breach of

Crime and Disorder Act 1998, s 1(10)

1 Anti-social behaviour orders

If without reasonable excuse a person does anything which he is prohibited from doing by an anti-social behaviour order, he is guilty of an offence.

EW

 Level 5 fine and/or 6 months'/5 years' imprisonment. When section 41 of the Crime and Security Act 2010 comes into force a parenting order must be made in certain circumstances following a conviction for breaching an anti-social behaviour order (see **D38.2**).

C2.1 Sentencing

Nature of failure and harm	Starting point	Sentencing range
Serious harassment, alarm, or distress has been caused or where such harm was intended	26 weeks' custody	Custody threshold to 2 years' custody
Lesser degree of harassment, alarm, or distress, where such harm was intended, or where it would have been likely if the offender had not been apprehended	6 weeks' custody	Medium level community order to 26 weeks' custody
No harassment, alarm, or distress was actually caused by the breach and none was intended by the offender	Low level community order	Band B fine to medium level community order

Aggravating factors	Mitigating factors
1. Offender has a history of disobedience to court orders 2. Breach was committed immediately or shortly after the order was made 3. Breach was committed subsequent to earlier breach proceedings arising from the same order 4. Targeting of a person the order was made to protect or a witness in the original proceedings	1. Breach occurred after a long period of compliance 2. The prohibition(s) breached was not fully understood, especially where an interim order was made without notice

C2.2 Key points

- The prosecution must be in a position to prove that the person before the court is the person in respect of whom the order was made (*Barber v Crown Prosecution Service* [2004] EWHC 2605 (Admin)).
- In *R v Nicholson* [2006] EWCA Crim 1518, the offender took part in a demonstration within a prohibited distance of a named property. She admitted, too, that she had not carefully checked the terms of the order, in particular the scheduled inclusion of premises named Halifax House. However, she maintained that she had a reasonable excuse for breaching the terms of the order within the statutory provision because she had no recollection of ever having heard before, or at the demonstration, of any reference to Halifax House as the address of the proposed laboratory, and she had mistakenly believed that she was entitled to attend the demonstration as she did. Held: forgetfulness, misunderstanding, or ignorance could amount in law to a reasonable excuse.
- The fact that a person is appealing against the imposition of an order does not give rise to a reasonable excuse (*West Midlands Probation Board v Daly* [2008] EWHC 15 (Admin)).
- A belief that the order has come to an end is capable of amounting to a reasonable excuse (*Barber v Crown Prosecution Service* [2004] EWHC 2605 (Admin)).
- Where conduct forming the breach would also be a criminal offence in its own right, a court was not bound by the maximum sentence available for that offence, but should have regard to proportionality. It would be wrong for a prosecutor to proceed with a breach of an anti-social behaviour order simply because it was thought that the penalty for the substantive offence was too lenient (*R v Stevens* [2006] EWCA Crim 255).
- The burden of negativing reasonable excuse, once raised by evidence by the defence, falls on the prosecution (*R v Charles* [2009] EWCA Crim 1570).

- A defendant's state of mind is relevant to the issue of reasonable excuse, notwithstanding the fact that the offence is one of strict liability (*JB v Crown Prosecution Service* [2012] EWHC 72 (Admin)).

 See *Blackstone's Criminal Practice 2014* **D25.17**

C3 **Bail: Failure to Surrender**

Bail Act 1976, s 6(1) and (2)

6 Offence of absconding by person released on bail

(1) If a person who has been released on bail in criminal proceedings fails without reasonable cause to surrender to custody he shall be guilty of an offence.

(2) If a person who—
   (a) has been released on bail in criminal proceedings, and
   (b) having reasonable cause therefor, has failed to surrender to custody,

   fails to surrender to custody at the appointed place as soon after the appointed time as is reasonably practicable he shall be guilty of an offence.

SO But with power to commit to the Crown Court

⊞ Level 5 fine and/or 3 months/12 months

C3.1 **Sentencing**

Offence seriousness (culpability and harm) A. Identify the appropriate starting point Starting points based on first-time offender pleading not guilty		
Example of nature of activity	**Starting point**	**Range**
Surrenders late on day but case proceeds as planned	Band A fine	Band A fine to band B fine
Negligent or non-deliberate failure to attend causing delay and/or interference with the administration of justice	Band C fine	Band B fine to medium level community order
Deliberate failure to attend causing delay and/or interference with the administration of justice. The type and degree of harm actually caused will affect where in the range the case falls	14 days' custody	Low level community order to 10 weeks' custody

SO Summary Only   **⊞** Sentence

Offence seriousness (culpability and harm)	
B. Consider the effect of aggravating and mitigating factors **(other than those within examples above)** The following may be particularly relevant but these lists are not exhaustive	
Factors indicating higher culpability 1. Serious attempts to evade justice 2. Determined attempt seriously to undermine the course of justice 3. Previous relevant convictions and/or breach of court orders or police bail **Factor indicating greater degree of harm** 1. Lengthy absence	**Factors indicating lower culpability** Where not amounting to a defence: 1. Misunderstanding 2. Failure to comprehend bail significance or requirements 3. Caring responsibilities **Factor indicating lesser degree of harm** 1. Prompt voluntary surrender

C3.2 Key points

- In *R v Scott* [2007] EWCA Crim 2757, the court rejected an argument that surrendering to bail 30 minutes late was *de minimis* so as to make proceeding with a Bail Act charge *Wednesbury* unreasonable. The court held:

  We are prepared for the sake of argument to accept the possibility that there could be circumstances where a defendant's late arrival at court was so truly marginal that it would be Wednesbury unreasonable to pursue it but it would be a rare case.

- In *R v Gateshead Justices, ex p Usher* [1981] Crim LR 491, DC, a period of seven minutes was held to be *de minimis*; however, in *Scott* the court said that no gloss should be placed on the clear wording in the Bail Act and *Usher* established no clear principle of law, observing that:

  there could be circumstances where a defendant's late arrival at court was so truly marginal that it would be Wednesbury unreasonable to pursue it but it would be a rare case . . . Even if a delay is small it can still cause inconvenience and waste of time. If a culture of lateness is tolerated the results can be cumulative and bad for the administration of justice.

- Proof of *bail* conditions: section 6 of the Bail Act 1976 provides:

Bail Act 1976, s 6(8) and (9)

6 Offence of absconding by person released on bail

(8) In any proceedings for an offence under subsection (1) or (2) above a document purporting to be a copy of the part of the prescribed record which relates to the time and place appointed for the person specified in the record to surrender to custody and to be duly certified to be a true copy of

that part of the record shall be evidence of the time and place appointed for that person to surrender to custody.

(9) For the purposes of subsection (8) above—

(a) 'the prescribed record' means the record of the decision of the court, officer or constable made in pursuance of section 5(1) of this Act;

(b) the copy of the prescribed record is duly certified if it is certified by the appropriate officer of the court or, as the case may be, by the constable who took the decision or a constable designated for the purpose by the officer in charge of the police station from which the person to whom the record relates was released.

- In *R v Liverpool Justices, ex p Santos* The Times, 23 January 1997, the court held that reliance on mistaken information provided by a solicitor may be found a reasonable excuse for failing to surrender. The court went on to say that all relevant factors would need to be considered, and a mistake on the part of a solicitor in calculating the bail date did not automatically excuse the defendant's non-attendance.

- A failure to give the defendant a written bail notice does not amount to a reasonable excuse.

- A genuine, albeit mistaken, belief that bail was to another date would not amount to a reasonable excuse (*Laidlaw v Atkinson* The Times, 2 August 1986).

- A reasonable excuse need be proved only to the civil standard (*R v Carr-Bryant* (1944) 29 Cr App R 76).

- A person who had overtly subjected himself to the court's direction (see *R v Central Criminal Court, ex p Guney* [1995] 2 All ER 577), or reported to court officials as directed, had surrendered to custody (see *Director of Public Prosecutions v Richards* [1988] QB 701 in relation to the magistrates' court). If the defendant later left court, no offence would be committed (although the court could issue a warrant for arrest). It is not essential that there be a formal surrender to an official (*R v Rumble* [2003] EWCA Crim 770), but simply arriving at the court at the proper time may not be enough (*R v Render* (1987) 84 Cr App R 294). In *Evans* [2011] EWCA Crim 2842, the court made clear that in the Crown Court a defendant who advises the usher and his own lawyer of his presence but then leaves, does not surrender to bail. He must be identified before the judge, or surrender to the dock officer.

- If a person is acquitted of the offence for which he was on bail, that does not mitigate the penalty for failing to surrender (*R v Maguire* [1993] RTR 306).

See *Blackstone's Criminal Practice 2014* **D7.97**

C4 **Communication Network Offences**

C4.1 Improper use of public electronic communications network

Communications Act 2003, s 127(1) and (2)

127 Improper use of public electronic communications network

(1) A person is guilty of an offence if he—
   (a) sends by means of a public electronic communications network a message or other matter that is grossly offensive or of an indecent, obscene or menacing character; or
   (b) causes any such message or matter to be so sent.
(2) A person is guilty of an offence if, for the purpose of causing annoyance, inconvenience or needless anxiety to another, he—
   (a) sends by means of a public electronic communications network, a message that he knows to be false,
   (b) causes such a message to be sent; or
   (c) persistently makes use of a public electronic communications network.

SO

🏛 Level 5 fine/6 months' imprisonment

C4.1.1 *Sentencing*

Offence seriousness (culpability and harm) **A. Identify the appropriate starting point** Starting points based on first-time offender pleading not guilty		
Sending grossly offensive, indecent, obscene, or menacing messages (s 127(1))		
Example of nature of activity	**Starting point**	**Range**
Single offensive, indecent, obscene, or menacing call of short duration, having no significant impact on receiver	Band B fine	Band A fine to band C fine
Single call where extreme language used, having only moderate impact on receiver	Medium level community order	Low level community order to high level community order

Single call where extreme language used and substantial distress or fear caused to receiver; OR One of a series of similar calls as described in box above	6 weeks' custody	High level community order to 12 weeks' custody

Sending false message/persistent use of communications network for purpose of causing annoyance, inconvenience, or needless anxiety (s 127(2))

Example of nature of activity	Starting point	Range
Persistent silent calls over short period to private individual, causing inconvenience or annoyance	Band B fine	Band A fine to band C fine
Single hoax call to public or private organization resulting in moderate disruption or anxiety	Medium level community order	Low level community order to high level community order
Single hoax call resulting in major disruption or substantial public fear or distress; OR One of a series of similar calls as described in box above	12 weeks' custody	High level community order to 18 weeks' custody

C4.1.2 Key points

- In *Director of Public Prosecutions v Collins* [2006] UKHL 40, the court held that to be guilty of an offence under section 127:
  - the defendant must have intended his words to be offensive to those to whom they related; or
  - must be aware that they might be taken to be so.
- It does not matter if the material sent was not received. The question of whether something is in fact offensive is to be determined by reference to whether or not reasonable persons would find the message grossly offensive, judged by the standards of an open and just multiracial society.
- Parliament cannot have intended to criminalize the conduct of a person using language which is, for reasons unknown to him, grossly offensive to those to whom it relates, or which may even be thought, however wrongly, to represent a polite or acceptable usage. On the other hand, a culpable state of mind will ordinarily be found where a message is couched in terms showing an intention to insult those to whom the message relates, or giving rise to the inference

that a risk of doing so must have been recognized by the sender. The same will be true where facts known to the sender of a message about an intended recipient render the message peculiarly offensive to that recipient, or likely to be so, whether or not the message in fact reaches the recipient.

- While it is an offence to send by public electronic communication network a message of a menacing character (Malicious Communications Act 2003, s 127(1)(a)), the mental element requires the sender either to have intended that the message be of a menacing character, or to have been aware or to have recognized the risk that it might create fear or apprehension in any reasonable member of the public who reads or sees it.
- If the message was intended as a joke, however poor, the offence will rarely be made out (*Chambers v DPP* [2012] EWHC 2157 (QB)).
- European Convention rights to freedom of expression will rarely provide a defence (see *Connolly v Director of Public Prosecutions* [2007] EWHC 237 (Admin), a case concerned with a different statute).

 See *Blackstone's Criminal Practice 2014* **B18.30**

C4.2 Sending indecent material through post

Postal Services Act 2000, s 85

85 Prohibition on sending certain articles by post

(1) A person commits an offence if he sends by post a postal packet which encloses any creature, article or thing of any kind which is likely to injure other postal packets in course of their transmission by post or any person engaged in the business of a postal operator.

(2) Subsection (1) does not apply to postal packets which enclose anything permitted (whether generally or specifically) by the postal operator concerned.

(3) A person commits an offence if he sends by post a postal packet which encloses—

(a) any indecent or obscene print, painting, photograph, lithograph, engraving, cinematograph film or other record of a picture or pictures, book, card or written communication, or

(b) any other indecent or obscene article (whether or not of a similar kind to those mentioned in paragraph (a)).

(4) A person commits an offence if he sends by post a postal packet which has on the packet, or on the cover of the packet, any words, marks or designs which are of an indecent or obscene character.

(5) A person who commits an offence under this section shall be liable—
   (a) on summary conviction, to a fine not exceeding the statutory maximum,
   (b) on conviction on indictment, to a fine or to imprisonment for a term not exceeding twelve months or to both.

EW

 Level 5 fine; 12 months' imprisonment

C4.2.1 Key points

Whether something is obscene is to be judged objectively.

In relation to Article 10 ECHR considerations, the court in *R v Kirk* [2006] EWCA Crim 725 held:

> We derive assistance, so far as the reference to the Convention is concerned, from the recent decision of the House of Lords in *K v London Borough of Lambeth* [2006] UKHL 10. We refer in particular to paragraph 110 of the opinion of Lord Hope. Article 10 protects the right of free speech; but the right is not absolute, and paragraph 2 of Article 10 permits restrictions on that right. It is not suggested, in the present case, that section 85 of the Postal Services Act 2000 is incompatible with the Convention. It follows that the restriction created by section 85 is accepted to be a restriction that is permitted by the Convention. That being so, the statute falls to be applied in the normal way: if a matter which is sent through the post is of an indecent or obscene character, there will be an offence under the Act.

📖 See *Blackstone's Criminal Practice 2014* **B18.25**

C4.3 Indecent or offensive or threatening letters, etc

Malicious Communications Act 1988, s 1

1 Offence of sending letters etc with intent to cause distress or anxiety

(1) Any person who sends to another person—
   (a) a letter, electronic communication or article of any description which conveys—
      (i) a message which is indecent or grossly offensive;
      (ii) a threat; or
      (iii) information which is false and known or believed to be false by the sender; or
   (b) any article or electronic communication which is, in whole or part, of an indecent or grossly offensive nature,

is guilty of an offence if his purpose, or one of his purposes, in sending it is that it should, so far as falling within paragraph (a) or (b) above, cause distress or anxiety to the recipient or to any other person to whom he intends that it or its contents or nature should be communicated.

(2) A person is not guilty of an offence by virtue of subsection (1)(a)(ii) above if he shows—

   (a) that the threat was used to reinforce a demand made by him on reasonable grounds; and

   (b) that he believed, and had reasonable grounds for believing, that the use of the threat was a proper means of reinforcing the demand.

(2A) In this section 'electronic communication' includes—

   (a) any oral or other communication by means of an electronic communications network; and

   (b) any communication (however sent) that is in electronic form.

(3) In this section references to sending include references to delivering or transmitting and to causing to be sent, delivered or transmitted and 'sender' shall be construed accordingly.

SO

▦ Fine level 5/6 months' imprisonment

C4.3.1 Key points

See *Connolly v Director of Public Prosecutions* [2008] 1 WLR 276 for Articles 9 (religion) and 10 (free speech) considerations. Articles 9(2) and 10(2) allow for restrictions on the relevant rights.

▢ See *Blackstone's Criminal Practice 2014* **B18.30**

C5 **Criminal Damage**

C5.1 Destroying or damaging property

Criminal Damage Act 1971, s 1

1 Destroying or damaging property

(1) A person who without lawful excuse destroys or damages any property belonging to another intending to destroy or damage any such property or being reckless as to whether any such property would be destroyed or damaged shall be guilty of an offence.

(2) A person who without lawful excuse destroys or damages any property, whether belonging to himself or another—

    (a) intending to destroy or damage any property or being reckless as to whether any property would be destroyed or damaged; and

    (b) intending by the destruction or damage to endanger the life of another or being reckless as to whether the life of another would be thereby endangered;

shall be guilty of an offence.

(3) An offence committed under this section by destroying or damaging property by fire shall be charged as arson.

EW (*Note*: Venue dictated by value)

SO If value does not exceed £5,000

▥ 3 months and/or fine level 4 (6 months if value > £5,000/10 years)

DO (s 1(2) offence)

C5.1.1 *Sentencing: criminal damage*

Offence seriousness (culpability and harm) **A. Identify the appropriate starting point** Starting points bases on first-time offender pleading not guilty		
Examples of nature of activity	**Starting point**	**Range**
Minor damage, eg breaking small window; small amount of graffiti	Band B fine	Conditional discharge to band C fine

Moderate damage, eg breaking large plate-glass or shop window; widespread graffiti	Low level community order	Band C fine to medium level community order
Significant damage up to £5,000, eg damage caused as part of a spree	High level community order	Medium level community order to 12 weeks' custody
Damage between £5,000 and £10,000	12 weeks' custody	6 to 26 weeks' custody
Damage over £10,000	Crown Court	Crown Cour

Offence seriousness (culpability and harm)
B. Consider the effect of aggravating and mitigating factors (other than those within examples above)
The following may be particularly relevant but these lists are not exhaustive

Factors indicating higher culpability	Factors indicating lower culpability
1. Revenge attack 2. Targeting vulnerable victim **Factors indicating greater degree of harm** 1. Damage to emergency equipment 2. Damage to public amenity 3. Significant public or private fear caused, eg in domestic context	1. Damage caused recklessly 2. Provocation

C5.1.2 *Sentencing: arson*

Offence seriousness (culpability and harm)
A. Identify the appropriate starting point
Starting points based on first-time offender pleading not guilty

Examples of nature of activity	Starting point	Range
Minor damage by fire	High level community order	Medium level community order to 12 weeks' custody
Moderate damage by fire	12 weeks' custody	6 to 26 weeks' custody
Significant damage by fire	Crown Court	Crown Court

Offence seriousness (culpability and harm)
B. Consider the effect of aggravating and mitigating factors
(other than those within examples above)
The following may be particularly relevant but these lists are not exhaustive

Factors indicating higher culpability	Factor indicating lower culpability
1. Revenge attack 2. Targeting vulnerable victim **Factors indicating greater degree** **of harm** 1. Damage to emergency equipment 2. Damage to public amenity 3. Significant public or private fear caused, eg in domestic context	1. Damage caused recklessly

C5.1.3 Key points

- There is no bar on charging attempted criminal damage where, due to value, the matter can be tried summarily only (*R v Bristol Justices, ex p E* [1999] 1 WLR 390).
- Lawful excuse is defined in section 5:

Criminal Damage Act 1971, s 5(2)–(5)

5 'Without lawful excuse'

(2) A person charged with an offence to which this section applies, shall, whether or not he would be treated for the purposes of this Act as having a lawful excuse apart from this subsection, be treated for those purposes as having a lawful excuse—

  (a) if at the time of the act or acts alleged to constitute the offence he believed that the person or persons whom he believed to be entitled to consent to the destruction of or damage to the property in question had so consented, or would have so consented to it if he or they had known of the destruction or damage and its circumstances; or

  (b) if he destroyed or damaged or threatened to destroy or damage the property in question or, in the case of a charge of an offence under section 3 above, intended to use or cause or permit the use of something to destroy or damage it, in order to protect property belonging to himself or another or a right or interest in property which was or which he believed to be vested in himself or another, and at the time of the act or acts alleged to constitute the offence he believed—

   (i) that the property, right or interest was in immediate need of protection; and

   (ii) that the means of protection adopted or proposed to be adopted were or would be reasonable having regard to all the circumstances.

(3) For the purposes of this section it is immaterial whether a belief is justified or not if it is honestly held.

(4) For the purposes of subsection (2) above a right or interest in property includes any right or privilege in or over land, whether created by grant, licence or otherwise.

(5) This section shall not be construed as casting doubt on any defence recognised by law as a defence to criminal charges.

- A person can avail himself of the defence of lawful excuse, notwithstanding the fact that he was intoxicated (*Jaggard v Dickinson* (1981) 72 Cr App R 33). The test is subjective, that is, whether the belief is held honestly, not whether it is justified or reasonable. However, whether a person is acting to protect property has an objective element (*R v Hunt* (1977) 66 Cr App R 105).

- It is clear that section 5(5) is intended to cover the situation whereby damage is caused to protect life or prevent injury (*R v Baker* The Times, 26 November 1996).

- Damage does not need to be destruction and encompasses harm that is not permanent, such as graffiti. If expense or inconvenience is involved in putting right the matter then damage will have been caused (eg stamping on a policeman's helmet so that it had to be pushed back into shape). Damaging something that can be restored (eg deleting a computer program) constitutes damage (*Cox v Riley* (1986) 83 Cr App R 54). Spitting on a police officer's uniform is unlikely to cause damage (*A v R* [1978] Crim LR 689). The soaking of a blanket and the flooding of the floor of a police cell were held to amount to damage in *R v Fiak* [2005] EWCA Crim 2381, and the daubing of water-soluble paint on a pavement was equally found to amount to damage in *Hardman v Chief Constable of Avon and Somerset* [1986] Crim LR 330.

- Determining whether something has been damaged is a matter of fact and degree to be determined by the magistrates or the jury (*Roe v Kingerlee* [1986] Crim LR 735).

- It is an offence to damage jointly-owned property. Section 10 provides:

Criminal Damage Act 1971, s 10

10 Interpretation

(1) In this Act 'property' means of a tangible nature, whether real or personal, including money and—

  (a) including wild creatures which have been tamed or are ordinarily kept in captivity, and any other wild creatures or their carcasses if, but only if, they have been reduced into possession which has not been lost or abandoned or are in the course of being reduced into possession; but

  (b) not including mushrooms growing wild on any land or flowers, fruit or foliage of a plant growing wild on any land.

For the purposes of this subsection 'mushroom' includes any fungus and 'plant' includes any shrub or tree.

(2) Property shall be treated for the purposes of this Act as belonging to any person—
  (a) having the custody or control of it;
  (b) having in it any proprietary right or interest (not being an equitable interest arising only from an agreement to transfer or grant an interest); or
  (c) having a charge on it.
(3) Where property is subject to a trust, the persons to whom it belongs shall be so treated as including any person having a right to enforce the trust.
(4) Property of a corporation sole shall be so treated as belonging to the corporation notwithstanding a vacancy in the corporation.

- The prosecution will have proved that the defendant was reckless if, having regard to all the available evidence, the court is sure:
  - that he was aware of a risk that property would be destroyed/damaged; and
  - that in the circumstances which were known to him it was unreasonable for him to take that risk.
- This test allows for some of the personal characteristics of a defendant to be taken into account (see *R v G* [2003] UKHL 50).

C5.1.4 *Criminal damage (by fire): Criminal Damage Act 1971, s 1(3)*

6 months and/or level 5 fine (regardless of value)—an offence under section 1(2) or (3) is triable only on indictment

See **C5.1**.

C5.1.5 *Racially or religiously aggravated criminal damage: Crime and Disorder Act 1998, s 30*

EW

6 months and/or level 5/14 years

C5.2 Threats to destroy or damage property

Criminal Damage Act 1971, s 2

2 Threats to destroy or damage property
A person who without lawful excuse makes to another a threat, intending that that other would fear it would be carried out—

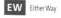

(a) to destroy or damage any property belonging to that other or a third person; or

(b) to destroy or damage his own property in a way which he knows is likely to endanger the life of that other or third person;

shall be guilty of an offence.

 Level 5 fine/6 months/10 years

C5.2.1 *Sentencing*

There are no sentencing guidelines for this offence.

C5.2.2 Key points

- Whether a threat has been made under section 2(a) is to be assessed objectively with reference to the words and actions of the defendant (*R v Cakmak* [2002] EWCA Crim 500).
- The term 'without lawful excuse' is defined in section 5 of the Act:

Criminal Damage Act 1971, s 5

5 'Without lawful excuse'

(1) This section applies to any offence under section 1(1) above and any offence under section 2 or 3 above other than one involving a threat by the person charged to destroy or damage property in a way which he knows is likely to endanger the life of another or involving an intent by the person charged to use or cause or permit the use of something in his custody or under his control so to destroy or damage property.

C5.3 Possessing anything with intent to destroy or damage property

Criminal Damage Act 1971, s 3

3 Possessing anything with intent to destroy or damage property

A person who has anything in his custody or under his control intending without lawful excuse to use it or cause or permit another to use it—

(a) to destroy or damage any property belonging to some other person; or

(b) to destroy or damage his own or the user's property in a way which he knows is likely to endanger the life of some other person;

shall be guilty of an offence.

 Level 5 fine/6 months/10 years

C5 Criminal Damage

C5.3.1 Key points

A conditional intent will suffice (*R v Buckingham* (1976) 63 Cr App R 159).

 See *Blackstone's Criminal Practice 2014* **B8**

C6 **Drugs**

C6.1 Key points

- A person must know that he is in possession of the drug; therefore a person holding drugs believing that they were something else would not be guilty (assuming the court believed the defendant). Note, however, that suspicion would be sufficient (see Misuse of Drugs Act 1971, s 28); and see later on containers.

- A person who 'forgot' that he had drugs would still be in possession of those drugs, but a person who had no knowledge at all would not (*R v Martindale* [1986] 3 All ER 25).

- A person need not be in physical possession of a drug, provided he is in control (sole or joint): see Misuse of Drugs Act 1971, section 37(3). It is not sufficient that the defendant might have knowledge of a confederate's possession of drugs; the test is whether the drugs were part of a common pool from which all could draw (*R v Searle* [1971] Crim LR 592).

- The fact that the quantity of drug was so miniscule as to be incapable of being used does not amount to a defence (*R v Boyesen* [1982] AC 768); it is merely an indication that the defendant may not have had knowledge of its presence.

- If a person is in possession of a container and he knows there is something inside, he will be in possession of the contents, even if he does not know their characteristics (*R v Lambert* [2002] 2 AC 545). If, however, the defendant had no right to open the container, he may not be in possession of its contents (*Warner v Metropolitan Police Commissioner* [1969] 2 AC 256), nor if he believed the contents to be different from what in fact they were (*R v McNamara* (1988) 87 Cr App R 246).

- Possession of drugs for religious purposes is not afforded any special protection under the European Convention (*R v Taylor* [2002] 1 Cr App R 519).

- Purchasing drugs on behalf of a third party, and passing those drugs to that party, even for no profit, amounts to supply.

- So-called social supply should be charged as simple possession. In *R v Denslow* [1998] Crim LR 566 the court observed:

  We wonder why it was thought necessary to charge supply in the circumstances of this case. How could it be possibly serve the interests of the public that there should be either a trial or if not a trial as conventionally understood a hearing to determine this matter of law? It was inevitable that the appellant would be dealt with at worst as though he were in possession of the drugs and, as turned out in this case, as though he were without any criminal responsibility for that particular part of the transaction. We are told that a plea had been offered to a charge of possession. It ought to have been accepted. We hope that those words will be borne in mind by prosecuting authorities in the future.

- A person who places drugs in the hands of a third party merely for safekeeping does not supply drugs (*R v Maginnis* [1987] AC 303).
- An offer to supply can be made by words or conduct, and once made cannot be withdrawn.
- It is the plant that must be cultivated, not the cannabis produced from the plant.
- The accused does not need to know that the plant was in fact cannabis (*R v Champ* (1981) 73 Cr App R 267).
- The defence of necessity (commonly pleaded by sufferers of certain illnesses) is not a defence available in law for this charge (*R v Quayle and others* [2006] 1 All ER 988).
- A statutory defence is provided by section 28 of the Misuse of Drugs Act 1971:

Misuse of Drugs Act 1971, s 28

28 Proof of lack of knowledge etc to be a defence in proceedings for certain offences

(1) This section applies to offences under any of the following provisions of this Act, that is to say section 4(2) and (3), section 5(2) and (3), section 6(2) and section 9.

(2) Subject to subsection (3) below, in any proceedings for an offence to which this section applies it shall be a defence for the accused to prove that he neither knew of nor suspected nor had reason to suspect the existence of some fact alleged by the prosecution which it is necessary for the prosecution to prove if he is to be convicted of the offence charged.

(3) Where in any proceedings for an offence to which this section applies it is necessary, if the accused is to be convicted of the offence charged, for the prosecution to prove that some substance or product involved in the alleged offence was the controlled drug which the prosecution alleges it to have been, and it is proved that the substance or product in question was that controlled drug, the accused—

(a) shall not be acquitted of the offence charged by reason only of proving that he neither knew nor suspected nor had reason to suspect that the substance or product in question was the particular controlled drug alleged; but

(b) shall be acquitted thereof—

(i) if he proves that he neither believed nor suspected nor had reason to suspect that the substance or product in question was a controlled drug; or

(ii) if he proves that he believed the substance or product in question to be a controlled drug, or a controlled drug of a description, such that, if it had in fact been that controlled drug or a controlled drug of that description, he would not at the material time have been committing any offence to which this section applies.

(4) Nothing in this section shall prejudice any defence which it is open to a person charged with an offence to which this section applies to raise apart from this section.

- In considering a defence under section 28(3)(b), self-induced intoxication should not be considered (*R v Young* [1984] 2 All ER 164).

C6.2 Key points Sentencing

- A minimum sentence of seven years must, unless not justified in all the circumstances, be imposed where an adult is convicted of a Class A drug trafficking offence (which excludes possession alone) if the offender has been convicted of two other drug trafficking offences in the circumstances set out in **D28**. Such offences may be tried on indictment only (Powers of Criminal Courts (Sentencing) Act 2000, s 110).
- Sentences are prescribed by Schedule 4 to the Misuse of Drugs Act 1971 in the following table.

C6.3 Drugs—Class A: fail to attend/remain for initial or follow-up assessment

Drugs Act 2005, s 12(1)–(3)

12 Attendance at initial assessment

(1) This section applies if a person is required to attend an initial assessment and remain for its duration by virtue of section 9(2).

(2) The initial assessor must inform a police officer or a police support officer if the person—
   (a) fails to attend the initial assessment at the specified time and place, or
   (b) attends the assessment at the specified time and place but fails to remain for its duration.

(3) A person is guilty of an offence if without good cause—
   (a) he fails to attend an initial assessment at the specified time and place, or
   (b) he attends the assessment at the specified time and place but fails to remain for its duration.

...

SO

▦ 6 months and/or level 4 fine

Misuse of Drugs Act 1971, Sch 4

Schedule 4

Prosecution and Punishment of Offences

Section Creation Offence	General Nature of Offence	Mode of Prosecution	Punishment			
			Class A drug involved	Class B drug involved	Class C drug involved	General
Section 4(2)	Production, or being concerned in the production, of a controlled drug.	(a) Summary	6 months or £5,000, or both.	6 months or £5,000, or both.	3 months or £2,500 or both	
		(b) On indictment	Life	14 years	14 years	
Section 4(3)	Supplying or offering to supply a controlled drug or being concerned in the doing of either activity by another.	(a) Summary	6 months or £5,000, or both.	6 months or £5,000, or both.	3 months or £2,500, or both.	
		(b) On indictment	Life.	14 years	14 years.	
Section 5(2)	Having possession of a controlled drug.	(a) Summary	6 months or £5,000, or both.	3 months or £2,500, or both.	3 months or £1,000, or both.	
		(b) On indictment	7 years	5 years	2 years	

Section Creation Offence	General Nature of Offence	Mode of Prosecution	Punishment		
Section 5(3)	Having possession of a controlled drug with intent to supply it to another.	(a) Summary	6 months or £5,000, or both. Life	6 months or £5,000, or both. 14 years	3 months or £2,500, or both. 14 years
		(b) On indictment			
Section 6(2)	Cultivation of cannabis plant.	(a) Summary			6 months or £5,000, or both. 14 years
		(b) On indictment			
Section 8	Being the occupier, or concerned in the management, of premises and permitting or suffering certain activities to take place there.	(a) Summary	6 months or £5,000, or both 14 years	6 months or £5,000, or both. 14 years	3 months or £2,500, or both. 14 years
		(b) On indictment			
⋮					

Drugs Act 2005, s 14(1) and (3)

14 Attendance at follow-up assessment

(1) This section applies if a person is required to attend a follow-up assessment and remain for its duration by virtue of section 10(2).

...

(3) A person is guilty of an offence if without good cause—

    (a) he fails to attend a follow-up assessment at the specified time and place, or

    (b) he attends the assessment at the specified time and place but fails to remain for its duration.

...

SO

🏛 6 months and/or level 4 fine

C6.3.1 *Sentencing*

Note that this guideline refers to section 12 offences only.

Offence seriousness (culpability and harm) A. Identify the appropriate starting point Starting points based on first-time offender pleading not guilty		
Examples of nature of activity	**Starting point**	**Range**
Failure to attend at the appointed place and time	Medium level community order	Band C fine to high level community order

Offence seriousness (culpability and harm) B. Consider the effect of aggravating and mitigating factors (other than those within examples above) The following may be particularly relevant but these lists are not exhaustive	
Factor indicating greater degree of harm	**Factors indicating lower culpability**
1. Threats or abuse to assessor or other staff	1. Offender turns up but at wrong place or time or fails to remain for duration of appointment 2. Subsequent voluntary contact to rearrange appointment

C6.4 Drugs—Class A: fail/refuse to provide a sample

Practitioners need to consider carefully section 63B of the Police and Criminal Evidence Act 1984 before allowing a client to plead guilty to an offence under this provision, as there are a considerable number of condition precedents that need to be satisfied before a lawful request for a sample can be made.

Police and Criminal Evidence Act 1984, s 63B

63B Testing for presence of Class A drugs

(1) A sample of urine or a non-intimate sample may be taken from a person in police detention for the purpose of ascertaining whether he has any specified Class A drug in his body if—

  (a) either the arrest condition or the charge condition is met;

  (b) both the age condition and the request condition are met; and

  (c) the notification condition is met in relation to the arrest condition, the charge condition or the age condition (as the case may be).

(1A) The arrest condition is that the person concerned has been arrested for an offence but has not been charged with that offence and either—

  (a) the offence is a trigger offence; or

  (b) a police officer of at least the rank of inspector has reasonable grounds for suspecting that the misuse by that person of a specified Class A drug caused or contributed to the offence and has authorised the sample to be taken.

(2) The charge condition is either—

  (a) that the person concerned has been charged with a trigger offence; or

  (b) that the person concerned has been charged with an offence and a police officer of at least the rank of inspector, who has reasonable grounds for suspecting that the misuse by that person of any specified Class A drug caused or contributed to the offence and has authorised the sample to be taken.

(3) The age condition is—

  (a) if the arrest condition is met, that the person concerned has attained the age of 18;

  (b) if the charge condition is met, that he has attained the age of 14.

(4) The request condition is that a police officer has requested the person concerned to give the sample.

(4A) ...

(4B) ...

(5) Before requesting the person concerned to give a sample, an officer must—

  (a) warn him that if, when so requested, he fails without good cause to do so he may be liable to prosecution, and

  (b) in a case within subsection (1A)(b) or (2)(b) above, inform him of the giving of the authorisation and of the grounds in question.

(5A) In the case of a person who has not attained the age of 17—

  (a) the making of the request under subsection (4) above;

  (b) the giving of the warning and (where applicable) the information under subsection (5) above; and

  (c) the taking of the sample,

  may not take place except in the presence of an appropriate adult.

(5B) ...

(5C) Despite subsection (1)(a) above, a sample may be taken from a person under this section if—

(a) he was arrested for an offence (the first offence),

(b) the arrest condition is met but the charge condition is not met,

(c) before a sample is taken by virtue of subsection (1) above he would (but for his arrest as mentioned in paragraph (d) below) be required to be released from police detention,

(d) he continues to be in police detention by virtue of his having been arrested for an offence not falling within subsection (1A) above, and

(e) the sample is taken before the end of the period of 24 hours starting with the time when his detention by virtue of his arrest for the first offence began.

(5D) A sample must not be taken from a person under this section if he is detained in a police station unless he has been brought before the custody officer.

(6) A sample may be taken under this section only by a person prescribed by regulations made by the Secretary of State by statutory instrument.

(6A) ...

(6B) ...

(7) ...

(8) A person who fails without good cause to give any sample which may be taken from him under this section shall be guilty of an offence.

▦ 3 months and/or level 4 fine

C6.4.1 *Sentencing*

Offence seriousness (culpability and harm) A. Identify the appropriate starting point Starting points based on first-time offender pleading not guilty		
Examples of nature of activity	**Starting point**	**Range**
Refusal to provide sample without good cause when required by police officer	Medium level community order	Band C fine to high level community order

Offence seriousness (culpability and harm) B. Consider the effect of aggravating and mitigating factors (other than those within examples above) The following may be particularly relevant but these lists are not exhaustive	
Factor indicating greater degree of harm	**Factors indicating lower culpability**
1. Threats or abuse to staff	1. Subsequent voluntary contact with drug workers 2. Subsequent compliance with testing on arrest/charge

C6.5 Drugs: fraudulent evasion of a prohibition by bringing into or taking out of the United Kingdom a controlled drug

Misuse of Drugs Act 1971, s 3

3 Restriction of importation and exportation of controlled drugs

(1) Subject to subsection (2) below—
  (a) the importation of a controlled drug; and
  (b) the exportation of a controlled drug, are hereby prohibited.

(2) Subsection (1) above does not apply—
  (a) to the importation or exportation of a controlled drug which is for the time being excepted from paragraph (a) or, as the case may be, paragraph (b) of subsection (1) above by regulations under section 7 of this Act or by provision made in a temporary class drug order by virtue of section 7A; or
  (b) to the importation or exportation of a controlled drug under and in accordance with the terms of a licence issued by the Secretary of State and in compliance with any conditions attached thereto.

Customs and Excise Management Act 1979, s 170(2)

170 Penalty for fraudulent evasion of duty, etc

(2) Without prejudice to any other provision of the Customs and Excise Acts 1979, if any person is, in relation to any goods, in any way knowingly concerned in any fraudulent evasion or attempt at evasion—
  (a) of any duty chargeable on the goods;
  (b) of any prohibition or restriction for the time being in force with respect to the goods under or by virtue of any enactment; or .
  (c) of any provision of the Customs and Excise Acts 1979 applicable to the goods,
he shall be guilty of an offence under this section and may be detained.

C6.5.1 *Sentencing*

STEP ONE: Determining the offence category

Culpability demonstrated by offender's role. One or more of these characteristics may demonstrate the offender's role. The list is not exhaustive.	Category of harm. Indicative output or potential output (upon which the starting point is based):
LEADING role: • directing or organizing production on a commercial scale; • substantial links to, and influence on, others in a chain; • expectation of substantial financial gain;	**Category 1** • heroin, cocaine—5kg; • ecstasy—10,000 tablets; • LSD—250,000 tablets; • amphetamine—20kg; • cannabis—200kg;

• uses business as cover; • abuses a position of trust or responsibility.	• ketamine—5kg.
SIGNIFICANT role: • operational or management function within a chain; • involves others in the operation whether by pressure, influence, intimidation, or reward; • motivated by financial or other advantage, whether or not operating alone; • some awareness and understanding of scale of operation.	**Category 2** • heroin, cocaine—1kg; • ecstasy—2,000 tablets; • LSD—25,000 squares; • amphetamine—4kg; • cannabis—40kg; • ketamine—1kg.
LESSER role: • performs a limited function under direction; • engaged by pressure, coercion, intimidation; • involvement through naivety/exploitation; • no influence on those above in a chain; • very little, if any, awareness or understanding of the scale of operation; • if own operation, solely for own use (considering reasonableness of account in all the circumstances).	**Category 3** • heroin, cocaine—150g; • ecstasy—300 tablets; • LSD—2,500 squares; • amphetamine—750g; • cannabis—6kg • ketamine—150g. **Category 4** • heroin, cocaine—5g; • ecstasy—20 tablets; • LSD—170 squares; • amphetamine—20g; • cannabis—100g • ketamine—5g

STEP TWO: Starting point and category range

CLASS A	Leading role	Significant role	Lesser role
Category 1	Crown Court	Crown Court	Crown Court
Category 2	Crown Court	Crown Court	Crown Court
Category 3	Crown Court	Crown Court	Crown Court
Category 4	Crown Court	Crown Court	Crown Court

CLASS B	Leading role	Significant role	Lesser role
Category 1	Crown Court	Crown Court	Crown Court
Category 2	Crown Court	Crown Court	1 year's custody Range: 26 weeks' to 3 years' custody

Category 3	Crown Court	Crown Court	Crown Court
Category 4	Crown Court	Crown Court	1 year's custody Range: 12 weeks' custody to 18 months' custody

CLASS C	Leading role	Significant role	Lesser role
Category 1	Crown Court	Crown Court	Crown Court
Category 2	Crown Court	Crown Court	26 weeks' custody Range: 12 weeks' to 18 months' custody
Category 3	Crown Court	26 weeks' custody Range: 12 weeks' to 18 months' custody	High level community order Range: Medium level com- munity order to 12 weeks' custody
Category 4	*	*	*

* Where the quantity falls below the indicative amount set out in the guideline for category 4, first identify the role for the importation offence, then refer to the starting point and ranges for possession or supply offences, depending on intent. Where the quantity is significantly larger than the indicative amounts for category 4 but below category 3 amounts, refer to the category 3 ranges.

Factors increasing seriousness	Factors reducing seriousness or reflecting personal mitigation
Statutory aggravating factors: Previous convictions, having regard to (a) nature of the offence to which conviction relates and relevance to current offence; and (b) time elapsed since offender used or permitted a person under 18 to deliver a controlled drug to a third person Offence committed on bail **Other aggravating factors include:** Sophisticated nature of concealment and/or attempts to avoid detection Attempts to conceal or dispose of evidence, where not charged separately Exposure of others to more than usual danger, for example drugs cut with harmful substances Presence of weapon, where not charged separately	Lack of sophistication as to nature of concealment Involvement due to pressure, intimidation, or coercion falling short of duress, except where already taken into account at step 1 Mistaken belief of the offender regarding the type of drug, taking into account the reasonableness of such belief in all the circumstances Isolated incident Low purity No previous convictions or no relevant or recent convictions Offender's vulnerability was exploited Remorse Good character and/or exemplary conduct Determination and/or demonstration of steps having been taken to address addiction or offending behaviour

High purity Failure to comply with current court orders Offence committed on licence	Serious medical conditions requiring urgent, intensive, or long-term treatment Age and/or lack of maturity where it affects the responsibility of the offender Mental disorder or learning disability Sole or primary carer for dependent relatives

Additional steps

Consider any factors which indicate a reduction, such as assistance to the prosecution; reduction for guilty plea; dangerousness; totality principle; compensation and ancillary orders; reasons; consideration for remand time.

C6.6 Drugs: supplying or offering to supply a controlled drug; possession of a controlled drug with intent to supply it to another

Misuse of Drugs Act 1971, ss 4(3) and 5(3)

4 Restriction of production and supply of controlled drugs

(3) Subject to section 28 of this Act, it is an offence for a person—

    (a) to supply or offer to supply a controlled drug to another in contravention of subsection (1) above; or

    (b) to be concerned in the supplying of such a drug to another in contravention of that subsection; or

    (c) to be concerned in the making to another in contravention of that subsection of an offer to supply such a drug.

. . .

5 Restriction of possession of controlled drugs

(3) Subject to section 28 of this Act, it is an offence for a person to have a controlled drug in his possession, whether lawfully or not, with intent to supply it to another in contravention of section 4(1) of this Act.

C6.6.1 *Sentencing*

STEP ONE: Determining the offence category

Culpability demonstrated by offender's role. One or more of these characteristics may demonstrate the offender's role. The list is not exhaustive.	Category of harm. Indicative output or potential output (upon which the starting point is based):
LEADING role: • directing or organizing production on a commercial scale; • substantial links to, and influence on, others in a chain; • expectation of substantial financial gain; • uses business as cover; • abuses a position of trust or responsibility. **SIGNIFICANT role:** • operational or management function within a chain; • involves others in the operation whether by pressure, influence, intimidation, or reward; • motivated by financial or other advantage, whether or not operating alone; • some awareness and understanding of scale of operation. **LESSER role:** • performs a limited function under direction; • engaged by pressure, coercion, intimidation; • involvement through naivety/exploitation; • no influence on those above in a chain; • very little, if any, awareness or under-standing of the scale of operation; • if own operation, solely for own use (considering reasonableness of account in all the circumstances).	**Category 1** • heroin, cocaine—5kg; • ecstasy—10,000 tablets; • LSD—250,000 tablets; • amphetamine—20kg; • cannabis—200kg; • ketamine—5kg. **Category 2** • heroin, cocaine—1kg; • ecstasy—2,000 tablets; • LSD—25,000 squares; • amphetamine—4kg; • cannabis—40kg; • ketamine—1kg. **Category 3** Where the offence is selling directly to users* ('street dealing'), the starting point is not based on quantity, OR Where the offence is suppy of drugs in prison by a prison employee, the starting point is not based on quantity. • heroin, cocaine—150g; • ecstasy—300 tablets; • LSD—2,500 squares; • amphetamine—750g; • cannabis—6kg; • ketamine—150g. **Category 4** • heroin, cocaine—5g; • ecstasy—20 tablets; • LSD—170 squares; • amphetamine—20g; • cannabis—100g • ketamine—5g OR Where the offence is selling directly to users* ('street dealing') the starting point is not based on quantity—go to category 3

* Including test purchase officers.

STEP TWO: Starting point and category range

CLASS A	Leading role	Significant role	Lesser role
Category 1	Crown Court	Crown Court	Crown Court
Category 2	Crown Court	Crown Court	Crown Court
Category 3	Crown Court	Crown Court	Crown Court
Category 4	Crown Court	Crown Court	18 months' custody Range: High level community order to 3 years' custody

CLASS B	Leading role	Significant role	Lesser role
Category 1	Crown Court	Crown Court	Crown Court
Category 2	Crown Court	Crown Court	1 year's custody Range: 26 weeks' to 3 years' custody
Category 3	Crown Court	1 year's custody. Range: 26 weeks' to 3 years' custody	High level community order Range: Band B fine to medium level community order
Category 4	18 months' custody Range: 16 weeks' to 3 years custody	High level community order. Range: medium level community order to 26 weeks' custody	Low level community order Range: Band B fine to medium level community order

CLASS C	Leading role	Significant role	Lesser role
Category 1	Crown Court	Crown Court	Crown Court
Category 2	Crown Court	Crown Court	26 weeks' custody Range: 12 weeks' to 18 months' custody
Category 3	Crown Court	26 weeks' custody Range: 12 weeks' to 18 months' custody	High level community order Range: low level community order to 12 weeks' custody

| Category 4 | 26 weeks' custody Range: high level community order to 18 months' custody | High level community order Range: low level community order to 12 weeks' custody | Low level community order Range: Band A fine to medium level community order |

Factors increasing seriousness	Factors reducing seriousness or reflecting personal mitigation
Statutory aggravating factors: Previous convictions, having regard to (a) nature of the offence to which conviction relates and relevance to current offence; and (b) time elapsed since conviction Offender used or permitted a person under 18 to deliver a controlled drug to a third person Offender 18 or over supplies or offers to supply a drug on, or in the vicinity of, school premises either when school in use as such or at a time between one hour before and one hour after they are to be used Offence committed on bail **Other aggravating factors include:** Targeting of any premises intended to locate vulnerable individuals or supply to such individuals and/or supply to those under 18 Exposure of others to more than usual danger, for example drugs cut with harmful substances Attempts to conceal or dispose of evidence, where not charged separately Presence of others, especially children and/ or non-users Presence of weapon, where not charged separately Charged as importation of a very small amount High purity Failure to comply with current court orders Offence committed on licence Established evidence of community impact	Involvement due to pressure, intimidation, or coercion falling short of duress, except where already taken into account at step 1 Supply only of drug to which offender addicted Mistaken belief of the offender regarding the type of drug, taking into account the reasonableness of such belief in all the circumstances Isolated incident Low purity No previous convictions or no relevant or recent convictions Offender's vulnerability was exploited Remorse Good character and/or exemplary conduct Determination and/or demonstration of steps having been taken to address addiction or offending behaviour Serious medical conditions requiring urgent, intensive, or long-term treatment Age and/or lack of maturity where it affects the responsibility of the offender Mental disorder or learning disability Sole or primary carer for dependent relatives

Additional steps

Consider any factors which indicate a reduction, such as assistance to the prosecution; reduction for guilty plea; dangerousness; totality principle; compensation and ancillary orders; reasons; consideration for remand time.

C6.7 Drugs: production of a controlled drug and cultivation of cannabis

C6.7.1 *Sentencing*

Misuse of Drugs Act 1971, ss 4(2)(a), (b) and 6

4 Restriction of production and supply of controlled drugs

(2) Subject to section 28 of this Act, it is an offence for a person—

    (a) to produce a controlled drug in contravention of subsection (1) above; or

    (b) to be concerned in the production of such a drug in contravention of that subsection by another.

6 Restriction of cultivation of cannabis plant

(1) Subject to any regulations under section 7 of this Act for the time being in force, it shall not be lawful for a person to cultivate any plant of the genus Cannabis.

(2) Subject to section 28 of this Act, it is an offence to cultivate any such plant in contravention subsection (1) above.

EW

STEP ONE: Determining the offence category

Culpability demonstrated by offender's role. One or more of these characteristics may demonstrate the offender's role. The list is not exhaustive.	Category of harm. Indicative output or potential output (upon which the starting point is based):
LEADING role: <ul><li>directing or organizing production on a commercial scale;</li><li>substantial links to, and influence on, others in a chain;</li><li>expectation of substantial financial gain;</li><li>uses business as cover;</li><li>abuses a position of trust or responsibility.</li></ul>	**Category 1** <ul><li>heroin, cocaine—5kg;</li><li>ecstasy—10,000 tablets;</li><li>LSD—250,000 tablets;</li><li>amphetamine—20kg;</li><li>cannabis—operation capable of producing industrial quantities for commercial use;</li><li>ketamine—5kg.</li></ul>

SIGNIFICANT role:	Category 2
• operational or management function within a chain; • involves others in the operation whether by pressure, influence, intimidation, or reward; • motivated by financial or other advantage, whether or not operating alone; • some awareness and understanding of scale of operation. **LESSER role:** • performs a limited function under direction; • engaged by pressure, coercion, intimidation; • involvement through naivety/exploitation; • no influence on those above in a chain; • very little, if any, awareness or under-standing of the scale of operation; • if own operation, solely for own use (considering reasonableness of account in all the circumstances).	• heroin, cocaine—1kg; • ecstasy—2,000 tablets; • LSD—25,000 squares; • amphetamine—4kg; • cannabis—operation capable of producing significant quantities for commercial use; • ketamine—1kg. **Category 3** • heroin, cocaine—150g; • ecstasy—300 tablets; • LSD—2,500 squares; • amphetamine—750g; • cannabis—28 plants;* • ketamine—150g. **Category 4** • heroin, cocaine—5g; • ecstasy—20 tablets; • LSD—170 squares; • amphetamine—20g; • cannabis—9 plants (domestic operation);* • ketamine—5g*with an assumed yield of 40g per plant

STEP TWO: Starting point and category range

CLASS A	Leading role	Significant role	Lesser role
Category 1	Crown Court	Crown Court	Crown Court
Category 2	Crown Court	Crown Court	Crown Court
Category 3	Crown Court	Crown Court	Crown Court
Category 4	Crown Court	Crown Court	Starting point 18 months' custody Range: High level community order to 3 years' custody

CLASS B	Leading role	Significant role	Lesser role
Category 1	Crown Court	Crown Court	Crown Court
Category 2	Crown Court	Crown Court	1 year's custody. Range: 26 weeks' to 3 years' custody

| Category 3 | Crown Court | 1 year's custody Range: 26 weeks' to 3 years' custody | High level community order. Range: low level community order to 26 weeks' custody |
| Category 4 | 1 year's custody Range: High level community order to 3 years' custody | High level community order Range: Medium level community order to 26 weeks' custody | Band C fine Range: Discharge to medium level community penalty |

CLASS C	Leading role	Significant role	Lesser role
Category 1	Crown Court	Crown Court	Crown Court
Category 2	Crown Court	Crown Court	26 weeks' custody Range: High level community order to 18 months' custody
Category 3	Crown Court	26 weeks' custody. Range: High level community order to 18 months' custody	High level community order Range: low level community order to 12 weeks' custody
Category 4	26 weeks' custody Range: High level Community order to 18 months' custody	High level community order. Range: low level community order to 12 weeks' custody	Band C fine Range: Discharge to medium level community penalty

Factors increasing seriousness	Factors reducing seriousness or reflecting personal mitigation
Statutory aggravating factors: Previous convictions, having regard to (a) nature of the offence to which conviction relates and relevance to current offence; and (b) time elapsed since conviction Offence committed on bail **Other aggravating factors include:** Nature of any likely supply	Involvement due to pressure, intimidation, or coercion falling short of duress, except where already taken into account at step 1 Isolated incident Low purity No previous convictions or no relevant or recent convictions

Level of any profit element	Offender's vulnerability was exploited
Use of premises accompanied by unlawful access to electricity/other utility supply of others	Remorse
	Good character and/or exemplary conduct
	Determination and/or demonstration of steps having been taken to address addiction or offending behaviour
Ongoing/large-scale operation as evidenced by presence and nature of specialist equipment	
	Serious medical conditions requiring urgent, intensive, or long-term treatment
Exposure of others to more than usual danger, for example drugs cut with harmful substances	Age and/or lack of maturity where it affects the responsibility of the offender
Attempts to conceal or dispose of evidence, where not charged separately	Mental disorder or learning disability
	Sole or primary carer for dependent relatives
Presence of others, especially children and/ or non-users	
Presence of weapon, where not charged separately	
High purity or high potential yield	
Failure to comply with current court orders	
Offence committed on licence	
Established evidence of community impact	

Additional steps

Consider any factors which indicate a reduction, such as assistance to the prosecution; reduction for guilty plea; dangerousness; totality principle; compensation and ancillary orders; reasons; consideration for remand time.

C6.8 Drugs: permitting premises to be used

Misuse of Drugs Act 1971, s 8

8 Occupiers etc of premises to be punishable for permitting certain activities to take place there

A person commits an offence if, being the occupier or concerned in the management of any premises, he knowingly permits or suffers any of the following activities to take place on those premises, that is to say—

(a) producing or attempting to produce a controlled drug in contravention of section 4(1) of this Act;

(b) supplying or attempting to supply a controlled drug to another in contravention of section 4(1) of this Act, or offering to supply a controlled drug to another in contravention of section 4(1);

(c) preparing opium for smoking;

(d) smoking cannabis, cannabis resin or prepared opium.

EW

C6.8.1 *Sentencing*

STEP ONE: Determining the offence category

Category 1	Higher culpability and greater harm
Category 2	Lower culpability and greater harm; or higher culpability and lesser harm
Category 3	Lower culpability and lesser harm

Factors indicating culpability (non-exhaustive)	Factors indicating harm (non-exhaustive)
Higher culpability: Permits premises to be used primarily for drug activity, for example crack house Permits use in expectation of substantial financial gain Uses legitimate business premises to aid and/or conceal illegal activity, for example public house or club **Lower culpability:** Permits use for limited or no financial gain No active role in any supply taking place Involvement through naivety	**Greater harm:** Regular drug-related activity Higher quantity of drugs, for example: heroin, cocaine—more than 5g; cannabis—more than 50g. **Lesser harm:** Infrequent drug-related activity Lower quantity of drugs, for example: heroin, cocaine—up to 5g; cannabis—up to 50g.

STEP TWO: Starting point and category range

Class A:

Offence category	Starting point	Category range
Category 1	Crown court	Crown court
Category 2	36 weeks' custody	High level community order to 18 months' custody
Category 3	Medium level community order	Low level community order to high level community order

Class B:

Offence category	Starting point	Category range
Category 1	12 weeks' custody	High level community order to 26 weeks' custody (max 12 weeks when tried summarily)
Category 2	Low level community order	Band C fine to high level community order
Category 3	Band A fine	Discharge to band C fine

Class C:

Offence category	Starting point	Category range
Category 1	1 year's custody	26 weeks' to 18 months' custody
Category 2	High level community order	Low level community order to 26 weeks' custody
Category 3	Band C fine	Band A fine to low level community order

Factors increasing seriousness	Factors reducing seriousness or reflecting personal mitigation
Statutory aggravating factors: Previous convictions, having regard to (a) nature of the offence to which conviction relates and relevance to current offence; and (b) time elapsed since conviction Offence committed on bail **Other aggravating factors include:** Length of time over which premises used for drug activity Volume of drug activity permitted Premises adapted to facilitate drug activity Location of premises, for example proximity to school Attempts to conceal or dispose of evidence, where not charged separately Presence of others, especially children and/ or non-users High purity Presence of weapons, where not charged separately Failure to comply with current court orders Offence committed on licence Established evidence of community impact	Involvement due to pressure, intimidation, or coercion falling short of duress Isolated incident Low purity No previous convictions or no relevant or recent convictions Offender's vulnerability was exploited Remorse Good character and/or exemplary conduct Determination and/or demonstration of steps having been taken to address addiction or offending behaviour Serious medical conditions requiring urgent, intensive or long-term treatment Age and/or lack of maturity where it affects the responsibility of the offender Mental disorder or learning disability Sole or primary carer for dependent relatives

Additional steps

Consider any factors which indicate a reduction, such as assistance to the prosecution; reduction for guilty plea; dangerousness; totality principle; compensation and ancillary orders; reasons; consideration for remand time.

C6.8.2 Key points

Where the allegation is permitting premises to be used for the supply of drugs, in order to establish the offence the Crown must prove not only that the defendant knowingly permitted the supply of the drugs, but also that a supply of the drugs had actually taken place on the premises (*R v McGee* [2012] EWCA Crim 613 (Class A); *R v Auguiste* [2003] EWCA Crim 3329 (Class B)).

C6.9 Drugs: possession of a controlled drug

> ### Misuse of Drugs Act 1971, s 5(2) and (4)
>
> **5 Restriction of possession of controlled drugs**
>
> (2) Subject to section 28 of this Act [see **C6.1**] and to subsection (4) below, it is an offence for a person to have a controlled drug in his possession in contravention of subsection (1) above.
>
> ...
>
> (4) In any proceedings for an offence under subsection (2) above in which it is proved that the accused had a controlled drug in his possession, it shall be a defence for him to prove—
>
> (a) that, knowing or suspecting it to be a controlled drug, he took possession of it for the purpose of preventing another from committing or continuing to commit an offence in connection with that drug and that as soon as possible after taking possession of it he took all such steps as were reasonably open to him to destroy the drug or to deliver it into the custody of a person lawfully entitled to take custody of it; or
>
> (b) that, knowing or suspecting it to be a controlled drug, he took possession of it for the purpose of delivering it into the custody of a person lawfully entitled to take custody of it and that as soon as possible after taking possession of it he took all such steps as were reasonably open to him to deliver it into the custody of such a person.

EW

C6.9.1 *Sentencing*

STEP ONE: Determine the offence category

Category 1: Class A drug

Category 2: Class B drug

Category 3: Class C drug

STEP TWO: Starting point and range

Offence category	Starting point	Category range
Category 1 (Class A)	Band C fine	Band A fine to 51 weeks' custody
Category 2 (Class B)	Band B fine	Discharge to 26 weeks' custody
Category 3 (Class C)	Band A fine	Discharge to medium level community order

 Either Way

Factors increasing seriousness	Factors reducing seriousness or reflecting personal mitigation
Statutory aggravating factors: Previous convictions, having regard to (a) nature of the offence to which conviction relates and relevance to current offence; and (b) time elapsed since conviction Offence committed on bail **Other aggravating factors include:** Possession of drug in prison Presence of others, especially children and/or non-users Possession of drug in school or licensed premises Failure to comply with current court orders Offence committed on licence Attempts to conceal or dispose of evidence, where not charged separately Charged as importation of a very small amount Established evidence of community impact	No previous convictions or no relevant or recent convictions Remorse Good character and/or exemplary conduct Offender is using cannabis to help with a diagnosed medical condition Determination and/or demonstration of steps having been taken to address addiction or offending behaviour Serious medical conditions requiring urgent, intensive, or long-term treatment Isolated incident Age and/or lack of maturity where it affects the responsibility of the offender Mental disorder or learning disability Sole or primary carer for dependent relatives

Additional steps

Consider any factors which indicate a reduction, such as assistance to the prosecution; reduction for guilty plea; dangerousness; totality principle; compensation and ancillary orders; reasons; consideration for remand time.

 See *Blackstone's Criminal Practice 2014* **B19**

C6.9.2 *Obstruction under the Misuse of Drugs Act 1971*

Section 23(4) of the Misuse of Drugs Act 1971 provides:

Misuse of Drugs Act 1971, s 23(4)

23 Powers to search and obtain evidence

(4) A person commits an offence if he—

(a) intentionally obstructs a person in the exercise of his powers under this section; or

(b) conceals from a person acting in the exercise of his powers under subsection (1) above any such books, documents, stocks or drugs as are mentioned in that subsection; or

(c) without reasonable excuse (proof of which shall lie on him) fails to produce any such books or documents as are so mentioned where their production is demanded by a person in the exercise of his power under that subsection.

C6 Drugs

 EW

 6 months and/or level 5 fine/2 years

For there to be obstruction, the officer must be acting in the execution of his office. The officer must comply strictly with the requirements of the Police and Criminal Evidence Act 1984 in relation to a stop and search (*R v Bristol* [2007] EWHC 3214 (Admin); *B v DPP* [2008] EWHC 1655 (Admin); *R (Michaels) v Highbury Corner Magistrates' Court* [2009] EWHC 2928 (Admin)).

C7 **Education Act**

C7.1 **School non-attendance**

Education Act 1996, s 444(1), (1A), (1B), (2), (2A), and (3)

444 Offence: failure to secure regular attendance at school of registered pupil

(1) If a child of compulsory school age who is a registered pupil at a school fails to attend regularly at the school, his parent is guilty of an offence.

(1A) If in the circumstances mentioned in subsection (1) the parent knows that his child is failing to attend regularly at the school and fails to cause him to do so, he is guilty of an offence.

(1B) It is a defence for a person charged with an offence under subsection (1A) to prove that he had a reasonable justification for his failure to cause the child to attend regularly at the school.

(2) Subsections (2A) to (6) below apply in proceedings for an offence under this section in respect of a child who is not a boarder at the school at which he is a registered pupil.

(2A) The child shall not be taken to have failed to attend regularly at the school by reason of his absence from the school at any time if the parent proves that at that time the child was prevented from attending by reason of sickness or any unavoidable cause.

(3) The child shall not be taken to have failed to attend regularly at the school by reason of his absence from the school—

  (a) with leave, or

  (b) [repealed]

  (c) on any day exclusively set apart for religious observance by the religious body to which his parent belongs.

SO

🏛 Level 3 fine (s 444(1)); level 4 fine and/or 3 months (s 444(1A))

C7.1.1 *Sentencing*

Offence seriousness (culpability and harm) A. Identify the appropriate starting point Starting points based on first-time offender pleading not guilty		
Example of nature of activity	**Starting point**	**Range**
Short period following previous good attendance (s 444(1))	Band A fine	Conditional discharge to band A fine

---

Erratic attendance for long period (s 444(1))	Band B fine	Band B fine to band C fine
Colluding in and condoning non-attendance or deliberately instigating non-attendance (s 444(1A))	Medium level community order	Low level community order to high level community order

Offence seriousness (culpability and harm) **B. Consider the effect of aggravating and mitigating factors** **(other than those within examples above)** The following may be particularly relevant but these lists are not exhaustive	
Factors indicating higher culpability 1. Parental collusion (s 444(1) only) 2. Lack of parental effort to ensure attendance (s 444(1) only) 3. Threats to teachers and/or officials 4. Refusal to cooperate with school and/or officials **Factors indicating greater degree of harm** 1. More than one child 2. Harmful effect on other children in family	**Factors indicating lower culpability** 1. Parent unaware of child's whereabouts 2. Parent tried to ensure attendance 3. Parent concerned by child's allegations of bullying/unable to get school to address bullying

C7.1.2 Key points

- The offence under section 444(1) is strict, and the prosecution have the duty to prove all four limbs. This is not contrary to the European Convention on Human Rights (*Barnfather v Islington Education Authority* [2003] EWHC 418 (Admin)).
- Difficulties in getting a child to school due to the child's behavioural and psychological difficulties did not equate to an unavoidable cause (s 444(1)), neither did it provide a defence under section 444(2A) (*Islington London Borough Council v D*, 23 March 2011 (Admin)). Unavoidable cause had to relate to the child, not the parent, and had to be something in the nature of an emergency.
- In relation to section 444(1A), the parent will have only an evidential burden to satisfy, the prosecution having then to prove to the criminal standard that the defence is not made out (*R (P) v Liverpool City Magistrates' Court* [2006] EWHC 2732 (Admin)).

C7.2 Education Act, failure to comply with school attendance order

Education Act 1996, s 443(1) and (2)

443 Offence: failure to comply with school attendance order

(1) If a parent on whom a school attendance order is served fails to comply with the requirements of the order, he is guilty of an offence, unless he proves that he is causing the child to receive suitable education otherwise than at school.

(2) If, in proceedings for an offence under this section, the parent is acquitted, the court may direct that the school attendance order shall cease to be in force.

SO

 Level 3 fine

C7.2.1 Key points

Where a parent asserts the defence contained in section 443(1), the burden of proving it remains with the parent (*Oxfordshire County Council v L*, 3 March 2010).

C8 **Immigration Offences**

C8.1 Offences

C8.1.1 *Illegal entry and deception*

Immigration Act 1971, ss 24 and 24A

24 Illegal entry and similar offences

(1) [It is an offence—]

    (a) if contrary to this Act he knowingly enters the United Kingdom in breach of a deportation order or without leave;

    (b) if, having only a limited leave to enter or remain in the United Kingdom, he knowingly either—

        (i) remains beyond the time limited by the leave; or

        (ii) fails to observe a condition of the leave;

    (c) if, having lawfully entered the United Kingdom without leave by virtue of section 8(1) above, he remains without leave beyond the time allowed by section 8(1);

    (d) if, without reasonable excuse, he fails to comply with any requirement imposed on him under Schedule 2 to this Act to report to a medical officer of health, or to attend, or submit to a test or examination, as required by such an officer;

    (e) if, without reasonable excuse, he fails to observe any restriction imposed on him under Schedule 2 or 3 to this Act as to residence, as to his employment or occupation or as to reporting to the police, to an immigration officer or to the Secretary of State;

    (f) if he disembarks in the United Kingdom from a ship or aircraft after being placed on board under Schedule 2 or 3 to this Act with a view to his removal from the United Kingdom;

    (g) if he embarks in contravention of a restriction imposed by or under an Order in Council under section 3(7) of this Act.

(1A) A person commits an offence under subsection (1)(b)(i) above on the day when he first knows that the time limited by his leave has expired and continues to commit it throughout any period during which he is in the United Kingdom thereafter; but a person shall not be prosecuted under that provision more than once in respect of the same limited leave.

(3) The extended time limit for prosecutions which is provided for by section 28 below shall apply to offences under subsection (1)(a) and (c) above.

(4) In proceedings for an offence against subsection (1)(a) above of entering the United Kingdom without leave,—

    (a) any stamp purporting to have been imprinted on a passport or other travel document by an immigration officer on a particular date for the purpose of giving leave shall be presumed to have been duly so imprinted, unless the contrary is proved;

    (b) proof that a person had leave to enter the United Kingdom shall lie on the defence if, but only if, he is shown to have entered within six months before the date when the proceedings were commenced.

24A Deception

(1) A person who is not a British citizen is guilty of an offence if, by means which include deception by him—
    (a) he obtains or seeks to obtain leave to enter or remain in the United Kingdom; or
    (b) he secures or seeks to secure the avoidance, postponement or revocation of enforcement action against him.

(2) 'Enforcement action', in relation to a person, means—
    (a) the giving of directions for his removal from the United Kingdom ('directions') under Schedule 2 to this Act or section 10 of the Immigration and Asylum Act 1999;
    (b) the making of a deportation order against him under section 5 of this Act; or
    (c) his removal from the United Kingdom in consequence of directions or a deportation order.

SO Section 24

EW Section 24A

▦ Fine level 5/6 months (s 24)

▦ 6 months/2 years (s 24A)

C8.1.2 *Assisting unlawful entry*

Immigration Act 1971, ss 25, 25A, and 25B

25 Assisting unlawful immigration to member State

(1) A person commits an offence if he—
    (a) does an act which facilitates the commission of a breach of immigration law by an individual who is not a citizen of the European Union,
    (b) knows or has reasonable cause for believing that the act facilitates the commission of a breach of immigration law by the individual, and
    (c) knows or has reasonable cause for believing that the individual is not a citizen of the European Union.

25A Helping asylum-seeker to enter United Kingdom

(1) A person commits an offence if—
    (a) he knowingly and for gain facilitates the arrival in, or the entry into, the United Kingdom of an individual, and
    (b) he knows or has reasonable cause to believe that the individual is an asylum-seeker.

25B Assisting entry to United Kingdom in breach of deportation or exclusion order

(1) A person commits an offence if he—

(a) does an act which facilitates a breach of a deportation order in force against an individual who is a citizen of the European Union, and

(b) knows or has reasonable cause for believing that the act facilitates a breach of the deportation order.

 Fine level 5/6 months/14 years

C8.1.3 *Possessing false passports, work permits, registration cards, etc*

Immigration Act 1971, ss 26 and 26A

26 General offences in connection with administration of Act

(1) A person shall be guilty of an offence punishable on summary conviction with a fine of not more than level 5 on the standard scale or with imprisonment for not more than six months, or with both, in any of the following cases—

(a) if, without reasonable excuse, he refuses or fails to submit to examination under Schedule 2 to this Act;

(b) if, without reasonable excuse, he refuses to fails to furnish or produce any information in his possession, or any documents in his possession or control, which he is on an examination under that Schedule required to furnish or produce;

(c) if on any such examination or otherwise he makes or causes to be made to an immigration officer or other person lawfully acting in the execution of a relevant enactment a return, statement or representation which he knows to be false or does not believe to be true;

(d) if, without lawful authority, he alters any certificate of entitlement, entry clearance, work permit or other document issued or made under or for the purposes of this Act, or uses for the purposes of this Act, or has in his possession for such use, any passport, certificate of entitlement, entry clearance, work permit or other document which he knows or has reasonable cause to believe to be false;

(e) if, without reasonable excuse, he fails to complete and produce a landing or embarkation card in accordance with any order under Schedule 2 to this Act;

(f) if, without reasonable excuse, he fails to comply with any requirement of regulations under section 4(3) or of an order under section 4(4) above;

(g) if, without reasonable excuse, he obstructs an immigration officer or other person lawfully acting in the execution of this Act.

(2) The extended time limit for prosecutions which is provided for by section 28 below shall apply to offences under subsection (1)(c) and (d) above.

26A Registration card

…

(3) A person commits an offence if he—
   (a) makes a false registration card,
   (b) alters a registration card with intent to deceive or to enable another to deceive,
   (c) has a false or altered registration card in his possession without reasonable excuse,
   (d) uses or attempts to use a false registration card for a purpose for which a registration card is issued,
   (e) uses or attempts to use an altered registration card with intent to deceive,
   (f) makes an article designed to be used in making a false registration card,
   (g) makes an article designed to be used in altering a registration card with intent to deceive or to enable another to deceive, or
   (h) has an article within paragraph (f) or (g) in his possession without reasonable excuse.
(4) In subsection (3) 'false registration card' means a document which is designed to appear to be a registration card.

EW

 Fine level 5/6 months/10 years (subs (3)(a), (b), (d), (e), (f), or (g)), 2 years (subs (3)(c) or (h))

C8.2 Defences

Immigration and Asylum Act 1999, s 31

31 Defences based on Article 31(1) of the Refugee Convention

(1) It is a defence for a refugee charged with an offence to which this section applies to show that, having come to the United Kingdom directly from a country where his life or freedom was threatened (within the meaning of the Refugee Convention), he—
   (a) presented himself to the authorities in the United Kingdom without delay;
   (b) showed good cause for his illegal entry or presence; and
   (c) made a claim for asylum as soon as was reasonably practicable after his arrival in the United Kingdom.
(2) If, in coming from the country where his life or freedom was threatened, the refugee stopped in another country outside the United Kingdom, subsection (1) applies only if he shows that he could not reasonably have expected to be given protection under the Refugee Convention in that other country.
(3) In England and Wales and Northern Ireland the offences to which this section applies are any offence, and any attempt to commit an offence, under—
   (a) Part I of the Forgery and Counterfeiting Act 1981 (forgery and connected offences);

    (b) section 24A of the 1971 Act (deception); or
    (c) section 26(1)(d) of the 1971 Act (falsification of documents).

...

(5) A refugee who has made a claim for asylum is not entitled to the defence provided by subsection (1) in relation to any offence committed by him after making that claim.

(6) 'Refugee' has the same meaning as it has for the purposes of the Refugee Convention.

(7) If the Secretary of State has refused to grant a claim for asylum made by a person who claims that he has a defence under subsection (1), that person is to be taken not to be a refugee unless he shows that he is.

C8.3 Key points

- Refugees are protected under Article 31 of the UN Convention relating to the status of refugees.
- The six-month time limit does not apply to offences under section 26(1)(c) and (d), or section 28(1)(a) and (c).
- The burden of proving that entry was legal falls upon the defendant in relation to prosecutions commenced within six months of that entry (s 24(4)(b)).

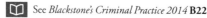 See *Blackstone's Criminal Practice 2014* **B22**

C9 **Prison Offences**

C9.1 **Conveyance of articles into prison**

The Prison Act 1952 lists the following prohibited articles (s 40A):

List A articles	List B articles
(a) a controlled drug (as defined for the purposes of the Misuse of Drugs Act 1971); (b) an explosive; (c) any firearm or ammunition (as defined in s 57 of the Firearms Act 1968); (d) any other offensive weapon (as defined in s 1(9) of the Police and Criminal Evidence Act 1984).	(a) alcohol (as defined for the purposes of the Licensing Act 2003); (b) a mobile telephone; (c) a camera; (d) a sound-recording device. 'camera' includes any device by means of which a photograph (as defined in s 40E) can be produced; 'sound-recording device' includes any device by means of which a sound-recording (as defined in s 40E) can be made. The reference in paragraph (b), (c), or (d) of List B to a device of any description includes a reference to— (a) a component part of a device of that description; or (b) an article designed or adapted for use with a device of that description (including any disk, film, or other separate article on which images, sounds or information may be recorded).

- A List C article is any article or substance prescribed for the purposes of this section by prison rules.
- Conveyance of an article in List A is triable only on indictment (Prison Act 1952, s 40B).

C9.1.1 *Conveyance of List B or C articles*

SO (For List C articles)

EW (For List B articles) (*Note*: List A items are indictable only)

▥ (For List B level 5 fine and/or 6 months/2 years; for List C articles, level 3 fine only

---

Prison Act 1952, s 40C

40C Conveyance etc of List B or C articles into or out of prison

(1) A person who, without authorisation—
  (a) brings, throws or otherwise conveys a List B article into or out of a prison,
  (b) causes another person to bring, throw or otherwise convey a List B article into or out of a prison,
  (c) leaves a List B article in any place (whether inside or outside a prison) intending it to come into the possession of a prisoner, or
  (d) knowing a person to be a prisoner, gives a List B article to him,
  is guilty of an offence.
(2) A person who, without authorisation—
  (a) brings, throws or otherwise conveys a List C article into a prison intending it to come into the possession of a prisoner,
  (b) causes another person to bring, throw or otherwise convey a List C article into a prison intending it to come into the possession of a prisoner,
  (c) brings, throws or otherwise conveys a List C article out of a prison on behalf of a prisoner,
  (d) causes another person to bring, throw or otherwise convey a List C article out of a prison on behalf of a prisoner,
  (e) leaves a List C article in any place (whether inside or outside a prison) intending it to come into the possession of a prisoner, or
  (f) while inside a prison, gives a List C article to a prisoner,
  is guilty of an offence.
(3) A person who attempts to commit an offence under subsection (2) is guilty of that offence.
(4) In proceedings for an offence under this section it is a defence for the accused to show that—
  (a) he reasonably believed that he had authorisation to do the act in respect of which the proceedings are brought, or
  (b) in all the circumstances there was an overriding public interest which justified the doing of that act.

C9.2 Other offences relating to prison security

Prison Act 1952, s 40D

40D Other offences relating to prison security

(1) A person who, without authorisation—
  (a) takes a photograph, or makes a sound-recording, inside a prison, or
  (b) transmits, or causes to be transmitted, any image, sound or information from inside a prison by electronic communications for simultaneous reception outside the prison,
  is guilty of an offence.
(2) It is immaterial for the purposes of subsection (1)(a) where the recording medium is located.

(3) A person who, without authorisation—

   (a) brings or otherwise conveys a restricted document out of a prison or causes such a document to be brought or conveyed out of a prison, . . .

   . . .

is guilty of an offence.

(3A) A person who, without authorisation, is in possession of any of the items specified in subsection (3B) inside a prison is guilty of an offence.

(3B) The items referred to in subsection (3A) are—

   (a) a device capable of transmitting or receiving images, sounds or information by electronic communications (including a mobile telephone);

   (b) a component part of such a device;

   (c) an article designed or adapted for use with such a device (including any disk, film or other separate article on which images, sounds or information may be recorded).

(4) In proceedings for an offence under this section it is a defence for the accused to show that—

   (a) he reasonably believed that he had authorisation to do the act in respect of which the proceedings are brought, or

   (b) in all the circumstances there was an overriding public interest which justified the doing of that act.

EW

Level 5 fine and/or 6 months/2 years

C10 **Protective Order, Breach of**

- Protection from Harassment Act 1997, section 5(5)
- Family Law Act 1996, section 42A
- Breach of restraining order: Protection from Harassment Act 1997, section 5(5)

EW

Level 5 fine and/or 6 months/5 years

DO

C10.1 **Sentencing**

Offence seriousness (culpability and harm) A. Identify the appropriate starting point Starting points based on first-time offender pleading not guilty		
Examples of nature of activity	**Starting point**	**Range**
Single breach involving no/ minimal direct contact	Low level community order	Band C fine to medium level community order
More than one breach involving no/ minimal contact or some direct contact	Medium level community order	Low level community order to high level community order
Single breach involving some violence and/or significant physical or psychological harm to the victim	18 weeks' custody	13 to 26 weeks' custody
More than one breach involving some violence and/or significant physical or psychological harm to the victim	Crown Court	26 weeks' custody to Crown Court
Breach (whether one or more) involving significant physical violence and significant physical or psychological harm to the victim	Crown Court	Crown Court

Offence seriousness (culpability and harm)
B. Consider the effect of aggravating and mitigating factors (other than those within examples above) The following may be particularly relevant but these lists are not exhaustive

Factors indicating higher culpability	**Factors indicating lower culpability**
1. Proven history of violence or threats by the offender	1. Breach occurred after long period of compliance
2. Using contact arrangements with a child to instigate offence	2. Victim initiated contact
3. Offence is a further breach, following earlier breach proceedings	
4. Offender has history of disobedience to court orders	
5. Breach committed immediately or shortly after order made	
Factors indicating greater degree of harm	
1. Victim is particularly vulnerable	
2. Impact on children	
3. Victim is forced to leave home	

 See *Blackstone's Criminal Practice 2014* **B14.130**

C11 **Public Order**

C11.1 **Affray**

> ### Public Order Act 1986, ss 3(1), (2), and (4), 6(2) and (5)
>
> #### 3 Affray
>
> (1) A person is guilty of affray if he uses or threatens unlawful violence towards another and his conduct is such as would cause a person of reasonable firmness present at the scene to fear for his personal safety.
>
> (2) Where 2 or more persons use or threaten the unlawful violence, it is the conduct of them taken together that must be considered for the purposes of subsection (1).
>
> (3) For the purposes of this section a threat cannot be made by the use of words alone...
>
> (4) No person of reasonable firmness need actually be, or be likely to be, present at the scene
>
> ...
>
> #### 6 Mental element: miscellaneous
>
> (2) A person is guilty of violent disorder or affray only if he intends to use or threaten violence or is aware that his conduct may be violent or threaten violence.
>
> (5) For the purposes of this section a person whose awareness is impaired by intoxication shall be taken to be aware of that of which he would be aware if not intoxicated, unless he shows either that his intoxication was not self-induced or that it was caused solely by the taking or administration of a substance in the course of medical treatment.

EW

 6 months and/or level 5 fine/3 years

DO

C11.1.1 *Sentencing*

Offence seriousness (culpability and harm) A. Identify the appropriate starting point Starting points based on first-time offender pleading not guilty		
Example of nature of activity	**Starting point**	**Range**
Brief offence involving low level violence, no substantial fear created	Low level community order	Band C fine to medium level community order
Degree of fighting or violence that causes substantial fear	High level community order	Medium level community order to 12 weeks' custody
Fight involving a weapon/ throwing objects, or conduct causing risk of serious injury	18 weeks' custody	12 weeks' custody to Crown Court

Offence seriousness (culpability and harm) B. Consider the effect of aggravating and mitigating factors (other than those within examples above) The following may be particularly relevant but these lists are not exhaustive	
Factors indicating higher culpability 1. Group action 2. Threats 3. Lengthy incident	**Factors indicating lower culpability** 1. Did not start the trouble 2. Provocation 3. Stopped as soon as police arrived
Factors indicating greater degree of harm 1. Vulnerable person(s) present 2. Injuries caused 3. Damage to property	

C11.1.2 Key points

- Section 6 provides that a threat cannot be made by the use of words alone.
- Affray may be committed in private as well as in public places. However, the fact that a third party could not be present may enable the court to hold that a hypothetical bystander would have viewed the threat as being restricted to the parties involved due to the turbulence of their relationship (*Leeson v Director of Public Prosecutions* [2010] EWHC 994 (Admin), where a conviction was quashed where L, who was drunk, had threatened a person with a knife in the bathroom of a private dwelling).

- In *R v Sanchez* (1996) 160 JP 321, the court approved the following academic commentary:

  The offence of affray envisages at least three persons: (i) the person using or threatening unlawful violence; (ii) a person towards whom the violence or threat is directed; and (iii) a person of reasonable firmness who need not actually be, or be likely to be, present at the scene. Thus the question in the present case was not whether a person of reasonable firmness in J's shoes would have feared for his personal safety but whether this hypothetical person, present in the room and seeing D's conduct towards J would have so feared.

- The definition of 'affray' is very wide, and in *Sanchez* the court agreed with D's counsel that care has to be taken to avoid extending it so widely that it would cover every case of common assault:

  A common assault may be very trivial, so that it would not cause anyone to fear for his 'personal safety'. But where the assault threatens serious harm to the victim, there may be evidence of affray depending on the circumstances. The person of reasonable firmness present in a small room as in the present case might fear for his personal safety whereas the same person, observing the same conduct in an open space, would not.

  The common law offence which it was intended to replace was, said the Law Commission, 'typically charged in cases of pitched street battles between rival gangs, spontaneous fights in public houses, clubs and at seaside resorts, and revenge attacks on individuals'.
- Reference should also be made to *R v Davison* [1992] Crim LR 31 and *R v Plavecz* [2002] Crim LR 837.
- The fact that a third party who is present does not feel afraid for their own safety is of evidential significance (*R v Blinkhorn* [2006] EWCA Crim 1416).

See *Blackstone's Criminal Practice 2014* **B11.37–B11.46**

C11.2 Alcohol sale offences

> Licensing Act 2003, s 141 (sale of alcohol to drunk person), s 146 (sale of alcohol to children), s 147 (allowing sale of alcohol to children), s 147A (persistently selling alcohol to children)

Section 147A of the Licensing Act 2003 makes it an offence if, on three or more different occasions within a period of three consecutive months, alcohol is sold unlawfully on the same premises to a person under 18.

SO

 Level 3 fine (s 141), level 5 fine (ss 146 and 147), £10,000 fine (s 147A)

SO Summary Only   Sentence

C11.2.1 *Sentencing (for Licensing Act 2003 offences only)*

Offence seriousness (culpability and harm) A. Identify the appropriate starting point Starting points based on first-time offender pleading not guilty		
Examples of nature of activity	**Starting point**	**Range**
Sale to a child (ie person under 18)/to a drunk person	Band B fine	Band A fine to band C fine

Offence seriousness (culpability and harm) **B. Consider the effect of aggravating and mitigating factors (other than those within examples above)** The following may be particularly relevant but these lists are not exhaustive	
Factors indicating higher culpability 1. No attempt made to establish age 2. Spirits/high-alcohol level of drink 3. Drunk person highly intoxicated 4. Large quantity of alcohol supplied 5. Sale intended for consumption by group of children/drunk people 6. Offender in senior or management position	
Factors indicating greater degree of harm 1. Younger child/children 2. Drunk person causing distress to others 3. Drunk person aggressive	

C11.2.2 Key points

- Provided a person has the authority to sell alcohol, it is irrelevant that he is unpaid (s 141).
- Section 146 provides:

Licensing Act 2003, s 146(4)–(6)

146 Sale of alcohol to children

(4) Where a person is charged with an offence under this section by reason of his own conduct it is a defence that—

    (a) he believed that the individual was aged 18 or over, and

    (b) either—

        (i) he had taken all reasonable steps to establish the individual's age, or

        (ii) nobody could reasonably have suspected from the individual's appearance that he was aged under 18.

(5) For the purposes of subsection (4), a person is treated as having taken all reasonable steps to establish an individual's age if—

(a) he asked the individual for evidence of his age, and

(b) the evidence would have convinced a reasonable person.

(6) Where a person ('the accused') is charged with an offence under this section by reason of the act or default of some other person, it is a defence that the accused exercised all due diligence to avoid committing it.

C11.3 Alcohol on coaches and trains

Sporting Events (Control of Alcohol etc) Act 1985, s 1(1)–(5)

1 Offences in connection with alcohol on coaches and trains

(1) This section applies to a vehicle which—

(a) is a public service vehicle or railway passenger vehicle, and

(b) is being used for the principal purpose of carrying passengers for the whole or part of a journey to or from a designated sporting event.

(2) A person who knowingly causes or permits alcohol to be carried on a vehicle to which this section applies is guilty of an offence—

(a) if the vehicle is a public service vehicle and he is the operator of the vehicle or the servant or agent of the operator, or

(b) if the vehicle is a hired vehicle and he is the person to whom it is hired or the servant or agent of that person.

(3) A person who has alcohol in his possession while on a vehicle to which this section applies is guilty of an offence.

(4) A person who is drunk on a vehicle to which this section applies is guilty of an offence.

(5) In this section 'public service vehicle' and 'operator' have the same meaning as in the Public Passenger Vehicles Act 1981.

SO

▦ Fine level 4 (s 1(2) offence), 3 months/fine level 3 (s 1(3) offence), fine level 2 (s 1(4) offence)

C11.4 Possession of bladed article or offensive weapon

Criminal Justice Act 1988, s 139(1)–(5) and (7)

139 Offence of having article with blade or point in public place

(1) Subject to subsections (4) and (5) below, any person who has an article to which this section applies with him in a public place shall be guilty of an offence.

(2) Subject to subsection (3) below, this section applies to any article which has a blade or is sharply pointed except a folding pocketknife.

(3) This section applies to a folding pocketknife if the cutting edge of its blade exceeds 3 inches.

(4) It shall be a defence for a person charged with an offence under this sectiojn to prove that he ahd good reason or lawful authority for having the article with him in a public place.

(5) Without prejudice to the generality of subsection (4) above, it shall be a defence for a person charged with an offence under this section to prove that he had the article with him—

    (a) for use at work;

    (b) for religious reasons; or

    (c) as part of any national costume.

...

(7) In this section 'public place' includes any place to which at the material time the public have or are permitted access, whether on payment or otherwise.

Prevention of Crime Act 1953, s 1(1) and (4)

1 Prohibition of the carrying of offensive weapons without lawful authority or reasonable excuse

(1) Any person who without lawful authority or reasonable excuse, the proof whereof shall lie on him, has with him in any public place any offensive weapon shall be guilty of an offence...

...

(4) In this section 'public place' includes any highway and any other premises or place to which at the material time the public have or are permitted to have access whether on payment or otherwise and 'offensive weapon' means any article made or adapted for use for causing injury to the person, or intended by the person having it with him for such use by him or some other person.

Criminal Justice Act 1988, s 139A(1) and (2)

139A Offence of having article with blade or point (or offensive weapon) on school premises

(1) Any person who has an article to which section 139 of this Act applies with him on school premises shall be guilty of an offence.

(2) Any person who has an offensive weapon within the meaning of section 1 of the Prevention of Crime Act 1953 with him on school premises shall be guilty of an offence. It shall be a defence for a person charged with an offence under this section to prove that he had good reason or lawful authority for having the article with him in a public place.

(3) ...

EW

  6 months and/or level 5 fine/4 years

C11.4.1 *Sentencing*

Offence seriousness (culpability and harm) A. Identify the appropriate starting point Starting points based on first-time offender pleading not guilty		
Examples of nature of activity	**Starting point**	**Range**
Weapon not used to threaten or cause fear	High level community order	Band C fine to 12 weeks' custody
Weapon not used to threaten or cause fear but offence committed in dangerous circumstances	6 weeks' custody	High level community order to Crown Court
Weapon used to threaten or cause fear and offence committed in dangerous circumstances	Crown Court	Crown Court

Offence seriousness (culpability and harm) B. Consider the effect of aggravating and mitigating factors (other than those within examples above) The following may be particularly relevant but these lists are not exhaustive	
Factors indicating higher culpability 1. Particularly dangerous weapon 2. Specifically planned use of weapon to commit violence, threaten violence, or intimidate 3. Offence motivated by hostility towards minority individual or group 4. Offender under influence of drink or drugs 5. Offender operating in group or gang **Factors indicating greater degree of harm** 1. Offence committed at school, hospital, or other place where vulnerable persons may be present 2. Offence committed on premises where people carrying out public services 3. Offence committed on or outside licensed premises 4. Offence committed on public transport 5. Offence committed at large public gathering, especially where there may be risk of disorder	1. Weapon carried only on temporary basis 2. Original possession legitimate, eg in course of trade or business

C11.4.2 **Key points**

- The Crown must prove that the person had the item with him and that it falls within the definition in the section. Only then must the defence establish a defence to the civil standard.
- 'Good reason' has been interpreted to mean the same as 'reasonable excuse' under the 1953 Act.
- A lock knife is not a folding knife, irrespective of the blade length (*Harris v Director of Public Prosecutions* [1993] 1 WLR 82).
- A screwdriver is not a bladed article (*R v Davis* [1998] Crim LR 564).
- A blade does not need to be sharp—a butter knife can be a bladed article (*Brooker v Director of Public Prosecutions* [2005] EWHC 1132 (Admin)).
- The fact that a defendant's employment was only casual was not a relevant consideration to prevent it being a good reason (*Chalal v Director of Public Prosecutions* [2010] EWHC 439 (Admin)).

C11.4.2.1 Prevention of Crime Act 1953

- The Crown must prove that the person had the weapon with him and that it falls within the definition in section 1(4), including proving any necessary intent. Only then must the defence establish the defence to the civil standard.
- It is necessary to show that the person knew that he was in possession of the offensive weapon (*R v Cugullere* [1961] 2 All ER 343).
- Weapons held by the appellate courts to be offensive per se include: a bayonet, a stiletto, a handgun, a butterfly knife, and a flickknife. Items that are inherently dangerous but manufactured for a lawful purpose are not offensive per se (eg razor blades, baseball bats, kitchen knives). It is likely that items prohibited for sale in England and Wales by virtue of the Criminal Justice Act 1988 (Offensive Weapons) (Amendment) Order 1988 (SI 1988/2019) are offensive per se. Whilst mere forgetfulness cannot amount to a reasonable excuse (or good reason) (*R v Glidewell* [1999] EWCA Crim 1221), the court must consider all the circumstances in which the forgetfulness arose (*R v Jolie* [2003] EWCA Crim 543).
- Fear of attack may amount to a reasonable excuse if the risk is imminent (*R v McAuley* [2009] EWCA Crim 2130).
- A court should not approach the issue of 'good reason' wholly objectively, nor hold that an angry, intoxicated, or traumatized state of mind could not contribute to good reason. A fear of attack can constitute good reason, the defendant's state of mind was relevant, and 'good reason' should be allowed a natural meaning. In this case the distorted thinking of the defendant following a sexual assault had to be considered. Only if the view was wholly unreasonable in all the

circumstances as perceived by her should a court dismiss the defence (*R v Clancy* [2012] EWCA Crim 8) (a decision under s 139 of the Criminal Justice Act 1988).

C11.4.2.2 Criminal Justice Act 1988

Regarding the section 139A offence of having an article with a blade or point (or offensive weapon) on school premises:

- school premises extend to surrounding land, playing fields, and yards;
- the offence can be committed when the school is closed;
- private schools premises fall within the Act.

See *Blackstone's Criminal Practice 2014* **B12.136–B12.177**

C11.5 Aggravated possession of bladed articles and offensive weaopns

Prevention of Crime Act 1953, s 1A

1A Offence of threatening with offensive weapon in public

(1) A person is guilty of an offence if that person—
  (a) has an offensive weapon with him or her in a public place,
  (b) unlawfully and intentionally threatens another person with the weapon, and
  (c) does so in such a way that there is an immediate risk of serious physical harm to that other person.

(2) For the purposes of this section physical harm is serious if it amounts to grievous bodily harm for the purposes of the Offences against the Person Act 1861.

(3) In this section 'public place' and 'offensive weapon' have the same meaning as in section 1.

...

(5) Where a person aged 16 or over is convicted of an offence under this section, the court must impose an appropriate custodial sentence (with or without a fine) unless the court is of the opinion that there are particular circumstances which—
  (a) relate to the offence or to the offender, and
  (b) would make it unjust to do so in all the circumstances.

(6) In this section 'appropriate custodial sentence' means—
  (a) in the case of a person who is aged 18 or over when convicted, a sentence of imprisonment (or detention)for a term of at least 6 months;
  (b) in the case of a person who is aged at least 16 but under 18 when convicted, a detention and training order of at least 4 months.

(7) In considering whether it is of the opinion mentioned in subsection (5) in the case of a person aged under 18, the court must have regard to its duty under section 44 of the Children and Young Persons Act 1933.

...

(10) If on a person's trial for an offence under this section (whether on indictment or not) the person is found not guilty of that offence but it is proved that the person committed an offence under section 1, the person may be convicted of the offence under that section.

Criminal Justice Act 1988, s 139 AA

139AA Offence of threatening with article with blade or point or offensive weapon

(1) A person is guilty of an offence if that person—
   (a) has an article to which this section applies with him or her in a public place or on school premises,
   (b) unlawfully and intentionally threatens another person with the article, and
   (c) does so in such a way that there is an immediate risk of serious physical harm to that other person.
(2) In relation to a public place this section applies to an article to which section 139 applies.
(3) In relation to school premises this section applies to each of these—
   (a) an article to which section 139 applies;
   (b) an offensive weapon within the meaning of section 1 of the Prevention of Crime Act 1953.
(4) For the purposes of this section physical harm is serious if it amounts to grievous bodily harm for the purposes of the Offences against the Person Act 1861.
(5) In this section—
   'public place' has the same meaning as in section 139;
   'school premises' has the same meaning as in section 139A.
(7) Where a person aged 16 or over is convicted of an offence under this section, the court must impose an appropriate custodial sentence (with or without a fine) unless the court is of the opinion that there are particular circumstances which—
   (a) relate to the offence or to the offender, and
   (b) would make it unjust to do so in all the circumstances.
(8) In this section 'appropriate custodial sentence' means—
   (a) in the case of a person who is aged 18 or over when convicted, a sentence of imprisonment(or detention) for a term of at least 6 months;
   (b) in the case of a person who is aged at least 16 but under 18 when convicted, a detention and training order of at least 4 months.
(9) In considering whether it is of the opinion mentioned in subsection (7) in the case of a person aged under 18, the court must have regard to its duty under section 44 of the Children and Young Persons Act 1933.
...
(12) If on a person's trial for an offence under this section (whether on indictment or not) the person is found not guilty of that offence but it is proved that the person committed an offence under section 139 or 139A, the person may be convicted of the offence under that section.

EW

6 months' imprisonment and/or level 5 fine/4 years *but* with a minimum obligatory sentence unless it would be unjust in all the circumstances. A 20 per cent reduction on that obligatory sentence is available for an early guilty plea, and there apears to be no statutory reason why a sentence on an adult should not be suspended.

C11.5.1 Key points

The defences available to the aggravated offences do not replicate those for the basic crimes.

C11.6 Sale of knives and certain articles with blade or point to persons under 18

Criminal Justice Act 1988, s 141A

141A Sale of knives and certain articles with blade or point to persons under eighteen

(1) Any person who sells to a person under the age of eighteen years an article to which this section applies shall be guilty of an offence and liable on summary conviction to imprisonment for a term not exceeding six months, or a fine not exceeding level 5 on the standard scale, or both.

(2) Subject to subsection (3) below, this section applies to—
(a) any knife, knife blade or razor blade,
(b) any axe, and
(c) any sword, and
(d) any other article which has a blade or which is sharply pointed and which is made or adapted for use for causing injury to the person.

(3) This section does not apply to any article described in—
(a) section 1 of the Restriction of Offensive Weapons Act 1959.
(b) an order made under section 141(2) of this Act, or
(c) an order made by the Secretary of State under this section.

(3A) It is not an offence under subsection (1) to sell a knife or knife blade to a person if—
(a) the person is aged 16 or over; and
(b) the knife or blade is designed for domestic use.

(4) It shall be a defence for a person charged with an offence under subsection (1) above to prove that he took all reasonable precautions and exercised all due diligence to avoid the commission of the offence.

SO

 6 months' imprisonment and/or level 5 fine

C11.6.1 Key points

A grapefruit knife is a knife for the purposes of section 141A (*R (Windsor and Maidenhead Royal Borough) v East Berkshire Justices* [2010] EWHC 3020 (Admin)).

C11.7 Disorderly behaviour (harassment, alarm, or distress)

Public Order Act 1986, s 5(1)

5 Harassment, alarm or distress

(1) A person is guilty of an offence if he—
  (a) uses threatening, abusive or insulting words or behaviour, or disorderly behaviour, or
  (b) displays any writing, sign or other visible representation which is threatening, abusive or insulting,
  within the hearing or sight of a person likely to be caused harassment, alarm or distress thereby.

SO

 Level 3 fine; level 4 fine if racially or religiously aggravated

C11.7.1 *Sentencing*

Offence seriousness (culpability and harm) A. Identify the appropriate starting point Starting points based on first-time offender pleading not guilty		
Examples of nature of activity	**Starting point**	**Range**
Shouting, causing disturbance for some minutes	Band A fine	Conditional discharge to band B fine
Substantial disturbance caused	Band B fine	Band A fine to band C fine

Offence seriousness (culpability and harm) B. Consider the effect of aggravating and mitigating factors (other than those within examples above) The following may be particularly relevant but these lists are not exhaustive	
Factors indicating higher culpability	**Factors indicating lower culpability**
1. Group action 2. Lengthy incident	1. Stopped as soon as police arrived 2. Brief/minor incident 3. Provocation

Factors indicating greater degree of harm	
1. Vulnerable person(s) present 2. Offence committed at school, hospital, or other place where vulnerable persons may be present 3. Victim providing public service	

C11.7.2 Key points

- Section 5 provides:

Public Order Act 1986, s 5(3)

5 Harassment, alarm or distress

(3) It is a defence for the accused to prove—

    (a) that he had no reason to believe that there was any person within hearing or sight who was likely to be caused harassment, alarm or distress, or

    (b) that he was inside a dwelling and had no reason to believe that the words or behaviour used, or the writing, sign or other visible representation displayed, would be heard or seen by a person outside that or any other dwelling, or

    (c) that his conduct was reasonable.

- Section 6 provides:

Public Order Act 1986, s 6(4) and (5)

6 Mental element: miscellaneous

(4) A person is guilty of an offence under section 5 only if he intends his words or behaviour, or the writing, sign or other visible representation, to be threatening, abusive or insulting, or is aware that it may be threatening, abusive or insulting or (as the case may be) he intends his behaviour to be or is aware that it may be disorderly.

(5) For the purposes of this section a person whose awareness is impaired by intoxication shall be taken to be aware of that of which he would be aware if not intoxicated, unless he shows either that his intoxication was not self-induced or that it was caused solely by the taking or administration of a substance in the course of medical treatment.

- An offence under section 5 may be committed in a public or a private place, except that no offence is committed where the words or behaviour are used, or the writing, sign, or other visible representation is displayed, by a person inside a dwelling and the other person is also inside that or another dwelling.

- A person can be harassed without emotional upset (*Southard v Director of Public Prosecutions* [2006] EWHC 3449 (Admin)). In *Southard*, the defendant intervened in his brother's arrest, shouting 'fuck off' and 'fuck you' at the officer. The conviction was upheld. The harassment must not, however, be trivial (eg *R (R) v Director of Public Prosecutions* [2006] EWHC 1375 (Admin)—another case involving a police officer where the conviction was quashed).
- Concealing a video camera in a changing room can amount to disorderly behaviour (*Vigon v Director of Public Prosecutions* (1997) 162 JP 115).
- For considerations under the European Convention on Human Rights (and in particular Art 10 ECHR), see *Abdul and others v Crown Prosecution Service* [2011] EWHC 247 (Admin)). The following principles emerge from Article 10 ECHR jurisprudence (para 49 of the judgment):

  (i) The starting point is the importance of the right to freedom of expression.

  (ii) In this regard, it must be recognised that legitimate protest can be offensive at least to some—and on occasions must be, if it is to have impact. Moreover, the right to freedom of expression would be unacceptably devalued if it did no more than protect those holding popular, mainstream views; it must plainly extend beyond that so that minority views can be freely expressed, even if distasteful. [The context of the remarks is a key factor.]

  (iii) The justification for interference with the right to freedom of expression must be convincingly established. Accordingly, while Art 10 does not confer an unqualified right to freedom of expression, the restrictions contained in Art 10.2 are to be narrowly construed.

  (iv) There is not and cannot be any universal test for resolving when speech goes beyond legitimate protest, so attracting the sanction of the criminal law. The justification for invoking the criminal law is the threat to public order. Inevitably, the context of the particular occasion will be of the first importance.

  (v) The relevance of the threat to public order should not be taken as meaning that the risk of violence by those reacting to the protest is, without more, determinative; sometimes it may be that protesters are to be protected. That said, in striking the right balance when determining whether speech is 'threatening, abusive or insulting', the focus on minority rights should not result in overlooking the rights of the majority.

(vi) Plainly, if there is no prima facie case that speech was 'threatening, abusive or insulting' or that the other elements of the s.5 offence can be made good, then no question of prosecution will arise. However, even if there is otherwise a prima facie case for contending that an offence has been committed under s.5, it is still for the Crown to establish that prosecution is a proportionate response, necessary for the preservation of public order.

If the line between legitimate freedom of expression and a threat to public order has indeed been crossed, freedom of speech will not have been impaired by 'ruling…out' threatening, abusive or insulting speech.

- *Harvey v DPP* [2011] EWHC 3992 (Admin) confirms that it is not an offence under section 5 of the Public Order Act to use swear words in the presence of a police officer. The Crown must produce evidence of the likelihood of harassment, alarm, or distress. This cannot be implied for police officers or young people for whom they are a regular feature of life.

 See *Blackstone's Criminal Practice 2014* **B11.69–B11.83**

C11.8 Disorderly behaviour with intent to cause harassment, alarm, or distress

Public Order Act 1986, s 4A(1)

4A Intentional harassment, alarm or distress

(1) A person is guilty of an offence if, with intent to cause a person harassment, alarm or distress, he—

(a) uses threatening, abusive or insulting words or behaviour, or disorderly behaviour, or

(b) displays any writing, sign or other visible representation which is threatening, abusive or insulting,

thereby causing that or another person harassment, alarm or distress.

SO

6 months and/or level 5 fine

Note: racially or religiously aggravated offence is triable either way (2 years on indictment).

Disorderly behaviour with intent to cause harassment C11.8

C11.8.1 *Sentencing*

Offence seriousness (culpability and harm) A. Identify the appropriate starting point Starting points based on first-time offender pleading not guilty		
Examples of nature of activity	**Starting point**	**Range**
Threats, abuse, or insults made more than once but on same occasion against the same person, eg while following down the street	Band C fine	Band B fine to low level community order
Group action or deliberately planned action against targeted victim	Medium level community order	Low level community order to 12 weeks' custody
Weapon brandished or used or threats against vulnerable victim—course of conduct over longer period	12 weeks' custody	High level community order to 26 weeks' custody

Offence seriousness (culpability and harm) B. Consider the effect of aggravating and mitigating factors (other than those within examples above) The following may be particularly relevant but these lists are not exhaustive	
Factors indicating higher culpability 1. High degree of planning 2. Offender deliberately isolates victim **Factors indicating greater degree of harm** 1. Offence committed in vicinity of victim's home 2. Large number of people in vicinity 3. Actual or potential escalation into violence 4. Particularly serious impact on victim	**Factors indicating lower culpability** 1. Very short period 2. Provocation

C11.8.2 Key points

- Section 4A(3) provides:

Public Order Act 1986, s 4A(3)

4A Intentional harassment, alarm or distress

(3) It is a defence for the accused to prove—
  (a) that he was inside a dwelling and had no reason to believe that the words or behaviour used, or the writing, sign or other visible representation displayed, would be heard or seen by a person outside that or any other dwelling, or
  (b) that his conduct was reasonable.

- An offence under this section may be committed in a public or a private place, except that no offence is committed where the words or behaviour are used, or the writing, sign, or other visible representation is displayed, by a person inside a dwelling and the person who is harassed, alarmed, or distressed is also inside that or another dwelling.
- For considerations under the European Convention on Human Rights (and in particular Art 10 ECHR), see *Abdul and others v Crown Prosecution Service* [2011] EWHC 247 (Admin)).

 See *Blackstones' Criminal Practice 2014* **B11.60–11.68**

C11.9 Drunk and disorderly in a public place

Criminal Justice Act 1967, s 91(1), (2), and (4)

91 Drunkenness in a public place

(1) Any person who in any public place is guilty, while drunk, of disorderly behaviour...shall be liable on summary conviction to a fine not exceeding [level 3 on the standard scale].
(2) The foregoing subsection shall have effect instead of any corresponding provision contained in section 12 of the Licensing Act 1872, section 58 of the Metropolitan Police Act 1839, section 37 of the City of London Police Act 1839, and section 29 of the Town Police Clauses Act 1847 (being enactments which authorise the imposition of a short term of imprisonment or of a fine not exceeding £10 or both for the corresponding offence) and instead of any corresponding provision contained in any local Act.
(3) ...
(4) In this section 'public place' includes any highway and any other premises or place to which at the material time the public have or are permitted to have access, whether on payment or otherwise.

SO Level 3 fine

C11.9.1 *Sentencing*

Offence seriousness (culpability and harm) A. Identify the appropriate starting point Starting points based on first-time offender pleading not guilty		
Examples of nature of activity	**Starting point**	**Range**
Shouting, causing disturbance for some minutes	Band A fine	Conditional discharge to band B fine
Substantial disturbance caused	Band B fine	Band A fine to band C fine

Offence seriousness (culpability and harm) B. Consider the effect of aggravating and mitigating factors (other than those within examples above) The following may be particularly relevant but these lists are not exhaustive	
Factors indicating higher culpability 1. Brandishing firearm 2. Carrying firearm in a busy place 3. Planned illegal use **Factors indicating greater degree of harm** 1. Person or people put in fear 2. Offender participating in violent incident	**Factors indicating lower culpability** 1. Firearm not in sight 2. No intention to use firearm 3. Firearm to be used for lawful purpose (not amounting to defence)

C11.9.2 Key points

- In *Carroll v Director of Public Prosecutions* [2009] EWHC 554 (Admin), the court stated that:

> 4. ... The offence requires proof of three elements, namely that (1) the defendant was drunk; (2) he was in a public place; and (3) he was guilty of disorderly behaviour. Only the first and third elements call for further comment:
>
> ...
>
> 9. As to the first element in *Neale v E (A Minor)* (1983) 80 Crim App R 20, this court (Robert Goff LJ and Mann J, as they each then were) decided that the word 'drunk' should be given its ordinary and natural meaning. In the end, therefore, whether a defendant was drunk is a simple question of fact in each case. On familiar principles it is the voluntary consumption of alcohol which is the requisite mens rea, such as it is, of this most basic offence. If that voluntary consumption results in the defendant becoming drunk then the first element of the offence is proved.
>
> 10. As to the third element, there is no requirement for mens rea at all. What is required is proof that objectively viewed the defendant was guilty of disorderly behaviour. Specific drunken intent and recklessness are nothing to the point. The words 'disorderly behaviour' are again to be given their ordinary

and natural meaning. In the end, therefore, it is a simple question of fact in each case: whether the defendant is guilty of disorderly behaviour.

 See *Blackstone's Criminal Practice 2014* **B11.202–B11.206**

C11.10 Firearm, carrying in public place

> ### Firearms Act 1968, s 19
>
> #### 19 Carrying a firearm in a public place
> A person commits an offence if, without lawful authority or reasonable excuse (the proof whereof lies on him) he has with him in a public place—
>
> (a) a loaded shot gun,
> (b) an air weapon (whether loaded or not),
> (c) any other firearm (whether loaded or not) together with ammunition suitable for use in that firearm, or
> (d) an imitation firearm.

EW (Summary only if an air weapon)

▦ 6 months and/or level 5 fine/7 years (12 months if imitation weapon)

C11.10.1 *Sentencing*

Offence seriousness (culpability and harm) A. Identify the appropriate starting point Starting points based on first-time offender pleading not guilty		
Examples of nature of activity	**Starting point**	**Range**
Carrying an unloaded air weapon	Low level community order	Band B fine to medium level community order
Carrying loaded air weapon/imitation firearm/ unloaded shot gun without ammunition	High level community order	Medium level community order to 26 weeks' custody (air weapon) Medium level community order to Crown Court (imitation firearm, unloaded shot gun)
Carrying loaded shot gun/ carrying shot gun or any other firearm together with ammunition for it	Crown Court	Crown Court

  EW Either Way ▦ Sentence

Offence seriousness (culpability and harm)
B. Consider the effect of aggravating and mitigating factors
(other than those within examples above)
The following may be particularly relevant but these lists are not exhaustive

Factors indicating higher culpability	Factors indicating lower culpability
1. Brandishing firearm	1. Firearm not in sight
2. Carrying firearm in a busy place	2. No intention to use firearm
3. Planned illegal use	3. Firearm to be used for lawful purpose
Factors indicating greater degree	(not amounting to defence)
of harm	
1. Person or people put in fear	
2. Offender participating in violent incident	

C11.10.2 Key points

- It is not necessary to show that the defendant knew that a gun was loaded (*R v Harrison* [1996] Crim LR 200).
- An item is an imitation firearm if it 'looked like' a firearm at the time of its use (*R v Morris and King* (1984) 149 JP 60).
- A part of the body (eg fingers pointed under clothing) could not constitute an imitation firearm (*R v Bentham* [2005] UKHL 18).

  See *Blackstone's Criminal Practice 2014* **B12.103**

C11.11 Football-related offences

The Sporting Events (Control of Alcohol etc) Act 1985, section 2 concerns possession of alcohol whilst entering or trying to enter a designated sports ground (s 2(1)), and being drunk in, or whilst trying to enter, a sports ground (s 2(2)); the Football Offences Act 1991 covers throwing of missiles (s 2), indecent or racialist chanting (s 3), and going onto prohibited areas (s 4); and the Criminal Justice and Public Order Act 1994 deals with the unauthorized sale or attempted sale of tickets (s 166).

> **Sporting Events (Control of Alcohol etc) Act 1985, s 2(1), (1A), (2), and (3)**
>
> **2 Offences in connection with alcohol, containers etc at sports grounds**
>
> (1) A person who has alcohol or an article to which this section applies in his possession—
> (a) at any time during the period of a designated sporting event when he is in any area of a designated sports ground from which the event may be directly viewed, or

    (b) while entering or trying to enter a designated sports ground at any time during the period of a designated sporting event at that ground, is guilty of an offence.

(1A) Subsection (1)(a) above has effect subject to section 5A(1) of this Act.

(2) A person who is drunk in a designated sports ground at any time during the period of a designated sporting event at that ground or is drunk while entering or trying to enter such a ground at any time during the period of a designated sporting event at that ground is guilty of an offence.

(3) This section applies to any article capable of causing injury to a person struck by it, being—

    (a) a bottle, can or other portable container (including such an article when crushed or broken) which—

        (i) is for holding any drink, and

        (ii) is of a kind which, when empty, is normally discarded or returned to, or left to be recovered by, the supplier, or

    (b) part of an article falling within paragraph (a) above;

but does not apply to anything that is for holding any medicinal product (within the meaning of the Medicines Act 1968) or any veterinary medicinal product (within the meaning of the Veterinary Medicines Regulations 2006).

Football Offences Act 1991, ss 2, 3, and 4

2 Throwing of missiles

It is an offence for a person at a designated football match to throw anything at or towards—

(a) the playing area, or any area adjacent to the playing area to which spectators are not generally admitted, or

(b) any area in which spectators or other persons are or may be present, without lawful authority or lawful excuse (which shall be for him to prove).

3 Indecent or racialist chanting

(1) It is an offence to engage or take part in chanting of an indecent or racialist nature at a designated football match.

(2) For this purpose—

    (a) 'chanting' means the repeated uttering of any words or sounds (whether alone or in concert with one or more others); and

    (b) 'of a racialist nature' means consisting of or including matter which is threatening, abusive or insulting to a person by reason of his colour, race, nationality (including citizenship) or ethnic or national origins.

4 Going onto the playing area

It is an offence for a person at a designated football match to go onto the playing area, or any area adjacent to the playing area to which spectators are not generally admitted, without lawful authority or lawful excuse (which shall be for him to prove).

Criminal Justice and Public Order Act 1994, s 166

166 Sale of tickets by unauthorised persons

(1) It is an offence for an unauthorised person to—
    (a) sell a ticket for a designated football match, or
    (b) otherwise to dispose of such a ticket to another person.

(2) For this purpose—
    (a) a person is 'unauthorised' unless he is authorised in writing to sell or otherwise dispose of tickets for the match by the organisers of the match;
    (aa) a reference to selling a ticket includes a reference to—
        (i)   offering to sell a ticket;
        (ii) exposing a ticket for sale;
        (iii) making a ticket available for sale by another;
        (iv) advertising that a ticket is available for purchase; and
        (v)   giving a ticket to a person who pays or agrees to pay for some other goods or services or offering to do so.
    (b) a 'ticket' means anything which purports to be a ticket;

...

 3 months/level 3 (s 2(1) offence), level 2 fine (s 2(2) offence)

Level 3 fine (throwing missile; indecent or racialist chanting; going onto prohibited areas)

Level 5 fine (unauthorized sale of tickets)

Level 3 fine and/or 3 months (possession of alcohol)

C11.11.1 *Sentencing*

Offence seriousness (culpability and harm) A. Identify the appropriate starting point Starting points based on first-time offender pleading not guilty		
Examples of nature of activity	**Starting point**	**Range**
Being drunk in, or whilst trying to enter, ground	Band A fine	Conditional discharge to band B fine
Going onto playing or other prohibited area; unauthorized sale or attempted sale of tickets	Band B fine	Band A fine to band C fine
Throwing missile; indecent or racialist chanting	Band C fine	Band C fine
Possession of alcohol whilst entering or trying to enter ground	Band C fine	Band B fine to high level community order

---

Offence seriousness (culpability and harm)
B. Consider the effect of aggravating and mitigating factors (other than those within examples above)
The following may be particularly relevant but these lists are not exhaustive

Factors indicating higher culpability
1. Commercial ticket operation; potential high cash value; counterfeit tickets
2. Inciting others to misbehave
3. Possession of large quantity of alcohol
4. Offensive language or behaviour (where not an element of the offence)

Factor indicating greater degree of harm
1. Missile likely to cause serious injury, eg coin, glass, bottle, stone

---

 See *Blackstone's Criminal Practice 2014* **B11.130–B11.133** and **B11.212–B11.216**

C11.12 Threatening behaviour, fear, or provocation of violence

Public Order Act 1986, ss 4(1), 6(3) and (5)

4 Fear or provocation of violence

(1) A person is guilty of an offence if he—
  (a) uses towards another person threatening, abusive or insulting words or behaviour, or
  (b) distributes or displays to another person any writing, sign or other visible representation which is threatening, abusive or insulting,

with intent to cause that person to believe that immediate unlawful violence will be used against him or another by any person, or to provoke the immediate use of unlawful violence by that person or another, or whereby that person is likely to believe that such violence will be used or it is likely that such violence will be provoked.

…

6 Mental element: miscellaneous

(3) A person is guilty of an offence under section 4 only if he intends his words or behaviour, or the writing, sign or other visible representation, to be threatening, abusive or insulting, or is aware that it may be threatening, abusive or insulting.

…

(5) For the purposes of this section a person whose awareness is impaired by intoxication shall be taken to be aware of that of which he would be aware if not intoxicated, unless he shows either that his intoxication was not self-induced or that it was caused solely by the taking or administration of a substance in the course of medical treatment.

SO (Racially or religiously aggravated offence is triable either way)

‖‖‖ 6 months and/or level 5 fine. Racially or religiously aggravated offence carries a maximum 2 years on indictment

C11.12.1 *Sentencing*

Offence seriousness (culpability and harm) A. Identify the appropriate starting point Starting points based on first-time offender pleading not guilty		
Examples of nature of activity	**Starting point**	**Range**
Fear or threat of low-level immediate unlawful violence such as push, shove, or spit	Low level community order	Band B fine to medium level community order
Fear or threat of medium-level immediate unlawful violence such as punch	High level community order	Low level community order to 12 weeks' custody
Fear or threat of high-level immediate unlawful violence such as use of weapon; missile thrown; gang involvement	12 weeks' custody	6 to 26 weeks' custody

Offence seriousness (culpability and harm) B. Consider the effect of aggravating and mitigating factors (other than those within examples above) The following may be particularly relevant but these lists are not exhaustive	
Factors indicating higher culpability 1. Planning 2. Offender deliberately isolates victim 3. Group action 4. Threat directed at victim because of job 5. History of antagonism towards victim **Factors indicating greater degree of harm** 1. Offence committed at school, hospital, or other place where vulnerable persons may be present 2. Offence committed on enclosed premises such as public transport 3. Vulnerable victim(s) 4. Victim needs medical help/counselling	**Factors indicating lower culpability** 1. Impulsive action 2. Short duration 3. Provocation

C11.12.2 Key points

- An offence under section 4 may be committed in a public or a private place, except that no offence is committed where the words or behaviour are used, or the writing, sign, or other visible representation is distributed or displayed, by a person inside a dwelling and the other person is also inside that or another dwelling.

- Subject to the Crown proving the use of threatening, etc words/behaviour and the mens rea, *Winn v DPP* (1992) 156 JP 881 confirmed that there are four ways in which the offence can be committed:
  - by intending to cause the person against whom the conduct is directed to believe that immediate unlawful violence will be used against him or another;
  - by intending to provoke the immediate use of unlawful violence by that person or another;
  - the person against whom the conduct is directed being likely to believe that immediate unlawful violence will be used; or
  - its being likely that immediate unlawful violence will be provoked.
- Actions taken in self-defence do not amount to unlawful violence.
- For the conduct to be used towards another, that other must be physically present (*Atkin v DPP* (1989) 89 Cr App R 199).
- The need for immediate unlawful violence means that it cannot be at some uncertain future time (*Horseferry Road Stipendiary Magistrate, ex p Siadatan* [1991] 1 QB 260), but it does not mean that it has to be instantaneous.
- For considerations under the European Convention on Human Rights (and in particular Art 10 ECHR), see *Abdul and others v Crown Prosecution Service* [2011] EWHC 247 (Admin)).

 See *Blackstone's Criminal Practice 2014* **B11.47–B11.58**

C11.13 Taxi touting/soliciting for hire

Criminal Justice and Public Order Act 1994, s 167

 Level 4 fine

C11.13.1 *Sentencing*

Offence seriousness (culpability and harm) A. Identify the appropriate starting point Starting points based on first-time offender pleading not guilty		
Examples of nature of activity	**Starting point**	**Range**
Licensed taxi-driver touting for trade (ie making approach rather than waiting for a person to initiate hiring)	Band A fine	Conditional discharge to band A fine and consider disqualification 1–3 months

PHV licence held but touting for trade rather than being booked through an operator; an accomplice to touting	Band B fine	Band A fine to band C fine and consider disqualification 3–6 months
No PHV licence held	Band C fine	Band B fine to band C fine and disqualification 6–12 months

Offence seriousness (culpability and harm) **B. Consider the effect of aggravating and mitigating factors** **(other than those within examples above)** The following may be particularly relevant but these lists are not exhaustive	
Factors indicating higher culpability 1. Commercial business/large-scale operation 2. No insurance/invalid insurance 3. No driving licence and/or no MOT 4. Vehicle not roadworthy **Factors indicating greater degree of harm** 1. Deliberately diverting trade from taxi rank 2. PHV licence had been refused/offender ineligible for licence	**Factor indicating lower culpability** 1. Providing a service when no licensed taxi available

C11.14 Violent disorder

Public Order Act 1986, s 2(1) and (2)

2 Violent disorder

(1) Where 3 or more persons who are present together use or threaten unlawful violence and the conduct of them (taken together) is such as would cause a person of reasonable firmness present at the scene to fear for his personal safety, each of the persons using or threatening unlawful violence is guilty of violent disorder.

(2) It is immaterial whether or not the 3 or more use or threaten unlawful violence simultaneously.

. . .

EW

6 months and/or level 5 fine/5 years

DO

C11.14.1 *Sentencing*

Offence seriousness (culpability and harm)
A. Identify the appropriate starting point
Starting points based on first-time offender pleading not guilty

The offences should normally be dealt with in the Crown Court
However, there may be rare cases involving minor violence or threats of violence leading to no or minor injury, with few people involved and no weapon or missiles, in which a custodial sentence within the jurisdiction of a magistrates' court may be appropriate.

C11.14.2 Key points

- The expression 'who are present together' was considered by the court in *R v NW* [2010] EWCA Crim 404, as follows:

  > [It] means no more than being in the same place at the same time. Three or more people using or threatening violence in the same place at the same time, whether for the same purpose or different purposes, are capable of creating a daunting prospect for those who may encounter them, simply by reason of the fact that they represent a breakdown of law and order which has unpredictable consequences. [The court is unable] to accept that the phrase requires any degree of cooperation between those who are using or threatening violence; all that is required is that they be present in the same place at the same time. The section is concerned with public disorder and is deliberately worded in a way that is apt to apply to anyone who uses or threatens violence of the requisite nature in a particular context, namely, in a public place where others are engaged in the same activity. . . . the requirement that the conduct of the participants taken together should be such as to cause members of the public to fear for their safety was included in order to direct attention to the overall effect of what may otherwise be unrelated acts or threats of violence.

- No person of reasonable firmness need actually be, or be likely to be, present at the scene.
- The use of words alone is not sufficient.
- A fight in public does not automatically become an affray (*R v Plavecz* [2002] EWCA Crim 1802).
- Section 6(2) of the Public Order Act 1986 provides:

Public Order Act 1986, s 6(2)

6 Mental element: miscellaneous

(2) A person is guilty of violent disorder or affray only if he intends to use or threaten violence or is aware that his conduct may be violent or threaten violence.

- Violent disorder may be committed in private as well as in public places.

 See *Blackstone's Criminal Practice 2014* **B11.28–B11.36**

C12 Road Traffic Offences—Definitions

C12.1 Accident

'Accident' is to be given its ordinary meaning (*Chief Constable of West Midlands v Billingham* [1979] 1 WLR 747). A deliberate act can amount to an accident (*Chief Constable of Staffordshire v Lees* [1981] RTR 506). A physical impact is not necessary (*R v Currie* [2007] EWCA Crim 927), but the *de minimis* principle applies (*R v Morris* [1972] 1 WLR 228).

C12.2 Causing

Causing requires a positive act (*Ross Hillman Ltd v Bond* [1974] QB 435) committed with prior knowledge.

C12.3 Driver

Section 192(1) of the Road Traffic Act 1988 provides:

> **Road Traffic Act 1988, s 192(1)**
>
> **192 General interpretation of Act**
>
> (1)…
> 'driver', where a separate person acts as a steersman of a motor vehicle, includes (except for the purposes of section 1 of this Act) that person as well as any other person engaged in the driving of the vehicle, and 'drive' is to be interpreted accordingly,
>
> …

A person supervising a driver will not be a driver unless he exercises some control over the vehicle (eg dual controls) (*Evans v Walkden* [1956] 1 WLR 1019).

C12.4 Driving

R v MacDonagh [1974] QB 448 defined 'driving' as use of the driver's controls for the purpose of directing the movement of the vehicle. The court gave the following guidance:

> There are an infinite number of ways in which a person may control the movement of a motor vehicle, apart from the orthodox one of sitting in the driving

seat and using the engine for propulsion. He may be coasting down a hill with the gears in neutral and the engine switched off; he may be steering a vehicle which is being towed by another. As has already been pointed out, he may be sitting in the driving seat whilst others push, or half sitting in the driving seat but keeping one foot on the road in order to induce the car to move. Finally, as in the present case, he may be standing in the road and himself pushing the car with or without using the steering wheel to direct it. Although the word 'drive' must be given a wide meaning, the Courts must be alert to see that the net is not thrown so widely that it includes activities which cannot be said to be driving a motor vehicle in any ordinary use of that word in the English language.

As a person may be driving a stationary vehicle, it is a matter of fact to be decided in each case, and factors such as the reason for the vehicle stopping and the duration of the stop will be relevant (*Planton v Director of Public Prosecutions* [2002] RTR 107).

Steering a vehicle being towed would amount to driving where there was an operational braking system (*McQuaid v Anderton* [1981] 1 WLR 154), as would freewheeling a vehicle down a hill while steering (*Saycell v Bool* [1948] 2 All ER 83). A person steering from the passenger seat is driving (*Tyler v Whatmore* [1976] RTR 83).

C12.5 **In charge**

In cases where the matter is not clear, the case of *Director of Public Prosecutions v Watkins* (1989) 89 Cr App R 112 should be considered in detail. The court laid down the following broad guidance:

> Broadly there are two distinct classes of case. (1) If the defendant is the owner or lawful possessor of the vehicle or has recently driven it, he will have been in charge of it, and the question for the Court will be whether he is still in charge or whether he has relinquished his charge. Usually such a defendant will be prima facie in charge unless he has put the vehicle in someone else's charge. However he would not be so if in all the circumstances he has ceased to be in actual control and there is no realistic possibility of his resuming actual control while unfit: eg if he is at home in bed for the night, if he is a great distance from the car, or if it is taken by another.

> (2) If the defendant is not the owner, the lawful possessor, or recent driver but is sitting in the vehicle or is otherwise involved with it, the question for the Court is, as here, whether he has assumed being in charge of it. In this class of case the defendant will be in charge if, whilst unfit, he is voluntarily in de facto control of the vehicle or if, in the circumstances, including his position, his intentions and his actions, he may be expected imminently to assume control. Usually this will involve his having gained entry to the car and evinced an intention to take control of it. But gaining entry may not be necessary if he has manifested that intention some other way, eg by stealing the keys of a car in circumstances which show he means presently to drive it.

The circumstances to be taken into account will vary infinitely, but the following will be usually relevant:

(i) Whether and where he is in the vehicle or how far he is from it.

(ii) What he is doing at the relevant time.

(iii) Whether he is in possession of a key that fits the ignition.

(iv) Whether there is evidence of an intention to take or assert control of the car by driving or otherwise

(v) Whether any other person is in, at or near the vehicle and if so, the like particulars in respect of that person.

It will be for the Court to consider all the above factors with any others which may be relevant and reach its decision as a question of fact and degree.

C12.6 **Motor vehicle**

There is no statutory definition of 'vehicle' and therefore its ordinary meaning of a carriage or conveyance should apply. Where the statute uses the phrase 'motor vehicle', the definition to be found in section 185 of the Road Traffic Act 1988 states that it is a 'mechanically propelled vehicle intended or adapted for use on roads'. The maximum speed of the vehicle is not a relevant factor (*Director of Public Prosecutions v King* [2008] EWHC 447 (Admin)).

C12.7 **Owner**

This includes a person in possession of a vehicle under a hire or hire-purchase agreement.

C12.8 **Permitting**

A person permits use when he allows or authorizes use, or fails to take reasonable steps to prevent use. For permitting use with no insurance, the prosecution do not need to show that the person knew the driver to be uninsured. If, however, use is conditional (eg on the person having insurance), the outcome would be different (*Newbury v Davis* [1974] RTR 367).

C12.9 **Public place**

This is a place to which the public have access. However, the law draws a distinction between general public access and access for a defined group of persons. The law in this area is complex and voluminous, and advocates should always seek an adjournment where the answer is not clear.

C12.10 **Road**

This is defined as any highway or road to which the public have access. The following have been held to be a road:

- pedestrian pavement (*Randall v Motor Insurers' Bureau* [1968] 1 WLR 1900);
- grass verge at the side of a road (*Worth v Brooks* [1959] Crim LR 855);
- bridges over which a road passes.

It will be a matter of fact and degree as to whether something is a road, and whether or not the public have access. A car park will not generally be a road, even if there are roads running through it. In *Barrett v Director of Public Prosecutions*, 10 February 2009, the court held that a roadway running through a private caravan park, and facilitating entry to a beach, constituted a road.

A vehicle will be 'on' a road when part of the vehicle protrudes over a road (*Avery v Crown Prosecution Service* [2011] EWHC 2388 (Admin)).

C12.11 **Highway**

This is defined as land over which there is a right of way on foot, by riding, or with vehicles and cattle. A highway includes: bridleways, footpaths, footways, walkways, carriageways, and driftways.

 See generally *Blackstone's Criminal Practice 2014* **C1**

C13 **Road Traffic Offences**

C13.1 Careless driving (drive without due care and attention)

> **Road Traffic Act 1988, s 3**
>
> **3 Careless, and inconsiderate, driving**
>
> If a person drives a mechanically propelled vehicle on a road or other public place without due care and attention, or without reasonable consideration for other persons using the road or place, he is guilty of an offence.

 Level 5 fine. Must endorse and may disqualify. If no disqualification, impose 3–9 points

C13.1.1 *Sentencing*

Offence seriousness (culpability and harm) A. Identify the appropriate starting point Starting points based on first-time offender pleading not guilty		
Example of nature of activity	**Starting point**	**Range**
Momentary lapse of concentration or misjudgement at low speed	Band A fine	Band A fine 3–4 points
Loss of control due to speed, mishandling, or insufficient attention to road conditions, or carelessly turning right across oncoming traffic	Band B fine	Band B fine 5–6 points
Overtaking manoeuvre at speed resulting in collision of vehicles, or driving bordering on the dangerous	Band C fine	Band C fine Consider disqualification OR 7–9 points

Offence seriousness (culpability and harm)
B. Consider the effect of aggravating and mitigating factors
(other than those within examples above)
The following may be particularly relevant but these lists are not exhaustive

Factors indicating higher culpability	Factors indicating lower culpability
1. Excessive speed	1. Minor risk
2. Carrying out other tasks while driving	2. Inexperience of driver
3. Carrying passengers or heavy load	3. Sudden change in road or weather
4. Tiredness	conditions
Factors indicating greater degree	
of harm	
1. Injury to others	
2. Damage to other vehicles or property	
3. High level of traffic or pedestrians in	
vicinity	
4. Location, eg near school when children	
are likely to be present	

C13.1.2 Key points

- Careless driving is defined in the Act.
- Section 3ZA(2)–(4) of the Road Traffic Act 1988 provides:

Road Traffic Act 1988, s 3ZA(2)–(4)

3ZA Meaning of careless, or inconsiderate, driving

...

(2) A person is to be regarded as driving without due care and attention if (and only if) the way he drives falls below what would be expected of a competent and careful driver.

(3) In determining for the purposes of subsection (2) above what would be expected of a careful and competent driver in a particular case, regard shall be had not only to the circumstances of which he could be expected to be aware but also to any circumstances shown to have been within the knowledge of the accused.

(4) A person is to be regarded as driving without reasonable consideration for other persons only if those persons are inconvenienced by his driving.

- Examples of careless or inconsiderate driving:
  Careless driving
  - overtaking on the inside or driving inappropriately close to another vehicle;
  - inadvertent mistakes, such as driving through a red light or emerging from a side road into the path of another vehicle;
  - short distractions such as tuning a car radio.

Inconsiderate driving

- flashing of lights to force other drivers in front to give way;
- misuse of any lane to avoid queuing or to gain some other advantage over other drivers;
- driving that inconveniences other road users or causes unnecessary hazards, such as unnecessarily remaining in an overtaking lane, unnecessarily slow driving or braking without good cause, driving with undipped headlights which dazzle oncoming drivers, or driving through a puddle causing pedestrians to be splashed.

- If death has resulted from the driving, any trial should await the conclusion of any inquest (*Smith v Director of Public Prosecutions* [2000] RTR 36).
- Failure to drive in accordance with the Highway Code will generally amount to careless driving.
- An offence of careless driving can be tried alongside an offence of dangerous driving as an alternative. However, it is not clear as to why this is done in the magistrates' court, as the offence is a statutory alternative in any event.
- If the facts are such that in the absence of an explanation put forward by the defendant, or where that explanation is objectively inadequate, the only possible conclusion is that he was careless, he should be convicted (*Director of Public Prosecutions v Cox* (1993) 157 JP 1044).
- A court does not need to consider an alternative inference from facts, such as mechanical defect, without hearing evidence of the same (*Director of Public Prosecutions v Tipton* (1992) 156 JP 172).

 See *Blackstone's Criminal Practice 2014* **C6.1–C6.8**

C13.2 Causing death by careless etc. driving

Road Traffic Act 1988, ss 2B and 3

Causing death by:

- careless or inconsiderate driving;
- unlicensed, disqualified, or uninsured drivers.

 5 years' imprisonment (2 years for unlicensed, disqualified, or uninsured), minimum disqualification of 12 months, discretionary re-test, 3–11 penalty points

C13.2.1 *Sentencing*

Death by careless or inconsiderate driving

Nature of offence	Starting point	Sentencing range
Careless or inconsiderate driving falling not far short of dangerous driving	15 months' custody	36 weeks to 3 years' custody
Other cases of careless or inconsiderate driving	36 weeks' custody	Community order (HIGH) to 2 years' custody
Careless or inconsiderate driving arising from momentary inattention with no aggravating factors	Community order (MEDIUM)	Community order (LOW) to Community order (HIGH)

Additional aggravating factors	Additional mitigating factors
1. Other offences committed at the same time, such as driving other than in accordance with the terms of a valid licence; driving while disqualified; driving without insurance; taking a vehicle without consent; driving a stolen vehicle 2. Previous convictions for motoring offences, particularly offences that involve bad driving 3. More than one person was killed as a result of the offence 4. Serious injury to one or more persons in addition to the death(s) 5. Irresponsible behaviour, such as failing to stop or falsely claiming that one of the victims was responsible for the collision	1. Offender was seriously injured in the collision 2. The victim was a close friend or relative 3. The actions of the victim or a third party contributed to the commission of the offence 4. The offender's lack of driving experience contributed significantly to the likelihood of a collision 5. The driving was in response to a proven and genuine emergency falling short of a defence

Causing death by unlicensed, disqualified, or uninsured drivers

Nature of offence	Starting point	Sentencing range
The offender was disqualified from driving; OR The offender was unlicensed or uninsured plus two or more aggravating factors from the list below	12 months' custody	36 weeks to 2 years' custody

The offender was unlicensed or uninsured plus at least one aggravating factor from the list below	26 weeks' custody	Community order (HIGH) to 36 weeks' custody
The offender was unlicensed or uninsured—no aggravating factors	Community order (MEDIUM)	Community order (LOW) to Community order (HIGH)

Additional aggravating factors	Additional mitigating factors
1. Previous convictions for motoring offences, whether involving bad driving or involving an offence of the same kind that forms part of the present conviction (ie unlicensed, disqualified, or uninsured driving) 2. More than one person was killed as a result of the offence 3. Serious injury to one or more persons in addition to the death(s) 4. Irresponsible behaviour such as failing to stop or falsely claiming that someone else was driving	1. The decision to drive was brought about by a proven and genuine emergency falling short of a defence 2. The offender genuinely believed that he or she was insured or licensed to drive 3. The offender was seriously injured as a result of the collision 4. The victim was a close friend or relative

C13.2.2 Key points

- Death must result from the act of driving.
- The driving must be more than a minimal cause of the death.
- It is not necessary that the driver be culpable or blameworthy in respect of an offence under section 3ZB. Where, therefore, a pedestrian walked in front of a vehicle and a collision occurred through no fault of the driver, a conviction would follow in the event that the driver was uninsured, disqualified, or driving otherwise than in accordance with a licence (*R v Williams* [2010] EWCA Crim 2552). However, notwithstanding *R v Williams*, *R v MH* [2011] EWCA Crim 1508 suggests it is open to the defence to argue that the defendant's contribution to the death was no more than minimal, for example in a stationary car or where the victim would have died anyway, say, because of a new act intervening.
- For an early sentencing decision in relation to this Act, see *R v Campbell* [2009] EWCA Crim 2459.
- See *R v Coe* [2009] EWCA Crim 1452 in relation to the admission of samples taken in relation to alcohol.

See *Blackstone's Criminal Practice 2014* **C3**

C13.3 Causing serious injury by dangerous driving

Road Traffic Act 1988, s 1A

1A Causing serious injury by dangerous driving

(1) A person who causes serious injury to another person by driving a mechanically propelled vehicle dangerously on a road or other public place is guilty of an offence.

(2) In this section 'serious injury' means— .

    (a) in England and Wales, physical harm which amounts to grievous bodily harm for the purposes of the Offences against the Person Act 1861,

    (b) ....

 6 months and/or level 5 fine/5 years

Obligatory disqualification for 12 months with obligatory re-test. If no disqualification then 3–11 penalty points.

C13.3.1 Key points

- Dangerous driving is defined by section 2A of the Road Traffic Act 1988. See **C13.4.2**.
- This provision applies to driving only on or after 3 December 2012.
- There is no specific sentencing guideline, but there have been decisions where there have been convictions under section 20 of the Offences Against the Person Act 1861.

 See *Blackstone's Criminal Practice 2014* **C3.33**

C13.4 Dangerous driving

Road Traffic Act 1988, s 2

2 Dangerous driving

A person who drives a mechanically propelled vehicle dangerously on a road or other public place is guilty of an offence.

 6 months and/or level 5 fine/2 years. Must endorse and disqualify for a minimum period of 12 months; must order extended re-test; must disqualify for at least 2 years if offender has had two or more disqualifications for periods of 56 days or more in preceding 3 years

C13.4.1 *Sentencing*

Offence seriousness (culpability and harm) A. Identify the appropriate starting point Starting points based on first-time offender pleading not guilty		
Example of nature of activity	**Starting point**	**Range**
Single incident where little or no damage or risk of personal injury	Medium level community order	Low level community order to high level community order Disqualify 12–15 months
Incident(s) involving excessive speed or showing off, especially on busy roads or in built-up area; OR Single incident where little or no damage or risk of personal injury but offender was disqualified driver	12 weeks' custody	High level community order to 26 weeks' custody Disqualify 15–24 months
Prolonged bad driving involving deliberate disregard for safety of others; OR Incident(s) involving excessive speed or showing off, especially on busy roads or in built-up area, by disqualified driver; OR Driving as described in box above while being pursued by police	Crown Court	Crown Court

Offence seriousness (culpability and harm) B. Consider the effect of aggravating and mitigating factors (other than those within examples above) The following may be particularly relevant but these lists are not exhaustive	
Factors indicating higher culpability	**Factors indicating lower culpability**
1. Disregarding warnings of others 2. Evidence of alcohol or drugs 3. Carrying out other tasks while driving 4. Carrying passengers or heavy load 5. Tiredness 6. Aggressive driving, such as driving much too close to vehicle in front, racing, inappropriate attempts to overtake, or cutting in after overtaking 7. Driving when knowingly suffering from a medical condition which significantly impairs the offender's driving skills 8. Driving a poorly maintained or dangerously loaded vehicle, especially where motivated by commercial concerns **Factors indicating greater degree of harm** 1. Injury to others 2. Damage to other vehicles or property	1. Genuine emergency 2. Speed not excessive 3. Offence due to inexperience rather than irresponsibility of driver

C13.4.2 Key points

- The Road Traffic Act 1988, section 2A provides:

Road Traffic Act 1988, s 2A

2A Meaning of dangerous driving

(1) For the purposes of sections 1 and 2 above a person is to be regarded as driving dangerously if (and, subject to subsection (2) below, only if)—
   (a) the way he drives falls far below what would be expected of a competent and careful driver, and
   (b) it would be obvious to a competent and careful driver that driving in that way would be dangerous.

(2) A person is also to be regarded as driving dangerously for the purposes of sections 1 and 2 above if it would be obvious to a competent and careful driver that driving the vehicle in its current state would be dangerous.

(3) In subsections (1) and (2) above 'dangerous' refers to danger either of injury to any person or of serious damage to property; and in determining for the purposes of those subsections what would be expected of, or obvious to, a competent and careful driver in a particular case, regard shall be had not only to the circumstances of which he could be expected to be aware but also to any circumstances shown to have been within the knowledge of the accused.

(4) In determining for the purposes of subsection (2) above the state of a vehicle, regard may be had to anything attached to or carried on or in it and to the manner in which it is attached or carried.

- The special skill (or indeed lack of skill) of a driver is an irrelevant circumstance when considering whether the driving is dangerous (*R v Bannister* [2009] EWCA Crim 1571).
- The fact that the defendant had consumed alcohol is an admissible factor (*R v Webster* [2006] 2 Cr App R 103). Where drink is a major plank of the prosecution case, advocates should have regard to *R v McBride* [1962] 2 QB 167.
- Where a vehicle's dangerous state is due to its official design and not use, it will not usually be appropriate to prosecute (*R v Marchant* [2004] 1 All ER 1187).
- A vehicle is being driven in a dangerous state if the driver is aware that his ability to control the vehicle might be impaired such that the standard of his driving might fall below the requisite standard (*R v Marison* [1997] RTR 457).

 See *Blackstone's Criminal Practice 2014* **C3.39**

C13.5 Driving whilst disqualified

> ### Road Traffic Act 1988, s 103(1)
>
> **103 Obtaining licence, or driving, while disqualified**
> (1) A person is guilty of an offence if, while disqualified for holding or obtaining a licence, he—
>   (a) obtains a licence, or
>   (b) drives a motor vehicle on a road.
>
> . . .

SO

 6 months and/or level 5 fine. Must endorse and may disqualify. If no disqualification, impose 6 points

C13.5.1 *Sentencing*

Offence seriousness (culpability and harm) A. Identify the appropriate starting point Starting points based on first-time offender pleading not guilty		
Example of nature of activity	**Starting point**	**Range**
Full period expired but re-test not taken	Low level community order	Band C fine to medium level community order 6 points or disqualify for 3–6 months
Lengthy period of ban already served	High level community order	Medium level community order to 12 weeks custody Lengthen disqualification for 6–12 months beyond expiry of current ban
Recently imposed ban	12 weeks' custody	High level community order to 26 weeks' custody Lengthen disqualification for 12–18 months beyond expiry of current ban

C13.5.2 Key points

- The prosecution do not need to prove that the defendant was aware of the prosecution that led to his being disqualified (*Taylor v Kenyon* [1952] 2 All ER 726); this is the case even where a driving licence has been returned to the defendant by mistake (*R v Bowsher* [1972] RTR 202). If the defendant was genuinely unaware of the disqualification and had no reason to anticipate one, prosecution is unlikely and an absolute discharge likely if one proceeds.
- Strict proof that the person disqualified by the court is the person now charged is required. This will normally arise from (a) admission, (b) fingerprints, (c) evidence of identity from someone in court when the disqualification was made (*R v Derwentside Justices, ex p Heaviside* [1996] RTR 384). Other evidence such as an unusual name will at least raise a prima facie case that the defendant will need to answer in order to avoid conviction (*Olakunori v Director of Public Prosecutions* [1998] COD 443).
- An admission made whilst giving evidence is sufficient to prove a disqualification, even in the absence of a certificate of conviction (*Moran v Crown Prosecution Service* (2000) 164 JP 562).
- A defendant's silence in interview (where he did not later rely on any fact) and his general attitude to the management of the case in accordance with the Criminal Procedure Rules, could not provide sufficient proof (*Mills v Director of Public Prosecutions* [2008] EWHC 3304 (Admin)).
- Consistency of personal details will normally be sufficient to raise a prima facie case. If the defendant calls no evidence to contradict that prima facie case, it will be open to the court to be satisfied that identity is proved (*Pattison v Director of Public Prosecutions* [2006] RTR 13).
- A solicitor could be called as a witness to confirm identity, although the practice is discouraged (*R (Howe) v South Durham Magistrates' Court* [2005] RTR 4).
- A mistaken belief by the defendant that he was not driving on a road will not amount to a defence (*R v Miller* [1975] 1 WLR 1222).
- The fact that a disqualification was later quashed on appeal does not provide a defence (*R v Thames Magistrates' Court, ex p Levy* The Times, 17 July 1997).
- A bad character application in relation to the disqualification is not necessary as it has to do with the facts of the alleged offence (Criminal Justice Act 2003, s 98) (*Director of Public Prosecutions v Agyemang* [2009] EWHC 1542 (Admin)).

 See *Blackstone's Criminal Practice 2014* **C6.40–C6.45**

C13.6 **Excess alcohol**

Road Traffic Act 1988, s 5(1)

5 Driving or being in charge of a motor vehicle with alcohol concentration above prescribed limit

(1) If a person—
  (a) drives or attempts to drive a motor vehicle on a road or other public place, or
  (b) is in charge of a motor vehicle on a road or other public place,
  after consuming so much alcohol that the proportion of it in his breath, blood, or urine exceeds the prescribed limit he is guilty of an offence.

SO

For driving 6 months and/or level 5. Must endorse and disqualify for at least 12 months. Must disqualify for at least 2 years if offender has had two or more disqualifications for periods of 56 days or more in preceding 3 years. Must disqualify for at least 3 years if offender has been convicted of a relevant offence in preceding 10 years

See **C13.17.2** for offence of being in charge.

C13.6.1 *Sentencing: driving with excess alcohol*

See the following table.

Offence seriousness(culpability and harm)
A. Identify the appropriate starting point
Starting points based on first-time offender pleading not guilty

Level of alcohol			Starting point	Range	Disqualification	Disqual. 2nd offence in 10 years—see note above
Breath (mg)	Blood (ml)	Urine (ml)				
36–59	81–137	108–183	Band C fine	Band C fine	12–16 months	36–40 months
60–89	138–206	184–274	Band C fine	Band C fine	17–22 months	36–46 months
90–119	207–275	275–366	Medium level community order	Low level community order to high level community order	23–28 months	36–52 months
120–150 and above	276–345 and above	367–459 and above	12 weeks' custody	High level community order to 26 weeks' custody	29–36 months	36–60 months

Offence seriousness (culpability and harm)	
B. Consider the effect of aggravating and mitigating factors (other than those within examples above)	
The following may be particularly relevant but these lists are not exhaustive	
Factors indicating higher culpability	**Factors indicating lower culpability**
1. LGV, HGV PSV, etc	1. Genuine emergency established*
2. Poor road or weather conditions	2. Spiked drinks*
3. Carrying passengers	3. Very short distance driven*
4. Driving for hire or reward	
5. Evidence of unacceptable standard of driving	
Factors indicating greater degree of harm	
1. Involved in accident	
2. Location, eg near school	
3. High level of traffic or pedestrians in the vicinity	

* even where not amounting to special reasons

C13.6.2 *Sentencing: in-charge*

 3 months and/or level 4 fine. Must endorse and may disqualify. If no disqualification, impose 10 points

Offence seriousness (culpability and harm)				
A. Identify the appropriate starting point				
Starting points based on first-time offender pleading not guilty				
Level of alcohol				
Breath (mg)	Blood (ml)	Urine (ml)	Starting point	Range
36–59	81–137	108–183	Band B fine	Band B fine 10 points
60–89	138–206	184–274	Band B fine	Band B fine 10 points OR consider disqualification
90–119	207–275	275–366	Band C fine	Band C fine to medium level community order Consider disqualification up to 6 months OR 10 points
120–150 and above	276–345 and above	367–459 and above	Medium level community order	Low level community order to 6 weeks' custody Disqualify 6–12 months

Offence seriousness (culpability and harm)	
B. Consider the effect of aggravating and mitigating factors (other than those within examples above)	
The following may be particularly relevant but these lists are not exhaustive	
Factors indicating higher culpability	**Factor indicating lower culpability**
1. LGV, HGV, PSV, etc	1. Low likelihood of driving
2. Ability to drive seriously impaired	
3. High likelihood of driving	
4. Driving for hire or reward	

C13.6.3 Key points

• Section 5(2)–(3) provides:

Road Traffic Act 1988, s 5(2)–(3)

5 Driving or being in charge of a motor vehicle with alcohol concentration above prescribed limit

(2) It is a defence for a person charged with an offence under subsection (1)(b) above to prove that at the time he is alleged to have committed the offence the circumstances were such that there was no likelihood of his driving the vehicle whilst the proportion of alcohol in his breath, blood or urine remained likely to exceed the prescribed limit.

(3) The court may, in determining whether there was such a likelihood as is mentioned in subsection (2) above, disregard any injury to him and any damage to the vehicle.

• The burden of proof falls on the defendant (*Sheldrake v Director of Public Prosecutions* [2005] RTR 2).

• Duress is available as a defence. The defence will be available only for as long as the threat is active and a sober and reasonable person would have driven (*Crown Prosecution Service v Brown* [2007] EWHC 3274 (Admin)).

• Automatism is available as a defence.

• Where there has been no consumption of alcohol between the incidence of driving and the testing, the alcohol reading is conclusive (Road Traffic Offences Act 1988, s 15(2), and *Griffiths v Director of Public Prosecutions* [2002] EWHC 792 (Admin)). However, the presumption in section 15(2) applies only to trials and does not extend to a *Newton* hearing (*Goldsmith v Director of Public Prosecutions* [2009] EWHC 3010 (Admin)).

• Where there is post-driving consumption of alcohol, the defendant is able to 'back calculate' to obtain a reading at the time of driving (Road Traffic Offences Act 1988, s 15(3)). The prosecution are also entitled to rely upon back calculations, but in practice rarely do so (*Gumbley v Cunningham* [1989] RTR 49).

- There will be no prosecution unless the alcohol level is at least 40 microgrammes (Home Office Circular 46/1982); it should be noted that this 'allowance' is already built into any blood or urine analysis.

 See *Blackstone's Criminal Practice 2014* **C5.57**

C13.7 Fail to give information of driver's identity as required

Road Traffic Act 1988, s 172

(1) This section applies—
    (a) to any offence under the preceding provisions of this Act except—
        (i) an offence under Part V, or
        (ii) an offence under section 13, 16, 51(2), 61(4), 67(9), 68(4), 96 or 120, and to an offence under section 178 of this Act,
    (b) to any offence under sections 25, 26 or 27 of the Road Traffic Offenders Act 1988,
    (c) to any offence against any other enactment relating to the use of vehicles on roads, and
    (d) to manslaughter, or in Scotland culpable homicide, by the driver of a motor vehicle.
(2) Where the driver of a vehicle is alleged to be guilty of an offence to which this section applies—
    (a) the person keeping the vehicle shall give such information as to the identity of the driver as he may be required to give by or on behalf of a chief officer of police, and
    (b) any other person shall if required as stated above give any information which it is in his power to give and may lead to identification of the driver.
(3) Subject to the following provisions, a person who fails to comply with a requirement under subsection (2) above shall be guilty of an offence.
(4) …
(5) Where a body corporate is guilty of an offence under this section and the offence is proved to have been committed with the consent or connivance of, or to be attributable to neglect on the part of, a director, manager, secretary or other similar officer of the body corporate, or a person who was purporting to act in any such capacity, he, as well as the body corporate, is guilty of that offence and liable to be proceeded against and punished accordingly.
(6) Where the alleged offender is a body corporate, or in Scotland a partnership or an unincorporated association, or the proceedings are brought against him by virtue of subsection (5) above or subsection (11) below, subsection (4) above shall not apply unless, in addition to the matters there mentioned, the alleged offender shows that no record was kept of the persons who drove the vehicle and that the failure to keep a record was reasonable.

(7) A requirement under subsection (2) may be made by written notice served by post; and where it is so made—

(a) it shall have effect as a requirement to give the information within the period of 28 days beginning with the day on which the notice is served, and

(b) the person on whom the notice is served shall not be guilty of an offence under this section if he shows either that he gave the information as soon as reasonably practicable after the end of that period or that it has not been reasonably practicable for him to give it.

(8) Where the person on whom a notice under subsection (7) above is to be served is a body corporate, the notice is duly served if it is served on the secretary or clerk of that body.

(9) For the purposes of section 7 of the Interpretation Act 1978 as it applies for the purposes of this section the proper address of any person in relation to the service on him of a notice under subsection (7) above is—

(a) in the case of the secretary or clerk of a body corporate, that of the registered or principal office of that body or (if the body corporate is the registered keeper of the vehicle concerned) the registered address, and

(b) in any other case, his last known address at the time of service.

(10) In this section—

'registered address', in relation to the registered keeper of a vehicle, means the address recorded in the record kept under the Vehicles Excise and Registration Act 1994 with respect to that vehicle as being that person's address, and

'registered keeper', in relation to a vehicle, means the person in whose name the vehicle is registered under that Act;

and references to the driver of a vehicle include references to the rider of a cycle.

SO 6 points (no endorsement for limited companies)

C13.7.1 Key points

- Section 172(4) provides:

Road Traffic Act 1988, s 172(4)

172 Duty to give information as to identity of driver etc in certain circumstances

(4) A person shall not be guilty of an offence by virtue of paragraph (a) of subsection (2) above if he shows that he did not know and could not with reasonable diligence have ascertained who the driver of the vehicle was.

- In *Duff v Director of Public Prosecutions* [2009] EWHC 675 (Admin), D's wife was served with a notice under section 172 of the Road Traffic Act 1988 requiring her to identify the name of the driver. D in fact replied to the notice, naming himself as the driver. As a result, a further section 172 notice was then served on D. Following legal advice, D did not respond to that notice and was subsequently convicted of failing to provide information. It was held that the conviction was sound, as the request to which he had in fact responded was a request of D's wife, not D himself.

- A driver is to be judged in relation to section 172(4) by the actions he did or did not take only from the time of the police request to ascertain the identity of the driver, not before (*Atkinson v Director of Public Prosecutions* [2011] EWHC 3363 (Admin)).

- For the defences available under section 172(7)(b), see *Purnell v Snaresbrook Crown Court* [2011] EWHC 934 (Admin) and *Whiteside v Director of Public Prosecutions* [2011] EWHC 3471 (Admin)). *Whiteside* held that a lack of personal knowledge of the request was not itself a defence. But the defendant may be able to show that it was not reasonably practicable for him to have been aware of the notice and to provide the information sought.

- In *Thomson v Jackson* [2010] HCJAC 96, the Scottish High Court ruled that the police cannot make more than one request for information directed to the same person. It is doubted whether this decision would be followed by an English court, but it is a significant issue in relation to prosecutions being time-barred.

 See *Blackstone's Criminal Practice 2014* **C2.12**

C13.8 Fail to provide specimen for analysis

Road Traffic Act 1988, s 7(6) and (7)

7 Provision of specimens for analysis

(6) A person who, without reasonable excuse, fails to provide a specimen when required to do so in pursuance of this section is guilty of an offence.

(7) A constable must, on requiring any person to provide a specimen in pursuance of this section, warn him that a failure to provide it may render him liable to prosecution.

SO

EW Driving/attempting to drive: 6 months and/or level 5 fine. Must endorse and disqualify for at least 12 months. Must disqualify for at least 2 years if offender has had two or more disqualifications for periods of 56 days or more in preceding 3 years. Must disqualify for at least 3 years if offender has been convicted of a relevant offence in preceding 10 years

EW In-charge: 3 months and/or level 4 fine. Must endorse and may disqualify. If no disqualification, impose 10 points

C13.8.1 *Sentencing: driving or attempting to drive*

Offence seriousness (culpability and harm) A. Identify the appropriate starting point Starting points based on first-time offender pleading not guilty				
Examples of nature of activity	Starting point	Range	Disqual.	Disqual. 2nd offence in 10 years
Defendant refused test when had honestly held but unreasonable excuse	Band C fine	Band C fine	12–16 months	36–40 months
Deliberate refusal or deliberate failure	Low level community order	Band C fine to high level community order	17–28 months	36–52 months
Deliberate refusal or deliberate failure where evidence of serious impairment	12 weeks' custody	High level community order to 26 weeks' custody	29–36 months	36–60 months

Offence seriousness (culpability and harm) B. Consider the effect of aggravating and mitigating factors (other than those within examples above) The following may be particularly relevant but these lists are not exhaustive	
Factors indicating higher culpability 1. Evidence of unacceptable standard of driving 2. LGV, HGV, PSV, etc 3. Obvious state of intoxication 4. Driving for hire or reward **Factor indicating greater degree of harm** 1. Involved in accident	**Factor indicating lower culpability** 1. Genuine but unsuccessful attempt to provide specimen

C13.8.2 *Sentencing: in-charge*

Offence seriousness (culpability and harm) A. Identify appropriate starting point Starting points based on first-time offender pleading not guilty		
Examples of nature of activity	Starting point	Range
Defendant refused test when had honestly held but unreasonable excuse	Band B fine	Band B fine 10 points

Deliberate refusal or deliberate failure	Band C fine	Band C fine to medium level community order Consider disqualification OR 10 points
Deliberate refusal or deliberate failure where evidence of serious impairment	Medium level community order	Low level community order to 6 weeks custody Disqualify 6–12 months

Offence seriousness (culpability and harm) **B. Consider the effect of aggravating and mitigating factors (other than those within examples above)** The following may be particularly relevant but these lists are not exhaustive	
Factors indicating higher culpability 1. Obvious state of intoxication 2. LGV, HGV, PSV, etc 3. High likelihood of driving 4. Driving for hire of reward	**Factors indicating lower culpability** 1. Genuine but unsuccessful attempt to provide specimen 2. Low likelihood of driving

C13.8.3 Key points

- A reasonable excuse for failing to provide must relate to inability due to physical or mental issues (*R v Lennard* [1973] RTR 252).
- The suspect need not in fact be the driver if relevant investigation is being conducted by the police.
- Failure to mention a medical reason at the time of refusal does not preclude a court from finding that a reasonable excuse existed, although it was a factor to be taken into account (*Piggott v Director of Public Prosecutions* [2008] RTR 16).
- Once a reasonable excuse is raised, it is for the prosecution to disprove it (*McKeon v Director of Public Prosecutions* [2008] RTR 14).
- A failure to understand the statutory warning relating to prosecution may amount to a reasonable excuse if the accused's understanding of English is poor (*Chief Constable of Avon and Somerset v Singh* [1988] RTR 107); but if an accredited interpreter is present there is an (rebuttable) inference that the warning was understood (*Bielecki v DPP* [2011] EWHC 2245 (Admin)). Failure to understand due to intoxication will not suffice.
- The taking of a specimen does not have to be delayed (over and above a couple of minutes) for the purpose of taking legal advice (*R v Gearing* [2008] EWHC 1695 (Admin)).

See *Blackstone's Criminal Practice 2014* **C5.9**

C13.9 Fail to stop/report road accident

Road Traffic Act 1988, s 170

170 Duty of driver to stop, report accident and give information or documents

(1) This section applies in a case where, owing to the presence of a mechanically propelled vehicle on a road or other public place, an accident occurs by which—

    (a) personal injury is caused to a person other than the driver of that mechanically propelled vehicle, or

    (b) damage is caused—

        (i) to a vehicle other than that mechanically propelled vehicle or a trailer drawn by that mechanically propelled vehicle, or

        (ii) to an animal other than an animal in or on that mechanically propelled vehicle or a trailer drawn by that mechanically propelled vehicle, or

        (iii) to any other property constructed on, fixed to, growing in or otherwise forming part of the land on which the road or place in question is situated or land adjacent to such land.

(2) The driver of the mechanically propelled vehicle must stop and, if required to do so by any person having reasonable grounds for so requiring, give his name and address and also the name and address of the owner and the identification marks of the vehicle.

(3) If for any reason the driver of the mechanically propelled vehicle does not give his name and address under subsection (2) above, he must report the accident.

(4) A person who fails to comply with subsection (2) or (3) above is guilty of an offence.

(5) If, in a case where this section applies by virtue of subsection (1)(a) above, the driver of a motor vehicle does not at the time of the accident produce such a certificate of insurance or security, or other evidence, as is mentioned in section 165(2)(a) of this Act—

    (a) to a constable, or

    (b) to some person who, having reasonable grounds for so doing, has required him to produce it,

the driver must report the accident and produce such a certificate or other evidence.

    This subsection does not apply to the driver of an invalid carriage.

(6) To comply with a duty under this section to report an accident or to produce such a certificate of insurance or security, or other evidence, as is mentioned in section 165(2)(a) of this Act, the driver—

    (a) must do so at a police station or to a constable, and

    (b) must do so as soon as is reasonably practicable and, in any case, within twenty-four hours of the occurrence of the accident.

(7) A person who fails to comply with a duty under subsection (5) above is guilty of an offence, but he shall not be convicted by reason only of a failure to produce a certificate or other evidence if, within seven days after the

occurrence of the accident, the certificate or other evidence is produced at a police station that was specified by him at the time when the accident was reported.

(8) In this section 'animal' means horse, cattle, ass, mule, sheep, pig, goat or dog.

EW 6 months and/or level 5 fine. Must endorse and may disqualify. If no disqualification, impose 5–10 points

C13.9.1 *Sentencing*

Offence seriousness (culpability and harm)		
A. Identify the appropriate starting point		
Starting points based on first-time offender pleading not guilty		
Examples of nature of activity	**Starting point**	**Range**
Minor damage/injury or stopped at scene but failed to exchange particulars or report	Band B fine	Band B fine 5–6 points
Moderate damage/injury or failed to stop and failed to report	Band C fine	Band C fine 7–8 points Consider disqualification
Serious damage/injury and/or evidence of bad driving	High level community order	Band C fine to 26 weeks custody Disqualify 6–12 months OR 9–10 points

Offence seriousness (culpability and harm)	
B. Consider the effect of aggravating and mitigating factors (other than those within examples above)	
The following may be particularly relevant but these lists are not exhaustive	
Factors indicating higher culpability	**Factors indicating lower culpability**
1. Evidence of drink or drugs/evasion of test 2. Knowledge/suspicion that personal injury caused (where not an element of the offence) 3. Leaving injured party at scene 4. Giving false details	1. Believed identity known 2. Genuine fear of retribution 3. Subsequently reported

C.13.9.2 <mark>Key points</mark>

A driver who is unaware of the accident cannot commit an offence under these provisons (*Harding v Price* [1948] 1 KB 695); but if he later becomes aware of the accident, he must report it personally if he becomes aware within 24 hours (*DPP v Drury* [1989] RTR 165).

 See *Blackstone's Criminal Practice 2014* **C6.51–C6.55**

C13.10 **No insurance, using, causing, or permitting**

Road Traffic Act 1988, s 143

SO

EW Fine level 5/discretionary disqualification/6–8 penalty points

C13.10.1 *Sentencing*

Offence seriousness (culpability and harm) A. Identify the appropriate starting point Starting points based on first-time offender pleading not guilty		
Examples of nature of activity	**Starting point**	**Range**
Using a motor vehicle on a road or other public place without insurance	Band C fine	Band C fine 6 points to 12 months' disqualification—see notes below

Offence seriousness (culpability and harm)
B. Consider the effect of aggravating and mitigating factors
(other than those within examples above)
The following may be particularly relevant but these lists are not exhaustive

Factors indicating higher culpability	**Factors indicating lower culpability**
1. Never passed test	1. Responsibility for providing insurance rests with another
2. Gave false details	
3. Driving LGV, HGV, PSV, etc	2. Genuine misunderstanding
4. Driving for hire or reward	3. Recent failure to renew or failure to transfer vehicle details where insurance was in existence
5. Evidence of sustained uninsured use	
Factors indicating greater degree of harm	
1. Involved in accident	4. Vehicle not being driven
2. Accident resulting in injury	

C13.10.2 Key points

- See **C12** for definitions.
- Proceedings may be brought within six months of a prosecutor forming the opinion that there is sufficient evidence of an offence having been committed (subject to an overall three-year time bar).
- It is for a defendant to show that he was insured, once it is established that a motor vehicle was used on a road or other public place.
- It is not necessary that the vehicle be capable of being driven (*Pumbien v Vines* [1996] RTR 37).
- Employed drivers have the following defence available to them:

Road Traffic Act 1988, s 143(3)

143 Users of motor vehicles to be insured or secured against third-party risks

(3) A person charged with using a motor vehicle in contravention of this section shall not be convicted if he proves—

   (a) that the vehicle did not belong to him and was not in his possession under a contract of hiring or of loan,

   (b) that he was using the vehicle in the course of his employment, and

   (c) that he neither knew nor had reason to believe that there was not in force in relation to the vehicle such a policy of insurance or security as is mentioned in subsection (1) above.

 See *Blackstone's Criminal Practice 2014* **C6.46–C6.51**

C13.11 Motorway offences

Offence	Maximum	Points	Starting point	Special considerations
Drive in reverse or wrong way on slip road	L4	3	B	
Drive in reverse or wrong way on motorway	L4	3	C	
Drive off carriageway (central reservation or hard shoulder)	L4	3	B	
Make U turn	L4	3	C	
Learner driver or excluded vehicle	L4	3	B	
Stop on hard shoulder	L4	–	A	
Vehicle in prohibited lane	L4	3	A	
Walk on motorway, slip road, or hard shoulder	L4	–	A	

C13.12 Offences concerning the driver

Offence	Maximum	Points	Starting point	Special considerations
Fail to cooperate with preliminary (roadside) breath test	L3	4	B	
Fail to give information of driver's identity as required	L3	6	C	For limited companies, endorsement is not available; a fine is the only available penalty
Fail to produce insurance certificate	L4	–	A	Fine per offence, not per document
Fail to produce test certificate	L3	–	A	
Drive otherwise than in accordance with licence (where could be covered)	L3	–	A	
Drive otherwise than in accordance with licence	L3	3–6	A	Aggravating factor if no licence ever held

 See *Blackstone's Criminal Practice 2014* **C6**

C13.13 Offences concerning the vehicle

The guidelines for some of the offences below differentiate between three types of offender when the offence is committed in the course of business: driver, owner-driver, and owner-company. For owner-driver, the starting point is the same as for driver; however, the court should consider an uplift of at least 25 per cent.

Offence	Maximum	Points	Starting point	Special considerations
No excise licence	L3 or 5 times annual duty, whichever is greater	–	A (1–3 months unpaid) B (4–6 months unpaid) C (7–12 months unpaid)	Add duty lost

Fail to notify change of ownership to DVLA	L3	–	A	If offence committed in course of business: A (driver) A* (owner-driver) B (owner-company)
No test certificate	L3	–	A	If offence committed in course of business: A (driver) A* (owner-driver) B (owner-company)
Brakes defective. Key points: It is sufficient only to prove that any part of the braking system is defective (*Kennett v British Airports Authority* [1975] Crim LR 106). The fact that everything possible (eg servicing) has been done in order to ensure that the vehicle is in good condition does not amount to a defence (*Hawkins v Holmes* [1974] RTR 436), as maintenance of the braking system is an absolute obligation on the driver (*Green v Burnett* [1954] 3 All ER 273).	L4	3	B	If offence committed in course of business: B (driver) B* (owner-driver) C (owner-company) L5 if goods vehicle
Steering defective	L4	3	B	If offence committed in course of business: B (driver) B* (owner-driver) C (owner-company) L5 if goods vehicle

Tyres defective. It is a defence if the vehicle is not being used and there was no intention to use when the tyres were defective, regardless of the fact that the vehicle was on a road (*Eden v Mitchell* [1975] RTR 425). There is no requirement for the prosecution to have had the tyre examined by an authorized examiner as the issue was a simple question of fact (*Phillips v Thomas* [1974] RTR 28).	L4	3	B	If offence committed in course of business: B (driver) B* (owner-driver) C (owner-company) L5 if goods vehicle Penalty per tyre
Condition of vehicle/accessories/ equipment involving danger of injury (Road Traffic Act 1988, s 40A)	L4	3	B	Must disqualify for at least 6 months if offender has one or more previous convictions for same offence within 3 years If offence committed in course of business: B (driver) B* (owner-driver) C (owner-company) L5 if goods vehicle
Exhaust defective	L3	–	A	If offence committed in course of business: A (driver) A* (owner-driver) B (owner-company)
Lights defective	L3	–	A	If offence committed in course of business: A (driver) A* (owner-driver) B (owner-company)

See *Blackstone's Criminal Practice 2014* **C6**

C13.14 Offences concerning use of the vehicle

The guidelines for some of the offences below differentiate between three types of offender when the offence is committed in the course of business: driver, owner-driver, and owner-company. For owner-driver, the starting point is the same as for driver; however, the court should consider an uplift of at least 25 per cent.

Offence	Maximum	Points	Starting point	Special considerations
Weight, position, or distribution of load or manner in which load secured involving danger of injury (Road Traffic Act 1988, s 40A). Many cases involve unsecured passengers on the back of vehicles which is objectively often viewed as involving danger of injury (eg *Gray v Director of Public Prosecutions* [1999] RTR 339)	L4	3	B	Must disqualify for at least 6 months if offender has one or more previous convictions for same offence within 3 years If offence committed in course of business: A (driver) A* (owner-driver) B (owner-company) L5 if goods vehicle
Number of passengers or way carried involving danger of injury (Road Traffic Act 1988, s 40A)	L4	3	B	If offence committed in course of business: A (driver) A* (owner-driver) B (owner-company) L5 if goods vehicle
Position or manner in which load secured (not involving danger) (Road Traffic Act 1988, s 42)	L3		A	L4 if goods vehicle

See *Blackstone's Criminal Practice 2014* **C6**

C13.15 Offences re buses/goods vehicles over 3.5 tonnes (GVW)

Offence	Maximum	Points	Starting point	Special considerations
No goods vehicle plating certificate	L3		A (driver) A* (owner-driver) B (owner-company)	
No goods vehicle test certificate	L4		B (driver) B* (owner-driver) C (owner-company)	
Brakes defective	L5	3	B (driver) B* (owner-driver) C (owner-company)	
Steering defective	L5	3	B (driver) B* (owner-driver) C (owner-company)	
Tyres defective	L5	3	B (driver) B* (owner-driver) C (owner-company)	Penalty per tyre
Exhaust emission	L4		B (driver) B* (owner-driver) C (owner-company)	
Condition of vehicle/accessories/equipment involving danger of injury (Road Traffic Act 1988, s 40A)	L5	3	B (driver) B* (owner-driver) C (owner-company)	Must disqualify for at least 6 months if offender has one or more previous convictions for same offence within 3 years
Number of passengers or way carried involving danger of injury (Road Traffic Act 1988, s 40A)	L5	3	B (driver) B* (owner-driver) C (owner-company)	Must disqualify for at least 6 months if offender has one or more previous convictions for same offence within 3 years
Weight, position, or distribution of load or manner in which load secured involving danger of injury (Road Traffic Act 1988, s 40A)	L5	3	B (driver) B* (owner-driver) C (owner-company)	Must disqualify for at least 6 months if offender has one or more previous convictions for same offence within 3 years

Position or manner in which load secured (not involving danger) (Road Traffic Act 1988, s 42)	L4	–	B (driver) B*(owner-driver) C (owner-company)	
Overloading/ exceeding axle weight	L5	–	B (driver) B* (owner-driver) C (owner-company)	Starting points cater for cases where the over-load is up to and including 10%. Thereafter, 10% should be added to the penalty for each additional 1% of overload. Penalty per axle
No operator's licence	L4		B (driver) B* (owner-driver) C (owner-company)	
Speed limiter not used or incorrectly calibrated	L4		B (driver) B* (owner-driver) C (owner-company)	
Tachograph not used/not working	L5		B (driver) B* (owner-driver) C (owner-company)	
Exceed permitted driving time/ periods of duty	L4		B (driver) B* (owner-driver) C (owner-company)	
Fail to keep/return written record sheets	L4		B (driver) B* (owner-driver) C (owner-company)	
Falsify or alter records with intent to deceive	L5/2 years		B (driver) B* (owner-driver) C (owner-company)	Either-way offence

C13.16 Speeding

Road Traffic Regulation Act 1984, s 89(1)

SO Level 3 fine (level 4 if motorway)

C13.16.1 *Sentencing*

Offence seriousness (culpability and harm) A. Identify the appropriate starting point Starting points based on first-time offender pleading not guilty			
Speed limit (mph)	**Recorded speed (mph)**		
20	21–30	31–40	41–50
30	31–40	41–50	51–60
40	41–55	56–65	66–75
50	51–65	66–75	76–85
60	61–80	81–90	91–100
70	71–90	91–100	101–110
Starting point	Band A fine	Band B fine	Band B fine
Range	Band A fine	Band B fine	Band B fine
Points/disqualification	3 points	4–6 points OR Disqualify 7–28 days	Disqualify 7–56 days OR 6 points

Offence seriousness (culpability and harm) B. Consider the effect of aggravating and mitigating factors (other than those within examples above) The following may be particularly relevant but these lists are not exhaustive	
Factors indicating higher culpability 1. Poor road or weather conditions 2. LGV, HGV, PSV, etc 3. Towing caravan/trailer 4. Carrying passengers or heavy load 5. Driving for hire or reward 6. Evidence of unacceptable standard of driving over and above speed **Factors indicating greater degree of harm** 1. Location, eg near school 2. High level of traffic or pedestrians in the vicinity	**Factor indicating lower culpability** 1. Genuine emergency established

C13.16.2 Key points

- Necessity is available as a defence (*Moss v Howdle* 1997 SLT 782).
- Check that a notice of intended prosecution has been served in time.
- Save where the road is a restricted road, there needs to be signage in accordance with the regulations. A failure to provide adequate signage is fatal to any conviction. In *Jones v Director of Public Prosecutions* [2011] EWHC 50 (Admin), the court held that the relevant question to be answered by the court was:

  Whether by the point on the road where the alleged offence took place (the point of enforcement) the driver by reference to the route taken thereto has been given (or drivers generally have been given) adequate guidance of the speed limit to be observed at that point on the road by the signs on the relevant part of parts of the road *in so far as (and thus to the extent that) those traffic signs comply with the 2002 Regulations?*

- In relation to restricted roads (where a 30 mph speed limit applies) there must be a system of street lighting not more than 200 yards apart. If this matter is put in issue (but not otherwise), the prosecution must establish this beyond reasonable doubt.
- The 200-yard rule relates to a 'system of street lighting', so some lights may be more than 200 yards apart, it being a question of fact whether the 'system of lighting' as a whole complies. In *Briere v Hailstone* (1968) 112 SJ 767, a conviction was upheld even though 50 per cent of the lamps were incorrectly distanced. Similarly, the fact that one lamp was in disrepair did not affect a conviction (*Spittle v Kent County Constabulary* [1985] Crim LR 744).

 See *Blackstone's Criminal Practice 2014* **C6.58–C6.62**

C13.17 Unfit through drink or drugs

Road Traffic Act 1988, s 4(1), (2), and (5)

4 Driving, or being in charge, when under influence of drink or drugs

(1) A person who, when driving or attempting to drive a mechanically propelled vehicle on a road or other public place, is unfit to drive through drink or drugs is guilty of an offence.

(2) Without prejudice to subsection (1) above, a person who, when in charge of a mechanically propelled vehicle which is on a road or other public place, is unfit to drive through drink or drugs is guilty of an offence.

…

(5) For the purposes of this section, a person shall be taken to be unfit to drive if his ability to drive properly is for the time being impaired.

C13 Road Traffic Offences

EW Drive/attempt to drive: 6 months and/or level 5 fine. Must endorse and disqualify for at least 12 months. Must disqualify for at least 2 years if offender has had two or more disqualifications for periods of 56 days or more in preceding years

Must disqualify for at least 3 years if offender has been convicted of a relevant offence in preceding 10 years

EW In-charge: 3 months and/or level 4 fine. Must endorse and may disqualify. If no disqualification, impose 10 points

C13.17.1 *Sentencing: driving or attempting to drive*

Offence seriousness (culpability and harm) A. Identify the appropriate starting point Starting points based on first-time offender pleading not guilty				
Examples of nature of activity	**Starting point**	**Range**	**Disqual.**	**Disqual. 2nd offence in 10 years**
Evidence of moderate level of impairment and no aggravating factors	Band C fine	Band C fine	12–16 months	36–40 months
Evidence of moderate level of impairment and presence of one or more aggravating factors listed below	Band C fine	Band C fine	17–22 months	36–46 months
Evidence of high level of impairment and no aggravating factors	Medium level community order	Low level Community order to high level community order	23–28 months	36–52 months
Evidence of high level of impairment and presence of one or more aggravating factors listed below	12 weeks' custody	High level Community order to 26 weeks' custody	29–36 months	36–60 months

Offence seriousness (culpability and harm)	
B. Consider the effect of aggravating and mitigating factors	
(other than those within examples above)	
The following may be particularly relevant but these lists are not exhaustive	
Factors indicating higher culpability	**Factors indicating lower culpability**
1. LGV, HGV, PSV, etc	1. Genuine emergency established*
2. Poor road or weather conditions	2. Spiked drinks*
3. Carrying passengers	3. Very short distance driven*
4. Driving for hire or reward	* even where not amounting to special
5. Evidence of unacceptable standard of driving	reasons
Factors indicating greater degree of harm	
1. Involved in accident	
2. Location, eg near school	
3. High level of traffic or pedestrians in the vicinity	

C13.17.2 *Sentencing: in-charge*

Offence seriousness (culpability and harm)		
A. Identify the appropriate starting point		
Starting points based on first-time offender pleading not guilty		
Examples of nature of activity	**Starting point**	**Range**
Evidence of moderate level of impairment and no aggravating factors	Band B fine	Band B fine 10 points
Evidence of moderate level of impairment and presence of one or more aggravating factors listed below	Band B fine	Band B fine 10 points or consider disqualification
Evidence of high level of impairment and no aggravating factors	Band C fine	Band C fine to medium level community order 10 points OR consider disqualification
Evidence of high level of impairment and presence of one or more aggravating factors listed below	High level community order	Medium level community order to 12 weeks' custody Consider disqualification OR 10 points

Offence seriousness (culpability and harm)	
B. Consider the effect of aggravating and mitigating factors (other than those within examples above)	
The following may be particularly relevant but these lists are not exhaustive	
Factors indicating higher culpability	**Factor indicating lower culpability**
1. LGV, HGV, PSV, etc	1. Low likelihood of driving
2. High likelihood of driving	
3. Driving for hire or reward	

C13.17.3 Key points

- No likelihood of driving whilst unfit provides a defence in law to the in-charge offence. Section 4(3) and (4) of the Road Traffic Act 1988 provides:

Road Traffic Act 1988, s 4(3) and (4)

4 Driving, or being in charge, when under influence of drink or drugs

(3) For the purposes of subsection (2) above, a person shall be deemed not to have been in charge of a mechanically propelled vehicle if he proves that at the material time the circumstances were such that there was no likelihood of his driving it so long as he remained unfit to drive through drink or drugs.

(4) The court may, in determining whether there was such a likelihood as is mentioned in subsection (3) above, disregard any injury to him and any damage to the vehicle.

- Drugs include normal medicines.
- Evidence of impairment to drive may be provided by both expert and lay witnesses. Note, however, that a lay witness can give evidence as to a person's demeanour (and how much he drank, for example) but not on the ultimate question of whether the person was 'fit' to drive.
- The results of any evidential specimens are admissible (Road Traffic Offenders Act 1988, ss 15 and 16).

 See *Blackstone's Criminal Practice 2014* **C5.57**

C14 **Sexual Offences**

C14.1 Child prostitution and pornography

Sexual Offences Act 2003, ss 48, 49, and 50

 6 months and/or level 5 fine/14 years

C14.1.1 *Sentencing*

Offence seriousness (culpability and harm)
A. Identify the appropriate starting point
Starting points based on first-time offender pleading not guilty

These offences should normally be dealt with in the Crown Court.
However, there may be rare cases of non-penetrative activity involving a victim aged 16 or 17 where the offender's involvement is minimal and not perpetrated for gain in which a custodial sentence within the jurisdiction of a magistrates' court may be appropriate.

Offence seriousness (culpability and harm)
B. Consider the effect of aggravating and mitigating factors
The following may be particularly relevant but these lists are not exhaustive

Factors indicating higher culpability	**Factor indicating lower culpability**
1. Background of threats or intimidation	1. Offender also being controlled in prostitution or pornography and subject to threats or intimidation
2. Large-scale commercial operation	
3. Use of drugs, alcohol, or other substance to secure the victim's compliance	
4. Forcing a victim to violate another person	
5. Abduction or detention	
6. Threats to prevent the victim reporting the activity	
7. Threats to disclose victim's activity to friends/relatives	
8. Image distributed to other children or persons known to the victim	
9. Financial or other gain	
Factors indicating greater degree of harm	
1. Induced dependency on drugs	

C14 Sexual Offences

2. Victim has been manipulated into physical and emotional dependence on the offender 3. Storing, making available, or distributing images in such a way that they can be inadvertently accessed by others	

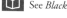 See *Blackstone's Criminal Practice 2014* **B3.221–B3.240**

C14.2 Exposure

Sexual Offences Act 2003, s 66(1)

66 Exposure

(1) A person commits an offence if—
  (a) he intentionally exposes his genitals, and
  (b) he intends that someone will see them and be caused alarm or distress.

EW

 6 months and/or level 5 fine/2 years

SO

C14.2.1 *Sentencing*

Offence seriousness (culpability and harm) A. Identify the appropriate starting point Starting points based on first-time offender pleading not guilty		
Examples of nature of activity	**Starting point**	**Range**
Basic offence as defined in the Act, assuming no aggravating or mitigating factors	Low level community order	Band B fine to medium level community order
Offence with an aggravating factor	Medium level community order	Low level community order to high level community order
Two or more aggravating factors	12 weeks' custody	6 weeks' custody to Crown Court

EW Either Way   Sentence   **SO** Summary Only

Offence seriousness (culpability and harm)
B. Consider the effect of aggravating and mitigating factors
(other than those within examples above)
The following may be particularly relevant but these lists are not exhaustive

Factors indicating higher culpability	
1. Threats to prevent the victim reporting an offence	
2. Intimidating behaviour/threats of violence	
Factor indicating greater degree of harm	
1. Victim is a child	

C14.2.2 Key points

- This offence is committed where an offender intentionally exposes his or her genitals and intends that someone will see them and be caused alarm or distress. It is gender neutral, covering exposure of male or female genitalia to a male or female witness.
- The Sentencing Guidelines Council guideline provides that when dealing with a repeat offender, the starting point should be 12 weeks' custody, with a range of four to 26 weeks' custody. The presence of aggravating factors may suggest that a sentence above the range is appropriate and that the case should be committed to the Crown Court.
- In accordance with section 80 of and Schedule 3 to the Sexual Offences Act 2003, automatic notification requirements apply upon conviction to an offender aged 18 or over where:
  - the victim was under 18; or
  - a term of imprisonment or a community sentence of at least 12 months is imposed.
- This guideline may be relevant by way of analogy to conduct charged as the common law offence of outraging public decency; the offence is triable either way and has a maximum penalty of a level 5 fine and/or 6 months' imprisonment when tried summarily.

 See *Blackstone's Criminal Practice 2014* **B3.295–B3.298**

C14.3 Indecent photographs of children

Protection of Children Act 1978, s 1(1)–(4)

1 Indecent photographs of children

(1) Subject to sections 1A and 1B, it is an offence for a person—
  (a) to take, or permit to be taken or to make, any indecent photograph or pseudo-photograph of a child; or

    (b) to distribute or show such indecent photographs or pseudo-photographs; or

    (c) to have in his possession such indecent photographs or pseudo-photographs, with a view to their being distributed or shown by himself or others; or

    (d) to publish or cause to be published any advertisement likely to be understood as conveying that the advertiser distributes or shows such indecent photographs or pseudo-photographs, or intends to do so.

(2) For purposes of this Act, a person is to be regarded as distributing an indecent photograph or pseudo-photograph if he parts with possession of it to, or exposes or offers it for acquisition by, another person.

(3) Proceedings for an offence under this Act shall not be instituted except by or with the consent of the Director of Public Prosecutions.

(4) Where a person is charged with an offence under subsection (1)(b) or (c), it shall be a defence for him to prove—

    (a) that he had a legitimate reason for distributing or showing the photographs or pseudo-photographs or (as the case may be) having them in his possession; or

    (b) that he had not himself seen the photographs or pseudo-photographs and did not know, nor had any cause to suspect, them to be indecent.

...

Criminal Justice Act 1988, s 160

160 Summary offence of possession of indecent photograph of child

(1) Subject to section 160A, it is an offence for a person to have any indecent photograph or pseudo-photograph of a child in his possession.

(2) Where a person is charged with an offence under subsection (1) above, it shall be a defence for him to prove—

    (a) that he had a legitimate reason for having the photograph or pseudo-photograph in his possession; or

    (b) that he had not himself seen the photograph or pseudo-photograph and did not know, nor had any cause to suspect, it to be indecent; or

    (c) that the photograph or pseudo-photograph was sent to him without any prior request made by him or on his behalf and that he did not keep it for an unreasonable time.

EW

 6 months and/or level 5 fine/10 years (5 if s 160)

C14.3.1 *Sentencing*

- The levels of seriousness (in ascending order) for sentencing for offences involving pornographic images are:
  - Level 1: images depicting erotic posing with no sexual activity.
  - Level 2: non-penetrative sexual activity between children, or solo masturbation by a child.

- Level 3: non-penetrative sexual activity between adults and children.
- Level 4: penetrative sexual activity involving a child or children, or both children and adults.
- Level 5: sadism or penetration of, or by, an animal.
- Pseudo-photographs generally should be treated less seriously than real photographs.
- Starting points should be higher where the subject of the indecent photograph(s) is a child under 13.
- In accordance with section 80 of and Schedule 3 to the Sexual Offences Act 2003, automatic notification requirements apply upon conviction to an offender aged 18 or over where the offence involved photographs of children aged under 16.

Offence seriousness (culpability and harm) A. Identify the appropriate starting point Starting points based on first-time offender pleading not guilty		
Examples of nature of activity	**Starting point**	**Range**
Possession of a large amount of level 1 material and/or no more than a small amount of level 2, and the material is for personal use and has not been distributed or shown to others	Medium level community order	Band C fine to high level community order
Offender in possession of a large amount of material at level 2 or a small amount at level 3 Offender has shown or distributed material at level 1 on a limited scale Offender has exchanged images at level 1 or 2 with other collectors, but with no element of financial gain	12 weeks' custody	4 to 26 weeks' custody
Possession of a large quantity of level 3 material for personal use Possession of a small number of images at level 4 or 5 Large number of level 2 images shown or distributed Small number of level 3 images shown or distributed	26 weeks' custody	4 weeks' custody to Crown Court
Possession of a large quantity of level 4 or 5 material for personal use only Large number of level 3 images shown or distributed Offender traded material at levels 1–3 Level 4 or 5 images shown or distributed	Crown Court	26 weeks' custody to Crown Court
Offender involved in the production of material of any level	Crown Court	Crown Court

Offence seriousness (culpability and harm)
B. Consider the effect of aggravating and mitigating factors (other than those within examples above)
The following may be particularly relevant but these lists are not exhaustive

Factors indicating higher culpability	Factors indicating lower culpability
1. Collection is systematically stored or organized, indicating a sophisticated approach to trading or a high level of personal interest 2. Use of drugs, alcohol, or other substance to facilitate the offence of making or taking 3. Background of intimidation or coercion 4. Threats to prevent victim reporting the activity 5. Threats to disclose victim's activity to friends/relatives 6. Financial or other gain **Factors indicating greater degree of harm** 1. Images shown or distributed to others, especially children 2. Images stored, made available, or distributed in such a way that they can be inadvertently accessed by others	1. A few images held solely for personal use 2. Images viewed but not stored 3. A few images held solely for personal use and it is established that the subject is aged 16 or 17 and that he or she was consenting

C14.3.2 Key points

- Photograph includes tracing or other image derived in whole or part from a photograph or pseudo-photograph.
- Whether a photograph is indecent depends on normally recognized standards of propriety.
- The age of the child may be relevant to the issue of indecency (*R v Owen* (1988) 88 Cr App R 291).
- The opening of an e-mail or viewing of an image on the screen would amount to the making of an image if the defendant has the requisite knowledge of what he is doing.
- A person is not in possession of images if they have been deleted, if he is not able to recover those images (*R v Porter* [2006] EWCA Crim 560).
- A child is a person under 18 years of age (Sexual Offences Act 2003, s 45).

 See *Blackstone's Criminal Practice 2014* **B3.320–B3.329**

C14.4 **Kerb crawling, loitering, and soliciting**

Sexual Offences Act 1985, ss 1(1) and 2(1)

1 Kerb-crawling

(1) A person commits an offence if he solicits another person (or different persons) for the purpose of prostitution—
   (a) from a motor vehicle while it is in a street or public place; or
   (b) in a street or public place while in the immediate vicinity of a motor vehicle that he has just got out of or off,

persistently or in such manner or in such circumstances as to be likely to cause annoyance to the person (or any of the persons) solicited, or nuisance to other persons in the neighbourhood.

2 Persistent soliciting

(1) A person commits an offence if in a street or public place he persistently solicits another person (or different persons) for the purpose of prostitution.

Street Offences Act 1959, s 1(1)

1 Loitering or soliciting for purposes of prostitution

(1) It shall be an offence for a person (whether male or female) persistently to loiter or solicit in a street or public place for the purpose of prostitution.

 SO

 Fine level 3 (for a first offence under Street Offences Act 1959, s 1, the fine is level 2)

 See *Blackstone's Criminal Practice 2014* **B3.316–B3.319**

C14.5 **Prohibited images of children**

Coroners and Justice Act 2009, s 62

62 Possession of prohibited images of children

(1) It is an offence for a person to be in possession of a prohibited image of a child.
(2) A prohibited image is an image which—
   (a) is pornographic,
   (b) falls within subsection (6), and
   (c) is grossly offensive, disgusting or otherwise of an obscene character.
(3) An image is 'pornographic' if it is of such a nature that it must reasonably be assumed to have been produced solely or principally for the purpose of sexual arousal.
(4) Where (as found in the person's possession) an image forms part of a series of images, the question whether the image is of such a nature as is mentioned in subsection (3) is to be determined by reference to—
   (a) the image itself, and

    (b) (if the series of images is such as to be capable of providing a context for the image) the context in which it occurs in the series of images.

(5) So, for example, where—

    (a) an image forms an integral part of a narrative constituted by a series of images, and

    (b) having regard to those images as a whole, they are not of such a nature that they must reasonably be assumed to have been produced solely or principally for the purpose of sexual arousal,

the image may, by virtue of being part of that narrative, be found not to be pornographic, even though it might have been found to be pornographic if taken by itself.

(6) An image falls within this subsection if it—

    (a) is an image which focuses solely or principally on a child's genitals or anal region, or

    (b) portrays any of the acts mentioned in subsection (7).

(7) Those acts are—

    (a) the performance by a person of an act of intercourse or oral sex with or in the presence of a child;

    (b) an act of masturbation by, of, involving or in the presence of a child;

    (c) an act which involves penetration of the vagina or anus of a child with a part of a person's body or with anything else;

    (d) an act of penetration, in the presence of a child, of the vagina or anus of a person with a part of a person's body or with anything else;

    (e) the performance by a child of an act of intercourse or oral sex with an animal (whether dead or alive or imaginary);

    (f) the performance by a person of an act of intercourse or oral sex with an animal (whether dead or alive or imaginary) in the presence of a child.

(8) For the purposes of subsection (7), penetration is a continuing act from entry to withdrawal.

(9) Proceedings for an offence under subsection (1) may not be instituted—

    (a) in England and Wales, except by or with the consent of the Director of Public Prosecutions;

    ...

EW

🏛 6 months and/or unlimited fine/3 years

C14.5.1 Key points

• Section 64 of the Act provides for the following defence:

Coroners and Justice Act 2009, s 64(1)

64 Defences

(1) Where a person is charged with an offence under section 62(1), it is a defence for the person to prove any of the following matters—

    (a) that the person had a legitimate reason for being in possession of the image concerned;

(b) that the person had not seen the image concerned and did not know, nor had any cause to suspect, it to be a prohibited image of a child;
(c) that the person—
   (i) was sent the image concerned without any prior request having been made by or on behalf of the person, and
   (ii) did not keep it for an unreasonable time.

- Section 65 of the Act defines the meaning of 'image' and 'child'.

See *Blackstone's Criminal Practice 2014* **B3.330–B3.335**

C14.6 Extreme pornography

Criminal Justice and Immigration Act 2008, s 63

63 Possession of extreme pornographic images

(1) It is an offence for a person to be in possession of an extreme pornographic image.
(2) An 'extreme pornographic image' is an image which is both—
   (a) pornographic, and
   (b) an extreme image.
(3) An image is 'pornographic' if it is of such a nature that it must reasonably be assumed to have been produced solely or principally for the purpose of sexual arousal.
(4) Where (as found in the person's possession) an image forms part of a series of images, the question whether the image is of such a nature as is mentioned in subsection (3) is to be determined by reference to—
   (a) the image itself, and
   (b) (if the series of images is such as to be capable of providing a context for the image) the context in which it occurs in the series of images.
(5) So, for example, where—
   (a) an image forms an integral part of a narrative constituted by a series of images, and
   (b) having regard to those images as a whole, they are not of such a nature that they must reasonably be assumed to have been produced solely or principally for the purpose of sexual arousal,
   the image may, by virtue of being part of that narrative, be found not to be pornographic, even though it might have been found to be pornographic if taken by itself.
(6) An 'extreme image' is an image which—
   (a) falls within subsection (7), and
   (b) is grossly offensive, disgusting or otherwise of an obscene character.
(7) An image falls within this subsection if it portrays, in an explicit and realistic way, any of the following—
   (a) an act which threatens a person's life,
   (b) an act which results, or is likely to result, in serious injury to a person's anus, breasts or genitals,
   (c) an act which involves sexual interference with a human corpse, or

    (d) a person performing an act of intercourse or oral sex with an animal (whether dead or alive), and a reasonable person looking at the image would think that any such person or animal was real.

(8) In this section 'image' means—
    (a) a moving or still image (produced by any means); or
    (b) data (stored by any means) which is capable of conversion into an image within paragraph (a).

(9) In this section references to a part of the body include references to a part surgically constructed (in particular through gender reassignment surgery).

(10) Proceedings for an offence under this section may not be instituted—
    (a) in England and Wales, except by or with the consent of the Director of Public Prosecutions;
    ...

EW

🏛 6 months and/or level 5 fine/3 years (2 years if the offence relates to an image that does not portray any act within s 63(7) (a) or (b))

📖 See *Blackstone's Criminal Practice 2014* **B3.331–B3.336**

C14.7 Exploitation of prostitution

Sexual Offences Act 2003, ss 52 and 53

EW

🏛 6 months and/or level 5 fine/7 years

DO

C14.7.1 *Sentencing*

Offence seriousness (culpability and harm) A. Identify the appropriate starting point Starting points based on first-time offender pleading not guilty		
Examples of nature of activity	**Starting point**	**Range**
No evidence victim was physically coerced or corrupted, and the involvement of the offender was minimal	Medium level community order	Band C fine to high level community order
No coercion or corruption but the offender is closely involved in the victim's prostitution	Crown Court	26 weeks' custody to Crown Court
Evidence of physical and/or mental coercion	Crown Court	Crown Court

   EW Either Way   🏛 Sentence   **DO** Dangerous Offender

Offence seriousness (culpability and harm) B. Consider the effect of aggravating and mitigating factors (other than those within examples above)	
Factors indicating higher culpability	**Factor indicating lower culpability**
1. Background of threats, intimidation, or coercion	1. Offender also being controlled in prostitution and subject to threats or intimidation
2. Large-scale commercial operation	
3. Substantial gain (in the region of £5,000 and up)	
4. Use of drugs, alcohol, or other substance to secure the victim's compliance	
5. Abduction or detention	
6. Threats to prevent the victim reporting the activity	
7. Threats to disclose victim's activity to friends/relatives	
Factor indicating greater degree of harm	
1. Induced dependency on drugs	

 See *Blackstone's Criminal Practice 2014* **B3.241–B3.255**

C14.8 Keeping a brothel used for prostitution

Sexual Offences Act 1956, ss 33 and 33A

EW

6 months and/or level 5 fine/7 years

C14.8.1 *Sentencing*

Offence seriousness (culpability and harm) A. Identify the appropriate starting point Starting points based on first-time offender pleading not guilty		
Examples of nature of activity	**Starting point**	**Range**
Involvement of the offender was minimal	Medium level community order	Band C fine to high level community order
Offender is the keeper of a brothel and is personally involved in its management	Crown Court	26 weeks to Crown Court
Offender is the keeper of a brothel and has made substantial profits in the region of £5,000 and upwards	Crown Court	Crown Court

C14 Sexual Offences

Offence seriousness (culpability and harm) B. Consider the effect of aggravating and mitigating factors (other than those within examples above) The following may be particularly relevant but these lists are not exhaustive	
Factors indicating higher culpability	**Factors indicating lower culpability**
1. Background of threats, intimidation, or coercion 2. Large-scale commercial operation 3. Personal involvement in the prostitution of others 4. Abduction or detention 5. Financial or other gain	1. Using employment as a route out of prostitution and not actively involved in exploitation 2. Coercion by third party

 See *Blackstone's Criminal Practice 2014* **B3.348–B3.363**

C14.9 Sexual activity in a public lavatory

Sexual Offences Act 2003, s 71(1) and (2)

71 Sexual activity in a public lavatory

(1) A person commits an offence if—
  (a) he is in a lavatory to which the public or a section of the public has or is permitted to have access, whether on payment or otherwise,
  (b) he intentionally engages in an activity, and,
  (c) the activity is sexual.
(2) For the purposes of this section, an activity is sexual if a reasonable person would, in all the circumstances but regardless of any person's purpose, consider it to be sexual.

 SO

 6 months and/or level 5 fine

C14.9.1 *Sentencing*

Offence seriousness (culpability and harm) A. Identify the appropriate starting point Starting points based on first-time offender pleading not guilty		
Examples of nature of activity	**Starting point**	**Range**
Basic offence as defined in the Act, assuming no aggravating or mitigating factors	Band C fine	Band C fine
Offence with aggravating factors	Low level community order	Band C fine to medium level community order

Offence seriousness (culpability and harm) B. Consider the effect of aggravating and mitigating factors (other than those within examples above) The following may be particularly relevant but these lists are not exhaustive	
Factors indicating higher culpability 1. Intimidating behaviour/threats of violence to member(s) of the public 2. Blatant behaviour	

C14.9.2 Key points

- This offence is committed where an offender intentionally engages in sexual activity in a public lavatory. It was introduced to give adults and children the freedom to use public lavatories for the purpose for which they are designed, without the fear of being an unwilling witness to overtly sexual behaviour of a kind that most people would not expect to be conducted in public. It is primarily a public order offence rather than a sexual offence.
- When dealing with a repeat offender, the starting point should be a low level community order, with a range of Band B and C fines to medium level community order. The presence of aggravating factors may suggest that a sentence above the range is appropriate.
- This guideline may be relevant by way of analogy to conduct charged as the common law offence of outraging public decency; the offence is triable either way and has a maximum penalty of a level 5 fine and/ or six months' imprisonment when tried summarily.

 See *Blackstone's Criminal Practice 2014* **B3.312–B3.314**

C14.10 Sexual assault

Sexual Offences Act 2003, ss 3(1)–(3), 4, 7(1), 8, and 9

3 Sexual assault

(1) A person (A) commits an offence if—
    (a) he intentionally touches another person (B),
    (b) the touching is sexual,
    (c) B does not consent to the touching, and
    (d) A does not reasonably believe that B consents.
(2) Whether a belief is reasonable is to be determined having regard to all the circumstances, including any steps A has taken to ascertain whether B consents.
(3) Sections 75 and 76 apply to an offence under this section.

4 Causing a person to engage in sexual activity without consent

(1) A person (A) commits an offence if—
    (a) he intentionally causes another person (B) to engage in an activity,

    (b) the activity is sexual,

    (c) B does not consent to engaging in the activity, and

    (d) A does not reasonably believe that B consents.

(2) Whether a belief is reasonable is to be determined having regard to all the circumstances, including any steps A has taken to ascertain whether B consents.

(3) Sections 75 and 76 apply to an offence under this section.

(4) A person guilty of an offence under this section, if the activity caused involved—

    (a) penetration of B's anus or vagina,

    (b) penetration of B's mouth with a person's penis,

    (c) penetration of a person's anus or vagina with a part of B's body or by B with anything else, or

    (d) penetration of a person's mouth with B's penis,

is liable, on conviction on indictment, to imprisonment for life.

7 Sexual assault of a child under 13

(1) A person commits an offence if—

    (a) he intentionally touches another person,

    (b) the touching is sexual, and

    (c) the other person is under 13.

8 Causing or inciting a child under 13 to engage in sexual activity

(1) A person commits an offence if—

    (a) he intentionally causes or incites another person (B) to engage in an activity,

    (b) the activity is sexual, and

    (c) B is under 13.

(2) A person guilty of an offence under this section, if the activity caused or incited involved—

    (a) penetration of B's anus or vagina,

    (b) penetration of B's mouth with a person's penis,

    (c) penetration of a person's anus or vagina with a part of B's body or by B with anything else, or

    (d) penetration of a person's mouth with B's penis,

is liable, on conviction on indictment, to imprisonment for life.

9 Sexual activity with a child

(1) A person aged 18 or over (A) commits an offence if—

    (a) he intentionally touches another person (B),

    (b) the touching is sexual, and

    (c) either—

        (i) B is under 16 and A does not reasonably believe that B is 16 or over, or

        (ii) B is under 13.

(2) A person guilty of an offence under this section, if the touching involved—

    (a) penetration of B's anus or vagina with a part of A's body or anything else,

    (b) penetration of B's mouth with A's penis,

    (c) penetration of A's anus or vagina with a part of B's body, or

    (d) penetration of A's mouth with B's penis.

EW Save for sections 4, 8, and 9 where penetration is involved and the offences become triable only on indictment with maximum sentences of life for both sections 4 and 8 and 14 years for section 9

IIII 6 months and/or level 5 fine/10 years (ss 3, 4), 14 years (ss 7, 8), 14 years (s 9), save for sections 4 and 8 where penetration is involved and the offence is triable only on indictment with a maximum of life imprisonment

DO

C14.10.1 *Sentencing*

Offence seriousness (culpability and harm) A. Identify the appropriate starting point Starting points based on first-time offender pleading not guilty		
Examples of nature of activity	**Starting point**	**Range**
Contact between part of offender's body (other than the genitalia) with part of the victim's body (other than the genitalia)	26 weeks' custody if the victim is under 13 Medium level community order if the victim is aged 13 or over	4 weeks' custody to Crown Court Band C fine to 6 weeks' custody
Contact between naked genitalia of offender and another part of victim's body Contact with naked genitalia of victim by offender using part of his or her body other than the genitalia, or an object Contact between either the clothed genitalia of offender and naked genitalia of victim or naked genitalia of offender and clothed genitalia of victim	Crown Court if the victim is under 13 Crown Court if the victim is aged 13 or over	Crown Court 26 weeks' custody to Crown Court
Contact between naked genitalia of offender and naked genitalia, face, or mouth of the victim	Crown Court	Crown Court

---

Offence seriousness (culpability and harm)
B. Consider the effect of aggravating and mitigating factors (other than those within examples opposite)
The following may be particularly relevant but these lists are not exhaustive

Factors indicating higher culpability	**Factors indicating lower culpability**
1. Background of intimidation or coercion	1. Youth and immaturity of the offender
2. Use of drugs, alcohol, or other substance to facilitate the offence	2. Minimal or fleeting contact
3. Threats to prevent the victim reporting the incident	*Where the victim is aged 16 or over*
4. Abduction or detention	3. Victim engaged in consensual activity with the offender on the same occasion and immediately before the offence
5. Offender aware that he or she is suffering from a sexually transmitted infection	*Where the victim is under 16*
6. Prolonged activity or contact	4. Sexual activity between two children (one of whom is the offender) was mutually agreed and experimental
Factors indicating greater degree of harm	
1. Offender ejaculated or caused victim to ejaculate	
2. Physical harm caused	

C14.10.2 Key points

- If a defendant does not reasonably know, or is mistaken about, the age of the child, it affords a defence to a section 7 offence (*B v Director of Public Prosecutions* [2000] AC 428).
- A person under 16 years of age cannot in law consent.

 See *Blackstone's Criminal Practice 2014* **B3.53–B3.70** and **B3.80–B3.94**

C14.11 Sex offenders register—fail to comply with notification requirements

Sexual Offences Act 2003, s 91(1)

91 Offences relating to notification

(1) A person commits an offence if he—

    (a) fails, without reasonable excuse, to comply with section 83(1), 84(1), 4(4)(b), 85(1), 87(4) or 89(2)(b) or any requirement imposed by regulations made under section 86(1); or

    (b) notifies to the police, in purported compliance with section 83(1), 4(1) or 85(1) or any requirement imposed by regulations made under section 86(1), any information which he knows to be false.

 EW

 Level 5 fine and/or 6 months/5 years

C14.11.1 *Sentencing*

Offence seriousness (culpability and harm) A. Identify the appropriate starting point Starting points based on first-time offender (see note below) pleading not guilty		
Example of nature of activity	**Starting point**	**Range**
Negligent or inadvertent failure to comply with requirements	Medium level community order	Band C fine to high level community order
Deliberate failure to comply with requirements OR Supply of information known to be false	6 weeks' custody	High level community order to 26 weeks' custody
Conduct as described in box above AND Long period of non-compliance OR Attempts to avoid detection	18 weeks' custody	6 weeks' custody to Crown Court

Offence seriousness (culpability and harm) B. Consider the effect of aggravating and mitigating factors (other than those within examples above) The following may be particularly relevant but these lists are not exhaustive	
Factor indicating higher culpability 1. Long period of non-compliance (where not in the examples above) **Factors indicating greater degree of harm** 1. Alarm or distress caused to victim 2. Particularly serious original offence	**Factor indicating lower culpability** 1. Genuine misunderstanding

C14.11.2 Key points

- A person who is subject to the notification requirements commits a criminal offence if he fails, without reasonable excuse, to:
  - make an initial notification in accordance with section 83(1);
  - notify a change of details in accordance with section 84(1);
  - make a weekly re-notification in accordance with section 85(1);
  - comply with any requirement imposed by regulations concerned with the notification of foreign travel (s 86(1));
  - notify the fact that a change did not happen as predicted when it had been notified in advance in accordance with section 84(4)(b);
  - allow a police officer to take his photograph or fingerprints (s 87(4));

- ensure that a young offender on whose behalf he is required by a parental direction to comply with the notification requirements attends a police station when a notification is made (s 89(2)(b));
- in the first four cases set out above, if he knowingly provides false information.

- The offence occurs on the first day of breach and continues—only one breach can be prosecuted in such circumstances.
- A conditional discharge cannot be imposed on breach.

 See *Blackstone's Criminal Practice 2014* **E23**

C14.12 Voyeurism

> **Sexual Offences Act 2003, s 67(1)–(4)**
>
> **67 Voyeurism**
> (1) A person commits an offence if—
>   (a) for the purpose of obtaining sexual gratification, he observes another person doing a private act, and
>   (b) he knows that the other person does not consent to being observed for his sexual gratification.
> (2) A person commits an offence if—
>   (a) he operates equipment with the intention of enabling another person to observe, for the purpose of obtaining sexual gratification, a third person (B) doing a private act, and
>   (b) he knows that B does not consent to his operating equipment with that intention.
> (3) A person commits an offence if—
>   (a) he records another person (B) doing a private act,
>   (b) he does so with the intention that he or a third person will, for the purpose of obtaining sexual gratification, look at an image of B doing the act, and
>   (c) he knows that B does not consent to his recording the act with that intention.
> (4) A person commits an offence if he installs equipment, or constructs or adapts a structure or part of a structure, with the intention of enabling himself or another person to commit an offence under subsection (1).

EW

6 months and/or level 5 fine/2 years

DO

C14.12.1 *Sentencing*

Offence seriousness (culpability and harm) A. Identify the appropriate starting point Starting points based on first-time offender pleading not guilty		
Examples of nature of activity	**Starting point**	**Range**
Basic offence as defined in the Act, assuming no aggravating or mitigating factors, eg the offender spies through a hole he has made in a changing room wall	Low level community order	Band B fine to high level community order
Offence with aggravating factors such as recording sexual activity and showing it to others	26 weeks' custody	4 weeks' custody to Crown Court
Offence with serious aggravating factors such as recording sexual activity and placing it on a website or circulating it for commercial gain	Crown Court	26 weeks to Crown Court

Offence seriousness (culpability and harm) B. Consider the effect of aggravating and mitigating factors (other than those within examples above) The following may be particularly relevant but these lists are not exhaustive	
Factors indicating higher culpability 1. Threats to prevent the victim reporting an offence 2. Recording activity and circulating pictures/videos 3. Circulating pictures or videos for commercial gain—particularly if victim is vulnerable, eg a child or a person with a mental or physical disorder **Factor indicating greater degree of harm** 1. Distress to victim, eg where the pictures/videos are circulated to people known to the victim	

C14.12.2 Key points

- Section 68 provides for the interpretation of key phrases:

Sexual Offences Act 2003, s 68

68 Voyeurism: interpretation

(1) For the purposes of section 67, a person is doing a private act if the person is in a place which, in the circumstances, would reasonably be expected to provide privacy, and—

(a) the person's genitals, buttocks or breasts are exposed or covered only with underwear,

(b) the person is using a lavatory, or
(c) the person is doing a sexual act that is not of a kind ordinarily done in public.
(2) In section 67, 'structure' includes a tent, vehicle or vessel or other temporary or movable structure.

- Consent is defined under section 74 of the Act:

Sexual Offences Act 2003, s 74

74 'Consent'

For the purposes of this Part, a person consents if he agrees by choice, and has the freedom and capacity to make that choice.

- Sections 75 and 76 deal with evidential presumptions in relation to consent.

 See *Blackstone's Criminal Practice 2014* **B3.299–B3.303**

C15 Dishonesty and Offences Against Property

C15.1 Aggravated vehicle-taking

Theft Act 1968, s 12A(1)–(3)

12A Aggravated vehicle-taking

(1) Subject to subsection (3) below, a person is guilty of aggravated taking of a vehicle if—

 (a) he commits an offence under section 12(1) above (in this section referred to as a 'basic offence') in relation to a mechanically propelled vehicle; and

 (b) it is proved that, at any time after the vehicle was unlawfully taken (whether by him or another) and before it was recovered, the vehicle was driven, or injury or damage was caused, in one or more of the circumstances set out in paragraphs (a) to (d) of subsection (2) below.

(2) The circumstances referred to in subsection (1)(b) above are—

 (a) that the vehicle was driven dangerously on a road or other public place;

 (b) that, owing to the driving of the vehicle, an accident occurred by which injury was caused to any person;

 (c) that, owing to the driving of the vehicle, an accident occurred by which damage was caused to any property, other than the vehicle;

 (d) that damage was caused to the vehicle.

(3) A person is not guilty of an offence under this section if he proves that, as regards any such proven driving, injury or damage as is referred to in subsection (1)(b) above, either—

 (a) the driving, accident or damage referred to in subsection (2) above occurred before he committed the basic offence; or

 (b) he was neither in nor on nor in the immediate vicinity of the vehicle when that driving, accident or damage occurred.

EW Summary if damage under £5,000

▦ Section 12A(2)(a) and (b): 6 months and/or level 5 fine/2 years (14 years if accident caused death). Must endorse and disqualify for at least 12 months. Must disqualify for at least 2 years if offender has had two or more disqualifications for periods of 56 days or more in preceding 3 years

▦ Section 12A(2)(c) and (d): 6 months and/or level 5 fine/2 years. Must endorse and disqualify for at least 12 months. Must disqualify for at least 2 years if offender has had 2 or more disqualifications for periods of 56 days or more in preceding 3 years

---

C15.1.1 *Sentencing: dangerous driving or accident causing injury*

Offence seriousness (culpability and harm) A. Identify the appropriate starting point Starting points based on first-time offender pleading not guilty		
Example of nature of activity	**Starting point**	**Range**
Taken vehicle involved in single incident of bad driving where little or no damage or risk of personal injury	High level community order	Medium community order to 12 weeks' custody
Taken vehicle involved in incident(s) involving excessive speed or showing off, especially on busy roads or in built-up area	18 weeks' custody	12 to 26 weeks' custody
Taken vehicle involved in prolonged bad driving involving deliberate disregard for safety of other	Crown Court	Crown Court

Offence seriousness (culpability and harm) B. Consider the effect of aggravating and mitigating factors (other than those within examples above) The following may be particularly relevant but these lists are not exhaustive	
Factors indicating higher culpability 1. Disregarding warnings of others 2. Evidence of alcohol or drugs 3. Carrying out other tasks while driving 4. Tiredness 5. Trying to avoid arrest 6. Aggressive driving, such as driving much too close to vehicle in front, inappropriate attempts to overtake, or cutting in after overtaking **Factors indicating greater degree of harm** 1. Injury to others 2. Damage to other vehicle or property	

C15.1.2 *Sentencing: damage caused*

Offence seriousness (culpability and harm) A. Identify the appropriate starting point Starting points based on first-time offender pleading not guilty		
Examples of nature of activity	**Starting point**	**Range**
Exceeding authorized use of, eg employer's or relative's, vehicle; retention of hire car beyond return date; minor damage to taken vehicle	Medium level community order	Low level community order to high level community order

Greater damage to taken vehicle and/or moderate damage to another vehicle and/or moderate damage to another vehicle and/or moderate damage to another vehicle and/or property	High level community order	Medium level community order to 12 weeks' custody
Vehicle taken as part of burglary or from private premises; severe damage	18 weeks' custody	12 to 26 weeks' custody (Crown Court if damage over £5,000)

Offence seriousness (culpability and harm)
B. Consider the effect of aggravating and mitigating factors (other than those within examples above)
The following may be particularly relevant but these lists are not exhaustive

Factors indicating higher culpability	Factors indicating lower culpability
1. Vehicle deliberately damaged/destroyed	1. Misunderstanding with owner
2. Offender under influence of alcohol/drugs	2. Damage resulting from actions of another (where this does not provide a defence)
Factors indicating greater degree of harm	
1. Passenger(s) carried	
2. Vehicle belonging to elderly or disabled person	
3. Emergency service vehicle	
4. Medium to large goods vehicle	
5. Damage caused in moving traffic accident	

C15.1.3 Key points

- If aggravating factor is solely damage, then the offence is triable summarily only if the damage does not exceed £5,000.
- A magistrates' court can convict a defendant of the alternative offence of vehicle taking if it does not find the aggravating feature(s) (*H v Liverpool Youth Court* [2001] Crim LR 897).

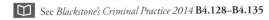 See *Blackstone's Criminal Practice 2014* **B4.128–B4.135**

C15.2 Alcohol/tobacco, fraudulently evade duty

Customs and Excise Management Act 1979, s 170

6 months and/or 3 times the duty evaded or level 5 fine, whichever is the greater/7 years

C15.2.1 *Sentencing*

See **Appendix 6**.

C15.2.2 Key points

- It is not sufficient for the prosecution to show that the defendant was merely reckless (*R v Panayi* [1989] 1 WLR 187).
- It is irrelevant that the defendant does not know the precise nature of the goods being imported (*R v Shivpuri* [1987] AC 1).
- The burden of proving that duty has been paid falls on the defendant (s 154).
- The prosecution have the right to appeal sentence (*Customs and Excise Commissioners v Brunt* (1998) 163 JP 161).

See *Blackstone's Criminal Practice 2014* **B16.36–B16.49**

C15.3 Burglary

Theft Act 1968, s 9(1) and (2)

9 Burglary

(1) A person is guilty of burglary if—
  (a) he enters any building or part of a building as a trespasser and with intent to commit any such offence as is mentioned in subsection (2) below; or
  (b) having entered any building or part of a building as a trespasser he steals or attempts to steal anything in the building or that part of it or inflicts or attempts to inflict on any person therein any grievous bodily harm.

(2) The offences referred to in subsection (1) (a) above are offences of stealing anything in the building or part of a building in question, of inflicting on any person therein any grievous bodily harm therein, and of doing unlawful damage to the building or anything therein.

EW

6 months and/or level 5 fine/10 years (14 if dwelling)

Offence *is indictable only* and must be sent to the Crown Court if:

- the offender:
  - was 18 or over when he committed the offence,
  - committed the offence on or after 1 December 1999,
  - had previously been convicted of two other domestic burglary offences in England and Wales; one of those offences has been committed after conviction for the other and both of the previous domestic burglaries had been committed on or after 1 December 1999;
- any person was subjected to violence or the threat of violence: Magistrates' Courts Act 1980, Sch 1.

C15.3.1 *Sentencing: non-dwelling*

STEP ONE: Determine the offence category

Category 1	Greater harm and higher culpability
Category 2	Greater harm and lower culpability or lesser harm and higher culpability
Category 3	Lesser harm and lower culpability

Factors indicating greater harm	Factors indicating higher culpability
Theft of/damage to property causing a significant degree of loss to the victim (whether economic, commercial, or personal value) Soiling, ransacking, or vandalism of property Victim on the premises (or returns) while offender present Trauma to the victim, beyond the normal inevitable consequence of intrusion and theft Violence used or threatened against victim Context of general public disorder	Premises or victim deliberately targeted (to include pharmacy or doctor's surgery and targeting due to vulnerability of victim or hostility based on disability, race, sexual orientation, and so forth) A significant degree of planning or organization Knife or other weapon carried (where not charged separately) Equipped for burglary (eg implements carried and/or use of vehicle) Member of a group or gang
Factors indicating lesser harm	**Factors indicating lower culpability**
Nothing stolen or only property of very low value to the victim (whether economic, commercial, or personal) Limited damage or disturbance to property	Offence committed on impulse, with limited intrusion into property Offender exploited by others Mental disorder or learning disability, where linked to the commission of the offence

STEP TWO : Starting point and category range

Offence category	Starting point	Category range
Category 1	Crown court	Crown Court
Category	18 weeks' custody	Low level community order to Crown Court (51 weeks' custody)
Category	Medium level community order	Band B fine to 18 weeks' custody

Factors increasing seriousness	Factors reducing seriousness or reflecting personal mitigation
Statutory aggravating factors: Previous convictions, having regard to (a) the nature of the offence to which the conviction relates and its relevance to the current offence; and (b) the time that has elapsed since the conviction Offence committed whilst on bail **Other aggravating factors include:** Offence committed at night, particularly where staff present or likely to be present Abuse of a position of trust Gratuitous degradation of the victim Any steps taken to prevent the victim reporting the incident or obtaining assistance and/or from assisting or supporting the prosecution Established evidence of community impact Commission of offence whilst under the influence of alcohol or drugs Failure to comply with current court orders Offence committed whilst on licence Offences taken into consideration (TICs)	Offender has made voluntary reparation to the victim Subordinate role in a group or gang No previous convictions or no relevant/recent convictions Remorse Good character and/or exemplary conduct Determination and/or demonstration of steps taken to address addiction or offending behaviour Serious medical conditions requiring urgent, intensive, or long-term treatment Age and/or lack of maturity where it affects the responsibility of the offender Lapse of time since the offence where this is not the fault of the offender Mental disorder or learning disability, where not linked to the commission of the offence Sole or primary carer for dependent relatives

Additional steps

Consider any factors which indicate a reduction, such as: assistance to the prosecution; reduction for guilty plea; dangerousness; totality principle; compensation and ancillary orders; reasons; consideration for remand time.

C15.3.2 *Sentencing: dwelling*

STEP ONE: Determine the offence category

Category 1	Greater harm and higher culpability
Category 2	Greater harm and lower culpability or lesser harm and higher culpability
Category 3	Lesser harm and lower culpability

Factors indicating greater harm	Factors indicating higher culpability
Theft of/damage to property causing a significant degree of loss to the victim (whether economic, sentimental, or personal value) Soiling, ransacking, or vandalism of property Occupier at home (or returns home) while offender present Trauma to the victim beyond the normal inevitable consequence of intrusion and theft Violence used or threatened against victim Context of general public disorder	Victim or premises deliberately targeted (eg due to vulnerability or hostility based on disability, race, or sexual orientation) A significant degree of planning or organization Knife or other weapon carried (where not charged separately) Equipped for burglary (eg implements carried and/or use of vehicle) Member of a group or gang
Factors indicating lesser harm	**Factors indicating lower culpability**
Nothing stolen or only property of very low value to the victim (whether economic, sentimental, or personal) Limited damage or disturbance to property	Offence committed on impulse, with limited intrusion into property Offender exploited by others Mental disorder or learning disability, where linked to the commission of the offence

STEP TWO: Starting point and category range

Where the defendant is dependent on or has a propensity to misuse drugs and there is sufficient prospect of success, a community order with a drug rehabilitation requirement under section 209 of the Criminal Justice Act 2003 may be a proper alternative to a short or moderate custodial sentence

Offence category	Starting point	Category range
Category 1	Crown court	Crown Court
Category 2	1 year's custody	High level community order to Crown Court (2 years' custody)
Category 3	High level community order	Low level community order to 26 weeks' custody

Factors increasing seriousness	Factors reducing seriousness or reflecting personal mitigation
Statutory aggravating factors: Previous convictions, having regard to (a) the nature of the offence to which the conviction relates and its relevance to the current offence; and (b) the time that has elapsed since the conviction* Offence committed whilst on bail Other aggravating factors include: Child at home (or returns home) when offence committed	Offender has made voluntary reparation to the victim Subordinate role in a group or gang No previous convictions or no relevant/ recent convictions Remorse Good character and/or exemplary conduct Determination and/or demonstration of steps taken to address addiction or offending behaviour

Offence committed at night Gratuitous degradation of the victim Any steps taken to prevent the victim reporting the incident or obtaining assistance and/or from assisting or supporting the prosecution Victim compelled to leave their home (in particular victims of domestic violence) Established evidence of community impact Commission of offence whilst under the influence of alcohol or drugs Failure to comply with current court orders Offence committed whilst on licence Offences taken into consideration (TICs)	Serious medical conditions requiring urgent, intensive, or long-term treatment Age and/or lack of maturity where it affects the responsibility of the offender Lapse of time since the offence where this is not the fault of the offender Mental disorder or learning disability, where not linked to the commission of the offence Sole or primary carer for dependent relatives

* Where sentencing an offender for a qualifying third domestic burglary, the court must apply section 111 of the Powers of the Criminal Courts (Sentencing) Act 2000 and impose a custodial term of at least three years, unless it is satisfied that there are particular circumstances which relate to any of the offences or to the offender, which would make it unjust to do so.

Additional steps

Consider any factors which indicate a reduction, such as: assistance to the prosecution; reduction for guilty plea; dangerousness; totality principle; compensation and ancillary orders; reasons; consideration for remand time.

C15.3.3 Key points

- Entry can be partial (*R v Brown* [1985] Crim LR 212), and may be effected without any part of the body entering the building (eg cane and hook burglaries).
- 'Building' is a factual not a legal issue, and will depend on all of the circumstances (*Brutus v Cozens* [1973] AC 854).
- Trespass can be committed knowingly or recklessly (*R v Collins* [1973] QB 100).

 See *Blackstone's Criminal Practice 2014* **B4.75–B4.96**

C15.4 Trespass against property

C15.4.1 *Squatting*

> **Legal Aid, Sentencing and Punishment of Offenders Act 2012, s 144**
>
> **144 Offence of squatting in a residential building**
> (1) A person commits an offence if—
>   (a) the person is in a residential building as a trespasser having entered it as a trespasser,
>   (b) the person knows or ought to know that he or she is a trespasser, and.
>   (c) the person is living in the building or intends to live there for any period.
> (2) The offence is not committed by a person holding over after the end of a lease or licence (even if the person leaves and re-enters the building).
> (3) For the purposes of this section—
>   (a) 'building' includes any structure or part of a structure (including a temporary or moveable structure), and
>   (b) a building is 'residential' if it is designed or adapted, before the time of entry, for use as a place to live.
> (4) For the purposes of this section the fact that a person derives title from a trespasser, or has the permission of a trespasser, does not prevent the person from being a trespasser.

SO

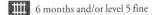 6 months and/or level 5 fine

C15.4.2 Key points

- The provision became effective on 1 September 2012 but applies to those who had entered before but remain after that date.
- It will be necessary to check that there was not even an informal licence; and whether a person intends to 'live' rather than stay temporarily will be a matter of fact in each case.

See *Blackstone's Criminal Practice 2014* **B13.31**

C15.4.3 *Aggravated trespass*

> **Criminal Justice and Public Order Act 1994, s 68(1) and (2)**
>
> **68 Offence of aggravated trespass**
> (1) A person commits the offence of aggravated trespass if he trespasses on land and, in relation to any lawful activity which persons are engaging in

or are about to engage in on that or adjoining land, does there anything
which is intended by him to have the effect—

(a) of intimidating those persons or any of them so as to deter them or any
of them from engaging in that activity,

(b) of obstructing that activity, or

(c) of disrupting that activity.

(2) Activity on any occasion on the part of a person or persons on land is 'lawful' for the purposes of this section if he or they may engage in the activity
on the land on that occasion without committing an offence or trespassing
on the land.

 SO

 3 months and/or level 4 fine

C15.4.4 Key points

- There are three elements to the offence (*Barnard v DPP* [2000] Crim LR 371):
  - trespass on land,
  - the intention to have any one of the three effects specified (*Tilly v DPP* [2001] EWHC 821 (Admin)),
  - an act done towards that end. This must be distinct from the act of trespass (*Peppersharp v DPP* [2012] EWHC 474 (Admin)).
- Actual disruption is not required if the necesasry intention is proved (*Winder v DPP* (1996) 160 JP 713).
- Activity takes place only if there is someone on the land who is not allowed to go on with what he is entitled to do (*Tilly v DPP* [2001] EWHC 821 (Admin)). The 'lawful activity' being carried on should not be explored by the court unless the activity itself gives rise to questions. Normal retail sales will not do so (*Richardson v DPP* [2012] EWHC 1238 (Admin)).

 See *Blackstone's Criminal Practice 2014* **B13.45**

C15.5 Electricity—abstract/use without authority

Theft Act 1968, s 13

13 Abstracting of electricity

A person who dishonestly uses without due authority, or dishonestly causes
to be wasted or diverted, any electricity shall be guilty of an offence.

 EW

 6 months and/or level 5 fine/5 years

C15.5.1 *Sentencing*

Offence seriousness (culpability and harm) A. Identify the appropriate starting point Starting points based on first-time offender pleading not guilty		
Examples of nature of activity	**Starting point**	**Range**
Where the offence results in substantial commercial gain, a custodial sentence may be appropriate		
Offence involving evidence of planning and indication that the offending was intended to be continuing, such as using a device to interfere with the electricity meter or rewiring to bypass the meter	Medium level community order	Band A fine to high level community order

Offence seriousness (culpability and harm) B. Consider the effect of aggravating and mitigating factors (other than those within examples above) The following may be particularly relevant but these lists are not exhaustive	
Factor indicating greater degree of harm 1. Risk of danger caused to property and/or life	

 See *Blackstone's Criminal Practice 2014* **B4.141–B4.146**

C15.6 **False accounting**

Theft Act 1968, s 17(1)

17 False accounting

(1) Where a person dishonestly, with a view to gain for himself or another or with intent to cause loss to another,—

    (a) destroys, defaces, conceals or falsifies any account or any record or document made or required for any accounting purpose; or

    (b) in furnishing information for any purpose produces or makes use of any account, or any such record or document as aforesaid, which to his knowledge is or may be misleading, false or deceptive in a material particular,

    (c) he shall on conviction...

EW

▥ 6 months and/or level 5 fine/7 years

C15.6.1 *Sentencing*

See **Appendix 6**.

See *Blackstone's Criminal Practice 2014* **B6.3–B6.13**

C15.7 Found on enclosed premises

> ### Vagrancy Act 1824, s 4
>
> #### 4 Persons committing certain offences to be deemed rogues and vagabonds
>
> [The following is an abbreviated version of the original]…[E]very person wandering abroad and lodging in any barn or outhouse, or in any deserted or unoccupied building, or in the open air, or under a tent, or in any cart or waggon, and not giving a good account of himself or herself; every person being found in or upon any dwelling house, warehouse, coach-house, stable, or outhouse, or in any inclosed yard, garden, or area, for any unlawful purpose;…is guilty of an offence.

C15.7.1 Key points

- An unlawful purpose is to commit an offence. Hiding from the police is therefore not enough (*L v CPS* [2007] EWHC 1843(Admin)).

SO

Level 3 fine/3 months

See *Blackstone's Criminal Practice 2014* **B4.95**

C15.8 Fraud

> ### Fraud Act 2006, ss 1(1) and (2), 2, 3, 4, and 5
>
> #### 1 Fraud
>
> (1) A person is guilty of fraud if he is in breach of any of the sections listed in subsection (2) (which provide for different ways of committing the offence).
> (2) The sections are—
>   (a) section 2 (fraud by false representation),
>   (b) section 3 (fraud by failing to disclose information), and
>   (c) section 4 (fraud by abuse of position).
>
> #### 2 Fraud by false representation
>
> (1) A person is in breach of this section if he—
>   (a) dishonestly makes a false representation, and

    (b) intends, by making the representation—
       (i) to make a gain for himself or another, or
       (ii) to cause loss to another or to expose another to a risk of loss.

(2) A representation is false if—
    (a) it is untrue or misleading, and
    (b) the person making it knows that it is, or might be, untrue or misleading.

(3) 'Representation' means any representation as to fact or law, including a representation as to the state of mind of—
    (a) the person making the representation, or
    (b) any other person.

(4) A representation may be express or implied.

(5) For the purposes of this section a representation may be regarded as made if it (or anything implying it) is submitted in any form to any system or device designed to receive, convey or respond to communications (with or without human intervention).

3 Fraud by failing to disclose information

(1) A person is in breach of this section if he—
    (a) dishonestly fails to disclose to another person information which he is under a legal duty to disclose, and
    (b) intends, by failing to disclose the information—
       (i) to make a gain for himself or another, or
       (ii) to cause loss to another or to expose another to a risk of loss.

4 Fraud by abuse of position

(1) A person is in breach of this section if he—
    (a) occupies a position in which he is expected to safeguard, or not to act against, the financial interests of another person,
    (b) dishonestly abuses that position, and
    (c) intends, by means of the abuse of that position—
       (i) to make a gain for himself or another, or
       (ii) to cause loss to another or to expose another to a risk of loss.

(2) A person may be regarded as having abused his position even though his conduct consisted of an omission rather than an act.

5 'Gain' and 'loss'

(1) The references to gain and loss in sections 2 to 4 are to be read in accordance with this section.

(2) 'Gain' and 'loss'—
    (a) extend only to gain or loss in money or other property;
    (b) include any such gain or loss whether temporary or permanent;
    and 'property' means any property whether real or personal (including things in action and other intangible property).

(3) 'Gain' includes a gain by keeping what one has, as well as a gain by getting what one does not have.

(4) 'Loss' includes a loss by not getting what one might get, as well as a loss by parting with what one has.

EW

 6 months and/or level 5 fine/10 years

C15 Dishonesty and Offences Against Property

C15.8.1 *Sentencing*

See **Appendix 6**.

 See *Blackstone's Criminal Practice 2014* **B5.4–B5.20**

C15.9 Handling stolen goods

> **Theft Act 1968, s 22(1)**
>
> **22 Handling stolen goods**
> (1) A person handles stolen goods if (otherwise than in the course of the stealing) knowing or believing them to be stolen goods he dishonestly receives the goods, or dishonestly undertakes or assists in their retention, removal, disposal or realisation by or for the benefit of another person, or if he arranges to do so.

 EW

 6 months and/or level 5 fine/14 years

C15.9.1 *Sentencing*

Offence seriousness (culpability and harm) A. Identify the appropriate starting point Starting points based on first-time offender pleading not guilty		
Examples of nature of activity	**Starting point**	**Range**
Property worth £1,000 or less acquired for offender's own use	Band B fine	Band B fine to low level community order
Property worth £1,000 or less acquired for resale; or property worth more than £1,000 acquired for offender's own use; or presence of at least one aggravating factor listed below—regardless of value	Medium level community order	Low level community order to 12 weeks' custody *Note:* the custody threshold is likely to be passed if the offender has a record of dishonesty offences
Sophisticated offending; or presence of at least two aggravating factors listed below	12 weeks' custody	6 weeks' custody to Crown Court
Offence committed in context of Offender Acts as organizer/distributor of proceeds of crime; or offender makes self available to other criminals as willing to handle the proceeds of thefts or burglaries; or offending highly organized, professional; or particularly serious original offence, such as armed robbery	Crown Court	Crown Court

Offence seriousness (culpability and harm)	
B. Consider the effect of aggravating and mitigating factors	
(other than those within examples above)	
The following may be particularly relevant but these lists are not exhaustive	
Factors indicating higher culpability	**Factors indicating lower culpability**
1. Closeness of offender to primary offence. Closeness may be geographical, arising from presence at or near the primary offence when it was committed, or temporal, where the handler instigated or encouraged the primary offence beforehand, or soon after provided a safe haven or route or disposal	1. Little or no benefit to offender
	2. Voluntary restitution to victim
	Factor indicating lower degree of harm
	1. Low value of goods
2. High level of profit made or expected by offender	
Factors indicating greater degree of harm	
1. Seriousness of the primary offence, including domestic burglary	
2. High value of goods to victim, including sentimental value	
3. Threats of violence or abuse of power by offender over others, such as an adult commissioning criminal activity by children, or a drug dealer pressurizing addicts to steal in order to pay for their habit	

C15.9.2 Key points

- Mere suspicion that goods are stolen will not suffice.
- In *R v Hall* (1985) 81 Cr App R 260, belief was said to be present when someone thought: 'I cannot say for certain that those goods are stolen, but there can be no other reasonable conclusion in the light of all the circumstances of all I have heard and seen.' Similarly if the person admits that 'my brain is telling me [they are stolen] despite what I have heard'.
- If the defendant argues that he has paid an adequate consideration for the goods, it falls upon the prosecution to disprove (*Hogan v Director of Public Prosecutions* [2007] EWHC 978 (Admin)).

See *Blackstone's Criminal Practice 2014* **B4.160–B4.186**

C15.10 **Money laundering**

Proceeds of Crime Act 2002, ss 327–329

327 Concealing etc

(1) A person commits an offence if he—
   (a) conceals criminal property;
   (b) disguises criminal property;
   (c) converts criminal property;
   (d) transfers criminal property;
   (e) removes criminal property from England and Wales or from Scotland or from Northern Ireland.

(2) But a person does not commit such an offence if—
   (a) he makes an authorised disclosure under section 338 and (if the disclosure is made before he does the act mentioned in subsection (1)) he has the appropriate consent;
   (b) he intended to make such a disclosure but had a reasonable excuse for not doing so;
   (c) the act he does is done in carrying out a function he has relating to the enforcement of any provision of this Act or of any other enactment relating to criminal conduct or benefit from criminal conduct.

(2A) Nor does a person commit an offence under subsection (1) if—
   (a) he knows, or believes on reasonable grounds, that the relevant criminal conduct occurred in a particular country or territory outside the United Kingdom, and
   (b) the relevant criminal conduct—
      (i) was not, at the time it occurred, unlawful under the criminal law then applying in that country or territory, and
      (ii) is not of a description prescribed by an order made by the Secretary of State.

(2B) In subsection (2A) 'the relevant criminal conduct' is the criminal conduct by reference to which the property concerned is criminal property.

(2C) A deposit-taking body that does an act mentioned in paragraph (c) or (d) of subsection (1) does not commit an offence under that subsection if—
   (a) it does the act in operating an account maintained with it, and
   (b) the value of the criminal property concerned is less than the threshold amount determined under section 339A for the act.

(3) Concealing or disguising criminal property includes concealing or disguising its nature, source, location, disposition, movement or ownership or any rights with respect to it.

328 Arrangements

(1) A person commits an offence if he enters into or becomes concerned in an arrangement which he knows or suspects facilitates (by whatever means) the acquisition, retention, use or control of criminal property by or on behalf of another person.

(2) But a person does not commit such an offence if—
   (a) he makes an authorised disclosure under section 338 and (if the disclosure is made before he does the act mentioned in subsection (1)) he has the appropriate consent;

(b) he intended to make such a disclosure but had a reasonable excuse for not doing so;

(c) the act he does is done in carrying out a function he has relating to the enforcement of any provision of this Act or of any other enactment relating to criminal conduct or benefit from criminal conduct.

329 Acquisition, use and possession

(1) A person commits an offence if he—

(a) acquires criminal property;

(b) uses criminal property;

(c) has possession of criminal property.

(2) But a person does not commit such an offence if—

(a) he makes an authorised disclosure under section 338 and (if the disclosure is made before he does the act mentioned in subsection (1)) he has the appropriate consent;

(b) he intended to make such a disclosure but had a reasonable excuse for not doing so;

(c) he acquired or used or had possession of the property for adequate consideration;

(d) the act he does is done in carrying out a function he has relating to the enforcement of any provision of this Act or of any other enactment relating to criminal conduct or benefit from criminal conduct.

(3) For the purposes of this section—

(a) a person acquires property for inadequate consideration if the value of the consideration is significantly less than the value of the property;

(b) a person uses or has possession of property for inadequate consideration if the value of the consideration is significantly less than the value of the use or possession;

(c) the provision by a person of goods or services which he knows or suspects may help another to carry out criminal conduct.

The critical definitions for these offences are contained in section 340 of the Proceeds of Crime Act 2002.

Proceeds of Crime Act 2002, s 340(2)–(4)(b)

340 Interpretation

(2) Criminal conduct is conduct which—

(a) constitutes an offence in any part of the United Kingdom, or

(b) would constitute an offence in any part of the United Kingdom if it occurred there.

(3) Property is criminal property if—

(a) it constitutes a person's benefit from criminal conduct or it represents such a benefit (in whole or part and whether directly or indirectly), and

(b) the alleged offender knows or suspects that it constitutes or represents such a benefit.

> (4) It is immaterial—
>   (a) who carried out the conduct;
>   (b) who benefited from it;
>   . . .

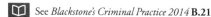 6 months' imprisonment and/or level 5 fine/14 years

C15.10.1 Key points

- For there to be criminal property, there must be an intent or a suspicion that there is a benefit from criminal conduct.
- In *Wilkinson v DPP* [2006] EWHC 3012 (Admin), the court discouraged the use of this offence (with its requirement only for suspicion rather than belief) when a handling charge would adequately have reflected the seriousness of the offence.
- For there to be an offence there must be actual criminal conduct and the proceeds must already be the product of that crime (*R v Gabriel* [2006] EWCA Crim 229).
- There are two ways in which the Crown can prove that the property derives from crime. Either:
  - by showing that it derives from criminal conduct of a specific kind; or
  - by proving that the circumstances in which it was handled create an irresistable inference that it can only have derived from crime (*R v Anwoir* [2008] EWCA Crim 1354).

See *Blackstone's Criminal Practice 2014* **B.21**

C15.11 Possession of false identity documents, etc without reasonable excuse

Identity Documents Act 2010, ss 6 and 7

6 Possession of false identity documents etc without reasonable excuse

(1) It is an offence for a person ('P'), without reasonable excuse, to have in P's possession or under P's control—
  (a) an identity document that is false,
  (b) an identity document that was improperly obtained,
  (c) an identity document that relates to someone else,

    (d) any apparatus which, to P's knowledge, is or has been specially designed or adapted for the making of false identity documents, or

    (e) any article or material which, to P's knowledge, is or has been specially designed or adapted to be used in the making of such documents.

7 Meaning of 'identity document'

(1) For the purposes of sections 4 to 6 'identity document' means any document that is or purports to be—

    (a) an immigration document,

    (b) a United Kingdom passport (within the meaning of the Immigration Act 1971),

    (c) a passport issued by or on behalf of the authorities of a country or territory outside the United Kingdom or by or on behalf of an international organisation,

    (d) a document that can be used (in some or all circumstances) instead of a passport,

    (e) a licence to drive a motor vehicle granted under Part 3 of the Road Traffic Act 1988 or under Part 2 of the Road Traffic (Northern Ireland) Order 1981, or

    (f) a driving licence issued by or on behalf of the authorities of a country or territory outside the United Kingdom.

(2) In subsection (1)(a) 'immigration document' means—

    (a) a document used for confirming the right of a person under the EU Treaties in respect of entry or residence in the United Kingdom,

    (b) a document that is given in exercise of immigration functions and records information about leave granted to a person to enter or to remain in the United Kingdom, or

    (c) a registration card (within the meaning of section 26A of the Immigration Act 1971).

(3) In subsection (2)(b) 'immigration functions' means functions under the Immigration Acts (within the meaning of the Asylum and Immigration (Treatment of Claimants, etc.) Act 2004).

(4) References in subsection (1) to the issue of a document include its renewal, replacement or re-issue (with or without modifications).

(5) In this section 'document' includes a stamp or label.

(6) The Secretary of State may by order amend the definition of 'identity document'.

EW

 6 months and/or level 5 fine/2 years

C15.11.1 *Sentencing*

Offence seriousness (culpability and harm) A. Identify the appropriate starting point Starting points based on first-time offender pleading not guilty		
Examples of nature of activity	**Starting point**	**Range**
Single document possessed	Medium level community order	Band C fine to high level community order
Small number of documents, no evidence of dealing	12 weeks' custody	6 weeks' custody to Crown Court
Considerable number of documents possessed, evidence of involvement in larger operation	Crown Court	Crown Court

Offence seriousness (culpability and harm) B. Consider the effect of aggravating and mitigating factors (other than those within examples above) The following may be particularly relevant but these lists are not exhaustive	
Factors indicating higher culpability 1. Clear knowledge that documents false 2. Number of documents possessed (where not in offence descriptions above) **Factor indicating greater degree of harm** 1. Genuine mistake or ignorance	**Factors indicating lower culpability** 1. Group activity 2. Potential impact of use (where not in offence descriptions above)

C15.11.2 Key points

- The offence under section 6 of the Identity Documents Act 2010 replaces the offence formerly charged under section 25 of the Identity Cards Act 2006. Sentencing guidelines have effect in relation to the new offence (s 13(2) of the 2010 Act).
- If the document itself is false then it is no defence in a case where the document was being used for establishing a registrable fact, that it bore the correct details of the defendant (*R v Jamalov* The Times, 17 March 2010), but the defendant's ignorance of a document's falsity could amount to a reasonable cause for possessing it (*R v Unah* [2011] EWCA Crim 1837).

 See *Blackstone's Criminal Practice 2014* **B6.59–B6.63**

C15.12 Making off without payment

Theft Act 1978, s 3

3 Making off without payment

(1) Subject to subsection (3) below, a person who, knowing that payment on the spot for any goods supplied or service done is required or expected from him, dishonestly makes off without having paid as required or expected and with intent to avoid payment of the amount due shall be guilty of an offence.

(2) For purposes of this section 'payment on the spot' includes payment at the time of collecting goods on which work has been done or in respect of which service has been provided.

(3) Subsection (1) above shall not apply where the supply of the goods or the doing of the service is contrary to law, or where the service done is such that payment is not legally enforceable.

EW

 6 months and/or level 5 fine/2 years

C15.12.1 *Sentencing*

Offence seriousness (culpability and harm) A. Identify the appropriate starting point Starting points based on first-time offender pleading not guilty		
Examples of nature of activity	**Starting point**	**Range**
Single offence committed by an offender acting alone with evidence of little or no planning, goods or services worth less than £200	Band C fine	Band A fine to high level community order
Offence displaying one or more of the following: — offender acting in unison with others — evidence of planning — offence part of a 'spree' — intimidation of victim — goods or services worth £200 or more	Medium level community order	Low level community order to 12 weeks' custody

C15.12.2 **Key points**

The intention to avoid making payment means a permanent intention not to pay, so a person who genuinely disputes a bill and challenges someone to bring legal action, cannot be said to have committed an offence.

 See *Blackstone's Criminal Practice 2014* **B5.34–B5.41**

C15.13 Obtaining services dishonestly

Fraud Act 2006, s 11(1) and (2)

11 Obtaining services dishonestly

(1) A person is guilty of an offence under this section if he obtains services for himself or another—
    (a) by a dishonest act, and
    (b) in breach of subsection (2).

(2) A person obtains services in breach of this subsection if—
    (a) they are made available on the basis that payment has been, is being or will be made for or in respect of them,
    (b) he obtains them without any payment having been made for or in respect of them or without payment having been made in full, and
    (c) when he obtains them, he knows—
        (i) that they are being made available on the basis described in paragraph (a), or
        (ii) that they might be,
    but intends that payment will not be made, or will not be made in full.

EW

 6 months and/or level 5 fine/5 years

C15.13.1 *Sentencing*

The offence of *obtaining services dishonestly* may be committed in circumstances that otherwise could be charged as an offence contrary to section 1 of the Fraud Act 2006, or may be more akin to *making off without payment*, contrary to section 3 of the Theft Act 1978. For this reason, it has not been included specifically within any of the guidelines for fraud, and one of the following approaches should be used:

• where it involves conduct which can be characterized as a fraud offence (such as obtaining credit through fraud or payment card fraud), the court should apply the guideline for the relevant type of fraud (see **Appendix 6**); or

• where the conduct could be characterized as *making off without payment* (ie where an offender, knowing that payment on the spot for any goods supplied or service done is required or expected, dishonestly makes off without having paid and with intent to avoid payment), the guideline for that offence should be used (see **C15.12.1**).

 See *Blackstone's Criminal Practice 2014* **B5.28–B5.33**

C15.14 Possession of articles for fraud

> **Fraud Act 2006, s 6**
>
> **6 Possession etc of articles for use in frauds**
> (1) A person is guilty of an offence if he has in his possession or under his control any article for use in the course of or in connection with any fraud.

 EW

 Level 5 fine/6 months/5 years

C15.14.1 *Sentencing*

See **Appendix 6**.

C15.14.2 Key points

Section 8 provides:

> **Fraud Act 2006, s 8**
>
> **8 'Article'**
> (1) For the purposes of—
>   (a) sections 6 and 7, and
>   (b) the provisions listed in subsection (2), so far as they relate to articles for use in the course of or in connection with fraud,
> 'article' includes any program or data held in electronic form.

📖 See *Blackstone's Criminal Practice 2014* **B5.21** and **B5.22**

C15.15 Making, adapting, supplying, or offering to supply articles for fraud

> **Fraud Act 2006, s 7**
>
> **7 Making or supplying articles for use in frauds**
> (1) A person is guilty of an offence if he makes, adapts, supplies or offers to supply any article—
>   (a) knowing that it is designed or adapted for use in the course of or in connection with fraud, or
>   (b) intending it to be used to commit, or assist in the commission of, fraud.

EW

Level 5 fine/6 months/10 years

C15 Dishonesty and Offences Against Property

C15.15.1 *Sentencing*

See **Appendix 6**.

C15.15.2 Key points

For definition of an 'article', see **C15.14.2**.

See *Blackstone's Criminal Practice 2014* **B5.23** and **B5.24**

C15.16 Income tax evasion

Finance Act 2000, s 144

144 Offence of fraudulent evasion of income tax

(1) A person commits an offence if he is knowingly concerned in the fraudulent evasion of income tax by him or any other person.

EW

Level 5 fine/6 months/7 years

C15.16.1 *Sentencing*

See **Appendix 6**.

See *Blackstone's Criminal Practice 2014* **B16.4**

C15.17 Railway fare evasion

Regulation of Railways Act 1889, s 5(1) and (3)

SO

Level 3 fine or 3 months (s 5(3)); level 2 fine (s 5(1))

C15.17.1 *Sentencing*

Offence seriousness (culpability and harm) A. Identify the appropriate starting point Starting points based on first-time offender pleading not guilty		
Examples of nature of activity	Starting point	Range
Failing to produce ticket or pay fare on request	Band A fine	Conditional discharge to band B fine

Travelling on railway without having paid the fare or knowingly and wilfully travelling beyond the distance paid for, with intent to avoid payment	Band B fine	Band A fine to band C fine

Offence seriousness (culpability and harm) **B. Consider the effect of aggravating and mitigating factors (other than those within examples above)** The following may be particularly relevant but these lists are not exhaustive	
Factor indicating higher culpability 1. Offensive or intimidating language or behaviour towards railway staff **Factor indicating greater degree of harm.** 1. High level of loss caused or intended to be caused	

C15.18 False statement/representation to obtain social security benefit

Social Security Administration Act 1992, ss 111A and 112

111A Dishonest representations for obtaining benefit etc

(1) If a person dishonestly—

    (a) makes a false statement or representation; or

    (b) produces or furnishes, or causes or allows to be produced or furnished, any document or information which is false in a material particular;

with a view to obtaining any benefit or other payment or advantage under the relevant social security legislation (whether for himself or for some other person), he shall be guilty of an offence.

(1A) A person shall be guilty of an offence if—

    (a) there has been a change of circumstances affecting any entitlement of his to any benefit or other payment or advantage under any provision of the relevant social security legislation;

    (b) the change is not a change that is excluded by regulations from the changes that are required to be notified;

    (c) he knows that the change affects an entitlement of his to such a benefit or other payment or advantage; and

    (d) he dishonestly fails to give a prompt notification of that change in the prescribed manner to the prescribed person.

(1B) A person shall be guilty of an offence if—

    (a) there has been a change of circumstances affecting any entitlement of another person to any benefit or other payment or advantage under any provision of the relevant social security legislation;

(b) the change is not a change that is excluded by regulations from the changes that are required to be notified;

(c) he knows that the change affects an entitlement of that other person to such a benefit or other payment or advantage; and

(d) he dishonestly causes or allows that other person to fail to give a prompt notification of that change in the prescribed manner to the prescribed person.

(1C) This subsection applies where—

(a) there has been a change of circumstances affecting any entitlement of a person ('the claimant') to any benefit or other payment or advantage under any provision of the relevant social security legislation;

(b) the benefit, payment or advantage is one in respect of which there is another person ('the recipient') who for the time being has a right to receive payments to which the claimant has, or (but for the arrangements under which they are payable to the recipient) would have, an entitlement; and

(c) the change is not a change that is excluded by regulations from the changes that are required to be notified.

(1D) In a case where subsection (1C) above applies, the recipient is guilty of an offence if—

(a) he knows that the change affects an entitlement of the claimant to a benefit or other payment or advantage under a provision of the relevant social security legislation;

(b) the entitlement is one in respect of which he has a right to receive payments to which the claimant has, or (but for the arrangements under which they are payable to the recipient) would have, an entitlement; and

(c) he dishonestly fails to give a prompt notification of that change in the prescribed manner to the prescribed person.

(1E) In a case where that subsection applies, a person other than the recipient is guilty of an offence if—

(a) he knows that the change affects an entitlement of the claimant to a benefit or other payment or advantage under a provision of the relevant social security legislation;

(b) the entitlement is one in respect of which the recipient has a right to receive payments to which the claimant has, or (but for the arrangements under which they are payable to the recipient) would have, an entitlement; and

(c) he dishonestly causes or allows the recipient to fail to give a prompt notification of that change in the prescribed manner to the prescribed person.

(1F) In any case where subsection (1C) above applies but the right of the recipient is confined to a right, by reason of his being a person to whom the claimant is required to make payments in respect of a dwelling, to receive payments of housing benefit—

(a) a person shall not be guilty of an offence under subsection (1D) or (1E) above unless the change is one relating to one or both of the following—

(i) the claimant's occupation of that dwelling;

      (ii) the claimant's liability to make payments in respect of that dwelling; but
   (b) subsections (1D)(a) and (1E)(a) above shall each have effect as if after 'knows' there were inserted 'or could reasonably be expected to know'.

(1G) For the purposes of subsections (1A) to (1E) above a notification of a change is prompt if, and only if, it is given as soon as reasonably practicable after the change occurs.

112 False representations for obtaining benefit etc

(1) If a person for the purpose of obtaining any benefit or other payment under the relevant social security legislation whether for himself or some other person, or for any other purpose connected with that legislation—
   (a) makes a statement or representation which he knows to be false; or
   (b) produces or furnishes, or knowingly causes or knowingly allows to be produced or furnished, any document or information which he knows to be false in a material particular, he shall be guilty of an offence.

(1A) A person shall be guilty of an offence if—
   (a) there has been a change of circumstances affecting any entitlement of his to any benefit or other payment or advantage under any provision of the relevant social security legislation;
   (b) the change is not a change that is excluded by regulations from the changes that are required to be notified;
   (c) he knows that the change affects an entitlement of his to such a benefit or other payment or advantage; and
   (d) he fails to give a prompt notification of that change in the prescribed manner to the prescribed person.

(1B) A person is guilty of an offence under this section if—
   (a) there has been a change of circumstances affecting any entitlement of another person to any benefit or other payment or advantage under any provision of the relevant social security legislation;
   (b) the change is not a change that is excluded by regulations from the changes that are required to be notified;
   (c) he knows that the change affects an entitlement of that other person to such a benefit or other payment or advantage; and
   (d) he causes or allows that other person to fail to give a prompt notification of that change in the prescribed manner to the prescribed person.

(1C) In a case where subsection (1C) of section 111A above applies, the recipient is guilty of an offence if—
   (a) he knows that the change affects an entitlement of the claimant to a benefit or other payment or advantage under a provision of the relevant social security legislation;
   (b) the entitlement is one in respect of which he has a right to receive payments to which the claimant has, or (but for the arrangements under which they are payable to the recipient) would have, an entitlement; and
   (c) he fails to give a prompt notification of that change in the prescribed manner to the prescribed person.

(1D) In a case where that subsection applies, a person other than the recipient is guilty of an offence if—

   (a) he knows that the change affects an entitlement of the claimant to a benefit or other payment or advantage under a provision of the relevant social security legislation;

   (b) the entitlement is one in respect of which the recipient has a right to receive payments to which the claimant has, or (but for the arrangements under which they are payable to the recipient) would have, an entitlement; and

   (c) he causes or allows the recipient to fail to give a prompt notification of that change in the prescribed manner to the prescribed person.

(1E) Subsection (1F) of section 111A above applies in relation to subsections (1C) and (1D) above as it applies in relation to subsections (1D) and (1E) of that section.

(1F) For the purposes of subsections (1A) to (1D) above a notification of a change is prompt if, and only if, it is given as soon as reasonably practicable after the change occurs.

Section 111A:

 6 months and/or level 5 fine/7 years

Section 112:

SO

 3 months and/or level 3 fine

C15.18.1 *Sentencing*

For offences under section 111A, refer to the 'Fraud Guideline' at **Appendix 6**.

Offence seriousness (culpability and harm) A. Identify the appropriate starting point Starting points based on first-time offender pleading not guilty		
Examples of nature of activity	**Starting point**	**Range**
Claim fraudulent from the start, up to £5,000 obtained (s 111A or s 112)	Medium level community order	Band B fine to high level community order
Claim fraudulent from the start, more than £5,000 but less than £20,000 obtained	12 weeks' custody	Medium level community order to Crown Court
Claim fraudulent from the start, large-scale, professional offending	Crown Court	Crown Court

Offence seriousness (culpability and harm)
B. Consider the effect of aggravating and mitigating factors
(other than those within examples above)
The following may be particularly relevant but these lists are not exhaustive

Factors indicating higher culpability	Factors indicating lower culpability
1. Offending carried out over a long period	1. Pressurized by others
2. Offender acting in unison with one or more others	2. Claim initially legitimate
3. Planning	**Factor indicating lesser degree of harm**
4. Offender motivated by greed or desire to live beyond his/her means	1. Voluntary repayment of amounts overpaid
5. False identities or other personal details used	
6. False or forged documents used	
7. Official documents altered or falsified	

R v Noel [2012] EWCA Crim 956 confirmed that a custodial sentence was not appropriate for an offence under section 112(1A)(2) (failing to notify change of circumstances) of the Social Security Amendment Act 1982 by a woman of good character, involving £12,500 over nearly five years. The committal to the Crown Court had been only for the purposes of confiscation.

C15.18.2 Key points

- In *R v Laku* [2008] EWCA Crim 1748, L made false representations in order to claim benefits and was prosecuted under sections 111A and 111A(1A) of the Social Security Administration Act 1992. On subsequent claims he did not correct the falsehoods. Held: convictions under section 111A(1A) quashed; he had not failed to notify a change in circumstances as the same false circumstances that founded the convictions under section 111A continued.
- An offence under section 111A(1B) requires a positive act on the part of the defendant. Sitting back and doing nothing does not amount to (allowing) an offence (*R v Tilley* [2009] EWCA Crim 1426).
- The offence under section 112(1A) of the Social Security Administration Act 1992 was interpreted in *Coventry City Council v Vassell* [2011] EWHC 1542 (Admin), and is committed if:
  - there is a change of circumstances affecting entitlement to benefit;
  - that change is not excluded from reporting by regulations; and
  - the defendant knows that change affects his entitlement to benefit. The court held this meant 'would' affect (not 'could' affect) that entitlement;

- In relation to the rrequirement that the defendant fails to give prompt notification in the prescribed manner to the prescribed person the court held that whether there was prompt notice is a matter of fact. In considering who is the prescribed person, the court confirmed that the DWP will not suffice if the regulations specify the local authority. However, the defendant must *know* who is the correct person for the offence to be committed. In considering that aspect, relevant issues include the information provided by the local authority and the unexpected continuation of benefit.

C15.18.3 *Time limits for prosecution*

The normal six-month time limit for summary only offences is extended in relation to section 112 by section 116(2):

Social Security Administration Act 1992, s 116(2)–(3)

116 Legal proceedings

(2) Notwithstanding anything in any Act—

  (a) proceedings for an offence under this Act (other than proceedings to which paragraph (b) applies), or for an offence under the Jobseekers Act 1995, may be begun at any time within the period of 3 months from the date on which evidence, sufficient in the opinion of the Secretary of State to justify a prosecution for the offence, comes to his knowledge or within a period of 12 months from the commission of the offence, whichever period last expires; and

  (b) proceedings brought by the appropriate authority for an offence under this Act relating to housing benefit or council tax benefit may be begun at any time within the period of 3 months from the date on which evidence, sufficient in the opinion of the appropriate authority to justify a prosecution for the offence, comes to the authority's knowledge or within a period of 12 months from the commission of the offence, whichever period last expires.

(2A) Subsection (2) above shall not be taken to impose any restriction on the time when proceedings may be begun for an offence under section 111A above.

(3) For the purposes of subsection (2) above—

  (a) a certificate purporting to be signed by or on behalf of the Secretary of State as to the date on which such evidence as is mentioned in paragraph (a) of that subsection came to his knowledge shall be conclusive evidence of that date; and.

  (b) a certificate of the appropriate authority as to the date on which such evidence as is mentioned in paragraph (b) of that subsection came to the authority's knowledge shall be conclusive evidence of that date.

  See *Blackstone's Criminal Practice 2014* **B5.8** and **B16.51–B16.55**

C15.19 **Tax credit fraud**

Tax Credits Act 2002, s 35

35 Offence of fraud

A person commits an offence if he is knowingly concerned in any fraudulent activity undertaken with a view to obtaining payments of a tax credit by him or any other person.

 6 months and/or level 5 fine/7 years

C15.19.1 *Sentencing*

See **Appendix 6**.

C15.19.2 Key points

- Disposing of the proceeds of fraud amounts to a fraudulent activity (*R v Kolapo* [2009] EWCA Crim 545).
- *R v Nolan and Howard* [2012] EWCA Crim 671 confirmed that the passive receipt of moneys and failure to report did not amount to 'fraudulent activity', which requires a positive act of misrepresentation with a view to gain. The statute requires behaviour calculated to achieve, rather than to capitalize on what had already been achieved.

 See *Blackstone's Criminal Practice 2014* **B16.5**

C15.20 **Theft**

Theft Act 1968, s 1(1) and (2)

1 Basic definition of theft

(1) A person is guilty of theft if he dishonestly appropriates property belonging to another with the intention of permanently depriving the other of it; and 'thief' and 'steal' shall be construed accordingly.

(2) It is immaterial whether the appropriation is made with a view to gain, or is made for the thief's own benefit.

C15 Dishonesty and Offences Against Property

C15.20.1 *Sentencing: theft, breach of trust*

Type/nature of activity	Starting point	Sentencing range
Theft of less than £2,000	Medium level community order	Band B fine to 26 weeks' custody
Theft of £2,000 or more but less than £20,000 OR Theft of less than £2,000 in breach of a high degree of trust	18 weeks' custody	High level community order to Crown Court
Theft of £20,000 or more OR Theft of £2,000 or more in breach of a high degree of trust	Crown Court	Crown Court

Additional aggravating factors
1. Long course of offending
2. Suspicion deliberately thrown on others
3. Offender motivated by intention to cause harm or out of revenge

C15.20.2 *Sentencing: theft from the person*

Type/nature of activity	Starting point	Sentencing range
Where the effect on the victim is particularly severe, the stolen property is of high value, or substantial consequential loss results, a sentence higher than the range into which the offence would fall may be appropriate.		
Theft from a vulnerable victim involving intimidation or the use or threat of force (falling short of robbery)	18 months' custody	12 months' to 3 years' custody
Theft from a vulnerable victim	18 weeks' custody	Community order (HIGH) to 12 months' custody
Theft from the person not involving vulnerable victim	Community order (MEDIUM)	Fine Band B to 18 weeks' custody

Additional aggravating factors
1. Offender motivated by intention to cause harm or out of revenge
2. Intimidation or face-to-face confrontation with victim [except where this raises offence into the higher sentencing range]
3. Use of force, or threat of force, against victim (not amounting to robbery) [except where this raises the offence into a higher sentencing range]
4. High level of inconvenience caused to victim, eg replacing house keys, credit cards, etc

C15.20.3 *Sentencing: theft from shop*

Type/nature of activity	Starting point	Sentencing range
Organized gang/group and Intimidation or the use or threat of force (short of robbery)	12 months' custody	36 weeks' to 4 years' custody
Significant intimidation or threats OR Use of force resulting in slight injury OR Very high level of planning OR Significant related damage	6 weeks' custody	Community order (HIGH) to 36 weeks' custody
Low level intimidation or threats OR Some planning, eg a session of stealing on the same day or going equipped OR Some related damage	Community order (LOW)	Fine to community order (MEDIUM)
Little or no planning or sophistication AND Goods stolen of low value	Fine	Conditional discharge to community order (LOW)

Additional aggravating factors

1. Child accompanying offender is involved in or aware of theft
2. Offender is subject to a banning order that includes the store targeted
3. Offender motivated by intention to cause harm or out of revenge
4. Professional offending
5. Victim particularly vulnerable (eg small independent shop)
6. Offender targeted high value goods

C15.20.4 Key points

- Dishonesty is a two-part test:

  1. Were the accused's actions dishonest according to the ordinary standards of reasonable and honest people?
  2. If so, did the accused know that those actions were dishonest according to those standards?

  (*R v Ghosh* [1982] QB 1058)

- 'Dishonestly' is considered in section 2 of the Theft Act 1968:

Theft Act 1968, s 2

2 'Dishonestly'

(1) A person's appropriation of property belonging to another is not to be regarded as dishonest—

   (a) if he appropriates the property in the belief that he has in law the right to deprive the other of it, on behalf of himself or of a third person; or

(b) if he appropriates the property in the belief that he would have the other's consent if the other knew of the appropriation and the circumstances of it; or

(c) (except where the property came to him as trustee or personal representative) if he appropriates the property in the belief that the person to whom the property belongs cannot be discovered by taking reasonable steps..

(2) A person's appropriation of property belonging to another may be dishonest notwithstanding that he is willing to pay for the property.

'Appropriation' means the assumption of any of the rights of an owner (*R v Gomez* [1993] AC 442).

The intention permanently to deprive is considered in section 6 of the Theft Act 1968:

Theft Act 1968, s 6

6 'With the intention of permanently depriving the other of it'

(1) A person appropriating property belonging to another without meaning the other permanently to lose the thing itself is nevertheless to be regarded as having the intention of permanently depriving the other of it if his intention is to treat the thing as his own to dispose of regardless of the other's rights; and a borrowing or lending of it may amount to so treating it if, but only if, the borrowing or lending is for a period and in circumstances making it equivalent to an outright taking or disposal.

(2) Without prejudice to the generality of subsection (1) above, where a person, having possession or control (lawfully or not) of property belonging to another, parts with the property under a condition as to its return which he may not be able to perform, this (if done for purposes of his own and without the other's authority) amounts to treating the property as his own to dispose of regardless of the other's rights.

C15.21 Going equipped for theft

Theft Act 1968, s 25(1)–(3), (5)

25 Going equipped for stealing etc

(1) A person shall be guilty of an offence if, when not at his place of abode, he has with him any article for use in the course of or in connection with any burglary or theft.

(2) A person guilty of an offence under this section shall on conviction on indictment be liable to imprisonment for a term not exceeding three years.

(3) Where a person is charged with an offence under this section, proof that he had with him any article made or adapted for use in committing a burglary or theft shall be evidence that he had it with him for such use.

(4) . . .

(5) For purposes of this section an offence under section 12(1) of this Act of taking a conveyance shall be treated as theft.

6 months and/or level 5 fine/3 years

C15.21.1 *Sentencing*

Offence seriousness (culpability and harm) A. Identify the appropriate starting point Starting points based on first-time offender pleading not guilty		
Examples of nature of activity	**Starting point**	**Range**
Possession of items for theft from shop or of vehicle	Medium level community order	Band C fine to high level community order
Possession of items for burglary, robbery	High level community order	Medium level community order to Crown Court

Offence seriousness (culpability and harm) B. Consider the effect of aggravating and mitigating factors (other than those within examples above) The following may be particularly relevant but these lists are not exhaustive	
Factors indicating higher culpability 1. Circumstances suggest offender equipped for particularly serious offence 2. Items to conceal identity	

C15.21.2 Key points

The article need not be intended for immediate use but it must be intended for future use (see *R v Ellames* [1974] 1 WLR 1391). Proof of intent is required and not mere contemplation of an offence (see *R v Hargreaves* [1985] Crim LR 243).

 See *Blackstone's Criminal Practice 2014* **B4.151–4.159**

C15.22 **Unauthorized used of trade mark, etc**

Trade Marks Act 1994, s 92(1)–(4)

92 Unauthorised use of trade mark, etc in relation to goods

(1) A person commits an offence who with a view to gain for himself or another, or with intent to cause loss to another, and without the consent of the proprietor—

(a) applies to goods or their packaging a sign identical to, or likely to be mistaken for, a registered trade mark, or

---

    (b) sells or lets for hire, offers or exposes for sale or hire or distributes goods which bear, or the packaging of which bears, such a sign, or

    (c) has in his possession, custody or control in the course of a business any such goods with a view to the doing of anything, by himself or another, which would be an offence under paragraph (b).

(2) A person commits an offence who with a view to gain for himself or another, or with intent to cause loss to another, and without the consent of the proprietor—

    (a) applies a sign identical to, or likely to be mistaken for, a registered trade mark to material intended to be used—

      (i)   for labelling or packaging goods,

      (ii) as a business paper in relation to goods, or

      (iii) for advertising goods, or

    (b) uses in the course of a business material bearing such a sign for labelling or packaging goods, as a business paper in relation to goods, or for advertising goods, or

    (c) has in his possession, custody or control in the course of a business any such material with a view to the doing of anything, by himself or another, which would be an offence under paragraph (b).

(3) A person commits an offence who with a view to gain for himself or another, or with intent to cause loss to another, and without the consent of the proprietor—

    (a) makes an article specifically designed or adapted for making copies of a sign identical to, or likely to be mistaken for, a registered trade mark, or

    (b) has such an article in his possession, custody or control in the course of a business,

knowing or having reason to believe that it has been, or is to be, used to produce goods, or material for labelling or packaging goods, as a business paper in relation to goods, or for advertising goods.

(4) A person does not commit an offence under this section unless—

    (a) the goods are goods in respect of which the trade mark is registered, or

    (b) the trade mark has a reputation in the United Kingdom and the use of the sign takes or would take unfair advantage of, or is or would be detrimental to, the distinctive character or the repute of the trade mark.

 6 months and/or level 5 fine/10 years

C15.22.1 *Sentencing*

Offence seriousness (culpability and harm) A. Identify the appropriate starting point Starting points based on first-time offender pleading not guilty		
Examples of nature of activity	**Starting point**	**Range**
Small number of counterfeit items	Band C fine	Band B fine to low level community order

Larger number of counterfeit items but no involvement in wider operation	Medium level community order, plus fine*	Low level community order to 12 weeks' custody, plus fine*
High number of counterfeit items or involvement in wider operation, eg manufacture or distribution	12 weeks' custody	6 weeks' custody to Crown Court
Central role in large-scale operation	Crown Court	Crown Court

* This may be an offence where it is appropriate to combine a fine with a community order.

Offence seriousness (culpability and harm) **B. Consider the effect of aggravating and mitigating factors** **(other than those within examples above)** The following may be particularly relevant but these lists are not exhaustive	
Factors indicating higher culpability 1. High degree of professionalism 2. High level of profit **Factor indicating greater degree of harm** 1. Purchasers at risk of harm, eg from counterfeit drugs	**Factor indicating lower culpability** 1. Mistake or ignorance about provenance of goods

C15.22.2 Key points

It is a defence for a person charged with an offence under section 92 to show that he believed on reasonable grounds that the use of the sign in the manner in which it was used, or was to be used, was not an infringement of the registered trade mark. In order to be able to satisfy the statutory defence under section 95(2) of the Trade Marks Act 1994, the defendant must show not only that he had an honest belief that the trade marks did not infringe registered trade marks, but also that he had reasonable grounds for so believing. Section 97 makes provision for the forfeiture of counterfeit goods and packaging.

 See *Blackstone's Criminal Practice 2014* **B6.102**

C15.23 TV licence payment evasion

Communications Act 2003, s 363

363 Licence required for use of TV receiver

Ⅲ Level 3 fine

C15.23.1 *Sentencing*

Offence seriousness (culpability and harm) A. Identify the appropriate starting point Starting points based on first-time offender pleading not guilty		
Examples of nature of activity	**Starting point**	**Range**
Up to 6 months' unlicensed use	Band A fine	Band A fine
Over 6 months' unlicensed use	Band B fine	Band A fine to band B fine

Offence seriousness (culpability and harm) B. Consider the effect of aggravating and mitigating factors (other than those within examples above) The following may be particularly relevant but these lists are not exhaustive	
	Factors indicating lower culpability 1. Accidental oversight or belief licence held 2. Confusion of responsibility 3. Licence immediately obtained

C15.24 TWOC (vehicle-taking without consent)

Theft Act 1968, s 12(1), (5), (6), and (7)

12 Taking motor vehicle or other conveyance without authority

(1) Subject to subsections (5) and (6) below, a person shall be guilty of an offence if, without having the consent of the owner or other lawful authority, he takes any conveyance for his own or another's use or knowing that any conveyance has been taken without such authority, drives it or allows himself to be carried in or on it.

(5) Subsection (1) above shall not apply in relation to pedal cycles; but, subject to subsection (6) below, a person who, without having the consent of the owner or other lawful authority, takes a pedal cycle for his own or another's use, or rides a pedal cycle knowing it to have been taken without such authority, shall on summary conviction be liable to a fine not exceeding level 3 on the standard scale.

---

(6) A person does not commit an offence under this section by anything done in the belief that he has lawful authority to do it or that he would have the owner's consent if the owner knew of his doing it and the circumstances of it.

(7) For purposes of this section—

(a) 'conveyance' means any conveyance constructed or adapted for the carriage of a person or persons whether by land, water or air, except that it does not include a conveyance constructed or adapted for use only under the control of a person not carried in or on it, and 'drive' shall be construed accordingly; and

(b) 'owner', in relation to a conveyance which is the subject of a hiring agreement or hire-purchase agreement, means the person in possession of the conveyance under that agreement.

SO

6 months and/or level 5 fine

C15.24.1 *Sentencing*

Offence seriousness (culpability and harm)		
A. Identify the appropriate starting point		
Starting points based on first-time offender pleading not guilty		
Examples of nature of activity	**Starting point**	**Range**
Exceeding authorized use of, eg employer's or relative's, vehicle; retention of hire car beyond return date	Low level community order	Band B fine to medium level community order
As above with damage caused to lock/ignition; OR Stranger's vehicle involved but no damage caused	Medium level community order	Low level community order to high level community order
Taking vehicle from private premises; OR Causing damage to, eg lock/ignition of stranger's vehicle	High level community order	Medium level community order to 26 weeks' custody

Offence seriousness (culpability and harm)	
B. Consider the effect of aggravating and mitigating factors	
(other than those within examples above)	
The following may be particularly relevant but these lists are not exhaustive	
Factors indicating greater degree of harm	**Factor indicating lower culpability**
1. Vehicle later burnt	1. Misunderstanding with owner

	Factor indicating lesser degree of harm
2. Vehicle belonging to elderly/ disabled person	1. Offender voluntarily returned vehicle to owner
3. Emergency services vehicle	
4. Medium to large goods vehicle	
5. Passengers carried	

C15.24.2 Key points

- This offence is summary only, but subject to the following exception in relation to limitation period. Section 12(4A)–(4C) of the Act provides:

Theft Act 1968, s 12(4A)–(4C)

(4A) Proceedings for an offence under subsection (1) above (but not proceedings of a kind falling within subsection (4) above) in relation to a mechanically propelled vehicle—

    (a) shall not be commenced after the end of the period of three years beginning with the day on which the offence was committed; but

    (b) subject to that, may be commenced at any time within the period of six months beginning with the relevant day.

(4B) In subsection (4A)(b) above 'the relevant day' means—

    (a) in the case of a prosecution for an offence under subsection (1) above by a public prosecutor, the day on which sufficient evidence to justify the proceedings came to the knowledge of any person responsible for deciding whether to commence any such prosecution;

    (b) in the case of a prosecution for an offence under subsection (1) above which is commenced by a person other than a public prosecutor after the discontinuance of a prosecution falling within paragraph (a) above which relates to the same facts, the day on which sufficient evidence to justify the proceedings came to the knowledge of the person who has decided to commence the prosecution or (if later) the discontinuance of the other prosecution;

    (c) in the case of any other prosecution for an offence under subsection (1) above, the day on which sufficient evidence to justify the proceedings came to the knowledge of the person who has decided to commence the prosecution.

(4C) For the purposes of subsection (4A)(b) above a certificate of a person responsible for deciding whether to commence a prosecution of a kind mentioned in subsection (4B)(a) above as to the date on which such evidence as is mentioned in the certificate came to the knowledge of any person responsible for deciding whether to commence any such prosecution shall be conclusive evidence of that fact.

- There must be movement for a vehicle to be taken (*R v Bogacki* [1973] QB 832). The vehicle must be taken as a conveyance (*R v Stokes* [1983] RTR 59). The burden of proving that the defendant did not have a belief that he had the authority of the owner lies on the Crown once the defendant has raised the issue by evidence (*R v Gannon* (1987) 87 Cr App R 254). The belief must exist at the time of the taking (*R v Ambler* [1979] RTR 217).

 See *Blackstone's Criminal Practice 2014* **B4.117–B4.127**

C15.25 **VAT evasion**

Value Added Tax Act 1994, s 72(1)

72 Offences

(1) If any person is knowingly concerned in, or in the taking of steps with a view to, the fraudulent evasion of VAT by him or any other person he shall be liable . . .

EW

Fine level 5 and/or 6 months/7 years

C15.25.1 *Sentence*

See **Appendix 6**.

C15.25.2 Key points

- Section 72(2) provides:

Value Added Tax Act 1999, s 72(2)

72 Offences

(2) Evasion of VAT includes a reference to the obtaining of—
  - (a) the payment of a VAT credit; or
  - (b) a refund under sections 35, 36 or 40 of this Act or section 22 of the 1983 Act; or
  - (c) a refund under any regulations made by virtue of section 13(5); or
  - (d) a repayment under section 39;

and any reference in those subsections to the amount of the VAT shall be construed—
  - (i) in relation to VAT itself or a VAT credit, as a reference to the aggregate of the amount (if any) falsely claimed by way of credit for input tax and the amount (if any) by which output tax was falsely understated, and

> (ii) in relation to a refund or repayment falling within paragraph (b),
> (c) or above, as a reference to the amount falsely claimed by way of
> refund or repayment.

- Turning a blind eye is sufficient to establish that a person 'knowingly did one of the prohibited acts' (*Ross v Moss* [1965] 2 QB 396).
- For an evasion there does not need to be any intention permanently to avoid payment (*R v Dealy* [1995] 1 WLR 658).

C15.26 Vehicle interference

Criminal Attempts Act 1981, s 9(1) and (2)

9 Interference with vehicles

(1) A person is guilty of the offence of vehicle interference if he interferes with a motor vehicle or trailer or with anything carried in or on a motor vehicle or trailer with the intention that an offence specified in subsection (2) below shall be committed by himself or some other person.

(2) The offences mentioned in subsection (1) above are—

    (a) theft of the motor vehicle or trailer or part of it;

    (b) theft of anything carried in or on the motor vehicle or trailer; and

    (c) an offence under section 12(1) of the Theft Act 1968 (taking and driving away without consent);

    and, if it is shown that a person accused of an offence under this section intended that one of those offences should be committed, it is immaterial that it cannot be shown which it was.

 SO

 3 months and/or fine level 4

C15.26.1 *Sentencing*

Offence seriousness (culpability and harm)		
A. Identify the appropriate starting point		
Starting points based on first-time offender pleading not guilty		
Examples of nature of activity	**Starting point**	**Range**
Trying door handles; no entry gained to vehicle; no damage caused	Band C fine	Band A fine to low level community order
Entering vehicle, little or no damage caused	Medium level community order	Band C fine to high level community order
Entering vehicle, with damage caused	High level community order	Medium level community order to 12 weeks' custody

Offence seriousness (culpability and harm)	
B. Consider the effect of aggravating and mitigating factors (other than those within examples above)	
The following may be particularly relevant but these lists are not exhaustive	
Factor indicating higher culpability	
1. Targeting vehicle in dark/isolated location	
Factors indicating greater degree of harm	
1. Emergency services vehicle	
2. Disabled driver's vehicle	
3. Part of series	

 See *Blackstone's Criminal Practice 2014* **B4.137–B4.140**

C15.27 Vehicle licence/registration fraud

Vehicle Excise and Registration Act 1994, s 44(1) and (2)

44 Forgery and fraud

(1) A person is guilty of an offence if he forges, fraudulently alters, fraudulently uses, fraudulently lends or fraudulently allows to be used by another person anything to which subsection (2) applies

(2) This subsection applies to—

    (a) a vehicle licence,

    (b) a trade licence,

    (c) a nil licence,

    (d) a registration mark,

    (e) a registration document, and

    (f) a trade plate (including a replacement trade plate).

EW

 Level 5 fine/2 years

C15.27.1 *Sentencing*

Offence seriousness (culpability and harm)		
A. Identify the appropriate starting point		
Starting points based on first-time offender pleading not guilty		
Examples of nature of activity	**Starting point**	**Range**
Use of unaltered licence from another vehicle	Band B fine	Band B fine

---

C15 Dishonesty and Offences Against Property

Forged licence bought for own use, or forged/altered for own use	Band C fine	Band C fine
Use of number plates from another vehicle; OR licence/number plates forged or altered for sale to another	High level community order (in Crown Court)	Medium level community order to Crown Court (*Note*: community order and custody available only in Crown Court)

Offence seriousness (culpability and harm)
B. Consider the effect of aggravating and mitigating factors (other than those within examples above)
The following may be particularly relevant but these lists are not exhaustive

Factors indicating higher culpability	Factors indicating lower culpability
1. LGV, PSV, taxi, etc 2. Long-term fraudulent use **Factors indicating greater degree of harm** 1. High financial gain 2. Innocent victim deceived 3. Legitimate owner inconvenienced	1. Licence/registration mark from another vehicle owned by defendant 2. Short-term use

 See *Blackstone's Criminal Practice 2014* **C4.10**

C16 **Offences Against the Person**

C16.1 **Assault occasioning actual bodily harm**

Offences Against the Person Act 1861, s 47

47 Assault occasioning bodily harm
Whosoever shall be convicted . . . of any assault occasioning actual bodily harm shall be liable . . .

 Maximum sentence

Level 5 fine and/or 6 months/5 years (7 years if racially aggravated)

C16.1.1 *Sentencing*
STEP ONE: Determining the offence category

Category 1	Greater harm (serious injury must normally be present) and higher culpability
Category 2	Greater harm (serious injury must normally be present) and lower culpability or lesser harm and higher culpability
Category 3	Lesser harm and lower culpability

Factors indicating greater harm	Factors indicating higher culpability
Injury (which includes disease transmission and/or psychological harm) which is serious in the context of the offence (must normally be present) Victim is particularly vulnerable because of personal circumstances Sustained or repeated assault on the same victim	**Statutory aggravating factors:** Offence motivated by, or demonstrating, hostility to, the victim based on his or her sexual orientation (or presumed sexual orientation) Offence motivated by, or demonstrating, hostility to, the victim's disability (or presumed disability) **Other aggravating factors:** A significant degree of premeditation Use of weapon or weapon equivalent (eg shod foot, head-butting, use of acid, use of animal) Intention to commit more serious harm than actually resulted from the offence

	Deliberately causes more harm than is necessary for commission of offence Deliberate targeting of vulnerable victim Leading role in group or gang Offence motivated by, or demonstrating, hostility based on, the victim's age, sex, gender identity (or presumed gender identity)
Factors indicating lesser harm	**Factors indicating lower culpability**
Injury which is less serious in the context of the offence	Subordinate role in group or gang A greater degree of provocation than normally expected Lack of premeditation Mental disorder or learning disability, where linked to commission of the offence Excessive self-defence

STEP TWO: Starting point and category range

Offence category	Starting point	Category range
Category 1	Crown court	Crown Court
Category 2	26 weeks' custody	Low level community order to Crown Court (51 weeks' custody)
Category 3	Medium level community order	Band A fine to high level community order

Factors increasing seriousness	Factors reducing seriousness or reflecting personal mitigation
Statutory aggravating factors: Previous convictions, having regard to (a) the nature of the offence to which the conviction relates and its relevance to the current offence; and (b) the time that has elapsed since the conviction Offence committed whilst on bail Other aggravating factors include: Location of the offence Timing of the offence Ongoing effect upon the victim Offence committed against those working in the public sector or providing a service to the public Presence of others including relatives, especially children or partner of the victim	No previous convictions or no relevant/recent convictions Single blow Remorse Good character and/or exemplary conduct Determination and/or demonstration of steps taken to address addiction or offending behaviour Serious medical conditions requiring urgent, intensive, or long-term treatment Isolated incident Age and/or lack of maturity where it affects the responsibility of the offender Lapse of time since the offence where this is not the fault of the offender

Gratuitous degradation of victim	Mental disorder or learning disability, where
In domestic violence cases, victim forced to	not linked to the commission of the offence
leave their home	Sole or primary carer for dependent relatives
Failure to comply with current court orders	
Offence committed whilst on licence	
Attempt to conceal or dispose of evidence	
Failure to respond to warnings or concerns	
expressed by others about the offender's	
behaviour	
Commission of offence whilst under the influ-	
ence of alcohol or drugs	
Abuse of power and/or position of trust	
Exploiting contact arrangements with a child	
to commit an offence	
Established evidence of community impact	
Any steps taken to prevent the victim report-	
ing an incident, obtaining assistance, and/or	
from assisting or supporting the prosecution	
Offences taken into consideration (TICs)	

Additional steps

Consider any factors which indicate a reduction, such as: assistance to the prosecution; reduction for guilty plea; dangerousness; totality principle; compensation and ancillary orders; reasons; consideration for remand time.

C16.1.2 Key points

- Action or words causing the person to apprehend imminent unlawful force. A conditional threat amounts to an assault, as does a threat to do something in the future (how far into the future is a matter of debate, see *R v Constanza* [1997] 2 Cr App R 492). Words in themselves could suffice, as could a gesture (eg using fingers to imitate a gun being fired, or a slashing action across the throat). An extreme example can be found in *R v Ireland* [1998] AC 147, a case where the appellant made silent phone calls to the victim. Conditional actions—for example, 'get out of my house or I will hurt you'—will amount to an assault. The words may also indicate that no assault is going to happen, as in the famous case of *Tuberville v Savage* (1669) 1 Mod Rep 3 ('if it were not assize time, I would not take such language from you'). Creating a danger can amount to an assault; for example if a prisoner knows that he has a needle secreted on him and dishonestly does not inform a police officer carrying out a search, he may be liable if the officer injures himself on that needle, such a risk being reasonably forseeable (*Director of Public Prosecutions v Santana-Bermudez* [2003] EWHC 2908 (Admin)).

- A battery involves the use of actual force being applied to the victim.
- Harm, which must be more than merely transient or trifling, encompasses not only injury but also hurt and damage. The concept of bodily harm is wide-ranging, and includes the cutting off of someone's hair (*DPP v Smith* [2006] 2 Cr App R 1). Psychiatric injury, in a medically diagnosed form, can amount to bodily harm, but anything short of this, for example upset or distress, will not.
- Mens rea is intention or recklessness. Note that the mens rea relates to the act of assault or battery; there is no requirement to prove that harm was intended, or that the defendant was reckless as to whether or not harm would be caused.

C16.1.3 *Defences*

The following defences should be considered:

- Consent, although *R v Brown* [1994] 1 AC 212 limits the application of this defence in sado-masochistic situations. It remains available, for instance, in sport or medical treatment, or where a wife agrees to be 'branded' (*R v Wilson* [1996] 2 Cr App R 241).
- Lawful correction or chastisement, but subject to section 58 of the Children Act 2004.

Children Act 2004, s 58(1)–(2)

58 Reasonable punishment

(1) In relation to any offence specified in subsection (2), battery of a child cannot be justified on the ground that it constituted reasonable punishment.

(2) The offences referred to in subsection (1) are—

    (a) an offence under section 18 or 20 of the Offences against the Person Act 1861 (c. 100) (wounding and causing grievous bodily harm);

    (b) an offence under section 47 of that Act (assault occasioning actual bodily harm);.

    (c) an offence under section 1 of the Children and Young Persons Act 1933 (c. 12) (cruelty to persons under 16).

- Self-defence. Because there must be an unlawful act, a person acting in self-defence cannot be guilty of an assault; and once the issue has been rasied by the defence in evidence, the Crown must prove that the defendant was not acting in self-defence. Householders enjoy a wider definition of self-defence under the amended s 76 of the Criminal Justice and Immigration Act 2008.
- Defence of property.
- Prevention of crime.

 See *Blackstone's Criminal Practice 2014* **B2.27–B2.35**

C16.2 Assault with intent to resist arrest

Offences Against the Person Act 1861, s 38

38 Assault with intent to resist apprehension, etc
Whosoever shall assault any person with intent to resist or prevent the lawful
apprehension or detainer of himself or of any other person for any offence,
shall be guilty of an offence.

EW

6 months and/or level 5 fine/2 years

DO

C16.2.1 *Sentencing*
STEP ONE: Determining the offence category

Category 1	Greater harm and higher culpability
Category 2	Greater harm and lower culpability; or lesser harm and higher culpability
Category 3	Lesser harm and lower culpability

Factors indicating lesser harm	Factors indicating lower culpability
Sustained or repeated assault on the same victim Injury which is less serious in the context of the offence	**Statutory aggravating factors:** Offence racially or religiously aggravated Offence motivated by, or demonstrating, hostility to the victim based on his or her sexual orientation (or presumed sexual orientation) Offence motivated by, or demonstrating, hostility to the victim based on the victim's disability (or presumed disability) **Other aggravating factors:** A significant degree of premeditation Use of weapon or weapon equivalent (eg shod foot, head-butting, use of acid, use of animal) Intention to commit more serious harm than actually resulted from the offence Deliberately causes more harm than is necessary for commission of offence Leading role in group or gang

Sentence

	Offence motivated by, or demonstrating, hostility based on the victim's age, sex, gender identity (or presumed gender identity)
	Subordinate role in group or gang
	Lack of premeditation
	Mental disorder or learning disability, where linked to commission of the offence

STEP TWO: Starting point and category range

Offence category	Starting point	Category range
Category 1	26 weeks' custody	12 weeks' custody to Crown Court (51 weeks' custody)
Category 2	Medium level community order	Low level community order to High level community order
Category 3	Band B fine	Band A fine to band C fine

Factors indicating greater harm	Factors indicating higher culpability
Statutory aggravating factors: Previous convictions, having regard to (a) the nature of the offence to which the conviction relates and its relevance to the current offence; and (b) the time that has elapsed since the conviction	No previous convictions or no relevant/recent convictions
Offence committed whilst on bail	Single blow
Other aggravating factors include:	Remorse
Location of the offence	Good character and/or exemplary conduct
Timing of the offence	Determination and/or demonstration of steps taken to address addiction or offending behaviour
Ongoing effect upon the victim	Serious medical conditions requiring urgent, intensive, or long-term treatment
Gratuitous degradation of victim	Isolated incident
Failure to comply with current court orders	Age and/or lack of maturity where it affects the responsibility of the defendant
Offence committed whilst on licence	Mental disorder or learning disability, where not linked to the commission of the offence
Attempt to conceal or dispose of evidence	Sole or primary carer for dependent relatives
Failure to respond to warnings or concerns expressed by others about the offender's behaviour	
Commission of offence whilst under the influence of alcohol or drugs	
Established evidence of community impact	
Any steps taken to prevent the victim reporting an incident, obtaining assistance, and/or assisting or supporting the prosecution	
Offences taken into consideration (TICs)	

Additional steps

Consider any factors which indicate a reduction, such as: assistance to the prosecution; reduction for guilty plea; dangerousness; totality principle; compensation and ancillary orders; reasons; consideration for remand time.

C16.2.2 Key points

- The arrest must be a lawful one, and the defendant's honest but mistaken belief in that regard does not afford a defence (*R v Lee* (2001) 165 JP 344).
- The prosecution do not need to prove that the defendant knew (in the case of a police officer) that the person was a police officer (*R v Brightling* [1991] Crim LR 364).

 See *Blackstone's Criminal Practice 2014* **B2.22–B2.26**

C16.3 Assaulting a police constable or resisting or obstructing a police constable

Police Act 1996, s 89(1)–(2)

89 Assaults on constables

(1) Any person who assaults a constable in the execution of his duty, or a person assisting a constable in the execution of his duty, shall be guilty of an offence . . .

(2) Any person who resists or wilfully obstructs a constable in the execution of his duty, or a person assisting a constable in the execution of his duty, shall be guilty of an offence . . .

SO

 6 months and/or level 5 fine (assaults), and/or 1 month/level 3 fine/(resist/obstruct)

C16.3.1 *Sentencing*

STEP ONE: Determining the offence category

Category 1	Greater harm and higher culpability
Category 2	Greater harm and lower culpability; or lesser harm and higher culpability
Category 3	Lesser harm and lower culpability

C16 Offences Against the Person

Factors indicating greater harm	Factors indicating higher culpability
Sustained or repeated assault on the same victim	**Statutory aggravating factors:** Offence racially or religiously aggravated Offence motivated by, or demonstrating, hostility to the victim based on his or her sexual orientation (or presumed sexual orientation) Offence motivated by, or demonstrating, hostility to the victim based on the victim's disability(or presumed disability) **Other aggravating factors:** A significant degree of premeditation Use of weapon or weapon equivalent (eg shod foot, headbutting, use of acid, use of animal) Intention to commit more serious harm than actually resulted from the offence Deliberately causes more harm than is necessary for commission of offence Leading role in group or gang Offence motivated by, or demonstrating, hostility based on the victim's age, sex, gender identity (or presumed gender identity)
Factors indicating lesser harm	**Factors indicating lower culpability**
Injury which is less serious in the context of the offence	Subordinate role in group or gang Lack of premeditation Mental disorder or learning disability, where linked to commission of the offence

STEP TWO: Starting point and category range

Offence category	Starting point	Category range
Category 1	12 weeks' custody	Low level community order to 26 weeks' custody
Category 2	Medium level community order	Low level community order to high level community order
Category 3	Band B fine	Band A fine to band C fine

Factors increasing seriousness	Factors reducing seriousness or reflecting personal mitigation
Statutory aggravating factors: Previous convictions, having regard to (a) the nature of the offence to which the conviction relates and its relevance to the current offence; and (b) the time that has elapsed since the conviction	No previous convictions or no relevant/recent convictions Single blow Remorse Good character and/or exemplary conduct

Offence committed whilst on bail	Determination and/or demonstration of
Other aggravating factors include:	steps taken to address addiction or offending
Location of the offence	behaviour
Timing of the offence	Serious medical conditions requiring urgent,
Ongoing effect upon the victim	intensive, or long-term treatment
Gratuitous degradation of victim	Isolated incident
Failure to comply with current court orders	Age and/or lack of maturity where it affects
Offence committed whilst on licence	the responsibility of the offender
Attempt to conceal or dispose of evidence	Lapse of time since the offence where this is
Failure to respond to warnings or concerns	not the fault of the offender
expressed by others about the offender's	Mental disorder or learning disability, where
behaviour	not linked to the commission of the offence
Commission of offence whilst under the	Sole or primary carer for dependent relatives
influence of alcohol or drugs	
Established evidence of community impact	
Any steps taken to prevent the victim report-	
ing an incident, obtaining assistance, and/or	
assisting or supporting the prosecution	
Offences taken into consideration (TICs)	

Additional steps

Consider any factors which indicate a reduction, such as: assistance to the prosecution; reduction for guilty plea; dangerousness; totality principle; compensation and ancillary orders; reasons; consideration for remand time.

C16.3.2 Key points

- The constable must be acting lawfully (ie in execution of his duty).
- The prosecution do not need to prove that the defendant knew that the person was a police officer (*R v Brightling* [1991] Crim LR 364).
- If officer A is not acting lawfully in arresting a suspect, officer B who in good faith seeks to assist officer A will not be acting lawfully (*Cumberbatch v Crown Prosecution Service* [2009] EWHC 3353 (Admin)).
- If a suspect is accused of trying to impede the arrest of a third party, it must be shown that the arrest of that third party was lawful (*Riley v Director of Public Prosecutions* (1990) 91 Cr App R 14).
- The court is entitled to convict on the basis of recklessness even where the Crown puts its case on the basis of an intentional assault (*D v Director of Public Prosecutions* [2005] Crim LR 962).
- For the lawfulness of a police officer entering premises to save life or limb, see *Baker v Crown Prosecution Service* [2009] EWHC 299 (Admin).

- For the situation where a police officer has had a licence to remain on property revoked, see *R (Fullard) v Woking Magistrates' Court* [2005] EWHC 2922 (Admin).
- An officer who had not yet established grounds for arrest was acting unlawfully in restraining a suspect (*Wood v Director of Public Prosecutions* [2008] EWHC 1056 (Admin)). It was unlawful to take hold of a woman to question her (*Collins v Wilcock* [1984] 1 WLR 1172), but not every interference with a citizen's liberty will be sufficient to take the officer outside the course of his duty. A police officer may take hold of a person's arm to attract his attention and calm him down (*Mepstead v DPP* (1996) 160 JP 175).
- The powers of the police to stop and search, and of entry under the Police and Criminal Evidence Act 1984, are interpreted strictly (see *R v Bristol* [2007] EWCA Crim 3214 and *B v Director of Public Prosecutions* [2008] EWHC 1655 (Admin)).

 See *Blackstone's Criminal Practice 2014* **B2.36–B2.46**

C16.4 Assaulting a court security officer

Courts Act 2003, s 57(1) and (3)

57 Assaulting and obstructing court security officers

(1) Any person who assaults a court security officer acting in the execution of his duty commits an offence.

...

(3) A person who resists or wilfully obstructs a court security officer acting in the execution of his duty commits an offence.

SO

 6 months and/or level 5 fine

C16.4.1 Key points

- A court officer must be appointed by the Lord Chancellor, and designated in that role (Courts Act 2003, s 51).
- Section 51(3) provides:

Courts Act 2003, s 51(3)

51 Court security officers

(3) ... a court security officer who is not readily identifiable as such (whether by means of his uniform or badge or otherwise), is not to be regarded as acting in the execution of his duty.

C16.5 Offences against designated and accredited persons

Police Reform Act 2002, s 46

46 Offences against designated and accredited persons etc.

(1) Any person who assaults—

    (a) a designated person in the execution of his duty,

    (b) an accredited person in the execution of his duty,

    (ba) an accredited inspector in the execution of his duty, or

    (c) a person assisting a designated or accredited person or an accredited inspector in the execution of his duty,

is guilty of an offence and shall be liable, on summary conviction, to imprisonment for a term not exceeding six months or to a fine not exceeding level 5 on the standard scale, or to both.

(2) Any person who resists or wilfully obstructs—

    (a) a designated person in the execution of his duty,

    (b) an accredited person or an accredited inspector in the execution of his duty,

    (ba) an accredited inspector in the execution of his duty, or

    (c) a person assisting a designated or accredited person in the execution of his duty,

is guilty of an offence and shall be liable, on summary conviction, to imprisonment for a term not exceeding one month or to a fine not exceeding level 3 on the standard scale, or to both.

(3) Any person who, with intent to deceive—

    (a) impersonates a designated person, an accredited person or an accredited inspector,

    (b) makes any statement or does any act calculated falsely to suggest that he is a designated person, that he is an accredited person or that he is an accredited inspector, or

    (c) makes any statement or does any act calculated falsely to suggest that he has powers as a designated or accredited person or as an accredited inspector that exceed the powers he actually has,

is guilty of an offence and shall be liable, on summary conviction, to imprisonment for a term not exceeding six months or to a fine not exceeding level 5 on the standard scale, or to both.

(4) In this section references to the execution by a designated person, accredited person or accredited inspector of his duty are references to his exercising any power or performing any duty which is his by virtue of his designation or accreditation.

 See above

C16.6 **Common assault**

Criminal Justice Act 1988, s 39

SO (Racially or religiously aggravated: either way)

░ 6 months and/or level 5 fine (racially or religiously aggravated: 2 years)

DO (Racially or religiously aggravated: common assault)

C16.6.1 *Sentencing*
STEP ONE: Determining the offence category

Category 1	Greater harm (injury or fear of injury must normally be present) and higher culpability
Category 2	Greater harm (injury or fear of injury must normally be present) and lower culpability; or lesser harm and higher culpability
Category 3	Lesser harm and lower culpability

Factors indicating greater harm	Factors indicating higher culpability
Injury or fear of injury which is serious in the context of the offence (must normally be present) Victim is particularly vulnerable because of personal circumstances Sustained or repeated assault on the same victim	**Statutory aggravating factors:** Offence motivated by, or demonstrating, hostility to the victim based on his or her sexual orientation (or presumed sexual orientation) Offence motivated by, or demonstrating, hostility to the victim based on the victim's disability (or presumed disability) **Other aggravating factors:** A significant degree of premeditation Threatened or actual use of weapon or weapon equivalent (eg shod foot, head-butting, use of acid, use of animal) Intention to commit more serious harm than actually resulted from the offence Deliberately causes more harm than is necessary for commission of offence Deliberate targeting of vulnerable victim Leading role in group or gang Offence motivated by, or demonstrating, hostility based on the victim's age, sex, gender identity (or presumed gender identity)

Factors indicating lesser harm	Factors indicating lower culpability
Injury which is less serious in the context of the offence	Subordinate role in group or gang A greater degree of provocation than normally expected Lack of premeditation Mental disorder or learning disability, where linked to commission of the offence Excessive self-defence

STEP TWO: Starting point and category range

Offence category	Starting point	Category range
Category 1	High level community order	Low level community order to 23 weeks' custody
Category 2	Medium level community order	Band A fine to high level community order
Category 3	Band A fine	Discharge to band C fine

Factors increasing seriousness	Factors reducing seriousness or reflecting personal mitigation
Statutory aggravating factors: Previous convictions, having regard to (a) the nature of the offence to which the conviction relates and its relevance to the current offence; and (b) the time that has elapsed since the conviction Offence committed whilst on bail **Other aggravating factors include:** Location of the offence Timing of the offence Ongoing effect upon the victim Offence committed against those working in the public sector or providing a service to the public Presence of others including relatives, especially children or partner of the victim Gratuitous degradation of victim In domestic violence cases, victim forced to leave their home Failure to comply with current court orders Offence committed whilst on licence Attempt to conceal or dispose of evidence Failure to respond to warnings or concerns expressed by others about the offender's behaviour	No previous convictions or no relevant/recent convictions Single blow Remorse Good character and/or exemplary conduct Determination and/or demonstration of steps taken to address addiction or offending behaviour Serious medical conditions requiring urgent, intensive, or long-term treatment Isolated incident Age and/or lack of maturity where it affects the responsibility of the offender Lapse of time since the offence where this is not the fault of the offender Mental disorder or learning disability, where not linked to the commission of the offence Sole or primary carer for dependent relative

| Commission of offence whilst under the influence of alcohol or drugs
Abuse of power and/or position of trust
Exploiting contact arrangements with a child to commit an offence
Established evidence of community impact
Any steps taken to prevent the victim reporting an incident, obtaining assistance, and/or assisting or supporting the prosecution
Offences taken into consideration (TICs) | |

Racially aggravated offences: the court should determine the appropriate sentence for the offence without taking account of the element of aggravation and then make an addition to the sentence, considering the level of aggravation involved. It may be appropriate to move outside the identified category range, taking into account the increased statutory maximum.

Additional steps

Consider any factors which indicate a reduction, such as: assistance to the prosecution; reduction for guilty plea; dangerousness; totality principle; compensation and ancillary orders; reasons; consideration for remand time.

C16.6.2 Key points

- Common assault comprises both assault (the intentional or reckless causing of another to apprehend immediate unlawful violence) and battery, and assault by beating (the intentional or reckless inflicting of unlawful force).
- Defences (see **C16.1.3**):
  - Consent: evidence of a lack of consent can be inferred from evidence in the case and need not come from the complainant (see *Director of Public Prosecutions v Shabbir* [2009] EWHC 2754 (Admin)).
  - Lawful correction or chastisement: this defence survives the implementation of section 58 of the Children Act 2004.
  - Self-defence.
  - Defence of property.
  - Prevention of crime.

 See *Blackstone's Criminal Practice 2014* **B2.1–B2.21**

C16.7 **Child neglect, etc**

Children and Young Persons Act 1933, s 1(1)

1 Cruelty to persons under 16

(1) If any person who has attained the age of sixteen years and has responsibility for any child or young person under that age, wilfully assaults, ill-treats, neglects, abandons, or exposes him, or causes or procures him to be assaulted, ill-treated, neglected, abandoned, or exposed, in a manner likely to cause him unnecessary suffering or injury to health (including injury to or loss of sight, or hearing, or limb, or organ of the body, and any mental derangement), that person shall be guilty of an offence.

EW

🏛 6 months and/or level 5 fine/10 years

DO

C16.7.1 *Sentencing*

- The same starting point and sentencing range are proposed for offences which might fall into the four categories (assault, ill-treatment or neglect, abandonment, and failure to protect). These are designed to take into account the fact that the victim is particularly vulnerable, assuming an abuse of trust or power and the likelihood of psychological harm, and are designed to reflect the seriousness with which society as a whole regards these offences.
- As noted above, the starting points have been calculated to reflect the likelihood of psychological harm, and this cannot be treated as an aggravating factor. Where there is an especially serious physical or psychological effect on the victim, even if unintended, this should increase sentence.
- The normal sentencing starting point for an offence of child cruelty should be a custodial sentence. The length of that sentence will be influenced by the circumstances in which the offence took place.
- However, in considering whether a custodial sentence is the most appropriate disposal, the court should take into account any available information concerning the future care of the child.
- Where the offender is the sole or primary carer of the victim or other dependants, this potentially should be taken into account for sentencing purposes, regardless of whether the offender is male or female. In such cases, an immediate custodial sentence may not be appropriate.
- The most relevant areas of personal mitigation are likely to be:
  - mental illness/depression;

- inability to cope with pressures of parenthood;
- lack of support;
- sleep deprivation;
- offender dominated by an abusive or a stronger partner;
- extreme behavioural difficulties in the child, often coupled with a lack of support;
- inability to secure assistance or support services in spite of every effort having been made by the offender.

- Some of the factors identified above, in particular sleep deprivation, lack of support, and an inability to cope, could be regarded as an inherent part of caring for children, especially when a child is very young, and could be put forward as mitigation by most carers charged with an offence of child cruelty. It follows that before being accepted as mitigation, there must be evidence that these factors were present to a high degree, and had an identifiable and significant impact on the offender's behaviour.

Offence seriousness (culpability and harm) A. Identify the appropriate starting point Starting points based on first-time offender pleading not guilty		
Example of nature of activity	**Starting point**	**Range**
(i) Short-term neglect or ill-treatment (ii) Single incident of short-term abandonment (iii) Failure to protect a child from any of the above	12 weeks' custody	Low level community order to 26 weeks' custody
(i) Assault(s) resulting in injuries consistent with ABH (ii) More than one incident of neglect or ill-treatment (but not amounting to long-term behaviour) (iii) Single incident of long-term abandonment OR regular incidents of short-term abandonment (the longer the period of long-term abandonment or the greater the number of incidents of short-term abandonment, the more serious the offence) (iv) Failure to protect a child from any of the above	Crown Court	26 weeks' custody to Crown Court
(i) Series of assaults (ii) Protracted neglect or ill-treatment (iii) Serious cruelty over a period of time (iv) Failure to protect a child from any of the above	Crown Court	Crown Court

Offence seriousness (culpability and harm) B. Consider the effect of aggravating and mitigating factors (other than those within examples above) The following may be particularly relevant but these lists are not exhaustive	
Factors indicating higher culpability	**Factor indicating lower culpability**
1. Targeting one particular child from the family 2. Sadistic behaviour 3. Threats to prevent the victim from reporting the offence 4. Deliberate concealment of the victim from the authorities 5. Failure to seek medical help	1. Seeking medical help or bringing the situation to the notice of the authorities

C16.7.2 Key points

- Section 1(2) of the Children and Young Persons Act 1933 provides that:
  - a parent or other person legally liable to maintain a child or young person, or the legal guardian of a child or young person, shall be deemed to have neglected him in a manner likely to cause injury to his health if he has failed to provide adequate food, clothing, medical aid, or lodging for him, or if, having been unable otherwise to provide such food, clothing, medical aid, or lodging, he has failed to take steps to procure it to be provided under the enactments applicable in that behalf;
  - where it is proved that the death of an infant under three years of age was caused by suffocation (not being suffocation caused by disease or the presence of any foreign body in the throat or air passages of the infant) while the infant was in bed with some other person who has attained the age of 16 years, that other person shall, if he was, when he went to bed, under the influence of drink, be deemed to have neglected the infant in a manner likely to cause injury to its health.
- Section 1(3) provides that a person may be convicted of an offence under this section:
  - notwithstanding that actual suffering or injury to health, or the likelihood of actual suffering or injury to health, was obviated by the action of another person;
  - notwithstanding the death of the child or young person in question.

See *Blackstone's Criminal Practice 2014* **B2.130–B2.141**

C16.8 Grievous bodily harm/unlawful wounding

Offences Against the Person Act 1861, s 20

20 Inflicting bodily injury, with or without weapon

Whosoever shall unlawfully and maliciously wound or inflict any grievous bodily harm upon any other person, either with or without any weapon or instrument, shall be guilty of an offence.

 6 months and/or level 5 fine/5 years (7 years if racially or religiously aggravated)

C16.8.1 *Sentencing*
STEP ONE: Determining the offence category

Category 1	Greater harm (serious injury must normally be present) and higher culpability
Category 2	Greater harm (serious injury must normally be present) and lower culpability; or lesser harm and higher culpability
Category 3	Lesser harm and lower culpability

Factors indicating greater harm	**Factors indicating higher culpability**
Injury (which includes disease transmission and/or psychological harm) which is serious in the context of the offence (must normally be present) Victim is particularly vulnerable because of personal circumstances Sustained or repeated assault on the same victim	**Statutory aggravating factors:** Offence motivated by, or demonstrating, hostility to. the victim based on his or her sexual orientation (or presumed sexual orientation) Offence motivated by, or demonstrating, hostility to the victim based on the victim's disability (or presumed disability) **Other aggravating factors:** A significant degree of premeditation Use of weapon or weapon equivalent (eg shod foot, head-butting, use of acid, use of animal) Intention to commit more serious harm than actually resulted from the offence Deliberately causes more harm than is necessary for commission of offence Deliberate targeting of vulnerable victim Leading role in group or gang Offence motivated by, or demonstrating, hostility based on the victim's age, sex, gender identity (or presumed gender identity

Factors indicating lesser harm	Factors indicating lower culpability
Injury which is less serious in the context of the offence	

STEP TWO: Starting point and category range

Offence category	Starting point	Category range
Category 1	Crown Court	Crown Court
Category 2	Crown Court	Crown Court
Category 3	High level community order	Low level community order to Crown Court (51 weeks' custody)

Factors increasing seriousness	Factors reducing seriousness or reflecting personal mitigation
Statutory aggravating factors: Previous convictions, having regard to (a) the nature of the offence to which the conviction relates and its relevance to the current offence; and (b) the time that has elapsed since the conviction Offence committed whilst on bail **Other aggravating factors include:** Location of the offence Timing of the offence Ongoing effect upon the victim Offence committed against those working in the public sector or providing a service to the public Presence of others including relatives, especially children or partner of the victim Gratuitous degradation of victim In domestic violence cases, victim forced to leave their home Failure to comply with current court orders Offence committed whilst on licence Attempt to conceal or dispose of evidence Failure to respond to warnings or concerns expressed by others about the offender's behaviour Commission of offence whilst under the influence of alcohol or drugs Abuse of power and/or position of trust Exploiting contact arrangements with a child to commit an offence Established evidence of community impact Any steps taken to prevent the victim reporting an incident, obtaining assistance, and/or assisting or supporting the prosecution Offences taken into consideration (TICs)	No previous convictions or no relevant/recent convictions Single blow Remorse Good character and/or exemplary conduct Determination and/or demonstration of steps taken to address addiction or offending behaviour Serious medical conditions requiring urgent, intensive, or long-term treatment Isolated incident Age and/or lack of maturity where it affects the responsibility of the offender Lapse of time since the offence where this is not the fault of the offender Mental disorder or learning disability, where not linked to the commission of the offence Sole or primary carer for dependent relatives

Additional steps

Consider any factors which indicate a reduction, such as: assistance to the prosecution; reduction for guilty plea; dangerousness; totality principle; compensation and ancillary orders; reasons; consideration for remand time.

C16.8.2 Key points

Wounding requires the breaking of the continuity of the whole of the skin. Although this may include relatively minor injuries, charging standards indicate that this offence should not be used in such cases. Harm can be inflicted without the need for an assault (*R v Ireland* [1998] AC 147). To be malicious there must be intention or subjective recklessness, but the harm foreseen need not be serious. This is a crime of basic intent.

 See *Blackstone's Criminal Practice 2014* **B2.47–B2.61**

C16.9 Harassment—putting people in fear of violence

> **Protection from Harassment Act 1997, s 4(1)**
>
> **4 Putting people in fear of violence**
>
> (1) A person whose course of conduct causes another to fear, on at least two occasions, that violence will be used against him is guilty of an offence if he knows or ought to know that his course of conduct will cause the other so to fear on each of those occasions.

 EW

 6 months and/or level 5 fine/5 years (7 years if racially or religiously aggravated)

 DO

C16.9.1 *Sentencing*

Offence seriousness (culpability and harm) A. Identify the appropriate starting point Starting points based on first-time offender pleading not guilty		
Examples of nature of activity	**Starting point**	**Range**
A pattern of two or more incidents of unwanted contact	6 weeks' custody	High level community order to 18 weeks' custody
Deliberate threats, persistent action over a longer period; or Intention to cause fear of violence	18 weeks' custody	12 weeks' custody to Crown Court
Sexual threats, vulnerable person targeted	Crown Court	Crown Court

Offence seriousness (culpability and harm) B. Consider the effect of aggravating and mitigating factors (other than those within examples above) The following may be particularly relevant but these lists are not exhaustive	
Factors indicating higher culpability 1. Planning 2. Offender ignores obvious distress 3. Visits in person to victim's home or workplace 4. Offender involves others 5. Using contact arrangements with a child to instigate offence **Factors indicating greater degree of harm** 1. Victim needs medical help/counselling 2. Physical violence used 3. Victim aware that offender has history of using violence 4. Grossly violent or offensive material sent 5. Children frightened 6. Evidence that victim changed lifestyle to avoid contact	**Factors indicating lower culpability** 1. Limited understanding of effect on victim 2. Initial provocation

C16.9.2 Key points

- The question of what constitutes a course of conduct has been considered in a number of cases, and the answer will always be fact-sensitive. In *R v Curtis* [2010] EWCA Crim 123, the court allowed a defence appeal where the defendant, in the context of there being a volatile relationship, had been responsible for six incidents over a period of nine months. The court held that the conduct must be unacceptable to a degree which would sustain criminal liability and also must be oppressive, and went on to say:

Courts are well able to separate the wheat from the chaff at an early stage of the proceedings. They should be astute to do so. In most cases courts should have little difficulty in applying the 'close connection' test. Where the claim meets that requirement, and the quality of the conduct said to constitute harassment is being examined, courts will have in mind that irritations, annoyances, even a measure of upset, arise at times in everybody's day-to-day dealings with other people. Courts are well able to recognise the boundary between conduct which is unattractive, even unreasonable, and conduct which is oppressive and unacceptable. To cross the boundary from the regrettable to the unacceptable the gravity of the misconduct must be of an order which would sustained [sic] criminal liability under section 2.

- References to harassing a person include alarming the person or causing the person distress (s 7). The person whose course of conduct is in question ought to know that it will cause another to fear that violence will be used against him on any occasion, if a reasonable person in possession of the same information would think the course of conduct would cause the other so to fear on that occasion.
- It is a defence for a person charged with an offence under this section to show that:
  - his course of conduct was pursued for the purpose of preventing or detecting crime;
  - his course of conduct was pursued under any enactment or rule of law, or to comply with any condition or requirement imposed by any person under any enactment; or
  - the pursuit of his course of conduct was reasonable for the protection of himself or another, or for the protection of his or another's property.
- In *R v Haque* [2011] EWCA Crim 1871, the following requirements were identified for there to be proof of harassment:
  - The conduct must be targeted at an individual.
  - Conduct must be calculated to produce the consequences in section 7 (alarm or distress).
  - Conduct must have been oppressive and unreasonable.
  - Provocation may possibly be relevant to causation and reasonableness.
  - There must also be proof that the defendant knew or ought to have known that conduct would cause the complainant to fear violence.
- In *R v Widdows* [2011] EWCA Crim 1500, the court held that in bringing a charge under section 4, the prosecutor (and the judge when summing up) should have in mind the concept of harassment which is at the core of the 1997 Act—though the word is not used in section 4—and the explanation of 'harassment' in *Majrowski v Guy's and St Thomas' NHS Trust* [2007] 1 AC 224 ('stalkers, racial abusers, disruptive neighbours, bullying at work and so forth') and

in *Thomas v News Group Newspapers Ltd* [2001] EWCA Civ 1233 (where the practice of stalking was said to be a prime example). The section is not normally appropriate for use as a means of criminalizing conduct, not charged as violence, during incidents in a long and predominantly affectionate relationship in which both parties persisted and wanted to continue.

• The naming of two complainants in one charge is not duplicitous, but at least one of the complainants must have feared violence on at least two occasions (*Caurti v Director of Public Prosecutions* [2002] EWHC 867 (Admin)).

 See *Blackstone's Criminal Practice 2014* **B2.174–B2.181**

C16.10 Harassment (without violence)

Protection from Harassment Act 1997, ss 1 and 2(1)

1 Prohibition of harassment

(1) A person must not pursue a course of conduct—
    (a) which amounts to harassment of another, and
    (b) which he knows or ought to know amounts to harassment of the other.

(2) For the purposes of this section, the person whose course of conduct is in question ought to know that it amounts to harassment of another if a reasonable person in possession of the same information would think the course of conduct amounted to harassment of the other.

(3) Subsection (1) does not apply to a course of conduct if the person who pursued it shows—
    (a) that it was pursued for the purpose of preventing or detecting crime,
    (b) that it was pursued under any enactment or rule of law or to comply with any condition or requirement imposed by any person under any enactment, or
    (c) that in the particular circumstances the pursuit of the course of conduct was reasonable.

2 Offence of harassment

(1) A person who pursues a course of conduct in breach of section 1 is guilty of an offence.

SO (Either way if racially or religiously aggravated)

⊞ 6 months and/or level 5 fine (2 years if racially or religiously aggravated)

C16.10.1 *Sentencing*

Offence seriousness (culpability and harm) A. Identify the appropriate starting point Starting points based on first-time offender pleading not guilty		
Examples of nature of activity	**Starting point**	**Range**
Small number of incidents	Medium level community order	Band C fine to high level community order
Constant contact at night, trying to come into workplace or home, involving others	6 weeks' custody	Medium level community order to 12 weeks' custody
Threatening violence, taking personal photographs, sending offensive material	18 weeks' custody	12 to 26 weeks' custody

Offence seriousness (culpability and harm) B. Consider the effect of aggravating and mitigating factors (other than those within examples above) The following may be particularly relevant but these lists are not exhaustive	
Factors indicating higher culpability 1. Planning 2. Offender ignores obvious distress 3. Offender involves others 4. Using contact arrangements with a child to instigate offence **Factors indicating greater degree of harm** 1. Victim needs medical help/counselling 2. Action over long period 3. Children frightened 4. Use or distribution of photographs	**Factors indicating higher culpability** 1. Limited understanding of effect on victim 2. Initial provocation

C16.10.2 Key points

- See key points at **C16.9.2**.
- The naming of two complainants in one charge is not duplicitous, but unlike the charge under section 4, there need only be conduct against at least two people on at least one occasion each (*Director of PublicProsecutions v Dunn* (2008) 165 JP 130).

📖 See *Blackstone's Criminal Practice 2014* **B2.156–B2.171**

C16.11 Stalking

The offences of stalking mirror the approach of the basic and aggravated forms of the harassment offences set out at **C16.9** and **C16.10.**

The defences in section 1(3) of the Protection from Harassment Act 1997 are available (see **C16.10**).

C16.11.1 *The basic offence*

Protection from Harassment Act 1997, s 2A

2A Offence of stalking

(1) A person is guilty of an offence if—
  (a) the person pursues a course of conduct in breach of section 1(1), and
  (b) the course of conduct amounts to stalking.
(2) For the purposes of subsection (1)(b) (and section 4A(1)(a)) a person's course of conduct amounts to stalking of another person if—
  (a) it amounts to harassment of that person,
  (b) the acts or omissions involved are ones associated with stalking, and
  (c) the person whose course of conduct it is knows or ought to know that the course of conduct amounts to harassment of the other person.
(3) The following are examples of acts or omissions which, in particular circumstances, are ones associated with stalking—
  (a) following a person,
  (b) contacting, or attempting to contact, a person by any means,
  (c) publishing any statement or other material—
    (i) relating or purporting to relate to a person, or
    (ii) purporting to originate from a person,
  (d) monitoring the use by a person of the internet, email or any other form of electronic communication,
  (e) loitering in any place (whether public or private),
  (f) interfering with any property in the possession of a person,
  (g) watching or spying on a person.
  …
(6) This section is without prejudice to the generality of section 2.

SO (Either way if racially or religiously aggravated)

▥ 6 months and/or level 5 fine (2 years if racially or religiously aggravated)

It is suggested that until a specific guideline is published, regard should be had to the guideline at **C16.10.1**, as both offences carry the same maximum penalty.

C16.11.2 *Aggravated stalking*

Protection from Harassment Act 1997, s 4A

4A Stalking involving fear of violence or serious alarm or distress

(1) A person ('A') whose course of conduct—
   (a) amounts to stalking, and
   (b) either—
      (i) causes another ('B') to fear, on at least two occasions, that violence will be used against B, or
      (ii) causes B serious alarm or distress which has a substantial adverse effect on B's usual day-to-day activities,

   is guilty of an offence if A knows or ought to know that A's course of conduct will cause B so to fear on each of those occasions or (as the case may be) will cause such alarm or distress

(2) For the purposes of this section A ought to know that A's course of conduct will cause B to fear that violence will be used against B on any occasion if a reasonable person in possession of the same information would think the course of conduct would cause B so to fear on that occasion.

(3) For the purposes of this section A ought to know that A's course of conduct will cause B serious alarm or distress which has a substantial adverse effect on B's usual day-to-day activities if a reasonable person in possession of the same information would think the course of conduct would cause B such alarm or distress.

(4) It is a defence for A to show that—
   (a) A's course of conduct was pursued for the purpose of preventing or detecting crime,
   (b) A's course of conduct was pursued under any enactment or rule of law or to comply with any condition or requirement imposed by any person under any enactment, or
   (c) the pursuit of A's course of conduct was reasonable for the protection of A or another or for the protection of A's or another's property.

. . .

(9) This section is without prejudice to the generality of section 4.

EW

🏛 6 months and/or level 5 fine/5 years (7 years if racially or religiously aggravated)

It is suggested that until a specific guideline is published, regard should be had to the guideline at **C16.9.1**, as both offences carry the same maximum penalty.

C16.12 Threats to kill

Offences Against the Person Act 1861, s 16

16 Threats to kill

A person who without lawful excuse makes to another a threat, intending that that other would fear it would be carried out, to kill that other or a third person shall be guilty of an offence.

 EW

 6 months and/or level 5 fine/10 years

DO

C16.12.1 *Sentencing*

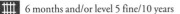

Offence seriousness (culpability and harm) A. Identify the appropriate starting point Starting points based on first-time offender pleading not guilty		
Examples of nature of activity	**Starting point**	**Range**
One threat uttered in the heat of the moment, no more than fleeting impact on victim	Medium level community order	Low level community order to high level community order
Single calculated threat or victim fears that threat will be carried out	12 weeks' custody	6 to 26 weeks' custody
Repeated threats or visible weapon	Crown Court	Crown Court

Offence seriousness (culpability and harm) B. Consider the effect of aggravating and mitigating factors (other than those within examples above) The following may be particularly relevant but these lists are not exhaustive	
Factors indicating higher culpability 1. Planning 2. Offender deliberately isolates victim 3. Group action 4. Threat directed at victim because of job 5. History of antagonism towards victim **Factors indicating greater degree of harm** 1. Vulnerable victim 2. Victim needs medical help/counselling	**Factor indicating lower culpability** 1. Provocation

See *Blackstone's Criminal Practice 2014* **B1.164**

C16.13 **Witness intimidation**

Criminal Justice and Public Order Act 1994, s 51(1)–(5)

51 Intimidation, etc of witnesses, jurors and others

(1) A person commits an offence if—
  (a) he does an act which intimidates, and is intended to intimidate, another person ('the victim'),
  (b) he does the act knowing or believing that the victim is assisting in the investigation of an offence or is a witness or potential witness or a juror or potential juror in proceedings for an offence, and
  (c) he does it intending thereby to cause the investigation or the course of justice to be obstructed, perverted or interfered with.

(2) A person commits an offence if—
  (a) he does an act which harms, and is intended to harm, another person or, intending to cause another person to fear harm, he threatens to do an act which would harm that other person,
  (b) he does or threatens to do the act knowing or believing that the person harmed or threatened to be harmed ('the victim'), or some other person, has assisted in an investigation into an offence or has given evidence or particular evidence in proceedings for an offence, or has acted as a juror or concurred in a particular verdict in proceedings for an offence, and
  (c) he does or threatens to do it because of that knowledge or belief.

(3) For the purposes of subsections (1) and (2) it is immaterial that the act is or would be done, or that the threat is made—
  (a) otherwise than in the presence of the victim, or
  (b) to a person other than the victim.

(4) The harm that may be done or threatened may be financial as well as physical (whether to the person or a person's property) and similarly as respects an intimidatory act which consists of threats.

(5) The intention required by subsection (1)(c) and the motive required by subsection (2)(c) above need not be the only or the predominating intention or motive with which the act is done or, in the case of subsection (2), threatened.

 EW

 6 months and/or level 5 fine/5 years

C16.13.1 *Sentencing*

Offence seriousness (culpability and harm) A. Identify the appropriate starting point Starting points based on first-time offender pleading not guilty		
Examples of nature of activity	**Starting point**	**Range**
Sudden outburst in chance encounter	6 weeks' custody	Medium level community order to 18 weeks' custody
Conduct amounting to a threat; staring at, approaching, or following witnesses; talking about the case; trying to alter or stop evidence	18 weeks' custody	12 weeks' custody to Crown Court
Threats of violence to witnesses and/ or their families; deliberately seeking out witnesses	Crown Court	Crown Court

Offence seriousness (culpability and harm) B. Consider the effect of aggravating and mitigating factors (other than those within examples above) The following may be particularly relevant but these lists are not exhaustive	
Factors indicating higher culpability 1. Breach of bail conditions 2. Offender involves others **Factors indicating greater degree of harm** 1. Detrimental impact on administration of justice 2. Contact made at or in vicinity of victim's home	

 See *Blackstone's Criminal Practice 2014* **B14.46**

Part D
Sentencing

D1 Age of Offender

D1.1 General principles

The age of the offender is important in relation to the court's power to impose different types of sentence. If age is in doubt, the court should consider all available evidence and make a determination before proceeding to sentence.

Generally speaking, the relevant age is the age of the offender on the date of conviction, not the date of offence. As a matter of public policy, however, the courts have been willing to sentence in relation to offence date, as opposed to conviction date. In *R v Ghafoor* [2002] EWCA Crim 1857, the court said:

> The approach to be adopted where a defendant crosses a relevant age threshold between the date of the commission of the offence and date of conviction should now be clear. The starting point is the sentence that the defendant would have been likely to receive if he had been sentenced at the date of the commission of the offence. It has been described as a 'powerful factor'. That is for the obvious reason that as Mr Emmerson points out, the philosophy of restricting sentencing powers in relation to young persons reflects both (a) society's acceptance that young offenders are less responsible for their actions and therefore less culpable than adults, and (b) the recognition that, in consequence, sentencing them should place greater emphasis on rehabilitation and less on retribution and deterrence than in the case of adults. It should be noted that the 'starting point' is not the maximum sentence that could lawfully have been imposed, but the sentence that the offender would have been likely to receive.

However, in *R v Bowker* [2007] EWCA Crim 1608, the court said that *Ghafoor* was a powerful starting point but other factors (such as the need for deterrent sentencing) may justify departing from it.

 See *Blackstone's Criminal Practice 2014* **E7.3** and **B1**

D1.2 Exceptions to general rule

Where a court revokes a community order made pursuant to the Criminal Justice Act 2003, the relevant age for the purpose of resentencing is the age of the offender when the order was made.

Where a court activates a conditional discharge, the relevant age for the purpose of resentencing is determined by the date on which the offender appears for sentence.

D2 Alteration of Sentence

D2.1 Section 142 of the Magistrates' Courts Act 1980

Section 142 of the Magistrates' Courts Act 1980 gives the court power
to reopen sentence. There are no time restrictions, but a court must
have regard to the principle of finality of sentence, meaning that in
many cases it will not be proper to interfere (*R (Trigger) v Northampton
Magistrates' Court* [2011] EWHC 149 (Admin)). Section 142(1)
provides:

> **Magistrates' Courts Act 1980, s 142(1)**
>
> **142 Power of magistrates' court to re-open cases to rectify
> mistakes etc**
>
> (1) A magistrates' court may vary or rescind a sentence or other order imposed
> or made by it when dealing with an offender if it appears to the court to be
> in the interests of justice to do so, and it is hereby declared that this power
> extends to replacing a sentence or order which for any reason appears to
> be invalid by another which the court has power to impose or make.

 See *Blackstone's Criminal Practice 2014* **D23.22–D23.25**

D3 **Anti-Social Behaviour Orders**

D3.1 **Age requirements**

An offender aged 10 years or over.

D3.2 **Notice**

Criminal Procedure Rule 50.3 requires the prosecutor to give notice, on a prescribed form, of his intention to apply for an anti-social behaviour order (ASBO). There are therefore no circumstances in which a defence lawyer should feel pressurized into dealing with what can be a complex area of law without adequate notice.

D3.3 **Criteria**

Anti-social behaviour orders may be made either on a free-standing basis, or following conviction. This book concentrates solely on the latter.

Section 1C of the Crime and Disorder Act 1998 provides:

> ### **Crime and Disorder Act 1998, s 1C**
> #### **1C Orders on conviction in criminal cases**
> (1) This section applies where a person (the 'offender') is convicted of a relevant offence.
> (2) If the court considers—
>   (a) that the offender has acted, at any time since the commencement date, in an anti-social manner, that is to say in a manner that caused or was likely to cause harassment, alarm or distress to one or more persons not of the same household as himself, and
>   (b) that an order under this section is necessary to protect persons in any place in England and Wales from further anti-social acts by him,
>   it may make an order which prohibits the offender from doing anything described in the order.
> (3) The court may make an order under this section—
>   (a) if the prosecutor asks it to do so, or
>   (b) if the court thinks it is appropriate to do so.
> (3A) For the purpose of deciding whether to make an order under this section the court may consider evidence led by the prosecution and the defence.
> (3B) It is immaterial whether evidence led in pursuance of subsection (3A) would have been admissible in the proceedings in which the offender was convicted.
> (4) An order under this section shall not be made except—
>   (a) in addition to a sentence imposed in respect of the relevant offence; or
>   (b) in addition to an order discharging him conditionally.

(4A) The court may adjourn any proceedings in relation to an order under this section even after sentencing the offender.

(4B) If the offender does not appear for any adjourned proceedings, the court may further adjourn the proceedings or may issue a warrant for his arrest.

(4C) But the court may not issue a warrant for the offender's arrest unless it is satisfied that he has had adequate notice of the time and place of the adjourned proceedings.

(5) An order under this section takes effect on the day on which it is made, but the court may provide in any such order that such requirements of the order as it may specify shall, during any period when the offender is detained in legal custody, be suspended until his release from that custody.

...

(9) Subsections (7), (10), (10C), (10D), (10E) and (11) of section 1 apply for the purposes of the making and effect of orders made by virtue of this section as they apply for the purposes of the making and effect of anti-social behaviour orders.

(9A) The council for the local government area in which a person in respect of whom an anti-social behaviour order has been made resides or appears to reside may bring proceedings under section 1(10) (as applied by subsection (9)above) for breach of an order under subsection (2) above.

(9AA) Sections 1AA and 1AB apply in relation to orders under this section, with any necessary modifications, as they apply in relation to anti-social behaviour orders.

(9AB) In their application by virtue of subsection (9AA), sections 1AA(1A)(b) and 1AB(6) have effect as if the words 'by complaint' were omitted.

(9AC) In its application by virtue of subsection (9AA), section 1AA(1A)(b) has effect as if the reference to the relevant authority which applied for the anti-social behaviour order were a reference to the chief officer of police, or other relevant authority, responsible under section 1K(2)(a) or (b) for carrying out a review of the order under this section.

(9B) Subsection (9C) applies in relation to proceedings in which an order under subsection (2) is made against a child or young person who is convicted of an offence.

(9C) In so far as the proceedings relate to the making of the order—

(a) section 49 of the Children and Young Persons Act 1933 (c 12) (restrictions on reports of proceedings in which children and young persons are concerned) does not apply in respect of the child or young person against whom the order is made;

(b) section 39 of that Act (power to prohibit publication of certain matter) does so apply.

(10) In this section—

'child' and 'young person' have the same meaning as in the Children and Young Persons Act 1933 (c 12);

'the commencement date' has the same meaning as in section 1 above;

'the court' in relation to an offender means—

(a) the court by or before which he is convicted of the relevant offence; or

(b) if he is committed to the Crown Court to be dealt with for that offence, the Crown Court; and

'relevant offence' means an offence committed after the coming into force of section 64 of the Police Reform Act 2002 (c 30).

D3.4   Relevant case law

Evidence of post-complaint behaviour is admissible to show both whether a person has acted in an anti-social manner and whether an order is necessary (*Birmingham City Council v Dixon* [2009] EWHC 761 (Admin)).

The following case studies and guidance are reproduced from *Anti-Social Behaviour Orders: A Guide for the Judiciary*, available from <http://www.judiciary.gov.uk>.

In *R v Gowan* [2007] EWCA Crim 1360, the court made an ASBO against the defendant's wife. The order was quashed because, the defendant's wife being of the same household as him, there was no power to make it. Anti-social behaviour orders are properly made for the protection of the general public.

In *S v Poole Borough Council* [2002] EWHC 244 (Admin), a youth aged 15 had been engaged in anti-social behaviour for 18 months up to the date of the application. The magistrates' court hearing was concluded five months later, and the Crown Court appeal seven and a half months after that. The defendant argued that there was no necessity for an order as there had been no anti-social behaviour for over a year. Describing this argument as hopeless, Simon Brown LJ said:

> It must be expected that, once an application of this sort is made, still more obviously once an ASBO has been made, its effect will be likely to deter future misconduct. That, indeed, is the justification for such orders in the first place... The conduct on which the magistrates' court, and in turn the Crown Court, should concentrate in determining whether such an order is necessary is that which underlay the authority's application for the order in the first place.

No prohibition may be imposed unless it is *necessary* for the purpose of protecting persons, whether relevant persons or persons elsewhere in England and Wales, from further anti-social acts by the defendant. The leading case is *R v Boness* [2005] EWCA Crim 2395. From that and other cases (notably *R v P (Shane Tony)* [2004] EWCA Crim 287, *R v McGrath* [2005] EWCA Crim 353, and *W v Director of Public Prosecutions* [2005] EWCA Civ 1333), the following principles emerge:

- The requirement that a prohibition must be necessary to protect persons from further anti-social acts by the defendant means that the use of an ASBO to punish a defendant is unlawful.
- Each separate prohibition must be targeted at the individual and the specific form of anti-social behaviour it is intended to prevent. The order must be tailored to the defendant and not designed on a word processor for generic use. Therefore the court must ask itself when considering a specific order, 'Is this order necessary to protect

persons in any place in England and Wales from further anti-social acts by the defendant?'

- Each prohibition must be precise and capable of being understood by the defendant. Therefore the court should ask itself before making an order: 'Are the terms of this order clear so that the defendant will know precisely what it is that he is prohibited from doing?' (So that unfamiliar words like 'curtilage' and 'environs' should be avoided, as should vague ones like 'implement' or 'paraphernalia'.) For example, a prohibition should clearly delineate any exclusion zone by reference to a map and clearly identify those whom the defendant must not contact or associate with.

- Each prohibition must be prohibitory and not mandatory: this means substantially and not just formally prohibitory.

- The terms of the order must be proportionate in the sense that they must be commensurate with the risk to be guarded against. This is particularly important where an order may interfere with a Convention right protected by the Human Rights Act 1998, for example Articles 8, 10, and 11 ECHR.

- There is no requirement that the prohibited acts should by themselves give rise to harassment, alarm, or distress.

- An ASBO should not be used merely to increase the sentence of imprisonment which an offender is liable to receive.

- Different considerations may apply if the maximum sentence is only a fine, but the court must still go through all the steps to make sure that an ASBO is necessary.

The fact that an order prohibits a defendant from committing a specified criminal offence does not automatically invalidate it. However, the court should not make such an order if the sentence which could be passed following conviction for the offence would be a sufficient deterrent. In addition, the Court of Appeal has indicated that prohibiting behaviour that is in any event a crime does not necessarily address the aim of an ASBO, which is to prevent anti-social behaviour. The better course is to make an anticipatory form of order, namely an order which prevents a defendant from doing an act preparatory to the commission of the offence, thereby helping to prevent the criminal offence from being committed in the first place. For example, an order might prevent a defendant from entering a shopping centre rather than stealing from shops.

In *Boness*, Hooper LJ gave other examples, drawing an analogy with bail conditions designed to prevent a defendant from committing further offences. He said:

> If, for example, a court is faced by an offender who causes criminal damage by spraying graffiti then the order should be aimed at facilitating action to be taken to prevent graffiti spraying by him and/or his associates before it takes

place. An order in clear and simple terms preventing the offender from being in possession of a can of spray paint in a public place gives the police or others responsible for protecting the property an opportunity to take action in advance of the actual spraying and makes it clear to the offender that he has lost the right to carry such a can for the duration of the order.

If a court wishes to make an order prohibiting a group of youngsters from racing cars or motor bikes on an estate or driving at excessive speed (anti-social behaviour for those living on the estate), then the order should not (normally) prohibit driving whilst disqualified. It should prohibit, for example, the offender whilst on the estate from taking part in, or encouraging, racing or driving at an excessive speed. It might also prevent the group from congregating with named others in a particular area of the estate. Such an order gives those responsible for enforcing order on the estate the opportunity to take action to prevent the anti-social conduct, it is to be hoped, before it takes place.

In *R (Cooke) v Director of Public Prosecutions* [2008] EWHC 2703 (Admin), the court held that an order was not appropriate in relation to an offender who due to mental incapacity was not able to understand its terms, as such an order would fail to protect the public and could therefore not be said to be necessary to protect others.

In *R (McGarrett) v Kingston Crown Court*, unreported, 8 June 2009, the court quashed an indefinite ASBO made against a defendant who had been convicted of a single offence of breaching a noise abatement notice. There were no other relevant offences or behaviour that had been considered by the court, and accordingly the test of necessity was not made out.

A condition not to cause harassment, alarm, or distress was too imprecise; conditions had to be clear as to what behaviour the order was seeking to discourage (*Heron v Plymouth City Council* [2009] EWHC 3562 (Admin)).

 See *Blackstone's Criminal Practice 2014* **D25.1–D25.44**

D4 Banning Orders (Football)

Banning orders are imposed under section 14A of the Football Spectators Act 1989.

D4.1 Criteria

Banning orders can be imposed when an offender is convicted of a relevant offence; and if the court is satisfied that there are reasonable grounds to believe that making a banning order would help to prevent violence or disorder at or in connection with any regulated football matches, it must make such an order in respect of the offender.

The core requirements of such an order are to prohibit the offender from attending regulated football matches in England and Wales. When matches are being played abroad, the order will require the offender to report to a police station and surrender his passport (unless there are exceptional circumstances certified by the court as to why this should not be done). Other requirements can be imposed, for example not to go within a certain distance of a football ground.

The order must be for a period of between three and five years, or six and ten years if a custodial sentence (including a sentence of detention) is imposed for the original offence.

In *Newman v Commissioner of Police for the Metropolis* [2009] EWHC 1642 (Admin), the court held that police were entitled to rely upon compilation witness statements and compilation video footage, and had no duty to disclose the underlying material from which they were drawn. There is no statutory disclosure regime applicable to the making of banning orders and a court should apply normal principles of 'fairness'. Advocates seeking disclosure should be careful to specify the material that they wish to view and the reasons why. An application that amounts to nothing more than a 'fishing expedition' ought to be refused.

D4.2 Relevant offences

Relevant offences are listed in Schedule 1 to the 1989 Act. For some offences, the court will need to make a declaration of relevance (see **D4.3**).

Football Spectators Act 1989, Sch 1

1. This Schedule applies to the following offences:
   (a) any offence under section 14J(1) or 21C(2) of this Act,
   (b) any offence under section 2 or 2A of the Sporting Events (Control of Alcohol etc.) Act 1985 (alcohol, containers, and fireworks) committed

by the accused at any football match to which this Schedule applies or while entering or trying to enter the ground,

(c) any offence under section 4A or 5 of the Public Order Act 1986 (harassment, alarm, or distress) or any provision of Part III of that Act (racial hatred) committed during a period relevant to a football match to which this Schedule applies at any premises while the accused was at, or was entering or leaving or trying to enter or leave, the premises,

(d) any offence involving the use or threat of violence by the accused towards another person committed during a period relevant to a football match to which this Schedule applies at any premises while the accused was at, or was entering or leaving or trying to enter or leave, the premises,

(e) any offence involving the use or threat of violence towards property committed during a period relevant to a football match to which this Schedule applies at any premises while the accused was at, or was entering or leaving or trying to enter or leave, the premises,

(f) any offence involving the use, carrying or possession of an offensive weapon or a firearm committed during a period relevant to a football match to which this Schedule applies at any premises while the accused was at, or was entering or leaving or trying to enter or leave, the premises,

(g) any offence under section 12 of the Licensing Act 1872 (persons found drunk in public places, etc) of being found drunk in a highway or other public place committed while the accused was on a journey to or from a football match to which this Schedule applies being an offence as respects which the court makes a declaration that the offence related to football matches,

(h) any offence under section 91(1) of the Criminal Justice Act 1967 (disorderly behaviour while drunk in a public place) committed in a highway or other public place while the accused was on a journey to or from a football match to which this Schedule applies being an offence as respects which the court makes a declaration that the offence related to football matches,

(j) any offence under section 1 of the Sporting Events (Control of Alcohol etc.) Act 1985 (alcohol on coaches or trains to or from sporting events) committed while the accused was on a journey to or from a football match to which this Schedule applies being an offence as respects which the court makes a declaration that the offence related to football matches,

(k) any offence under section 4A or 5 of the Public Order Act 1986 (harassment, alarm, or distress) or any provision of Part III of that Act (racial hatred) committed while the accused was on a journey to or from a football match to which this Schedule applies being an offence as respects which the court makes a declaration that the offence related to football matches,

(l) any offence under section 4 or 5 of the Road Traffic Act 1988 (driving etc when under the influence of drink or drugs or with an alcohol concentration above the prescribed limit) committed while the accused was on a journey to or from a football match to which this Schedule applies being an offence as respects which the court makes a declaration that the offence related to football matches,

(m) any offence involving the use or threat of violence by the accused towards another person committed while one or each of them was on a journey to or from a football match to which this Schedule applies being an offence as respects which the court makes a declaration that the offence related to football matches,

(n) any offence involving the use or threat of violence towards property committed while the accused was on a journey to or from a football match to which this Schedule applies being an offence as respects which the court makes a declaration that the offence related to football matches,

(o) any offence involving the use, carrying or possession of an offensive weapon or a firearm committed while the accused was on a journey to or from a football match to which this Schedule applies being an offence as respects which the court makes a declaration that the offence related to football matches,

(p) any offence under the Football (Offences) Act 1991,

(q) any offence under section 4A or 5 of the Public Order Act 1986 (harassment, alarm, or distress) or any provision of Part 3 or 3A of that Act (hatred by reference to race etc)—
  (i) which does not fall within paragraph (c) or (k) above,
  (ii) which was committed during a period relevant to a football match to which this Schedule applies, and
  (iii) as respects which the court makes a declaration that the offence related to that match or to that match and any other football match which took place during that period,

(r) any offence involving the use or threat of violence by the accused towards another person—
  (i) which does not fall within paragraph (d) or (m) above,
  (ii) which was committed during a period relevant to a football match to which this Schedule applies, and
  (iii) as respects which the court makes a declaration that the offence related to that match or to that match and any other football match which took place during that period,

(s) any offence involving the use or threat of violence towards property—
  (i) which does not fall within paragraph (e) or (n) above,
  (ii) which was committed during a period relevant to a football match to which this Schedule applies, and
  (iii) as respects which the court makes a declaration that the offence related to that match or to that match and any other football match which took place during that period,

(t) any offence involving the use, carrying or possession of an offensive weapon or a firearm—
  (i) which does not fall within paragraph (f) or (o) above,
  (ii) which was committed during a period relevant to a football match to which this Schedule applies, and
  (iii) as respects which the court makes a declaration that the offence related to that match or to that match and any other football match which took place during that period.

(u) any offence under section 166 of the Criminal Justice and Public Order Act 1994 (sale of tickets by unauthorised persons) which relates to tickets for a football match.

D4.3 Declaration of relevance

The prosecution must give five days' notice that they intend to invite a court to make a declaration of relevance. That notice period may be waived by the defence; it can also be dispensed with by the court if the interests of justice do not require a longer notice period to be given. Note that the court can grant an adjournment to facilitate the five-day notice period.

The declaration is that the offence related to that match, or to that match and any other football match which took place during that period.

Each of the following periods is 'relevant to' a football match to which Schedule 1 applies:

- in the case of a match which takes place on the day on which it is advertised to take place, the period:
  - beginning 24 hours before whichever is the earlier of the start of the match and the time at which it was advertised to start, and
  - ending 24 hours after it ends;
- in the case of a match which does not take place on the day on which it was advertised to take place, the period:
  - beginning 24 hours before the time at which it was advertised to start on that day, and
  - ending 24 hours after that time.

In *R v Arbery* [2008] EWCA Crim 702, the offenders were drinking in a public house following a football match, waiting for their train home, when violence broke out with rival supporters. A football banning order was quashed on appeal, as the court held that the offence arose out of a disagreement in the pub, completely unrelated to football.

In *R v Eliot* [2007] EWCA Crim 1002, the court gave a helpful insight into how the issue of 'relevance' might be approached:

> Did the offences committed in the present case relate to the match? Clearly, the presence of the applicants in London and indeed at Leicester Square related to the match. But it is not their presence, or their allegiance, which is the touchstone of the declaration; it is the relationship between the offence and the match. Here, the offences were sparked by the presence of a group of football supporters in London. The spark, however, had nothing to do with the match itself on the facts as found by the judge. The violence took place, not because of anything that had happened at the football match, or between supporters but because of disparaging remarks made to a lady who had nothing to do with the football match and remarks which had nothing to do with the football match. In those circumstances, we do not consider that, in this case, the statutory requirement was satisfied.

In *Director of Public Prosecutions v Beaumont* [2008] EWHC 523 (Admin), the court rejected an argument that there was a temporal limit to the making of a banning order. In that case the violence erupted more than one hour after the end of the match.

A travel restriction, imposed as part of a banning order, does not infringe EU law, or the European Convention on Human Rights (*Gough v Chief Constable of Derbyshire* [2002] EWCA Civ 351).

Reviewing the law in *R v Doyle* [2012] EWCA Crim 1869, the court said that two requirements must be met in order to require the mandatory imposition of an order:

- Conviction of a relevant offence (Sch 1—see **D4.2**). These offences must 'relate' to football matches, which is an issue of fact—one match will suffice. Merely being on a journey to a match is not enough. Groups of fans will more easily meet the test. It is not enough that the violence would not have occurred 'but for' the journey to the football match.
- There are reasonable grounds to believe that the making of an order would help to prevent violence or disorder at or in connection with a regulated football match. One match can raise an inquiry, but there must be a risk of repetition.

D4.4 Appeals

An appeal lies to the Crown Court in respect to the making of a banning order or dismissal of prosecution application (Football Spectators Act 1989, s 14D).

 See *Blackstone's Criminal Practice 2014* **E21.3–E21.7**

D5 **Bind Over**

D5.1 Criteria

Any person before the court, as defendant or witness (provided that he has given evidence), may be bound over.

A bind over can be made only by consent, and the court should, as a matter of good practice, hear representations (but see *R v Woking Justices, ex p Gossage* [1973] QB 448, where the court held that there was no duty to hear representations if the court was binding over a person in his own recognizance for a 'just and suitable' sum); refusal can result in committal to prison. The order is to keep the peace and be of good behaviour; further conditions are not permitted.

The court will set a recognizance to be forfeit on breach. If the sum set is more than trivial, inquiry should be made in relation to means; a failure to do so may give rise to a successful challenge (*R v Lincoln Crown Court, ex p Jude* The Times, 30 April 1997).

Generally, a binding over to keep the peace is typically warranted only where there is evidence of likely personal danger to others, involving violence or the threat of violence (see, eg, *Percy v Director of Public Prosecutions* [1995] 3 All ER 124).

In *R v Middlesex Crown Court, ex p Khan* (1997) 161 JP 240, the court held that:

> if a judge is going to require a man to be bound over in circumstances where he has been acquitted, it is particularly important that he should be satisfied beyond a reasonable doubt that the man poses a potential threat to other persons and that he is a man of violence.

D5.2 Practice Direction

The Consolidated Criminal Practice Direction states, at paragraph III.31:

Consolidated Criminal Practice Direction, para III.31.2, III.31.3, III.31.4, and III.31.8

Binding over to keep the peace

III.31.2

Before imposing a binding over order, the court must be satisfied that a breach of the peace involving violence, or an imminent threat of violence, has occurred, or that there is a real risk of violence in the future.

D5 Bind Over

Such violence may be perpetrated by the individual who will be subject to the order, or by a third party as a natural consequence of the individual's conduct.

III.31.3

In light of the judgment in Hashman and Harrup, courts should no longer bind an individual over 'to be of good behaviour'. Rather than binding an individual over to 'keep the peace' in general terms, the court should identify the specific conduct or activity from which the individual must refrain.

Written order

III.31.4

When making an order binding an individual over to refrain from specified types of conduct or activities, the details of that conduct or those activities should be specified by the court in a written order served on all relevant parties. The court should state its reasons for the making of the order, its length and the amount of the recognisance. The length of the order should be proportionate to the harm sought to be avoided and should not generally exceed 12 months.

Burden of proof

III.31.8

The court should be satisfied beyond reasonable doubt of the matters complained of before a binding over order may be imposed. Where the procedure has been commenced on complaint, the burden of proof rests on the complainant. In all other circumstances the burden of proof rests on the prosecution.

 See *Blackstone's Criminal Practice 2014* **E13**

D6 **Committal for Sentence**

D6.1 Criteria

A magistrates' court may commit an offender for sentence following a guilty plea (Powers of Criminal Courts (Sentencing) Act 2000 (PCC(S)A 2000), s 3). When a magistrates' court has retained jurisdiction for an offence and the offender is convicted, it will require exceptional circumstances to do so. See **A4**.

A magistrates' court will commit for sentence if the court is of the opinion:

- that the offence or the combination of the offence and one or more offences associated with it was so serious that greater punishment should be inflicted for the offence than the court has power to impose; or
- in the case of a violent or sexual offence, that a custodial sentence for a term longer than the court has power to impose is necessary to protect the public from serious harm from the offender.

Additional committal powers are provided for under sections 4 and 6 of the PCC(S)A 2000. The powers of the Crown Court depend on the use of the correct section.

Powers of Criminal Courts (Sentencing) Act 2000, ss 3–6

3 Committal for sentence on summary trial of offence triable either way

(1) Subject to subsection (4) below, this section applies where on the summary trial of an offence triable either way a person aged 18 or over is convicted of the offence.

(2) If the court is of the opinion—

   (a) that the offence or the combination of the offence and one or more offences associated with it was so serious that greater punishment should be inflicted for the offence than the court has power to impose, or

   (b) in the case of a violent or sexual offence, that a custodial sentence for a term longer than the court has power to impose is necessary to protect the public from serious harm from him,

   the court may commit the offender in custody or on bail to the Crown Court for sentence in accordance with section 5(1) below.

(3) Where the court commits a person under subsection (2) above, section 6 below (which enables a magistrates' court, where it commits a person under this section in respect of an offence, also to commit him to the Crown Court to be dealt with in respect of certain other offences) shall apply accordingly.

---

(4) This section does not apply in relation to an offence as regards which this section is excluded by section 33 of the Magistrates' Courts Act 1980 (certain offences where value involved is small).

(5) The preceding provisions of this section shall apply in relation to a corporation as if—

  (a) the corporation were an individual aged 18 or over; and

  (b) in subsection (2) above, paragraph (b) and the words 'in custody or on bail' were omitted.

4   Committal for sentence on indication of guilty plea to offence triable either way

(1) This section applies where—

  (a) a person aged 18 or over appears or is brought before a magistrates' court ('the court') on an information charging him with an offence triable either way ('the offence');

  (b) he or his representative indicates that he would plead guilty if the offence were to proceed to trial; and

  (c) proceeding as if section 9(1) of the Magistrates' Courts Act 1980 were complied with and he pleaded guilty under it, the court convicts him of the offence.

(2) If the court has committed the offender to the Crown Court for trial for one or more related offences, that is to say, one or more offences which, in its opinion, are related to the offence, it may commit him in custody or on bail to the Crown Court to be dealt with in respect of the offence in accordance with section 5(1) below.

(3) If the power conferred by subsection (2) above is not exercisable but the court is still to inquire, as examining justices, into one or more related offences—

  (a) it shall adjourn the proceedings relating to the offence until after the conclusion of its inquiries; and

  (b) if it commits the offender to the Crown Court for trial for one or more related offences, it may then exercise that power.

(4) Where the court—

  (a) under subsection (2) above commits the offender to the Crown Court to be dealt with in respect of the offence, and

  (b) does not state that, in its opinion, it also has power so to commit him under section 3(2) above,

  section 5(1) below shall not apply unless he is convicted before the Crown Court of one or more of the related offences.

(5) Where section 5(1) below does not apply, the Crown Court may deal with the offender in respect of the offence in any way in which the magistrates' court could deal with him if it had just convicted him of the offence.

(6) Where the court commits a person under subsection (2) above, section 6 below (which enables a magistrates' court, where it commits a person under this section in respect of an offence, also to commit him to the Crown Court to be dealt with in respect of certain other offences) shall apply accordingly.

(7) For the purposes of this section one offence is related to another if, were they both to be prosecuted on indictment, the charges for them could be joined in the same indictment.

5 Power of Crown Court on committal for sentence under sections 3 and 4

(1) Where an offender is committed by a magistrates' court for sentence under section 3 or 4 above, the Crown Court shall inquire into the circumstances of the case and may deal with the offender in any way in which it could deal with him if he had just been convicted of the offence on indictment before the court.

(2) In relation to committals under section 4 above, subsection (1) above has effect subject to section 4(4) and (5) above.

6 Committal for sentence in certain cases where offender committed in respect of another offence

(1) This section applies where a magistrates' court ('the committing court') commits a person in custody or on bail to the Crown Court under any enactment mentioned in subsection (4) below to be sentenced or otherwise dealt with in respect of an offence ('the relevant offence').

(2) Where this section applies and the relevant offence is an indictable offence, the committing court may also commit the offender, in custody or on bail as the case may require, to the Crown Court to be dealt with in respect of any other offence whatsoever in respect of which the committing court has power to deal with him (being an offence of which he has been convicted by that or any other court).

(3) Where this section applies and the relevant offence is a summary offence, the committing court may commit the offender, in custody or on bail as the case may require, to the Crown Court to be dealt with in respect of—

  (a) any other offence of which the committing court has convicted him, being either—

    (i) an offence punishable with imprisonment; or

    (ii) an offence in respect of which the committing court has a power or duty to order him to be disqualified under section 34, 35 or 36 of the Road Traffic Offenders Act 1988 (disqualification for certain motoring offences); or

  (b) any suspended sentence in respect of which the committing court has under paragraph 11(1) of Schedule 12 to the Criminal Justice Act 2003 power to deal with him.

(4) The enactments referred to in subsection (1) above are—

  (a) the Vagrancy Act 1824 (incorrigible rogues);

  (b) sections 3 to 4A above (committal for sentence for offences triable either way);

  (c) section 13(5) below (conditionally discharged person convicted of further offence);

  (d) paragraph 11(2) of Schedule 12 to the Criminal Justice Act 2003 (committal to Crown Court where offender convicted during operational period of suspended sentence).

 See *Blackstone's Criminal Practice 2014* **D23.30**

D7 Community Orders and Sentences: General

D7.1 Criteria

Section 148 of the Criminal Justice Act 2003 (as amended) provides:

> ### Criminal Justice Act 2003, s 148
>
> **148 Restrictions on imposing community sentences**
>
> (1) A court must not pass a community sentence on an offender unless it is of the opinion that the offence, or the combination of the offence and one or more offences associated with it, was serious enough to warrant such a sentence.
>
> (2) Where a court passes a community sentence which consists of or includes a community order—
>
>   (a) the particular requirement or requirements forming part of the community order must be such as, in the opinion of the court, is, or taken together are, the most suitable for the offender, and
>
>   (b) the restrictions on liberty imposed by the order must be such as in the opinion of the court are commensurate with the seriousness of the offence, or the combination of the offence and one or more offences associated with it.
>
> (3) Subsections (1) and (2) (b) have effect subject to section 151(2).
>
> (4) The fact that by virtue of any provision of this section—
>
>   (a) a community sentence may be passed in relation to an offence; or
>
>   (b) particular restrictions on liberty may be imposed by a community order or youth rehabilitation order,
>
> does not require a court to pass such a sentence or to impose those restrictions.

Because a court is not required to impose a community sentence in cases where the offence is serious enough to justify such a sentence, there is a wider discretion to impose financial penalties. Section 150A of the Criminal Justice Act 2003 restricts community orders for those aged 18 or above to offences that are punishable with imprisonment:

> ### Criminal Justice Act 2003, s 150A
>
> **150A Community order available only for offences punishable with imprisonment or for persistent offenders previously fined**
>
> (1) The power to make a community order is only exercisable in respect of an offence if—
>
>   (a) the offence is punishable with imprisonment; or
>
>   (b) in any other case, section 151(2) confers power to make such an order.

(2) For the purposes of this section and section 151 an offence triable either way that was tried summarily is to be regarded as punishable with imprisonment only if it is so punishable by the sentencing court (and for this purpose section 148(1) is to be disregarded).

D7.2 Reports

The court must obtain a report unless the court is of the view that one is unnecessary. (See **D30**.)

No custodial sentence or community sentence is invalidated by the failure of a court to obtain and consider a pre-sentence report (Criminal Justice Act 2003, s 156(6)).

D7.3 Sentencing guidelines

The Council's guideline provides that the seriousness of the offence should be the initial factor in determining which requirements to include in a community order. It establishes three sentencing ranges within the community order band based on offence seriousness (low, medium, and high), and identifies non-exhaustive examples of requirements that might be appropriate in each. These are set out below. The examples focus on punishment in the community; other requirements of a rehabilitative nature may be more appropriate in some cases.

The particular requirements imposed within the range must be suitable for the individual offender and will be influenced by a wide range of factors, including the stated purpose(s) of the sentence, the risk of reoffending, the ability of the offender to comply, and the availability of the requirements in the local area. Sentencers must ensure that the sentence strikes the right balance between proportionality and suitability. The resulting restriction on liberty must be a proportionate response to the offence that was committed.

D7.4 Community order made after long remand in custody

It is not uncommon in a magistrates' court for the offender to have served time on remand equivalent to the maximum custodial sentence available. Some courts, instead of imposing a custodial sentence that allows for immediate release, go on to sentence the offender to a community penalty, effectively visiting upon the offender a greater punishment than is deserved for the crime. In *R v Hemmings* [2008] 1 Cr App R (S) 106, the court held:

A sentence of a community order, and all the more so one coupled with requirements which have a real impact on the offender's liberty, is a form of punishment. It does not seem to us to be right that the appellant should receive a substantial further punishment in circumstances where he has already received what was in practice the maximum punishment by way of imprisonment which the law could have imposed. That reasoning seems to us to be in line with the reasoning in [earlier cases where] . . . the court took the course of imposing a conditional discharge.

The court went on to impose a conditional discharge that expired immediately upon sentence to ensure that the appellant could not fall foul of the consequences of any breach of the order. In *R v Rakib* [2011] EWCA Crim 870, the court, considering *Hemmings*, held that time spent in custody was not a determinative factor, and the rehabilitative aims of sentencing (s 142(1) of the Criminal Justice Act 2003) may in some cases justify a community penalty even if the offender had served on remand the equivalent of the maximum custodial sentence.

Low	Medium	High
Offences only just cross community order threshold, where the seriousness of the offence or the nature of the offender's record means that a discharge or fine is inappropriate.	Offences that obviously fall within the community order band.	Offences only just fall below the custody threshold or the custody threshold is crossed but a community order is more appropriate in the circumstances.
In general, only one requirement will be appropriate and the length may be curtailed if additional requirements are necessary.		More intensive sentences which combine two or more requirements may be appropriate.
Suitable requirements might include: • 40–80 hours' unpaid work • curfew requirement within the lowest range (eg up to 12 hours per day for a few weeks) • exclusion requirement, without electronic monitoring, for a few months • prohibited activity requirement • attendance centre requirement (where available).	Suitable requirements might include: • greater number of hours of unpaid work (eg 80–150 hours) • curfew requirement within the middle range (eg up to 12 hours per day for 2–3 months) • exclusion requirement lasting in the region of 6 months • prohibited activity requirement.	Suitable requirements might include: • 150–300 hours' unpaid work • activity requirement up to the maximum of 60 days • curfew requirement up to 12 hours per day for 4–6 months • exclusion order lasting in the region of 12 months.

D7.5 Requirements

When imposing requirements on the offender as part of the community order, a court should balance the requirements, or combination of requirements, with the offender's personal circumstances, and avoid conflict with work, schooling, or religious beliefs.

The available requirements are:

- unpaid work of betwen 40 and 300 hours;
- activity for up to 60 days;
- programme;
- prohibited activity;
- curfew for up to 16 hours a day for up to 12 months;
- exclusion, normally with electronic monitoring; such a requirement to exclude the offender from the UK is unlawful (*R (Dragoman) v Camberwell Green Magistrates' Court* [2012] EWHC 4105 (Admin);
- residence;
- mental health treatment;
- drug treatment;
- alcohol treatment;
- supervision;
- (if under 25) attendance centre;
- foreign travel restriction for up to 12 months;
- alcohol abstinence and monitoring (not fully in force), if alcohol an element of the offence or a factor contributing to it.

 See *Blackstone's Criminal Practice 2014* **E8**

D7.6 Breach of and offences while on a community order

D7.6.1 *Criteria*

Breach of community orders imposed under the Criminal Justice Act 2003 is dealt with in accordance with Schedule 8 to that Act (as amended). A general defence of reasonable excuse is open to the defendant. The fact that a person is appealing against a community order does not give him a reasonable excuse not to comply (*West Midlands Probation Board v Sutton Coldfield Magistrates' Court* [2008] EWHC 15 (Admin)).

On breach of a community order due to the offender's having failed to comply with the terms of the order, the court has a number of options open to it:

- take no action;
- impose a fine of up to £2,500;
- impose more onerous requirements than the original order (having taken into account the offender's level of cooperation with the order) and let the order continue (including, on one occasion, lengthening the order by up to six months beyond its original date);
- if the order was made by the Crown Court, commit the offender for sentence;
- revoke the order and deal with the offender in any manner in which it could deal with him if he had just been convicted by the court of the offence (having taken into account the offender's level of cooperation with the order).

It should be noted that with respect to an offender aged 18 years or older, imprisonment for a term of up to six months can be imposed following a wilful and persistent failure to comply, even if the original offence is not in itself imprisonable.

A court must be 'satisfied' that a breach has occurred to the criminal standard of proof (*West Yorkshire Probation Board v Boulter* (2005) 169 JP 601).

If the breach has occurred due to the offender's ill-health, a court should not resentence (*R v Bishop* [2004] EWCA Crim 2956).

If a person breaches an order that does not already include an unpaid work requirement, and the court is minded to impose such a requirement, the minimum hours to be worked shall be 20 (Criminal Justice Act 2003, Sch 8, para 9(3A)).

There is no power to commence breach proceedings once the operational period has expired (*West Yorkshire Probation Board v Cruickshanks* [2010] EWHC 615 (Admin)).

D7.6.2 *Further offences whilst subject to a community order*

If the offender has committed a further offence during the life of the community order and is convicted whilst that order is in force, the court has three options open to it in respect to the original order:

- do nothing, and sentence for the new offence; or
- if the order was made by the Crown Court, commit the offender for sentence; or
- revoke the order and deal with the offender in any manner in which it could deal with him if he had just been convicted by the court of

the offence (having taken into account the offender's level of cooperation with the order).

D7.6.3 *Approach to be taken by the court*

The Sentencing Guidelines Council issued guidance (*Guideline: New Sentences: Criminal Justice Act 2003*):

- When increasing the onerousness of requirements, the court must consider the impact on the offender's ability to comply and the possibility of precipitating a custodial sentence for further breach. For that reason, and particularly where the breach occurs towards the end of the sentence, the court should take account of compliance to date and may consider that extending the supervision or operational periods will be more sensible; in other cases it might choose to add punitive or rehabilitative requirements instead. In making these changes the court must be mindful of the legislative restrictions on the overall length of community sentences and on the supervision and operational periods allowed for each type of requirement.
- The court dealing with breach of a community sentence should have as its primary objective ensuring that the requirements of the sentence are finished, and this is important if the court is to have regard to the statutory purposes of sentencing. A court that imposes a custodial sentence for breach without giving adequate consideration to alternatives is in danger of imposing a sentence that is not commensurate with the seriousness of the original offence and is solely a punishment for breach. This risks undermining the purposes it has identified as being important. Nonetheless, courts will need to be vigilant to ensure that there is a realistic prospect of the purposes of the order being achieved.
- A court sentencing for breach must take account of the extent to which the offender has complied with the requirements of the community order, the reasons for breach, and the point at which the breach has occurred. Where a breach takes place towards the end of the operational period and the court is satisfied that the offender's appearance before the court is likely to be sufficient in itself to ensure future compliance, then given that it is not open to the court to make no order, an approach that the court might wish to adopt could be to resentence in a way that enables the original order to be completed properly—for example, a differently constructed community sentence that aims to secure compliance with the purposes

of the original sentence. (Note the restriction on making no order has now been removed.)

- If the court decides to make the order more onerous, it must give careful consideration, with advice from the Probation Service, to the offender's ability to comply. A custodial sentence should be the last resort, where all reasonable efforts to ensure that an offender completes a community sentence have failed.

 See *Blackstone's Criminal Practice 2014* **E8.29**

D8 Compensation Order

D8.1 Age requirements

Any offender, subject to means.

D8.2 Criteria

Powers of Criminal Courts (Sentencing) Act 2000, s 130(1)–(10)

130 Compensation orders against convicted persons

(1) A court by or before which a person is convicted of an offence, instead of or in addition to dealing with him in any other way, may, on application or otherwise, make an order (in this Act referred to as a 'compensation order') requiring him—

  (a) to pay compensation for any personal injury, loss or damage resulting from that offence or any other offence which is taken into consideration by the court in determining sentence; or

  (b) to make payments for funeral expenses or bereavement in respect of a death resulting from any such offence, other than a death due to an accident arising out of the presence of a motor vehicle on a road; but this is subject to the following provisions of this section and to section 131 below.

(2) Where the person is convicted of an offence the sentence for which is fixed by law or falls to be imposed under 110(2) or 111(2) above, section 51A(2) of the Firearms Act 1968, section 225, 226, 227 or 228 of the Criminal Justice Act 2003 or section 29(4) or (6) of the Violent Crime Reduction Act 2006, subsection (1) above shall have effect as if the words 'instead of or' were omitted.

(2A) A court must consider making a compensation order in any case where this section empowers it to do so.

(3) A court shall give reasons, on passing sentence, if it does not make a compensation order in a case where this section empowers it to do so.

(4) Compensation under subsection (1) above shall be of such amount as the court considers appropriate, having regard to any evidence and to any representations that are made by or on behalf of the accused or the prosecutor.

(5) In the case of an offence under the Theft Act 1968 or Fraud Act 2006, where the property in question is recovered, any damage to the property occurring while it was out of the owner's possession shall be treated for the purposes of subsection (1) above as having resulted from the offence, however and by whomever the damage was caused.

(6) A compensation order may only be made in respect of injury, loss or damage (other than loss suffered by a person's dependants in consequence of

his death) which was due to an accident arising out of the presence of a motor vehicle on a road, if—

(a) it is in respect of damage which is treated by subsection (5) above as resulting from an offence under the Theft Act 1968 or Fraud Act 2006; or

(b) it is in respect of injury, loss or damage as respects which—

    (i) the offender is uninsured in relation to the use of the vehicle; and

    (ii) compensation is not payable under any arrangements to which the Secretary of State is a party.

(7) Where a compensation order is made in respect of injury, loss or damage due to an accident arising out of the presence of a motor vehicle on a road, the amount to be paid may include an amount representing the whole or part of any loss of or reduction in preferential rates of insurance attributable to the accident.

(8) A vehicle the use of which is exempted from insurance by section 144 of the Road Traffic Act 1988 is not uninsured for the purposes of subsection (6) above.

(9) A compensation order in respect of funeral expenses may be made for the benefit of any one who incurred the expenses.

(10) A compensation order in respect of bereavement may be made only for the benefit of a person for whose benefit a claim for damages for bereavement could be made under section 1A of the Fatal Accidents Act 1976; and the amount of compensation in respect of bereavement shall not exceed the amount for the time being specified in section 1A (3) of that Act.

D8.3 Principles

A magistrates' court can order compensation up to a maximum of £5,000 for each offence, and may also award compensation in relation to offences taken into consideration (but may not exceed the total arrived at by multiplying offences x £5,000).

In relation to motor vehicle damage, the maximum payable will generally be the excess not paid by the Motor Insurers Bureau (MIB) (currently £300), save where it is in respect to a vehicle stolen or taken without consent and there is damage to that vehicle, or the claim is not covered by the MIB.

If the amount of compensation is not agreed, the prosecution must be in a position to call evidence. In cases where the loss is unclear or subject to complex argument, the best course of action is to leave the matter to the civil courts to resolve (*R v Horsham Justices, ex p Richards* [1985] 2 All ER 1114); the Court of Appeal did, however, uphold a compensation order made in respect of injuries occasioned as a result of health and safety-related failures, in the sum of £90,000 (*R v Pola* [2009] EWCA Crim 655). In *R v Bewick* [2007] EWCA Crim 3297, the court observed that it would generally not be appropriate to resolve compensation applications where it was necessary to hear from a third party in evidence. A court can, however, make a commonsense determination (eg £50 for a small broken window).

D8.4 Assessment of means

In determining whether to make a compensation order against any person, and in determining the amount to be paid by any person under such an order, the court shall have regard to his means so far as they appear or are known to the court. An order made in the absence of a means inquiry is at risk of being ruled unlawful (*R v Gray* [2011] EWCA Crim 225).

Where the court considers:

- that it would be appropriate both to impose a fine and to make a compensation order; but
- that the offender has insufficient means to pay both an appropriate fine and appropriate compensation,

the court shall give preference to compensation (though it may impose a fine as well).

Save where a sentence of custody impacts on the offender's ability to pay, there is nothing wrong in principle with imposing compensation in addition to a custodial penalty.

D8.5 Suggested levels of compensation

The Magistrates' Court Sentencing Guidelines set out the following scales for the award of compensation:

Physical injury		
Type of injury	**Description**	**Starting point**
Graze	Depending on size	Up to £75
Bruise	Depending on size	Up to £100
Cut: no permanent scar	Depending on size and whether stitched	£100–500
Black eye		£125
Eye	Blurred or double vision lasting up to 6 weeks	Up to £1,000
	Blurred or double vision lasting for 6–13 weeks	£1,000
	Blurred or double vision lasting for more than 13 weeks (recovery expected)	£1,750
Brain	Concussion lasting one week	£1,500
Nose	Undisplaced fracture of nasal bone	£1,000

D8 Compensation Order

	Displaced fracture requiring manipulation	£2,000
	Deviated nasal septum requiring septoplasty	£2,000
Loss of non-front tooth	Depending on cosmetic effect	£1,250
Loss of front tooth		£1,750
Facial scar	Minor disfigurement (permanent)	£1,500
Arm	Fractured humerus, radius, ulna (substantial recovery)	£3,300
Shoulder	Dislocated (substantial recovery)	£1,750
Wrist	Dislocated/fractured—including scaphoid fracture (substantial recovery)	£3,300
	Fractured—colles type (substantial recovery)	£4,400
Sprained wrist, ankle	Disabling for up to 6 weeks	Up to £1,000
	Disabling for 6–13 weeks	£1,000
	Disabling for more than 13 weeks	£2,500
Finger	Fractured finger other than index finger (substantial recovery)	£1,000
	Fractured index finger (substantial recovery)	£1,750
	Fractured thumb (substantial recovery)	£2,000
Leg	Fractured fibula (substantial recovery)	£2,500
	Fractured femur, tibia (substantial recovery)	£3,800
Abdomen	Injury requiring laprotomy	£3,800

Mental injury	
Description	**Starting point**
Temporary mental anxiety (including terror, shock, distress), not medically verified	Up to £1,000
Disabling mental anxiety, lasting more than 6 weeks, medically verified	£1,000
Disability mental illness, lasting up to 28 weeks, confirmed by psychiatric diagnosis	£2,500

Physical and sexual abuse		
Type of abuse	Description	Starting point
Physical abuse of adult	Intermittent physical assaults resulting in accumulation of healed wounds, burns, or scalds, but with no appreciable disfigurement	£2,000
Physical abuse of child	Isolated or intermittent assault(s) resulting in weals, hair pulled from scalp etc	£1,000
	Intermittent physical assaults resulting in accumulation of healed wounds, burns, or scalds, but with no appreciable disfigurement	£2,000
Sexual abuse of adult	Non-penetrative indecent physical acts over clothing	£1,000
	Non-penetrative indecent act(s) under clothing	£2,000
Sexual abuse of child (under 18)	Non-penetrative indecent physical act(s) over clothing	£1,000
	Non-penetrative frequent assaults over clothing or non-penetrative indecent act under clothing	£2,000
	Repetitive indecent acts under clothing	£3,300

See *Blackstone's Criminal Practice 2014* **E16**

D9 Confiscation: Proceeds of Crime Act 2002

D9.1 Criteria

A magistrates' court has no power to make a confiscation order. However, in some cases it will be appropriate to accept jurisdiction for an offence but find that the prosecution or court later consider that confiscation proceedings are appropriate (a common example is in relation to counterfeit goods). A magistrates' court may commit an offender to the Crown Court for the purposes of activating the confiscation regime under the Proceeds of Crime Act 2002, even where a discharge is considered the proper sentence (see *R v Varma* [2012] UKSC 42 and **D15**).

In the event that the prosecution wish to proceed with confiscation proceedings, the court *must* commit the offender to the Crown Court for sentence.

Proceeds of Crime Act 2002, s 70

70 Committal by magistrates' court

(1) This section applies if—
   (a) a defendant is convicted of an offence by a magistrates' court, and
   (b) the prosecutor asks the court to commit the defendant to the Crown Court with a view to a confiscation order being considered under section 6.

(2) In such a case the magistrates' court—
   (a) must commit the defendant to the Crown Court in respect of the offence, and
   (b) may commit him to the Crown Court in respect of any other offence falling within subsection (3).

(3) An offence falls within this subsection if—
   (a) the defendant has been convicted of it by the magistrates' court or any other court, and
   (b) the magistrates' court has power to deal with him in respect of it.

(4) If a committal is made under this section in respect of an offence or offences—
   (a) section 6 applies accordingly, and
   (b) the committal operates as a committal of the defendant to be dealt with by the Crown Court in accordance with section 71.

(5) If a committal is made under this section in respect of an offence for which (apart from this section) the magistrates' court could have committed the defendant for sentence under section 3(2) of the Sentencing Act (offences triable either way) the court must state whether it would have done so.

(6) A committal under this section may be in custody or on bail.

Particular note should be made of section 70(5), with the court being invited to confirm that it would not otherwise have committed for sentence. Later clarification cannot be relied upon and it is therefore essential that a full contemporaneous note is taken *(R v Blakeburn* [2007] EWCA Crim 1803).

 See *Blackstone's Criminal Practice 2014* **E19**

D10 **Custodial Sentences**

D10.1 **Age requirements**

See the table in **D10.2**.

D10.2 **Criteria**

The court must not pass a custodial sentence unless it is of the opinion that the offence, or the combination of the offence and one or more offences associated with it, was so serious that neither a fine alone nor a community sentence can be justified for the offence.

Nothing prevents the court from passing a custodial sentence on the offender if:

- he fails to express his willingness to comply with a requirement which is proposed by the court to be included in a community order and which requires an expression of such willingness; or
- he fails to comply with an order under section 161(2) of the Criminal Justice Act 2003 (pre-sentence drug testing).

The custodial sentence must be for the shortest term (not exceeding the permitted maximum) that in the opinion of the court is commensurate with the seriousness of the offence, or the combination of the offence and one or more offences associated with it.

Type of sentence	Age requirement	Notes
Detention in young offender institution	18–20 years	Minimum sentence of 21 days. Maximum 6 months for any one offence. Maximum 12 months for two or more either way offences. Subject always to the statutory maximum for the offences in question. See **D14**.
Imprisonment	21 years+	Minimum 5 days save for imprisonment imposed under Magistrates' Courts Act 1980, ss 135 and 136. Maximum 6 months for any one offence. Maximum 12 months for two or more either way offences. Subject always to the statutory maximum for the offences in question.

 See *Blackstone's Criminal Practice 2014* **E2**

D11 **Dangerous Offenders**

D11.1 Criteria

Generally speaking, the dangerous offender provisions are of concern to the magistrates' court only when determining venue. The only sentence now available is an extended sentence, and this is available for those who commit a specified violent or sexual offence, as listed in **Appendix 5**, where the court is of the opinion that 'there is a significant risk to members of the public of serious harm occasioned by the commission by him of further specified offences' (Criminal Justice Act 2003, s 227). If new information becomes available during a summary trial, there is a residuary power to commit for sentence under these dangerous offender provisons (PCC(S)A 2000, s 3A).

D11.2 Specified offences

Specified offences are those listed in Schedule 15 to the Criminal Justice Act 2003 and appear in **Appendix 5**.

 See *Blackstone's Criminal Practice 2014* **D24.37–D24.40**

D12 **Deferment of Sentence**

D12.1 Age requirements

None.

D12.2 Criteria

The magistrates' court can defer sentence, on one occasion, for a maximum period of six months, to enable the court to assess the offender's capacity to change or carry out reparation to the victim. Such cases are simply adjourned (not on bail), and a warrant can be issued (PCC(S)A 2000, s 1(7)(b)) if the offender fails to attend for sentence (the court also has the option of issuing a summons, and the court should always be invited to try this option first). If the offender reoffends before the period of deferment has expired, he may be dealt with for the deferred matter.

The power to defer shall be exercisable only if:

- the offender consents;
- the offender undertakes to comply with any requirements as to his conduct during the period of the deferment that the court considers it appropriate to impose; and
- the court is satisfied, having regard to the nature of the offence and the character and circumstances of the offender, that it would be in the interests of justice to exercise the power.

See **D12.4** for legislative framework.

D12.3 Sentencing Council Guideline on use of deferred sentences

Under the new framework, there is a wider range of sentencing options open to the courts, including the increased availability of suspended sentences, and deferred sentences are likely to be used in very limited circumstances. A deferred sentence enables the court to review the conduct of the defendant before passing sentence, having first prescribed certain requirements. It also provides several opportunities for an offender to have some influence as to the sentence passed—

(a) it tests the commitment of the offender not to re-offend;

(b) it gives the offender an opportunity to do something where progress can be shown within a short period;

(c) it provides the offender with an opportunity to behave or refrain from behaving in a particular way that will be relevant to sentence.

Given the new power to require undertakings and the ability to enforce those undertakings before the end of the period of deferral, the decision to defer sentence should be predominantly for a small group of cases at either the custody threshold or the community sentence threshold where the sentencer feels that there would be particular value in giving the offender the opportunities listed because, if the offender complies with the requirements, a different sentence will be justified at the end of the deferment period.

This could be a community sentence instead of a custodial sentence or a fine or discharge instead of a community sentence. It may, rarely, enable a custodial sentence to be suspended rather than imposed immediately.

> The use of deferred sentences should be predominantly for a small group of cases close to a significant threshold where, should the defendant be prepared to adapt his behaviour in a way clearly specified by the sentencer, the court may be prepared to impose a lesser sentence.

A court may impose any conditions during the period of deferment that it considers appropriate. These could be specific requirements as set out in the provisions for community sentences, or requirements that are drawn more widely. These should be specific, measurable conditions so that the offender knows exactly what is required and the court can assess compliance; the restriction on liberty should be limited to ensure that the offender has a reasonable expectation of being able to comply whilst maintaining his or her social responsibilities.

Given the need for clarity in the mind of the offender and the possibility of sentence by another court, the court should give a clear indication (and make a written record) of the type of sentence it would be minded to impose if it had not decided to defer and ensure that the offender understands the consequences of failure to comply with the court's wishes during the deferral period.

> When deferring sentence, the sentencer must make clear the consequence of not complying with any requirements and should indicate the type of sentence it would be minded to impose. Sentencers should impose specific, measurable conditions that do not involve a serious restriction on liberty.

D12.4 Legislation

Sections 1–1D of the PCC(S)A 2000 provide:

Powers of Criminal Courts (Sentencing) Act 2000, ss 1, 1A(1)–(2), 1B, 1C, and 1D

1 Deferment of sentence

(1) The Crown Court or a magistrates' court may defer passing sentence on an offender for the purpose of enabling the court, or any other court to which it falls to deal with him, to have regard in dealing with him to—

    (a) his conduct after conviction (including, where appropriate, the making by him of reparation for his offence); or

---

    (b) any change in his circumstances;

    but this is subject to subsections (3) and (4) below.

(2) Without prejudice to the generality of subsection (1) above, the matters to which the court to which it falls to deal with the offender may have regard by virtue of paragraph (a) of that subsection include the extent to which the offender has complied with any requirements imposed under subsection (3)(b) below.

(3) The power conferred by subsection (1) above shall be exercisable only if—

    (a) the offender consents;

    (b) the offender undertakes to comply with any requirements as to his conduct during the period of the deferment that the court considers it appropriate to impose; and

    (c) the court is satisfied, having regard to the nature of the offence and the character and circumstances of the offender, that it would be in the interests of justice to exercise the power.

(4) Any deferment under this section shall be until such date as may be specified by the court, not being more than six months after the date on which the deferment is announced by the court; and, subject to section 1D(3) below, where the passing of sentence has been deferred under this section it shall not be further so deferred.

(5) Where a court has under this section deferred passing sentence on an offender, it shall forthwith give a copy of the order deferring the passing of sentence and setting out any requirements imposed under subsection (3)(b) above—

    (a) to the offender,

    (b) ...

(6) Notwithstanding any enactment, a court which under this section defers passing sentence on an offender shall not on the same occasion remand him.

(7) Where—

    (a) a court which under this section has deferred passing sentence on an offender proposes to deal with him on the date originally specified by the court, or

    (b) the offender does not appear on the day so specified,

    the court may issue a summons requiring him to appear before the court at a time and place specified in the summons, or may issue a warrant to arrest him and bring him before the court at a time and place specified in the warrant.

(8) Nothing in this section or sections 1A to 1D below shall affect—

    (a) the power of the Crown Court to bind over an offender to come up for judgment when called upon; or

    (b) the power of any court to defer passing sentence for any purpose for which it may lawfully do so apart from this section.

1A Further provision about undertakings

(1) Without prejudice to the generality of paragraph (b) of section 1(3) above, the requirements that may be imposed by virtue of that paragraph include requirements as to the residence of the offender during the whole or any part of the period of deferment.

(2) Where an offender has undertaken to comply with any requirements imposed under section 1(3)(b) above the court may appoint—

    (a) an officer of a local probation board or an officer of a provider of probation services, or

    (b) any other person whom the court thinks appropriate, to act as a supervisor in relation to him.

1B Breach of undertakings

(1) A court which under section 1 above has deferred passing sentence on an offender may deal with him before the end of the period of deferment if—

    (a) he appears or is brought before the court under subsection (3) below; or

    (b) the court is satisfied that he has failed to comply with one or more requirements imposed under section 1(3)(b) above in connection with the deferment.

(2) Subsection (3) below applies where—

    (a) a court has under section 1 above deferred passing sentence on an offender;

    (b) the offender undertook to comply with one or more requirements imposed under section 1(3)(b) above in connection with the deferment; and

    (c) a person appointed under section 1A(2) above to act as a supervisor in relation to the offender has reported to the court that the offender has failed to comply with one or more of those requirements.

(3) Where this subsection applies, the court may issue—

    (a) a summons requiring the offender to appear before the court at a time and place specified in the summons; or

    (b) a warrant to arrest him and bring him before the court at a time and place specified in the warrant.

1C Conviction of offence during period of deferment

(1) A court which under section 1 above has deferred passing sentence on an offender may deal with him before the end of the period of deferment if during that period he is convicted in Great Britain of any offence.

(2) Subsection (3) below applies where a court has under section 1 above deferred passing sentence on an offender in respect of one or more offences and during the period of deferment the offender is convicted in England and Wales of any offence ('the later offence').

(3) Where this subsection applies, then (without prejudice to subsection (1) above and whether or not the offender is sentenced for the later offence during the period of deferment), the court which passes sentence on him for the later offence may also, if this has not already been done, deal with him for the offence or offences for which passing of sentence has been deferred, except that—

    (a) the power conferred by this subsection shall not be exercised by a magistrates' court if the court which deferred passing sentence was the Crown Court; and

    (b) the Crown Court, in exercising that power in a case in which the court which deferred passing sentence was a magistrates' court, shall not pass any sentence which could not have been passed by a magistrates' court in exercising that power.

(4) Where a court which under section 1 above has deferred passing sentence on an offender proposes to deal with him by virtue of subsection (1) above before the end of the period of deferment, the court may issue—

    (a) a summons requiring him to appear before the court at a time and place specified in the summons; or

    (b) a warrant to arrest him and bring him before the court at a time and place specified in the warrant.

1D   Deferment of sentence: supplementary

(1) In deferring the passing of sentence under section 1 above a magistrates' court shall be regarded as exercising the power of adjourning the trial conferred by section 10(1) of the Magistrates' Courts Act 1980, and accordingly sections 11(1) and 13(1) to (3A) and (5) of that Act (non-appearance of the accused) apply (without prejudice to section 1(7) above) if the offender does not appear on the date specified under section 1(4) above.

(2) Where the passing of sentence on an offender has been deferred by a court ('the original court') under section 1 above, the power of that court under that section to deal with the offender at the end of the period of deferment and any power of that court under section 1B(1) or 1C(1) above, or of any court under section 1C(3) above, to deal with the offender—

    (a) is power to deal with him, in respect of the offence for which passing of sentence has been deferred, in any way in which the original court could have dealt with him if it had not deferred passing sentence; and

    (b) without prejudice to the generality of paragraph (a) above, in the case of a magistrates' court, includes the power conferred by section 3 below to commit him to the Crown Court for sentence.

(3) Where—

    (a) the passing of sentence on an offender in respect of one or more offences has been deferred under section 1 above, and

    (b) a magistrates' court deals with him in respect of the offence or any of the offences by committing him to the Crown Court under section 3 below,

the power of the Crown Court to deal with him includes the same power to defer passing sentence on him as if he had just been convicted of the offence or offences on indictment before the court.

(4) Subsection (5) below applies where—

    (a) the passing of sentence on an offender in respect of one or more offences has been deferred under section 1 above;

    (b) it falls to a magistrates' court to determine a relevant matter; and

    (c) a justice of the peace is satisfied—

        (i) that a person appointed under section 1A(2)(b) above to act as a supervisor in relation to the offender is likely to be able to give evidence that may assist the court in determining that matter; and

        (ii) that that person will not voluntarily attend as a witness.

(5) The justice may issue a summons directed to that person requiring him to attend before the court at the time and place appointed in the summons to give evidence.

(6) For the purposes of subsection (4) above a court determines a relevant matter if it—

(a) deals with the offender in respect of the offence, or any of the offences, for which the passing of sentence has been deferred; or

(b) determines, for the purposes of section 1B(1)(b) above, whether the offender has failed to comply with any requirements imposed under section 1(3)(b) above.

 See *Blackstone's Criminal Practice 2014* **D20.103–D20.109**

D13 **Deprivation Order**

D13.1 **Age requirements**

None.

D13.2 **Criteria**

Orders of this kind should not be made without warning the defendant in advance and inviting representations, otherwise they are liable to be quashed on appeal (*R v Ball* [2002] EWCA Crim 2777). The court should not proceed without first ascertaining the value of the property, and should also ensure that an order made against just one offender does not result in an overly disproportionate sentence (*Ball*). Such an order will be invalid if the financial consequences and the value of the property have not been considered (*Trans Berckx BVBA v North Avon and Swindon Magistrates' Court* [2011] EWHC 2605 (Admin)).

The power can be used to forfeit property intended to be used for any offence, not just the particular offence before the court (*R v O'Farrell* [1988] Crim LR 387). Deprivation orders are intended only for straightforward cases involving unencumbered property (*R v Troth* [1980] Crim LR 249).

> ## **Powers of Criminal Courts (Sentencing) Act 2000, s 143**
>
> ### 143 **Powers to deprive offenders of property used etc. for purposes of crime**
>
> (1) Where a person is convicted of an offence and the court by or before which he is convicted is satisfied that any property which has been lawfully seized from him, or which was in his possession or under his control at the time when he was apprehended for the offence or when a summons in respect of it was issued—
>
>   (a) has been used for the purpose of committing, or facilitating the commission of, any offence, or
>
>   (b) was intended by him to be used for that purpose,
>
> the court may (subject to subsection (5) below) make an order under this section in respect of that property.
>
> (2) Where a person is convicted of an offence and the offence, or an offence which the court has taken into consideration in determining his sentence, consists of unlawful possession of property which—
>
>   (a) has been lawfully seized from him, or

    (b) was in his possession or under his control at the time when he was apprehended for the offence of which he has been convicted or when a summons in respect of that offence was issued,

the court may (subject to subsection (5) below) make an order under this section in respect of that property.

(3) An order under this section shall operate to deprive the offender of his rights, if any, in the property to which it relates, and the property shall (if not already in their possession) be taken into the possession of the police.

(4) Any power conferred on a court by subsection (1) or (2) above may be exercised—

    (a) whether or not the court also deals with the offender in any other way in respect of the offence of which he has been convicted; and

    (b) without regard to any restrictions on forfeiture in any enactment contained in an Act passed before 29th July 1988.

(5) In considering whether to make an order under this section in respect of any property, a court shall have regard—

    (a) to the value of the property; and

    (b) to the likely financial and other effects on the offender of the making of the order (taken together with any other order that the court contemplates making).

(6) Where a person commits an offence to which this subsection applies by—

    (a) driving, attempting to drive, or being in charge of a vehicle, or

    (b) failing to comply with a requirement made under section 7 or 7A of the Road Traffic Act 1988 (failure to provide specimen for analysis or laboratory test or to give permission for such a test) in the course of an investigation into whether the offender had committed an offence while driving, attempting to drive or being in charge of a vehicle, or

    (c) failing, as the driver of a vehicle, to comply with subsection (2) or (3) of section 170 of the Road Traffic Act 1988 (duty to stop and give information or report accident),

the vehicle shall be regarded for the purposes of subsection (1) above (and section 144(1)(b) below) as used for the purpose of committing the offence (and for the purpose of committing any offence of aiding, abetting, counselling or procuring the commission of the offence).

(7) Subsection (6) above applies to—

    (a) an offence under the Road Traffic Act 1988 which is punishable with imprisonment;

    (b) an offence of manslaughter; and

    (c) an offence under section 35 of the Offences Against the Person Act 1861 (wanton and furious driving).

(8) Facilitating the commission of an offence shall be taken for the purposes of subsection (1) above to include the taking of any steps after it has been committed for the purpose of disposing of any property to which it relates or of avoiding apprehension or detection.

 See *Blackstone's Criminal Practice 2014* **E18**

D14 Detention in Young Offender Institution

D14.1 Age requirements

Aged 18 to 20 years.

D14.2 Criteria

The general requirements for the imposition of a custodial sentence (see **D10**) must be met. A minimum sentence of 21 days must be imposed.

A suspended sentence order (see **D43**) may be imposed.

 See *Blackstone's Criminal Practice 2014* **E7.4**

D15 **Discharges; Conditional and Absolute**

D15.1 **Age requirements**

Any offender.

D15.2 **Criteria**

An order can be imposed where it is inexpedient to inflict any punishment. A conditional discharge can be for up to three years. Only the orders mentioned in section 12(7) of the PCC(S)A 2000 can be made alongside a discharge, but a magistrates' court may commit an offender to the Crown Court for the purposes of activating the confiscation regime under the Proceeds of Crime Act 2002 even where a discharge is considered the proper sentence (*R v Varma* [2012] UKSC 42).

> ## **Powers of Criminal Courts (Sentencing) Act 2000, s 12(7)**
>
> ### **12 Absolute and conditional discharge**
>
> (7) Nothing in this section shall be construed as preventing a court, on discharging an offender absolutely or conditionally in respect of any offence, from making an order for costs against the offender or imposing any disqualification on him or from making in respect of the offence an order under section 130, 143 or 148 below (compensation orders, deprivation orders and restitution orders).

Where a person who has received a warning under section 65 of the Crime and Disorder Act 1998 or a youth caution is convicted of an offence committed within two years of the warning or caution, the court by or before which he is so convicted:

- shall not impose a conditional discharge in respect of the offence unless it is of the opinion that there are exceptional circumstances relating to the offence or the offender which justify its doing so; and
- where it does so, shall state in open court that it is of that opinion and why it is.

A person convicted of breaching an ASBO may not receive a conditional discharge (Crime and Disorder Act 1998, s 1(11)).

If a person commits an offence during the life of a conditional discharge, he may be resentenced for that original offence even if the period of discharge has expired at the date of sentence. The offender will be sentenced with reference to his age at the date of sentence, not the date of the previous offence, and can be sentenced in any way as if he had just been convicted of the offence. If the conditional discharge was imposed by the Crown Court, the offender can be committed to that court for resentence.

There is no requirement to resentence, and a court could sentence for a new offence and leave the conditional discharge in place if it saw fit to do so.

See also section 12 of the PCC(S)A 2000.

 See *Blackstone's Criminal Practice 2014* **E12**

D16 **Discounts for Early Plea**

D16.1 **Age requirements**
None.

D16.2 **Criteria**

A court must discount a sentence in return for a guilty plea. A magistrates' court may impose a maximum sentence as an alternative to committing the case for sentence to the Crown Court. A reduced discount must be given even if the prosecution case is overwhelming. The amount of discount will depend upon the timing of the plea. The *Magistrates' Sentencing Guidelines* state:

> The reduction has no impact on sentencing decisions in relation to ancillary orders, including disqualification. The level of the reduction should reflect the stage at which the offender indicated a willingness to admit guilt and will be gauged on a sliding scale, ranging from a recommended one third (where the guilty plea was entered at the first reasonable opportunity), reducing to a recommended one quarter (where a trial date has been set) and to a recommended one tenth (for a guilty plea entered at the 'door of the court' or after the trial has begun). There is a presumption that the recommended reduction will be given unless there are good reasons for a lower amount. The application of the reduction may affect the type, as well as the severity, of the sentence. It may also take the sentence below the range in some cases. The court must state that it has reduced a sentence to reflect a guilty plea. It should usually indicate what the sentence would have been if there had been no reduction as a result of the plea.

In each category, there is a presumption that the recommended reduction will be given unless there are good reasons for a lower amount		
First reasonable opportunity	After a trial date is set	Door of the court/after trial has begun
recommended 1/3	**recommended 1/4**	**recommended 1/10**

The issue has been comprehensively reviewed in *R v Caley* [2012] EWCA Crim 2821. The court held that the following points should apply:

- The Sentencing Council's Guideline on discount for guilty plea remains the starting point for the consideration of the relevant issues.

- The discount is given for the indication of the guilty plea. This is based on the need to alleviate the anxieties of victims and witnesses, and to contribute to an effective criminal justice system.
- It is separate to the issue of remorse.

D16.2.1 *First reasonable opportunity*

When the first reasonable opportunity arises is a matter for the judge.

For the police interview to be the first reasonable opportunity would require a significant adjustment to general practice. It may affect the caution and rules of practice on how interviews are conducted. The charge will not have been formulated. An admission in interview is, however, very relevant as mitigation prior to the application of the discount.

It is necessary to distinguish cases where the defendant will know of his guilt and where he needs advice. The discount is not for knowing that the case can be proved. Relevant facts can be admitted if not specific charges. Case management forms seek an indication of plea at a sending. Early guilty plea schemes have this in mind. An indication at the magistrates' court or immediately on arrival at the Crown Court, and certainly by the plea and case management hearing (PCMH), is desirable. However the PCMH is not usually the first reasonable opportunity. It will usually allow a discount of 25 per cent. The other two opportunities will ordinarily attract the maximum one-third discount. An indication may be to indicate a plea to a lesser charge where that is reasonable.

D16.2.2 *Overwhelming evidence*

Discount should be given in accordance with the guideline and *R v Wilson* [2012] EWCA Crim 386. In any event, a case may not be as overwhelming as part of the evidence only suggests. Twenty per cent is the minimum appropriate discount.

D16.2.3 *Available penalties*

A low maximum sentence is not relevant.

D16.2.4 *Unsuccessful* Newton *hearings*

A normal reduction is not appropriate. The actual discount will depend on the circumstances and number of issues in dispute.

D16.2.5 *Residual flexibility*

There is a residual discretion to deal with the facts of individual cases such as the following:

- Where expert evidence is involved in a serious case, if the significance of the act is in dispute but not the occurrence of the act itself (*R v Peters* [2005] EWCA Crim 605).
- To blame poor advice on plea to an inexperienced defendant rather than an experienced one, but there may have to be a full waiver of privilege.
- The avoidance of an exceptionally long or complex trial may also lead to an exceptional discount. Care is needed to ensure those who plead early see a benefit.

There is not to be a detailed investigation of the savings in individual cases.

Because all relevant documents had not been served, a full discount was given when they were (*R v Thompson* [2012] EWCA Crim 1431). In *R v Carlisle* [2012] EWCA Crim 2501, a 20 per cent discount was appropriate when the defence prevaricated after the Crown had refused to accept a plea to a lesser charge.

Thus to secure a maximum discount at the Crown Court, an indication of plea should be given at or immediately after a sending if a guilty plea has not been entered in the magistrates' court.

D17 **Disqualification from Driving**

D17.1 **Age requirements**

None.

D17.2 **Criteria**

Disqualification (or in the fifth example, more accurately a revocation) may arise in one of five ways:

1. Offence carrying obligatory disqualification (see **D17.4**).
2. Offence carrying discretionary disqualification (see **D17.6**).
3. As a result of accumulating 12 or more penalty points (see **D17.7**).
4. As a result of conviction for any offence, or an offence where a vehicle was used for crime (PCC(S)A 2000, ss 146, 147) (see **D17.9**).
5. As a result of a 'new driver' accumulating six penalty points (see **D17.10**).

D17.3 **Interim disqualification**

An interim disqualification can be imposed when the court commits an offender for sentence to the Crown Court, remits the case to another court, or defers or adjourns sentence (Road Traffic Offenders Act 1988, s 26). More than one interim disqualification may be imposed, but the total term must not exceed six months.

 See *Blackstone's Criminal Practice 2014* **C7.11**

D17.4 **Obligatory disqualification**

Where a person is convicted of an offence involving obligatory disqualification, the court must order him to be disqualified for such period not less than 12 months as the court thinks fit, unless the court for special reasons (see **D17.5**) thinks fit to order him to be disqualified for a shorter period or not to order him to be disqualified (Road Traffic Offenders Act 1988, s 34).

A person disqualified for dangerous driving must also be ordered to undertake an extended driving test.

A mandatory disqualification does not have the effect of removing any penalty points existing on the licence.

There are certain exceptions to the minimum 12-month period that are applicable to those sentenced in the magistrates' court, as set out in **D17.4.1–D17.4.3**.

D17.4.1 *Minimum three-year disqualification*

A minimum three-year disqualification follows where, within the ten years immediately preceding the commission of the offence, a person has been been convicted of any such offence, and is again convicted of an offence under any of the following provisions of the Road Traffic Act 1988, that is:

- section 3A (causing death by careless driving when under the influence of drink or drugs);
- section 4(1) (driving or attempting to drive while unfit);
- section 5(1)(a) (driving or attempting to drive with excess alcohol);
- section 7(6) (failing to provide a specimen) where that is an offence involving obligatory disqualification;
- section 7A(6) (failing to allow a specimen to be subjected to laboratory test) where that is an offence involving obligatory disqualification.

D17.4.2 *Minimum two-year disqualification*

A minimum two-year disqualification follows in relation to a person on whom more than one disqualification for a fixed period of 56 days or more has been imposed within the three years immediately preceding the commission of the offence.

D17.4.3 *Minimum six months' disqualification*

A minimum six months' disqualification follows where a person convicted of an offence under section 40A of the Road Traffic Act 1988 (using vehicle in dangerous condition, etc) has, within the three years immediately preceding the commission of the offence, been convicted of any such offence.

D17.5 Special reasons

There is no statutory definition of 'special reasons', but it must not amount to a defence in law, must be directly connected with the offence in question (not the offender), and must be a mitigating or extenuating circumstance. The burden (civil standard) falls on the defendant. Good character, personal service to the community (eg being a doctor), financial hardship as a result of a disqualification, and the fact the offence was not particularly serious have all been held not to amount to special reasons.

An ignorance of the terms of motor insurance cannot generally amount to special reasons (*Rennison v Knowler* [1947] 1 All ER 302), unless the person was misled or there is a particularly good reason for the ignorance (eg illness, confusion brought about by others).

D17 Disqualification from Driving

If special reasons are found, the court has a discretion not to endorse points, and to reduce or not impose a mandatory period of disqualification. Note, however, that for an offence involving mandatory disqualification, where special reasons are found and the court does not disqualify, it must impose points, unless it finds special reasons also for not doing so.

Common special reasons are:

- spiked drinks or mistake as to item drunk;
- shortness of distance driven;
- medical or other emergencies.

In *R v Mander*, unreported, 13 May 2008, CA, the court found special reasons where a taxi driver, upon three of five passengers alighting without paying, drove dangerously for approximately nine-tenths of a mile. The court declined, however, to exercise its discretion to reduce the period of disqualification on the grounds that the defendant had overreacted to the circumstances.

In *Warring-Davies v Director of Public Prosecutions* [2009] EWHC 1172 (Admin), the court emphasized the need to find a causal link between any alleged medical condition and the driving in question.

In *Director of Public Prosecutions v Harrison* [2007] EWHC 556 (Admin), the court held it wrong to find special reasons where a drunken person drove 446 yards in order to find youths who had harassed him earlier.

In *Director of Public Prosecutions v Oram* [2005] EWHC 964 (Admin), the court held that special reasons would not be arguable to a drunk driver who relied upon shortness of distance driven alone.

Taylor v Rajan [1974] RTR 304 deals with the principles involved in 'emergency' cases:

> This is not the first case in which the court has had to consider whether driving in an emergency could justify a conclusion that there are special reasons for not disqualifying the driver. If a man, in the well-founded belief that he will not drive again, puts his car in the garage, goes into his house and has a certain amount to drink in the belief that he is not going to drive again, and if thereafter is an emergency which requires him in order to deal with it to take his car out despite his intention to leave it in the garage, then that is a situation which can in law amount to a special reason for not disqualifying a driver. On the other hand, Justices who are primarily concerned with dealing with this legislation should approach the exercise of the resulting discretion with great care. The mere fact that the facts disclose a special reason does not mean that the driver is to escape disqualification as a matter of course. There is a very serious burden upon the Justices, even when a special reason has been disclosed, to decide whether in their discretion they should decline to disqualify a particular case. The Justices should have very much in mind that

> if a man deliberately drives when he knows he has consumed a considerable quantity of drink, he presents a potential source of danger to the public which no private crisis can likely excuse. One of the most important matters which Justices have to consider in the exercise of this discretion is whether the emergency (and I call it such for want of a more convenient word) was sufficiently acute to justify the driver taking his car out. The Justices should only exercise a discretion in favour of the driver in clear and compelling circumstances . . . The Justices therefore must consider the whole of the circumstances. They must consider the nature and degree of the crisis or emergency which has caused the defendant to take the car out. They must consider with particular care whether there were alternative means of transport or methods of dealing with the crisis other than and alternative to the use by the defendant of his own car. They should have regard to the manner in which the defendant drove . . . and they should generally have regard to whether the defendant acted responsibly or otherwise . . . The matter must be considered objectively and the quality and gravity of the crisis must be assessed in that way. Last, but by no means least, if the alcohol content in the defendant's blood and body is very high, that is a powerful reason for saying that the discretion should not be exercised in his favour. Indeed, if the alcohol content exceeds 100 milligrammes per hundred millilitres of blood, the Justices should rarely, if ever, exercise this discretion in favour of the defendant driver . . .

In *DPP v Heathcote* [2011] EWHC 2536 (Admin), it was held that in deciding whether an 'emergency' justified driving, the court should ask whether a sober, reasonable, and responsible friend would have advised the defendant to drive. Relevant factors included:

- amount drunk;
- threat to others;
- state of the roads;
- distance to be driven;
- nature of the emergency;
- what alternatives were available.

The court confirmed that the use of an emergency as a special reason was not limited to life and limb cases; but on the facts, to chase the thieves of a relative's car was not acceptable.

Chatters v Burke [1986] 3 All ER 168 details the seven factors relevant to a 'shortness of distance driven' argument:

- distance;
- manner of driving;
- state of the vehicle;
- whether there was an intention to drive further;
- road and traffic conditions;
- possibility of danger to road users and pedestrians;
- reason for the driving.

In order to establish a spiked drinks defence, it will be necessary to prove that the drink was laced, the defendant did not know it was laced, and that but for the lacing of the drink his alcohol level would not have exceeded the legal limit. It will normally be necessary to call expert evidence in relation to the last point. The higher the reading, the less likely it is that a defendant will be able to prove he had no knowledge. If a court is of the view that the defendant ought to have realized his drink was spiked, it will not find special reasons (*Pridge v Grant* [1985] RTR 196).

 See *Blackstone's Criminal Practice 2014* **C7.8** and **C7.55**

D17.6 Discretionary disqualification

Where an offence carries discretionary disqualification, the court must consider disqualification before it considers the imposition of penalty points. This is the case even if the offender would be liable to disqualification under the 'totting-up' provisions.

Practitioners will consider the tactical considerations of inviting a court to impose a discretionary disqualification as opposed to points that could trigger a totting-up disqualification. The benefit of a discretionary disqualification is that it can be for as short a period as the court directs; the negative side is that any previous points remain on the licence. If a totting-up disqualification were imposed, all the points would be removed but the defendant would face a minimum six-month period of disqualification. This applies only if the court is minded to impose a shorter period, as a defendant may prefer to tot up and clear his licence after a six-month disqualification, rather than have, say, four months disqualified and still have the existing points hanging over him. If a court disqualifies then no additional penalty points are imposed. The period of disqualification can be for any period the court thinks proper.

D17.7 As a result of accumulating 12 or more penalty points

Under section 35 of the Road Traffic Offenders Act 1988 (see **D17.8**), if a driver has accumulated 12 or more points on his licence, the court must order him to be disqualified for not less than the minimum period, unless it is satisfied, having regard to all the circumstances, that there are grounds for disqualifying him for a shorter period or not to disqualify him. In calculating the points on the licence ('totting up'), the court will have regard to:

- the points to be imposed for the new offence, and
- any points on the licence for offences committed no longer than three years from the date of commission of the new offence

(therefore, points run from date of the old offence to the date of new offence) (Road Traffic Offenders Act 1988, s 29).

If there has been in the three-year period a disqualification under the totting-up provisions, then points imposed prior to that disqualification would be disregarded.

The minimum period of disqualification is:

- six months if no previous disqualification;
- 12 months if one previous disqualification (for 56 days or more);
- two years if two or more previous disqualifications (for 56 days or more).

The previous disqualifications must have been imposed within three years of the date of the new offence to count.

D17.8 Mitigating circumstances

'Mitigating circumstances' may be argued in order to escape disqualification as a result of totting-up (see **D17.7**).

Section 35 of the Road Traffic Offenders Act 1988 provides:

Road Traffic Offenders Act 1988, s 35

35 Disqualification for repeated offences

(1) Where—
  (a) a person is convicted of an offence to which this subsection applies, and
  (b) the penalty points to be taken into account on that occasion number twelve or more,
  the court must order him to be disqualified for not less than the minimum period unless the court is satisfied, having regard to all the circumstances, that there are grounds for mitigating the normal consequences of the conviction and thinks fit to order him to be disqualified for a shorter period or not to order him to be disqualified.

(1A) Subsection (1) above applies to—
  (a) an offence involving discretionary disqualification and obligatory endorsement, and
  (b) an offence involving obligatory disqualification in respect of which no order is made under section 34 of this Act.

(2) The minimum period referred to in subsection (1) above is—
  (a) six months if no previous disqualification imposed on the offender is to be taken into account, and
  (b) one year if one, and two years if more than one, such disqualification is to be taken into account;
  and a previous disqualification imposed on an offender is to be taken into account if it was for a fixed period of 56 days or more and was imposed within the three years immediately preceding the commission of the latest offence in respect of which penalty points are taken into account under section 29 of this Act.

---

(3) Where an offender is convicted on the same occasion of more than one offence to which subsection (1) above applies—

    (a) not more than one disqualification shall be imposed on him under subsection (1) above,

    (b) in determining the period of the disqualification the court must take into account all the offences, and

    (c) for the purposes of any appeal any disqualification imposed under subsection (1) above shall be treated as an order made on the conviction of each of the offences.

(4) No account is to be taken under subsection (1) above of any of the following circumstances—

    (a) any circumstances that are alleged to make the offence or any of the offences not a serious one,

    (b) hardship, other than exceptional hardship, or

    (c) any circumstances which, within the three years immediately preceding the conviction, have been taken into account under that subsection in ordering the offender to be disqualified for a shorter period or not ordering him to be disqualified.

(5) References in this section to disqualification do not include a disqualification imposed under section 26 of this Act or section 147 of the Powers of Criminal Courts (Sentencing) Act 2000 or section 223A or 436A of the Criminal Procedure (Scotland) Act 1975 (offences committed by using vehicles) or a disqualification imposed in respect of an offence of stealing a motor vehicle, an offence under section 12 or 25 of the Theft Act 1968, an offence under section 178 of the Road Traffic Act 1988, or an attempt to commit such an offence.

(5A) The preceding provisions of this section shall apply in relation to a conviction of an offence committed by aiding, abetting, counselling, procuring, or inciting to the commission of, an offence involving obligatory disqualification as if the offence were an offence involving discretionary disqualification.

It should be noted that the burden of establishing mitigating circumstances is on the defendant; and those circumstances will generally need to be proved by way of evidence as opposed to submission.

 See *Blackstone's Criminal Practice 2014* **C7.28**

D17.9 As a result of conviction for any offence, or an offence where a vehicle was used for crime

Section 146 of the PCC(S)A 2000 gives a court the power to disqualify an offender from holding a driving licence following a conviction for any offence. There need be no nexus between driving and the offence in question, and nothing additional should be written into the statute over and above what is already present; this allows a court to use the provision whenever it feels it to be appropriate in all of the circumstances (*R v Sofekun* [2008] EWCA Crim 2035).

Section 147 of the PCC(S)A 2000 gives courts a narrower power to disqualify where a motor vehicle was involved in the commission of the offence. In the magistrates' court the power is limited solely to the offences of assault:

Powers of Criminal Courts (Sentencing) Act 2000, s 147(1) and (3)

147 Driving disqualification when vehicle used for purposes of crime

(1) This section [...] applies where a person is convicted by or before any court of common assault or of any other offence involving an assault (including an offence of aiding, abetting, counselling or procuring, or inciting to the commission of, an offence).

(2) [...]

(3) If, in a case to which this section applies by virtue of subsection (2) above, the court is satisfied that the assault was committed by driving a motor vehicle, the court may order the person convicted to be disqualified, for such period as the court thinks fit, for holding or obtaining a driving licence.

 See *Blackstone's Criminal Practice 2014* **E21.11** and **E21.12**

D17.10 Road Traffic (New Drivers) Act 1995

Newly qualified drivers are subject to a two-year probationary period. If at any time during that period the points to be endorsed on a driving licence amount to six or more, the licence will be automatically revoked. The relevant date is the date of offence not conviction, so revocation cannot be avoided by delaying court proceedings.

In appropriate cases, advocates may seek to invite courts to disqualify instead of endorse points, in order to try to avoid the draconian consequences of accumulating six or more penalty points.

 See *Blackstone's Criminal Practice 2014* **C7.44**

D17.11 Return of driving licence

D17.11.1 *Overview*

Section 42 of the Road Traffic Offenders Act 1988 provides for a disqualified driver to apply to the court for the return of his driving licence, prior to the expiry of the disqualification period. These proceedings may be funded at the magistrates' court by way of a means-tested representation order.

Period of disqualification	Minimum period of disqualification that must have elapsed before court can consider an application
Less than 4 years	2 years
4 years, but less than 10 years	One half of the disqualification period
10 years or more	5 years

If a disqualification is imposed by virtue of section 36(1) of the Act (disqualification until test is passed), there is no power to return a licence under section 43.

D17.11.2 *Criteria to be applied*

On any such application the court may, as it thinks proper having regard to:

- the character of the person disqualified and his conduct subsequent to the order;
- the nature of the offence; and
- any other circumstances of the case,

either by order remove the disqualification as from such date as may be specified in the order, or refuse the application.

D17.11.3 *Further application following refusal*

Where an application is refused, a further application shall not be entertained if made within three months after the date of the refusal.

 See *Blackstone's Criminal Practice 2014* **C7.42**

D18 **Disqualification of Company Directors**

D18.1 **Age requirements**

None.

D18.2 **Criteria**

Section 2 of the Company Directors Disqualification Act 1986 provides:

> ### Company Directors Disqualification Act 1986, s 2(1)
>
> **2 Disqualification on conviction of indictable offence**
>
> (1) The court may make a disqualification order against a person where he is convicted of an indictable offence (whether on indictment or summarily) in connection with the promotion, formation, management, liquidation or striking off of a company with the receivership of a company's property or with his being an administrative receiver of a company.

Section 5 provides:

> ### Company Directors Disqualification Act 1986, s 5
>
> **5 Disqualification on summary conviction**
>
> (1) An offence counting for the purposes of this section is one of which a person is convicted (either on indictment or summarily) in consequence of a contravention of, or failure to comply with, any provision of the companies legislation requiring a return, account or other document to be filed with, delivered or sent, or notice of any matter to be given, to the registrar of companies (whether the contravention or failure is on the person's own part or on the part of any company).
>
> (2) Where a person is convicted of a summary offence counting for those purposes, the court by which he is convicted (or, in England and Wales, any other magistrates' court acting in the same local justice area) may make a disqualification order against him if the circumstances specified in the next subsection are present.
>
> (3) Those circumstances are that, during the 5 years ending with the date of the conviction, the person has had made against him, or has been convicted of, in total not less than 3 default orders and offences counting for the purposes of this section; and those offences may include that of which he is convicted as mentioned in subsection (2) and any other offence of which he is convicted on the same occasion.

(4) For the purposes of this section—

    (a) the definition of 'summary offence' in Schedule 1 to the Interpretation Act 1978 applies for Scotland as for England and Wales, and

    (b) 'default order' means the same as in section 3(3)(b).

(5) The maximum period of disqualification under this section is 5 years.

The effect of the order (s 1) is that the offender:

- will not be a director of a company, act as receiver of a company's property, or in any way, whether directly or indirectly, be concerned or take part in the promotion, formation, or management of a company unless (in each case) he has the leave of a court; and
- will not act as an insolvency practitioner.

The management of the company relates to both internal and external activities, so a director who obtains goods from another during the course of his business can properly be made subject to an order for disqualification (*R v Corbin* (1984) 6 Cr App R (S) 17).

A magistrates' court can make such an order for a maximum period of five years. An order cannot run consecutively to an existing order. It is wrong to also impose compensation if the defendant has, by virtue of being disqualified as a director, been deprived of his means to earn money in order to pay compensation (*R v Holmes* (1992) 13 Cr App R (S) 29).

📖 See *Blackstone's Criminal Practice 2014* **E21.8**

D19 **Drinking Banning Order**

D19.1 **Age requirements**

16 years or over.

D19.2 **Criteria**

Following conviction for any offence, the court must determine whether the offence was committed while under the influence of alcohol and, if so, whether a banning order is necessary for the purpose of protecting others from further criminal or disorderly conduct by the offender while he is under the influence of alcohol.

An order may last between two months and two years, and may impose any prohibition on the offender which is necessary to prevent criminal or disorderly conduct while under the influence of alcohol, and must include prohibitions as the court considers necessary on the offender's entering licensed premises. Breach of an order carries a maximum penalty of a fine (level 4). Note that these orders are not available in all criminal justice areas.

Violent Crime Reduction Act 2006, s 6

6 Orders on conviction in criminal proceedings

(1) This section applies where—
   (a) an individual aged 16 or over is convicted of an offence (the 'offender'); and
   (b) at the time he committed the offence, he was under the influence of alcohol.
(2) The court must consider whether the conditions in section 3(2) are satisfied in relation to the offender.
(3) If the court decides that the conditions are satisfied in relation to the offender, it may make a drinking banning order against him.
(4) If the court—
   (a) decides that the conditions are satisfied in relation to the offender, but
   (b) does not make a drinking banning order,
   it must give its reasons for not doing so in open court.
(5) If the court decides that the conditions are not satisfied in relation to the offender, it must state that fact in open court and give its reasons.

Section 3(2) sets out the conditions:

Violent Crime Reduction Act 2006, s 3(2)

3 Orders on an appliation to magistrates' court

(2) The conditions are—

(a) that the individual has, after the commencement of this section, engaged in criminal or disorderly conduct while under the influence of alcohol; and

(b) that such an order is necessary to protect other persons from further conduct by him of that kind while he is under the influence of alcohol.

The section 7 supplementary provision about orders on conviction provides:

Violent Crime Reduction Act 2006, s 7

7 Supplementary provisions about orders on conviction

(1) For the purpose of deciding whether to make a drinking banning order under section 6 the court may consider evidence led by the prosecution and evidence led by the defence.

(2) it is immaterial whether the evidence would have been admissible in the proceedings in which the offender was convicted.

(3) A drinking banning order under section 6 must not be made except—

(a) in addition to a sentence imposed in respect of the offence; or

(b) in addition to an order discharging the offender conditionally.

(4) The court may adjourn any proceedings in relation to a drinking banning order under section 6 even after sentencing the offender.

(5) If the offender does not appear for any adjourned proceedings, the court may further adjourn the proceedings or may issue a warrant for his arrest.

(6) But the court may not issue a warrant for the offender's arrest unless it is satisfied that he has had adequate notice of the time and place of the adjourned proceedings.

(7) A drinking banning order under section 6 takes effect on—

(a) the day on which it is made; or

(b) if on that day the offender is detained in legal custody, the day on which he is released from that custody.

(8) Subsection (9) applies in relation to proceedings in which a drinking banning order is made under section 6 against a young person.

(9) In so far as the proceedings relate to the making of the order—

(a) section 49 of the Children and Young Persons Act 1933 (c 12) (restrictions on reports of proceedings in which children and young persons are concerned) does not apply in respect of the young person against whom the order is made; and

(b) section 39 of that Act (power to prohibit publication of certain matters) does so apply.

(10) In section 3(2)(fa) of the Prosecution of Offences Act 1985 (c 23) (functions of the Director), after the first occurrence of 'conviction of certain

offences)' insert, 'section 6 of the Violent Crime Reduction Act 2006 (orders on conviction in criminal proceedings)'.
(11) In this section and section 6 'the court' in relation to an offender means—
   (a) the court by or before which he is convicted of the offence; or
   (b) if he is committed to the Crown Court to be dealt with for the offence, the Crown Court.

 See *Blackstone's Criminal Practice 2014* **E21.2**

D20 **Exclusion from Licensed Premises**

D20.1 **Age requirements**

None.

D20.2 **Criteria**

The term of the order must be between three months and two years. Section 1 of the Licensed Premises (Exclusion of Certain Persons) Act 1980 provides:

Licensed Premises (Exclusion of Certain Persons) Act 1980, s 1(1) and (2)

1 Exclusion Orders

(1) Where a court by or before which a person is convicted of an offence committed on licensed premises is satisfied that in committing that offence he resorted to violence or offered or threatened to resort to violence, the court may, subject to subsection (2) below, make an order (in this Act referred to as an 'exclusion order') prohibiting him from entering those premises or any other specified premises, without the express consent of the licensee of the premises or his servant or agent.

(2) An exclusion order may be made either—

    (a) in addition to any sentence which is imposed in respect of the offence of which the person is convicted; or

    (b) where the offence was committed in England and Wales, notwithstanding the provisions of sections 12 and 14 of the Powers of Criminal Courts (Sentencing) Act 2000 (cases in which absolute and conditional discharges may be made, and their effect), in addition to an order discharging him absolutely or conditionally.

 See *Blackstone's Criminal Practice 2014* **E21.1**

D21 **Financial Circumstances Order**

D21.1 **Age requirements**

None.

D21.2 **Criteria**

Section 162 of the Criminal Justice Act 2003 provides:

> ### Criminal Justice Act 2003, s 162
>
> #### 162 Powers to order statment as to offender's financial circumstances
>
> (1) Where an individual has been convicted of an offence, the court may, before sentencing him, make a financial circumstances order with respect to him.
>
> (2) Where a magistrates' court has been notified in accordance with section 12(4) of the Magistrates' Courts Act 1980 (c 43) that an individual desires to plead guilty without appearing before the court, the court may make a financial circumstances order with respect to him.
>
> (3) In this section 'a financial circumstances order' means, in relation to any individual, an order requiring him to give to the court, within such period as may be specified in the order, such a statement of his financial circumstances as the court may require.
>
> (4) An individual who without reasonable excuse fails to comply with a financial circumstances order is liable on summary conviction to a fine not exceeding level 3 on the standard scale.
>
> (5) If an individual, in furnishing any statement in pursuance of a financial circumstances order—
>
>   (a) makes a statement which he knows to be false in a material particular,
>
>   (b) recklessly furnishes a statement which is false in a material particular, or
>
>   (c) knowingly fails to disclose any material fact, he is liable on summary conviction to a fi ne not exceeding level 4 on the standard scale.
>
> (6) Proceedings in respect of an offence under subsection (5) may, notwithstanding anything in section 127(1) of the Magistrates' Courts Act 1980 (c 43) (limitation of time), be commenced at any time within two years from the date of the commission of the offence or within six months from its first discovery by the prosecutor, whichever period expires the earlier.

 See *Blackstone's Criminal Practice 2014* **E15.14** and **E15.15**

D22 **Fines**

D22.1 **Age requirements**

None.

D22.2 **Criteria**

The Magistrates' Court Sentencing Guidelines set out the following approach to fines:

Fine band starting points and ranges

In these guidelines, where the starting point or range for an offence is or includes a fine, it is expressed as one of three fine bands (A, B, or C). Each fine band has both a starting point and a range.

On some offence guidelines, both the starting point and the range are expressed as a single fine band; see, for example, careless driving, where the starting point and range for the first level of offence activity are 'fine band A'. This means that the starting point will be the starting point for fine band A (50 per cent of the offender's relevant weekly income) and the range will be the range for fine band A (25–75 per cent of relevant weekly income). On other guidelines, the range encompasses more than one fine band; see, for example, drunk and disorderly in a public place on page 55 of the Sentencing Guidelines, where the starting point for the second level of offence activity is 'fine band B' and the range is 'fine band A to fine band C'. This means that the starting point will be the starting point for fine band B (100 per cent of relevant weekly income) and the range will be the lowest point of the range for fine band A to the highest point of the range for fine band C (125–175 per cent of relevant weekly income).

1. The amount of a fine must reflect the seriousness of the offence.

2. The court must also take into account the financial circumstances of the offender; this applies whether it has the effect of increasing or reducing the fine. Normally a fine should be of an amount that is capable of being paid within 12 months.

3. The aim is for the fine to have an equal impact on offenders with different financial circumstances; it should be a hardship but should not force the offender below a reasonable 'subsistence' level.

4. The guidance below aims to establish a clear, consistent, and principled approach to the assessment of fines that will apply fairly in the majority of cases. However, it is impossible to anticipate every situation that may be encountered and in each case the court will need to exercise its judgement to ensure that the fine properly reflects the seriousness of the offence and takes into account the financial circumstances of the offender.

5. For the purpose of the offence guidelines, a fine is based on one of three bands (A, B, or C). The selection of the relevant fine band, and the position

of the individual offence within that band, is determined by the seriousness of the offence.

	Starting point	**Range**
Fine band A	50% of relevant weekly income	25–75% of relevant weekly income
Fine band B	100% of relevant weekly income	75–125% of relevant weekly income
Fine band C	150% of relevant weekly income	125–175% of relevant weekly income

Definition of relevant weekly income

6. The seriousness of an offence determines the choice of fine band and the position of the offence within the range for that band. The offender's financial circumstances are taken into account by expressing that position as a proportion of the offender's relevant weekly income.

7. Where an offender is in receipt of income from employment or is self-employed and that income is more than £110 per week after deduction of tax and national insurance (or equivalent where the offender is self-employed), the actual income is the relevant weekly income.

8. Where an offender's only source of income is state benefit (including where there is relatively low additional income as permitted by the benefit regulations) or the offender is in receipt of income from employment or is self-employed but the amount of income after deduction of tax and national insurance is £110 or less, the relevant weekly income is deemed to be £110.

9. In calculating relevant weekly income, no account should be taken of tax credits, housing benefit, child benefit, or similar.

No reliable information

10. Where an offender has failed to provide information, or the court is not satisfied that it has been given sufficient reliable information, it is entitled to make such determination as it thinks fit regarding the financial circumstances of the offender. Any determination should be clearly stated on the court records for use in any subsequent variation or enforcement proceedings. In such cases, a record should also be made of the applicable fine band and the court's assessment of the position of the offence within that band based on the seriousness of the offence.

11. Where there is no information on which a determination can be made, the court should proceed on the basis of an assumed relevant weekly income of £400. This is derived from national median pre-tax earnings; a gross figure is used as, in the absence of financial information from the offender, it is not possible to calculate appropriate deductions.

12. Where there is some information that tends to suggest a significantly lower or higher income than the recommended £400 default sum, the court should make a determination based on that information.

13. A court is empowered to remit a fine in whole or part if the offender subsequently provides information as to means. The assessment of offence seriousness and, therefore, the appropriate fine band and the position of the offence within that band is not affected by the provision of this information.

Assessment of financial circumstances

14. While the initial consideration for the assessment of a fine is the offender's relevant weekly income, the court is required to take account of the offender's financial circumstances more broadly. Guidance on important parts of this assessment is set out below.

15. An offender's financial circumstances may have the effect of increasing or reducing the amount of the fine; however, they are not relevant to the assessment of offence seriousness. They should be considered separately from the selection of the appropriate fine band and the court's assessment of the position of the offence within the range for that band.

Out-of-the-ordinary expenses

16. In deciding the proportions of relevant weekly income that are the starting points and ranges for each fine band, account has been taken of reasonable living expenses. Accordingly, no further allowance should normally be made for these. In addition, no allowance should normally be made where the offender has dependants.

17. Outgoings will be relevant to the amount of the fine only where the expenditure is out of the ordinary and substantially reduces the ability to pay a financial penalty so that the requirement to pay a fine based on the standard approach would lead to undue hardship.

Unusually low outgoings

18. Where the offender's living expenses are substantially lower than would normally be expected, it may be appropriate to adjust the amount of the fine to reflect this. This may apply, for example, where an offender does not make any financial contribution towards his or her living costs.

Savings

19. Where an offender has savings these will not normally be relevant to the assessment of the amount of a fine although they may influence the decision on time to pay.

20. However, where an offender has little or no income but has substantial savings, the court may consider it appropriate to adjust the amount of the fine to reflect this.

Household has more than one source of income

21. Where the household of which the offender is a part has more than one source of income, the fine should normally be based on the income of the offender alone.

22. However, where the offender's part of the income is very small (or the offender is wholly dependent on the income of another), the court may have regard to the extent of the household's income and assets which will be available to meet any fine imposed on the offender.

Potential earning capacity

23. Where there is reason to believe that an offender's potential earning capacity is greater than his or her current income, the court may wish to adjust the amount of the fine to reflect this. This may apply, for example, where an unemployed offender states an expectation to gain paid employment within a short time. The basis for the calculation of fine should be recorded in order to ensure that there is a clear record for use in variation or enforcement proceedings.

High income offenders

24. Where the offender is in receipt of very high income, a fine based on a proportion of relevant weekly income may be disproportionately high when compared with the seriousness of the offence. In such cases, the court should adjust the fine to an appropriate level; as a general indication, in most cases the fine for a first time offender pleading not guilty should not exceed 75 per cent of the maximum fine.

Offence committed for 'commercial' purposes

25. Some offences are committed with the intention of gaining a significant commercial benefit. These often occur where, in order to carry out an activity lawfully, a person has to comply with certain processes which may be expensive. They include, for example, 'taxitouting' (where unauthorized persons seek to operate as taxi drivers) and 'fly-tipping' (where the cost of lawful disposal is considerable).

26. In some of these cases, a fine based on the standard approach set out above may not reflect the level of financial gain achieved or sought through the offending.

Accordingly:

(a) where the offender has generated income or avoided expenditure to a level that can be calculated or estimated, the court may wish to consider that amount when determining the financial penalty;

(b) where it is not possible to calculate or estimate that amount, the court may wish to draw on information from the enforcing authorities about the general costs of operating within the law.

Reduction for a guilty plea

27. Where a guilty plea has been entered, the amount of the fine should be reduced by the appropriate proportion.

D22 Fines

Maximum fines

28. A fine must not exceed the statutory limit. Where this is expressed in terms of a 'level', the maxima are:

Level 1	£200
Level 2	£500
Level 3	£1,000
Level 4	£2,500
Level 5	£5,000

Victims' surcharge

29. Whenever a court imposes a fine in respect of an offence committed after 1 April 2007, it must order the offender to pay a surcharge

30. Where the offender is of adequate means, the court must not reduce the fine to allow for imposition of the surcharge. Where the offender does not have sufficient means to pay the total financial penalty considered appropriate by the court, the order of priority is: compensation, surcharge, fine, costs.

[See also **D42**.]

Costs

31. Where the offender does not have sufficient means to pay the total financial penalty considered appropriate by the court, the order of priority is: compensation, surcharge, fine, costs.

Multiple offences

32. Where an offender is to be fined for two or more offences that arose out of the same incident, it will often be appropriate to impose on the most serious offence a fine which reflects the totality of the offending where this can be achieved within the maximum penalty for that offence. 'No separate penalty' should be imposed for the other offences.

33. Where compensation is being ordered, that will need to be attributed to the relevant offence as will any necessary ancillary orders.

Fine bands D and E

34. Two further fine bands are provided to assist a court in calculating a fine where the offence and general circumstances would otherwise warrant a community order (band D) or a custodial sentence (band E) but the court has decided that it need not impose such a sentence and that a financial penalty is appropriate. See pages 160 and 163 of the *Magistrates' Court Sentencing Guidelines* for further guidance.

35. The following starting points and ranges apply:

	Starting point	Range
Band D	250% of relevant weekly income	200–300% of relevant weekly income
Band E	400% of relevant weekly income	300–500% of relevant weekly income

Imposition of fines with custodial sentences

36. A fine and a custodial sentence may be imposed for the same offence, although there will be few circumstances in which this is appropriate, particularly where the custodial sentence is to be served immediately. One example might be where an offender has profited financially from an offence but there is no obvious victim to whom compensation can be awarded. Combining these sentences is most likely to be appropriate only where the custodial sentence is short and/or the offender clearly has, or will have, the means to pay.

37. Care must be taken to ensure that the overall sentence is proportionate to the seriousness of the offence and that better-off offenders are not able to 'buy themselves out of custody'.

Payment

38. A fine is payable in full on the day on which it is imposed. The offender should always be asked for immediate payment when present in court and some payment on the day should be required wherever possible.

39. Where that is not possible, the court may, in certain circumstances, require the offender to be detained. More commonly, a court will allow payments to be made over a period set by the court:

(a) if periodic payments are allowed, the fine should normally be payable within a maximum of 12 months. However, it may be unrealistic to expect those on very low incomes to maintain payments for as long as a year;

(b) compensation should normally be payable within 12 months. However, in exceptional circumstances it may be appropriate to allow it to be paid over a period of up to three years.

40. Where fine bands D and E apply (see paras 35–36 above), it may be appropriate for the fine to be of an amount that is larger than can be repaid within 12 months. In such cases, the fine should normally be payable within a maximum of 18 months (band D) or two years (band E).

41. It is generally recognized that the maximum weekly payment by a person in receipt of state benefit should rarely exceed £5.

42. When allowing payment by instalments by an offender in receipt of earned income, the following approach may be useful. If the offender has

dependants or larger than usual commitments, the weekly payment is likely to be decreased.

Net weekly income	Starting point for weekly payment
£60	£5
£120	£10
£200	£25
£250	£30
£300	£50
£400	£80

The rate of payment for fines in bands D and E was approved in *R (Purnell) v South Western Magistrates' Court* [2013] EWHC 64 (Admin), which confirmed also that the responsibilty to advise the court of other fines outstanding falls upon the offender. *R v Rance* [2012] EWCA Crim 2023 confirmed that it was for the defendant to provide the court with all releavant financial information, but that fines must have regard only to the means of the offender—there is no concept of a 'tainted gift'.

If the defendant fails to put all relevant information before the court, he cannot later complain that the court has failed to take account of financial circumstances as required by section 164 of the Criminal Justice Act 2003.

R v Rance also held that whilst the court should have regard to any financial benefit from the crime, this is merely one consideration and does not mean that an equivalent or large proportion of the amount should be included in the fine.

D22.3 The detention alternative

Section 135 of the Magistrates' Courts Act 1980 provides:

Magistrates' Courts Act 1980, s 135

135 Detention of offender for one day in court-house or police station

(1) A magistrates' court that has power to commit to prison a person convicted of an offence, or would have that power but for section 82 or 88 above, may order him to be detained within the precincts of the court-house or at any police station until such hour, not later than 8 o'clock in the evening of

the day on which the order is made, as the court may direct, and, if it does so, shall not, where it has power to commit him to prison [or detention if aged 18–20 years], exercise that power.

(2) A court shall not make such an order under this section as will deprive the offender of a reasonable opportunity of returning to his abode on the day of the order.

 See *Blackstone's Criminal Practice 2014* **E15**

D23 **Forfeiture Order**

D23.1 **Age requirements**

None.

D23.2 **Criteria**

Section 27 of the Misuse of Drugs Act 1971 provides:

> ### Misuse of Drugs Act 1971, s 27
>
> **27 Forfeiture**
> (1) Subject to subsection (2) below, the court by or before which a person is convicted of an offence under this Act or an offence falling within subsection (3) below or an offence to which section 1 of the Criminal Justice (Scotland) Act 1987 relates may order anything shown to the satisfaction of the court to relate to the offence, to be forfeited and either destroyed or dealt with in such other manner as the court may order.
> (2) The court shall not order anything to be forfeited under this section, where a person claiming to be the owner of or otherwise interested in it applies to be heard by the court, unless an opportunity has been given to him to show cause why the order should not be made.
> (3) An offence falls within this subsection if it is an offence which is specified in—
>   (a) paragraph 1 of Schedule 2 to the Proceeds of Crime Act 2002 (drug trafficking offences), or
>   (b) so far as it relates to that paragraph, paragraph 10 of that Schedule.

There are also powers of forfeiture in other statutes, such as the Knives Act 1997 and the Obscene Publications Act 1959.

Section 1 of the Prevention of Crime Act 1953 provides that where any person is convicted of an offence under that section, the court may make an order for the forfeiture or disposal of any weapon in respect of which the offence was committed.

 See *Blackstone's Criminal Practice 2014* **E18.7** and, in relation to deprivation orders, **D21**

D24 **Guardianship and Hospital Orders**

D24.1 **Age requirements**

None.

D24.2 **Criteria**

Section 37 of the Mental Health Act 1983 provides:

> ### Mental Health Act 1983, s 37
>
> #### 37 Powers of court to order hospital admission or guardianship
>
> (1) Where a person is convicted ... by a magistrates' court of an offence punishable on summary conviction with imprisonment, and the conditions mentioned in subsection (2) below are satisfied, the court may by order authorise his admission to and detention in such hospital as may be specified in the order or, as the case may be, place him under the guardianship of a local social services authority or of such other person approved by a local social services authority as may be so specified.
>
> (1A) ...
>
> (1B) ...
>
> (2) The conditions referred to in subsection (1) above are that—
>
> (a) the court is satisfied, on the written or oral evidence of two registered medical practitioners, that the offender is suffering from mental illness, psychopathic disorder, severe mental impairment or mental impairment and that either—
>
> (i) the mental disorder from which the offender is suffering is of a nature or degree which makes it appropriate for him to be detained in a hospital for medical treatment and, in the case of psychopathic disorder or mental impairment, that such treatment is likely to alleviate or prevent a deterioration of his condition; or
>
> (ii) in the case of an offender who has attained the age of 16 years, the mental disorder is of a nature or degree which warrants his reception into guardianship under this Act; and
>
> (b) the court is of the opinion, having regard to all the circumstances including the nature of the offence and the character and antecedents of the offender, and to the other available methods of dealing with him, that the most suitable method of disposing of the case is by means of an order under this section.
>
> (3) Where a person is charged before a magistrates' court with any act or omission as an offence and the court would have power, on convicting him of that offence, to make an order under subsection (1) above in his case as being a person suffering from mental illness or severe mental impairment, then, if the court is satisfied that the accused did the act or

made the omission charged, the court may, if it thinks fit, make such an order without convicting him.

(4) An order for the admission of an offender to a hospital (in this Act referred to as 'a hospital order') shall not be made under this section unless the court is satisfied on the written or oral evidence of the registered medical practitioner who would be in charge of his treatment or of some other person representing the managers of the hospital that arrangements have been made for his admission to that hospital, and for his admission to it within the period of 28 days beginning with the date of the making of such an order; and the court may, pending his admission within that period, give such directions as it thinks fit for his conveyance to and detention in a place of safety.

(8) Where an order is made under this section, the court shall not—

    (a) pass sentence of imprisonment or impose a fine or make a community order (within the meaning of Part 12 of the Criminal Justice Act 2003) in respect of the offence,

    (b) if the order under this section is a hospital order, make a referral order (within the meaning of the Powers of Criminal Courts (Sentencing) Act 2000) in respect of the offence, or

    (c) make in respect of the offender an order under section 150 of that Act (binding over of parent or guardian),

but the court may make any other order which it has power to make apart from this section; and for the purposes of this subsection 'sentence of imprisonment' includes any sentence or order for detention.

See *Blackstone's Criminal Practice 2014* **E22**

D25 *Newton* Hearings

D25.1 Age requirements

None.

D25.2 The rule in *Newton*

The rule in *R v Newton* (1982) 77 Cr App R 13 indicates that an offender will be sentenced on the prosecution's version of the facts unless the defence make clear that they are pleading on an alternative basis. In that situation, the Crown must prove its version of the facts by admissible evidence to the criminal standard of proof.

D25.3 Criteria

Updated guidance in relation to the holding of *Newton* hearings were set down in *R v Underwood* [2004] EWCA Crim 2256:

(1) The starting point has to be the defendant's instructions. His advocate will appreciate whether any significant facts about the prosecution evidence are disputed and the factual basis on which the defendant intends to plead guilty. Responsibility for taking initiative and alerting the prosecutor to the disputed areas rests with the defence.

(2) Where the Crown accepts the defendant's account of the disputed facts, the agreement should be written down and signed by both advocates. It should then be made available to the judge. If pleas have already been accepted and approved then it should be available before the sentencing hearing begins. If the agreed basis of plea is not signed by both advocates, the judge is entitled to ignore it. The Crown might reject the defendant's version. If so, the areas of dispute should be identified in writing, focusing the court's attention on the precise facts in dispute.

(3) The prosecution's position might be that they have no evidence to contradict the defence's assertions. In those circumstances, particularly if the facts relied on by the defendant arise from his personal knowledge and depend on his own account of the facts, the Crown should not normally agree the defendant's account unless supported by other material. The court should be notified at the outset in writing of the points in issue and the Crown's responses.

(4) After submissions, the judge will decide how to proceed. If not already decided, he would address the question of whether he should approve the Crown's acceptance of pleas. Then he would address the proposed basis of plea. It should be emphasized that whether or not the basis of plea is agreed, the judge is not bound by any such agreement and is entitled of his own motion to insist that any evidence relevant to the facts in dispute should be called before him, paying appropriate regard to any

agreement reached by the advocates and any reasons which the Crown, in particular, might advance to justify him proceeding immediately to sentence. The judge is responsible for the sentencing decision and may order a Newton hearing to ascertain the truth about disputed facts.

(5) Relevant evidence should be called by prosecution and defence, particularly where the issue arises from facts which are within the exclusive knowledge of the defendant. If the defendant is willing to give evidence he should be called and, if not, subject to any explanation offered, the judge may draw such inference as he sees fit. The judge can reject the evidence called by the prosecution or by the defendant or his witnesses even if the Crown has not called contradictory evidence. The judge's conclusions should be explained in the judgment.

(6) There are occasions when a Newton hearing would be inappropriate. Some issues require a jury's verdict; if a defendant denies that a specific criminal offence has been committed, the tribunal for deciding whether the offence has been proved is the jury. At the end of a Newton hearing the judge cannot make findings of fact and sentence on a basis which is inconsistent with the pleas to counts which have already been accepted and approved by the court. Particular care is needed in relation to a multicount indictment involving one defendant or, an indictment involving a number of defendants. Where there are a number of defendants to a joint enterprise, the judge, while reflecting on the individual basis of pleas, should bear in mind the relative seriousness of the joint enterprise on which the defendants were involved.

(7) Normally, matters of mitigation are not dealt with by way of a Newton hearing but it is always open to the court to allow a defendant to give evidence on matters of mitigation which are within his own knowledge. The judge is entitled to decline to hear evidence about disputed facts if the case advanced is, for good reason, to be regarded as absurd or obviously untenable.

(8) If the issues at the Newton hearing are wholly resolved in the defendant's favour, mitigation for guilty pleas should not be reduced. If the defendant is disbelieved or obliges the prosecution to call evidence from the victim, who is then subjected to cross-examination which, because it is entirely unfounded, causes unnecessary and inappropriate distress, or if the defendant conveys that he has no insight into the consequences of his offence, and no genuine remorse, the judge might reduce the discount for the guilty pleas. There may be a few exceptional cases in which the normal entitlement to credit for a plea of guilty is wholly dissipated by the Newton hearing, and, in such cases, the judge should explain his reasons.

 See *Blackstone's Criminal Practice 2014* **D20.8–D20.29**

D26 **Offences Taken into Consideration**

D26.1 **Age requirements**

None.

D26.2 **Criteria**

In *R v Miles* [2006] EWCA Crim 256, the court made the following observations:

> [T]he sentence is intended to reflect a defendant's overall criminality. Offences cannot be taken into consideration without the express agreement of the offender. That is an essential prerequisite. The offender is pleading guilty to the offences. If they are to be taken into account (and the court is not obliged to take them into account) they have relevance to the overall criminality. When assessing the significance of TICs, as they are often called, of course the court is likely to attach weight to the demonstrable fact that the offender has assisted the police, particularly if they are enabled to clear up offences which might not otherwise be brought to justice. It is also true that cooperative behaviour of that kind will often provide its own very early indication of guilt, and that usually means that no further proceedings at all need be started. They may also serve to demonstrate a genuine determination by the offender (and we deliberately use the colloquialism) to wipe the slate clean, so that when he emerges from whatever sentence is imposed on him, he can put his past completely behind him, without having worry or concern that offences may be revealed and that he is then returned to court. As in so many aspects of sentencing, of course, the way in which the court deals with offences to be taken into consideration depends on context. In some cases the offences taken into consideration will end up by adding nothing or nothing very much to the sentence which the court would otherwise impose. On the other hand, offences taken into consideration may aggravate the sentence and lead to a substantial increase in it. For example, the offences may show a pattern of criminal activity which suggests careful planning or deliberate rather than casual involvement in a crime. They may show an offence or offences committed on bail, after an earlier arrest. They may show a return to crime immediately after the offender has been before the court and given a chance that, by committing the crime, he has immediately rejected. There are many situations where similar issues may arise. One advantage to the defendant, of course, is that if once an offence is taken into consideration, there is no likely risk of any further prosecution for it. If, on the other hand, it is not, that risk remains. In short, offences taken into consideration are indeed taken into consideration. They are not ignored or expunged or disregarded.

The Sentencing Council has issued a definitive guideline in relation to offences taken into consideration (TICs), which was intended to reflect the existing law. It confirms that when sentencing an offender who requests offences to be taken into consideration, courts should pass a total sentence which reflects all the offending behaviour. The sentence must be just and proportionate, and must not exceed the statutory maximum for the conviction offence.

The court is likely to consider that the fact that the offender has assisted the police (particularly if the offences would not otherwise have been detected) and avoided the need for further proceedings demonstrates a genuine determination by the offender to wipe the slate clean.

The sentence imposed on the offender should, in most circumstances, be increased to reflect the fact that other offences have been taken into consideration. The court should:

- determine the sentencing starting point for the conviction offence;
- consider aggravating and mitigating circumstances. The presence of TICs should generally be treated as an aggravating feature that justifies an upward adjustment from the starting point. Where there is a large number of TICs, it may be appropriate to move outside the category range, although this must be considered in the context of the case and subject to the principle of totality. The court is limited to the statutory maximum for the conviction offence;
- consider whether the frank admission of a number of offences is an indication of a defendant's remorse or determination and/or demonstration of steps taken to address addiction or offending behaviour.

Any reduction for guilty plea should be applied to the total sentence, as should the totality principle.

Ancillary orders may take account of TICs to the limit allowed by the offences for which there is a conviction.

See *Blackstone's Criminal Practice 2014* **D20**

D27 **Penalty Points for Driving Offences**

(See the Road Traffic Offenders Act 1988, sections 28 et seq.)

D27.1 **Criteria**

Penalty points must be imposed for all offences that are subject to obligatory endorsement, unless the court finds special reasons for not imposing points (see Road Traffic Offenders Act 1988, s 44(2)).

A person who acts as a secondary party to an offence carrying obligatory disqualification is liable to 10 penalty points.

If a person is found guilty, on one or more occasions, of more than one offence committed on the same occasion, the range of penalty points is taken as being whichever is the highest available for any one offence (eg a person convicted of speeding (3–6 points) and no insurance (6–8 points) is liable to receive up to 8 points). A court does, however, have discretion to disapply this rule if reasons are given (Road Traffic Act 1988, s 28).

Where a court orders obligatory disqualification and there are further offences to be sentenced, it should not order points for the further offences

 See *Blackstone's Criminal Practice 2014* **C7.10–C7.23**

D28 **Prescribed Minimum Sentences**

D28.1 Criteria

Burglary	• Latest offence committed on or after 1 December 1999. • Offender aged 18 or over at date of this offence. • Convicted of two previous domestic burglaries, both of which occurred after 1 December 1999, and had been convicted of the first burglary before he committed the second. Must have been sentenced to a penalty greater than a discharge. • Minimum three-year sentence (discount of 20% permissible for guilty plea) • The case must be sent to the Crown Court.
DrugTrafficking	• Latest offence committed on or after 1 October 1997. • Offender aged 18 or over at date of this offence. • Convicted of two previous drug trafficking offences and had been convicted of the first offence before he committed the second but the dates of conviction are not relevant. Must have been sentenced to a penalty greater than a discharge. • Minimum seven-year sentence (discount of 20% permissible for guilty plea). • The case must be sent to the Crown Court.

Firearms	Minimum five years, or three years (depending on whether offender aged under or over 18 years at time of commission of offence):
	
	Firearms Act 1968, s 51A
	(1) This section applies where—
	  (a) an individual is convicted of—
	    (i) an offence under section 5(1)(a), (ab), (aba), (ac), (ad), (ae), (af) or (c) of this Act,
	    (ii) an offence under section 5(1A)(a) of this Act, or
	    (iii) an offence under any of the provisions of this Act listed in subsection (1A) in respect of a firearm or ammunition specified in section 5(1)(a), (ab), (aba), (ac), (ad), (ae), (af) or (c) or section 5(1A)(a) of this Act, and
	  (b) the offence was committed after the commencement of this section and at a time when he was aged 16 or over.
	(1A) The provisions are—
	  (a) section 16 (possession of firearm with intent to injure);
	  (b) section 16A (possession of firearm with intent to cause fear of violence);
	  (c) section 17 (use of firearm to resist arrest);
	  (d) section 18 (carrying firearm with criminal intent);
	  (e) section 19 (carrying a firearm in a public place);
	  (f) section 20(1) (trespassing in a building with firearm).

	(2) The court shall impose an appropriate custodial sentence (or order for detention) for a term of at least the required minimum term (with or without a fine) unless the court is of the opinion that there are exceptional circumstances relating to the offence or to the offender which justify its not doing so. The relevant date for the section 51(1A) offences is 6 April 2007. For all other offences, it is 22 January 2004.
Aggravated possession of weapons (Prevention of Crime Act 1953, s 1A; Criminal Justice Act 1988, s 139AA)	• Offence committed on or after 3 December 2012. • Minimum 6-month sentence unless unjust in all the circumstances of the offence or of the offender, with a 20% discount available for a guilty plea. • A suspended sentence appears to be available.

 See *Blackstone's Criminal Practice 2014* **E5** and **B12.157**

D29 **Pre-Sentence Drug Testing**

D29.1 **Age requirements**

14 years or over.

D29.2 **Criteria**

Note: not in force at time of writing.

Section 161 of the Criminal Justice Act 2003 provides:

Criminal Justice Act 2003, s 161(1)–(4)

161 Pre-sentence drug testing

(1) Where a person is convicted of an offence and the court is considering passing a community sentence or a suspended sentence, it may make an order under subsection (2) for the purpose of ascertaining whether the offender has any specified Class A drug in his body.

(2) The order requires the offender to provide, in accordance with the order, samples of any description specified in the order.

(3) Where the offender has not attained the age of 17, the order must provide for the samples to be provided in the presence of an appropriate adult.

(4) If it is proved to the satisfaction of the court that the offender has, without reasonable excuse, failed to comply with the order it may impose on him a fine of an amount not exceeding level 4.

D30 **Pre-Sentence Reports**

D30.1 **Age requirements**

None.

D30.2 **Criteria**

Section 156 of the Criminal Justice Act 2003 provides:

> ### Criminal Justice Act 2003, s 156
>
> #### 156 Pre-sentence reports and other requirements
>
> (1) In forming any such opinion as is mentioned in section 148(1) or (2)(b), section 152(2) or section 153(2), or in section 1 (4)(b) or (c) of the Criminal Justice and Immigration Act 2008 (youth rehabilitation orders with intensive supervision and surveillance or fostering), a court must take into account all such information as is available to it about the circumstances of the offence or (as the case may be) of the offence and the offence or offences associated with it, including any aggravating or mitigating factors.
>
> (2) In forming any such opinion as is mentioned in section 148(2)(a), the court may take into account any information about the offender which is before it.
>
> (3) Subject to subsection (4), a court must obtain and consider a pre-sentence report before—
>
>   (a) in the case of a custodial sentence, forming any such opinion as is mentioned in section 152(2), section 153(2), section 225(1)(b), section 226(1)(b), section 227(1)(b) or section 228(1)(b)(i), or
>
>   (b) in the case of a community sentence, forming any such opinion as is mentioned in section 148(1) or (2)(b), or in section 1(4)(b) or (c) of the Criminal Justice and Immigration Act 2008, or any opinion as to the suitability for the offender of the particular requirement or requirements to be imposed by the community order or youth rehabilitation order.
>
> (4) Subsection (3) does not apply if, in the circumstances of the case, the court is of the opinion that it is unnecessary to obtain a pre-sentence report.
>
> (5) In a case where the offender is aged under 18, the court must not form the opinion mentioned in subsection (4) unless—
>
>   (a) there exists a previous pre-sentence report obtained in respect of the offender, and
>
>   (b) the court has had regard to the information contained in that report, or, if there is more than one such report, the most recent report.
>
> (6) No custodial sentence or community sentence is invalidated by the failure of a court to obtain and consider a pre-sentence report before forming an opinion referred to in subsection (3), but any court on an appeal against such a sentence—
>
>   (a) must, subject to subsection (7), obtain a pre-sentence report if none was obtained by the court below, and

    (b) must consider any such report obtained by it or by that court.

(7) Subsection (6)(a) does not apply if the court is of the opinion—

    (a) that the court below was justified in forming an opinion that it was unnecessary to obtain a pre-sentence report, or

    (b) that, although the court below was not justified in forming that opinion, in the circumstances of the case at the time it is before the court, it is unnecessary to obtain a pre-sentence report.

(8) In a case where the offender is aged under 18, the court must not form the opinion mentioned in subsection (7) unless—

    (a) there exists a previous pre-sentence report obtained in respect of the offender, and

    (b) the court has had regard to the information contained in that report, or, if there is more than one such report, the most recent report.

D30.3 Judicial guidance in early guilty plea cases

(1) This guidance on the preparation of pre-sentence reports for early guilty plea (EGP) cases should be considered at magistrates' courts and Crown Court when ordering an EGP hearing.

(2) The guidance suggests that the following questions may assist the decision process:

> Is a report necessary at all?
>
> If a report is necessary should it be a pre-sentence report (PSR) or a fast delivery report (FDR)?
>
> If a report is necessary has there been a PSR or FDR on this defendant in the last 12 months?
>
> If there has been any report in the last 12 months is there any need for either a fresh report or an update?

(3) To assist in answering these questions the following factors are said to be relevant.

It will usually be appropriate to order a report where (in some of these cases a recent report may be sufficient):

> The defendant is 17 and under.
>
> The defendant is under 21 and is a first-time offender/has not served a prison sentence.
>
> The defendant falls to be assessed for 'dangerousness' (Sch 15 cases).

It will *not* usually be appropriate to order a report (or have a recent report available) in the cases where:

> The defendant has a previous prison sentence (s).
>
> The defence have asked for report to assist in determining the 'length of sentence'.

Supply of Class A offences.
False passport/ID docs.
3rd strike burglary.
Cultivation of cannabis.
Offences in breach of a suspended sentence order.
High level frauds (in excess of £100K).
'Custody inevitable' cases where dangerousness is not a consideration and defendant is not under 18 (cf 'length of sentence' cases).

(4) The timely preparation of reports, when reports are essential, is central to the EGP scheme. If ordered reports are not available at EGP hearing much of the benefit of the system is lost. Accordingly, when magistrates' courts consider the need for reports, they should record their decision as 'PSR' or 'FDR' or 'No Report'. This will ensure, at later hearings, that it is clear that the court did indeed consider the need for a report and what its decision was. In like manner, the CPS and defence should assume a duty to assist the magistrates by ensuring that the decision is addressed and should note their files. Where a report has been ordered, defence solicitors should be alert to check with and ensure that Probation has indeed been made aware of the need for the report and that they have the defendant's details.

Solicitors will also be aware of the ability to make representations to the Crown Court in any particular case where a decision has been made that no report is required, or where the court has not been asked to make such a decision.

 See *Blackstone's Criminal Practice 2014* **E1.27** and **E1.28**

D31 **Previous Convictions**

D31.1 **Age requirements**

None.

D31.2 **Criteria**

Section 143 of the Criminal Justice Act 2003 provides:

> ### Criminal Justice Act 2003, s 143
>
> #### 143 Determining the seriousness of an offence
>
> (1) In considering the seriousness of any offence, the court must consider the offender's culpability in committing the offence and any harm which the offence caused, was intended to cause or might forseeably have caused.
>
> (2) In considering the seriousness of an offence ('the current offence') committed by an offender who has one or more previous convictions, the court must treat each previous conviction as an aggravating factor if (in the case of that conviction) the court considers that it can reasonably be so treated having regard, in particular, to—
>
>   (a) the nature of the offence to which the conviction relates and its relevance to the current offence, and
>
>   (b) the time that has elapsed since the conviction.
>
> (3) In considering the seriousness of any offence committed while the offender was on bail, the court must treat the fact that it was committed in those circumstances as an aggravating factor.
>
> (4) Any reference in subsection (2) to a previous conviction is to be read as a reference to—
>
>   (a) a previous conviction by a court in the United Kingdom,
>
>   (aa) a previous conviction by a court in another member State of a relevant offence under the law of that State,
>
>   (b) a previous conviction of a service offence within the meaning of the Armed Forces Act 2006 ('conviction' here including anything that under section 376(1) and (2) of that Act is to be treated as a conviction), or
>
>   (c) a finding of guilt in respect of a member State service offence.
>
> (5) Subsections (2) and (4) do not prevent the court from treating—
>
>   (a) a previous conviction by a court outside both the United Kingdom and any other member State, or
>
>   (b) a previous conviction by a court in any member State (other than the United Kingdom) of an offence which is not a relevant offence,
>
> as an aggravating factor in any case where the court considers it appropriate to do so.
>
> (6) For the purposes of this section—
>
>   (a) an offence is 'relevant' if the offence would constitute an offence under the law of any part of the United Kingdom if it were done in that part at the time of the conviction of the defendant for the current offence,

(b) 'member State service offence' means an offence which—
  (i) was the subject of proceedings under the service law of a member State other than the United Kingdom, and
  (ii) would constitute an offence under the law of any part of the United Kingdom, or a service offence (within the meaning of the Armed Forces Act 2006), if it were done in any part of the United Kingdom, by a member of Her Majesty's forces, at the time of the conviction of the defendant for the current offence,

(c) 'Her Majesty's forces' has the same meaning as in the Armed Forces Act 2006, and

(d) 'service law', in relation to a member State other than the United Kingdom, means the law governing all or any of the naval, military or air forces of that State.

 See Blackstone's Criminal Practice 2014 **D20.45** and **D20.51**

D32 **Prosecution Costs**

D32.1 **Age requirements**

None.

D32.2 **Criteria**

The following principles may be derived from the *Criminal Practice Direction* and *R v Northallerton Magistrates' Court, ex p Dove* [2000] 1 Cr App R (S) 136:

(1) An order to pay costs to the prosecutor should never exceed the sum which, having regard to the defendant's means and any other financial order imposed upon him, the defendant was able to pay and which it was reasonable to order the defendant to pay.

(2) Such an order should never exceed the sum that the prosecutor had actually and reasonably incurred (or was liable to a third party to pay, for example, when that third party commissions a report on behalf of the prosecution).

(3) The purpose of such an order was to compensate the prosecutor and not punish the defendant. Where the defendant had by his conduct put the prosecutor to avoidable expense he might, subject to his means, be ordered to pay some or all of that sum to the prosecutor. However, he was not to be punished for exercising his constitutional right to defend himself.

(4) Whilst there was no requirement that any sum ordered by justices to be paid to a prosecutor by way of costs should stand in any arithmetical relationship to any fine imposed, the costs ordered to be paid should not in any ordinary way be grossly disproportionate to the fine. Justices should ordinarily begin by deciding on the appropriate fine to reflect the criminality of the defendant's offence, always bearing in mind his means and ability to pay, and then consider what, if any, costs he should be ordered to pay to the prosecutor. If, when the costs sought by the prosecutor were added to the proposed fine, the total exceeded the sum which in the light of the defendant's means and all other relevant circumstances the defendant could reasonably be ordered to pay, it was preferable to achieve an acceptable total by reducing the sum of costs which the defendant was ordered to pay rather than by reducing the fine.

(5) If the offender fails to disclose properly his means to the court, reasonable inferences can be drawn as to his means from evidence they had heard and all the circumstances of the case.

In determining the amount of costs to be paid by an offender, consideration should be given to any time that the offender has spent in custody on remand, if the court is to go on to impose any further punishment (eg a community order) (*R v Rakib* [2011] EWCA Crim 870).

 See Blackstone's Criminal Practice 2014 **D33.16**

D33 Racially and Religiously Aggravated Crimes

D33.1 Age requirements

None.

D33.2 Criteria

Section 145 of the Criminal Justice Act 2003 provides:

Criminal Justice Act 2003, s 145

145 Increase in sentences for racial or religious aggravation

(1) This section applies where a court is considering the seriousness of an offence other than one under sections 29 to 32 of the Crime and Disorder Act 1998 (c 37) (racially or religiously aggravated assaults, criminal damage, public order offences and harassment etc).

(2) If the offence was racially or religiously aggravated, the court—
   (a) must treat that fact as an aggravating factor, and
   (b) must state in open court that the offence was so aggravated.

(3) Section 28 of the Crime and Disorder Act 1998 (meaning of 'racially or religiously aggravated') applies for the purposes of this section as it applies for the purposes of sections 29 to 32 of that Act. An offence is racially or religiously aggravated if—
   (a) at the time of committing the offence, or immediately before or after doing so, the offender demonstrates towards the victim of the offence hostility based on the victim's membership (or presumed membership) of a racial or religious group; or
   (b) the offence is motivated (wholly or partly) by hostility towards members of a racial or religious group based on their membership of that group.

Following the guidance given by the court in *R v Kelly and Donnelly* [2001] 2 Cr App R (S) 73, the court should follow a two-stage process, identifying first the sentence it would have passed if the offence had not been racially aggravated and then adding an appropriate uplift to reflect the racial element, so that the sentencing process is transparent and the public can see to what extent the racial element has been reflected. There is no fixed uplift, but in *Kelly and Donnelly*, an uplift of 50 per cent was applied.

For other aggravating factors, see **D41**.

 See *Blackstone's Criminal Practice 2014* **B11.149–B11.155** and **E1.16**

D34 Remand to Hospital for Reports

D34.1 Age requirements

None.

D34.2 Criteria

Section 35 of the Mental Health Act 1983 provides:

Mental Health Act 1983, s 35

35 Remand to hospital for report on accused's mental condition

(1) Subject to the provisions of this section, the Crown Court or a magistrates' court may remand an accused person to a hospital specified by the court for a report on his mental condition.

(2) For the purposes of this section an accused person is—

    (a) ...

    (b) in relation to a magistrates' court, any person who has been convicted by the court of an offence punishable on summary conviction with imprisonment and any person charged with such an offence if the court is satisfied that he did the act or made the omission charged or he has consented to the exercise by the court of the powers conferred by this section.

(3) Subject to subsection (4) below, the powers conferred by this section may be exercised if—

    (a) the court is satisfied, on the written or oral evidence of a registered medical practitioner, that there is reason to suspect that the accused person is suffering from mental disorder; and

    (b) the court is of the opinion that it would be impracticable for a report on his mental condition to be made if he were remanded on bail; but those powers shall not be exercised by the Crown Court in respect of a person who has been convicted before the court if the sentence for the offence of which he has been convicted is fixed by law.

(4) The court shall not remand an accused person to a hospital under this section unless satisfied, on the written or oral evidence of the registered medical practitioner who would be responsible for making the report or of some other person representing the managers of the hospital, that arrangements have been made for his admission to that hospital and for his admission to it within the period of seven days beginning with the date of the remand; and if the court is so satisfied it may, pending his admission, give directions for his conveyance to and detention in a place of safety.

(5) Where a court has remanded an accused person under this section it may further remand him if it appears to the court, on the written or oral evidence of the approved clinician responsible for making the report, that a

---

further remand is necessary for completing the assessment of the accused person's mental condition.

(6) The power of further remanding an accused person under this section may be exercised by the court without his being brought before the court if he is represented by an authorised person who is given an opportunity of being heard.

(7) An accused person shall not be remanded or further remanded under this section for more than 28 days at a time or for more than 12 weeks in all; and the court may at any time terminate the remand if it appears to the court that it is appropriate to do so.

(8) An accused person remanded to hospital under this section shall be entitled to obtain at his own expense an independent report on his mental condition from a registered medical practitioner or approved clinician chosen by him and to apply to the court on the basis of it for his remand to be terminated under subsection (7) above.

(9) Where an accused person is remanded under this section—

(a) a constable or any other person directed to do so by the court shall convey the accused person to the hospital specified by the court within the period mentioned in subsection (4) above; and

(b) the managers of the hospital shall admit him within that period and thereafter detain him in accordance with the provisions of this section.

(10) If an accused person absconds from a hospital to which he has been remanded under this section, or while being conveyed to or from that hospital, he may be arrested without warrant by any constable and shall, after being arrested, be brought as soon as practicable before the court that remanded him; and the court may thereupon terminate the remand and deal with him in any way in which it could have dealt with him if he had not been remanded under this section.

 See Blackstone's Criminal Practice 2014 **D20.74**

D35 **Restitution Order**

D35.1 **Age requirements**

None.

D35.2 **Criteria**

A court passing sentence in handling cases should always have in mind the power to make restitution orders (*R v Webbe and others* [2002] 1 Cr App R (S) 22), but section 148 of the PCC(S)A 2000 provides:

> ### Powers of Criminal Courts (Sentencing) Act 2000, s 148(1)–(5)
>
> **148 Restitution Orders**
>
> (1) This section applies where goods have been stolen, and either—
>   - (a) a person is convicted of any offence with reference to the theft (whether or not the stealing is the gist of his offence); or
>   - (b) a person is convicted of any other offence, but such an offence as is mentioned in paragraph (a) above is taken into consideration in determining his sentence.
> (2) Where this section applies, the court by or before which the offender is convicted may on the conviction (whether or not the passing of sentence is in other respects deferred) exercise any of the following powers—
>   - (a) the court may order anyone having possession or control of the stolen goods to restore them to any person entitled to recover them from him; or
>   - (b) on the application of a person entitled to recover from the person convicted any other goods directly or indirectly representing the stolen goods (as being the proceeds of any disposal or realisation of the whole or part of them or of goods so representing them), the court may order those other goods to be delivered or transferred to the applicant; or
>   - (c) the court may order that a sum not exceeding the value of the stolen goods shall be paid, out of any money of the person convicted which was taken out of his possession on his apprehension, to any person who, if those goods were in the possession of the person convicted, would be entitled to recover them from him;
>
>   and in this subsection 'the stolen goods' means the goods referred to in subsection (1) above.
> (3) Where the court has power on a person's conviction to make an order against him both under paragraph (b) and under paragraph (c) of subsection (2) above with reference to the stealing of the same goods, the court may make orders under both paragraphs provided that the person in whose favour the orders are made does not thereby recover more than the value of those goods.

(4) Where the court on a person's conviction makes an order under subsection (2)(a) above for the restoration of any goods, and it appears to the court that the person convicted—

(a) has sold the goods to a person acting in good faith, or

(b) has borrowed money on the security of them from a person so acting, the court may order that there shall be paid to the purchaser or lender, out of any money of the person convicted which was taken out of his possession on his apprehension, a sum not exceeding the amount paid for the purchase by the purchaser or, as the case may be, the amount owed to the lender in respect of the loan.

(5) The court shall not exercise the powers conferred by this section unless in the opinion of the court the relevant facts sufficiently appear from evidence given at the trial or the available documents, together with admissions made by or on behalf of any person in connection with any proposed exercise of the powers.

 See Blackstone's Criminal Practice 2014 **E17**

D36 **Restraining Order**

D36.1 **Age requirements**

None.

D36.2 **Criteria**

Under the Protection from Harassment Act 1997, a court may impose a restraining order following conviction or acquittal (acquittal includes where the prosecution offer no evidence on a charge). Section 5 provides:

Protection from Harassment Act 1997, s 5(2)–(6)

5 Restraining orders

(1) …

(2) The order may, for the purpose of protecting the victim or victims of the offence, or any other person mentioned in the order, from further conduct which—

    (a) amounts to harassment, or

    (b) will cause a fear of violence,

    prohibit the defendant from doing anything described in the order.

(3) The order may have effect for a specified period or until further order.

(4) The prosecutor, the defendant or any other person mentioned in the order may apply to the court which made the order for it to be varied or dis-charged by a further order.

(5) If without reasonable excuse the defendant does anything which he is pro-hibited from doing by an order under this section, he is guilty of an offence.

(6) A person guilty of an offence under this section is liable—

    (a) on conviction on indictment, to imprisonment for a term not exceeding five years, or a fine, or both, or

    (b) on summary conviction, to imprisonment for a term not exceeding six months, or a fine not exceeding the statutory maximum, or both.

The terms of the order must be proportionate and not violate the offender's human rights. However, a person can harass someone by publishing truthful things (eg that someone is gay), and an order may be made preventing publication of information that is the truth; such an order will not violate a person's right to freedom of expression under the European Convention (*R v Debnath* [2006] 2 Cr App R (S) 25).

An order must name the person it is seeking to protect (*R v Mann* The Times, 11 April 2000), but there is no reason in principle why an order cannot be made to protect a group of individuals or a company (*R v Buxton* [2010] EWCA Crim 2023).

In relation to restraining orders after acquittal, a new legal aid order should be sought from the court and the matter billed separately (as a CRM 7 non-standard claim). The following points emerge from *R v Major* [2010] EWCA Crim 3016:

- It was not Parliament's intention that orders be made only when the facts are uncontested, nor that orders should be made only rarely.
- The civil standard of proof applies.
- There is no contradiction in making an order post-acquittal, as the standard of proof required for a conviction is higher than that for making a restraining order.
- The evidence did not have to establish on the balance of probabilities that there had been harassment; it was enough if the evidence established conduct which fell short of harassment but which might well, if repeated in the future, amount to harassment and so make an order necessary.
- The court should set out the factual basis for making an order. Section 5A of the Protection from Harassment Act 1997 provides:

Protection from Harassment Act 1997, s 5A(1), (2), and (5)

5A Restraining orders on acquittal

(1) A court before which a person ('the defendant') is acquitted of an offence may, if it considers it necessary to do so to protect a person from harassment by the defendant, make an order prohibiting the defendant from doing anything described in the order.

(2) Subsections (3) to (7) of section 5 apply to an order under this section as they apply to an order under that one.

(3) …

(4) …

(5) A person made subject to an order under this section has the same right of appeal against the order as if—

    (a) he had been convicted of the offence in question before the court which made the order, and

    (b) the order had been made under section 5.

In making an order on acquittal, the court must ensure that the defendant is not denied the opportunity to make submissions on the propriety and the terms of an order. See *R v Trott* [2011] EWCA Crim 2395, following *R v Kapotra* [2011] EWCA Crim 1843 (see also Criminal Procedure Rules Part 50). In *R v M J Smith* [2012] EWCA Crim 2566, the court quashed an order on acquittal following a finding that the defendant was not guilty by reason of insanity, as that meant there was no sufficient intent and it unnecessarily criminalized acts that were otherwise lawful; and held that that the order was not for the benefit of a sufficiently identifiable group of persons.

R v Brown [2012] EWCA Crim 1152 confirms that a court should not make an order preventing contact with a complainant who had capacity to decide and who genuinely (and not in fear) wished the relationship to continue, notwithstanding a course of violence against her.

Even though the defendant had been convicted of an offence against a neighbour under section 3 of the Sexual Offences Act 2003, an order excluding him from his home, where he cared for elderly parents, for five years could not be justified. The order already prevented him from contacting the neighbour directly or indirectly. Neither the fact of knowing he was living next door nor anxiety from knowing there might be a sighting of him, made this part of the order necessary for the protection of the victim from conduct of the defendant which would cause fear of violence (see *R v M* [2012] EWCA Crim 1144).

 See Blackstone's Criminal Practice 2014 **E21.28** and **E21.29**

D37 **Return to Custody**

This power has ceased to exist. Section 116 of the PCC(S)A 2000 has now been fully repealed with effect from 3 December 2012 (Criminal Justice Act 2003 (Commencement No 30 and Consequential Amendments) Order 2012 (SI 2012/2905)).

D38 Sentencing Guidelines Issued by the Sentencing Council

D38.1 Age requirements

None.

D38.2 Criteria

On 5 April 2010 the Sentencing Council took over the role previously carried out by the Sentencing Guidelines Council and Sentencing Advisory Panel. A court must follow sentencing guidelines issued by the Sentencing Council, unless it is contrary to the interests of justice to do so (Coroners and Justice Act 2009, s 125).

Section 174(2) of the Criminal Justice Act 2003 provides:

Criminal Justice Act 2003, s 174(2)

174 Duty to give reasons for, and explain effect of, sentence

(2) ... the court must—
   (a) identify any definitive sentencing guidelines relevant to the offender's case and explain how the court discharged any duty imposed on it by section 125 of the Coroners and Justice Act 2009,
   (aa) where the court did not follow any such guidelines because it was of the opinion that it would be contrary to the interests of justice to do so, state why it was of that opinion,

   ...

 See Blackstone's Criminal Practice 2014 **E1.3-E1.6**

D39 Sexual Offences Notification Requirements

D39.1 Age requirements

None.

D39.2 Criteria

It is not a requirement that a court 'orders' a notification requirement, as it will follow automatically as a result of a qualifying conviction (ie those offences specified in Sch 3 to the Sexual Offences Act 2003).

An offender will be given a notice to sign and be provided with his own copy that sets down the requirements to be satisfied. For some offences a specific sentence is required before the liability arises. In *R v Davison* [2008] EWCA Crim 2795, D was ordered to complete 220 hours of unpaid work within a 12-month period. An issue arose as to whether the defendant was, therefore, subject to notification requirements (Sexual Offences Act 2003). D submitted that a community order which contains solely an unpaid work requirement to be completed within 12 months is not a community sentence of at least 12 months' duration, as it is open to the offender to complete the work within the 12-month period and on completion of the work the community order ceases. He relied on *Odam* [2008] EWCA Crim 1087. The court held:

> We have had the benefit of helpful written and oral argument on behalf of both the applicant and the respondent which were not available to the court in *Odam*. These have led us to the conclusion that the length of a community order must be capable of being determined on the date it is made. In our judgement the period specified under section 177(5) of the Criminal Justice Act 2003 by a court when imposing a community order is the relevant period for the purpose of determining the duration of the order under paragraph 18(b)(ii)(c) of Schedule 3 to the Sexual Offences Act 2003 however long it in fact takes the offender to carry out the requirements under the order. It follows that in our judgement the opinion expressed in *Odam* was wrong.

Penalty	Notification period for an adult (Sexual Offences Act 2003, s 82)
Conditional discharge	Period of discharge
A person sentenced otherwise than as mentioned elsewhere	5 years

Imprisonment for a term of 6 months or less	7 years
Imprisonment for a minimum term of 6 months but less than 30 months	10 years
A person sentenced to imprisonment for life or for 30 months or more	Indeterminate
Note: Where the registration is indeterminate there is a power to apply for removal once 15 years has been served and then every 8 years	

 See Blackstone's Criminal Practice 2014 **E23**

D40 Sexual Offences Prevention Order

D40.1 Age requirements

None.

D40.2 Criteria

Following conviction for an offence specified in Schedule 3 (other than paragraph 60) or 5 to the Sexual Offences Act 2003, the court may go on to consider whether or not to make a sexual offences prevention order (Sexual Offences Act 2003, s 104). Schedule 5 contains a wide range of non-sexual offences.

A court may make such an order if satisfied that it is necessary to make such an order for the purpose of protecting the public or any particular members of the public from serious sexual harm from the defendant, and only prohibitions necessary to achieve that purpose may be included. The offence in question may pre-date 1 May 2004. There is nothing in section 104 to indicate that a court must believe a defendant to be 'dangerous' (within the meaning of the sentencing regime) before it can make such an order (*R v Richards* [2006] EWCA Crim 2519).

A sexual offences prevention order:

- prohibits the defendant from doing anything described in the order; and
- has effect for a fixed period (not less than five years) specified in the order or until further order.

Notice of an application for a sexual offences prevention order should always be given under Part 50 of the Criminal Procedure Rules.

The burden of proof for obtaining such an order is the criminal standard (*MPC v Ebanks*, 4 July 2012, DC).

The order must be capable of being complied with without unreasonable difficulty, and free of the risk of unintended breach (*R v Hemsley* [2012] EWCA Crim 225). It must be clear and necessary, and avoid a total ban on the use of the Internet, though it can require a history of use of the Internet to be kept (*R v Smith* [2012] EWCA Crim 1772; *Mortimer* [2010] EWCA Crim 1303).

R v Smith [2011] EWCA Crim 3142 confirms that if it is intended to allow access to children under 16 only with the consent of their parent/guardian, provision should be made for accidental or inadvertent contact: see also *R v Jackson* [2012] EWCA Crim 2602, confirming that to order that the police have access at all times to any computer is too great an invasion of privacy.

In *R v Christopher James* [2012] EWCA Crim 81, where a defendant was convicted of offences of making indecent photographs, it was not on the facts necessary, whilst controlling the use of the Internet, to insert non-contact provisions with children as there was no identified risk, and a ten-year order substituted for lifetime control.

 See Blackstone's Criminal Practice 2014 **E21.24–E21.27**

D41 **Sexual Orientation, Disability, or Transgender Identity**

Section 146 of the Criminal Justice Act 2003 provides:

Criminal Justice Act 2003, s 146

146 Increase in sentences for aggravation related to disability or sexual orientation

(1) This section applies where the court is considering the seriousness of an offence committed in any of the circumstances mentioned in subsection (2).

(2) Those circumstances are—

  (a) that, at the time of committing the offence, or immediately before or after doing so, the offender demonstrated towards the victim of the offence hostility based on—

    (i) the sexual orientation (or presumed sexual orientation) of the victim, or

    (ii) a disability (or presumed disability) of the victim,

    (iii) the victim being or being presumed to be transgender; or

  (b) that the offence is motivated (wholly or partly)—

    (i) by hostility towards persons who are of a particular sexual orientation, or

    (ii) by hostility towards persons who have a disability or a particular disability,

    (iii) by hostility to persons who are transgender.

(3) The court—

  (a) must treat the fact that the offence was committed in any of those circumstances as an aggravating factor, and

  (b) must state in open court that the offence was committed in such circumstances.

(4) It is immaterial for the purposes of paragraph (a) or (b) of subsection (2) whether or not the offender's hostility is also based, to any extent, on any other factor not mentioned in that paragraph.

(5) In this section 'disability' means any physical or mental impairment

(6) In this section references to being transgender include references to being transsexual, or undergoing, proposing to undergo or having undergone a process or part of a process of gender reassignment.

See *Blackstone's Criminal Practice 2014* **E1.17**

D42 **Surcharge Order**

D42.1 Age requirements

None. It is the offender's age at the date of the offence that decides the level of surcharge.

D42.2 Criteria

In any case relating to an offence committed on or after 1 October 2012, the court must impose a surcharge order in accordance with the following table if a fine is imposed (Criminal Justice Act 2003, s 161A and the Criminal Justice Act 2003 (Surcharge) Order 2012 (SI 2012/1696)). The surcharge may be reduced if the offender would not be able to pay both the surcharge and compensation. If the offender would not be able to pay both a surcharge and a fine, the surcharge takes precedence and the fine should be reduced.

Sentence	Adult	Youths	Company
Conditional discharge	£15	£10	£15
Fine	10% in range £20 to £120	£15	10% in range £20 to £120
YRO/Referral order		£15	
Community order	£60		
Suspended sentence	£80 if 6 months or less		

At present there is no surcharge if an immediate custodial sentence is imposed in the magistrates' court.

One surcharge (at the highest rate) is payable if more than one sentence (including more than one fine) is imposed.

If any one offence was committed as a youth then the youth court figures apply.

 See *Blackstone's Criminal Practice 2014* **E15.24**

D43 **Suspended Sentences**

See section 189 of the Criminal Justice Act 2003.

D43.1 **Age requirements**

None.

D43.2 **Length of suspended sentences**

A magistrates' court may suspend a sentence of not less than 14 days and not more than six months (Criminal Justice Act 2003, s 189). Where a person has served such time on remand that a custodial sentence would result in immediate release, it is not appropriate to impose a suspended sentence order (*R v Waters and Young* [2008] EWCA Crim 2538).

The court may suspend the sentence for between six months and two years, and may add appropriate requirement(s) to be completed as part of the order.

D43.3 **Breach of suspended sentence order**

See Schedule 12 to the Criminal Justice Act 2003.

An order will be breached if the offender does not comply with any community requirement during the period of suspension, or commits a further offence during the operational period. Following conviction for a new offence, a magistrates' court has no jurisdiction to deal with breach of a suspended sentence order imposed by the Crown Court; it must either commit the offender for sentence upon conviction for the new offence, or notify the Crown Court of the breach so that that court can take action if it so wishes. A Crown Court order will specify whether or not any breach of its requirements should result in a return to the Crown Court or be left to the magistrates' court (it is the norm for a Crown Court to order any breach be reserved to itself).

Upon a breach being proved the court has the following options open to it:

- order the sentence to take effect (ie send the offender to prison); or
- order the sentence to take effect but with a reduced term of imprisonment; or
- impose more onerous community requirements; or
- impose a fine of up to £2,500.

Note: the court must order one of the first two options unless it would be unjust to do so in all the circumstances. A court must give reasons for so ordering.

 See *Blackstone's Criminal Practice 2014* **E6**

D44 **Time on Remand**

D44.1 **Age requirements**

None.

D44.2 **Criteria**

Section 240ZA of the Criminal Justice Act 2003 provides that any immediate custodial sentence shall be reduced automatically by any time spent on remand in custody.

Section 240A of the Criminal Justice Act 2003 enables the sentencing court to direct that time spent on bail under an electronically-monitored curfew should be credited against an immediate custodial sentence in a similar way. A person will receive credit at the rate of a half a day for every day spent subject to a qualifying electronically-monitored curfew (ie a curfew of nine hours a day or more). The section sets out the procedure as follows:

Criminal Justice Act 2003, s 240A(3)

240A Crediting periods of remand on bail: terms of imprisonment and detention

(3) The credit period is calculated by taking the following steps.

> *Step 1*
> Add—
> (a) the day on which the offender's bail was first subject to the relevant conditions (and for this purpose a condition is not prevented from being a relevant condition by the fact that it does not apply for the whole of the day in question), and
> (b) the number of other days on which the offender's bail was subject to those conditions (but exclude the last of those days if the offender spends the last part of it in custody).
>
> *Step 2*
> Deduct the number of days on which the offender, whilst on bail subject to the relevant conditions, was also—
> (a) subject to any requirement imposed for the purpose of securing the electronic monitoring of the offender's compliance with a curfew requirement, or
> (b) on temporary release under rules made under section 47 of the Prison Act 1952.
>
> *Step 3*
> From the remainder, deduct the number of days during that remainder on which the offender has broken either or both of the relevant conditions.

Step 4
Divide the result by 2.

Step 5
If necessary, round up to the nearest whole number.

(3A) A day of the credit period counts as time served—
    (a) in relation to only one sentence, and
    (b) only once in relation to that sentence.

(3B) A day of the credit period is not to count as time served as part of any period of 28 days served by the offender before automatic release (see section 255B(1)).

Appendices

Appendix 1

Case Management and Standard Case Preparation Time Limits

Case management

These notes are prepared by reference to questions for the defence raised by the current Preparation for Trial form.

6 Advice on plea and absence

The current law on discount for guilty plea is summarized at **D16**. The law on trials in the absence of a defendant is at **A2.2.2**.

7 Partial or different guilty plea

There is a risk that any admission of a lesser offence may be used in evidence to prove ingredients of the greater. However, consideration should be given to *R v Newell* [2012] EWCA Crim 650:

Whilst an answer by a lawyer on a case management form may be admissible as hearsay under the agency rule, a discretion should be exercised to exclude the answer from evidence under section 78 of the Police and Criminal Evidence Act 1984, provided that the case is conducted in accordance with the letter and spirit of the Criminal Procedure Rules. It would be otherwise if there was an ambush.

The *Newton* principles in relation to a basis of plea appear at **D25**.

8 Case management information

8.1–8.3 *Agreed facts*

Facts agreed in section 8.3 may be used in evidence by the Crown. There was again a risk that other responses might be used by the Crown in evidence, but that risk has been largely removed by the decision in *R v Newell* (above). However, care should be taken before admissions are made, and specific authority obtained from the client. The tape summary cannot be agreed unless the solicitor was present or the tape has been played. Information about the defendant's previous convictions held by a solicitor is confidential and must not be disclosed to the client's detriment, but great care must be taken not to mislead the court. It is for the Crown to prove to the criminal standard the existence of previous convictions if they are not agreed.

Appendix 1

8.4 Disputed issues

A defendant is entitled to put the Crown to proof without giving any indication of the issues in dispute. The form should indicate that the defence put the Crown to proof or do not raise any positive defence. Care should be taken, as these statements may be used in cross-examination should the defendant later raise a specific issue. The law is set out in *R v Rochford* [2010] EWCA Crim 1928. The words in square brackets are so marked because defence statements are not obligatory in the magistrates' court:

> What is the duty of the lawyer if the defendant has no positive case to advance at trial but declines to plead guilty? That is a realistic (if rare) practical possibility. It may occur in at least two situations. It might happen that a defendant within the cloak of privilege confides in his lawyer that he is in fact guilty of the offence charged but refuses to plead guilty. He cannot be prevented from taking that course and his instructions to his lawyer are covered by privilege. He is entitled in those circumstances to sit through the trial and to see whether the Crown can prove the case or not. What he is not entitled to do is to conduct the trial by the putting in issue of specific matters and advancing either evidence or argument towards them without giving notice [in his defence statement] that he is going to do it. A less extreme but equally possible example is the defendant who refuses to give instructions either at all or on specific points. That too can occur. In neither of those situations can it possibly be the obligation of the defendant to put in [to his defence statement] an admission of guilt or a refusal to give instructions. What are the lawyers to do? It seems to us that we can give an answer only in general terms because it would be unhelpful for us to attempt the impossible task of foreseeing every factual scenario that might occur in future. They will have to be dealt with as they arise, case by case. But in general terms our answer is this. The defence [statement] must say that the defendant does not admit the offence or the relevant part of it as the case may be, and calls for the Crown to prove it. But it must also say that he advances no positive case because if he is going to advance a positive case [that must appear in the defence statement and] notice of it must be given.

In its guidance on the Criminal Procedure Rules, the Law Society states:

> Your client is entitled to put the prosecution to proof and you are not required by the CPR to cease acting simply because you are unable to assist the court further. However you will note the consequent limitation on your client's ability to raise any positive case at his trial.

8.5 Defence statements

These are not obligatory in the magistrates' court but will be required if there are disclosure issues, and such issues cannot be raised without one. A defence statement cannot be filed without the defendant's consent. *R v Rochford* (above) has made clear that compliance with the requirement for a defence statement cannot require a breach of privilege.

9 Application for directions

Check that you will be able to comply with the standard time limits, or apply to vary them. Consider particularly issues around disclosure, CCTV, and tapes.

10 Prosecution witnesses

Appropriate assistance should be given in identifying the relevant witnesses and witnesses whose evidence can be read, but this should always be checked with the client. Nothing that is said, including by the court, can make hearsay evidence admissible upon the completion of the form. Either there must be agreement under section 10 of the Criminal Justice Act 1967, or there must be compliance with section 9 of the Criminal Justice Act 1967 or section 114 of the Criminal Justice Act 2003. (See **A20**.)

11 Defence witnesses

An estimate of the number of defence witnesses can be given, but it is unlikely that they can be named at this stage as they are unlikely to have been proofed. The defence can comply with their obligations to notify the details of witnesses once there is an intention to call them (see **A10.4**).

Consideration should also be given to special measures required for the defendant or defence witnesses. See **B10** and **A31**.

Standard case preparation time limits[1]

*The court can vary any of these time limits. Time limits marked * are not prescribed by rules. **The total time needed to comply with all these time limits is 6 weeks (9 weeks if paragraph m applies)**.*

Written admissions (Criminal Procedure Rules, r 37.6; Criminal Justice Act 1967, s 10)

a. The parties must serve any written admissions of agreed facts within **14 days**.*

Defence statement (Criminal Procedure Rules, r 22.4; Criminal Procedure and Investigations Act 1996, s 6)

b. Any defence statement must be served within **14 days** of the prosecutor completing or purporting to complete initial disclosure.

---

[1] <http://www.justice.gov.uk/courts/procedure-rules/criminal/docs/crim-pr-part-3-magistrates-courts-preparation-for-trial-form-aug-2010.pdf>.

Appendix 1

Defence witnesses (Criminal Procedure and Investigations Act 1996, s 6C)

c. Defence witness names, etc must be notified within **14 days** of the prosecutor completing or purporting to complete initial disclosure.

Application for disclosure (Criminal Procedure Rules, rr 22.2 & 22.5; Criminal Procedure and Investigations Act 1996, s 8)

d. The defendant must serve any application for prosecution disclosure when serving any defence statement.*

e. The prosecutor must serve any representations in response within **14 days** after that.

Witness statements (Criminal Procedure Rules, r 27.4; Criminal Justice Act 1967, s 9)

f. The The defendant must serve any defence witness statement to be read at trial at least **14 days before the trial.***

g. Any objection to a witness statement being read at trial must be made within **7 days of service of the statement.** *This does not apply to the statements listed in paragraph 10.1.*

Measures to assist a witness or defendant to give evidence (Criminal Procedure Rules, rr 29.3, 29.13, 29.17, 29.22, 29.26)

h. Any [further] application for special or other measures must be served within 14 **days.**

i. Any representations in response must be served within **14 days after that.**

Cross-examination where defendant not represented (Criminal Procedure Rules, rr 31.1, 31.4)

j. The defendant must serve notice of any representative appointed to cross-examine within **7 days.**

k. The prosecutor must serve any application to prohibit cross-examination by the defendant in person as soon as reasonably practicable.

l. Any representations in response must be served within **14 days after that.**

Expert evidence (Criminal Procedure Rules, rr 33.4, 33.6)

m. If either party relies on expert evidence, the directions below apply.

    (i)   The expert's report must be served within **28 days**.*
    (ii)   A party who wants that expert to attend the trial must give notice within **7 days after (i)**.*
    (iii)   A party who relies on expert evidence in response must serve it within **14 days after (ii)**.*
    (iv)   There must be a meeting of experts under rule 33.6 within **14 days after (iii)**.*
    (v)   The parties must notify the court **immediately after (iv)** if the length of the trial is affected by the outcome of the meeting.*

Case Management and Standard Case Preparation Time Limits

Hearsay evidence (Criminal Procedure Rules, rr 34.2, 34.3)

n. The prosecutor must serve any notice to introduce hearsay evidence within **14 days.**

o. The defendant must serve any notice to introduce hearsay evidence as soon as reasonably practicable.

p. Any application to determine an objection to hearsay evidence must be served within **14 days of service** of the notice or evidence.

Bad character evidence (Criminal Procedure Rules, rr 35.2, 35.3, 35.4)

q. The prosecutor must serve any notice to introduce evidence of the defendant's bad character within **14 days.**

r. Any application to determine an objection to that notice must be served within **14 days after that.**

s. Any application to introduce evidence of a non-defendant's bad character must be served within **14 days** of prosecution disclosure.

t. Any notice of objection to that evidence must be served within **14 days after that**[CM2]**.**

Previous sexual behaviour evidence (Criminal Procedure Rules, rr 36.2, 36.3, 36.4. 36.5)

u. The defendant must serve any application for permission to introduce evidence of a complainant's previous sexual behaviour within **28 days** of prosecution disclosure.

v. The prosecutor must serve any representations in response within **14 days after that.**

Point of law (Criminal Procedure Rules, rr 3.3, 3.9)

w. Any skeleton argument must be served at least **14 days before the trial.***

x. Any skeleton argument in reply must be served within **7 days after that.***

Trial readiness (Criminal Procedure Rules, rr 3.3, 3.9)

y. The parties must certify readiness for trial at least **14 days before the trial,** confirming which witnesses will give evidence in person and the trial time estimate.*

Extracts from the Criminal Procedure Rules 2012

Extracts from the following rules are reproduced in this appendix:

- rule 1 (the overriding objective); and
- rule 3 (case management).

Part 1 The Overriding Objective

The overriding objective

1.1—(1) The overriding objective of this new code is that criminal cases be dealt with justly.

(2) Dealing with a criminal case justly includes—

(a) acquitting the innocent and convicting the guilty;

(b) dealing with the prosecution and the defence fairly;

(c) recognising the rights of a defendant, particularly those under Article 6 of the European Convention on Human Rights;

(d) respecting the interests of witnesses, victims and jurors and keeping them informed of the progress of the case;

(e) dealing with the case efficiently and expeditiously;

(f) ensuring that appropriate information is available to the court when bail and sentence are considered; and

(g) dealing with the case in ways that take into account—

(i) the gravity of the offence alleged,

(ii) the complexity of what is in issue,

(iii) the severity of the consequences for the defendant and others affected, and

(iv) the needs of other cases.

The duty of the participants in a criminal case

1.2—(1) Each participant, in the conduct of each case, must—

(a) prepare and conduct the case in accordance with the overriding objective;

(b) comply with these Rules, practice directions and directions made by the court; and

(c) at once inform the court and all parties of any significant failure (whether or not that participant is responsible for that failure) to take any procedural step required by these Rules, any practice direction or any direction of the court. A failure is significant if it might hinder the court in furthering the overriding objective.

(2) Anyone involved in any way with a criminal case is a participant in its conduct for the purposes of this rule.

Extracts from the Criminal Procedure Rules 2012

The application by the court of the overriding objective

1.3 The court must further the overriding objective in particular when—

    (a) exercising any power given to it by legislation (including these Rules);

    (b) applying any practice direction; or

    (c) interpreting any rule or practice direction.

Part 3 Case Management

The scope of this Part

3.1 This Part applies to the management of each case in a magistrates' court and in the Crown Court (including an appeal to the Crown Court) until the conclusion of that case.

[Note. Rules that apply to procedure in the Court of Appeal are in Parts 65 to 73 of these Rules.]

The duty of the court

3.2—(1) The court must further the overriding objective by actively managing the case.

    (2) Active case management includes—

        (a) the early identification of the real issues;

        (b) the early identification of the needs of witnesses;

        (c) achieving certainty as to what must be done, by whom, and when, in particular by the early setting of a timetable for the progress of the case;

        (d) monitoring the progress of the case and compliance with directions;

        (e) ensuring that evidence, whether disputed or not, is presented in the shortest and clearest way;

        (f) discouraging delay, dealing with as many aspects of the case as possible on the same occasion, and avoiding unnecessary hearings;

        (g) encouraging the participants to co-operate in the progression of the case; and

        (h) making use of technology.

    (3) The court must actively manage the case by giving any direction appropriate to the needs of that case as early as possible.

Case preparation and progression

3.8—(1) At every hearing, if a case cannot be concluded there and then the court must give directions so that it can be concluded at the next hearing or as soon as possible after that.

    (2) At every hearing the court must, where relevant—

        (a) if the defendant is absent, decide whether to proceed nonetheless;

        (b) take the defendant's plea (unless already done) or if no plea can be taken then find out whether the defendant is likely to plead guilty or not guilty;

        (c) set, follow or revise a timetable for the progress of the case, which may include a timetable for any hearing including the trial or (in the Crown Court) the appeal;

(d) in giving directions, ensure continuity in relation to the court and to the parties' representatives where that is appropriate and practicable; and

(e) where a direction has not been complied with, find out why, identify who was responsible, and take appropriate action.

(3) In order to prepare for a trial in the Crown Court, the court must conduct a plea and case management hearing unless the circumstances make that unnecessary.

(4) In order to prepare for the trial, the court must take every reasonable step—

(a) to encourage and to facilitate the attendance of witnesses when they are needed; and

(b) to facilitate the participation of any person, including the defendant.

Indictable Only Offences and Offences Carrying Life Imprisonment

Class	Sub Class	Offence	Act	Max Sentence
Burglary	31 Burglary in a building other than a dwelling	Aggravated burglary in building other than a dwelling	Theft Act 1968, s 10	life
Burglary	28A/B/C/D Burglary in a dwelling	Burglary—indictable	Theft Act 1968, s 9	14
Burglary	28A/B/C/D Burglary in a dwelling	Burglary—violence	Theft Act 1968, s 9	14
Burglary	30A/B Burglary in a building other than a dwelling	Burglary in a building other than a dwelling—indictable only	Theft Act 1968, s 9	10
Burglary	29 Aggravated Burglary in a dwelling	Aggravated burglary in a dwelling	Theft Act 1968, s 10	life
Criminal Damage	56A Arson endangering life	Arson endangering life	Criminal Damage Act 1971, s 1	life
Criminal Damage	56A Arson	Arson to other building endangering life	Criminal Damage Act 1971, s 1	life
Criminal Damage	56A Arson	Arson to motor vehicle endangering life	Criminal Damage Act 1971, s 1	life
Criminal Damage	56A Arson	Arson to other property endangering life	Criminal Damage Act 1971, s 1	life
Criminal Damage	58A Criminal damage to a dwelling	Criminal damage to a dwelling endangering life	Explosive Substances Act 1883, ss 2, 3 Criminal Damage Act 1971, s 1(2)	life

Appendix 3

Class	Sub Class	Offence	Act	Max Sentence
Criminal Damage	58B Criminal damage to a building other than a dwelling	Criminal damage to a building other than a dwelling endangering life	Explosive Substances Act 1883, ss 2, 3 Criminal Damage Act 1971, s 1(2)	life
Criminal Damage	58C Criminal damage to a vehicle	Criminal damage to a vehicle endangering life	Explosive Substances Act 1883, ss 2, 3 Criminal Damage Act 1971, s 1(2)	life
Criminal Damage	58D Other criminal damage	Criminal damage endangering life other	Explosive Substances Act 1883, ss 2, 3 Criminal Damage Act 1971, s 1(2)	life
Criminal Damage	59 Threat or possession with intent to commit criminal damage	Making or possessing explosives etc with intent	Offences Against the Person Act 1861, s 64 Explosive Substances Act 1883, s 3	life
Fraud & Forgery	53C Fraud by false representation cheque, plastic card, and online bank accounts (not eBay or PayPal)	Conspiracy to commit cheque or credit card fraud	Common Law Criminal Justice Act 1987, s 12	life
Fraud & Forgery	53D Fraud by false representation Other fraud	Conspiracy to defraud (apart from cheque & credit card fraud)	Common Law Criminal Justice Act 1987, s 12	life
Fraud & Forgery	61A Possession of false documents	Possess/control identity documents with intent	Identity Documents Act 2010, s 4	10
Fraud & Forgery	61A Possession of false documents	Make/possess/control apparatus/article/material designed/adapted for making false identity documents	Identity Documents Act 2010, s 5	10

Class	Sub Class	Offence	Act	Max Sentence
Fraud & Forgery	53B Preserved other fraud and repealed fraud offences	Frauds in connection with sale of land etc	Law of Property Act 1925, s 183	2
Other Offences	66 Other offences against the state or public order	Compelling by threatening to destroy or damage ship or sea platform or property used in navigation	Aviation and Maritime Security Act 1990, s 13	life
Other Offences	36 Kidnapping	Hijacking	Aviation Security Act 1982, ss 1, 6	life
Other Offences	36 Kidnapping	Destroying, damaging, or endangering safety of aircraft	Aviation Security Act 1982, ss 2, 6	life
Other Offences	36 Kidnapping	Other acts endangering safety of aircraft	Aviation Security Act 1982, ss 3, 6	life
Other Offences	99 Other notifiable offences	Census official contravening provisions	Census Act 1920, s 8(2)	2
Other Offences	36 Kidnapping	Hijacking, destroying, or damaging Channel Tunnel train or system	Channel Tunnel (Security) Order 1994, arts 4, 5, 7, 8 Channel Tunnel Act 1987, s 1(7))	life
Other Offences	36 Kidnapping	Kidnapping	Common Law	life
Other Offences	36 Kidnapping	False imprisonment	Common Law	life
Other Offences	79 Perverting the course of justice	Attempting to pervert the course of public justice	Common Law	life
Other Offences	80 Absconding from lawful custody	Absconding from lawful custody	Common Law	life
Other Offences	99 Other notifiable offences	Blasphemous libel	Common Law	life

Appendix 3

Class	Sub Class	Offence	Act	Max Sentence
Other Offences	99 Other notifiable offences	Conspiracy to outrage public decency	Common Law	life
Other Offences	99 Other notifiable offences	Conspiracy to corrupt public morals	Common Law	life
Other Offences	99 Other notifiable offences	Embracery	Common Law	life
Other Offences	99 Other notifiable offences	Obstructing coroner in the execution of his duty	Common Law	life
Other Offences	99 Other notifiable offences	Duty to aid constables	Common Law	life
Other Offences	99 Other notifiable offences	Rescuing a prisoner in custody	Common Law	life
Other Offences	99 Other notifiable offences	Showing an indecent exhibition	Common Law	life
Other Offences	99 Other notifiable offences	Removing corpse from grave	Common Law	life
Other Offences	99 Other notifiable offences	Common Law offences not listed separately	Common Law	life
Other Offences	99 Other notifiable offences	Libel	Common Law Libel Acts 1792 and 1843	2
Other Offences	99 Other notifiable offences	Organization convicted of corporate manslaughter/ homicide fail to comply with order to publish particulars of offences	Corporate Manslaughter and Corporate Homicide Act 2007, s 10	fine
Other Offences	99 Other notifiable offences	Organization convicted of corporate manslaughter/ homicide fail to comply with remedial order	Corporate Manslaughter and Corporate Homicide Act 2007, s 9	fine

Class	Sub Class	Offence	Act	Max Sentence
Other Offences	95 Disclosure, obstruction, false or misleading statements	Knowingly or recklessly providing false information or a document to obtain grant of an exemption licence	Counter-Terrorism Act 2008, Sch 7, para 31	2
Other Offences	99 Other notifiable offences	Assist offender (offences triable on indictment only)	Criminal Law Act 1967, s 4(1) in part	7
Other Offences	99 Other notifiable offences	Enforcement provisions relating to newspaper mergers	Fair Trading Act 1973, s 62	2
Other Offences	81 Other firearms offences	Possessing or distributing prohibited weapons or ammunition	Firearms Act 1968, s 5(1), as amended by Criminal Justice and Public Order Act 1994, s 157, Sch 8, Pt III	10
Other Offences	83 Bail offences	Acknowledging bail in false name	Forgery Act 1861, s 34	7
Other Offences	99 Other notifiable offences	Destroying, forging, or falsifying registers of births, marriages, deaths, burials etc	Forgery Act 1861, s 36	life
Other Offences	99 Other notifiable offences	Forgery of copy of registrar's record	Forgery Act 1861, s 37	life
Other Offences	99 Other notifiable offences	Prevention and punishment of the crime of genocide	Genocide Act 1969, s 1(1)	life
Other Offences	99 Other notifiable offences	Placing in a women a human embryo which has been created otherwise than by fertilization	Human Reproductive Cloning Act 2001, s 1	10
Other Offences	67 Perjury	False written statements tendered in evidence	Magistrates' Court Act 1980, s 106 Criminal Justice Act 1967, s 89	2

Appendix 3

Class	Sub Class	Offence	Act	Max Sentence
Other Offences	99 Other notifiable offences	Selling abroad wreck found in British waters	Merchant Shipping Act 1995, s 245	5
Other Offences	99 Other notifiable offences	Prohibition of sale of medical practices	National Health Service Act 2006, s 259 and Sch 21	indefinite
Other Offences	67 Perjury	Perjury—judicial proceedings	Perjury Act 1911, s 1	7
Other Offences	99 Other notifiable offences	Falsification by the registrar	Pharmacy Act 1954, s 18	1
Other Offences	99 Other notifiable offences	Piracy with violence	Piracy Act 1837, s 2	life
Other Offences	99 Other notifiable offences	Piracy	Piracy Acts 1698–1721 and Piracy Act 1837, s 3	life
Other Offences	69 Offender Management Act	Assisting a prisoner to escape	Prison Act 1952, as inserted by Offender Management Act 2007	10
Other Offences	69 Offender Management Act	Conveyance etc of List A articles into or out of prison	Prison Act 1952, as inserted by Offender Management Act 2007	10
Other Offences	99 Other notifiable offences	Assisting prisoners to escape	Prison Act 1952, s 39	5
Other Offences	99 Other notifiable offences	Prison mutiny	Prison Security Act 1992, s 1	10
Other Offences	80 Absconding from lawful custody	Participating in prison mutiny with or without failing to submit to lawful authority	Prison Security Act 1992, s 1(1) and (4)	10
Other Offences	62A Violent disorder	Riot	Public Order Act 1986, s 1	10
Other Offences	99 Other notifiable offences	Conspiracy to commit a listed sexual offence	Sexual Offences (Conspiracy and Incitement) Act 1996	life

Class	Sub Class	Offence	Act	Max Sentence
Other Offences	99 Other notifiable offences	Unqualified person acting as a solicitor	Solicitors Act 1974, s 20	2
Other Offences	76 Aiding suicide	Intentionally doing an act capable of encouraging or assisting the suicide or attempted suicide of another	Suicide Act 1961, s 2(1)	14
Other Offences	36 Kidnapping	Detaining and threatening to kill or injure a hostage	Taking of Hostages Act 1982, s 1	life
Other Offences	66 Other offences against the state or public order	Use radioactive device/material in the course of/in connection with commission/purposes of terrorism	Terrorism Act 2006, s 10	life
Other Offences	66 Other offences against the state or public order	In course of/in connection with commission/purposes of terrorism use/damage nuclear facility to cause release/ask of release of radioactive material	Terrorism Act 2006, s 10	life
Other Offences	66 Other offences against the state or public order	Terrorist make demand relating to devices/materials/facilities	Terrorism Act 2006, s 11	life
Other Offences	66 Other offences against the state or public order	Terrorist make threat to use radioactive device/material	Terrorism Act 2006, s 11	life
Other Offences	66 Other offences against the state or public order	With intent that self/to assist another to commit act of terrorism engage in preparation	Terrorism Act 2006, s 5	life

Appendix 3

Class	Sub Class	Offence	Act	Max Sentence
Other Offences	66 Other offences against the state or public order	Possess radioactive material with intent use it in commission/preparation for terrorism	Terrorism Act 2006, s 9	life
Other Offences	66 Other offences against the state or public order	Make/possess radioactive device with intent use it in commission/preparation for terrorism.	Terrorism Act 2006, s 9(1)(a)	life
Other Offences	35 Blackmail	Blackmail	Theft Act 1968, s 21	14
Other Offences	62A Violent disorder	Attempting to injure or alarm the sovereign	Treason Act 1842, s 2	life
Other Offences	62A Violent disorder	Treason	Treason Acts 1351–1814	life
Other Offences	62A Violent disorder	Treason—felony	Treason Felony Act 1848	life
Other Offences	66 Other offences against the state or public order	Threats of attack on United Nations workers	United Nations Personnel Act 1997, ss 2, 3	10
Other Offences	99 Other notifiable offences	Meeting for training or drilling to the use of arms or for practising military exercise movement or evolution without lawful authority	Unlawful Drilling Act 1819, s 1	7
Robbery	34B Robbery of personal property	Robbery—personal	Theft Act 1968, s 8	life
Robbery	34A Robbery of business property	Robbery—business	Theft Act 1968, s 8	life
Robbery	34B Robbery of personal property	Assault with intent to rob—personal	Theft Act 1968, s 8	life
Robbery	34A Robbery of business property	Assault with intent to rob—business	Theft Act 1968, s 8	life
Sexual Offences	19D Rape of a female child under 16	Rape of a female aged under 16	Sexual Offences Act 2003, s 1	life

Class	Sub Class	Offence	Act	Max Sentence
Sexual Offences	19C Rape of a female aged 16 and over	Rape of a female aged 16 or over	Sexual Offences Act 2003, s 1	life
Sexual Offences	19G Rape of a male child under 16	Rape of a male aged under 16	Sexual Offences Act 2003, s 1	life
Sexual Offences	19F Rape of a male aged 16 and over	Rape of a male aged 16 or over	Sexual Offences Act 2003, s 1	life
Sexual Offences	19D Rape of a female child under 16	Attempted rape of a female aged under 16	Sexual Offences Act 2003, s 1	life
Sexual Offences	19C Rape of a female aged 16 and over	Attempted rape of a female aged 16 or over	Sexual Offences Act 2003, s 1	life
Sexual Offences	19G Rape of a male child under 16	Attempted rape of a male aged under 16	Sexual Offences Act 2003, s 1	life
Sexual Offences	19F Rape of a male aged 16 and over	Attempted rape of a male aged 16 or over	Sexual Offences Act 2003, s 1	life
Sexual Offences	22B Sexual activity involving a child under 16	Causing or inciting a child under 16 to engage in sexual activity—female child	Sexual Offences Act 2003, s 10	14
Sexual Offences	22B Sexual activity involving a child under 16	Causing or inciting a child under 16 to engage in sexual activity—male child	Sexual Offences Act 2003, s 10	14
Sexual Offences	17A Sexual assault on a male aged 13 and over	Assault on a male by penetration	Sexual Offences Act 2003, s 2	life
Sexual Offences	20A Sexual assault on a female aged 13 or over	Assault on a female by penetration	Sexual Offences Act 2003, s 2	life
Sexual Offences	23 Incest or familial sexual offences	Sexual activity with a child family member—penetration—offender 18 or over—victim female 13 to 17	Sexual Offences Act 2003, s 25	14

Appendix 3

Class	Sub Class	Offence	Act	Max Sentence
Sexual Offences	23 Incest or familial sexual offences	Sexual activity with a child family member—penetration—offender 18 or over—victim male 13 to 17	Sexual Offences Act 2003, s 25	14
Sexual Offences	23 Incest or familial sexual offences	Sexual activity with a child family member—penetration—offender 18 or over—victim female under 13	Sexual Offences Act 2003, s 25	14
Sexual Offences	23 Incest or familial sexual offences	Sexual activity with a child family member—penetration—offender 18 or over—victim male under 13	Sexual Offences Act 2003, s 25	14
Sexual Offences	23 Incest or familial sexual offences	Inciting a child family member to engage in sexual activity—penetration—offender 18 or over—victim female 13 to 17	Sexual Offences Act 2003, s 26	14
Sexual Offences	23 Incest or familial sexual offences	Inciting a child family member to engage in sexual activity—penetration—offender 18 or over—victim male 13 to 17	Sexual Offences Act 2003, s 26	14
Sexual Offences	23 Incest or familial sexual offences	Inciting a child family member to engage in sexual activity—penetration—offender 18 or over—victim female under 13	Sexual Offences Act 2003, s 26	14

Class	Sub Class	Offence	Act	Max Sentence
Sexual Offences	23 Incest or familial sexual offences	Inciting a child family member to engage in sexual activity—penetration—offender 18 or over—victim male under 13	Sexual Offences Act 2003, s 26	14
Sexual Offences	70 Sexual activity etc with a person with a mental disorder	Sexual activity with a person with a mental disorder impeding choice—male person	Sexual Offences Act 2003, s 30	life
Sexual Offences	70 Sexual activity etc with a person with a mental disorder	Sexual activity with a person with a mental disorder impeding choice—female person	Sexual Offences Act 2003, s 30	life
Sexual Offences	70 Sexual activity etc with a person with a mental disorder	Causing or inciting a person with a mental disorder impeding choice to engage in sexual activity—male person	Sexual Offences Act 2003, s 31	life
Sexual Offences	70 Sexual activity etc with a person with a mental disorder	Causing or inciting a person with a mental disorder impeding choice to engage in sexual activity—female person	Sexual Offences Act 2003, s 31	life
Sexual Offences	70 Sexual activity etc with a person with a mental disorder	Inducement, threat or deception to procure sexual activity with a person with a mental disorder—penetration	Sexual Offences Act 2003, s 34	life
Sexual Offences	70 Sexual activity etc with a person with a mental disorder	Causing a person with a mental disorder to engage in sexual activity by inducement, threat or deception—penetration	Sexual Offences Act 2003, s 35	life

Appendix 3

Class	Sub Class	Offence	Act	Max Sentence
Sexual Offences	70 Sexual activity etc with a person with a mental disorder	Care workers: sexual activity with a person with a mental disorder—male person	Sexual Offences Act 2003, s 38	14
Sexual Offences	70 Sexual activity etc with a person with a mental disorder	Care workers: sexual activity with a person with a mental disorder—female person	Sexual Offences Act 2003, s 38	14
Sexual Offences	70 Sexual activity etc with a person with a mental disorder	Care workers: causing or inciting sexual activity (person with mental disorder)—penetration	Sexual Offences Act 2003, s 39	14
Sexual Offences	22A Causing sexual activity without consent	Causing a person to engage in sexual activity without consent—female person	Sexual Offences Act 2003, s 4	life
Sexual Offences	22A Causing sexual activity without consent	Causing a person to engage in sexual activity without consent—male person	Sexual Offences Act 2003, s 4	life
Sexual Offences	71 Abuse of children through prostitution & pornography	Paying for the sexual services of a child —female child under 13	Sexual Offences Act 2003, s 47	life
Sexual Offences	71 Abuse of children through prostitution & pornography	Paying for the sexual services of a child—male child under 13	Sexual Offences Act 2003, s 47	life
Sexual Offences	71 Abuse of children through prostitution & pornography	Paying for the sexual services of a child—female child under 16	Sexual Offences Act 2003, s 47	14
Sexual Offences	71 Abuse of children through prostitution & pornography	Paying for the sexual services of a child—male child under 16	Sexual Offences Act 2003, s 47	14

Class	Sub Class	Offence	Act	Max Sentence
Sexual Offences	19E Rape of a female child under 13	Rape of a female child under 13 by a male	Sexual Offences Act 2003, s 5	life
Sexual Offences	19H Rape of a male child under 13	Rape of a male child under 13 by a male	Sexual Offences Act 2003, s 5	life
Sexual Offences	19E Rape of a female child under 13	Attempted rape of a female child under 13 by a male	Sexual Offences Act 2003, s 5	life
Sexual Offences	19H Rape of a male child under 13	Attempted rape of a male child under 13 by a male	Sexual Offences Act 2003, s 5	life
Sexual Offences	17B Sexual assault on a male child under 13	Assault on a male child under 13 by penetration	Sexual Offences Act 2003, s 6	life
Sexual Offences	20B Sexual assault on a female child under 13	Assault of a female child under 13 by penetration	Sexual Offences Act 2003, s 6	life
Sexual Offences	21 Sexual activity involving a child under 13	Causing or inciting a child under 13 to engage in sexual activity—female child	Sexual Offences Act 2003, s 8	life
Sexual Offences	21 Sexual activity involving a child under 13	Causing or inciting a child under 13 to engage in sexual activity—male child	Sexual Offences Act 2003, s 8	life
Sexual Offences	22B Sexual activity involving a child under 16	Sexual activity with a child under 16—female child	Sexual Offences Act 2003, s 9	14
Sexual Offences	22B Sexual activity involving a child under 16	Sexual activity with a child under 16—male child	Sexual Offences Act 2003, s 9	14
Violence Against the Person	5E Endangering life	Use etc of nuclear weapons	Anti-Terrorism, Crime and Security Act 2001, s 47	life
Violence Against the Person	5E Endangering life	Weapons-related acts overseas	Anti-Terrorism, Crime and Security Act 2001, s 50	life

Appendix 3

Class	Sub Class	Offence	Act	Max Sentence
Violence Against the Person	5E Endangering life	Inducing commission of offence relating to safety of ship, cargo, or sea platform outside UK	Aviation and Maritime Security Act 1990, s 14(4)	life
Violence Against the Person	5E Endangering life	Assisting commission of offence relating to safety of ship, cargo, or sea platform outside UK	Aviation and Maritime Security Act 1990, s 14(4)	life
Violence Against the Person	5E Endangering life	Endangering safety at aerodromes	Aviation and Maritime Security Act 1990, s 1	life
Violence Against the Person	5E Endangering life	Destroying ships or fixed platforms endangering their safety	Aviation and Maritime Security Act 1990, s 11	life
Violence Against the Person	5E Endangering Life	Other acts endangering or likely to endanger safe navigation	Aviation and Maritime Security Act 1990, s 12	life
Violence Against the Person	5E Endangering life	Destroying, damaging etc a Channel Tunnel train or the Tunnel system or committing acts of violence likely to endanger safety of operation	Channel Tunnel Act 1987, s 1(7) Channel Tunnel (Security) Order 1994, art 6	life
Violence Against the Person	5E Endangering life	Premises or equipment for producing chemical weapons	Chemical Weapons Act 1996, s 11	life
Violence Against the Person	5E Endangering life	Use of chemical weapons	Chemical Weapons Act 1996, s 2	life
Violence Against the Person	1 Murder	Murder of persons aged 1 yr or over	Common Law	life

Class	Sub Class	Offence	Act	Max Sentence
Violence Against the Person	1 Murder	Murder of persons under 1 yr of age	Common Law	life
Violence Against the Person	2 Attempted Murder	Attempted murder	Common Law Criminal Attempts Act 1981	life
Violence Against the Person	4/1 Manslaughter	Manslaughter	Common Law Offences against the Person Act 1861, s 5	life
Violence Against the Person	4/10 Corporate manslaughter	Corporate manslaughter	Corporate Homicide Act 2007, s 1(1)	unlimited fine
Violence Against the Person	5D Assault with intent to cause serious harm	Torture	Criminal Justice Act 1988, s 134	life
Violence Against the Person	3A Conspiracy to commit murder	Assisting offender by impeding his apprehension or prosecution in a case of murder	Criminal Law Act 1967, s 4(1)	10
Violence Against the Person	3A Conspiracy to commit murder	Conspiracy to commit murder	Criminal Law Act 1977, s 1	life
Violence Against the Person	5E Endangering life	Shooting at naval or revenue vessels	Customs & Excise Management Act 1979, s 85(2)	5
Violence Against the Person	4/7 Cause or allow death or serious physical harm to child or vulnerable person	Cause or allow a child or vulnerable adult to suffer serious physical harm	Domestic Violence, Crime and Victims Act 2004, as added by the Domestic Violence, Crime and Victims (Amendment) Act 2012	10
Violence Against the Person	4/7 Cause or allow death or serious physical harm to child or vulnerable person	Causing or allowing death of child or vulnerable person	Domestic Violence, Crime and Victims Act 2004, s 5	14

Appendix 3

Class	Sub Class	Offence	Act	Max Sentence
Violence Against the Person	5E Endangering life	Possession of explosives with intent to endanger life	Explosive Substances Act 1883, s 3(1)(b)	life
Violence Against the Person	5E Endangering life	Possession of firearm with intent to injure (Group I)	Firearms Act 1968, s 16	life
Violence Against the Person	5E Endangering life	Possession of firearm with intent to injure (Group II)	Firearms Act 1968, s 16	life
Violence Against the Person	5E Endangering life	Possession of firearm with intent to injure (Group III)	Firearms Act 1968, s 16	life
Violence Against the Person	10A Possession of firearms with intent	Possessing firearm or imitation firearm with intent to cause fear of violence	Firearms Act 1968, s 16A	10
Violence Against the Person	10A Possession of firearms with intent	Possessing firearm or imitation firearm with intent to cause fear of violence	Firearms Act 1968, s 16A	10
Violence Against the Person	10A Possession of firearms with intent	Possessing firearm or imitation firearm with intent to cause fear of violence	Firearms Act 1968, s 16A	10
Violence Against the Person	5E Endangering life	Use of firearm to resist arrest	Firearms Act 1968, s 17(1)	life
Violence Against the Person	5E Endangering life	Use of firearm to resist arrest	Firearms Act 1968, s 17(1)	life
Violence Against the Person	5E Endangering life	Use of firearm to resist arrest	Firearms Act 1968, s 17(1)	life
Violence Against the Person	10A Possession of firearms with intent	Possessing firearm or imitation firearm while committing or being arrested for offence specified below	Firearms Act 1968, s 17(2)	life

Class	Sub Class	Offence	Act	Max Sentence
Violence Against the Person	10A Possession of firearms with intent	Possessing firearm or imitation firearm while committing or being arrested for offence specified below	Firearms Act 1968, s 17(2)	life
Violence Against the Person	10A Possession of firearms with intent	Possessing firearm or imitation firearm while committing or being arrested for offence specified below	Firearms Act 1968, s 17(2)	life
Violence Against the Person	10A Possession of firearms with intent	Possessing firearm or imitation firearm with intent to commit indictable offence or resist arrest	Firearms Act 1968, s 18(1)	life
Violence Against the Person	10A Possession of firearms with intent	Possessing firearm or imitation firearm with intent to commit indictable offence or resist arrest	Firearms Act 1968, s 18(1)	life
Violence Against the Person	10A Possession of firearms with intent	Possessing firearm or imitation firearm with intent to commit indictable offence or resist arrest	Firearms Act 1968, s 18(1)	life
Violence Against the Person	10B Possession of firearms offences	Possessing or distributing firearm designed as other object	Firearms Act 1968, s 5(1A)(a), as amended by the Criminal Justice Act 2003, s 288	10
Violence Against the Person	4/3 Intentional destruction of a viable unborn child	Child destruction	Infant Life (Preservation) Act 1929, s 1	life
Violence Against the Person	4/2 Infanticide	Infanticide	Infanticide Act 1938, s 1(1)	life

Appendix 3

Class	Sub Class	Offence	Act	Max Sentence
Violence Against the Person	1 Murder	Genocide or crime against humanity	International Criminal Court Act 2001, ss 51, 53	life
Violence Against the Person	3A Conspiracy to commit murder	Conspiring, aiding, abetting, counselling, procuring, or inciting commission of genocide or crime against humanity	International Criminal Court Act 2001, ss 52, 53, and 55	life
Violence Against the Person	2 Attempted murder	Attempted genocide or crime against humanity	International Criminal Court Act 2001, ss 52, 53, 55	life
Violence Against the Person	5E Endangering life	Administering poison so as to endanger life	Offences Against the Person Act 1861, s 23	10
Violence Against the Person	5E Endangering life	Impeding the saving of life from shipwreck	Offences Against the Person Act 1861, s 17	life
Violence Against the Person	5D Assault with intent to cause serious harm	Wounding with intent to do grievous bodily harm	Offences Against the Person Act 1861, s 18	life
Violence Against the Person	5E Endangering life	Attempting to choke etc in order to commit indictable offence	Offences Against the Person Act 1861, s 21	life
Violence Against the Person	5E Endangering life	Using chloroform etc to commit indictable offence	Offences Against the Person Act 1861, s 22	life
Violence Against the Person	5D Assault with intent to cause serious harm	Causing bodily injury by explosion	Offences Against the Person Act 1861, s 28	life
Violence Against the Person	5E Endangering life	Causing explosions, sending explosive substance or throwing corrosive fluids with intent to do grievous bodily harm	Offences Against the Person Act 1861, s 29	life

Class	Sub Class	Offence	Act	Max Sentence
Violence Against the Person	5E Endangering life	Placing explosives in or near buildings with intent to do bodily harm	Offences Against the Person Act 1861, s 30	14
Violence Against the Person	5E Endangering life	Endangering railway passengers by placing anything on railway, taking up rails, changing points and signals etc	Offences Against the Person Act 1861, s 32	life
Violence Against the Person	5E Endangering life	Endangering railway passengers by throwing anything at railway carriages etc	Offences Against the Person Act 1861, s 33	life
Violence Against The Person	3A Conspiracy to commit murder	Soliciting to commit murder	Offences Against the Person Act 1861, s 4 Criminal Law Act 1977, s 1	life
Violence Against the Person	8N Assault with injury	Administering poison with intent to injure or annoy	Offences Against the Person Act 1861, s 24	5
Violence Against the Person	8N Assault with injury	Drivers injuring persons by furious driving	Offences Against the Person Act 1861, s 35	2
Violence Against the Person	8N Assault with injury	Assault on person preserving wreck	Offences Against the Person Act 1861, s 37	7
Violence Against the Person	14 Procuring illegal abortion	Administering drugs or using instruments to procure abortion	Offences Against the Person Act 1861, s 58	life
Violence Against the Person	14 Procuring illegal abortion	Procuring drugs etc to cause abortion	Offences Against the Person Act 1861, s 59	5
Violence Against the Person	4/4 Causing death by dangerous driving	Causing death by dangerous driving	Road Traffic Act 1988, s 1, as added by the Road Traffic Act 1991, s 1 and Criminal Justice Act 1993, s 67	14

Appendix 3

Class	Sub Class	Offence	Act	Max Sentence
Violence Against the Person	4/6 Causing death by careless driving under influence of drink or drugs	Causing death by careless driving when under the influence of drink or drugs	Road Traffic Act 1988, s 3A, as added by the Road Traffic Act 1991, s 3 and amended by the Criminal Justice Act 1993, s 67	14
Violence Against the Person	3A Conspiracy to commit murder	Intentionally encouraging or assisting commission of murder	Serious Crime Act 2007, s 44 (pt)	life
Violence Against the Person	3A Conspiracy to commit murder	Encouraging or assisting in the commission of murder believing it will be committed	Serious Crime Act 2007, s 45 (pt)	life
Violence Against the Person	3A Conspiracy to commit murder	Encouraging or assisting in the commission of one or more offences of murder believing one or more will be committed	Serious Crime Act 2007, s 46 (pt)	life
Violence Against the Person	10C Possession of other weapons	Using someone to look after a dangerous weapon—offensive/weapon/knife/bladed weapon	Violent Crime Reduction Act 2006, s 28	4
Violence Against the Person	10A Possession of firearms with intent	Using someone to look after a dangerous weapon—firearm	Violent Crime Reduction Act 2006, s 28	10
Violence Against the Person	3A Conspiracy to commit murder	Concealing commission of genocide or crime against humanity	International Criminal Court Act 2001, ss 52, 53, 55	life

Relevant Offences for the Purposes of Special Measures Direction

Schedule 14 Coroners and Justice Act 2009
RELEVANT OFFENCES FOR THE
PURPOSES OF SECTION 17

Murder and manslaughter

1 Murder in a case where it is alleged that a firearm or knife was used to cause the death in question.

2 Manslaughter in a case where it is alleged that a firearm or knife was used to cause the death in question.

3 Murder or manslaughter in a case (other than a case falling within paragraph 1 or 2) where it is alleged that—
   (a) the accused was carrying a firearm or knife at any time during the commission of the offence, and
   (b) a person other than the accused knew or believed at any time during the commission of the offence that the accused was carrying a firearm or knife.

Offences Against the Person Act 1861 (c. 100)

4 An offence under section 18 of the Offences against the Person Act 1861 (wounding with intent to cause grievous bodily harm etc) in a case where it is alleged that a firearm or knife was used to cause the wound or harm in question.

5 An offence under section 20 of that Act (malicious wounding) in a case where it is alleged that a firearm or knife was used to cause the wound or inflict the harm in question.

6 An offence under section 38 of that Act (assault with intent to resist arrest) in a case where it is alleged that a firearm or knife was used to carry out the assault in question.

7 An offence under section 47 of the Offences against the Person Act 1861 (assault occasioning actual bodily harm) in a case where it is alleged that a firearm or knife was used to inflict the harm in question.

8 An offence under section 18, 20, 38 or 47 of the Offences against the Person Act 1861 in a case (other than a case falling within any of paragraphs 4 to 7) where it is alleged that—
   (a) the accused was carrying a firearm or knife at any time during the commission of the offence, and

(b) a person other than the accused knew or believed at any time during the commission of the offence that the accused was carrying a firearm or knife.

Prevention of Crime Act 1953 (c. 14)

9　An offence under section 1 of the Prevention of Crime Act 1953 (having an offensive weapon in a public place).

Firearms Act 1968 (c. 27)

10　An offence under section 1 of the Firearms Act 1968 (requirement of firearm certificate).

11　An offence under section 2(1) of that Act (possession etc of a shot gun without a certificate).

12　An offence under section 3 of that Act (business and other transactions with firearms and ammunition).

13　An offence under section 4 of that Act (conversion of weapons).

14　An offence under section 5(1) of that Act (weapons subject to general prohibition).

15　An offence under section 5(1A) of that Act (ammunition subject to general prohibition).

16　An offence under section 16 of that Act (possession with intent to injure).

17　An offence under section 16A of that Act (possession with intent to cause fear of violence).

18　An offence under section 17 of that Act (use of firearm to resist arrest).

19　An offence under section 18 of that Act (carrying firearm with criminal intent).

20　An offence under section 19 of that Act (carrying firearm in a public place).

21　An offence under section 20 of that Act (trespassing with firearm).

22　An offence under section 21 of that Act (possession of firearms by person previously convicted of crime).

23　An offence under section 21A of that Act (firing an air weapon beyond premises).

24　An offence under section 24A of that Act (supplying imitation firearms to minors).

Criminal Justice Act 1988 (c. 33)

25　An offence under section 139 of the Criminal Justice Act 1988 (having article with blade or point in public place).

26　An offence under section 139A of that Act (having article with blade or point (or offensive weapon) on school premises).

Violent Crime Reduction Act 2006 (c. 38)

27 An offence under section 28 of the Violent Crime Reduction Act 2006 (using someone to mind a weapon).

28 An offence under section 32 of that Act (sales of air weapons by way of trade or business to be face to face).

29 An offence under section 36 of that Act (manufacture, import and sale of realistic imitation firearms).

General

30 A reference in any of paragraphs 1 to 8 to an offence ('offence A') includes—
   (a) a reference to an attempt to commit offence A in a case where it is alleged that it was attempted to commit offence A in the manner or circumstances described in that paragraph,
   (b) a reference to a conspiracy to commit offence A in a case where it is alleged that the conspiracy was to commit offence A in the manner or circumstances described in that paragraph,
   (c) a reference to an offence under Part 2 of the Serious Crime Act 2007 in relation to which offence A is the offence (or one of the offences) which the person intended or believed would be committed in a case where it is alleged that the person intended or believed offence A would be committed in the manner or circumstances described in that paragraph, and
   (d) a reference to aiding, abetting, counselling or procuring the commission of offence A in a case where it is alleged that offence A was committed, or the act or omission charged in respect of offence A was done or made, in the manner or circumstances described in that paragraph.

31 A reference in any of paragraphs 9 to 29 to an offence ('offence A') includes—
   (a) a reference to an attempt to commit offence A,
   (b) a reference to a conspiracy to commit offence A,
   (c) a reference to an offence under Part 2 of the Serious Crime Act 2007 in relation to which offence A is the offence (or one of the offences) which the person intended or believed would be committed, and
   (d) a reference to aiding, abetting, counselling or procuring the commission of offence A.

Interpretation

32 In this Schedule—
   'firearm' has the meaning given by section 57 of the Firearms Act 1968;
   'knife' has the meaning given by section 10 of the Knives Act.

Specifed Offences under the Criminal Justice Act 2003, Schedule 15 (Dangerous Offender Provisions)

SCHEDULE 15 Specified offences for purposes of Chapter 5 of Part 12

Part 1 Specified violent offences

1. Manslaughter.
2. Kidnapping.
3. False imprisonment.
4. An offence under section 4 of the Offences against the Person Act 1861 (c 100) (soliciting murder).
5. An offence under section 16 of that Act (threats to kill).
6. An offence under section 18 of that Act (wounding with intent to cause grievous bodily harm).
7. An offence under section 20 of that Act (malicious wounding).
8. An offence under section 21 of that Act (attempting to choke, suffocate, or strangle in order to commit or assist in committing an indictable offence).
9. An offence under section 22 of that Act (using chloroform etc to commit or assist in the committing of any indictable offence).
10. An offence under section 23 of that Act (maliciously administering poison etc so as to endanger life or inflict grievous bodily harm).
11. An offence under section 27 of that Act (abandoning children).
12. An offence under section 28 of that Act (causing bodily injury by explosives).
13. An offence under section 29 of that Act (using explosives etc with intent to do grievous bodily harm).
14. An offence under section 30 of that Act (placing explosives with intent to do bodily injury).
15. An offence under section 31 of that Act (setting spring guns etc with intent to do grievous bodily harm).
16. An offence under section 32 of that Act (endangering the safety of railway passengers).
17. An offence under section 35 of that Act (injuring persons by furious driving).

18. An offence under section 37 of that Act (assaulting officer preserving wreck).

19. An offence under section 38 of that Act (assault with intent to resist arrest).

20. An offence under section 47 of that Act (assault occasioning actual bodily harm).

21. An offence under section 2 of the Explosive Substances Act 1883 (c 3) (causing explosion likely to endanger life or property).

22. An offence under section 3 of that Act (attempt to cause explosion, or making or keeping explosive with intent to endanger life or property).

23. An offence under section 1 of the Infant Life (Preservation) Act 1929 (c 34) (child destruction).

24. An offence under section 1 of the Children and Young Persons Act 1933 (c 12) (cruelty to children).

25. An offence under section 1 of the Infanticide Act 1938 (c 36) (infanticide).

26. An offence under section 16 of the Firearms Act 1968 (c 27) (possession of firearm with intent to endanger life).

27. An offence under section 16A of that Act (possession of firearm with intent to cause fear of violence).

28. An offence under section 17(1) of that Act (use of firearm to resist arrest).

29. An offence under section 17(2) of that Act (possession of firearm at time of committing or being arrested for offence specified in Schedule 1 to that Act).

30. An offence under section 18 of that Act (carrying a firearm with criminal intent).

31. An offence under section 8 of the Theft Act 1968 (c 60) (robbery or assault with intent to rob).

32. An offence under section 9 of that Act of burglary with intent to—inflict grievous bodily harm on a person, or do unlawful damage to a building or anything in it.

33. An offence under section 10 of that Act (aggravated burglary).

34. An offence under section 12A of that Act (aggravated vehicle-taking) involving an accident which caused the death of any person.

35. An offence of arson under section 1 of the Criminal Damage Act 1971 (c 48).

36. An offence under section 1(2) of that Act (destroying or damaging property) other than an offence of arson.

37. An offence under section 1 of the Taking of Hostages Act 1982 (c 28) (hostage-taking).

38. An offence under section 1 of the Aviation Security Act 1982 (c 36) (hijacking).
39. An offence under section 2 of that Act (destroying, damaging or endangering safety of aircraft).
40. An offence under section 3 of that Act (other acts endangering or likely to endanger safety of aircraft).
41. An offence under section 4 of that Act (offences in relation to certain dangerous articles).
42. An offence under section 127 of the Mental Health Act 1983 (c 20) (illtreatment of patients).
43. An offence under section 1 of the Prohibition of Female Circumcision Act 1985 (c 38) (prohibition of female circumcision).
44. An offence under section 1 of the Public Order Act 1986 (c 64) (riot).
45. An offence under section 2 of that Act (violent disorder).
46. An offence under section 3 of that Act (affray).
47. An offence under section 134 of the Criminal Justice Act 1988 (c 33) (torture).
48. An offence under section 1 of the Road Traffic Act 1988 (c 52) (causing death by dangerous driving).
49. An offence under section 3A of that Act (causing death by careless driving when under influence of drink or drugs).
50. An offence under section 1 of the Aviation and Maritime Security Act 1990 (c 31) (endangering safety at aerodromes).
51. An offence under section 9 of that Act (hijacking of ships).
52. An offence under section 10 of that Act (seizing or exercising control of ffxed platforms).
53. An offence under section 11 of that Act (destroying ffxed platforms or endangering their safety).
54. An offence under section 12 of that Act (other acts endangering or likely to endanger safe navigation).
55. An offence under section 13 of that Act (offences involving threats).
56. An offence under Part II of the Channel Tunnel (Security) Order 1994 (SI 1994/570) (offences relating to Channel Tunnel trains and the tunnel system).
57. An offence under section 4 of the Protection from Harassment Act 1997 (c 40) (putting people in fear of violence).
58. An offence under section 29 of the Crime and Disorder Act 1998 (c 37) (racially or religiously aggravated assaults).
59. An offence falling within section 31(1) (a) or (b) of that Act (racially or religiously aggravated offences under section 4 or 4A of the Public Order Act 1986 (c 64)).

Specifed Offences under the Criminal Justice Act 2003

59A. An offence under section 54 of the Terrorism Act 2000 (weapons training).

59B. An offence under section 56 of that Act (directing terrorist organisation).

59C. An offence under section 57 of that Act (possession of article for terrorist purposes).

59D. An offence under section 59 of that Act (inciting terrorism overseas).

60. An offence under section 51 or 52 of the International Criminal Court Act 2001 (c 17) (genocide, crimes against humanity, war crimes and related offences), other than one involving murder.

60A. An offence under section 47 of the Anti-terrorism, Crime and Security Act 2001 (use etc of nuclear weapons).

60B. An offence under section 50 of that Act (assisting or inducing certain weapons-related acts overseas).

60C. An offence under section 113 of that Act (use of noxious substance or thing to cause harm or intimidate).

61. An offence under section 1 of the Female Genital Mutilation Act 2003 (c 31) (female genital mutilation).

62. An offence under section 2 of that Act (assisting a girl to mutilate her own genitalia).

63. An offence under section 3 of that Act (assisting a non-UK person to mutilate overseas a girl's genitalia).

63A. An offence under section 5 of the Domestic Violence, Crime and Victims Act 2004 (causing or allowing the death of a child or vulnerable adult).

63B. An offence under section 5 of the Terrorism Act 2006 (preparation of terrorist acts).

63C. An offence under section 6 of that Act (training for terrorism).

63D. An offence under section 9 of that Act (making or possession of radioactive device or material).

63E. An offence under section 10 of that Act (use of radioactive device or material for terrorist purposes etc).

63F. An offence under section 11 of that Act (terrorist threats relating to radioactive devices etc).

64. An offence of—
    (a) aiding, abetting, counselling, procuring or inciting the commission of an offence specified in this Part of this Schedule,
    (b) conspiring to commit an offence so specified, or
    (c) attempting to commit an offence so specified.

65. An attempt to commit murder or a conspiracy to commit murder.

Appendix 5

Part 2 Specified sexual offences

66. An offence under section 1 of the Sexual Offences Act 1956 (c 69) (rape).
67. An offence under section 2 of that Act (procurement of woman by threats).
68. An offence under section 3 of that Act (procurement of woman by false pretences).
69. An offence under section 4 of that Act (administering drugs to obtain or facilitate intercourse).
70. An offence under section 5 of that Act (intercourse with girl under 13).
71. An offence under section 6 of that Act (intercourse with girl under 16).
72. An offence under section 7 of that Act (intercourse with a defective).
73. An offence under section 9 of that Act (procurement of a defective).
74. An offence under section 10 of that Act (incest by a man).
75. An offence under section 11 of that Act (incest by a woman).
76. An offence under section 14 of that Act (indecent assault on a woman).
77. An offence under section 15 of that Act (indecent assault on a man).
78. An offence under section 16 of that Act (assault with intent to commit buggery).
79. An offence under section 17 of that Act (abduction of woman by force or for the sake of her property).
80. An offence under section 19 of that Act (abduction of unmarried girl under 18 from parent or guardian).
81. An offence under section 20 of that Act (abduction of unmarried girl under 16 from parent or guardian).
82. An offence under section 21 of that Act (abduction of defective from parent or guardian).
83. An offence under section 22 of that Act (causing prostitution of women).
84. An offence under section 23 of that Act (procuration of girl under 21).
85. An offence under section 24 of that Act (detention of woman in brothel).
86. An offence under section 25 of that Act (permitting girl under 13 to use premises for intercourse).
87. An offence under section 26 of that Act (permitting girl under 16 to use premises for intercourse).

88. An offence under section 27 of that Act (permitting defective to use premises for intercourse).
89. An offence under section 28 of that Act (causing or encouraging the prostitution of, intercourse with or indecent assault on girl under 16).
90. An offence under section 29 of that Act (causing or encouraging prostitution of defective).
91. An offence under section 32 of that Act (soliciting by men).
92. An offence under section 33 of that Act (keeping a brothel).
93. An offence under section 128 of the Mental Health Act 1959 (c 72) (sexual intercourse with patients).
94. An offence under section 1 of the Indecency with Children Act 1960 (c 33) (indecent conduct towards young child).
95. An offence under section 4 of the Sexual Offences Act 1967 (c 60) (procuring others to commit homosexual acts).
96. An offence under section 5 of that Act (living on earnings of male prostitution).
97. An offence under section 9 of the Theft Act 1968 (c 60) of burglary with intent to commit rape.
98. An offence under section 54 of the Criminal Law Act 1977 (c 45) (inciting girl under 16 to have incestuous sexual intercourse).
99. An offence under section 1 of the Protection of Children Act 1978 (c 37) (indecent photographs of children).
100. An offence under section 170 of the Customs and Excise Management Act 1979 (c 2) (penalty for fraudulent evasion of duty etc) in relation to goods prohibited to be imported under section 42 of the Customs Consolidation Act 1876 (c 36) (indecent or obscene articles).
101. An offence under section 160 of the Criminal Justice Act 1988 (c 33) (possession of indecent photograph of a child).
102. An offence under section 1 of the Sexual Offences Act 2003 (c 42) (rape).
103. An offence under section 2 of that Act (assault by penetration).
104. An offence under section 3 of that Act (sexual assault).
105. An offence under section 4 of that Act (causing a person to engage in sexual activity without consent).
106. An offence under section 5 of that Act (rape of a child under 13).
107. An offence under section 6 of that Act (assault of a child under 13 by penetration).
108. An offence under section 7 of that Act (sexual assault of a child under 13).
109. An offence under section 8 of that Act (causing or inciting a child under to engage in sexual activity).

110. An offence under section 9 of that Act (sexual activity with a child).
111. An offence under section 10 of that Act (causing or inciting a child to engage in sexual activity).
112. An offence under section 11 of that Act (engaging in sexual activity in the presence of a child).
113. An offence under section 12 of that Act (causing a child to watch a sexual act).
114. An offence under section 13 of that Act (child sex offences committed by children or young persons).
115. An offence under section 14 of that Act (arranging or facilitating commission of a child sex offence).
116. An offence under section 15 of that Act (meeting a child following sexual grooming etc).
117. An offence under section 16 of that Act (abuse of position of trust: sexual activity with a child).
118. An offence under section 17 of that Act (abuse of position of trust: causing or inciting a child to engage in sexual activity).
119. An offence under section 18 of that Act (abuse of position of trust: sexual activity in the presence of a child).
120. An offence under section 19 of that Act (abuse of position of trust: causing a child to watch a sexual act).
121. An offence under section 25 of that Act (sexual activity with a child family member).
122. An offence under section 26 of that Act (inciting a child family member to engage in sexual activity).
123. An offence under section 30 of that Act (sexual activity with a person with a mental disorder impeding choice).
124. An offence under section 31 of that Act (causing or inciting a person with a mental disorder impeding choice to engage in sexual activity).
125. An offence under section 32 of that Act (engaging in sexual activity in the presence of a person with a mental disorder impeding choice).
126. An offence under section 33 of that Act (causing a person with a mental disorder impeding choice to watch a sexual act).
127. An offence under section 34 of that Act (inducement, threat or deception to procure sexual activity with a person with a mental disorder).
128. An offence under section 35 of that Act (causing a person with a mental disorder to engage in or agree to engage in sexual activity by inducement, threat or deception).
129. An offence under section 36 of that Act (engaging in sexual activity in the presence, procured by inducement, threat or deception, of a person with a mental disorder).

130. An offence under section 37 of that Act (causing a person with a mental disorder to watch a sexual act by inducement, threat or deception).
131. An offence under section 38 of that Act (care workers: sexual activity with a person with a mental disorder).
132. An offence under section 39 of that Act (care workers: causing or inciting sexual activity).
133. An offence under section 40 of that Act (care workers: sexual activity in the presence of a person with a mental disorder).
134. An offence under section 41 of that Act (care workers: causing a person with a mental disorder to watch a sexual act).
135. An offence under section 47 of that Act (paying for sexual services of a child).
136. An offence under section 48 of that Act (causing or inciting child prostitution or pornography).
137. An offence under section 49 of that Act (controlling a child prostitute or a child involved in pornography).
138. An offence under section 50 of that Act (arranging or facilitating child prostitution or pornography).
139. An offence under section 52 of that Act (causing or inciting prostitution for gain).
140. An offence under section 53 of that Act (controlling prostitution for gain).
141. An offence under section 57 of that Act (trafficking into the UK for sexual exploitation).
142. An offence under section 58 of that Act (trafficking within the UK for sexual exploitation).
143. An offence under section 59 of that Act (trafficking out of the UK for sexual exploitation).
144. An offence under section 61 of that Act (administering a substance with intent).
145. An offence under section 62 of that Act (committing an offence with intent to commit a sexual offence).
146. An offence under section 63 of that Act (trespass with intent to commit a sexual offence).
147. An offence under section 64 of that Act (sex with an adult relative: penetration).
148. An offence under section 65 of that Act (sex with an adult relative: consenting to penetration).
149. An offence under section 66 of that Act (exposure).
150. An offence under section 67 of that Act (voyeurism).
151. An offence under section 69 of that Act (intercourse with an animal).

152. An offence under section 70 of that Act (sexual penetration of a corpse).
153. An offence of—
    (a) aiding, abetting, counselling, procuring or inciting the commission of an offence specified in this Part of this Schedule,
    (b) conspiring to commit an offence so specified, or
    (c) attempting to commit an offence so specified.

Fraud Guideline (Note: the Sentencing Council is presently consulting on a new edition of this guideline)

Fraud—banking and insurance fraud, and obtaining credit through fraud, benefit fraud, and revenue fraud—factors to take into consideration

This guideline and accompanying notes are taken from the Sentencing Guidelines Council's definitive guideline *Sentencing for Fraud—Statutory Offences*, published 26 October 2009.

The starting points and ranges for fraud against HM Revenue and Customs, for benefit fraud and for banking and insurance and obtaining credit through fraud are the same since the seriousness of all offences of organisational fraud derives from the extent of the fraudulent activity (culpability) and the financial loss caused or likely to be caused (harm).

Key factors common to these types of fraud

(a) As the determinants of seriousness include the 'value of property or consequential loss involved', the table provides both a fixed amount (on which the starting point is based) and a band (on which the sentencing range is based). Where the value is larger or smaller than the amount on which the starting point is based, this should lead to upward or downward movement from the starting point as appropriate. Where the amount the offender intended to obtain cannot be established, the appropriate measure will be the amount that was likely to be achieved in all the circumstances. Where the offender was entitled to part or all of the amount obtained, the starting point should be based on the amount to which they were not entitled.

(b) A further determinant of seriousness is whether the fraud was a single fraudulent transaction or a multiple fraud. Where one false declaration or a failure to disclose a change in circumstances results in multiple payments, this should be regarded as multiple fraud.

(c) In general terms, the greater the loss, the more serious will be the offence. However, the financial value of the loss may not reflect the full extent of the harm caused. The court should also take into account; the impact of the offence on the victim (particularly where the loss may be significantly greater than the monetary value); harm to persons other than the direct victim (including the aggravation and stress of unscrambling the consequences of an offence); erosion of public confidence; and the difference between the loss intended and that which results (which may involve adjusting the assessment of seriousness to reflect the degree of loss caused).

(d) When the offending involves a number of people acting cooperatively, this will aggravate an offence as it indicates planning or professional activity, and may also increase the degree of loss caused or intended. The role of each offender is important in determining the appropriate level of seriousness and movement above or below the starting point within the applicable level.

(e) Use of another person's identity is an aggravating factor; the extent to which it aggravates an offence will be based on the degree of planning and the impact that the offence has had on the living victim or relatives of the deceased—whether the identity belongs to a living or deceased person is neutral for this purpose.

(f) Matters of offender mitigation which may be particularly relevant to these types of fraud include:

— *Voluntary cessation of offending*—a claim, supported by objective evidence, that an offender stopped offending before being apprehended should be treated as mitigation, particularly where accompanied by a genuine expression of remorse. The lapse of time since commission of the last offence is relevant to whether the claim is genuine, and reasons for the cessation will assist the court in determining whether it amounts to mitigation and if so, to what degree.

— *Complete and unprompted disclosure of the extent of the fraud*—An admission that a greater sum has been obtained than that known to the authorities ensures that an offender is sentenced for the complete extent of the fraud. This is ready co-operation with the authorities and should be treated as mitigation. Provision of information about others involved in the fraud should also be treated as mitigation. Generally, the earlier the disclosure is given and the higher the degree of assistance, the greater the allowance for mitigation.

— *Voluntary restitution*—the timing of the voluntary restitution will indicate the degree to which it reflects genuine remorse. Generally, the earlier the property or money is returned the greater the degree of mitigation the offender should receive. If circumstances beyond the control of the offender prevent return of defrauded items, the degree of mitigation will depend on the point in time at which, and the determination with which the offender tried to return the items.

— *Financial pressure*—financial pressure neither increases nor diminishes an offender's culpability. However, where such pressure is exceptional and not of the offender's own making, it may in very rare circumstances constitute mitigation.

(g) A court should be aware that a confiscation order is an important sanction. Such an order may only be made in the Crown Court. The court must commit the offender to the Crown Court where this is requested by the prosecution with a view to an order being considered.

(h) Ancillary orders should be considered in all cases, principally compensation, deprivation and disqualification from driving, as well as other powers particular to the type of offending behaviour.

Additional notes:

Banking and insurance fraud and obtaining credit through fraud

(i) A payment card or bank account fraud is unlikely to be committed in circumstances where the offender's intention was not fraudulent from the outset.

(ii) Use of another person's identity is a feature of nearly all payment card and bank account frauds since in most cases the offender claims to be the account holder or a person authorised to deal with the account. Courts should therefore increase the starting point to reflect the presence of this aggravating factor.

Benefit fraud

(i) This guideline is based on an understanding that the prosecutor will generally seek summary trial for appropriate benefit fraud cases involving sums up to £35,000.

(ii) The fact that defrauded sums may have been recovered is not relevant to the choice of the type of sentence to be imposed.

(iii) The court should have regard to personal and family circumstances of offenders which will vary greatly and may be particularly significant to sentencing this type of fraud.

Revenue fraud

(i) The proposals for the sentencing of revenue fraud take as a starting point an offender who acts intentionally. Where the offender has acted recklessly (relevant only to offences under the Value Added Tax Act 1994), courts should adjust the assessment ofseriousness to take account of this lower level of culpability.

(ii) Payments to HMRC may be evaded in order to increase the profitability of a legitimate business or the level of an individual's legitimate remuneration; payments may be fraudulently obtained from HMRC without any underlying legitimate activity at all as in a Carousel Fraud. Although the type of harm is the same since both result in a loss to HMRC, where payment is sought from HMRC in such circumstances, culpability is likely to be higher. Accordingly, such offences are likely to be regarded as more serious.

All offences: Triable either way:

Maximum when tried summarily: Level 5 fine and/or 6 months

Maximum when tried on indictment: Fraud 10 years, other offences, 7 years

Offences under s 112, Social Security Administration Act 1992 are not covered by this guideline.

This guideline does not apply to offences under s 50 or s 170, Customs and Excise Management Act 1979 which involve prohibited weapons and have a maximum penalty of 10 years.

Offence seriousness (culpability and harm) A. Identify the appropriate starting point Starting points based on first time offender pleading not guilty		
Examples of nature of activity	**Starting point**	**Range**
Single fraudulent transaction, not fraudulent from the outset	Value £2,500*—Band B fine Value £12,500*—Medium level community order Value £60,000*—12 weeks custody	Value less than £5,000—Band A fine to low level community order Value £5,000 to less than £20,000—Band B fine to 6 weeks custody Value £20,000 to less than £100,000—Medium level community order to Crown Court
Single fraudulent transaction, fraudulent from the outset	Value £2,500*—Low level community order Value £12,500*—High level community order Value £60,000*—26 weeks custody	Value less than £5,000—Band A fine to medium level community order Value £5,000 to less than £20,000—Band C fine to 18 weeks custody Value £20,000 to less than £100,000—6 weeks custody to Crown Court
Not fraudulent from the outset, **and either** • fraud carried out over a significant period of time or • multiple frauds	Value £2,500*—Medium level community order Value £12,500*—6 weeks custody Value £60,000*—Crown Court	Value less than £5,000—Band B fine to high level community order Value £5,000 to less than £20,000—Medium level community order to 26 weeks custody Value £20,000 to less than £100,000—12 weeks custody to Crown Court
Where value exceeds £100,000	Crown Court	Crown Court

Offence seriousness (culpability and harm)		
A. Identify the appropriate starting point		
Starting points based on first time offender pleading not guilty		
Examples of nature of activity	**Starting point**	**Range**
Fraudulent from the outset, **and either** • fraud carried out over a significant period of time or • multiple frauds	Value £2,500*—High level community order	Value less than £5,000—Low level community order to 6 weeks custody
	Value £12,500*—12 weeks custody Value £60,000*—Crown Court	Value £5,000 to less than £20,000—High level community order to Crown Court Value £20,000 to less than £100,000—18 weeks custody to Crown Court
Where value £100,000 or more or fraud was professionally planned	Crown Court	Crown Court

* Where the actual amount is greater or smaller than the value on which the starting point is based, that is likely to be one of the factors which will move the sentence within range (see (a) on page 62b)

Offence seriousness (culpability and harm)	
B. Consider the effect of aggravating and mitigating factors	
(other than those within examples above)	
Common aggravating and mitigating factors are identified in the pullout card— the following may be particularly relevant but **these lists are not exhaustive**	
Factors indicating higher culpability	**Factors indicating lower culpability**
1. Number involved in the offence and role of the offender 2. Making repeated importations, particularly in the face of warnings from the authorities 3. Dealing in goods with an additional health risk	1. Peripheral involvement 2. Misleading or incomplete advice
Factors indicating greater degree of harm	
1. Use of another person's identity 2. Disposing of goods to under-aged purchasers	

Form a preliminary view of the appropriate sentence,
then consider offender mitigation
Common factors are identified in the pullout card

Consider a reduction for a guilty plea

Appendix 6

| **Consider ancillary orders** |
| Refer to pages 168–174 for guidance on available ancillary orders |

| **Decide sentence** |
| **Give reasons** |

Fraud—confidence—factors to take into consideration

This guideline and accompanying notes are taken from the Sentencing Guidelines Council's definitive guideline *Sentencing for Fraud—Statutory Offences*, published October 2009.

Key factors

(a) This type of offending involves a victim transferring money and/ or property as a result of being deceived or misled by the offender. An example of a simple confidence fraud is a person claiming to be collecting money for charity when, in fact, he or she intends to keep the money. Other examples of common confidence frauds are *Advance fee frauds* (such as lottery/prize draw scams and foreign money-making frauds) and *Fraudulent sales of goods and services* (where goods or services are never received/performed or are worth less than represented.

(b) As the determinants of seriousness include the 'value of property or consequential loss involved', the table provides both a fixed amount (on which the starting point is based) and a band (on which the sentencing range is based). Where the value is larger or smaller than the amount on which the starting point is based, this should lead to upward or downward movement as appropriate. Where the amount the offender intended to obtain cannot be established, the appropriate measure will be the amount that was likely to be achieved in all the circumstances.

(c) A further determinant of seriousness is whether the fraud was a single fraudulent transaction or a multiple fraud. Most confidence frauds will by their nature involve many actual or potential victims and multiple transactions and should be regarded as multiple fraud.

(d) Targeting a vulnerable victim is also a determinant of seriousness. A victim might be vulnerable as a result of old age, youth or disability. In addition, some victims of advance fee frauds may have personalities which make them 'vulnerable in a way and to a degree not typical of the general population' because they fall for scams many times and may be targeted using 'sucker lists' of people who have previously fallen victim to scams. Care should be taken to ensure that where targeting a vulnerable victim is used to determine the appropriate level of seriousness and starting point, that it is not used again as an aggravating factor to move within the sentencing range.

(e) In general terms, the greater the loss, the more serious will be the offence. However, the financial value of the loss may not reflect the full extent of the harm caused. The court should also take into account; the impact of the offence on the victim (particularly where the loss may be significantly greater than the monetary value); harm to persons other than the direct victim (including the aggravation and stress of unscrambling the consequences of an offence); erosion of public confidence; and the difference between the loss intended and that which results (which may involve adjusting the assessment of seriousness to reflect the degree of loss caused).

(f) When the offending involves a number of people acting co-operatively, this will aggravate an offence as it indicates planning or professional activity, and may also increase the degree of loss caused or intended. The role of each offender is important in determining the appropriate level of seriousness and movement above or below the starting point within the applicable level.

(g) Use of another person's identity is an aggravating factor; the extent to which it aggravates an offence will be based on the degree of planning and the impact that the offence has had on the living victim or relatives of the deceased—whether the identity belongs to a living or deceased person is neutral for this purpose.

(h) Matters of offender mitigation which may be particularly relevant to this type of fraud include:

— *Voluntary cessation of offending*—a claim, supported by objective evidence, that an offender stopped offending before being apprehended should be treated as mitigation, particularly where accompanied by a genuine expression of remorse. The lapse of time since commission of the last offence is relevant to whether the claim is genuine, and reasons for the cessation will assist the court in determining whether it amounts to mitigation and if so, to what degree.

— *Complete and unprompted disclosure of the extent of the fraud*— an admission that a greater sum has been obtained than that known to the authorities ensures that an offender is sentenced for the complete extent of the fraud. This amounts to ready co-operation with the authorities and should be treated as mitigation. Provision of information about others involved in the fraud should also be treated as mitigation. Generally, the earlier the disclosure is given and the higher the degree of assistance, the greater the allowance for mitigation.

— *Voluntary restitution*—the timing of the voluntary restitution will indicate the degree to which it reflects genuine remorse. Generally, the earlier the property or money is returned the greater the degree of mitigation the offender should receive. If circumstances beyond the control of the offender prevent return of defrauded items, the degree of mitigation will depend on the point in time at which, and the determination with which the offender tried to return the items.

— *Financial pressure*—financial pressure neither increases nor diminishes an offenders culpability. However, where such pressure is exceptional and not of the offenders own making, it may in very rare circumstances constitute mitigation.

(i) A court should be aware that a confiscation order is an important sanction. Such an order may only be made in the Crown Court. The court must commit the offender to the Crown Court where this is requested by the prosecution with a view to an order being considered.

(j) Ancillary orders should be considered in all cases, principally compensation and deprivation.

All Offences: Triable either way:

Maximum when tried summarily: Level 5 fine and/or 6 months

Maximum when tried on indictment: Fraud 10 years, other offences, 7 years

Offence seriousness (culpability and harm) A. Identify the appropriate starting point Starting points based on first time offender pleading not guilty		
Examples of nature of activity	**Starting point**	**Range**
Single fraudulent transaction confidence fraud not targeting a vulnerable victim, and involving no or limited planning	Value £10,000*— Medium level community order Value £60,000*— 12 weeks custody	Value less than £20,000—Band B fine to 6 weeks custody Value £20,000 to less than £100,000—Medium level community order to Crown Court
Single fraudulent transaction confidence fraud involving targeting of a vulnerable victim	Value £10,000*— 6 weeks custody Value £60,000*— 26 weeks custody	Value less than £20,000— Medium level community order to 26 weeks custody Value £20,000 to less than £100,000—High level community order to Crown Court

Offence seriousness (culpability and harm)		
A. Identify the appropriate starting point		
Starting points based on first time offender pleading not guilty		
Examples of nature of activity	**Starting point**	**Range**
Lower scale advance fee fraud **or** other confidence fraud characterised by a degree of planning and/or multiple transactions	Value £10,000*— Crown Court Value £60,000*— Crown Court	Value less than £20,000—26 weeks custody to Crown Court Value £20,000 to less than £100,000—Crown Court
Large scale advance fee fraud or other confidence fraud involving the deliberate targeting of a large number of vulnerable victims	Value £10,000*— Crown Court Value £60,000*— Crown Court	Value less than £20,000— Crown Court Value £20,000 to less than £100,000—Crown Court

* Where the actual amount is greater or smaller than the value on which the starting point is based, that is likely to be one of the factors which will move the sentence within range (see (b) on page 62f)

Offence seriousness (culpability and harm)	
B. Consider the effect of aggravating and mitigating factors	
(other than those within examples above)	
Common aggravating and mitigating factors are identified in the pullout card—the following may be particularly relevant **but these lists are not exhaustive**	
Factors indicating higher culpability	**Factors indicating lower culpability**
1. Number involved in the offence and role of the offender 2. Offending carried out over a significant period of time	1. Peripheral involvement 2. Behaviour not fraudulent from the outset 3. Misleading or inaccurate advice
Factors indicating greater degree of harm	
1. Use of another person's identity 2. Offence has lasting effect on the victim	

Form a preliminary view of the appropriate sentence, then consider offender mitigation
Common factors are identified in the pullout card

Consider a reduction for a guilty plea

Consider ancillary orders
Refer to pages 168–174 for guidance on available ancillary orders

> Decide sentence
> Give reasons

Fraud—possessing, making or supplying articles for use in fraud—factors to take into consideration

This guideline and accompanying notes are taken from the Sentencing Guidelines Council's definitive guideline *Sentencing for Fraud—Statutory Offences*, published 26 October 2009.

Key factors

(a) There are many ways in which offenders may commit this group of offences. 'Articles' will include any electronic programs or data stored electronically, false fronts for cash machines, computer programs for generating credit card numbers, lists of credit card or bank account details, 'sucker lists' and draft letters or emails for use in advance fee frauds.

(b) Offenders who possess, make or supply articles for use in fraud intend their actions to lead to a fraud, and therefore have the highest level of culpability. The three offences in this group all involve an element of planning (whether by the offender or by another person) which indicates a higher level of culpability; this has been incorporated into the proposed starting points.

(c) In relation to harm, the value of the fraud (either that intended by the offender where that can be ascertained, or that which was likely to be achieved) is not a determinant of seriousness for these offences but is a factor that should be taken into account in determining the appropriate sentence within the sentencing range.

(d) Whilst in many cases no financial harm will have been caused, in some cases, particularly where the 'article' is a list of credit card or bank account details, the victim(s) may have been inconvenienced despite not suffering any financial loss. In all cases, the harm must be judged in light of the offender's culpability.

(e) When the offending involves a number of people acting co-operatively, this will aggravate an offence as it indicates planning or professional activity, and may also increase the degree of loss caused or intended. The role of each offender is important in determining the appropriate level of seriousness and movement above or below the starting point within the applicable level.

(f) Matters of offender mitigation which may be particularly relevant to this type of fraud include:

— *Voluntary cessation of offending*—a claim, supported by objective evidence, that an offender stopped offending before being apprehended should be treated as mitigation, particularly where accompanied by a genuine expression of remorse. The lapse of time since commission of the last offence is relevant to whether the claim is genuine, and reasons for the cessation will assist the court in determining whether it amounts to mitigation and if so, to what degree.

— *Complete and unprompted disclosure of the extent of the fraud*—An admission that a greater sum has been obtained than that known to the authorities ensures that an offender is sentenced for the complete extent of the fraud. This amounts to ready co-operation with the authorities and should be treated as mitigation. Provision of information about others involved in the fraud should also be treated as mitigation. Generally, the earlier the disclosure is given and the higher the degree of assistance, the greater the allowance for mitigation.

— *Voluntary restitution*—the timing of the voluntary restitution will indicate the degree to which it reflects genuine remorse. Generally, the earlier the property or money is returned the greater the degree of mitigation the offender should receive. If circumstances beyond the control of the offender prevent return of defrauded items, the degree of mitigation will depend on the point in time at which, and the determination with which the offender tried to return the items.

— *Financial pressure*—financial pressure neither increases nor diminishes an offender's culpability. However, where such pressure is exceptional and not of the offender's own making, it may in very rare circumstances constitute mitigation.

(g) A court should be aware that a confiscation order is an important sanction. Such an order may only be made in the Crown Court. The court must commit the offender to the Crown Court where this is requested by the prosecution with a view to an order being considered.

(h) Ancillary orders should be considered in all cases, principally compensation and deprivation.

Possession of articles: Triable either way
Maximum when tried summarily: Level 5 fine and/or 6 months
Maximum when tried on indictment: 5 years

Making or supplying articles, and Fraud (s 1): Triable either way
Maximum when tried summarily: Level 5 fine and/or 6 months
Maximum when tried on indictment: 10 years

Offence seriousness (culpability and harm)		
A. Identify the appropriate starting point		
Starting points based on first time offender pleading not guilty		
Examples of nature of activity	**Starting point**	**Range**
Possessing articles intended for use in a less extensive and less skillfully planned fraud	Medium level community order	Low level community order to 26 weeks custody
Possessing articles for use in an extensive and skillfully planned fraud	Crown Court	6 weeks custody to Crown Court
Making or adapting, supplying or offering to supply articles intended for use in a less extensive and less skillfully planned fraud	26 weeks custody	High level community order to Crown Court
Making or adapting, supplying or offering to supply articles for use in an extensive and skillfully planned fraud	Crown Court	Crown Court

Offence seriousness (culpability and harm)	
B. Consider the effect of aggravating and mitigating factors	
(other than those within examples above)	
Common aggravating and mitigating factors are identified in the pullout card— the following may be particularly relevant but **these lists are not exhaustive**	
Factors indicating higher culpability	**Factor indicating**
1. Number involved in the offence and role of the offender	**lower culpability**
2. Offending carried out over a significant period of time	1. Peripheral involvement
Factors indicating greater degree of harm	
1. Use of another person's identity	
2. Offence has lasting effect on the victim	

**Form a preliminary view of the appropriate sentence,
then consider offender mitigation**

Common factors are identified in the pullout card

Consider a reduction for a guilty plea

Consider ancillary orders

Refer to pages 168–174 for guidance on available ancillary orders

---

**Decide sentence
Give reasons**

Rehabilitation Periods

Legal Aid, Sentencing and Punishment of Offenders Act 2012, s 139(1), (4), (6), and (7), amending the Rehabilitation of Offenders Act 1974

139 Establishment or alteration of rehabilitation periods

(1) The Rehabilitation of Offenders Act 1974 is amended as follows.

…

(4) For section 5(2) to (11) (rehabilitation periods) substitute—

'(2) For the purposes of this Act and subject to subsections (3) and (4), the rehabilitation period for a sentence is the period—

(a) beginning with the date of the conviction in respect of which the sentence is imposed, and

(b) ending at the time listed in the following Table in relation to that sentence:

Sentence	End of rehabilitation period for adult offenders	End of rehabilitation period for offenders under 18 at date of conviction
A custodial sentence of more than 30 months and up to, or consisting of, 48 months	The end of the period of 7 years beginning with the day on which the sentence (including any licence period) is completed	The end of the period of 42 months beginning with the day on which the sentence (including any licence period) is completed
A custodial sentence of more than 6 months and up to, or consisting of, 30 months	The end of the period of 48 months beginning with the day on which the sentence (including any licence period) is completed	The end of the period of 24 months beginning with the day on which the sentence (including any licence period) is completed
A custodial sentence of 6 months or less	The end of the period of 24 months beginning with the day on which the sentence (including any licence period) is completed	The end of the period of 18 months beginning with the day on which the sentence (including any licence period) is completed
Removal from Her Majesty's service	The end of the period of 12 months beginning with the date of the conviction in respect of which the sentence is imposed	The end of the period of 6 months beginning with the date of the conviction in respect of which the sentence is imposed

A sentence of service detention	The end of the period of 12 months beginning with the day on which the sentence is completed	The end of the period of 6 months beginning with the day on which the sentence is completed
A fine	The end of the period of 12 months beginning with the date of the conviction in respect of which the sentence is imposed	The end of the period of 6 months beginning with the date of the conviction in respect of which the sentence is imposed
A compensation order	The date on which the payment is made in full	The date on which the payment is made in full
A community or youth rehabilitation order	The end of the period of 12 months beginning with the day provided for by or under the order as the last day on which the order is to have effect	The end of the period of 6 months beginning with the day provided for by or under the order as the last day on which the order is to have effect
A relevant order	The day provided for by or under the order as the last day on which the order is to have effect	The day provided for by or under the order as the last day on which the order is to have effect

(3) Where no provision is made by or under a community or youth rehabilitation order or a relevant order for the last day on which the order is to have effect, the rehabilitation period for the order is to be the period of 24 months beginning with the date of conviction.

(4) There is no rehabilitation period for—

    (a) an order discharging a person absolutely for an offence, or

    (b) any other sentence in respect of a conviction where the sentence is not dealt with in the Table or under subsection (3),

and, in such cases, references in this Act to any rehabilitation period are to be read as if the period of time were nil.

(5) See also—

    (a) section 8AA (protection afforded to spent alternatives to prosecution), and

    (b) Schedule 2 (protection for spent cautions).

(6)–(8) . . .'

(5) . . .

(6) After section 8A (protection afforded to spent cautions) insert—

'8AA Protection afforded to spent alternatives to prosecution

(1) The following provisions of this Act apply, with the modifications specified in subsection (3), to a spent alternative to prosecution as they apply to a spent caution—

(a) section 9A (unauthorised disclosure of spent cautions), and

(b) paragraphs 2 to 6 of Schedule 2 (protection relating to spent cautions and ancillary circumstances).

(3) The modifications mentioned in subsection (1) are—

    (a) references to cautions are to be read as references to alternatives to prosecution (and references to cautioned are to be read accordingly),

    (b) references to the offence which was the subject of the caution are to be read as references to the offence in respect of which the alternative to prosecution was given,

    (c) paragraphs (e) and (f) of paragraph 2(1) of Schedule 2 are to be read as if they were—

      "(e)anything done or undergone in pursuance of the terms of the alternative to prosecution,",

    (d) references to cautions for an offence are to be read as references to alternatives to prosecution in respect of an offence, and

    (e) the reference in paragraph 5 of Schedule 2 to the rehabilitation period applicable to the caution is to be read as a reference to the time at which the alternative to prosecution becomes spent.'

(7) In paragraph 1 of Schedule 2 (protection for spent cautions)—

    (a) in sub-paragraph (1)(a) (when conditional cautions to be regarded as spent cautions) for ', at the end of the relevant period for the caution;' substitute '—

      (i) at the end of the period of three months from the date on which the caution is given, or

      (ii) if earlier, when the caution ceases to have effect; and', and

    (b) omit sub-paragraphs (2) and (3) (meaning of 'the relevant period for the caution').

The (Criminal Record Certificates: Relevant Matters) (Amendment) (England and Wales) Order 2013 (SI 2013/1200); Police Act 1997 (Criminal Records) (Amendment) Regulations 2013 (SI 2013/1194); and Rehabilitation of Offenders Act 1974 (Exceptions) Order 1975 (Amendment) (England and Wales) Order 2013 (SI 2013/1198) make further amendments.

The effect of these amendments in relation to convictions is that:

(1) convictions that resulted in a custodial sentence, convictions for serious sexual or violent offences, and convictions for certain other specified offences will always be disclosed;

(2) in relation to all other convictions for persons aged 18 or over, convictions that fall within an 11-year period ending with the day on which the certificate is issued will be disclosed;

(3) in relation to all other convictions for persons aged under 18, convictions that fall within a five-and-a-half-year period ending with the day on which the certificate is issued will be disclosed; but

(4) persons with more than one conviction will have all their convictions disclosed.

Appendix 7

The effect of the amendments in relation to cautions is that—

(1) cautions for serious sexual and violent offences and certain other offences will always be disclosed;
(2) in relation to all other cautions for persons aged 18 or over, cautions that fall within a six-year period ending with the day on which the certificate is issued will be disclosed; and
(3) in relation to all other cautions for person aged under 18, cautions that fall within a two-year period ending with the day on which the certificate is issued will be disclosed.

The 1974 Act is no longer disapplied (and so no disclosure need be made), save in defined circumstances, in respect of a 'protected caution' or a 'protected conviction' (as defined in Rehabilitation of Offenders Act 1974 (Exceptions) Order 1975 (SI 1975/1023), art 2A) when a question is asked to assess a person's suitability for certain purposes, or when a decision is made for certain purposes.

Index

Index

Index

Index

Index

Index

Index

Index

Index

Index

Index

Index

Index

Index

Index

Index

Index

Index

Index

Index

2013

January
M		7	14	21	28
T	1	8	15	22	29
W	2	9	16	23	30
T	3	10	17	24	31
F	4	11	18	25	
S	5	12	19	26	
S	6	13	20	27	

February
M		4	11	18	25
T		5	12	19	26
W		6	13	20	27
T		7	14	21	28
F	1	8	15	22	
S	2	9	16	23	
S	3	10	17	24	

March
M		4	11	18	25
T		5	12	19	26
W		6	13	20	27
T		7	14	21	28
F	1	8	15	22	29
S	2	9	16	23	30
S	3	10	17	24	31

April
M	1	8	15	22	29
T	2	9	16	23	30
W	3	10	17	24	
T	4	11	18	25	
F	5	12	19	26	
S	6	13	20	27	
S	7	14	21	28	

May
M		6	13	20	27
T		7	14	21	28
W	1	8	15	22	29
T	2	9	16	23	30
F	3	10	17	24	31
S	4	11	18	25	
S	5	12	19	26	

June
M		3	10	17	24
T		4	11	18	25
W		5	12	19	26
T		6	13	20	27
F		7	14	21	28
S	1	8	15	22	29
S	2	9	16	23	30

July
M	1	8	15	22	29
T	2	9	16	23	30
W	3	10	17	24	31
T	4	11	18	25	
F	5	12	19	26	
S	6	13	20	27	
S	7	14	21	28	

August
M		5	12	19	26
T		6	13	20	27
W		7	14	21	28
T	1	8	15	22	29
F	2	9	16	23	30
S	3	10	17	24	31
S	4	11	18	25	

September
M		2	9	16	23	30
T		3	10	17	24	
W		4	11	18	25	
T		5	12	19	26	
F		6	13	20	27	
S		7	14	21	28	
S	1	8	15	22	29	

October
M		7	14	21	28
T	1	8	15	22	29
W	2	9	16	23	30
T	3	10	17	24	31
F	4	11	18	25	
S	5	12	19	26	
S	6	13	20	27	

November
M		4	11	18	25
T		5	12	19	26
W		6	13	20	27
T		7	14	21	28
F	1	8	15	22	29
S	2	9	16	23	30
S	3	10	17	24	

December
M		2	9	16	23	30
T		3	10	17	24	31
W		4	11	18	25	
T		5	12	19	26	
F		6	13	20	27	
S		7	14	21	28	
S	1	8	15	22	29	

Index

Index